Institutional Economics Perspectives on African Agricultural Development

Institutional Economics Perspectives on African Agricultural Development

Edited by Johann F. Kirsten, Andrew R. Dorward,
Colin Poulton, and Nick Vink

INTERNATIONAL FOOD POLICY
RESEARCH INSTITUTE
sustainable solutions for ending hunger and poverty

Supported by the CGIAR

International Food Policy Research Institute
2033 K Street, NW
Washington, D.C. 20006-1002, U.S.A.
Telephone +1-202-862-5600
www.ifpri.org

Figure 3.1 adapted from E. Ostrom, R. Gardner, and J. Walker, *Rules, games, and common-pool resources,* Figure 2.2, p. 37, copyright © 1994 the University of Michigan Press, and E. Ostrom, Doing institutional analysis: Digging deeper than markets and hierarchies, in *Handbook of New Institutional Economics,* ed. Claude Ménard and Mary M. Shirley, Figure 2, p. 829, copyright © 2005 Springer Science and Business Media. Adapted and reproduced with kind permission of the University of Michigan Press and Springer Science and Business Media.

DOI: 10.2499/9780896297814BK

Library of Congress Cataloging-in-Publication Data

Institutional economics perspectives on African agricultural development / edited by Johann F. Kirsten . . . [et al.].
     p. cm.
    Includes bibliographical references and index.
    ISBN 978-0-89629-781-4 (alk. paper)
    1. Agriculture and state—Africa.   2. Economic development—Africa.
3. Agricultural development projects—Africa.   I. Kirsten, Johann.
HD2118.I57   2009
338.1096—dc22   2009014462

Contents

Tables

Figures

Boxes

Foreword

The economics professions have been paying increasing attention to institutional issues, and they have developed strong concepts and analytical tools that are particularly relevant to the problems of agricultural change in Africa. This book represents an effort to consolidate lessons learned from applying an "institutional lens" to these challenges. It presents a framework for thinking about the institutional challenges facing African agriculture and identifies the tools of economic analysis that can be used to address them. The combination of theoretical chapters on core themes, supported by case studies from a wide range of countries, makes an important contribution to existing literature. Through an accessible synthesis of new institutional economics theory and research, the authors develop a better understanding of African agriculture and how to improve it.

The focus throughout is on Sub-Saharan Africa (especially Eastern and Southern Africa), and on policies and institutions affecting smallholder agriculture, the predominant livelihood in the region. The book's focus on institutional issues is by no means at the expense of essential complementary issues such as infrastructural development or technical change, but the emphasis on institutions is warranted, for two reasons. First, too little analysis of institutional processes and constraints in agricultural development has been done in the past. Second, institutional change is often a prerequisite for effective investment in infrastructural and technical change.

The International Food Policy Research Institute (IFPRI) has in recent years paid increased attention to capacity strengthening of higher education in agricultural economics for improved policymaking. For instance, IFPRI was an important partner in the development of the collaborative master's degree in Agricultural and Applied Economics in Eastern and Southern Africa. This book can serve as a key resource for the core course in such degree programs, and we hope that it will make an important contribution to helping students apply institutional analysis to many of Africa's agricultural development challenges.

Joachim von Braun
Director General, IFPRI

Acknowledgments

The idea for this book emerged from two concurrent initiatives. First, in 2003 a group of African universities initiated a process to establish a new collaborative master's degree in Agricultural and Applied Economics, for which the participating universities would share resources to teach a relevant, cutting-edge degree program to train agricultural economic professionals on the African continent. In designing the degree program, the participating departments agreed that this degree should have a strong focus on institutional economics. The book is therefore directly related to this initiative, because no core textbook was available to support the presentation of the Institutional Economics module, one of the foundation modules of this degree program. In this regard we acknowledge the support and leadership of Willis Oluoch-Kosura, the program director of the African Agricultural Economics Education Network (AAEEN), and of all other members of the Network. At the same time we also appreciate the efforts of the International Development Research Centre (IDRC) and the Rockefeller Foundation's Africa office, in particular Akin Adesina, for providing the moral and financial support to AAEEN during the planning phase of the master's program. Another important partner in the design process was the International Food Policy Research Institute (IFPRI), which has a particular interest in capacity building in developing countries for improved policymaking. This interest made IFPRI a natural partner to the AAEEN initiative and thus provided intellectual support for developing the collaborative master's degree and the writing of this book.

The second initiative running parallel to the AAEEN process was the agreement between the University of Pretoria (one of the participating universities in AAEEN) and the Agrarian Development Group at the Wye campus of Imperial College, England (the group has recently joined the School of African and Oriental Studies, at the University of London) to jointly develop a module on institutional economics for the Distance Learning Programmes in agricultural and rural development and poverty reduction offered by the University of London and co-tutored by staff at the University of Pretoria.

These two initiatives came to together when the Rockefeller Foundation granted the core team of authors a residency period at the Rockefeller Study and Conference Centre at Bellagio, Italy, to draft the text for this book. A group of African academics, colleagues from Imperial College at Wye, and colleagues from IFPRI who all work on the institutional economic aspects of African agriculture spent July 6–15, 2005, at Bellagio working on the draft text for this book.

We thank the Rockefeller Foundation for allowing us to use the beautiful and inspiring facilities at Bellagio and for funding the travels of our colleagues from Africa. Thanks also go to IFPRI and to Imperial College at Wye for supporting their staff members' travel costs to Bellagio.

Following the residency period at Bellagio one member of the editorial team, Johann Kirsten, spent two months at the French Agricultural Research Centre for International Development (CIRAD) in Montpellier, France, and four months at the Agricultural and Development Economics Division (ESA) of the Food and Agricultural Organization of the United Nations (FAO) in Rome, where he worked on the draft text generated at Bellagio. Thus we also thank Rolland Guis, director of the Territories, Environment, and People Department (TERA) at CIRAD; Prabhu Pingali, director of ESA at FAO; and Randy Stringer, service chief of ESAC; for providing the financial support, office infrastructure, and the peace and tranquillity necessary to accomplish this task.

The book would not have been possible without the dedication and long hours of debate and writing provided by all volume contributors. The enthusiasm during the meeting at Bellagio and afterward through various email exchanges showed a true commitment from the contributors to assist in improving our tools and approaches to analyze economic phenomena in developing-country agriculture. We hope that this volume will make a difference for tomorrow's generation of analysts, managers, and policymakers and that it will help lead to improved decisionmaking in government and agribusiness, which will ensure sustainable agricultural growth in Africa and in other parts of the developing world.

Introduction

Professionals in economics and agricultural economics have been paying increasing attention to institutional issues and have developed strong concepts and analytical tools to do so. The core message of this book is that this new focus is particularly relevant to the problems of agricultural development in Africa. As a result, there is a need to consolidate the lessons learned into a textbook to illustrate the relevance and application of these concepts and tools. The core purpose of the book is, therefore, to provide an accessible text on the economics of institutions relevant to agricultural development in the African context. However, the book cannot be regarded as exhaustive: it should be used by the discerning student as a text to be supplemented by the reading lists and the large volume of literature cited throughout the volume.

The book is divided into four parts. The first part provides a conceptual framework for looking at the problems of agricultural development in Africa from an institutional perspective, and the next three parts address the institutional aspects of problems of exchange, natural resource management, and the state, respectively. The analysis in each of the latter three parts is supplemented by case studies.

The focus throughout the book is on Sub-Saharan Africa and on policies and institutions affecting smallholder agriculture, reflecting the predominance of smallholder farming in the subcontinent and long-standing arguments that in poor agrarian economies smallholder agricultural development has a critical role to play in poverty-reducing economic growth (for example, Hazell 2005). Although the issues raised in the book apply to large parts of Sub-Saharan Africa, the geographic coverage of the case studies is not uniform (with a bias toward East and Southern Africa, and away from central and West Africa), as the studies were selected to illustrate specific themes arising from the conceptual analysis. It is important, therefore, to recognize that there are significant modes of agricultural production and regions not represented in the case studies. The book's focus on institutional issues should also not be taken to imply that other issues (such as infrastructural development or technical change) are not important; indeed it is reiterated throughout the book that infrastructural and technical changes are essential complements to institutional change. Explicit attention to institutions is warranted, however, for two reasons. First, there has in the past been too little analysis of institutional processes and constraints on agricultural development, and greater understanding of institutions is needed to remedy this shortcoming. Second, institutional change is often a prerequisite for effective investment in infrastructural and technical changes.

Our consideration of the challenges facing agricultural development in Africa emerges from the recognition that criticisms of the market-liberalization policies pursued in many African countries over the past 20 years are growing and that pressures are rising for governments and international agencies to do more for agriculture, do it differently, and do it fast. The resultant calls for increased government spending on agricultural development suggest a more active role for the state, but this trend sits uneasily with both the dominant market-liberalization paradigm and the generally negative African experience with earlier state-led development. As a result, there is growing interest in the development of new institutional frameworks involving the state, the private sector, and stakeholder groups in agricultural development.[1]

This new trend in turn requires, as we argue in this volume, a sound application of economics and other social sciences. However, two difficulties facing both theorists and policy analysts are first, identifying appropriate theoretical frameworks for analysis, and second, striking the appropriate trade-off between identification of generalizable causal relationships on the one hand and, on the other, context-specific analysis of the complex web of variables and relationships that are important in particular cases. The latter dilemma, which might be parodied as the choice between generally right but precisely wrong on the one hand or precisely right but generally wrong on the other, requires greater attention to both detailed analysis of specific cases and theoretical synthesis of findings from these cases. The theoretical tools that graduate students in agricultural economics usually study are necessary but insufficient for these tasks. This book therefore aims to supplement the traditional core training of agricultural economics students with additional perspectives and disciplines necessary for them to undertake these tasks in their professional careers.

Note

1. The meaning of the term "institutions" as used in this book is discussed in Chapter 2, where it is defined as the rules of society that provide a framework of incentives that shape economic, political, and social organization and behavior.

Part 1

Theoretical and Conceptual Framework

Chapter 1

Institutions and the Agricultural Development Challenge in Africa

Andrew R. Dorward, Johann F. Kirsten,
S. Were Omamo, Colin Poulton, and Nick Vink

The purpose of this chapter is to introduce some of the major themes of the book and to discuss their importance to the challenges facing agricultural development and policy analysis in Africa. The chapter starts with a broad overview of the agricultural development policy challenges, noting some of the successes and failures in agricultural development. Section 1.2 provides an overview of past policy trends in agricultural development. In Section 1.3 the importance of complementary technical, infrastructural, and institutional changes in economic development is recognized, with a focus on the role that institutions play in this process. A distinction is drawn between the institutional environment and institutional arrangements and, within the latter, between gift exchange, hierarchies, and markets. Section 1.4 concludes.

1.1 Agricultural Policy Challenges in Africa

Millions of Africans are born, live, and die poor, hungry, and malnourished. Most of these unfortunate people live in rural areas and directly or indirectly depend for a large part of their livelihoods on agriculture. Although dramatic agricultural growth has been a critical driver of poverty reduction in some parts of the world, in large parts of Africa its performance has been disappointing, with low or negative per capita growth over much of the past 40 years or so.[1]

Parts of this chapter, notably Sections 1.3 and 1.4, draw heavily on work by Jonathan Kydd. Sections also draw on Dorward, Kydd, and Poulton (2005a). These contributions are gratefully acknowledged, while any errors or omissions remain the responsibility of the authors.

This state of affairs has not arisen because agriculture has been ignored by policymakers (Box 1.1). Policy establishments across Africa have consistently recognized the importance of agriculture to the poor of the continent and have stressed the significance of agriculture to African economies and people. Pick up almost any food policy statement, agricultural development strategy, or national economic development plan produced in almost any African country over the past 40 years, and almost surely the first sentence will read something like "agriculture is the mainstay of the economy," or "agriculture is the economic backbone of the country." These documents then set out in great detail actions for the government of the day to do for agriculture because of what agriculture could or should do for the country—but in these same countries, shares of public investment in agriculture will usually be low and often declining. This mismatch between the rhetoric of policy on the one hand and the reality of rural poverty and public investment in agriculture on the other is widely recognized—by the people of Africa, by their political leaders, by international agencies, and by policy analysts.

Box 1.1 If economists are so smart, why is Africa so poor?

President Bush's new Africa initiative, and the recent events unfolding in Liberia, raise the question why, despite decades of aid, Africa remains impoverished. Over the years, the continent has been the site of large-scale experiments to reform its economies. But however ambitious, these projects have failed to generate sustained economic growth. Most African nations today are poorer than they were in 1980, sometimes by very wide margins. And of the continent's three-dozen countries, only two (Botswana and Uganda) have managed to grow at rates exceeding 3% per annum since 1980. More shocking, two-thirds of African countries have either stagnated or shrunk in real per capita terms since the onset of independence in the early 1960s.

A major reason for the failure of reform is that the market-based policies—the so-called "Washington consensus"—that underpinned the African experiments had a fatal flaw: they assumed that economic reforms can create efficient markets without simultaneous reform of the political institutions. Without a limit on government and a guarantee of property rights and individual liberty, "efficient markets" cannot exist. Economists have made an impressive start on the types of economic institutions needed to support efficient markets, but have not made equal strides in devising political institutions that will accomplish that objective. . . .

The efficient functioning of markets requires that some organization enforce contracts and property rights. As Thomas Hobbes warned in "Leviathan," the absence of an enforcer implies a free-for-all: everybody knows that everybody else can behave in an opportunistic fashion, therefore everybody behaves opportunistically. (How like the Congo that looks—or Liberia.) To be credible, the organization that enforces contract and property rights must have the power to force people to adhere to its decisions. This necessarily implies that the enforcer is the government. History offers us no case of a well-developed market system that was not embedded in a well-developed political system. Even under apartheid, South Africa prospered—relative to the rest of Africa—because of the rule of law (however unpalatable and discriminatory some laws were)....

The necessary connection between government and the market creates a thorny problem. Any government strong enough to enforce contract and property rights is also strong enough, presumably, to expropriate its citizens' wealth —witness the confiscation of white farms in Zimbabwe. Undemocratic African governments have powerful incentives to do this. First, they need revenue for their political survival. Second, to survive, they must also serve politically crucial constituents. Too often governments exchange political support for monopoly rights, protection from competition, or special privileges. The fundamental political problem of economic development is therefore that of devising the appropriate means for channeling government action into support of markets, rather than predatoriness....

In effect, solving the development problem in Africa requires the crafting of political institutions that limit the discretion and authority of government and, more saliently, of individual actors within the government. No simple recipe for limiting government exists. Yet two principles are clear. First, the countries of Africa must create mechanisms and incentives for different branches and levels of government to impose sanctions on one another if they exceed the authority granted to them by the law. Second, these sanctions cannot be imposed in an arbitrary or ad hoc fashion: the sanction mechanisms themselves must be limited by the law.

Source: Haber, North, and Weingast (2003).

1.1.1 Successes and Failures in African Agriculture

Agriculture plays a key role in the economies of most African countries, in terms of such standard economic indicators as contribution to gross domestic product (GDP) and foreign exchange earnings, in terms of the number and distribution of people employed as farmers or farm workers, and in terms of the importance of food expenditures for poor people. The potential contribution of agricultural development to economic growth and poverty reduction beyond the agricultural sector through a variety of multiplier effects has also been recognized in an extensive literature (see World Bank 2007 for a recent restatement). There are therefore sound reasons for investments in the large numbers of agricultural development projects and programs that have been implemented across the subcontinent for decades. What is disappointing is the decidedly mixed results of these investments.

There have been some important agricultural successes in African agriculture. In the precolonial and colonial periods widespread adoption of new crops and practices by African farmers was quite remarkable (for example, the spread of maize across the continent; the use of ox ploughs in Uganda; and the cultivation of such new cash crops as cocoa, coffee, cotton, and groundnuts across the continent; see, for example, Carr 2001). Under postindependence state-led policies there were significant successes in the development, release, and adoption of improved high-yielding maize varieties in East and Southern Africa (Smale and Jayne 2003), perhaps most notably in Malawi and Zimbabwe (Heisey and Smale 1995; Eicher and Kupfuma 1998). Smallholder cotton production in a number of francophone countries in West Africa provides another example of dramatic success with state-led development policies. More recent successes include horticulture and cut-flower exports from Kenya, smallholder dairying in Kenya, urban and peri-urban agriculture in West Africa and Kenya (Tiffen, Mortimer, and Gichuki 1994; Tiffen 2003), and cotton production in several countries in East and Southern Africa (Poulton et al. 2004). Major research successes include the development of new rice varieties (New Rice for Africa [NERICA]) and the control of cassava mosaic virus and cassava mealybug in a pan-African action that benefited millions of farmers and consumers. Gabre-Madhin and Haggblade (2003) report these and other notable successes in African agriculture. Wiggins (1995) and Turner, Hyden, and Kates (1993) provide instructive examples of African farming systems responding successfully to new opportunities and challenges. Turner, Hyden, and Kates (1993) note that African agriculture is facing unprecedented demands to respond to rapid and fundamental changes in population growth and in economic and social systems—changes that took centuries in Europe and Asia are occurring over mere decades in Africa. These researchers also note that often institutions, and institutional change, are critical in determining the ability of farmers to respond positively to new challenges and opportunities.

However, these successes are too often the exception and have been too limited in scope to significantly increase overall agricultural productivity and the welfare of farmers and consumers across the continent. They also fall far short of achievements in other parts of the world. Fertilizer use per hectare of arable land in Africa, for example, was stagnant from 1980 to 2005 and is far below that of other continents (9 kg/ha compared to 70–150 kg/ha in Latin America and South and Southeast Asia; Crawford et al. 2003; Crawford, Jayne, and Kelly 2005). Agricultural development policies in Africa have not generally worked—neither the state-led policies of the postindependence period nor the market-liberalization policies that followed. Many policies have not been implemented or have been implemented only in part or very poorly; those that have been implemented well have often not delivered sustainable benefits.

1.1.2 Technical and Institutional Challenges in African Agricultural Development

A widely accepted objective for agricultural development in Africa is to achieve sustainable intensification (Reardon 1998) with the adoption of new technologies that use purchased inputs (such as improved seeds and inorganic fertilizers) to increase land and labor productivity. There are, however, a daunting set of generic and often mutually reinforcing problems that commonly inhibit such processes in poor rural areas that need them most. These problems include poor roads and telecommunications; poor human health; lack of a well-developed and diversified monetary economy; and thin markets for agricultural inputs, outputs, and finance, despite significant direct and indirect dependence of the local economy on agriculture. Thin markets contribute to and are the result of a business environment generally characterized by weak information (on prices, new technologies, and other potential market players), by difficult and weak contract enforcement, by high risks (not only in production and prices but also in access to inputs and markets and in enforcing contracts), and by high transaction costs (as buyers and sellers protect themselves against risks of a transaction failing by searching for and screening potential suppliers or buyers and their goods and services, then negotiating and contracting with them, and monitoring and enforcing their adherence to the contract).

Nested within these general challenges facing poor rural areas are a set of issues specific to agriculture and, in particular, to small-scale farming (and farm labor). Particular challenges to small-scale farmers include:

- the absence, in many cases, of markets because of low purchasing power in the domestic market and poor access to global markets caused by trade distortions (such as rich-country agricultural subsidies);

- production and sales cycles that are long by the standards of other small businesses (exacerbating climate, pest, price, and transaction risks; leading to significant seasonality in labor use, cash flow, food availability, prices, and risks; and affecting whole communities and their economies);

- high returns to timely labor at periods of peak labor demand, so that often it makes sense even for poor farmers to supplement their own family labor with hired help if they have the means, even though they may seek to hire their own labor out just a few weeks or days later;

- insufficient allocation of labor to their own land during labor peaks for some farmers because of poverty, forgoing valuable increases in their harvest, as shortages of food drive them to work for others;

- small-scale individual input purchases that therefore have high transaction costs in situations where markets are poorly developed and risky, even though technical progress and population pressure on land increase farmers' needs for inputs;

- technical choices that involve discontinuous switches between technologies and crops, with threshold prices and levels of performance above (below) which certain activities are (are not) profitable or viable, with these thresholds determining whether significant numbers of farmers demand or supply particular services and/or commodities;

- need for seasonal financing of farmers' input purchases, raising issues of how such purchases can be financed and how the risks of such finance to poor farmers can be mitigated;

- use of significant shares of output for subsistence, generating welfare but not cash, so that sales of outputs often fail to fully cover purchased input and labor costs; and

- land tenure arrangements that affect farmers' ability to borrow, expand, or exit with a lump sum, by land-market transactions, and that also influence incentives for land improvement.

There are also particular off-farm challenges in the development of input supply systems. Key inputs, such as fertilizer, are purchased by farmers in fairly narrow time windows. Their uncertain input demands depend on assessment of input profitability (affected by relative input and output prices and by unfolding climatic and pest behavior during the season) and on their ability to finance purchases. The latter depends not only on the general wealth and income status of individual farmers but also on their vulnerability to shocks affecting incomes and expenditure, their access to credit, more general price and economic changes, and events in the community. However, if input suppliers are left with excess inventory, then it often cannot be disposed of for another year and deteriorates in storage. Input suppliers therefore face incentives to be cautious in stocking and to cover their risks with high margins.

The challenges to greater input supply are related to challenges in delivery of financial services to support farmers' input purchases—small-scale lending to dispersed farmers with uncertain credit demand and engagement in risky enterprises leads to high transaction costs for lenders and high risks of default. These risks have to be covered by high interest rates, which make borrowing more risky for farmers and hence both depress demand (reducing the scale of lending) and increase incentives to default—further increasing the costs of lending (Binswanger and Rosenzweig 1986).

In addition to these general problems of small-scale agriculture, substantial numbers of poor farmers in Africa face problems that are unique to their circumstances:

- human health issues, including but not restricted to the HIV/AIDS pandemic, and other debilitating diseases (such as malaria and other insect- and waterborne diseases) in the face of weak healthcare systems in rural areas;

- poor animal and plant healthcare systems that exacerbate the impact of problems caused by trypanosomiases, foot and mouth disease, East Coast fever, Newcastle disease, maize striga, rust in legumes, and the like (problems often caused by specific seasonal factors);

- heterogeneous patterns of population density, with the result that rural markets are small and fragmented (hence demand for agricultural products, whether from food processors or consumers directly, is also weak and fragmented);

- relative scarcity of water, both for human basic needs and for direct production in irrigation agriculture (the latter exacerbated by the low level of investment in irrigation infrastructure);

- additional constraints faced by women because of their low level of de facto and de jure rights to land and other resources, as well as discrimination in access to financial services and other means of production;

- deleterious effects of a history of successive phases of colonial exploitation, manipulation by one or the other superpower during the Cold War, and (especially in Southern Africa) destabilization caused by the apartheid regime in South Africa;

- environmental degradation that causes, among other things, soil nutrient depletion, soil erosion, destruction of water catchment areas, and salinization;

- fragile and weak states, often induced by the particular type of development aid dispensed by developed countries; and

- competition with "food aid" whose main purpose is to get rid of rich-country food surpluses and whose main effect is to crowd local farmers out of markets, even where justifiable emergency needs are being met.

Just as problems in input supply and financial service delivery to small-scale subsistence farmers in poor rural areas of Africa are mutually reinforcing, so they can also have negative effects on output market development: without greater use of purchased inputs and seasonal finance, farmers' marketed surpluses will be relatively small (in terms of both individual and aggregate transactions), leading to higher transaction costs and risks for output buyers. This difficulty is compounded because small, often residual, surpluses tend to fluctuate considerably from year to year in response to climatic variations, thereby raising buyers' search costs. Thus higher trading margins are required, and these—together with low profits that depress investment and competition—depress farmgate prices, further reducing farmers' demand for inputs and seasonal finance. Small and variable residual surpluses also reduce incentives for larger firms to enter output markets. As a result markets play a greater allocative role in African agriculture than in developed economies. In the grain trade of the United States, for example, there are far fewer intermediaries between producer and consumer than in liberalized markets in Africa: in other words the grain trade in Africa is generally more market intensive (Fafchamps 2004). However, Fafchamps (2004, 11–12) goes further by highlighting why market exchange in Africa is much more costly, cumbersome, time consuming, and unpredictable than elsewhere:

- Search costs are high because of the large number of participants (no printed catalogs, no phone listings, yellow pages, or the like).

- Most transactions are small and cash-based with limited and highly personalized credit arrangements, because contracts are difficult to enforce.

- The quality of goods and services is uneven, and as a result traders choose to inspect the quality of products at each transaction.

- Few, if any, government standards are available to facilitate quality verification. This lack of transparency on product quality makes it difficult to distinguish bona fide producers from fly-by-night operators selling inferior products.

- Because of no proper personal identification systems, the transparency problem also applies to the selection of customers.

Dorward, Kydd, and Poulton (2005a, 3) argue that

> the key point that emerges from an examination of institutional and economic development is that low income economies are characterised by situations with high transaction costs and risks, weak information flows and a weak institutional environment. Actors, particularly those with little financial and social resources or political leverage, then face high (all too often prohibitive) costs in accessing information and in enforcing property rights. These costs inhibit both market development and access to existing markets.

As a result of these conditions:

• Insurance markets fail because of covariance of risk and high costs of monitoring behavior to protect against moral hazard and adverse selection.

• Credit markets fail because of the inability to insure borrowers, lack of collateral, difficulties of recovering loans, and limited diversification of local economies, all of which impede the development of a sustainable model of rural financial services.

• Output markets are weak because of poor infrastructure, limited surpluses (caused by lack of credit), and consequent disincentives for private trade.

These weak or failed markets in turn inhibit economic and technological development. Low levels of economic activity themselves lead to thin markets, inadequate coordination, high transaction costs and risks, and high unit costs for infrastructural development. The result can easily be a low-level equilibrium trap. In such a trap constraints, lack of investment incentives, and a stagnant rural economy reinforce one another.

According to this analysis the major challenge for smallholder agricultural development policy is to ascertain the seriousness of the various problems outlined above as barriers to the economic and institutional changes needed for adoption of technologies for sustainable intensification, and then to identify, design, and put in place cost-effective mechanisms for addressing them. Such mechanisms involve the development of systems of coordinated exchange that allow smallholder farmers and the economies they participate in to escape from the low-level equilibrium trap. Specifically they involve processes of political, social, and economic change that enable supply-chain systems to provide smallholders with access to the range of pre- and postharvest services required for sustainable intensification.

Cash crop development offers some opportunities for meeting these challenges, as higher output values provide more incentives for buyer and farmer investments in technology and in the institutions needed to coordinate, by means of inter-locking contracts, input and credit provision with output market purchases.[2] Unfortunately the challenges to sustainable intensification are most acute where such intensification is most urgently needed: in the production of staple food crops. The widespread production, trading, and consumption of staple foods makes them critically important for development (their low productivity contributing to the disproportionate use of household and national resources in their production and consumption). At the same time, it makes their sustainable intensification difficult (large numbers of producers, small-scale traders, and consumers make coordination difficult and, with variable and often small margins, discourage investment in tech-nology and in coordinating institutions).

The result is that outside of major cash crop growing areas and peri-urban areas, there tends to be a strong subsistence orientation with a high proportion of cultivat-ed areas devoted to low-yield staple food production. The limited use of purchased inputs or organic manures, combined with increasing population pressure, leads to soil mining and declining soil fertility on declining holding sizes. Large numbers of rural households are net deficit in food staples, despite the high share of land devoted to their cultivation. The high proportion of subsistence production and the low proportion of staples traded then lead to thin staple markets which, with high trans-port costs and restrictive international trade policies, may show marked intra- and inter-seasonal instability in the face of weather and policy shocks. Such instability strengthens incentives for subsistence production (the risks of low prices discourage production of surplus for sale, whereas risks of high prices discourage reliance on market purchases for consumption). Consequent prioritization of land, labor, and capital allocation to low-productivity staples then impedes allocation of resources to higher value crops for market (even though these crops may be comparatively advantageous). Although this scenario is most evident in more densely populated and poverty-stricken areas, such as southern Malawi and western Kenya (Marenya et al. 2003; Dorward and Kydd 2004; Poulton and Ndufa 2005; Imperial College et al. 2007), it may be that such areas are simply harbingers on a path of increasing popula-tion pressure, environmental degradation, and poverty, as evidenced by general find-ings of low fertilizer use, low per capita agricultural growth rates, low cereal yields, and high proportions of food-deficit food producers (Jayne, Zulu, and Nijhoff 2006; Omamo et al. 2006; Morris et al 2007; Barrett 2008).

This scenario poses major challenges for agricultural development policy, as simultaneous development and stabilization of input, credit, and output markets is needed. These challenges are reduced where cassava is the major staple food crop, because it has fewer input requirements and its capacity for storage in the field reduces its price instability.[3] Where cereals are the major staple, we have to ask how simultaneous development and stabilization can be achieved in input, credit, and output markets. The large scale of coordination and investment required suggests key roles for the state and agricultural development policy. How does the history of agricultural policy in Africa over the past 40 or so years fare when analyzed in the context of these challenges?

1.2   Smallholder Agricultural Development Policy in Africa

The predominant agricultural development policy in poor rural economies over the past 40 years or so can be (simplistically) divided into two broad phases: state- and then market-led development.[4] Most countries have undergone an extended period of adjustment between the two phases. These two policy phases reflect changes in the dominant paradigms of economic policy: the first phase emphasized problems of market failure in poor economies (and promoted state interventions to address these market failures) and the second phase emphasizes state failures when intervening in markets (and promotes reliance on the private sector and markets and encourages state withdrawal from market interventions). Continuing difficulties with agricultural growth in liberalizing economies in Africa have led more recently to increasing recognition of another sphere of state failure—failing to support the conditions necessary for markets to work (see Section 1.2.3, Box 1.1, and Chapter 20).

1.2.1   State-Led Development Policy

At independence most African governments were acutely aware of the importance of smallholder agriculture to their aspirations for rapid development. Some saw it as a long-term driver of growth in their fledgling economies, some as a foreign-exchange earner with a large reserve of unused labor, ripe to be taxed to fund the development of industries on which to build a modern economy, and still others as a means of achieving the politically important goal of food self-sufficiency. Whatever its role, rapid increases in the productivity of smallholder agriculture were needed. The private sector, however, was generally considered too weak to take on the task: it lacked organizational capacity; access to capital and human resources; and incentives to make large, risky, and unattractive investments in rural areas. (These investments were considered unattractive partly because simultaneous investments were needed in communications infrastructure, input and output trading, research and extension, and farmers' input purchases and production.) The private sector was also not trusted by nationalist leaders with socialist leanings, associated as it was with exploitation by colonial or other elites. State intervention, however, was considered an effective instrument for development. The state was able to access public-sector financial resources to invest in organizational and human-resource development; infrastructure;

and the coordinated delivery of research, extension, financial, and input and output marketing services. State action also offered opportunities for personal and political patronage.

Similar thinking was found across much of Asia, and as a result there were massive government investments in Asian and African agriculture in the second half of the twentieth century. Models of intervention varied widely across regions, crops, and time periods. They generally involved price interventions (through input and finance subsidies and produce price stabilization and support) and organizational interventions (through parastatals, state-sponsored cooperatives, and agricultural finance organizations), the latter going well beyond what was necessary to administer price interventions (Dorward et al. 2004b). The subsidies to agriculture, however, were generally provided in the context of economywide policies that led to an overall bias against agriculture. These policies, notably exchange rate overvaluation, generally swamped the benefits that farmers received from interventions in the agricultural sector.

The results of these state-activist policies were mixed. In some (mainly Asian) countries) they led to the spectacular successes of the Green Revolution, resulting in the most dramatic and widespread agricultural growth and poverty reduction in history. In other (mainly African) countries, however, large government expenditures in agricultural development led to very little agricultural growth and were a major drain on government budgets (although there were some notable and instructive African successes; see Chapter 20). Realization of the scale of these problems coincided with increasing questions about the ability and intentions of state interventions and shifts from Keynesian to monetarist macroeconomic policies in developed economies. As a result donor support waned with increasing hostility toward the state-led development approach.[5] Government intervention was then seen as causing distortions in the economy (by protecting inefficient local industries) that depressed efficiency by limiting local competition and private-sector development. It was considered to be a corrupt and expensive drain on already overspent government budgets (leading to difficulties in macroeconomic management). And all the while it rendered poor services to farmers and, through overvalued exchange rates, taxed them and removed incentives for investment in agriculture. This analysis was applied both to (mainly Asian) countries that had succeeded in transforming their smallholder agriculture (where it was considered that even greater success would have been achieved without distorting and inefficient government interventions) and to those (mainly African) countries where agricultural development policies had largely failed.

1.2.2 Market-Led Development Policies

Critics of parastatals and overvalued exchange rates were correct in these observations and, in the African case at least, the status quo in the 1980s was indefensible and often unsustainable. The standard structural adjustment prescription of privatization and liberalization, based largely on what is increasingly recognized as a naive application of neoclassical economic theories about the efficiency of competitive markets, often provided some quick fiscal relief. These prescriptions involved the limitation of state activities to the provision of nonexcludable and nonsubtractable public goods to overcome conventional market failures. In agriculture, therefore, the state was limited to research into pro-poor technologies; technical extension and market information; market regulation; and provision of physical infrastructure, such as telecommunications and roads. International donors—sometimes with the acquiescence of, and sometimes in the face of opposition from, nongovernmental organizations (NGOs)—promoted the privatization or dismantling of agricultural marketing parastatals (generally delinking credit, input, and output markets); deregulation of these markets; and elimination of credit, input, and output subsidies. These agricultural sector reforms tied in with economywide policies reducing public expenditure and overvalued exchange rates. With time increasing emphasis was given to the development of institutions supporting markets (see, for example, World Bank 2000, 2002, 2003).

The outcome of the market liberalization and structural adjustment (or market-led) policies was, however, equally mixed. These policies appear to have successfully stimulated growth in poor countries with dense populations, good infrastructure, and a diversified agriculture and rural economy (Bangladesh, for example). They also appear to have benefited lower- to middle-income countries, where staples production is no longer the basis of the livelihoods of most of the poor. In most of Africa, however, the record is not so bright: these policies have not generally succeeded in jump-starting agriculture in poor rural economies that have not already transformed their agriculture. Despite some benefits, such as reduced food prices for processed staples for poor consumers in Southern Africa (Jayne and Jones 1997) and positive impacts on the supply chains for some cash crops in some countries (Shepherd and Farolfi 1999), there has been a notable failure to develop input, output, and financial markets offering attractively priced, timely, and reliable services that are critical for food crop (particularly cereal) intensification.

Although few would argue that the preliberalization situation could or should have been sustained, it is widely recognized that liberalization has not delivered the substantial agricultural growth needed to drive rural poverty reduction and increased food security. Thus, it is fair to ask why both state- and market-led approaches to development appear to have generally failed in Africa, whereas both have worked in parts of Asia. Further, it is necessary to ask what insights, if any, the earlier analysis of the institutional problems of poor rural areas can provide into explanations of these patterns of success and failure.

1.2.3   Explanations of Policy Success and Failure

A large number of broad explanations have been propounded for the mixed and disappointing results of liberalization. These explanations are not mutually incompatible (they can explain different and compounding factors contributing to the disappointing results of liberalization), but they are often based on different understandings of the importance and nature of institutional change in development, and in some areas they lead to very different policy recommendations:

- The "partial implementation" view argues that the poor results can be attributed to government failures to fully liberalize their agricultural sectors (for example, Kherallah et al. 2000; Jayne et al. 2002). This view does not recognize that there are important institutional constraints to market development in poor rural areas. It points to successes in those sectors where liberalization has been more pronounced but blames piecemeal, start-stop liberalization and frequent policy reversals (or fears of policy reversals) for depressing the returns and raising the risks associated with private-sector investment. Another element of this may also be the sequencing of liberalization policies.

- "The weak institutions" view attributes the failure of market liberalization in delivering expected benefits to weak institutional support for market and private-sector development, with cultural, political, and legal factors undermining clear contract enforcement and property rights and hence private investment incentives (for example, World Bank 2000, 2002, 2003).

- The "lack of productive investments" view complements the two previous views. This argument explains agricultural development failures as the result of a lack of long-term productive investments in agricultural research, agricultural extension, and rural infrastructure. These shortfalls in investments are explained by declining overall investment in agriculture together with crowding out of long-term productive investments by fertilizer subsidies and price supports, which yield few long-term benefits and are motivated by immediate political concerns and patronage (see, for example, Maxwell and Heber-Percy 2001; Jayne et al. 2002; Africa Commission 2005).

- The "coordination failure" view is more radical than the abovementioned arguments in its questions about perceptions of the pervasive failure of state activism and the superiority of liberalized markets. Adherents of this view note that whereas activist state intervention in agricultural markets in poor rural economies has a record of both dramatic successes and dramatic failures, experience with market liberalization in poor rural economies shows limited success in stimulating significant broad-based growth and poverty reduction (Dorward et al. 2004b). This view calls for a more nuanced approach to policy that recognizes the different conditions and demands of economies with varying characteristics and at different stages of development. Policy is directed toward promoting change in institutional arrangements (for example, in the development of hierarchies) and in the institutional environment (Dorward, Kydd, and Poulton 2005b; Poulton, Dorward, and Kydd 2005).

- The "state failure" view brings together important aspects of the abovementioned views, with emphasis on the weakness of the state in many African countries, as evidenced by a lack of strong institutions to foster exchange and protect property and a lack of capacity to implement policy. In such countries the state is commonly too weak to prevent theft of property by private actors, and/or itself misuses power and threatens property rights. Entrepreneurs and organizations then face high risks that they will not be able to realize a return if they invest in knowledge, skills, or capital, so they refrain from such expenditures. The state is not only weak in providing these fundamental institutions but also fails to provide other public goods (hard and soft infrastructure, such as roads; communication infrastructure; and general access to information) that shape the institutional environment in which farmers and entrepreneurs need to operate. The state also lacks the capacity to effectively and impartially intervene in economic activities. These problems are not restricted to failed states marked by conflict and complete breakdown of the state apparatus.

- The "high service delivery costs" view argues that the high costs of service delivery to smallholder farmers limit the supply of and their access to input, finance, and produce markets and to technical and management information (see, for example, Poulton, Dorward, and Kydd 2005). Some observers, therefore, argue that farmer organizations are needed to allow smallholder farmers and their service suppliers to achieve economies of scale in service access and delivery (see, for example, Peacock et al. 2004).

- The "poverty/soil-fertility trap" view contends that poverty, combined with declining soil fertility and incomes, locks smallholder farmers into a spiral of increasing poverty and an inability to afford purchased inputs needed to increase productivity. Substantial external investments are therefore needed in subsidised fertilizer delivery to rejuvenate soil fertility and lift farm productivity out of the vicious poverty spiral (see, for example, UN Millennium Project 2005a,b).[6]

- The "trade liberalization" view argues that there are major national and international demand (and trade) constraints that limit the actual and potential returns to agricultural investment in Africa (see, for example, Diao, Dorosh, and Rahman 2003). Actions are therefore needed both to stimulate demand (for example, through international trade liberalization) and to improve the efficiency of markets in transmitting demand to producers (as in the weak institutions view described above).

- The "agricultural skeptic" view argues that there is overdependence on rainfed agriculture, which, because of its inherent limited productive potential, is unable to support an increasing rural population. Thus diversification out of agriculture is needed, as are investments to create nonagricultural employment and income opportunities (see, for example, Ashley and Maxwell 2001; Ellis 2005).

Both the partial-liberalization and weak-institutions views are essentially supportive of the liberalization agenda and are consistent with its basic neoclassical tenets. These views (particularly the latter) recognize the importance of state support for those institutional public goods necessary for functioning markets. Both views subscribe to the basic narrative of orthodox market economics, which sees the market as the dominant mode of organization and by implication the most efficient. The central challenge is then to extend this organization to poor rural economies—to make markets work for the poor.

This leads to a policy agenda aimed at completing the market-liberalization process, accompanied by other measures to address problems in financial markets and those affecting remote producers. These measures include addressing problems identified in the lack-of-productive-investments view: increased investment in infrastructure, legal institutions, market institutions, and agricultural support organizations (research and extension); promotion of smallholder production of export crops; removal of advanced countries' protectionism and poor countries' restrictions on external and internal trade (as in the trade-liberalization view); tackling concentrations of local power that force the poor to access markets (such as credit) on highly adverse terms; short-term targeted support to vulnerable groups in remote areas (for example, safety-net transfers); credible sustainable macroeconomic policies; and institutional innovations for input credit, such as contract farming and group approaches (World Bank 2000),[7] as in the high-service-delivery-cost view. This analysis also leads to an emphasis on governance, which focuses on how to improve the implementation of liberalization policies, facilitate delivery of public goods, and reduce associated rent seeking. In this sense, governance then becomes an integral part of market-liberalization policies for economic development, as well as being a goal in its own right. The centerpiece of some versions of the markets-for-the-poor paradigm is an emphasis on replacement of nontradable rights to resources based on community membership with tradable property rights to land, water, and buildings. Tradable property rights, it is argued, can be leveraged to provide the poor with the finances to develop business or invest in their human capital (as argued, for example, by De Soto 2000).[8]

In contrast, the institutional critique of market liberalization in the coordination-failure view recognizes that it is important to improve poor peoples' interactions with markets but is also more critical of the conceptualization of markets as efficient exchange mechanisms in poor rural areas. Here, it is argued, markets are particularly prone to transaction failures (as discussed earlier) so that the development of other nonmarket or hybrid exchange and coordination mechanisms is needed: markets are only one mechanism for allocation and exchange (albeit a very important one), so it is also important to investigate others and ask how they can be made to complement market development in pro-poor ways.

Complementing their different views about markets, the explanations of agricultural liberalization failures outlined above differ in regard to the appropriate role for the state. Nevertheless many of them share a concern about the weakness of the state and a lack of capacity to perform critical functions: in the first view the state has failed to implement liberalization policies and to control rent seeking, whereas in the second view it has also failed to enforce critical property rights and provide critical public goods. According to the coordination-failure view, liberalization has precluded the state from providing critical support to nonmarket coordination, and indeed state efforts to promote market coordination have sometimes critically weakened nonmarket coordination. Other views suggest a failure of the economy to adapt or invest in certain ways, suggesting a role for policy (and implicitly the state) to promote certain adaptations or investments (or to remove constraints to such efforts). There is therefore agreement that improved governance and government capacity are critical for agricultural growth; nonetheless no agreement exists on the appropriate scope and reach of state responsibilities.

These explanations of agricultural liberalization failures also pose questions about why policies and institutions have evolved or failed to evolve in particular ways, and thus about how policies and institutions change. Thus the partial-liberalization view raises implicit questions about why African states have not implemented market-liberalization policies. The weak-institutions view explicitly addresses further questions about the processes of change in the institutional environment. The lack-of-productive-investments view raises questions about the political economy reasons for this lack of investment. The coordination-failure view extends these questions with explicit concerns about processes of change in the institutional arrangements.

Similar questions are raised by the other explanations of agricultural liberalization failures. These issues are discussed further in Chapter 20.

These sets of complementary questions about the role of markets and that of the state in promoting coordinated exchange, and about processes of institutional change, lie at the heart of debates about agricultural development policy in Africa. Their resolution is critical for the welfare of Africa's poor and is the major challenge facing agricultural policy analysts.

1.3   Institutional Change as a Critical Process in Economic Development

How does the analysis of the previous section, emphasizing institutional change as a critical process in agricultural development and identifying the promotion of institutional change as a critical role for the state, relate to broader understandings of development? We begin this section by setting out a simple analytical framework demonstrating the potential importance of institutional change in development, and then we examine empirical evidence supporting this model. We conclude by considering different roles and types of institutions.

1.3.1   Importance of Institutional Change in Economic Development

Development is a multifaceted process that involves change in a wide variety of economic, social, and physical factors as they affect people's opportunities and constraints to participate in society and make choices. Poverty is similarly multifaceted and related to communities' and individuals' social, physical, and economic relations and the constraints on the choices they can make. Economic growth is an important element of both development and poverty reduction in its own right (through its relationships with income opportunities) and because other important components—such as the building of human and social capital, of infrastructure, and of improved governance—are unlikely to be sustained or accessible without it. What then does economic growth or development involve?

Early writings in development economics largely attributed underdevelopment to deficiencies in factor endowments, specifically physical and human capital, and to the lack of technology. Using this framework gives a simple traditional microeconomic view of development as a widespread process of change across different sectors and communities that shifts supply and demand curves to the right, increasing supply and demand (and their elasticities) and consumer and producer surpluses. This transformation is shown in Figure 1.1. Initially the supply curve (S_1) is relatively inelastic. Development involves an outward shift and increased elasticity in the supply curve (S_1 moves to S_2). Increased producer and consumer incomes throughout

Figure 1.1   Changes in supply and demand during economic development

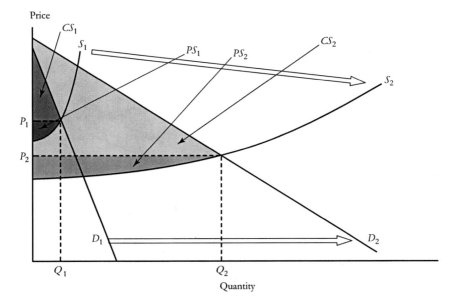

the economy lead to expanded demand (which shifts from D_1 to D_2). The result of these changes is a new equilibrium with much greater volumes bought and sold (Q_1 increases to Q_2), a fall in prices (P_1 falls to P_2) and large increases in consumer and producer welfare (as indicated by expansions in consumer and producer surpluses: CS_1 and PS_1 increase to CS_2 and PS_2, respectively).

What is involved in this expansion in the producer supply curve? The comparative static approach implicit in this analysis cannot, of course, answer this question in any detail; hence it is necessary to dig a little deeper. Figure 1.2 distinguishes between two sets of supply curves describing producer supply (S_1 and S_2) and supply to consumers (S_1' and S_2'), the first resulting from costs of production (up to the farm gate) and the second resulting from the costs and risks both of production and of getting produce purchased and paid for by consumers. The differences between S_1 and S_1' and between S_2 and S_2' therefore represent transaction costs and risks of consumer supply—the costs and risks of doing business—and transport costs in less-developed and more-developed economies, respectively. These differences in the figure suggest that development involves (1) an outward shift and increasing elasticity in the producer supply curves and (2) a reduction in the transport, communication, and transaction costs and risks per unit supply to consumers. Development research and

Figure 1.2   Changes in supply and demand during technical and institutional development

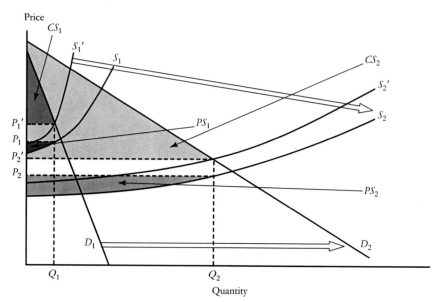

policy analysis therefore needs to be concerned with both of these processes, the relationship between them, and the means of promoting them. "The escape routes out of poverty are often blocked by various kinds of institutional impediments that go far beyond deficiencies in factor endowments" (Bardhan 2001, 139), and removal of these impediments should be a prime focus of policy analysis and action.

Reductions in transport, communication, and transaction costs and risks are achieved by technical change, infrastructural investment, and institutional changes (for example, standardized weights and measures; the structure and enforcement of business laws; and the relationships between producers, consumers, and market-chain intermediaries), as all these efforts can make it easier, cheaper, and less risky for buyers and sellers to communicate and trade with one another over longer distances. Since many transaction costs are fixed per transaction or per transaction relationship, increasing traded volumes can also reduce transaction costs per unit good or service transacted.

The shift in the producer supply curve (S_1 to S_2) arises largely as a result of new production technology and specialization, which together lower basic production costs per unit, particularly at higher volumes of production (because of increased economies of scale). Higher volumes of production and specialization themselves are encouraged by the larger markets that are opened up by cheaper transport and communications; better institutions; and lower costs of capital, capital equipment, and materials. These are also encouraged by lower transport, communication, and transaction costs and risks, this time in producers' purchases as opposed to sales.

Technical and institutional change and infrastructural development are critical drivers in this process, stimulating and also benefiting from factor accumulation, which also provides important positive feedbacks in the development process if institutions provide appropriate investment incentives. Later chapters in the book explore the relationship between technical change and infrastructural development on the one hand and institutional change on the other. For the purposes of this introductory discussion, however, it is important to note (1) the importance of institutional change, (2) the role that institutional change plays in economic development, and (3) the different types of institutional change that may be involved.

This discussion has examined economic growth processes involving the use, production, and consumption of private goods and services. There are, however, further challenges to agricultural development where it depends on natural resources that are not only used by large numbers of small-scale farmers but are also important in providing other goods and services to rural people (for example, water, fish, fuel wood, construction materials, grazing, and wild foods). Such resources have often been particularly important to women and poorer, more disadvantaged groups in rural society. Traditional institutions have managed these as common-property resources and have balanced the costs and benefits of using and maintaining them among different users. The development of institutions that coordinate efficient and equitable management, use, and exchange of these resources poses a different, but related, set of challenges to those discussed above. As with private goods, solutions require an appropriate balance of and integration among infrastructural development and institutional and technical change. These solutions must recognize that effective institutions in developed countries often do not work in Africa, which has lower volumes and densities of economic activity, smaller economic units, poorer infrastructure, and different traditions in common-property resource management.

It should be apparent from this discussion that institutional change potentially plays a significant role in economic development. Its actual importance is an empirical question, which may be conceptualized in terms of the relative contribution of institutional change to its direct and indirect effects in shifting S_1 and S_1' to S_2 and S_2' (see Figure 1.2). Although there are significant difficulties in making such estimates, a study of changes in transaction costs in the U.S. economy suggests that institutional change played a critical role in U.S. economic growth over the period 1900–1970, and by 1970 the transaction sector made up 45 percent of GNP (Wallis and North 1986). Cross-country work on comparative economic growth in the twentieth century also suggests that the quality of institutions, and therefore implicitly institutional change, is a critical factor in economic growth (Rodrik, Subramanian, and Trebbi 2004; Pande and Udry 2005). Acemoglu, Johnson, and Robinson (2001) also provide evidence that the institutional hypothesis explains the differences in prosperity and levels of economic growth among countries. According to this view some societies have "good institutions" that encourage investment in machinery, human capital, and improved technologies; consequently these countries achieve economic prosperity. Good institutions according to Acemoglu, Johnson, and Robinson (2001) are those that (1) enforce property rights for a broad cross-section of society; (2) constrain the actions of elites and other powerful groups; and (3) provide some degree of equal opportunity for broad segments of society. Whether one can be prescriptive and apply normative analysis to institutions, however, remains open to debate.[9]

The literature on the institutional hypothesis largely relies on cross-country analysis and is rather limited in its explanation of the role of institutions. For this reason Pande and Udry (2005) argue for a greater exploitation of synergies between research on specific institutions based on microdata and the big questions posed by the literature on institutions and growth. They recommend two research programs based on microdata to understand how these institutions influence economic activity and how the incentives provided by a given institutional context often vary with the individual's economic and political status. This approach should help in understanding how institutional change comes about in response to changing economic and demographic pressures.

1.3.2   Role of Institutions in Economic Development

The empirical findings presented above are not surprising if the role of institutions in economic activity is considered as being one of facilitating exchange and managing natural resources, again using the simple analysis presented in Section 1.3.1.

The role of effective institutions in facilitation has three components:

1. Institutions facilitate *coordinated* exchange and resource management. Coordination is needed at several levels. At its most basic level, coordinated exchange involves the reliable bringing together of buyers and sellers. If an economy is to include more complex economic activities and support specialization, however, another level of coordination is needed: entrepreneurs must be able to obtain their various requisite resources and to exchange their products with buyers. Access to these transactions must be reliable (in terms of price, quality, and timing) if activities are not to be too risky. This second level of coordination may be termed "complementary coordination," and economic development, with increasingly

technical processes and specialization, generally involves an increasingly complex, dense, and extensive web of complementary relationships.

2. Institutions facilitate *low-cost* exchange and resource management and encourage trust. This set of institutions includes contracts and enforcement mechanisms, commercial norms and rules, and habits and beliefs favoring shared values and the accumulation of human capital.

3. Institutions *provide incentives* for exchange and resource management in that they create profitable opportunities for investment and exchange. In so doing, they encourage entrepreneurs and society more broadly to look for and invest in these opportunities—and in particular to invest in infrastructure development and technical and institutional innovation. This role of institutions in driving (or conversely holding back) development is explored in more detail in Chapter 5.

An alternative way of looking at the role of institutions in agricultural development is in terms of three widely recognized pillars of agricultural development and poverty-reduction policy: expanding access to assets (such as land and capital), development of markets, and investment in basic public goods (such as rural roads and research). These respectively involve the development of institutions concerning property rights, markets, and the management of public good investments (through state organizations or private contractors, for example). There are also downstream and upstream institutional issues, regarding respectively the utilization of investment or policy outputs (for example, newly acquired or redistributed assets, market services, and new knowledge or technology) and allocation of financial and other resources to these (and other) alternative activities and investments. Upstream and public-good institutional issues are addressed in chapters on the role of the state in Part 4; issues in access to assets and market development downstream are more closely aligned with topics covered in Parts 2 and 3.

1.3.3 Types of Institutions and Institutional Change in Economic Development

The final point to note about institutional change and development is that, in considering the many different types of institution and institutional change, it is also helpful to draw a distinction among different types of institution, the institutional environment, and institutional (or contractual) arrangements (Davis and North 1971). Here the term "institutional environment" describes property rights, enforcement mechanisms, human behaviors, and power relations in an economy. It also includes beliefs, such as religions; norms, such as trust and lawfulness; constitutionally determined government structures; and legal systems. These elements of the institutional environment provide the structures in which economic decisions, actions (selling, buying, and negotiating), transactions, and flows (resulting from the aggregation of these transactions) are embedded. Three evolving structures can be identified:

1. formal economic institutions and rules (the political dimension);

2. culture, values, and conventions (that give sense to economic actions, define what is good and great, and supply common knowledge for facing the uncertainty of economic behavior); and

3. social networks (density and forms of the networks, and the position of each economic agent in the network).

Institutional arrangements, as distinct from the institutional environment, describe the sets of rules and structures governing the allocation and exchange of resources through specific transactions. Three broad categories of institutional arrangement can also be distinguished—namely gift exchange, hierarchies, and markets—with many hybrid forms combining elements from each so that the distinctions among these forms are often blurred. These forms of course are found in different elements of the institutional environment described above.

Gift exchange, hierarchies, and markets may be seen as lying on a continuum of institutional arrangements with increasing emphasis on precision in the content of exchange, decreasing emphasis on the relationship between parties in exchange, decreasing interactions between different transactions involving the same parties (over time and across different goods and services), and increasing demands on the wider institutional environment. Gift exchange is based on shared values that stress shared responsibilities in social groups with deliberately imprecise terms of mutual obligations that are heavily reliant on investment in social values and social capital. Hierarchies use organizational command and control to allocate resources. Hierarchies are the basis for operations by governments, parastatal agencies, most NGOs, and anything other than the smallest private firms.

In present-day economies, hierarchies coexist with markets and gift exchange and indeed use markets and (to a lesser extent) gift exchange to transact with one another and with final consumers and to organize their own activities and resources.[10] The boundaries between hierarchy and market are fluid and restless, for example when firms merge, hierarchy takes over from market allocation but, in contrast, when successful business start-ups compete with existing players, ground is regained for the market.

Market transactions usually have more precise (in terms of quantity, quality, location, and time) terms of exhange than do gift transactions. Market transactions facilitate competition (spurring gains in quality and production efficiency) by requiring money (which is not only an essential condition for wider exchange but also the critical medium for savings, loans, and investment) and by being voluntary (in the sense that both sides have to expect to gain from each transaction).

This classification of institutions is important in understanding the processes of institutional change in economic development. Three important and related propositions that are developed further in later chapters can be made:

1. The efficiency and effectiveness of particular institutional arrangements vary according to interactions between the specific characteristics of the transaction on the one hand and the institutional environment on the other (as elaborated in Chapter 4).

2. Economic development generally involves declining reliance on gift exchange and increasing reliance on hierarchies. The efficiency and effectiveness of competitive markets, as one particular type of institutional arrangement, varies in comparison to other types of institutional arrangement (for example, hybrids between gift exchange, hierarchy, and market arrangements) depending on the characteristics of different transactions and of the institutional environment, and on the interests and resources of the transacting parties (see the case studies in Chapters 6–12). The appropriateness of competitive markets is therefore conditional on the specific conditions under which they must operate, and the development of such markets cannot be assumed to be a generally applicable short- or medium-term policy goal. The same holds for developed countries, where a substantial proportion of transactions are not conducted in competitive markets but within firms and through long-term relationships between firms (see, for example, Williamson 1991; Coase 1992; Hall and Soskice 2001). Globally the proportion and number of transactions occurring within firms is growing, as two-thirds of world trade is either within transnational corporations or associated with them (United Nations 1999; Yusuf 2001).

3. Economic development depends on change in both the institutional environment and institutional arrangements. These are endogenous development processes and must co-evolve with each other, with technical and infrastructural change, and with wider social and economic change (see Chapter 3). Understanding this co-evolution is critical to the design and implementation of agricultural development policy.

These points are discussed and their implications for policy developed further as a major theme running through the book. They are stressed here as they are relevant to a discussion about the particular difficulties facing agricultural development in poor rural areas in Africa, the successes and failures of different policy approaches, and the challenges facing agricultural policy analysis in this region.

1.4   Analytical Challenges

Conventional theory and wider empirical evidence suggest good reasons for giving markets a prominent role in Africa's agricultural development. By linking production and consumption sectors, creating jobs, and connecting domestic and international sources of supply and demand, efficient agricultural markets can be a means to achieving several social ends: efficient economic growth, equitable distributions of income, widespread nutritional well-being, and increased food security.

However, the development and operation of agricultural markets in poor rural economies is fraught with difficulties. Where dramatic poverty-reducing growth in poor rural economies has been achieved outside Africa, it has not generally been in the context of liberalized markets or liberalized market development: there is in fact little empirical evidence of the benefits of liberalized market development in stimulating poverty-reducing growth in such economies. There are good institutional reasons for this disconnect. There are also wider concerns about rural markets that have not been discussed here: markets do not always function in the best interests of a broad cross-section of society, especially where communication and transportation facilities are poor, markets are highly segmented, access is restricted to particular groups, and highly unequal financial bargaining power exists in the relationship between seller and buyer.

The realities of institutions and political economy as well as the nature of agricultural production in Africa therefore make market development very difficult. Innovative private-sector solutions can overcome some but not all problems. Although these observations suggest that market development requires a proactive state role, such a role carries its own difficulties. As outlined earlier, the record of state intervention in African agriculture is not generally good, and weaknesses in state capacity present problems for both market- and state-led development.

The stakes in resolving these dilemmas are high. Some African governments, frustrated by the meager returns from painful agricultural market liberalization, are reinstating key elements of state intervention in agricultural markets. Marketing boards are being resuscitated, top-down cooperatives resurrected, and agricultural finance corporations granting cheap credit revived. It is important that the outcomes of such interventions will not repeat those of the earlier era of state-led development: widespread failure at great cost to public treasuries and damage to hard-won confidence in the private sector in agriculture policy.

A new approach is therefore needed to agricultural development policy that goes beyond what has become an unhelpful, increasingly artificial, and obsolete but persistent divide between state- and market-led approaches to development. A pragmatic and inclusive approach is needed that may be described as "developmental coordination" (Dorward, Kydd, and Poulton 2005a). The profession of agricultural development economics bears a heavy responsibility in this effort. Omamo (2003) suggests that the failure of agricultural development policies based on market liberalization represents a fundamental failure of the policy research community—in particular, the agricultural economics profession. He argues that agricultural economists have failed to engage with Africa's agricultural problems outside abstract conceptualizations and have not come to grips with the real problems facing agricultural policymakers: how to assess the operational feasibility of alternative policy options and how to promote the best alternatives. He therefore suggests a different approach to agricultural policy research, focusing more on "how" and less on "what" and "why" questions, and emphasizing action research in case studies of initiatives involving promising institutional innovations.

The widespread adoption of such an approach, however, requires that agricultural policy analysts acquire broader theoretical understanding and practical skills that include both neoclassical and institutional theories that can draw lessons from the experiences of both state- and market-led development policies. In the remainder of this book we provide the foundations for such an approach. The following chapters provide first an introduction to the economics of institutional analysis, building on more familiar neoclassical foundations, and then develop a general framework for the analysis of institutions and institutional issues in development. Subsequent chapters set out the theoretical underpinnings and case studies with regard to institutional aspects of problems of exchange, natural resource management, and state interventions in agricultural development.

Notes

1. There are, however, some signs of recent improved performance of African agriculture (see, for example, World Bank 2007).

2. See Poulton et al. (2004) and Chapter 5 for further discussion of these issues.

3. For this reason cassava performs well relative to other staples in Africa. It is also the reason West Africa outperforms Southern and East Africa in overall agricultural production. West Africa's outperformance of the other two regions in cereals may also be due in part to West Africa's greater reliance on roots and tubers, which reduces cereal price instability and allows cereals to be treated more like a cash crop.

4. These two phases of thinking, about the role and nature of the state and markets in development, of course interact with other progressions—concerning the goals of development, the relative importance of different sectors of the economy, the nature of growth needed for development, and the like.

5. The Berg report (World Bank 1981), for example, marked a watershed in the development of the Washington consensus on economic policies in Africa.

6. Poverty traps also arise for a variety of other reasons, associated with, for example, lack of assets, transaction costs, or lack of infrastructure (see, for example, Barrett 2008).

7. Ironically, support for such institutional innovations as contract farming, group approaches, and microfinance sits uneasily with more general support for competitive markets, as these innovations rely on nonmarket and/or hybrid exchange and coordination systems (involving hierarchy and gift exchange). Although justified by the special problems facing poor and remote producers, these innovations implicitly raise questions about the appropriateness and performance of competitive market exchange in agricultural supply chains in poor rural areas and indeed in developed economies where farmers also sometimes engage in contract farming and use hierarchies to access markets.

8. Such thinking underlies the emergence in the early 2000s of the effort to make markets work for the poor as a way forward out of the impasse of the 1990s, emphasizing the need for explicit establishment and development of markets that the poor can access and benefit from. However this idea has evolved to include an increasing emphasis on the institutional issues that are the focus of this book (see http://www.dfid.gov.uk/news/files/trade_news/adb-workshop.asp).

9. However, Schmid (2005) argues against both the use of econometric studies to investigate the influence of institutions and the primacy of simplistic property rights enforcement. Schmid suggests that (1) institutions affect the structure of relations in production functions and cannot be simply inserted into them and (2) growth may be related to selective confiscation of property rights. This second point is implicit in the juxtaposition by Acemoglu, Johnson, and Robinson (2001) of property rights enforcement for a broad cross-section of society with (sometimes conflicting) constraints on the actions of some members of society and the provision of some degree of equal opportunity in society. Readers are encouraged to peruse the series of articles in the June 2003 issue of *Finance & Development*, which provide a perspective on the role of institutions in economic growth. These articles are nontechnical summaries of the various studies referenced here.

10. Gift exchange includes firms' investments to establish reputation with consumers and to cultivate relations with key personnel in other firms (for example, corporate hospitality and other elements of social interaction in business relationships). It can serve as the basis for sharing responsibilities, tasks, resources, and rewards by teams in a hierarchy.

References

Acemoglu, D., S. Johnson, and J. A. Robinson. 2001. Colonial origins of comparative development: An empirical investigation. *American Economic Review* 91 (9): 1369–1401.

Africa Commission. 2005. *Our common interest: Report of the Commission for Africa*. London: Africa Commission.

Ashley, C., and S. Maxwell. 2001. Rethinking rural development. *Development Policy Review* 19 (4): 395–425.

Bardhan, P. K. 2001. Institutions, reforms and agricultural performance. In *Current and emerging issues for economic analysis and policy research*, ed. K. G. Stamoulis. Rome: Economic and Social Department, Food and Agriculture Organization of the United Nations.

Barrett, C. B. 2008. Smallholder market participation: Concepts and evidence from Eastern and Southern Africa. *Food Policy* 33 (4): 299–317.

Binswanger, H., and M. Rosenzweig. 1986. Behavioural and material determinants of production relations in agriculture. *Journal of Development Studies* 22: 503–539.

Carr, S. 2001. Changes in African smallholder agriculture in the twentieth century and the challenges of the twenty first. *Africa Crop Science Journal* 9 (1): 331–338.

Coase, R. H. 1992. The institutional structure of production. *American Economic Review* 82 (4): 713–719.

Crawford, E., T. S. Jayne, and V. A. Kelly. 2005. *Alternative approaches for promoting fertiliser use in Africa with particular reference to the role of fertiliser subsidies*. East Lansing: Michigan State University.

Crawford, E., V. Kelly, T. S. Jayne, and J. Howard. 2003. Input use and market development in Sub-Saharan Africa: An overview. *Food Policy* 28 (4): 277–292.

Davis, L. E., and D. C. North. 1971. *Institutional change and American economic growth*. Cambridge: Cambridge University Press.

De Soto, H. 2000. *The mystery of capital: Why capitalism triumphs in the West and fails everywhere else*. New York: Basic Books.

Diao, X., P. Dorosh, and S. Rahman. 2003. *Market opportunities for African agriculture: An examination of demand-side constraints on agricultural growth*. Development Strategy and Governance Division Discussion Paper 1. Washington, D.C.: International Food Policy Research Institute. Available at http://www.ifpri.org/divs/dsgd/dp/papers/dsgdp01.pdf.

Dorward, A. R., and J. Kydd. 2004. The Malawi 2002 food crisis: The rural development challenge. *Journal of Modern Africa Studies* 42 (3): 343–361.

Dorward, A. R., J. Kydd, and C. Poulton. 2005a. Coordination risk and cost impacts on economic development in poor rural areas. Paper presented at the Agricultural Economics Society Conference, Nottingham, U.K., April.

————. 2005b. Beyond liberalisation: "Developmental coordination" policies for African smallholder agriculture. *IDS Bulletin* 36 (2): 80–85.

Dorward, A. R., J. G. Kydd, J. A. Morrison, and I. Urey. 2004b. A policy agenda for pro-poor agricultural growth. *World Development* 32: 73–89.

Eicher, C. K., and B. Kupfuma. 1998. Zimbabwe's maize revolution: Insights for closing Africa's food gap. In *International agricultural development*, ed. C. K. Eicher and J. Staatz. Baltimore: Johns Hopkins University Press.

Ellis, F. 2005. Small farms, livelihood diversification and rural–urban transitions: Strategic issues in Sub-Saharan Africa. In *The future of small farms: Proceedings of a research workshop, Wye, U.K., June 26–29th 2005.* Washington, D.C.: International Food Policy Research Institute. Available at http://www.ifpri.org/events/seminars/2005/smallfarms/sfproc.asp.

Fafchamps, M. 2004. *Market institutions and Sub-Saharan Africa: Theory and evidence.* Cambridge, Mass., U.S.A.: MIT Press.

Gabre-Madhin, E. Z., and S. Haggblade. 2003. *Successes in African agriculture: Results of an expert survey.* Markets and Structural Studies Division Discussion Paper 53. Washington, D.C., International Food Policy Research Institute.

Haber, S., D. C. North, and B. R. Weingast. 2003. If economists are so smart, why is Africa so poor? *Hoover Digest* 4. Available at http://www.hoover.org/publications/digest/3050836.html. Accessed April 2009.

Hall, P. A., and D. Soskice, eds. 2001. *Varieties of capitalism: The institutional foundations of comparative advantage.* Oxford: Oxford University Press.

Hazell, P. B. R. 2005. The role of agriculture and small farms in economic development. Paper presented at the Conference on the Future of Small Farms, Wye, U.K., June.

Heisey, P. W., and M. Smale. 1995. *Maize technology in Malawi: A Green Revolution in the making?* Research Report 4. Mexico City: International Maize and Wheat Improvement Centre.

Imperial College, Wadonda Consult, Michigan State University, and Overseas Development Institute. 2007. *Evaluation of the 2006/7 Agricultural Input Supply Programme, Malawi: Interim report.* London: Imperial College.

Jayne, T. S., and S. Jones. 1997. Food marketing and pricing policy in Eastern and Southern Africa: A survey. *World Development* 25: 1505–1527.

Jayne, T. S., B. Zulu, and J. Nijhoff. 2006. Stabilizing food markets in Eastern and Southern Africa. *Food Policy* 31 (4): 328–341.

Jayne, T. S., J. Govereh, A. Mwanaumo, A. Chapoto, and J. K. Nyoro. 2002. False promise or false premise? The experience of food and input market reform in Eastern and Southern Africa. *World Development* 30: 1967–1985.

Kherallah, M., C. L. Delgado , E. Z. Gabre-Madhin, N. Minot, and M. Johnson. 2000. *The road half-travelled: Agricultural market reform in Sub-Saharan Africa.* Food Policy Report 10. Washington, D.C.: International Food Policy Research Institute.

Marenya, P., W. Oluoch-Kosura, F. Place, and C. Barrett. 2003. *Education, nonfarm income and farm investment in land-scarce western Kenya.* Broadening Access and Strengthening Input Market Systems Brief 14. Madison: University of Wisconsin.

Maxwell, S., and R. Heber-Percy 2001. New trends in development thinking and implications for agriculture. In *Food agriculture and rural development: Current and emerging issues for economic analysis and policy research,* ed. K. Stamoulis. Rome: Food and Agriculture Organization of the United Nations.

Morris, M., V. Kelly, R. Kopicki, and D. Byerlee 2007. *Promoting increased fertilizer use in Africa.* Washington, D.C.: World Bank.

Omamo, S. W. 2003. Policy research on African agriculture: Trends, gaps, and challenges. ISNAR Research Report 21. The Hague: International Service for National Agricultural Research.

Omamo, S. W., X. Diao, S. Wood, J. Chamberlin, L. You, S. Benin, U. Wood-Sichra, and A. Tatwangire. 2006. Strategic priorities for agricultural development in eastern and central Africa. Research Report 150. Washington, D.C.: International Food Policy Research Institute.

Pande, R., and C. R. Udry. 2005. *Institutions and development: A view from below.* Economic Growth Center Discussion Paper 928. New Haven, Conn., U.S.A.: Yale University.

Peacock, C., A. Jowett, A. R. Dorward, C. Poulton, and I. Urey. 2004. Reaching the poor: A call to action. Investment in smallholder agriculture in Sub-Saharan Africa. Unpublished report, FARM-Africa, London.

Poulton, C., and J. Ndufa 2005. *Linking soil fertility and improved cropping strategies to development interventions: Final technical report Annex A.* Wye, U.K.: Department for International Development Natural Resources Systems Programme, Imperial College, and Kenya Forestry Research Institute.

Poulton, C., A. R. Dorward, and J. Kydd. 2005. The future of small farms: New directions for services, institutions and intermediation. Paper presented at The Future of Small Farms Workshop, Imperial College, Wye, U.K., June.

Poulton, C., J. Kydd, and A. R. Dorward. 2004. Overcoming market constraints to pro-poor agricultural growth in Sub-Saharan Africa. Paper prepared for the Africa Commission, Imperial College, Wye, U.K., November.

Poulton, C., P. Gibbon, B. Hanyani-Mlambo, J. Kydd, M. Nylandset Larsen, W. Maro, A. Osario, D. Tschirley, and B. Zulu. 2004. Competition and coordination in liberalized African cotton market systems. *World Development* 32: 519–536.

Poulton, C., J. Kydd, S. Wiggins, and A. R. Dorward. 2005. State intervention for food price stabilisation in Africa: Can it work? Paper presented at the World Bank–Department for International Development workshop Managing Food Price Risks and Instability, Washington, D.C., February 28–March 1.

Reardon, T. 1998. African agriculture: Productivity and sustainability issues. In *International agricultural development,* ed. C. K. Eicher and J. Staatz. Baltimore: Johns Hopkins University Press.

Rodrik, D., A. Subramanian, and F. Trebbi. 2004. Institutions rule: The primacy of institutions over geography and integration in economic development. *Journal of Economic Growth* 9: 131–165.

Schmid, A. A. 2005. An institutional economics perspective on economic growth. Paper presented at the Seventh International Workshop on Institutional Economics, University of Hertfordshire, Hertfordshire, U.K., June. Available at http://www.msu.edu/user/schmid/institutional%20perspective.htm.

Shepherd, A., and S. Farolfi. 1999. *Export crop liberalization in Africa: A review.* Rome: Food and Agriculture Organization of the United Nations.

Smale, M., and T. S. Jayne. 2003. *Maize in eastern and southern Africa: "Seeds" of success in retrospect.* Environment and Production Technology Paper Division Discussion Paper 97. Washington, D.C.: International Food Policy Research Institute.

Tiffen, M. 2003. Transition in Sub-Saharan Africa: Agriculture, urbanization and income growth. *World Development* 31: 1343–1366.

Tiffen, M., M. Mortimore, and F. Gichuki. 1994. *More people less erosion: Environmental recovery in Kenya.* Chichester, U.K.: John Wiley and Sons.

Turner, B. L. I., G. Hyden, and R. W. Kates, eds. 1993. *Population growth and agricultural change in Africa.* Gainesville, Fla., U.S.A.: University of Florida Press.

United Nations. 1999. *World investment report.* New York.

UN Millennium Project. 2005a. *Halving hunger: It can be done.* New York: UN Task Force on Hunger.

———. 2005b. *Investing in development: A practical plan to achieve the Millennium Development Goals.* New York.

Wallis, J. J., and D. C. North. 1986. Measuring the transaction sector in the American economy. In *Long-term factors in American economic growth,* ed. S. L. Engerman and R. E. Gallmann. Chicago: University of Chicago Press.

Wiggins, S. 1995. Change in African farming systems between the mid-1970s and the mid-1980s. *Journal of International Development* 7 (6): 807–848.

Williamson, O. E. 1991. Comparative economic organisation: The analysis of discrete structural alternatives. *Administrative Science Quarterly* 36: 269–296.

World Bank. 1981. *Accelerated development in Sub-Saharan Africa: An agenda for action.* Washington, D.C.

———. 2000. *Can Africa claim the 21st century?* Washington, D.C.: World Bank, African Development Bank, and United Nations Economic Commission for Africa.

———. 2002. *Institutions for markets. World development report 2001/2002.* Washington, D.C.

———. 2003. *Sustainable development in a dynamic world: Transforming institutions, growth, and quality of life. World development report 2003.* Washington, D.C.

———. 2007. *World development report 2008: Agriculture for development.* Washington, D.C.

Yusuf, S. 2001. *Globalisation and the challenge for developing countries.* Washington, D.C.: World Bank.

Chapter 2

Introduction to the
Economics of Institutions

Johann F. Kirsten, A. S. Mohammad Karaan,
and Andrew R. Dorward

D ifferent schools of economic theory have been developed over the years to interpret economic phenomena, behaviors, and outcomes. It is generally acknowledged that these phenomena, behaviors, and outcomes (decisions, transactions, and welfare impacts) are shaped by (1) formal economic institutions and rules; (2) culture, values, and conventions; and (3) social networks.

Works associated with the various schools of theory place differing emphases on these contextual variables and make different assumptions about their relative importance and the degree to which they are endogenous or exogenous to the problems being examined. Thus, for example, the neoclassical tradition places less emphasis on institutions, taking them largely as given, but focuses on the analysis of efficiency, often abstracting from particular institutional contexts. In contrast, approaches using New Institutional Economics (NIE) explore institutional structures at different levels and examine efficiency and welfare with respect to these structures. Network (and economic) sociology emphasizes assessment of the influence of relational dimensions but are more limited in their analysis of economic efficiency and formal economic institutions.

The focus of this book is on understanding economic institutions to facilitate institutional development that will lead to more efficient economic outcomes in the agricultural sectors of poor rural economies. To this end we use a broad set of approaches that fall in the category of NIE. NIE draws on the theoretical and empirical

We are indebted to Eleni Gabre-Madhin, Mike Lyne, Ruth Meinzen-Dick, Andrew Mude, and Esther Mwangi for providing useful inputs to this chapter.

tools of neoclassical economics in analyses of both the evolution of institutions and their effects on economic behavior and outcomes in different circumstances. NIE also draws on a variety of schools of thought in other social sciences; consequently NIE is not a well-defined school of thought but rather a loose collection of related research interests and methodologies (Heltberg 2002). The main purpose of this chapter is to familiarize the reader with insights from different schools of thought associated with NIE.

Therefore we begin by showing how core NIE approaches have developed by removing some key assumptions that underlie the basic neoclassical model in Section 2.3. Applying and developing neoclassical analysis to address real-life situations where perfectly competitive conditions do not apply has been the dominant project of neoclassical economics from the time of its inception. However the particular focus and contribution of NIE approaches have been their emphasis on (1) the problems that economic actors face as a result of imperfect information in transactions and (2) the role of institutions in addressing (or exacerbating) such problems.

Following this exploration of the neoclassical roots of NIE and of different NIE approaches, Section 2.2 deals with questions about the definition and nature of institutions, the functions of different types of institutions in economic activity, the determinants of their effectiveness in performing these functions for different actors and stakeholders, and the processes of institutional change. The chapter concludes with a brief discussion of the relevance of some of these issues to agricultural development economics.

2.1   Adding Institutions to Neoclassical Economics

Assumptions are important tools in scientific enquiry, because they allow analysts to focus on one set of issues at a time. Introductory physics courses often begin with assuming a frictionless plane; but during the course the assumption is lifted to deal with the effects of friction in reality. Similarly, training in neoclassical economics starts with the development of basic theorems of individual behavior and market interactions under controlled conditions in a virtual laboratory provided by the assumptions of perfect competition. A critical feature of the successful development and application of neoclassical economics is therefore an understanding of its basic assumptions and the ability to extend its analysis to situations in which particular assumptions, or sets of assumptions, do not hold.

Core assumptions of the perfect competition model are:

- Profit and utility maximization: These are the dominant objectives motivating producers and consumers, respectively (or these actors behave as though this is the case).

- Perfect information: Economic actors (individuals, households, firms, or government) have complete information about all aspects of business profits and consumption utility, including market opportunities, available technology, costs of production under alternative production arrangements, prices, natural resources, quality of goods produced, and (critically) the intentions of fellow actors.

- Homogenous products: Goods that are bought and sold in a given market are identical in all respects, including quality.

- Ease of entry and exit: Firms can enter and withdraw from all markets without cost. There are no initial investment costs and no costs associated with shutting down. The assumption of costless entry and exit provides the necessary discipline to discourage existing firms in a market from colluding to raise the prices of goods sold, as this action would trigger new competition to undercut them.

- Large numbers of firms and buyers: No buyer or seller is large enough to influence the market price of the good or services being transacted—all economic agents are price takers.

- No economies of scale or production externalities: This assumption ensures that all production takes place to equate (private and social) marginal cost and marginal benefit with no externalities (including environmental externalities). It also means that large producers do not enjoy any competitive advantage over smaller firms.

- Complete set of markets: Perfect markets exist for all commodities, including goods to be exchanged in the future and insurance against all risks. Completeness also implies well-defined and well-protected private property rights.

Taken together, these assumptions generate a world of market-clearing equilibria with costless adjustments to shocks; therefore, no risk of loss attached to current investment decisions. Goods are homogenous and exchange is anonymous, based purely on the price being charged for different goods and taking place in spot markets. In such a world there is no particular role for organizations and management (Dorward, Kydd, and Poulton 1998). But this scenario is not the real world in which most economic activity takes place.

The major thrust of neoclassical economics has always been the extension of its analysis to address conditions in which some of these assumptions do not hold. Thus, for example, there are extensive literatures, both within and beyond the agricultural sector, on nonprofit objectives of producers and the effects of corporate governance on firms' objectives; consumer behavior; price and production risk and uncertainty; product differentiation and branding; monopoly, oligopoly, and other market structures; public goods, externalities, and related market failures; and household economics.

The specific contribution of NIE arises from its recognition that (1) economic actors face a particular problem as a result of imperfect information about the behavior of other actors in transactions and (2) institutions play an important role in addressing these problems (with varying benefits for different actors in a transaction and for wider participants in an economy; North 1994, 1995). This recognition demands explicit attention to the ways that actors and societies address problems arising from imperfect information in transactions. However it also allows NIE to retain the methodological and analytical foundations of neoclassical economics in its consideration of self-seeking individuals who attempt to maximize an objective function subject to constraints.

The NIE focus on imperfect transaction information and its analysis of associated institutional issues (related to nonstandard behavior of actors, lack of complete markets or well-defined property rights, and high information costs) is particularly relevant to the challenges to agricultural development in poor rural economies in Africa as discussed in Chapter 1. In the rest of this section we therefore examine the implications of relaxing assumptions of perfect transactional information. What are the economic, behavioral, and system implications of removing assumptions of perfect transactional information, particularly in the context of high information costs and weak contract enforcement? Several closely related strands of economic literature address these issues: the economics of imperfect information, transaction-costs economics, moral hazard and agency theory, property rights, and incomplete-contracts theory. These are all important developments of the standard economic tools and are sometimes classified as part of the NIE body of thought. The classification of these literatures under NIE or as part of the expansion of the standard theory is however not critical. It is merely important to recognize that these are important schools of thought in economics and can be useful in addressing key developmental problems.

2.1.1 The Economics of Imperfect Information

The literature on the economics of information includes seminal papers by Akerlof (1970), Stigler (1961, 1967), and Stiglitz and associates (Stigliz 1985a,b; Greenwald and Stiglitz 1986; Arnott, Greenwald, and Stiglitz 1993). The main argument is that lack of perfect and freely available information leads to risk and uncertainty in transactions. Information is incomplete and asymmetrical in that sellers have more information than do buyers about the availability and characteristics of the supply of products that they are offering for sale, while buyers have more information than sellers about the nature of their demand and their ability and intentions to pay for products that they purchase. Searching for and obtaining information about products and sellers and about demand and buyers is then necessary for buyers and sellers, respectively, to reduce the risks of transaction failure. However, searching and obtaining information is not costless: it is an important source of transaction costs.

The dilemma this asymmetry poses for buyers is well illustrated in Akerlof's (1970) paper on the secondhand car market in the United States (Box 2.1). Akerlof explains how quality guarantees (labels, certificates), reputation, and trust are useful tools to ensure the production of quality goods and project information about them. His analysis also implies that government intervention to increase information flow can make all parties better off.

These relatively simple observations regarding imperfect transactional information have wide-ranging consequences. First, recognition that imperfect information

---

Box 2.1 Adverse selection and moral hazard

Adverse selection describes a situation in which buyers have more information than sellers prior to purchase. It is especially relevant in the insurance market (and the credit market), where people who take out insurance are more likely to file claims than the individuals used by the insurer to set their rates. The sellers of insurance thus face the risk of selecting buyers with above-average probabilities of making claims. The seller therefore faces information costs in discerning and discriminating between potential good and bad clients.

Akerlof (1970) developed the concept of adverse selection in the context of the "market for lemons." People buying used cars do not know whether the cars are "lemons" (bad cars) or "cherries" (good cars), so they are willing to pay a price that lies between the price for lemons and cherries, a willingness based on the probability that a given car is a lemon or a cherry. Sellers respond by offering for sale fewer good cars because the price is too low, but they offer more bad cars, because they get a better price for them. After a while the buyers recognize this trend and no longer want to pay the old price for the used car. Thus prices will drop, reinforcing the tendency for fewer cherries and more lemons being offered for sale.

Moral hazard refers to the risk that results from a change in conduct caused by an expectation of compensation for a negative outcome. A contract can itself change the behavior of one party to that contract to the detriment of the other party. Crop insurance, for example, gives farmers an incentive not to invest in the prevention of crop failure but rather to rely on cash income from the insurance proceeds of the failed crop.

leads to substantial transaction costs in most forms of economic activity has profound implications for welfare economics and hence economic development and management policy: it is exceptional to find markets that approximate the conditions necessary for efficiency (Stiglitz and Grossman 1980). Transaction costs impede exchange and hence impede competitive markets' ability to reach efficient equilibria even for private goods not normally considered prone to market failure.[1] This complication leads to multiple possible equilibria in an economy, dependent on institutional arrangements governing different markets in the economy. Modification of institutions to allow more efficient resource allocation and exchange then becomes an important subject of policy, one that has long been recognized implicitly in policy practice but has not generally been given sufficient attention by conventional economic policy analysis.

Second, Akerlof's analysis provides insights into the extent and importance of the difficulties posed by imperfect transactional information in different situations. These difficulties will vary with

- the nature of the product or service being exchanged;

- the institutions governing the transaction;

- the nature and extent of investments in the transaction;

- the characteristics of transacting parties (for example, their power, wealth, risk aversion, and access to information); and

- the characteristics of the economy, sector, and society of the transacting parties.

Consideration of these issues then gives rise to different but closely related approaches to analyzing institutional issues in transactions. We consider these in turn, beginning with moral hazard and agency theory and then moving on to consider transaction-cost economics, property rights, and incomplete-contracts theory.

2.1.2 Moral Hazard and Agency

The literature on the economics of information initially found an important application to two problems observed in the insurance industry: adverse selection and moral hazard (Akerlof 1970). In addition Stiglitz illustrated the role of imperfect information, adverse selection, and moral hazard on the performance of credit and labor markets, and the behavior of firms.

Agency theory (or principal-agent theory), as developed by Jensen and Meckling (1976), Fama (1980), and Fama and Jensen (1983), is a closely related field that is concerned with the effects of institutions on reducing transaction risks (Box 2.2) and costs arising from imperfect transactional information. Agency theory studies the design of ex ante incentive-compatible mechanisms to reduce agency costs in the face of potential moral hazard by agents: it addresses the question of how a principal (for example, an owner of capital or manager of labor) can structure contracts, incentives, and sanctions to encourage, at low cost, agents (users of capital, or laborers) to behave in ways that will lead to the achievement of the principal's goals.

Agency costs are defined by Jensen and Meckling (1976, 308) as the sum of "(1) the monitoring expenditures of the principal, (2) the bonding expenditures by the agent and (3) the residual loss." The residual loss represents the potential gains from trade not realized because principals cannot provide perfect incentives for agents when the agents' actions are unobservable. There are close parallels between agency costs and transaction costs.

The problem of motivating one party to act on behalf of another is known as the principal-agent problem. It arises when a principal compensates an agent for performing certain acts that are useful to the principal and costly to the agent and there

---

Box 2.2 Transaction costs versus transaction risks

Dorward (2001) and Dorward, Kydd, and Poulton (2005a) consider transaction costs and transaction risks together, as actors are presumed to invest in transaction costs to reduce transaction risks. Thus transaction costs refer to the costs originating from the various actions taken to reduce the risk of transaction failure. Despite these actions (or costs), actors are not able to eliminate transaction risks, so costs are incurred to provide an optimal trade-off where the marginal transaction costs are equal to the marginal utility of risk reduction.

Transaction costs therefore involve (1) the establishment and enforcement of exclusive property rights and/or (2) the definition and enforcement of the attributes of the good or service being exchanged. However, transaction risks represent the losses incurred because of failure to (1) enforce exclusive property rights, (2) enforce required attributes, or (3) complete the transaction.

Problems of enforcing exclusive property rights arise with public goods and externalities. Problems of enforcing the attributes of goods or services or failure to complete the transaction arise when there are difficulties in obtaining information about goods, services, and the actors involved in the exchange (commitment problems) or difficulties relating to enforcing the agreements (opportunism) (Dorward, Kydd, and Poulton 2005a,b).

are elements of the performance that are costly to observe. This is the case to some extent for all contracts, given that we live in a world of information asymmetry, uncertainty, and risk. Principals do not know enough about whether (or to what extent) a contract is being or has been satisfied. The solution to this information problem, closely related to the moral hazard problem, is to ensure (as far as possible) the provision of appropriate incentives so that agents act in the way principals wish them to. It involves changing the institutional arrangement (rules of the game) so that the choices that the principal predicts the agent will make coincide with the choices the principal desires.

A large body of literature in this field is about employment contracts, in which it is shown that the challenge is to structure incentives by optimally connecting the information available about employee performance and the compensation for that performance. The structural details of individual contracts vary widely, however, because of differences in (1) the quantity and quality of information available about the performance of individual employees, (2) the ability of employees to bear risk, and (3) the ability of employees to manipulate evaluation methods.[2]

Milgrom and Roberts (1992) identify four basic principles of contract design:

1. The informativeness principle: Holmstrom (1979) states that any measure of performance that (on the margin) reveals information about the effort level chosen by the agent should be included in the compensation contract.

2. The incentive-intensity principle: An optimal intensity of effort is devoted to solving the principal-agent problem, so it will to some extent always be "not fully resolved," and thus principal-agent issues are always subject to further experiment and contest in the public and private sectors.

3. The monitoring intensity principle: Situations in which the optimal intensity of incentives is high correspond to those in which the optimal level of monitoring is also high.

4. The equal-compensation principle: Activities equally valued by the employer should be equally valuable (in terms of compensation, including such nonfinancial aspects as pleasantness) to the employee. This principle relates to the problem that employees may be engaged in several activities, and if some of these are not monitored or are monitored less heavily, they will be neglected, as activities with higher marginal returns to the employee are favored. Targeting certain measurable variables may cause others to suffer. For example, if agricultural extension workers are rewarded by the volume of input packages sold to farmers or the number of loans

granted to farmers, they may de-emphasize equally or more important aspects of their role that were not explicitly targeted in their performance contract.

In the agency literature, the firm itself is not the subject of attention. According to Alchian and Demsetz (1972) and Jensen and Meckling (1976), "firm" is simply a convenient label for the collection of contracts between owners and managers, managers and employees, and the firm and its customers and suppliers.

These issues are particularly important in agriculture (especially in the risk-prone, extensive agricultural systems common in many parts of Africa), as the dispersed nature of agriculture and its exposure to multiple sources of risk and uncertainty frequently make the monitoring of inputs and their relationship to outputs problematic. As a result imperfect information and agency theory have been used to explain the emergence of key agrarian institutions, which have been analyzed as substitutes for missing credit or insurance markets in an environment of pervasive risk, information asymmetry, and high transaction costs (Binswanger and Rosenzweig 1986; Bardhan 1989). These institutions include sharecropping and other forms of interlocked contracts among land, labor, credit, inputs, and outputs. Bardhan (1989), for example, argues that these agrarian institutions may serve a real economic function under a set of informational constraints and missing markets. Such institutions as sharecropping, whose persistence was formerly considered a major development puzzle, can then be seen as an institutional response to the absence of markets for risk insurance (Stiglitz 1989). This strand of thinking has led to a large literature on sharecropping (for example, Stiglitz 1974; Eswaran and Kotwal 1985). Other applications of such analysis include interlinked contracts in credit and land lease (Braverman and Stiglitz 1982); labor hiring, output sales, and institutions for hedging risk (Zusman 1976; Newberry 1977); interlocking credit, input, and produce transactions (Dorward, Kydd, and Poulton 1998); and cooperative institutions in production and credit (Putterman 1980). Further insights into such institutions can be gained from a more explicit examination of transaction costs.

2.1.3 Transaction-Cost Economics

The general hypothesis of transaction-cost economics (TCE) is that institutions are transaction-cost–reducing arrangements that may change and evolve with changes in the nature and sources of transaction costs. Coase (1937) pioneered this work in his article "The Nature of the Firm," in which he argued that market exchange is not costless. Coase underlined the important role of transaction costs in the organization of firms and other contracts. He explained that firms emerge to economize on the transaction costs of market exchange and that the boundary of a firm or the extent of vertical integration depends on the magnitude of these transaction costs.

Coase was not the first to use the term "transaction costs" (the term is attributed to Arrow) but expanded on this concept in his paper "The Problem of Social Cost" (Coase 1960). His insight that the costs of reaching, modifying, and implementing agreements restrain the potential gains from trade provided the foundation for analyzing organizations and governance in terms of transaction cost. Thus, in a world of transaction costs, the relative merits of different organizational forms depend on a comparison of the costs of transacting under each (Masten 1996). Arrow (1969, 68) defined transaction costs as the "costs of running the economic system." These transaction costs are distinguished as ex ante and ex post—the first includes those of drafting, negotiating, and monitoring an agreement, whereas the second includes the costs of maladaption, haggling, setup, and running associated with governance and the bonding costs of securing commitment (Williamson 1985). Moreover, unlike market price, transaction costs are unique to each agent or firm and are related to the process of exchange itself.

Eggertson (1990, 15) provides perhaps one of the more comprehensive discussions on the reasons for the existence of transaction costs, also emphasizing that information costs and transaction costs are not identical:

> When information is costly various activities related to the exchange of property rights between individuals give rise to transaction costs. These activities include:
>
> 1. The search for information about the distribution of price and quality of commodities and labour inputs, and the search for potential buyers and sellers and for relevant information about their behaviour and circumstances.
>
> 2. The bargaining that is needed to find the true position of buyers and sellers when prices are endogenous.
>
> 3. The making of contracts.
>
> 4. The monitoring of contractual partners to see whether they abide by the terms of the contract.
>
> 5. The enforcement of a contract and the collection of damages when partners fail to observe their contractual obligations.
>
> 6. The protection of property rights against third party encroachment.

The uncertainty of the behavior of trading partners and the costs of contract nego-tiation identified by Eggertson are key sources of transaction costs identified in the literature. Schmid (2004), however, adds another two to the list: the uncertainty of future states of the world (particularly the general level of demand and new technol-ogy) and the inability of the brain to deal with complex decisionmaking (people find it difficult to deal with complexities and therefore rely on routines).

As developed by Williamson (1975, 1985, 1996); Klein, Crawford, and Alchian (1978); Grossman and Hart (1986); and Hart and Moore (1999), TCE main-tains that the implication of positive transaction costs is that contracts are typically incomplete.

Therefore, parties that invest in relationship-specific assets expose themselves to the hazard that, if circumstances change, their trading partners may try to expropri-ate the rents accruing to specific assets (assets that have been committed to a particu-lar transaction), a hazard known as the hold-up problem (Shelanski and Klein 1995). Transaction costs are then costs incurred by parties to protect themselves against the hold-up problem, and institutions are sets of rules, arrangements, and relation-ships that parties invest in to economize on such costs (Box 2.2). Thus institutions are a means to reduce information and transaction costs. Alternatively, to follow Dorward's (2001) argument, institutions are formed to reduce uncertainty in human exchange (or risk). Markets are only one type of social device for settling the terms of transactions.

The focus here is thus on the costs of doing business, specifically, the making, monitoring, and enforcing of contracts. The ease or difficulty of contracting and the types of contract made are determined by the level and nature of transaction costs. These costs are influenced by the extent of imperfect information involved in mak-ing a transaction and the risks involved in transaction failure.

Williamson (1991) identifies three major determinants of transaction costs and of transaction cost–reducing governance structures: the specificity of assets involved, the uncertainties surrounding the transaction, and the frequency of that transaction. Ménard (2005) notes that these three variables are notoriously difficult to measure, and almost all the empirical literature avoids any attempt at measuring transaction costs directly, using instead reduced-form models in which transac-tion costs are assumed to be minimized. However, Williamson (1991) argues that transaction costs increase with a higher degree of asset specificity, a higher degree of uncertainty, and lower frequency of transaction. Furthermore, Williamson reasons that increases in these three variables are associated with shifts from spot markets to hybrid to hierarchical forms of governance, the last form involving vertical integra-tion or a variety of alternative governance structures or institutional arrangements of economic organization.[3]

Box 2.3 Private, merit, toll, public, and common pool goods and resources

Conventional analysis of market failures makes use of two attributes to distinguish among four basic types of goods and services: excludability and subtractability (or rivalness) of use. *Excludability* relates to the difficulty of restricting those who benefit from the provision of a good or a service. *Subtractability* or *rivalness* refers to the extent to which one individual's use subtracts from (or rivals) the availability of a good or service for consumption by others. Both of these attributes can range from low to high and can be used as the defining attributes of the following basic types of goods:

- *Private goods* have both high excludability (through private property rights) and high subtractability. When a private good (or service) is consumed, there is nothing left for the next consumer. Examples include food, clothing, and consumer goods.

- *Toll goods* (sometimes referred to as club goods) have high excludability (people can be excluded through payment of tolls or memberships) and low subtractability. Examples include roads and various services for which fixed costs are high relative to variable costs and use is low relative to capacity. Subtractability generally increases as utilization increases.

- *Public goods* yield nonsubtractive benefits that can be enjoyed jointly by many people who are hard to exclude from obtaining these benefits. Examples include enjoyment and use of general environmental services, such as clean air, and institutional services, such as law and order.

- *Common pool resources* have low excludability, but the use of such a resource subtracts from that resource. Examples include natural fisheries and common lands used for grazing, hunting, or extraction of other natural resources.

- In addition, *merit goods* are those with private good characteristics but that yield further nonexcludable positive externalities. Examples include education and health services, which provide immediate excludable and subtractable benefits to individuals, but their use by individuals provides further benefits to society as a whole (by raising the productivity of labor).

Note that increasing population pressure and/or economic growth often cause subtractability or rivalness to increase, whereas technical and institutional changes can lead to changes in exclusion costs. Thus, for example, subtractability in the use of fisheries increases with increasing fishing intensity. With regard to excludability, although digital technology has made the copying of music much easier and hence reduced excludability in the music industry, new electronic surveillance and tracking technologies allow better low-cost control of access to fisheries and toll goods, such as roads. Increases in excludability may also be achieved by changes in institutional arrangements. These issues are discussed further in Chapter 13.

The working hypothesis of TCE is thus that economic organization is an effort to align transactions, which have different attributes, with governance structures, with different costs and competencies, in a cost-economizing way (Williamson 1991). More precisely, it is an effort to maximize profits allowing for trade-offs among risks of contracting; transaction costs required to reduce those risks; and normal production (or transformation) costs, risks, and revenues (Dorward 2001).

2.1.4 Property Rights

Property rights are a fundamental institution governing who can do what with resources. Property rights may be defined as "the capacity to call upon the collective to stand behind one's claim to a benefit stream" (Bromley 1991, 15), or "the claims, entitlements and related obligations among people regarding the use and disposition of a scarce resource" (Furubotn and Pejovich 1972). Property rights are found in the oldest written laws, and they equate the expectation of use or profit to some payment from the very beginning. Property rights usually also refer to a bundle of rights. These rights include:

- use rights (usufruct): controlling the use of the property;

- extraction rights: the right to capture the benefits from the property through, for example, mining or agriculture;

- transfer rights: the right to sell or lease the property to someone else;

- exclusion rights: the right to exclude someone from the property;

- encumbrance rights: the right to use property as security or for other purposes.

Although exact definitions of these rights vary, there are several key elements. First, property rights are fundamentally a social relation: they are not about the link between a person and a thing (object of property), but rather about the relations between people with regard to a thing, or more particularly, with regard to the benefit stream that is generated. Unless others respect one's property rights, they are meaningless. Thus, all property rights are associated with corresponding duties of others to observe them. They are also frequently associated with specific duties of the rights-holder to do certain things to maintain the right to the resource.

According to Coase (1960), relatively well-defined property rights and institutions for implementing them form a prerequisite for making the transfer of rights possible and the trade-off among arrangements meaningful. Property rights thus affect contractual hazards and embed transactions into specific institutional environments. If property rights are well established and there are no transaction costs, an externality can be internalized between two private parties through bargaining and negotiations (Coase 1960). This observation is the essence of what has been labeled the Coase Theorem. Coase's argument was used to counter Arthur Pigou's call for government taxes to curb negative externalities. Coase showed that government involvement is in fact not necessary if property rights are well established. He also showed that, in the absence of transaction costs, the outcome would be efficient and equitable regardless of who owns the property right. In the presence of transaction costs, however, different systems of property rights may yield different outcomes in terms of efficiency and equity.

The property-rights school (see, for example, Demsetz 1967; Alchian and Demsetz 1973) hypothesizes that potential collective efficiency gains in adaptation to changes in relative prices are the key determinant factor for changes in property rights (Demsetz 1967; Hayami and Ruttan 1985). However, this approach does not deal with the distribution of property rights, and it cannot explain why efficient regimes of property rights are the exception rather than the rule (Libecap 1989; Eggertson 1990; North 1990). Which property rights eventually evolve is a function of their economic consequences, ideology regarding the proper distribution of benefits that accrue from property rights, and the bargaining power of the various interest groups (Ensminger 1992, 29).

The property-rights school argues for the formalization of property rights in land, which is argued to be the most important step toward intensification of agricultural practices and thus critical for agricultural and economic growth. It is argued that well-defined (implying private) property rights guide incentives to achieve a greater internalization of externalities and thereby create opportunities to access finance and enhance efficiency in land markets. For economic specialization to develop, it is thus important that well-defined property rights are established and that suspicion and fear of fraud do not pervade transactions.

There is, however, considerable opposition to this argument in the context of a long tradition of communal land ownership in many African societies. Access to land in such societies, through membership in the group or tribe, brings with it a number of associated rights and livelihood opportunities that might be endangered by parceling or privatizing land (see Platteau 1995; Chapter 15). In addition, it is important to note that in developing countries, insecurity; high transaction costs; poor, partial, and arbitrary enforcement of rights; and lack of infrastructure can seriously constrain the efficiency of individual property rights, especially if those rights do not enjoy the support of custom and a general sense of fairness (Platteau 1996).

The property-rights school also argues that rights, institutions, and technologies should adapt in some optimal manner to population pressure and growing resource scarcity, which are undermining the sustainability of open access and unregulated common-property resources. However, those changes need not always be in the direction of privatization, as assumed by the property-rights school (as illustrated by the case study in Chapter 15). Heltberg (2002) envisages a move toward better regulation of the commons, for example, in the form of effective management of use rights or yield-enhancing investments. The choice between individual rights and regulated common property would probably depend on such factors as transaction and enforcement costs, environmental and technological factors, and distributional considerations. The conclusion is that the common implicit assumption that individual and transferable property rights are the end goal of development may not be warranted.

2.1.5 Incomplete Contract Theory

Property rights issues are also embedded in incomplete contract theory (ICT). ICT of the firm combines the insights of TCE regarding the importance of bounded rationality and contracting costs with the rigor of agency theory. This theory focuses on the way different organizational structures assign property rights to resolve the issues that arise when contracts are incomplete. It provides a basis for defining different organizational structures by the ownership and control of key assets.

ICT was pioneered by Oliver Hart (Grossman and Hart 1986), building on initial insights from Williamson. Hart departed from the Coasian premise that firms arise when people write incomplete contracts and instead proposed that the allocation of power and control subsequently becomes necessary. Contracts (whether written or unwritten, and whether linked to business or to the use of natural resources) are essentially incomplete because of the bounded rationality of the contracting parties and the nonverifiability of relevant variables necessary to make the contract complete. It is thus accepted that contracts are perpetually renegotiated and redesigned to gain greater efficacy despite the renegotiation cost. These notions of contractual incompleteness and power can be used to understand economic institutions and arrangements.

Four aspects are particularly relevant when considering incomplete contracts: (1) ownership, (2) the boundaries of firms, (3) securities, and (4) power distribution (Saussier 2000). The first two refer to property rights and are concerned with why ownership of assets (human and physical) matters. Generally ownership matters because it provides power when contracts are incomplete. In addition, ownership allows residual control (that is, the right to decide about asset use outside of a given contract) and appropriation of residual income (that is, entrepreneurial profit).

ICT predicts that asset ownership has an effect on parties' incentives to invest, because it is impossible to write comprehensive contingent contracts for relationship-specific investments and the resulting potential for opportunistic behavior and ex post renegotiation over the trade benefits. This risk of hold-up leads to underinvestment. Changing the allocation of asset ownership between the trading parties may partially solve the hold-up problem.

2.1.6 Theory of Collective Action

An area of considerable interest in NIE literature concerns collective action. Indeed, Schmid (2000) goes as far as to argue that "the main agenda of institutional economics is collective action."

Collective action arises when people collaborate on joint action and decisions to accomplish an outcome that involves their interests or well-being (Sandler 1992). Collective-action problems are typically characterized by interdependency among the participants, so that the contributions or efforts of one individual influences the contributions or efforts of others, no wider benefits are produced, and all are worse off if they each act to maximize their own narrow self-interests.

The economic theory of collective action is concerned with the provision of public goods (and other goods and services that are collectively consumed) through the collaboration of two or more individuals and with the impact of externalities on group behavior. Although there are many instances in which individuals would be better off if they cooperated, collective action often does not emerge. Problems typically arise over imbalances among contributions to the effort and the distribution of benefits from the creation of public or collective goods, known as the free-rider problem.[4]

The foundation of this work was Olson's (1965) book *The Logic of Collective Action*. The theory of collective action is a useful tool to analyze how to overcome free-rider problems and fashion cooperative solutions for the management of common resources or the provision of public goods.

Collective action differs from other coordination mechanisms in that it involves pooled decisions within a group, whereas in hierarchies (such as firms) delegated decisions are made, and individuals operate in terms of independent decisions.

An important field of investigation in the theory and application of collective action concerns the use of common-pool resources, such as water, land, fisheries, and forests. In the past, the solution to the so-called tragedy of the commons was the establishment of enforceable property rights over the resources. However, recent work by Ostrom (2005b) and others has shown that local institutional arrangements, including customs and social conventions designed to induce cooperative solutions, can overcome the difficulties of collective action and help achieve efficiency in the use of such resources (Nabli and Nugent 1989). The key distinction here is between commons (or common-property resources) and open-access resources—an aspect that is discussed in more detail in Part 3 of this book.

According to Olson (1971), important determinants of success in collective action include the size, homogeneity, and purpose of the group. Building on this observation, Gaspart and Platteau (2002) argue that the success of collective action depends on two sets of factors:

1. characteristics of the people concerned:

   • the size of the group,

   • the extent of heterogeneity in the group,[5] and

   • social capital in the group (specifically, the tradition of cooperation in other areas) and

2. characteristics of the environment that bear on the enforcement costs of a collective scheme:

   • technical characteristics (including the physical attributes of the resource and its location),

   • economic characteristics (especially market conditions), and

   • political characteristics (the role played by state institutions).

TCE also provides a useful tool to evaluate collective schemes by assessing monitoring and enforcement costs and aspects of market power. Gaspart and Platteau's (2002) study of collective schemes in the Senegalese fishing industries show how an assessment of the rate of infraction of the rules adopted versus rule abidance can also predict the success or failure of collective action.

2.2   Beyond Institutions and Neoclassical Economics

The various approaches to institutional economics described in the previous section can be criticized in a number of ways. An important set of criticisms relates to difficulties with operationalizing the concept of transaction costs in meaningful empirical work. Considerable work remains in precisely measuring key transaction costs and variables that influence transaction costs and governance (uncertainty, asset specificity, and opportunism). Transaction costs are difficult to define and measure, and variables that influence transaction costs and governance are subject to endogeneity bias (Boerner and Macher 2001). Moreover, reduced-form tests of transaction-cost propositions are limited in that they provide evidence only on the differential costs of organizing and do not allow identification of the underlying structural relations. They also do not disclose the magnitude of transaction costs, leaving open the question of the scale of costs of inefficient organization (Masten 1996).

TCE has also been criticized on theoretical grounds (Harriss-White 1999). First, some argue that its main proposition is tautological: institutions minimize transaction costs because it is rationalized ex post that minimization is their function. Second, there may be some inconsistency: agents are required to devise institutions that are transaction-cost efficient while also having bounded rationality as a constraint. Such concerns lead Platteau (2000) to argue that the core idea that efficient institutions minimize transaction costs is flawed. The Coase Theorem asserts that efficiency alone determines the choice of organization, yet this presumes the absence of wealth effects, costless bargaining, the existence of a solution to the bargaining problem, and the absence of transaction costs related to private information and bounded rationality. Finally, it has been noted that, although the TCE approach is adequate for a comparative static analysis, it does not serve the purposes of grasping the dynamics of institutional change (Beije 1996; Nooteboom 1996). It may also be argued, however, that although these criticisms may relate to particular applications or developments of TCE, they can be addressed by more precise specifications of transactions and greater investigation and recognition of the importance of some of these issues for understanding transaction costs and institutions. This observation then points to the need for greater integration of institutional analysis as described here with complementary theories drawn from other, noneconomic, social sciences.

This amalgamation generally requires further departure from the core assumptions and methodological approaches of conventional economics.

Edgeworth (1881, 15) asserted in his *Mathematical Psychics* that "the first principle of economics is that every agent is actuated only by self interest." This view of human behavior has been a persistent feature of most economic models, despite strong critiques from within the economics professions (for example, Sen 1977) and from other social sciences.

Although much work in NIE continues to adopt the assumption of the rational, utility-maximizing behavior of economic agents, some authors have questioned this fundamental assumption (see, for example, Platteau 2000). These concerns are the primary focus of the behavioral economics school, which recognizes that when making decisions, people face constraints with regard to time, information, and cognitive abilities, and they may also have limited willpower and changing preferences as their circumstances and perceptions change (see, for example, Mullainathan and Thaler 2000; Bernheim and Rangel 2007).

In behavioral economics, the recognition of cognitive and informational limits in decisionmaking and of changing and context-specific preferences is linked to psychological research on human behavior. This research suggests different interpretations of human choice and the ways in which utility functions can be modified to make them more realistic (Rabin 1998). Evidence from neuroscience also suggests that individuals may be dually motivated with conflicted "self-interested" egoistic and "others-interested" homonymous motivations in different parts of the brain (Lynne and Hitzhusen 2002). This emphasis on socially framed preferences ties in with sociological insights that fundamental aspects of social relationships characterize economic actions (Richter 2001). It also accords with the emphasis of sociology on the interactions between groups and individuals, and with the concept of economic agents[6] influenced by social, cultural, and economic structures that need to be analyzed. The interface between the individual and society means that economic agents are socially embedded and cannot be treated as individuals who make decisions independent of other actors. We return later in this chapter to consider Williamson's concept of embeddedness in institutional analysis, but we note here that there is an increasing appreciation for this concept and acceptance that "economic action takes place within the networks of social relations that make up the social structure" (Richter 2001, 6). Such concepts should be particularly important in explaining crucial forms of economic behavior, such as cooperation, innovation, and action under conditions of uncertainty (Beckert 2002).

Scholars in economic sociology are also critical of more naive constructs of NIE that focus on transaction costs without considering the issues of power; trust; embeddedness; social relationships; networks; and concepts of fairness, altruism, and status.

Power has begun to take on broader meaning in institutional economics, and it holds a more salient place in the theories of sociologists than does the conventional concept of market power in imperfect competition.[7] Sociology and anthropology also make contributions to the analysis of evolving and sometimes multiple and competing social norms (that is, institutions), culture, and ideologies. These fields consider, for example, social identity and customary land tenure rights, income sharing, reciprocity, and social (for example, age and gender) differentiation (Ensminger 1992, 2000; Platteau 2000). The importance of social relations, trust, and power to the way that people relate to institutions implies that concepts of social capital are also relevant to understanding processes of institutional change and access to different institutions (see, for example, Putnam 2000; Durlauf and Fafchamps 2005; Cox and Fafchamps 2007).

2.3   The Definition and Nature of Institutions

It is hard to make much progress in the study of institutions if scholars define the term to mean almost anything. (Ostrom 2005a, 820)

Williamson (2000b, 595) makes the point that despite enormous progress, "we are still very ignorant about institutions," mainly because institutions are complex, neoclassical economics has been largely dismissive of them, and much institutional theory lacks scientific ambition. The purpose of this section is to provide a thorough understanding of the concept of institutions.

The simplest way of defining institutions is as "the rules of the game" (North 1994), rules that provide a framework of incentives that shape economic, political, and social organization. Institutions are composed of (1) formal rules (for example, laws and constitutions), (2) informal constraints (conventions, codes of conduct, and norms of behavior), and (3) their enforcement. Enforcement is carried out by third parties (law enforcement, social ostracism), second parties (retaliation), or by the first party (self-imposed codes of conduct).

Schmid (2004) qualifies this definition by arguing that institutions are more than just the rules of the game providing constraints. They are also enablement to do what the individual cannot do alone. They also affect beliefs and preferences and provide cues to uncalculated action.

In her definition of institutions Ostrom (1990, 1998, 2005a) refers to the rules, norms, and strategies used by humans in repetitive situations:

- Rules refer to shared prescriptions (must, must not, or may) that are mutually understood and enforced in particular situations in a predictable way by agents responsible for monitoring conduct and for imposing sanctions.

- Norms are prescriptions that are known and accepted yet involve intrinsic costs and benefits rather than material sanctions or inducements.

- Strategies represent the regularized plans that individuals make within the structure of incentives produced by rules, norms, and expectations of the likely behavior of others in a situation affected by physical and material conditions.

The early institutionalists understood institutions as essentially "collective action in control of individual action" (Commons 1934, 69). In this tradition institutions are understood to supplement markets where markets cannot function, and in a world of imperfect information institutions carry information about the expected behavior of other agents to better coordinate economic activity. (In a market economy with perfect information, such coordination would instead be directed by the price mechanism.) Institutions are created by human design through explicit bargaining or by evolution.

In defining the nature of his institutional economics, Commons (1934, 52, 91, 97, 107) identified some key features that underpin much of the institutional approach:

- "Conflict of issues" as opposed to "harmony" is its starting point.

- "Duty and debt" as opposed to "liberty and love" are its foundations.

- "Activity" as opposed to "pleasure and pain" is its focus.

To understand and define institutions it is also important to distinguish between "institutions" and "organizations," although these terms are often used interchangeably in everyday language. In the context of institutional analysis, however, institutions are complexes of norms and behaviors that persist over time by serving some collectively valued purposes, whereas organizations are structures of recognized and accepted roles, formal or informal (Uphoff 1986, 8–10). Examples of organizations include trade unions, producer groups, and government agencies. Although there is a great deal of overlap between institutions and organizations, many cultural and market institutions do not have a corresponding organization, and certain organizations may exist "on paper" only and have not been fully institutionalized through the creation of accepted rules. North (1993b, 3) helps to clarify this link between institutions and organizations:

> It is the interaction between institutions and organizations that shapes the institutional evolution of an economy. If institutions are the rules of the game, organizations and their entrepreneurs are the players. Organizations

are made up of groups of individuals bound together by some common purpose to achieve certain objectives. Organizations include political bodies (political parties, the senate, a city council, regulatory bodies), economic bodies (firms, trade unions, family farms, cooperatives), social bodies (churches, clubs, athletic associations), education bodies (schools, universities). The organizations that come into existence will reflect the opportunities provided by the institutional matrix. That is if the institutional framework rewards piracy then piratical organizations will come into existence; and if the institutional framework rewards productive activities then organizations—firms—will come in to existence to engage in productive activities.

Clearly, institutions can be many things: they can be organizations or sets of rules within organizations; they can be markets or particular rules about the way a market operates; they can refer to the set of property rights and rules governing exchanges in a society; they may be formally written down or unwritten and informally sanctioned. Institutions can also be defined as "agreed and policed regularity in social behaviour for specific recurrent situations," "complexes of norms of behaviour that persist by serving collectively valued purposes," "patterned forms of human interaction," "rules, their enforcement and norms of behaviour for repeated human interaction," "rights and obligations," or "constraints on behaviour" (Nabli and Nugent 1989, 1334–1335, citing various authors).

Following from these definitions, institutions can be considered as the mechanisms used to structure human interactions in the face of uncertainty, and they are formed to reduce uncertainty and risk in human exchange. In the economic exchange of goods and services, then, institutions act as a set of constraints that govern the relations among individuals or groups in the exchange process. Institutions thus help human beings to form expectations of what other people will do. Markets are only one type of social device for settling the terms of transactions.

There are, therefore, many concepts that are grouped under the rubric of institutions; as a result the definition of institutions is usually relatively broad (Hodgson 1998). As this generality leads to confusion, it is important to unpack the different aspects of institutions. This can be done by first considering the different levels of institutions, then considering the different types of institutions, and finally considering the functions and scope of institutions.

2.3.1   Levels of Institutions

Davis and North (1970), North (1990), and Williamson (1993, 2000b) consider that institutions operate at both the macro- and microlevels. The macrolevel deals with the institutional environment, or the rules of the game, which affect the behavior and performance of economic actors and in which organizational forms and transactions are embedded. Davis and North (1970) describe the environment as the set of fundamental political, social, and legal ground rules that establish the basis for production, exchange, and distribution.

In contrast, the microlevel analysis (also known as the level of institutional arrangements) deals with the institutions of governance, which North (1990) considers as a subclass of the institutional environment. These, according to Williamson (1993), refer more to the modes of managing transactions and include market, quasi-market, and hierarchical modes of contracting. The focus here is on the individual transaction, and questions regarding organizational forms (for example, vertical integration versus outsourcing) are analyzed. An institutional arrangement is an arrangement between economic units that governs the ways in which its members can cooperate and/or compete. For Williamson, the institutional arrangement is probably the closest counterpart to the most popular use of the term "institution."

Williamson (1999) later, after conceding the importance of embeddedness (Box 2.4), expanded these levels of institutions by considering institutional analysis in a framework with four levels (Table 2.1). At the lowest level (level 4), actors operate in existing institutions, making marginal decisions that are amenable to neoclassical microeconomic analyses of performance. These decisions are made in the context of governance structures (level 3)—the institutional arrangements governing rights over resources, goods, and services, and the structure and terms of exchange and access to

Table 2.1 The economics of institutions

Level		Purpose	Theory
1	Embeddedness: social environment (for example, informal institutions, traditions, norms, religion, culture, sociopolitical imperatives)	Protect, preserve, and empower	Social theory
2	Institutional environment: formal rules of the game (for example, property rights, laws, and constitutions)	First-order economizing: create appropriate institutional environment	Economics of property rights; positive political theory
3	Governance: play of the game (aligning governance structures with transactions)	Second-order economizing: create appropriate governance structure	Transaction-cost economics
4	Neoclassical analysis: performance (for example, optimality, prices, quantities, and incentives)	Third-order economizing: create appropriate marginal conditions	Neoclassical economics; agency theory

Source: Adapted from Williamson (1999).

Box 2.4 Origins and meanings of "embeddedness"

The concept of embeddedness relates to Granovetter's (1985) argument that the economy is structurally embedded in social networks that affect its functioning. Embeddedness has deep roots in social science, tracing back to Polanyi (1957), who argued that the human economy is embedded and enmeshed in institutions, economic and noneconomic. For Polanyi the inclusion of the noneconomic in the analysis is vital. The concept of embeddedness is also central to research in economic sociology and is typically treated as synonymous with the notion that organizations and the economy are part of a larger institutional structure. Granovetter (1985) uses the term in a more specific way to mean that economic action takes place in networks of social relations that make up the social structure. Dimaggio (1994), however, argues that economic action is embedded not only in social structure but also in culture.

---

resources. Governance or institutional arrangements are determined (in part at least, as discussed in later chapters) by the institutional environment (level 2), that is, the wider rules of the game set out in formal property rights and laws, for example. This institutional environment is then itself embedded in deeper traditions; norms; and cultural, religious, and sociopolitical systems (level 1).

Level 1 is associated with social theory, level 2 and 3 with NIE, and level 4 with neoclassical economics. Most advances in economics have been made in levels 2–4, and relatively little has been accomplished in level 1. However, for economic development and theory, we need to be aware of the implications of level 1, which may require drawing on other disciplines, such as anthropology and history, which deal with this level in depth. Although level 1 does not strictly fall in the realm of economics but rather in that of social theory, its profound impact on the economic functioning of institutions necessitates that it be considered as integral to a comprehensive understanding of the origins and roles of institutions. It is precisely for this reason that this chapter also addresses the other disciplines associated with level 1.

Ostrom (2005b) refined the point about different levels of institutions (or rules) by showing that multiple sources of structure are located at diverse analytical levels as well as diverse geographic domains. Besides multiple and nested action arenas at any one level of analysis, nesting of arenas also occurs across several levels of analysis. Ostrom's multiple levels of analysis refer to operational situations, collective choice, and constitutional choice, with sets of rules in the three arenas being nested within one another. For example, decisions made at the constitutional level (or the macrolevel) affect collective-choice decisions, as these impinge on the operational decisions of individuals.

Thus, decisions made about rules at any one level are usually made within a structure of rules existing at a different level. It is for this reason that institutional studies need to encompass multiple levels of analysis. At any one level of analysis, combinations of prescriptions, attributes of the world, and communities of the individuals involved work together in a configurative, rather than an additive, manner (Ostrom 2005b).

The framework of Williamson (1999) discussed above also corresponds with Scott's (2001) interpretation of three basic elements (or pillars) that can be identified as vital ingredients of institutions: regulative systems, normative systems, and cultural-cognitive systems:

- The regulatory pillar is legally sanctioned and includes rules, laws, and sanctions. It uses coercion as a mechanism for enforcement and compliance.

- The normative pillar is morally governed and includes such indicators as certification and accreditation.

- The cultural-cognitive pillar is culturally supported and has the common beliefs and shared logics of action as indicators. Shared understanding is the basis for compliance. This pillar also corresponds with Clague's (1997) category of institutions as cultural endowments, including the normative behavioral codes of society and the mental models that people use to interpret their experiences. The cultural endowment aspect of institutions links closely to the concepts of social capital and embeddedness of institutions.

These three elements of institutions form a continuum moving from the conscious to the unconscious, from the legally enforced to the taken for granted (Scott 2001). Scott (2001, xxi) also reminds us that most scholars underscore the regulatory aspects of institutions that constrain and regularize behavior: "Society's institutions—the rules of the game—largely determine the incentives of the entrepreneurs and thereby guide their actions." Economists are particularly likely to view institutions as resting primarily on the regulatory pillar. North's definition presented earlier, which builds on his Nobel Prize lecture (North 1993b) and has been quoted in virtually every piece on institutional economics since 1994, illustrates the point. Scott (2001) argues that this emphasis may stem in part from the fact that economists are used to focusing attention on the behavior of individuals and firms in competitive situations, where contending interests are more common and, hence, explicit rules and referees are necessary to preserve order. It is perhaps for this reason that private property rights are considered one of the most important institutions.

There has, however, been a greater recognition among economists that cultural aspects, ethical and moral issue (values), and informal constraints (such as conventions, norms, and ideologies) also shape human behavior. Thus the second and third pillars of institutions have increasingly been woven into economists' work about the role of institutions, as Williamson has also explained in his abovementioned four-level schema. This approach is stressed in this chapter (and indeed throughout the book) by demonstrations of the relevance of such disciplines as economic sociology, anthropology, and psychology when the standard assumptions of orthodox neo-classical economics are relaxed.

2.3.2   Types of Institutions: Formal and Informal

A common theme in the different analytical frameworks discussed above is the distinction between formal and informal institutions. Although Williamson's framework of four levels of institutional analysis may appear to suggest that formal rules (level 2) are embedded in informal rules (level 1), both formal and informal rules exist in levels 2 and 3, and formal and informal rules are embedded in each other, as argued earlier by Ostrom (2005b).

Formal institutions.   Formal rules (for example, legal environment and property rights) are formally written down and enforced by the state. Of these, the law has received the most attention from economists interested in the economic effects of the legal environment. Economics has been used to study not only the character and effects of law but also the mechanisms by which legal rules change. Contract law and property law is of particular interest to NIE scholars.

The constitutional order is the fundamental set of rules that govern the way societies and states are organized, and within this order institutional arrangements are devised by the collective and individual actions of members (Clague 1997). However, the constitutional order changes slowly (except in revolutionary periods), and for that reason it is usually considered as a given. Out of this constitutional order then flow statutes, common law, and various regulations. At various levels of government different laws and bylaws shape the way business, natural resources, and social activity are organized. In the case of food products, for example, the rules regarding food safety, grades, and standards are specified in regulations and enforced by government officials.

Furthermore, the formal rules and, by definition, the legal system and its effectiveness also determine the incentive structure in an economy through their influence on the protection of property rights and contract enforcement. Property rights are a key economic institution, but the effectiveness of property rights depends on the nature of the legal system, because these rights are meaningless if not enforced. This argument also extends to contracts, although in that case self-enforcing institutions may apply.

Informal institutions.   Informal rules (such as norms and conventions) are unwritten and informally sanctioned. These informal and often tacit rules are as important as formal rules in structuring social conduct. As North (1990, 36) emphasizes: "formal rules . . . make up a small part of the sum of constraints that shape choices . . . the governing structure is overwhelmingly defined by codes of conduct, norms of behaviour and conventions." Such (informal) rules, once established, form constraints for individual actors. One fundamental component here is cultural endowments. Cultural endowments include the normative behavioral codes of society and the mental models that people use to interpret their experiences. Similar to constitutional order, the cultural endowments of society change slowly. Norms and conventions are different types of informal rules. These are often considered loosely as interchangeable terms, but some authors draw a distinction between them.

Conventions are related to such concepts as habits, customs, routines, and standard practices, including honoring queues, access by seniority, and basic ideas of honesty and fair dealing. Biggart and Beamish (2003, 444) define them as "understandings, often tacit but also conscious, that organize and coordinate action in predictable ways. Conventions are agreed-upon, if flexible, guides for economic interpretation and interaction." Conventions thus refer to values, rules, and representations that influence economic behavior and include such practices as driving on the right (Favereau and Lazega 2002), although this goes beyond a convention, as it is enshrined in formal laws.

Customs need to be distinguished from conventions and routines. Individuals adhere to certain customs even if costly because of their emotional commitment and self-identity. Theorists of conventions see institutions as bundles of conventions that have emerged as pragmatic solutions to economic problems and have become reified as normal. Institutional arrangements may serve elite interests, but theorists also leave open the possibility that arrangements are merely congealed successful solutions to economic problems.

Although conventions are used by individuals as they buy, bargain, and sell, conventions do not reside in individuals. Theorists of conventions explain economic order as the product of socially knowledgeable actors working within collective understandings of what is possible, probable, and likely to result in fiscal and social gains and losses. Conventions are shared templates for interpreting situations and planning courses of action in mutually comprehensible ways that involve social accountability; that is, they provide a basis for judging the appropriateness of acts by self and others. Conventions thus are a means of economic coordination among actors that are inherently collective, social, and even moral in nature (Biggart and Beamish 2003).

Social conventions, which tend to be embedded in culture (or specific contexts), serve the common welfare and can be interpreted as noncooperative Nash-equilibrium[8] solutions to a variety of repeated games (supergames) faced by individuals in social settings. These social conventions can assist with important coordination problems in communities.

Norms are considered to be shared prescriptions known and accepted by most of the participants themselves. They involve intrinsic costs and benefits rather than material sanctions or inducements (Ostrom 2005b). Social norms such as "customary law" can in some cases be superior to administrative or judicial dispute resolution among people with close social ties. Local disputes are often resolved by appealing to generally accepted social rules, not by bargaining over legal rights. Through repeated interaction, agents tend to converge on strategies of cooperation that improve joint well-being. These strategies replace traditional legal remedies, and in some cases relationships prevail over law.

Barbara Harriss-White (2000) identifies what she calls "social institutions of markets" as part of informal institutions or constraints. This definition includes aspects related to class and markets, which have to do with exchange relations, political alignments, habituated collective action, and gender.

2.3.3 Scope and Function of Institutions

The function of institutions is to help agents or groups of agents to improve their welfare, but many different institutions can often serve the same function. The type of institution that emerges depends on various factors, including (1) power relations, (2) information structures, (3) the legal environment, and (4) historical accident and path dependence. North (1993a) summarizes the main function of institutions as forming the incentive structure of a society; political and economic institutions consequently are the underlying determinants of economic performance. Institutions are, therefore, critical to determining economic performance by influencing the cost of production, which includes input and transaction costs.

Hall and Soskice (2001) go to great lengths to show how the institutions of the political economy perform a most important function in shaping the behavior of firms. There are three ways to understand the relationship between the political institutions and behavior:

1. Institutions can be considered as socializing agencies that instill a particular set of norms or attitudes in those who operate within them.

2. The effects of institutions can be considered as stemming from the power they confer on particular actors.

3. Institutions of the political economy can be considered as a matrix of sanctions and incentives to which the relevant actors respond.

In the tradition of NIE, institutions are seen as governance tools. They help individuals cooperate, or they overcome market failures. Many institutions serve a different purpose, however: they manage conflict. Conflict has many causes, for example, a difference of interests, a clash of ideology, identity, honor, or irrational elements in human behavior.

However, individuals are not merely constrained and influenced by institutions. As social beings, humans are jointly shaped by the natural environment, biotic inheritance, and institutions. Nevertheless, this notion of institutions must coexist with the equally valid notion that institutions are formed and changed by individuals (Hodgson 1998).

2.3.4 Path Dependence and Institutional Change

In their efforts to achieve a deeper understanding of institutional change, scholars are continuously faced with the dilemma of whether current changes are unique and separable from long-run processes. Some argue that institutional change is incremental: any change occurs within the parameters of existing or prior institutions (Libecap 1989, 1998; North 1990; Ostrom 1990). History thus helps explain institutional transformation. To understand today's choices, it is necessary to track the incremental evolution of institutions. Path dependence is a common phenomenon in evolving systems, such as biological systems or ecosystems, and is an important feature in the development of social and political institutions.

How does history matter? North (1990) provides the conceptual foundation for a path-dependent framework. He suggests that actors are faced with making choices, both political and economic, at each point in the development of institutions. Although these choices may provide alternatives, previously viable options may be foreclosed because of positive feedback in an existing institutional pattern. Thus change and/or reform may be difficult to achieve. Positive feedback may be sustained by actors' subjective models derived from past learning (North 1990) or, where individuals benefit from existing institutional frameworks, they will have an interest in perpetuating the system (Libecap 1989; North 1990). These self-reinforcing (also referred to as positive feedback or increasing returns) properties of institutions are particularly potent in politics because of an absence of efficiency-enhancing mechanisms (such as competition), the relatively short time horizons of political actors, and the strong status quo bias built into political institutions (Pierson 2000). Policy reversal becomes ever more difficult.

North provides a historical perspective on the influence of different paths of institutional change on economic development (Davis and North 1971; North and Weingast 1989; North 1990, 1995). Institutional change is explained in terms of the responses of powerful groups to changes in relative prices, technologies, and transaction costs. These groups respond by modifying institutions in ways that they perceive to be in their interest. In different countries the same sets of changes to relative prices and to transaction technology may stimulate radically different types of institutional change. The results depend sensitively on (1) the perceptions of different groups of the possible opportunities and threats posed to their interests by alternative paths of institutional change or stagnation and (2) their political effectiveness (locally, nationally, and internationally) in influencing the paths and pace of institutional change. Institutional change can take a broad "antidevelopment" form (structuring transactions to create rents), or a "prodevelopment" form (structuring transactions to reduce costs and thus promote trade and investment). There is a strong path dependency in these processes, as initial conditions play an important role in determining both the relative perceptions and power of different groups on the one hand, and the institutional and technological options that they face on the other (Dorward et al. 2005). Population density (along with other geographical dimensions) is often a crucial factor in these processes of technical, economic, and institutional change (Boserup 1965; Platteau 2000).

Recent attempts to specify the dynamics of path dependence more carefully identify three sequential and interrelated processes (Thelen 1999, 2003; Mahoney 2000; Pierson 2000). First, a critical juncture occurs in which events trigger a move. Second, positive feedback reinforces movement along a path for some period while maintaining a given institutional pattern. Third, an end to the path finally occurs when new events dislodge the long-standing equilibrium.

It is reasonable to specify the period just prior to a critical juncture as the beginning of a sequence (Mahoney 2000, 2001). During this time different institutional arrangements are available, one of which is ultimately selected at the critical juncture. What is analytically significant at this moment is that the outcome of the critical juncture should be only stochastically related to the initial—precritical—juncture conditions. Thus the outcome should be unpredictable, thereby qualifying a critical juncture as a point in time when an unpredictable, contingent outcome sets in motion a largely irreversible set of events.

How are critical junctures translated into lasting legacies? What are the mechanisms of reproduction of a given institutional path over time? How does a given institutional pattern become locked-in? Mahoney (2000) describes four mechanisms:

- Rational actors may choose to reproduce institutions, including suboptimal ones, as the costs of transformation outweigh the benefits.

- Institutions may persist because they serve certain beneficial functions.

- Actors may perpetuate institutions based on their subjective understandings and beliefs of appropriateness and morality.

- An institution may persist if its beneficiaries have sufficient strength to sustain it. Institutions are not neutral, and they distribute benefits and costs unevenly across society. Differentially endowed actors have conflicting interests with regard to the perpetuation of institutions.

Consequently, it is important to establish who has invested in particular institutional arrangements, how this investment is sustained over time, and how those who are not invested in the institutions are excluded (Thelen 1999).

Each institutional path is characterized by a set of constraints and incentives, which in turn generates characteristic strategies and shared decision rules that produce a pattern of behavior among actors (Thelen 1999). Changes in institutions that preserve these elements of the path's pre-existing logic constitute a path of bounded innovation, and actors' decisions thus become linked across time. Consequently a narrow focus on current outcomes alone is at best incomplete and is sometimes misleading, because the necessary conditions for current outcomes may have occurred in the past. Specifying these longer run mechanisms of reproduction and feedback is key to understanding institutional evolution.

Although this notion of increasing returns for some actors is useful in explaining why institutions may follow a set pattern, some authors acknowledge that even though lock-in may occur, it is not necessarily irrevocable, because further choice points may exist (Thelen 2003). Those actors disadvantaged by prevailing institutions do not necessarily disappear. They may bide their time as conditions change, or they may even work within existing frameworks in pursuit of goals different from (or even subversive to) those of the institution's crafters.

2.4 Implications for the Agricultural Economics Paradigm

The arguments presented in this chapter have important implications for how agricultural economists get involved in policy prescriptions for the development of agriculture in Africa. It is critical that policy be developed on the basis of an understanding of what is likely to be the broad outlines of appropriate institutional arrangements for a given context. The question is whether this basis is enough to make a meaningful difference. The bottom line is that research on poverty and the agricultural development challenge in Africa needs to be institutionally informed. The challenge is to provide insights on how to design nonstandard institutional arrangements, nonmarket coordination, and the role of government.

In the final instance it is important that institutional analysis incorporate the idea that the institutions of a country or a region are embedded in the culture in which their logic is symbolically grounded, organizationally structured, and politically defended. All the institutions and structures of a country are integrated into its social configuration (and influenced by culture and history) to shape the social system of production (Hollingsworth and Boyer 1997). The way a nation organizes its economic activity and how its transactions take place are functions of culture and society. Thus it is important to be sensitive to the social context in which transactions are embedded and to understand the degree to which social bonds exist among economic actors. Given that there are many institutional arrangements for effectively organizing modern societies, the challenge is to find and understand the institutional arrangements that will deliver viable economic performance.

In this chapter we argue that institutional schools of thought in economics and other social sciences both demonstrate the need for and provide some of the tools for appropriate institutional analysis and design in addressing the types of agricultural development challenges outlined in Chapter 1.

At the end of his Nobel Prize lecture, Douglas North (1993b) stated that "we cannot account for the rise and decline of the Soviet Union and world communism with the tools of neo-classical analysis, but we should with an institutional/cognitive approach to contemporary problems of development." This remark is equally applicable to the problems of agricultural development outlined in Chapter 1: We cannot address the problems of the (agricultural) economies of developing countries with the tools of neoclassical analysis, but we can do so with an institutional and/or cognitive approach to contemporary problems of agricultural development.

Development and application of a practical paradigm or analytical framework for agricultural economics is therefore required to address these issues, building on the extensive research and analytical insights outlined in this chapter. The following chapters provide such a framework and illustrate how the relevant issues may be examined and the potential benefits of such analysis.

Notes

1. See Box 2.3 for a discussion of private goods and of other forms of goods that are more prone to market failure.

2. Of course, a purely financial calculus does not provide the whole picture: variation in incentive structures and supervisory mechanisms may be attributable to variation in the level of psychological satisfaction to be had from different types of work.

3. These forms of governance or institutional arrangement were introduced in Chapter 1. The effects of these variables on forms of governance is explained in more detail in Chapter 3.

4. In the analyses of economics and political science, free riders are actors who take more than their fair share of the benefits or do not shoulder their fair share of the costs of their use of a resource, involvement in a project, or the like. The free-rider problem is the question of how to prevent free riding from taking place, or at least limit its effects.

5. Apart from race, sex, age, and culture, heterogeneity is influenced by different exit opportunities, time horizons, skill levels, capital endowments, resources, and techniques.

6. The term "agent" is used to refer to any actor or player in a transaction, in a supply chain, or in a group or community deciding on the use and management of natural resources.

7. Narrowly defined, "power" implies the ability to act effectively and impose one's will on others. In economic terms it refers to the strength that a person or group has by exercising control over others.

8. In game theory, the Nash equilibrium (named after John Nash) is a kind of optimal strategy in a game involving two or more players, in which no player has anything to gain by changing only their own strategy. If each player has chosen a strategy and no player can benefit by changing strategy while the other players keep theirs unchanged, then the current set of strategy choices and the corresponding payoffs constitute a Nash equilibrium.

Further Reading

Drobak, J., and J. Nye. 1997. *Frontiers of the New Institutional Economics*. San Diego: Academic Press.

Furubotn, E. G., and R. Richter. 2005. *Institutions and economic theory: The contribution of the NIE*, second edition. Ann Arbor: University of Michigan Press.

Schmid, A. A. 2004. *Conflict and cooperation: Institutional and behavioral economics*. Malden, Mass., U.S.A.: Blackwell.

References

Akerlof, G. 1970. The market for lemons: Quality uncertainty and the market mechanism. *Quarterly Journal of Economics* 83 (3): 488–500.

Alchian, A. A., and H. Demsetz. 1972. Production information costs and economic organization. *American Economic Review* 62 (9): 777–795.

———. 1973. The property rights paradigm. *Journal of Economic History* 33 (1): 16–27.

Arnott, R., B. C. Greenwald, and J. E. Stiglitz. 1993. *Information and economic efficiency*. Working Paper 4533. Cambridge, Mass., U.S.A.: National Bureau of Economic Research.

Arrow, K. J. 1969. The organization of economic activity: Issues pertinent to the choice of market versus non-market allocation. In *The analysis and evaluation of public expenditures: The PBB-*

system. Joint Economic Committee, 91st Congress, first session, vol.1. Washington, D.C.: U.S. Government Printing Office.

Bardhan, P. K. 1989. Alternative approaches to the theory of institutions in economic development. In *The economic theory of agrarian institutions*, ed. P. Bardhan. Oxford: Clarendon Press.

Beckert, J. 2002. *Beyond the market: The social foundations of economic efficiency*. Princeton, N.J., U.S.A.: Princeton University Press.

Beije, P. R. 1996. Transaction costs and technological learning. In *Transaction cost economics and beyond*, ed. J. Groenewegen. Boston: Kluwer.

Bernheim, B. D., and A. Rangel. 2007. Toward choice-theoretic foundations for behavioral welfare economics. *American Economic Review* 97 (2): 464–470.

Biggart, N. W., and T. D. Beamish. 2003. The economic sociology of conventions: Habit, custom, practice, and routine in market order. *Annual Review of Sociology* 29: 443–464.

Binswanger, H., and M. Rosenzweig. 1986. Behavioural and material determinants of production relations in agriculture. *Journal of Development Studies* 22: 503–539.

Boerner, C., and J. Macher. 2001. Transaction cost economics: An assessment of empirical research in the social sciences. Working paper. http://www.msb.georgetown.edu/faculty/jtm4. Accessed June 2005.

Boserup, E. 1965. *Conditions of Agricultural growth*. Chicago: Aldine.

Braverman, A., and J. Stiglitz. 1982. Sharecropping and inter-linking of agrarian markets. *American Economic Review* 72 (4): 695–715.

Bromley, D. W. 1991. *Environment and economy: Property rights and public policy*. Cambridge, Mass., U.S.A.: Blackwell.

Clague, C. 1997. *Institutions and economic development: Growth and governance in less-developed and post-socialist countries*. Baltimore: Johns Hopkins University Press.

Coase, R. H. 1937. The nature of the firm. *Economica* 4 (16): 386–405.

———. 1960. The problem of social cost. *Journal of Law and Economics* 3 (October): 1–44.

Commons, J. R. 1934. *Institutional economics. Its place in political economy*. Basingstoke, U.K.: Macmillan.

Cox, D., and M. Fafchamps. 2007. Extended family and kinship networks. In *Handbook of Development Economics*, vol. 4, ed. M. Rosenzweig and P. Schultz. Amsterdam: North-Holland.

Davis, L. E., and D. C. North. 1970. Institutional change and American economic growth: A first step towards a theory of innovation. *Journal of Economic History* 30: 131–149.

———. 1971. *Institutional change and American economic growth*. Cambridge: Cambridge University Press.

Demsetz, H. 1967. Toward a theory of property rights. *American Economic Review* 57 (2): 347–359.

Dimaggio, P. J. 1994. Culture and economy. In *The handbook of economic sociology,* ed. N. J. Smelser and R. Swedberg. Princeton, N.J., U.S.A.: Princeton University Press.

Dorward, A. R. 2001. The effects of transaction costs, power and risk on contractual arrangements: A conceptual framework for quantitative analysis. *Journal of Agricultural Economics* 52 (2): 59–74.

Dorward, A. R., J. Kydd, and C. Poulton. 1998. *Smallholder cash crop production under market liberalization: A New Institutional Economics perspective.* Wallingford, U.K.: CAB International.

————. 2005a. Coordination risk and cost impacts on economic development in poor rural areas. Paper presented at the Agricultural Economics Society Conference, Nottingham, U.K., April.

————. 2005b. Beyond liberalisation: "Developmental coordination" policies for African smallholder agriculture. *IDS Bulletin* 36 (2): 80–85.

Dorward, A. R., J. G. Kydd, J. A. Morrison, and C. Poulton. 2005. Institutions, markets and economic coordination: Linking development policy to theory and praxis. *Development and Change* 36 (1): 1–25.

Drobak, J. N., and J. V. C. Nye. 1997. *The frontiers of the New Institutional Economics.* New York: Academic Press.

Durlauf, S. N., and M. Fafchamps. 2005. Social capital. In *Handbook of economic growth,* vol. 1, ed. P. Aghion and S. N. Durlauf. Amsterdam: Elsevier.

Edgeworth, F.Y. 1881. *Mathematical Psychics: An essay on the application of mathematics to the moral sciences.* London: Kegan Paul & Co.

Eggertson, T. 1990. *Economic behaviour and institutions.* Cambridge: Cambridge University Press.

Ensminger, J. 1992. *Making a market: The institutional transformation of an African society.* New York: Cambridge University Press.

————. 2000. Experimental economics in the bush: Why institutions matter. In *Institutions, contracts, and organizations: Perspectives from the new institutional economics,* ed. C. Ménard. Cheltenham, U.K.: Edward Elgar

Eswaran, M., and A. Kotwal. 1985. A theory of contractual choice in agriculture. *American Economic Review* 75 (3): 352–367.

Fama, E. F. 1980. Agency problems and the theory of the firm. *Journal of Political Economy* 88 (2): 288–307.

Fama, E. F., and M. C. Jensen. 1983. Separation of ownership and control. *Journal of Law and Economics* 26 (June): 301–325.

Favereau, O., and E. Lazega, eds. 2002. *Conventions and structures in economic organisation: Markets, networks and hierarchies.* Cheltenham, U.K.: Edward Elgar.

Furubotn, E. G., and S. Pejovich. 1972. Property rights and economic theory: A survey of recent literature. *Journal of Economic Literature* 10 (4): 1137–1162.

Gaspart, F., and J.-P. Platteau. 2002. Collective action for local-level effort regulation: An assessment of recent experiences in Senegalese small-scale fisheries. In *Group behaviour and development: Is the market destroying cooperation?* ed. J. Heyer, F. Stewart, and R. Thorp. Queen Elizabeth House Series in Development Studies. New York: Oxford University Press.

Granovetter, M. 1985. Economic action and social structure: The problem of embeddedness. *American Journal of Sociology* 91 (3): 481–510.

Greenwald, B. C., and J. E. Stiglitz. 1986. Externalities in economies with imperfect information and incomplete markets. *Quarterly Journal of Economics* 101 (2): 229–264.

Grossman, S., and O. Hart. 1986. The costs and benefits of ownership: A theory of vertical and lateral integration. *Journal of Political Economy* 94 (4): 691–719.

Hall, P. A., and D. Soskice, eds. 2001. *Varieties of capitalism: The institutional foundations of comparative advantage.* Oxford: Oxford University Press.

Harriss-White, B., ed. 1999. *Agricultural markets from theory to practice: Field experience in developing countries.* New York: St. Martin's Press.

———. 2000. Taking gender: Social institutions as regulators of markets. In *Agricultural markets beyond liberalisation,* ed. A. Van Tilburg and H. Moll. Dordrecht: Kluwer Academic.

Hart, O., and J. Moore. 1999. Foundations of incomplete contracts. *Review of Economic Studies* 66 (1): 115–138.

Hayami, Y., and V. Ruttan. 1985. *Agricultural development. An international perspective.* Baltimore: Johns Hopkins University Press.

Heltberg, R. 2002. Property rights and natural resource management in the developing countries. *Journal of Economic Surveys* 16 (2): 189–214.

Hodgson, G. 1998. The approach of institutional economics. *Journal of Economic Literature* 36: 166–192.

Hollingsworth, J. R., and R. Boyer, eds. 1997. *Contemporary capitalism: The embeddedness of institutions.* Cambridge: Cambridge University Press.

Holmstrom, B. 1979. Moral hazard and observability. *Bell Journal of Economics* 10 (1): 74–91.

Jensen, M., and W. Meckling. 1976. Theory of the firm: Managerial behaviour, agency costs, and ownership structure. *Journal of Financial Economics* 3: 305–360.

Klein, B., V. P. Crawford, and A. Alchian. 1978. Vertical integration, appropriable quasi-rents and the competitive contracting process. *Journal of Law and Economics* 21: 297–326.

Libecap, G. D. 1989. *Contracting for property rights.* New York: Cambridge University Press.

———. 1998. Distributional and political issues modifying traditional common-property institutions. In *Law and the governance of renewable resources: Studies from Northern Europe and Africa,* ed. E. Berge and C. Stenseth. Oakland, Calif., U.S.A.: ICS Press.

Lynne, G. B., and F. J. Hitzhusen. 2002. Toward an institutional and behavioral (agricultural) economics: Assessing progress. Working paper. Lincoln: University of Nebraska–Lincoln. Available at http://agecon.unl.edu/Lynne/IBES2002.pdf. Accessed July 2005.

Mahoney, J. 2000. Path dependence in historical sociology. *Theory and Society* 29 (4): 507–548.

———. 2001. Path-dependent explanations of regime change: Central America in comparative perspective. *Studies in Comparative International Development* 36 (1): 111–141.

Masten, S. E. 1996. *Case studies in contracting and organization.* New York: Oxford University Press.

Ménard, C. 2005. A new institutional approach to organization. In *Handbook of New Institutional Economics,* ed. C. Ménard and M. M. Shirley. Dordrecht: Springer.

Milgrom, P., and J. Roberts. 1992. *Economics, organisation and management.* London: Prentice-Hall.

Mullainathan, S., and R. H. Thaler. 2000. Behavioral economics. NBER Working Paper 7948. Cambridge, Mass., U.S.A.: National Bureau of Economic Research.

Nabli, M. K., and J. B. Nugent. 1989. The New Institutional Economics and its applicability to development. *World Development* 17: 1333–1347.

Newberry, D. M. G. 1977. Risk-sharing, sharecropping, and uncertain labor markets. *Review of Economic Studies* 44: 585–594.

Nooteboom, B. 1996. Towards a learning based model of transactions. In *Transaction cost economics and beyond,* ed. J. Groenewegen. Boston: Kluwer.

North, D. C. 1990. *Institutions, institutional change and economic performance.* Cambridge: Cambridge University Press.

———. 1993a. New Institutional Economics and economic development. Working paper. Washington University, St Louis. http://129.3.20.41/eps/eh/papers/9309/9309002.pdf. Accessed July 17, 2005.

———. 1993b. Economic performance through time. Lecture to the memory of Alfred Nobel, Stockholm, December 1993. http://www.nobelprize.org/economics/laureates/1993/northlecture.html. Accessed June 25, 2005.

———. 1994. Economic performance through time. *American Economic Review* 84 (3): 359–368.

———. 1995. The New Institutional Economics and Third World development. In *The New Institutional Economics and Third World development,* ed. J. Harriss, J. Hunter, and C. M. Lewis. London: Routledge.

North, D. C., and B. W. Weingast. 1989. The evolution of institutions governing public choice in 17th-century England. *Journal of Economic History* 49: 803–832.

Olson, M. 1965. *The logic of collective action: Public goods and the theory of groups.* Cambridge, Mass., U.S.A.: Harvard University Press.

————. 1971. *The logic of collective action: Public goods and the theory of groups.* New York: Shocken Books.

Ostrom, E. 1990. *Governing the commons. The evolution of institutions for collective action.* Cambridge: Cambridge University Press.

————. 1998. The institutional analysis and development approach. In *Designing institutions for environment and natural resource management,* ed. E. T. Loehman and D. M. Kilgour. Cheltenham, U.K.: Edward Elgar.

————. 2005a. Doing institutional analysis: Digging deeper than markets and hierarchies. In *Handbook of New Institutional Economics,* ed. C. Ménard and M. Shirley. Dordrecht: Springer.

————. 2005b. *Understanding institutional diversity.* Princeton, N.J., U.S.A.: Princeton University Press.

Pierson, P. 2000. Increasing returns, path dependence, and the study of politics. *American Political Science Review* 94 (2): 251–267.

Platteau, J.-P. 1995. *Reforming land rights in Sub-Saharan Africa: Issues of efficiency and equity.* Discussion Paper 60. Geneva: United Nations Research Institute for Social Development.

————. 1996. The evolutionary theory of land rights as applied to Sub-Saharan Africa: A critical assessment. *Development and Change* 27 (1): 29–86.

————. 2000. *Institutions, social norms, and economic development. Fundamentals of development economics.* Amsterdam: Harwood Academic.

Polanyi, K. 1957. The economy as an instituted process. In *Trade and market in the early empires: Economies in history and theory,* ed. K. Polanyi, C. M. Arensberg, and H. W. Pearson. New York: Free Press.

Putnam, R. 2000. *Bowling alone: The collapse and revival of American community.* New York: Simon and Schuster.

Putterman, L. 1980. Voluntary collectivization: A model of producers' institutional choice. *Journal of Comparative Economics* 4: 125–157.

Rabin, M. 1998. Psychology and economics. *Journal of Economic Literature* 36 (1): 11–46.

Richter, R. 2001. New economic sociology and New Institutional Economics. Paper presented at the 2001 conference of the International Society for New Institutional Economics, Berkeley, Calif., U.S.A., September 13–15. Available at http://ww16srv.wiwi.uni-sb.de/richter/home-eng.htm.

Sandler, T. 1992. *Collective action: Theory and applications.* Ann Arbor: University of Michigan Press.

Saussier, S. 2000. When incomplete contract theory meets transaction cost economics: A test on contract form. In *Institutions, contracts, and organizations: Perspectives from the New Institutional Economics,* ed. C. Ménard. Cheltenham, U.K.: Edward Elgar.

Schmid, A. A. 2000. Is there any theory in institutional economics? http://www.msu.edu/user/ schmid/commons.htm. Accessed October 7, 2000.

———. 2004. *Conflict and cooperation: Institutional and behavioral economics.* Malden, Mass., U.S.A.: Blackwell.

Scott, W. R. 2001. *Institutions and organisations.* London: Sage.

Sen, A. 1977. Rational fools: A critique of the behavioural foundations of economic theory. *Philosophy and Public Affairs* 6 (4): 317–344.

Shelanski, H. A., and P. G. Klein. 1995. Empirical research in transaction cost economics: A survey and assessment. *Journal of Law, Economics and Organization* 11 (2): 335–361.

Stigler, G. J. 1961. The economics of information. *Journal of Political Economy* 69: 213–225.

———. 1967. Imperfections in the capital market. *Journal of Political Economy* 75: 287–292.

Stiglitz, J. E. 1974. Incentives and risk sharing in sharecropping. *Review of Economic Studies* 41 (2): 219–256.

———. 1985a. Information and economic analysis: A perspective. *Economic Journal* 95 (issue supplement): 21–41.

———. 1985b. *Economics of information and the theory of economic development.* NBER Working Paper 1566. Cambridge, Mass., U.S.A.: National Bureau of Economic Research.

———. 1989. Rational peasants, efficient institutions and the theory of rural organization: Methodological remarks for development economics. In *The economic theory of agrarian institutions,* ed. P. Bardhan. Oxford: Clarendon Press.

Stiglitz, J. E., and S. J. Grossman. 1980. On the impossibility of informationally efficient markets. *American Economic Review* 70 (3): 393–408.

Thelen, K. 1999. Historical institutionalism in comparative politics. *Annual Review of Political Science* 2: 369–404.

———. 2003. How institutions evolve: Insights from comparative historical analysis. In *Comparative historical analysis in the social sciences,* ed. J. Mahoney and D. Rueschemeyer. New York: Cambridge University Press.

Uphoff, N. 1986. *Local institutional development: An analytical sourcebook with cases.* West Hartford, Conn., U.S.A.: Kumarian Press.

Williamson, O. E. 1975. *Markets and hierarchies: Analysis and anti-trust implications.* New York: Free Press.

———. 1985. *The economic institutions of capitalism.* New York: Free Press.

———. 1991. Comparative economic organisation: The analysis of discrete structural alternatives. *Administrative Science Quarterly* 36: 269–296.

———. 1993. The evolving science of organization. *Journal of Institutional and Theoretical Economics* 149: 36–63.

———. 1996. *The mechanisms of governance.* New York: Oxford University Press.

———. 1999. The New Institutional Economics: Taking stock and looking ahead. Address to the International Society for New Institutional Economics. *ISNIE Newsletter* 2 (2): 9–20.

———. 2000a. Ronald Harry Coase: Institutional economist/institution builder. In *Institutions, contracts, and organizations: Perspectives from the New Institutional Economics,* ed. C. Ménard. Cheltenham, U.K.: Edward Elgar.

———. 2000b. The New Institutional Economics: Taking stock, looking ahead. *Journal of Economic Literature* 38 (September): 595–613.

Zusman, P. 1976. The incorporation and measurement of social power in economic models. *International Economic Review* 17: 447–462.

Chapter 3

A Framework for Analyzing Institutions

Andrew R. Dorward and S. Were Omamo

T he opening chapter in this book introduced the role of institutions in natural resource management and the coordinated exchange of goods and services, different types of institutions and institutional change, and particular problems of agricultural development in poor areas in Africa. It was argued that understanding and influencing institutional change are fundamental to understanding and influencing the processes of social, economic, and technical change in agricultural development.

Chapter 2 set out the main theoretical elements of the economics of institutions, dealing with questions about the definition and nature of institutions, the functions that different types of institutions play in economic activity, influences on their effectiveness in performing these functions for different stakeholders, and the processes of institutional change.

The remainder of this book develops and applies this theory to address the challenges set out in Chapter 1, examining practical issues regarding the roles and effectiveness of markets, state action, and collective action in promoting agricultural developmental in different circumstances. Before embarking on this effort, however, we need to develop a conceptual framework for applying the theories described in Chapter 2 to analyze the evolution, functions, and economic and social outcomes of specific institutions, such as those governing the management of common property resources, those bringing players together in market exchange, or

Ruth Meinzen-Dick, Esther Mwangi, and Eleni Gabre-Madhin made substantial contributions to this chapter, notably in the development of the framework in Figure 3.2 and in reading and commenting on drafts.

those assisting in the enforcement of credit contracts. Analysts may wish to know the answers to such questions as:

- How effectively do these institutions perform their functions?

- Are there trade-offs between the performance of these functions and, for example, other aspects of market efficiency?

- Do these arrangements have the potential to generate corruption or rent seeking?

- Are there winners and losers from the particular configuration of institutional arrangements that are observed and, if so, who are these winners and losers?

- Can the design of a particular institution—or a set of institutional arrangements— be modified to improve its effectiveness, efficiency, equity, or sustainability?

The purpose of this chapter is to develop a conceptual framework for conducting this type of analysis. The framework introduced here will provide a unifying structure for the analysis of different institutions illustrated in the case study chapters in Parts 2 and 3 of the book.

3.1   Framework—Origins and Layout

In this section, a framework for institutional analysis is set out. The framework is intended to identify the main elements that need to be considered when undertaking institutional analysis. The framework is intentionally abstract, to allow its application to a wide variety of situations and enable it to accommodate different theories about the roles of and influences on institutions. The framework draws on the general agreement between these theories regarding the core structural elements in all social and economic relations.

The framework presented here has its roots in two branches of New Institutional Economics (NIE). First, there has been a flourishing literature that initially emphasized understanding collective action in natural resource management but has been broadened to integrate the application of different theoretical approaches to the study of a wide range of institutions in different spheres of economic activity, namely, the Institutional Analysis and Development (IAD) approach. The framework is developed by unpacking and extending the basic building blocks: exogenous variables are broken down into physical/material conditions, community attributes, and rules in use; actors and action situations are set in an action arena; and the feedback of outcomes to the exogenous variables and action arena is mediated through patterns of interactions and evaluative criteria. The IAD approach (Ostrom, Gardner, and Walker 1994) is a widely known framework. The basic structure of the IAD framework involves (1) an exogenous set of variables that influence (2) situations of actors (or players in the game) and (3) the behavior of actors in those situations, leading to outcomes, which then feed back to modify both the exogenous variables and the actors and their situations.

An IAD framework diagram is set out in Figure 3.1. The blocks can be unpacked further into clusters of variables in the action situation and with different theoretical assumptions about actors' behavior. The IAD framework can be used to help develop predictions about actor behavior and outcomes from changes in the exogenous variables, assuming that the variables specifying the situation and the motivational and cognitive structure of actors do not change. Further analysis can investigate factors affecting the structure of the action arena in terms of interrelationships among institutions, actors, and their activities and resources.

The second branch of NIE from which the framework has developed is transaction-cost economics (TCE). The primary focus of TCE is the analysis of institutions for the exchange of goods and services (Davis and North 1971; Williamson 1985, 1991; North 1990; Jaffee and Morton 1995). Frameworks in this branch emphasize (1) the influences of the environment; (2) characteristics of goods or services being exchanged; and (3) characteristics of potential parties to a transaction, as they determine the outcomes of bargaining over the form and terms of particular

Figure 3.1   The IAD framework

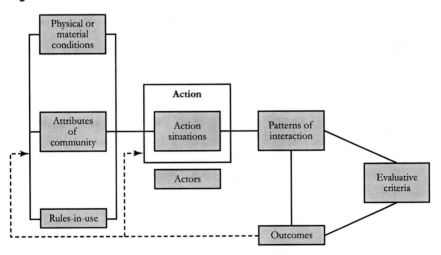

Source: Adapted from Ostrom, Gardner, and Walker (1994) and Ostrom (2005a).

institutional arrangements. The environment is further separated into the physical/infrastructural environment, institutional environment (following Davis and North 1971), and social/economic environment.

The framework presented here draws on these two branches, recognizing their common structure (an environment or exogenous variables influencing actor behavior in and through institutions) but also playing on their respective strengths (the emphasis in the IAD framework on the action arena and on feedbacks from the outcomes to the environment; the emphasis on actor, institutional, and activity attributes in the TCE frameworks). Figure 3.2 provides an overview of (1) the main elements in the theoretical and practical analysis of institutions and (2) broad relationships among these elements. The paragraphs below provide a brief overview of the diagram; the rest of the chapter discusses in detail each element of Figure 3.2.

The heart of the framework is the identification of the action domain, which defines the spheres of activity and interest of the analysis (such as economic exchange of goods and services, the management of natural resources, or insurance and safety nets). The action domain is discussed in more detail in Section 3.2. It comprises the institutions to be analyzed, the activities that the institutions engage in (see the left and right sides of Figure 3.2), and the actors in those institutions and activities.[1] An important part of institutional analysis is the identification of the institutions, activities, and actors that are important in a particular action domain. This identification must be accompanied by examination of the attributes of these elements.

The structure and behavior of the action domain is not, however, determined solely by the elements in it. The action domain is set in and affected by a wider environment (see the top of Figure 3.2), which is considered in three parts—the physical and infrastructural, the socioeconomic, and the policy and governance environments (see Section 3.3). Institutions, activities, and actors are affected by (and in turn affect) their wider environment.

The interactions among institutions, actors, and activities involve actions that lead to outcomes. The outcomes of these actions may reinforce or change the environment, institutions, activities, and actors. Impacts may be direct or indirect, the latter occurring, for example, when the outcome of particular actions is a change in the scarcity or value of a particular resource, which leads to changes in the environment, in the aspirations and wealth of actors, and in the attributes of actors. These changes lead to institutional change.

The remainder of this chapter describes in more detail the elements of this framework and the interactions among them. These are discussed in a particular sequence, but institutional analysis need not follow a neat linear approach—it is likely to be iterative and cumulative, as consideration of one element leads to identification of another, or to the realization of the importance of another set of institutional,

Figure 3.2   A conceptual framework for institutional analysis

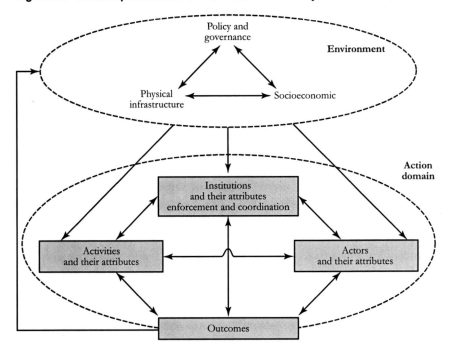

activity, or actor attributes. The framework should be used more as a checklist of the major elements and interactions that should be considered in institutional analysis. The application of this framework must be adapted to suit the specific situation, type of analysis, and the analyst, and different elements and relationships will be found to be important in different situations. This flexibility is illustrated in the case studies in later chapters for the two types of action domain that are the major focus of this book: exchange of goods and services and natural resource management.[2]

3.2   Action Domain

The framework begins with the definition of action domains, which draws on the IAD concept of action arenas as social spaces in which actors (individuals and organizations) interact in social and economic exchange (Ostrom, Gardner, and Walker 1994; Ostrom 2005b). It can also be related to Aoki's (2001) discussion of the six basic types of domain in which institutions operate: commons, economic exchange, organization, social exchange, polity, and generic organizational fields. In this book the primary concern is with applying institutional economics to two types of domain that are important to agricultural development in Africa: the economic exchange of goods and services (the focus of Part 2 of this book), and natural resource management (considered in Part 3).[3] Application of the framework to specific situations requires the definition of specific action domains.

As discussed earlier, there are four major parts of the action domain—institutions, activities, actors, and outcomes. Institutional analysis requires

- identification of which institutions, activities, actors, and outcomes are important and significantly affect the behavior of the action domain; and

- consideration of the attributes of institutions, activities, and actors that significantly affect interactions among them and wider behavior in the action domain.

The action domain lies in an environment (discussed in Section 3.3), and a critical part of institutional analysis is the identification of the boundaries between the action domain and its environment—which elements are in the action domain, and which are outside it, in its environment? Action-domain boundaries are determined by the purposes of the analysis and the specific research or policy question to be addressed in the institutional analysis: Does the analysis seek to investigate the way that existing institutions influence actors' behavior and hence their responses to and the outcomes of exogenous changes (with institutions largely fixed as exogenous variables)? Or does it seek to go further and investigate the impact of exogenous factors on changes in institutions? A critical issue in determining which elements should be included in the action domain is the level of institutions at which change is to be investigated. This issue is discussed in Section 3.2.1.

Just as some institutions, actors, and activities will be included in the action domain (Box 3.1), there will be others that affect the action domain but are largely exogenous to it: these should be considered as part of the environment. They should be defined as part of the environment if

- they operate at a much larger scale than the action domain and are therefore hardly affected by changes in it (for example, national markets or large river flows may be hardly affected by changes in small community markets or small catchment areas, respectively);

- they respond slowly to feedback effects and can thus be ignored in short- to medium-term analyses (for example, it will take a long time before improved school enrollments of children affect literacy and educational attainments of the working population or before a reduction in livestock numbers ameliorates the severe effects of gully erosion); and

- they are unaffected by changes in the action domain and there are no feedback effects (for example, wages in tasks reserved for men may be largely unaffected by changes in the burden of women's activities).

The boundaries of environment should therefore be sensitive to aggregation effects, the time scale of analysis, and structural changes in the environment or action domain. Thus in the examples above:

- National markets may well be affected by changes in small community markets if all (or many) of these markets change in the same way, just as large river flows may be significantly affected by changes in small catchment areas if all (or many) catchment areas change in the same way.

- Actors' education levels should be treated as endogenous and included in the action domain as attributes, if long-term analysis is being conducted.

- Removal of restrictions on women's participation in activities previously reserved for men may mean that wages in these tasks are now more sensitive to changes in the burden of women's activities.

Box 3.1 Action domains

An *action domain* concerned with the exchange of particular goods and services includes those actors involved in the exchange of these goods and services in locations or social groups that are the subject of the analysis. It also includes activities that directly interact with these exchanges and actors, and the institutions that govern these interactions. Similarly an action domain concerned with the management of natural resources includes those actors with property rights over these resources as well as other stakeholders in locations or social groups that are the subject of the analysis. It also includes activities and actors directly interacting with the application of those rights (in use, control, and usufruct, as explained in Chapter 2). These interactions may involve social, economic, or natural (biological, chemical, or physical) relations.

Decisions about what lies in the action domain and what lies in the environment are also likely to change in the process of analysis, as interactions that were not initially recognized are seen to be important.

Institutions, actors, and activities outside the action domain (Box 3.2) but affecting it still need to be analyzed, as discussed in Section 3.3. Note that action domains are not distinct entities that can be analyzed in isolation: interactions among domains are a major feature of social and economic systems, and their analytical separation is made to simplify analysis of a highly complex and interrelated system. As a result, selection of one domain of study means that other domains become part of the first domain's environment.

3.2.1 Institutions and Their Attributes

A major task in the analysis of institutions in an action domain is the identification of the institutions that are important in the domain. This effort begins with an initial

---

Box 3.2 Examples of the boundaries of action domains used for institutional analysis

The boundaries of action domains are constructs—artificial limits on analysis set by the analyst to suit the particular interests of analysis and the system under study.

Exchange of goods and services. In the analysis of the exchange of goods and services, the action domain may be defined by social or economic variables. Thus emphasis on sociopolitical issues might lead, for example, to the action domain being limited to a village, an administrative district, or an area occupied by an ethnic group. Emphasis on economic variables might result in defining the boundary of the action domain as being an area that serves and is served by a particular market or set of markets. Geographical features may determine administrative districts and markets: agro-ecology (affecting areas where particular crops are produced) or topography and communications infrastructure (for example, roads serving certain areas, or rivers acting as boundaries or transport and communications routes).

Natural resource management. In an area with settled farmers and transhumant pastoralists, the action domain may be bounded by the local village (so that events concerning migrant pastoral groups elsewhere are treated as external influences), or it may be bounded by a larger area that encompasses the territory covered by the pastoralists. The latter may even span national borders.

identification of the boundaries of the domain and continues iteratively as actors and activities are identified and the attributes of these elements and their interactions are considered.

Identifying institutions and their attributes is no easy task. Ostrom (2005a) notes that institutions are invisible, there are multiple definitions of institutions, there are multiple interactions among them, and they operate at multiple levels and are inter-nested. Institutions also perform a variety of social and economic functions, and they connect and affect different sets of actors. Identifying institutions that are significant influences in the action domain, and the attributes that make them significant, can be considered by addressing questions about what institutions are, who they connect and affect, why they exist (the social, economic or other functions they perform or have performed in the past for particular stakeholders), and how they work (Figure 3.3). Analysis should move between these questions (and between similar sets of questions about actors and activities) in an iterative fashion. These questions are now considered in turn, although the question about who they connect and affect is left to the discussion of the actors and their attributes in Section 3.2.3.

What institutions are.   In Chapter 2, institutions were defined as formal or informal rules that govern people's behavior by providing a framework of incentives that shape economic, political, and social organization. Williamson's (1999) identification of four levels of institutions was also discussed in Chapter 2 (see Table 2.1). Kiser and Ostrom (1982) identify three levels of rules or institutions: *operational rules* affecting people's everyday decisions, higher level *collective-choice rules* influencing the structure and use of operational rules by different actors, and *constitutional choice rules* influencing the structure and use of collective-choice rules by different actors. This categorization has similarities with the distinction by Davis and North (1971) between lower level institutional arrangements and their higher level institutional environment. Higher level rules generally have wider scope and are more resistant to change than lower level rules. For these reasons higher level rules often lie outside the action domain and are considered as elements of the socioeconomic or policy governance environment.

This discussion of institutional levels links with—but is distinct from—earlier consideration of the boundaries of the action domain, and of the distinction between institutions (and actors and activities) that lie in the action domain and those that are considered part of the environment. This distinction was concerned with the scale of institutions. Institutional scales and levels are often related (for example, operational rules tend to operate at smaller scales than collective-choice and constitutional-choice rules), but there are nevertheless operational rules that operate at very large scales and constitutional-choice rules that operate at small scales. As discussed earlier, one approach to addressing the question of action-domain boundaries is to consider the

Figure 3.3   Institutions and their attributes

What?   **Definition**
Formal or informal rules that govern people's behavior by providing a framework of incentives that shape eonomic, political, and social organization

Level

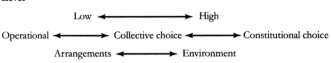

Why?   **Functions**
Enforcement and coordination

Who?   **Actors**
Different social, human, natural, financial, and physical resources, and different aspirations; with different scales, scopes, and mechanisms of aggregation

How?   **Types of rule**
Boundary, position, scope, authority, aggregation, information, and payoff

Types of structure

Arrangement:	Social capital–based exchange, hierarchy, market, hybrid
Sector:	Collective action, state, market, hybrid
Incentive:	Normative, coercive, remunerative
Property rights:	Common, public, private, hybrid, open access
Cost sharing:	Collective, public, individual, hybrid

Source: From Ostrom (2005a).

purpose and scope of the analysis with respect to the relationship between institutions and actors. Pertinent questions include whether the analysis deals with any of the following:

- The access of particular actors to existing local institutions that are considered to be fixed and thus exogenous (for example, considering how poor people's ability to obtain a license to access a resource could be improved by improved literacy, or how their ability to participate in a market might be enhanced by some change in the productivity of their assets or access to assets).

- The terms of access of particular actors to existing local institutions, where these terms might be negotiable (for example, local operational rules considering how poor people's access to a resource could be improved by reducing license fees or literacy requirements, or their participation in a market improved by better prices or reduced transaction costs).

- The form of local institutions (for example, local constitutional choice rules involving the replacement of licensed access from local authorities by resource-user associations or private ownership and markets, or the abolition of local market regulations).

- The terms and forms of wider, higher-level, or more embedded institutions (wider operational or constitutional-choice rules, such as international and national laws and policies, or local cultural norms defining local institutions).

These different levels and scales of analysis require the boundaries of the action domain to be drawn in different places. In the first case local institutions governing resource access are considered fixed and thus analyzed as part of the environment (although local institutions governing access to literacy or productive assets would probably be considered as part of the action domain). If all institutions are considered fixed, then analysis can be considered in terms of level 4 in Williamson's schema in Table 2.1. The subsequent cases above represent a moving up levels of institutions in Williamson's and Ostrom's schemas, with higher level institutions becoming endogenous and thus part of the action domain.

Why institutions exist and their social and economic functions. Institutions exhibit path dependency, as discussed in Chapter 2, and their functions and the benefits they offer to different stakeholders evolve over time. Nevertheless definitions of institutions are often helpfully expressed in terms of their general functions.

Institutions perform two fundamental (and related) functions in social and economic interactions between actors—enforcement and coordination:

- Enforcement (an activity conducted to ensure compliance) concerns the informal and formal rules that define interaction; the monitoring and sanctioning mechanisms through which rules and contracts for interaction between actors are enforced; and the roles of trust, community norms, morality, and social capital in enforcement. Further issues in enforcement concern the motivation, or incentive compatibility, of enforcement and the impact of limitations of enforcement mechanisms on markets and other forms of exchange.

- Coordination (a process encouraging parties to take common or complementary actions necessary to achieve individual goals) may be viewed primarily as an information and transaction-cost/risk problem. Here analysis is concerned with information access and the sources and extent of transaction costs and risks related to search, negotiation, monitoring, and enforcing property rights and exchange; the ways that transaction costs determine contractual forms; and the economic organization of actors in collective, private, or state-dominated arrangements. In many agricultural development situations transaction costs and risks are high, and analysts need to consider how they can be reduced and the likely impacts on market organization and performance of different ways of reducing them.

Institutions can also be considered in terms of a more detailed classification of closely linked rule functions or types. Within the IAD framework seven types of rule are commonly identified (Ostrom 2005a):

- *Boundary rules* (or entry and exit rules) affect the number of actors with roles and influence in a situation, the attributes and resources needed for these roles, actors' ability to enter and exit these roles, and the terms of entry and exit.

- *Position rules* (which are closely related to boundary rules) establish the particular (and relative) roles and influence of actors in the situation.

- *Authority rules* (associated with the abovementioned rules) assign sets of actions that actors in given positions should, may, or should not take (the set of decisions open to them).

- *Scope rules* determine the range of outcomes that can be affected by these actions.

- *Aggregation rules* affect the degree of control that actors are able to exercise in initiating actions.

- *Information rules* affect the information that actors acquire and use.

- *Payoff rules* determine the costs and benefits associated with particular actions, outcomes, and actors.

These types of rule interact closely and can be analyzed in terms of the way that they reflect (1) power relations and (2) individual and collective mechanisms for dealing with problems of imperfect information, bounded rationality, and asymmetric information. In any situation there are also generally several different rules of each type.

How institutions work.   There is some overlap between the functions of institutions and the way that institutions provide incentives, sanctions, and information to promote particular types of behavior. There are other dimensions that can be considered in terms of different structural elements: contractual forms, institutional sectors, incentive systems, property rights, and cost sharing.[4] In each of these dimensions particular types with specific characteristics are identified, but it must be recognized that although consideration of these types is useful in setting out basic institutional variations, many (perhaps most) institutions do not conform to these pure types and are best understood as hybrids. Furthermore, the different types overlap in different ways across the various structural elements discussed below. The purpose of this discussion, therefore, is not to define particular combinations of structural elements in different action domains but to set out in broad terms the ways in which different functions may be performed by different institutions.

Three basic types of *contractual form* are recognized in the transaction-cost literature: market, hierarchy, and gift exchange.[5] Williamson (1991) in particular analyzes the influence of asset specificity, frequency of exchange, and uncertainty in influencing actors' choice of spot-market, hierarchy, or hybrid (bilateral contractual) contracts to reduce transaction costs and risks in industrial economies.[6] In some other literatures gift exchange is described more in terms of investment in and utilization of social capital; thus here it is referred to as social reciprocity where investment in social capital (through gifts and participation in social activities) leads to direct and indirect claims on others (such as for labor, food, money, and political or social support).

The importance of social reciprocity is widely recognized in traditional rural communities: economic development is often considered to involve declining reliance on social reciprocity and increasing reliance on markets, because markets, when they work well, provide more efficient information and incentives for efficient resource allocation and exchange. However, the important roles of both hierarchies and social reciprocity in supporting market exchange are often overlooked. Hierarchies are particularly important in developed market economies, where a substantial proportion of transactions are not conducted in competitive markets but within firms and in long-term relationships between firms (see, for example, Williamson 1991; Coase 1992; Hall and Soskice 2001). This situation is particularly relevant to modern supermarket procurement systems (Reardon and Timmer 2005). Globally the proportion of transactions occurring within firms is growing, and two-thirds of world trade is either within transnational corporations or associated with them (see Yusuf 2001). Similarly, the importance of social reciprocity in market economies is often underestimated: this effort includes firms' investments in reputation with consumers and in personal relations with key personnel in other firms they work with (for example, through corporate hospitality and other social interactions in business relationships). It also includes gift exchange by teams in hierarchies to promote working together and effective sharing of responsibilities, tasks, resources, and rewards. Social reciprocity may be particularly important in the development of supply chains and market, hierarchy, and hybrid relations in rural areas (Johnson, Suarez, and Lundy 2002). Such exchange underpins collective action in which individuals and groups manage resources to meet shared goals. Collective action can, therefore, be considered as a particular contractual form closely related to and reliant on social capital–based exchange.

Just as there are three types of contractual forms (and a range of hybrids), there are also three typical *institutional sectors* of actors[7] and action in enforcement and coordination in a domain—the private, state, and collective-action sectors (Uphoff 1993a). These are loosely related with the contractual forms discussed above. As already noted, market forms of exchange are most commonly found in the private sector, hierarchy may be the predominant contractual form in the state sector, and social reciprocity may be closely related to collective action. However, private-sector firms that interact through the market are themselves hierarchies (unless they are very small), and social reciprocity and collective action may be important for both their internal and external relations. Many private-sector market operations also depend on and are nested in hierarchical contracts by which states regulate markets and limit opportunistic behavior. Similarly although the state sector may involve predominantly hierarchical command-and-control contracts both within state agencies and between the state and other agents, market contracts may also be important (as the state contracts out services, for example, and is also a significant player in financial and other markets). These relationships also use social reciprocity and collective action (as discussed above), and indeed the power and capacity of the state depends on its social capital. Similarly, players in the collective-action sector enter into markets and may, like firms, use hierarchical contracts in their own structures and engage in hierarchical relations with other players in the collective-action sector.

The third structural element of institutions relates to the *incentive systems* that support and are used by the contractual forms and institutional sectors discussed above. What is it that encourages actors to behave in accordance with institutions? Uphoff (1993a) loosely aligns the different sectors with different incentive systems. He characterizes these incentive systems as remunerative (actors gain from interactions with one another), coercive (actors are forced to interact in particular ways by threats), and normative (actors are induced to behave in certain ways by personal or collective norms of behavior). Market interactions in the private sector are considered to involve primarily remunerative incentives; the collective-action sector to involve both normative and remunerative (with emphasis on the former); and the state sector to involve all three forms of incentives. These can also be mapped against social capital–based exchange, hierarchy, and market contracts.

The fourth structural element relates to the way that the *property-rights system* works. Property rights are defined and discussed more fully in Chapters 13 and 14. They can involve collective, public, and private rights (and of course hybrids among them). Although the mechanisms of establishment and enforcement of rights are loosely correlated with the collective-action, public, and private sectors, private property rights are normally embedded in wider state and collective rights, and actors in different sectors may hold a range of types of property rights.

The question of the embeddedness of property rights is closely related to the final structural element in this discussion of how institutions work: the *cost-sharing system*. This system refers to the way that enforcement and coordination costs are shared in society. Again, private, public, and collective costs are considered. In the last case the costs of establishing, operating, maintaining, and adapting institutions are borne by specific social or economic groups. This case largely pertains to isolated and traditional rural communities. Market activity in such communities would probably rely significantly on group and individual social capital. Where wider institutions (beyond the community) are weakly developed, individuals wishing to engage in private-sector markets would have to bear much of the coordination and enforcement costs. These high private costs would likely lead to market failure for many goods and services and the development of hybrid rather than spot-market contracts where these could be established. Some of these contracts would involve collective action among producers and traders, with a transfer of costs from individuals to producer and trader associations, which are able to achieve economies of scale in transaction costs. Further development of the economy would involve improved provision of communications infrastructure, information, trading standards, and the rule of law by the state, with a transfer of collective and private costs to the public sector. The improved institutional environment that this transfer provides allows the expansion of market exchanges across wider geographic areas without large increases in the private costs of exchange. The private costs of operating large hierarchies also fall, allowing hierarchies to grow and larger hierarchies to become more common—although market arrangements would still have lower private transaction costs than would hierarchical arrangements (but often with the disadvantage of higher transaction risks).

Application of these principles in natural resource management, however, is more problematic. Isolated and traditional communities often have property rights over natural resources that are defined and enforced by the group, with a combination of individual and collective use and management rights. With increasing contact with outsiders—whether the state or other individuals, firms, or groups—the locally defined rights that are vested, at some level (whether use or allocation level) in the local community may not be recognized by the outsiders. If those outsiders also wish to use the resource, the existing customary rights may not stand up to the increased competition. The result has often been policies to either nationalize the resource or to privatize it so that it can be transferred to outsiders. The latter has been associated, in theory, with higher efficiency, because resources can be transferred to more productive users and used as collateral to obtain credit. However, allowing unfettered sales of natural resources often ignores overlapping claims on the resource, as well as power and wealth differentials between local and external interests. The result can be negative third-party effects and the overall loss of value of output as secondary uses are cut off. These issues are returned to in Section 3.2.2, where the importance of resource attributes in determining appropriate cost-sharing systems and contractual forms is discussed.

The efficient distribution of enforcement and coordination costs varies with the extent and distribution of economic activity, the attributes of the activities, and the attributes of the actors. This important theme lies at the heart of this book (see, for example, the discussion concerning Figures 1.1 and 1.2 in Chapter 1). It is taken up again, in different ways, later in this chapter and subsequent ones.

Our discussion of institutions and their attributes has provides some order to a complex set of arrangements that cannot be described in any neat and linear structure. The discussion above has also regularly used the term "actors" without defining it—actors are discussed in more detail in Section 3.2.3. Before leaving this discussion of institutions and their attributes, however, note that the term "actor" has been used to describe a decisionmaking entity. In this sense, although individuals are important actors in an action domain, they often work with and are part of aggregate groups that are also actors—households, different social groups, economic and user associations, firms and state agencies—though their behavior is influenced by the interactions among their constituent actors. It is this interaction of institutions and actors at multiple levels, sometimes inter-nested, that leads to many of the difficulties analysts face in understanding institutions and their attributes.

3.2.2 Activities and Attributes

This section examines the nature of activities in the action domain. Production and exchange *processes* that actors engage in and the *resources* and *products* (goods and services) that are managed, used, produced, and exchanged are included under the term "activities." Understanding the attributes of these processes, resources, and products is important when (1) these attributes affect the benefits, costs, and risks to actors (and hence their ability to invest and engage in them), and (2) these benefits, costs, and risks can be modified by different contractual forms and terms, property-rights systems, and incentive systems. Actors are expected to craft contractual arrangements that maximize the risk-adjusted net benefits that adhere to limits determined by the wider policy and governance environment, past experience and path dependency, and power relations.

Jaffee and Morton (1995) treat the distinctive techno-economic characteristics of the individual commodities as major determinants of institutional arrangements developed and adopted by transacting parties. Dorward (2001) draws on Jaffee and Morton (1995) to break these "techno-economic characteristics" into commodity and transaction characteristics. Transaction characteristics include volume and frequency, uncertainty and bounded rationality, asset specificity, and scope for opportunism. These traits relate to one another and depend significantly on commodity characteristics—price and volume (production) uncertainty, perishability, processing and storage requirements, quality, seasonality, economies of scale, the supply chain and the commodity's place in it, and government interventions. Further commodity (or resource) characteristics identified by Ostrom (1990, 1992) as being of great relevance to natural resource management include the ease of resource use by multiple users (subtractability or rivalness); the ease of exclusion of potential users (excludability); the importance of interactions and interdependence in use, management, and benefits across natural resources (externalities); the degree to which benefits can be divided among users (divisibility); the degree to which benefits can be transferred between users (transferability); the size and dispersion of benefits (boundedness); the temporal distribution of the resource and predictability across time and space; the mobility of resources (for example, of fish or wildlife); and the extent to which different items or bundles of resources can be distinguished from one another or identified.

Activities (products, processes, and resources) also differ in the value that actors place on them. In many societies, for example, land has social and spiritual significance that is more important than its productive or monetary value. Similar observations may be made about the keeping of animals, growing of some crops, and particular aspects of labor use by different social groups.

The nature and importance of many of the activity characteristics listed above are examined in more detail in the case study chapters in Parts 2 and 3 of the book. Here they are considered in terms of five broad and related dimensions that determine the institutional arrangements maximizing risk-adjusted net benefits to actors. Four of these dimensions have their primary influence on the institutional arrangements governing relations among actors who are stakeholders in the same activities (for example, among farmers, fishers, workers, or traders). These dimensions are the relative costs and returns of excluding others from the benefits of using a resource, product, or service; the economies of scale in a process or in transactions associated with a process; the importance and nature of externalities; and the importance and characteristics of renewable natural resources in the activity. The fifth dimension— the relative transaction risks and returns of a process—has its primary influence on the institutional arrangements governing relations among actors using the same supply chain (for example, among fishers, fish processors, and fish traders or among farm-input suppliers, farmers, and agricultural produce buyers). Each of these dimensions is explained in turn below.

Relative costs and returns of exclusion. Resources, goods, and services differ in the ease with which their owners or producers can exclude others from benefiting from their use. Excludability depends upon the extent to which resources, their products, or their use are bounded, divisible, dispersed, identifiable, mobile, and rival (or subtractable).[8] Excludability relates to the cost of preventing others from using the resource, whereas subtractability refers to situations in which use of the resource by one individual reduces the amount available to others. Resources that have high excludability can be managed efficiently as private property; those with low excludability but also low subtractability are public goods that the state can provide. Those with low excludability and high subtractability are common pool resources, which are the most susceptible to degradation through the "tragedy of the commons" if management institutions are weak or lacking.[9]

When excludability is high, the costs of exclusion are low and can largely be ignored by investors: production costs and sales revenues are the main items to be considered in investment decisions. When excludability is low, however, the costs of enforcing exclusion also need to be taken into account in investment decisions. If these costs are sufficiently high relative to potential returns, they may make otherwise profitable investments unprofitable. The result will be market failure (that is, profits from engaging in the activity are insufficient to justify transaction risks and costs, even though underlying prices and input–output relations suggest transactions should be profitable), unless:

1. The state intervenes to enforce property rights or subsidize production.

2. Potential investors are able to take some collective nonmarket action to enforce property rights at lower cost than would be possible were they to act individually.

3. A small number of individual investors are able to invest on a sufficiently large scale to make it worthwhile to take on the costs of nonmarket action to enforce property or use rights.

This analysis therefore suggests that in a spectrum of activities with increasing costs of enforcing exclusion relative to returns, those with lower exclusion cost/return ratios are amenable to smaller scale market exchange (with all the efficiencies of well-functioning markets), whereas higher exclusion costs lead to increased activity coordination and integration through collective action or larger firms (hierarchies). Very high exclusion costs, however, lead to market failure or, if the state considers it worthwhile, to state action (another form of hierarchy) to overcome market failure.

Economies of scale in a process or in transactions associated with a process.   The relative costs and benefits of excluding other parties from using resources, goods or services have been shown to be an important attribute determining both the benefits of activity coordination (whether achieved through hierarchies or collective action) and, in more extreme situations, the occurrence of market failure (and possibly state intervention to overcome market failure). However, this relation is largely a special case of a more general pattern: higher economies of scale in activities lead to a shift from independent market exchanges to activity coordination and integration (with larger scales of production, management, or transaction) and to market failure (or state intervention). Economies of scale may arise because of exclusion costs as discussed above, transaction costs,[10] or high fixed costs of management or machinery. Natural resources that are highly variable over time and space have economies of scale, as seen in many rangeland areas. The production of multiple products from the same resource may also create economies of scale (or of scope), as seen in community forests that provide a range of products used with different frequency (as opposed to private monocropped woodlots that might provide only timber or firewood).

Importance and nature of externalities.   *Externalities* are nonexcludable costs or benefits arising from the existence or use of a resource. They are therefore closely associated with issues of excludability. Although economies of scale in general (and more specifically the relative costs and benefits of excluding other parties from using resources, goods, or services) are important determinants of the scale and form of institutional arrangements for the management of activities, these arrangements are also affected by the extent and nature of externalities associated with them. Their management, however, goes beyond the consideration of relative costs and returns of exclusion: coordination is needed among actors owning or managing activities with externalities and others affected by these externalities, and market mechanisms on their own will not provide such coordination. When the number of actors involved is relatively small, they may be managed by collective action (perhaps involving some collective-action/market hybrid arrangements). As the number of actors increases and coordination becomes more complex, collective action becomes more difficult, and more hierarchical arrangements are needed for coordination. Again these may involve some hybrid arrangement, mixing collective action and hierarchy, but in complex multi-stakeholder situations the state likely needs to be involved to provide some element of hierarchical coordination.

Natural resources.   Natural resources are a dimension that influences the institutional arrangements governing relations among actors who are stakeholders in the same activities for two reasons. First, externalities associated with multiple-use rights are particularly important and complex for many, particularly renewable, natural resources. This factor leads to the general importance of collective and state action in natural resource management.

Second, the general pattern of private-market contracts giving way to hierarchical or collective contractual forms of activity coordination (or to market failure or state intervention as exclusion costs rise relative to returns) can take on a particular form in natural resources management activities, as these resources generally exist without any investment (where levels of utilization are low). The returns to enforcement of exclusive-use rights depends on the value of losses incurred if these rights are not enforced. These losses (and the returns to enforcement of exclusive-use rights) are generally low for nonrival (or nonsubtractable) goods or services, or for rival (subtractable) goods or services when exploitation is low compared to natural stocks or rates of use.[11] Under such conditions open access prevails (the equivalent to market failure for capital items and services not provided by the natural environment) unless the state regulates access and use. If there are increased losses from nonenforcement, however, there may be increased gains from establishing and enforcing property rights. Increasing losses from nonenforcement encourage common property arrangements or large-scale hierarchical management units and then, with high returns to exclusive-rights enforcement, private management of small-scale units.

Relative transaction risks and returns.   The four dimensions of activity attributes discussed above are important because they affect contractual arrangements and property rights for particular resources, goods, or services in terms of the relations among different (potential) users, owners, producers, and managers of these elements. The ways in which activity attributes affect contractual arrangements between resource owners, process managers, and buyers and sellers along a supply chain are now considered.

As noted earlier, Williamson has identified uncertainty, asset specificity, and frequency of exchange as key influences of actors' preferences for market, hybrid, and hierarchical contractual forms (see Williamson 1985, 1991). Uncertainty and asset specificity are important for the way that they affect the risks of loss from transaction failure compared with the potential gains from successful transactions. This can be considered in terms of an investment's transaction risk/return ratio. This ratio is high in conditions of uncertainty and for large investments in more specific assets (assets whose returns are specific to and dependent on a particular set of transactions).

Uncertainty is linked to imperfect information, bounded rationality, and opportunism. Bounded rationality (an inability to make use of all information available) and opportunism (which can lead to unpredictable and potentially damaging behavior by transaction partners) both contribute to uncertainty and risk of transaction failure. Actors also face a third source of uncertainty and risk of failure: some aspects of the environment are highly variable and unpredictable (climate, yields, disease and pest attacks, and prices, for example). This type of uncertainty is sometimes known as *substantive* uncertainty, whereas uncertainty due to bounded rationality is known as *procedural* uncertainty. These three types of uncertainty interact, as substantive and procedural uncertainties often make it more difficult to control opportunism (for example, crop buyers can give farmers poor prices for their produce under the pretext that central market prices are very low, when this may not be the case).

However, uncertainty alone does not lead to risk of financial loss in a transaction. Such losses are only incurred if an adverse event leads to transaction failure and an actor has invested in specific assets (those that cannot easily or cheaply be redirected to other uses if the transaction fails). General examples of specific assets in agriculture include tree crops, specialized technical knowledge, and fixed specialized processing facilities. Dorward and Kydd (2004) note that asset specificity is primarily the result of thin markets for an asset. As a result, in the weak markets that are common in poor rural areas in Africa, many assets have high specificity, although such assets would not generally be considered as specific assets in economies with thicker functioning markets that would allow redeployment. This circumstance has important implications for agricultural supply-chain development, as discussed in Chapter 5.

Uncertainty and asset specificity are together important codeterminants of transaction risks, because uncertainty increases the probability of transaction failure, and large investments in specific assets increase the scale of potential losses from transaction failure. Potentially high returns from transactions, however, reduce the transaction risk/return ratio. This ratio is important for actors' institutional preferences as, with higher risks, actors look for ways to reduce transaction risks. In particular they are likely to look for contractual forms that reduce risks by establishing longer term (hybrid or hierarchy) arrangements that bind buyers and sellers in a transaction, with improved communication (to reduce substantive and procedural uncertainty) and monitoring and incentive systems to control opportunism. The establishment and maintenance of such arrangements involve transaction costs. If it is not possible to establish such arrangements at reasonable costs, then potential investors may decide not to invest. The result is market failure, unless the state steps in to enforce or subsidize transactions (that is, by reducing transaction risks and/or costs or increasing returns).

The third activity attribute identified by Williamson as influencing contractual forms is frequency of exchange: when buyers and sellers of a good or service have an interest in repeated transactions, the establishment of hybrid or hierarchical relationships is likely to yield higher returns than is the case for individual transactions. These higher returns arise because (1) the fixed costs of the relationship are spread over more transactions (with lower cost per transaction), (2) the prospect of continuing gains from future transactions creates incentives for parties to fulfil their obligations in each transaction and not behave opportunistically, and (3) greater exchange frequency is also often associated with reduced procedural uncertainty as repetition increases familiarity with transaction procedures. Frequency of exchange can therefore moderate the transaction risk/return ratio—more frequent exchanges can, with hybrid or hierarchical relations, reduce risks and raise returns.

Figure 3.4 shows the stylized relationships among frequency of transaction, the transaction risk/return ratio, and contractual forms. Figure 3.4a shows how the

Figure 3.4   Frequency of exchange, transaction risk/return ratio, and contractual forms

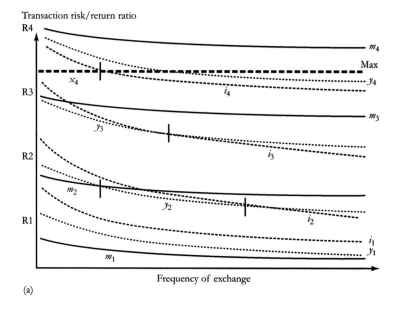

(a)

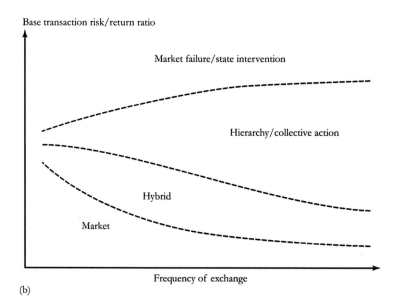

(b)

transaction risk/return ratio for different contractual forms changes with frequency of exchange under different risk/return scenarios. These scenarios are labeled R1 to R4 in order of increasing risk, and for each scenario three sets of lines show how the risk/return ratio changes for the three main types of contractual form (with a solid line for market transactions, a dotted line for hybrid transactions, and a dashed line for hierarchy transactions). Contracting parties should choose the contractual form that gives the lowest risk/return ratio for a particular frequency of exchange under each scenario. These are indicated by m, y, or i (to represent market, hybrid, and hierarchy, respectively) for each scenario. In scenario R1 market arrangements give the lowest risk/return ratio; in scenario R2 the same applies at low frequency of exchange, but with increasing frequency first hybrid and then hierarchy forms have the lowest ratio. In scenario R3 hybrid arrangements have a lower ratio than do market arrangements even at low frequency of exchange, but with higher frequency, hierarchy forms have a lower ratio. Finally in the highest risk/return scenario (R4) there are no contractual forms that can yield an acceptable risk/return ratio (below the dashed line marked "Max") at low frequency of exchange, leading to market failure (indicated by x_4 on the figure). With high frequency of exchange, however, hierarchy arrangements can reduce the risk/return ratio sufficiently to make them viable.[12]

Figure 3.4b generalizes the analysis of Figure 3.4a to show how preferred types of contractual arrangement vary with different combinations of frequency of exchange (on the horizontal axis) and base transaction risk/return ratio[13] (on the vertical axis). The figure shows (1) how increases in transaction risk (indicated by the base transaction risk/return ratio) make market relations less attractive relative to hybrid relations, so that further increases in the risk/return ratio lead to hierarchy and then to market failure (as discussed earlier) and (2) how the advantages of hybrid and then hierarchical relations relative to market relations grow with higher frequency of exchange, which may also reduce the likelihood of market failure as the risk/return ratio increases.

The stylized relationships in Figure 3.4 will, however, be modified by a number of factors: the institutional environment (including institutional attributes, as discussed in Section 3.2.1), actor characteristics (discussed in Section 3.2.3), the physical/infrastructural and political/governance environment (discussed in Section 3.3), and other activity attributes.[14] The importance of other activity attributes is illustrated by the existence of common property resource and open access regimes for high-exclusion cost/return natural resources, as discussed earlier. Supply chains also involve a variety of activities that may have different techno-economic characteristics (suggesting different contractual forms) but that need to be bound together in the same contractual arrangements. Similarly one resource may be used in different supply chains with different activity characteristics. When multiple use rights exist, they introduce another level of complexity to institutional development and analysis. Finally path dependency —the historical context that shapes institutions, actors, and their attributes—is a major influence on institutional arrangements and may lead to deviations from what might appear to be optimal or least-cost institutional arrangements. Complex and overlapping mixes of institutional arrangements are therefore common.

3.2.3   Actors and Their Attributes

As with institutions and activities, the analysis of actors and attributes involves an iterative process of identification in the context of institutions, activities, and their respective attributes. The analysis starts with a discussion of different types of actors, followed by a consideration of the types of attributes that may be important to them.

Types of actors.   From the earlier discussion of institutions it should be apparent that actors in an action domain can be in the private, public, or collective-action sectors. There are also actors who do not fall neatly into any of these sectors and are best considered as hybrids. Uphoff (1993a) provides a useful analysis of the continuum of different types of local organizations (Table 3.1).[15]

Table 3.2 provides another perspective on a similar set of issues. It highlights the multiple involvement of members as owners and suppliers of capital, as clients and (for some) as employees in multiple membership organizations. These roles can lead to conflicting interests that do not arise in the same way in nongovernmental organizations (NGOs) or private companies. The nature of these conflicts vary with the rules under which farmer organizations operate—their norms of behavior, their articles or by-laws, their relationships with other organizations, and national laws relating to different forms of association. (A distinction needs to be recognized between de jure and de facto laws and regulations, the former existing in name whether or not they are implemented, the latter being those that are actually applied.) Tables 3.1 and 3.2 identify the multiple roles of different individuals in the various types of organization.

Table 3.1   Continuum of types of local organization by sector

Type of organization	Public sector		Collective action sector		Private sector	
	Local administration	Local government	Membership	Cooperative	Service	Private business
Orientation of local organization	Bureaucratic	Political	Self-help (common interests)	Self-help (resource pooling)	Charitable (nonprofit enterprise)	Profit making (business enterprise)
Role of individuals in organization	Citizens or subjects	Voters and constituents	Members	Members (or owners), clients, and employees	Clients (or beneficiaries) and employees	Owners clients, and employees

Adapted from Uphoff (1986, Figure 1.2; 1993b, Figure 3).

Table 3.2 Principal roles of individuals in farmer organizations, private companies, and NGOs

Role in organization	Farmer organization	NGO	Private company
Suppliers of capital	Members, donors, banks, and trading partners	Donors	Equity: shareholders Loans: banks and trading partners
Clients	Members and nonmembers	Beneficiaries	Customers
Employees	Members and nonmembers	Not owners	Not generally owners

Source: Adapted from Stockbridge et al. (2003).
Note: NGO, nongovernmental organization.

Uphoff (1993a) also makes an important distinction between organizations or actors that operate at different levels and involve different degrees of aggregation among individuals (Table 3.3). It is important that institutional analysis explicitly consider these different levels when defining the boundaries of the action domain and the allocation of institutions and organizations or actors between the action domain and the environment. However, institutional changes (such as deconcentration, devolution, and decentralization—discussed in Chapters 14 and 17) may shift the boundaries of the action domain as well as change the institutions and actors with responsibilities for particular activities.

Uphoff's (1993a) identification of sectors and levels or scope of activities is helpful in classifying organizational actors, but at the lowest level he does not categorize individual people into his three sectors—most individuals have multiple roles and relationships among the different sectors. It is therefore often more helpful to categorize individuals by social or economic characteristics that relate to their roles in the action domain (their interests and aspirations, resources, and social grouping).

Attributes of actors. At the outset of analysis it is important to remember the general characteristics of economic actors that affect their economic behavior: imperfect information, bounded rationality, self-interest, and opportunism. The extent to which these characteristics are present varies among actors and is affected by the attributes of their activities as well as by their own attributes discussed below.

In Section 3.2.2 it was noted that when actors are exposed to high risks of loss from transaction failure due to significant investments in specific assets and uncertainty in prices or transaction partners, they often wish to engage in bilateral (hybrid) contracts or even in vertically integrated hierarchical contracts rather than spot-market transactions to reduce risks. In this case, therefore, asset attributes appear to be major influences on contractual forms. This conclusion, however, depends upon actors' aversion to risk—more risk-averse actors will have a greater preference for risk-reducing contractual forms, and therefore actor attributes that reduce or increase risk aversion may influence preferences for different contractual forms. Furthermore, because actors who are party to the same activities may have different risk preferences and may use different resources and processes (for example, farmers and crop buyers

Table 3.3   Institutional sectors, levels of action, and decisionmaking

Level	Sector		
	Public	Collective action	Private
International	United Nations agency; multilateral and bilateral donor agencies	Society for International Development	Multinational corporation; PVO
National	Central government ministry; parastatal corporation	National cooperative federation; national women's association	National corporation; national PVO; PVO coordinating body
Regional	Regional administrative body; regional development authority	Regional cooperative federation; watershed consultative assembly	Regional company; regional PVO; PVO council
District	District council; district administrative office	District supply cooperative; soil conservation educational forum	District firm; charitable organization
Subdistrict	Subdistrict council; sub-district administrative office	Subdistrict marketing cooperative; area sports club	Rural enterprise; private hospital; bank branch office
Local	Division council; health clinic; secondary school; extension office	Wholesale cooperative society; forest protection association	Market town business; service club (for example, Rotary)
Community	Village council; post office; primary school; extension worker	Primary cooperative society; village dike patrol; parent-teachers association	Village shop; mosque committee for village welfare
Group	Caste panchayat; ward or neighborhood assembly	Tubewell Users Association; mothers' club; savings group	Microenterprise
Individual	Citizen, voter, taxpayer, partaker of services	Member	Customer, client, beneficiary, employee

Source: Uphoff (1993).
Note: PVO, external private voluntary organization.

may be partners in crop-purchase transactions but may have different specific assets and risk exposure), these actors' contractual arrangement preferences may differ. In this case the terms and forms of transaction will be subject to bargaining. The result of this bargaining depends on the relative power of the different parties (Dorward 2001), where power may be a function of such attributes as access to information; social status and relations; alternative livelihood options; links to urban centers; political and other connections; willingness to bargain; education and literacy; self-confidence; previous experience; access to capital, land, and labor; gender, age, caste, and ethnicity; and willingness to engage in protracted bargaining processes.

Particular resources that confer actors with power to bargain are termed "action resources" (Di Gregorio et al. 2005). Examples of action resources that may be amenable to rapid change are information (for example, through access to mobile phones), and cognitive schema in which people view themselves and the limits of their ability to act.

Actor attributes may also be affected by membership in social groups, whose members can act together to improve their bargaining position. Such groups may provide social support or material resources to represent their members' interests. These groups, when effective, can be considered as actors in their own right.

3.3 Environment

Three categories of factors define the environment in which action domains are embedded: physical and technical factors, socioeconomic factors, and policy and governance factors. The interactive impacts of these three categories of environmental factors condition how institutions and attributes of actors and activities combine to shape outcomes (see Figure 3.2). Identifying and analyzing these interrelationships is therefore crucial. The main elements to be considered in the environment and their attributes are briefly discussed below, followed by some illustrations of how the environment can interact with other elements in institutional analysis. The boundaries between the environment and the action domain have been discussed in Sections 3.2 and 3.2.1.

3.3.1 Physical and Technical Environment

In agriculture, geography and climate are central features of the physical environment. Biophysical conditions—such as levels and variability (seasonality) of rainfall and temperature, soil quality, and access to surface and ground water—are crucial determinants of production potential and risk (for example, from drought; flooding; and human, animal, and crop pests and diseases). The more favorable these conditions, the higher the potential of agricultural sectors, and vice versa. Biophysical conditions vary widely across Africa, suggesting corresponding diversity in production potential. Also important is the level of infrastructural development in the form of roads, transport services, telecommunications, marketplaces, and irrigation systems. The relationship between population density and the level and quality of infrastructure is crucial. As argued in Chapter 1, in many African countries population growth has far outstripped infrastructure development.

The degree of technological advancement relative to the frontier represented by the newest and most promising technologies defines the technical limits of production and exchange. The diversified subsistence-oriented production systems that dominate agriculture in most of Africa are based on technical and organizational routines poorly suited to the requirements of agro-industrialization built on commercialized agriculture. The interactions of these physical and technical conditions with those in the socioeconomic and policy spheres delineate actual opportunities.

3.3.2 Socioeconomic Environment

Socioeconomic conditions refer to the demographic, sociocultural, and economic underpinnings of societies. Population levels and distributions define land/labor ratios, with important consequences for land management, the choice of production technology, and supply of goods and services; they also influence patterns of demand and thus scope for trade in matching supply and demand. Birth, mortality, and morbidity rates influence a range of investment choices, most notably in education, thereby influencing long-term prospects for growth and poverty reduction.

Distributions of human, financial, and social assets (or capital) have major implications for levels and distributions of income, wealth, and power. Highly unequal distributions of these variables in many African countries thus reflect deeper disparities in asset holdings.

Cultural heterogeneity and interactions across ethnic groups impact importantly on several key determinants of social welfare, including the size and behavior of markets, the scope and nature of collective action, the performance of public organizations, and the form of political discourse. Cultural norms shape values as well as behavioral patterns. Cultural habits tend to be deeply held and highly resilient to change, suggesting major challenges in effecting long-lasting change in many societies.

The socioeconomic environment thus represents the milieu in which physical and technical realities express themselves. It is the underlying context for broader policy and governance regimes.

3.3.3 Policy and Governance Environment

Policy and governance conditions comprise the set of fundamental political, social, and legal ground rules that establish the basis for production, exchange, and distribution. Rules governing political elections and representation determine long-term political stability. Judicial systems—especially the availability of courts to resolve disputes—define property rights, rights to contract, and the scope for contract enforcement. The nature and stability (predictability) of macroeconomic, sectoral, and trade regimes influence investment climates, most notably through interest and inflation rates. Legislation and related administrative processes establish channels of authority for the use of public, communal, and private resources, especially land. Contracts related to concessions, disciplinary actions, and personnel rules affect recruitment, retention, promotion, and discipline of human resources in public and private agencies. In many cases these formal systems coexist with customary institutions that may not only inform them but also sometimes provide an alternative, competing forum for the allocation and distribution of productive resources as well as for conflict resolution.

Together these policy and governance factors condition how physical, technical, and socioeconomic factors are articulated in given settings, thereby establishing links through which prevailing conditions influence the future and determining the direction and pace of change in societies. Clearly, some of these policy and governance conditions might also be defined as institutions within some action domains. The key recognition is that environments and action domains are nested. Decisions about whether conditions belong in or outside action domains depend on the scale of analysis and the set of issues under consideration. These issues are discussed in Chapter 20.

3.3.4   Action Domain–Environment Interactions

Some of the impacts of the environment on elements in the action domain need little discussion. It is, for example, apparent that climatic, price, or macroeconomic uncertainty tends to increase uncertainty among activities related to these elements, which has consequences for contractual forms, as discussed in Section 3.2.2. This influence is important, given the many sources of uncertainty and risk in smallholder agriculture in Africa.

Other interactions among the environment, institutions, and agricultural development in Africa may be less obvious. Some of the forms that these can take can be illustrated with reference to three further characteristics of poor rural economies in Africa: thin markets, weak institutions, and a low level of economic activity among dispersed populations.

It was noted earlier that asset specificity as defined by Williamson (1985) is the result of thin markets, as it represents an investment in an asset that cannot easily or cheaply be transferred to another use. Limited opportunities for transferring the asset to another use arise because there is limited demand for use of the asset outside the transaction that justified the investment. Many assets that would be easily transferred to other uses in a more developed economy can therefore take on the characteristics of specific assets in poor rural economies with low levels of economic activity and thin markets. Examples might include fertilizers and other agricultural inputs and investments in general storage facilities (for input or produce traders). The consequent increased importance of asset specificity in agricultural supply chains means that small players in atomistic markets are less likely to find it worthwhile to engage in activities in these supply chains. Apart from traditional export crop supply chains, however, these rural economies tend to lack large firms that are able to engage in supply-chain coordination, and hybrid contractual arrangements are often slow to develop, limited in extent, and fragile.

The tendency for thin markets to increase the importance of asset specificity in poor rural economies, and hence demand a greater role for hybrid and hierarchy (as opposed to market) contractual forms, can be reinforced by a weak institutional environment. Dorward et al. (2005) note that highly productive technologies require intensive and effective mechanisms for complex coordination and exchange, to allow investment in and operation of different specialized activities with increasing input purchases and output sales. Increased exchange places demands on the institutional environment, with the highest demands for market exchange and lower demands for hybrid and hierarchy exchange (because hybrid and hierarchical contractual forms internalize more transaction-enforcement mechanisms and costs compared to market exchanges), although as noted in Section 3.2.1 the costs of running hierarchies are also reduced with stronger institutional environments.

Dorward et al. (2005) explore this dynamic with a diagram that maps technological development on the horizontal axis and the strength or effectiveness of the institutional environment on the vertical axis (Figure 3.5). Economic development involves movement from the lower left to the upper right of the diagram, with complementary progress in institutional and technological development. This stylized representation yields several useful insights about the interactions between technological and institutional change in economic development. A poorly developed institutional environment cannot support highly advanced technologies, and therefore market failure occurs in the lower right of the diagram. In the upper left corner, however, a highly developed institutional environment allows effective competitive markets to support relatively simple technologies. Along the diagonal from the lower left to the upper right there is a zone of ambiguity: here the institutional environment may not be sufficiently developed to support increasingly intensive markets that are required for the coordination and exchange needed by more productive technologies. Hybrid and hierarchical arrangements, however, may be more effective for supporting these technologies in such conditions.

This analysis suggests that there is no a priori reason for expecting economic development to involve the promotion of competitive market arrangements—more emphasis may be needed on promoting hybrid and hierarchical arrangements that serve development interests. Dorward et al. (2005) argue that this pattern of development is indeed what has been generally been observed in successful economic development in the twentieth century.

Our final illustration of the interaction between the environment and the development of institutional arrangements concerns the effects of dispersed populations and low levels of economic development on poor rural people's access to services. As noted in Chapter 1, many poor rural areas in Africa have dispersed populations with poor communications and low levels of economic activity. Together these conditions

Figure 3.5   Technology, institutional environment, and contractual arrangements in economic development

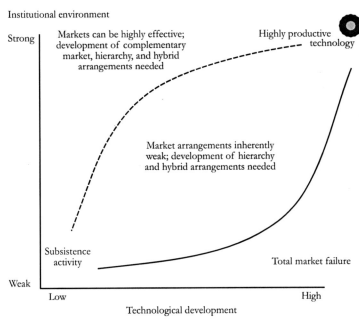

Source: Adapted from Dorward et al. (2005).

lead to a low density of economic activity and high transaction costs (and risks) for providers of services, as it takes time and other resources to search, screen, and monitor transaction partners. Dorward, Poulton, and Kydd (2001) apply this analysis in a review of rural and agricultural financial services and extend Von Pischke's (1993) concept of a financial frontier to map out a low-cost financial service frontier (Figure 3.6). This map shows how market access to financial services is more difficult for small, poor businesses or households (with smaller, more costly transactions than for large businesses) and for lower levels of economic development and density. As a result, the low-cost financial service frontier slopes down from left to right in Figure 3.6: businesses or households located to the right and above this frontier can access such services; those to the left and below the frontier cannot, and their only access to financial services (if any) is to high-cost services that are generally too expensive for financing productive investments and are only used in emergencies.

Figure 3.6 also shows how microfinance systems can be seen as an institutional innovation that shifts the low-cost financial service frontier downward, establishing new institutional arrangements that reduce transaction costs and risks for both

Figure 3.6 The low-cost financial service frontier and institutional innovation

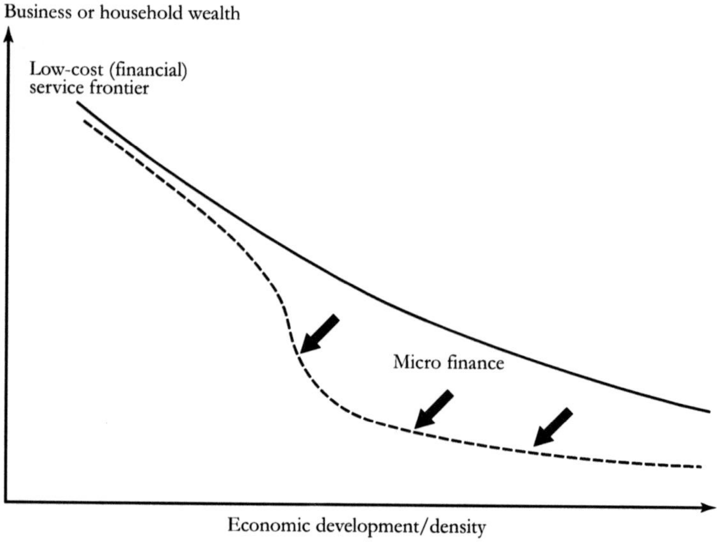

Source: Adapted from Dorward, Poulton, and Kydd (2001).

financial service providers and poor people accessing these services. However, micro-finance systems do not normally reach the very poor, nor do they extend into poorer rural areas. They are also not well suited to seasonal rainfed crop production.

The analysis of Figure 3.6 can be generalized to other types of service delivery and economic activity by recognizing (1) the concept of low-cost service delivery frontiers and (2) the need for new institutional arrangements to push these frontiers down.

3.4 Action Outcomes

We conclude this discussion of the analytical framework by considering action outcomes. These may be actions by actors in the action domain or changes in states in the action domain (for example, changes in the attributes of activities or actors, such as increases or reductions in resource stocks, supply, demand, or prices). These outcomes may impact directly on other elements in the action domain, and they may have feedback effects into the socioeconomic, policy-governance, or physical-infrastructural environment (for example, by affecting prices in wider markets).

Outcomes can also be considered in terms of general outcome measures for the action domain (its efficiency, equity, and sustainability), and the welfare of particular interest groups (such as the poor, landless, or women), and specific attributes of products of the action domain (such as adherence to quality standards).

3.5 Conclusions

This chapter provides a conceptual framework for institutional analysis, linking the elements of the action domain (institutions, actors, and activities) with the physical-infrastructural, socioeconomic, and policy-governance environments. The framework provides a checklist of some of the types of elements and attributes that may be important in institutional analysis, and it also considers ways in which these elements interact. It is clear that institutions, actors, and activities influence one another: activities and their attributes interact with different actors' attributes to shape institutions governing access to resources or opportunities. However, these institutions themselves also shape other attributes of actors and activities.

Agricultural development is embedded in these relationships, but different natural resources, agricultural production processes, and agricultural products have different inherent techno-economic attributes. These attributes tend to promote certain types of contractual arrangement in enforcement and coordination of use and exchange. The effects of existing path-dependent institutions and actors, however, may moderate these tendencies. The result is considerable variability in the way that institutions develop in otherwise similar systems of resource management and production. The way that this variability is manifested in various institutions and processes of institutional change, and the implications for rural people and for agricultural development analysis, are the subjects of the chapters and case studies that follow.

Notes

1. The term "activities" is used here to encompass various production and exchange activities and the resources and products (goods and services) that are involved.

2. The research methods for fieldwork and analysis required for conducting institutional analysis are not discussed here. This topic is important, but it is beyond the scope of this book.

3. There are of course other domains that are important in agricultural development in Africa (insurance and safety nets, for example), but the discussion is restricted to illustrating the application of institutional economics to these two domains.

4. In keeping with the overall framework for analyzing institutions, this section integrates concepts and terminology that are often used differently by those working in transaction-cost economics and collective action/natural resource management and analysis. In integrating these branches into one framework, new terminology is sometimes developed.

5. These are defined in Chapter 1. Note also that the use of the term "contractual" does not imply the use of formal written contracts and can be applied to informal (and sometimes implicit) agreements.

6. The influence of these activity attributes on contractual forms is discussed in more detail in Section 3.2.2 and Chapter 5.

7. The characteristics of actors in these sectors are discussed more fully in Section 3.2.

8. These concepts are explained in more detail in Chapter 2.

9. Although many common pool resources are managed under common property regimes, it is essential to distinguish the two. Common pool resources refer to the characteristics of the resource, which may be managed under public, private, or common property regimes, or they may be open access (Oakerson 1992).

10. An important reason for the establishment of smallholder farmer organizations, for example, is the opportunity to achieve economies of scale in buying inputs, obtaining financial services, or selling produce.

11.. Products or services that are not derived from natural resources have zero rates of natural production and hence have potentially high returns to enforcement of exclusive-use rights.

12. The stylized relationships shown in Figure 3.4a have characteristics described by the equation

$$(R/Y)_{as} = R_{bs}(1 - z_a)/(Y_{bs} - v_a - [c_a/f]),$$

where $(R/Y)_{as}$ is the risk/return ratio for scenario s and contractual arrangement a; R_{bs} and Y_{bs} are, respectively, the base risk and base return (under basic market arrangements with minimal transaction costs and single transactions) for s; z_a is the proportion of base risk that is removed by adopting a; v_a is the additional variable transaction cost per transaction under a; c_a is the additional fixed transaction cost under a; and f is the number of transactions covered by a.

In addition, R_{bs} is increasing from R1 to R4 with constant Y_{bs}; z_a, $(c_a + v_a)$, and $c_a/(c_a + v_a)$ are all increasing from market to hybrid to hierarchy arrangements. (Note that $(c_a + v_a)$ is the total transaction costs for all transactions under contractual arrangement a, and $c_a/(c_a + v_a)$ represents fixed transaction costs as a proportion of total transaction costs.)

13. The base transaction risk/return ratio on the vertical axis of Figure 3.4b is defined as the ratio that would prevail for a single market transaction under basic market arrangements with minimal transaction costs.

14. These factors affect the values of R_{bs}, Y_{bs}, z_a, v_a, and c_a in note 12.

15. More detailed discussion and the definition of cooperatives are provided in Chapter 5.

Further Reading

Explanation of the IAD

Ostrom, E. 2005. Doing institutional analysis: Digging deeper than markets and hierarchies. In *Handbook of New Institutional Economics,* ed. C. Ménard and M. Shirley. Dordrecht: Springer.

———. 2005. *Understanding institutional diversity.* Princeton, N.J., U.S.A.: Princeton University Press.

Applications of the IAD

Gibson, C. C., M. A. McKean, and E. Ostrom. 2000. *People and forests: Communities, institutions and governance.* Cambridge, Mass., U.S.A: MIT Press.

Lam, W. F. 1998. *Governing irrigation systems in Nepal: Institutions, infrastructure and collective action.* San Francisco: ICS Press.

Tang, S. Y. 1992. *Institutions and collective action: Self-governance in irrigation.* San Francisco: ICS Press.

Institutional arrangements

Fafchamps, M. 2004. *Market institutions and Sub-Saharan Africa: Theory and evidence.* Cambridge, Mass., U.S.A.: MIT Press.

Jaffee, S., and J. Morton, eds. 1995. *Marketing Africa's high value foods.* Dubuque, Iowa, U.S.A.: Kendall Hunt.

Williamson, O. E. 1991. Comparative economic organisation: The analysis of discrete structural alternatives. *Administrative Science Quarterly* 36: 269–296.

References

Aoki, M. 2001. *Toward a comparative institutional analysis.* Cambridge, Mass., U.S.A.: MIT Press.

Coase, R. H. 1992. The institutional structure of production. *American Economic Review* 82 (4): 713–719.

Davis, L. E., and D. C. North. 1971. *Institutional change and American economic growth.* Cambridge: Cambridge University Press.

Di Gregorio, M., K. Hagedorn, M. Kirk, B. Korf, N. McCarthy, R. S. Meinzen-Dick, and B. Swallow. 2005. The role of property rights and collective action for poverty reduction. In *Unlocking human potential: Concepts and policies for linking the informal and formal sectors,* ed. B. Guha-Khasnobis, R. Kanbur, and E. Ostrom. Helsinki: United Nations University–World Institute for Development Economics Research.

Dorward, A. R. 2001. The effects of transaction costs, power and risk on contractual arrangements: A conceptual framework for quantitative analysis. *Journal of Agricultural Economics* 52 (2): 59–74.

Dorward, A. R., and J. Kydd. 2004. The Malawi 2002 food crisis: The rural development challenge. *Journal of Modern Africa Studies* 42 (3): 343–361.

Dorward, A., C. Poulton, and J. Kydd. 2001. Rural and farmer finance: An international perspective (with particular reference to Sub-Saharan Africa). Paper presented at the Annual Conference of the Agricultural Economics Association of South Africa, Drakensberg Mountains, South Africa, September 19–20.

Dorward, A. R., J. G. Kydd, J. A. Morrison, and C. Poulton. 2005. Institutions, markets and economic coordination: Linking development policy to theory and praxis. *Development and Change* 36 (1): 1–25.

Hall, P. A., and D. Soskice, eds. 2001. *Varieties of capitalism: The institutional foundations of comparative advantage.* Oxford: Oxford University Press.

Jaffee, S., and J. Morton, eds. 1995. *Marketing Africa's high value foods.* Dubuque, Iowa, U.S.A.: Kendall Hunt.

Johnson, N., R. Suarez, and M. Lundy. 2002. The importance of social capital in Colombian rural agroenterprises. CAPRi Working Paper 26. Washington, D.C.: International Food Policy Research Institute.

Kiser, L. L., and E. Ostrom. 1982. The three worlds of action: A meta-theoretical synthesis of institutional approaches. *Strategies of political inquiry,* ed. E. Ostrom. Beverly Hills, Calif., U.S.A.: Sage.

North, D. C. 1990. *Institutions, institutional change and economic performance.* Cambridge: Cambridge University Press.

Oakerson, R. J. 1992. Analyzing the commons: A framework. In *Making the commons work: Theory, practice and policy,* ed. D. W. Bromley. San Francisco: ICS Press.

Ostrom, E. 1990. *Governing the commons: The evolution of institutions for collective action.* Cambridge: Cambridge University Press.

———. 1992. *Crafting institutions for self-governing irrigation systems.* San Francisco: ICS Press.

———. 2005a. Doing institutional analysis: Digging deeper than markets and hierarchies. In *Handbook of New Institutional Economics,* ed. C. Ménard and M. Shirley. Dordrecht: Springer.

———. 2005b. *Understanding institutional diversity.* Princeton, N.J., U.S.A.: Princeton University Press.

Ostrom, E., R. Gardner, and J. Walker. 1994. *Rules, games, and common-pool resources.* Ann Arbor: University of Michigan Press.

Reardon, T., and C. P. Timmer. 2005. Transformation of markets for agricultural output in developing countries since 1950: How has thinking changed? In *Handbook of agricultural economics,* vol. 3: *Agricultural development: Farmers, farm production and farm markets,* ed. R. E. Evenson, P. Pingali, and T. P. Schultz. Amsterdam: Elsevier.

Stockbridge, M., A. R. Dorward, J. Kydd, J. Morrison, and N. Poole. 2003. *Farmer organisations for market access: Issues from a literature review on global experience and theoretical analysis.* London: Department of Agricultural Sciences, Imperial College.

Uphoff, N. 1986. *Local institutional development: An analytical sourcebook with cases.* West Hartford, Conn., U.S.A.: Kumarian Press.

———. 1993a. Grassroots organizations and NGOs in rural development: Opportunities with diminishing states and expanding markets. *World Development* 21: 607–622.

———. 1993b. *Local institutions and participation for sustainable development.* Gatekeeper Series 31. London: International Institute for Environment and Development.

Von Pischke, J. D. 1993. *Finance at the frontier: Debt capacity and the role of credit in the private economy.* Washington, D.C., World Bank.

Williamson, O. E. 1985. *The economic institutions of capitalism.* New York: Free Press.

———. 1991. Comparative economic organisation: The analysis of discrete structural alternatives. *Administrative Science Quarterly* 36: 269–296.

———. 1999. The New Institutional Economics: Taking stock and looking ahead. Address to the International Society for New Institutional Economics. *ISNIE Newsletter* 2 (2): 9–20.

Yusuf, S. 2001. *Globalisation and the challenge for developing countries.* Washington, D.C.: World Bank.

Exchange in Goods and Services

Institutional Aspects Related to the Exchange of Goods and Services

In this section of the book the action domain is the market for goods and services in the context of agriculture and rural markets in developing countries. The focus of the theoretical chapters and the case studies in Part 2 is on addressing a key development problem, namely, the development of coordinated exchange systems in poor rural areas. The core problem relates to the existence of thin markets and low density of economic activity in these areas, resulting in the failure of competitive markets to be effective and efficient mechanisms for coordinated exchange. The use of nonmarket coordination mechanisms develops from this failure but is not unique to developing countries. Under conditions of market failure and for other reasons, nonmarket coordination mechanisms are also often preferred in the developed nations of the world.

One critical aspect related to the exchange of goods (and services, to some extent) is the establishment and enforcement of exclusive property rights and/or the definition and enforcement of attributes of the good or service being exchanged (Dorward, Kydd, and Poulton 2005a,b; Dorward et al. 2005). It is for this reason that one of the theoretical chapters (Chapter 4) in this section is devoted to the issue of enforcement. Chapter 4 develops the basis for a thorough understanding of the various institutions that have emerged to enable contract enforcement and of the conditions under which particular institutions emerge. Enforcement is not only concerned with formal enforcement institutions, such as rules and laws, but also includes other forms of enforcement, such as trust, guilt, reputation, repeated interaction, and joint sanctioning in communities. Enforcement is therefore addressed from a broad, multidisciplinary approach.

Because legal enforcement of formal contracts is problematic in most poor economies due to weak states and poor legal and juristic systems, many agreements facilitating exchange take on the form of relational contracts that are usually not legally enforceable but rely on social relations between the contracting parties. It is in this respect that trust, reputation, and networks are relevant. Trust is one important self-enforcement mechanism facilitating exchange and is discussed in detail in Chapter 4 and illustrated by the case study in Chapter 6.

In Chapter 2 North's (1994) definition of institutions as "the rules of the game" defining the incentives and sanctions shaping people's behavior was adopted. A distinction between the institutional environment and institutional arrangements is made in this part of the book as well. The term "institutional arrangements" largely refers to the sets of rules and structures that govern contracts and agreements. It is these institutional arrangements that are vital for the coordination required for efficient exchange.

The institutional economics literature concerning economic coordination seeks to explain why market systems are structured as they are, thereby revealing fundamental challenges that have to be addressed if efficient and competitive markets (for goods and services) are to develop. The second theoretical chapter in this section (Chapter 5) therefore explains the framework underlying coordination. In essence coordination is discussed as a move away from atomistic competition and spot-market transactions to a range of deliberately structured relationships among market players. These relationships are designed to reduce transaction costs and guard against potential transaction risks and opportunistic behavior associated with the standard problems of asymmetric information, adverse selection, and moral hazard.

The institutions that emerge in agricultural markets to deal with these coordination problems are not only shaped by (or embedded in) the institutional environment (for example, property rights, legal systems, enforcement mechanisms, infrastructure, power relations, and culture) but also by the characteristics of the contracted goods and services together with the characteristics and attributes of the actors. The framework developed in Chapter 3 explained this well, and it is for this reason that the case studies discussing the various coordination mechanisms for exchange in goods and services apply this framework. Thus the case studies described in Chapters 6–12, building on the theoretical discussions of Chapters 3, 4, and 5, provide a useful illustration of how an institutional analysis using the new institutional economics can provide a good understanding of the role of nonmarket institutions in enabling transactions and reducing costs for the sake of market development.

Case Study Chapters

Chapters 6–12 present case studies to illustrate how an institutional approach to the analysis of the markets for agricultural goods and agricultural and rural services bring us much closer to understanding the real life problems of African agricultural development. The studies also highlight the policy interventions as well as the appropriate governance structures for producers, firms, and agro-food supply chains in an African context.

The case studies all seek to shed light on key institutional features of African agriculture specifically related to the exchange of goods and services. In the process the case studies employ concepts and methods related to institutions as well as the analytical framework developed in Chapter 3. Coordination of exchange and the enforcement of agreements and contracts to do so are central themes through most of these chapters. Collective action, an important aspect of horizontal coordination, is another theme that features mainly in Chapters 7–9.

To the extent possible, each of the chapters discusses the characteristics and attributes of the commodity or product in question and the characteristics of the actors engaging in the transaction. This description is set against a specific context—the environment—which shapes the specific institutions. These are discussed in terms of attributes and how they assist enforcement and coordination in the exchange process to ultimately realize the specific economic and social outcomes.

A common theme that runs through the majority of the cases in this section is the changing coordination mechanisms in agricultural commodity markets in Africa that have emerged following the liberalization of the economies of these countries. The case studies all highlight the nature of these new arrangements and the transaction costs, risks, and structural issues related to these changes. In some cases an effort is made to show how transaction costs inform the establishment of these new arrangements or assist in organizational design (for example, Chapter 10). Another theme in most of the case studies is the issue of enforcement—an important issue in the coordination of exchange, as discussed in Chapters 4 and 5. The mechanisms of enforcement and the performance of contractual agreements among growers, processors, and traders for a variety of commodities (sugar, coffee, and tea) in several countries are highlighted.

Some of the commodity markets analyzed in the case studies are related to the traditional agricultural exports of African countries, namely, sugar (Chapter 6), coffee (Chapter 9), and tea (Chapter 8). There are also, however, a case study on the mussel industry in South Africa (Chapter 10), two studies on the provision of services—Chapter 11 on the market for animal health services and Chapter 12 on a social or safety-net service provided through social networks in rural Ethiopia—and a study on group organization of land reform (Chapter 7). Both Chapters 11 and 12 provide interesting and unconventional applications of the NIE (New Institutional Economics) paradigm. The case study of networks in Ethiopia (Chapter 12) illustrates the importance of social capital (established through networks) for rural households as mechanisms for coping with shocks that can adversely affect their well-being. It is thus a form of social insurance—an important service for many households in risk-prone rural areas.

These case studies provide a useful illustration of how different situations, decisions, arrangements, and economic outcomes can be analyzed and explained through an institutional lens. All the case studies highlight the critical role that institutions play in influencing productive behavior, market efficiency, and market power. How, then, does one design, or even define, a research effort that seeks to approach a particular question of interest in the institutional economic framework? As the various case studies indicate, there are several possibilities. Many of the case studies show that there are often many similarities in survey methodology and approach with standard economic or agricultural economic studies. However, most of the studies make it evident that researchers who collect firsthand information through fieldwork are better able to tell "the story behind the story" and interpret the analytical results in terms of the institutional dynamics. They are thus able to relate the realities of the environment to outcomes.

In the process of unpacking the institutional issues influencing the behavior of agents, a variety of data collection techniques can be used. These techniques include questionnaire surveys, participant observation, informal interviews, kinship and biographical descriptions, and follow-up questionnaires with variable frequencies.

The case studies generally put less stress on the sophistication of their mathematical models and econometric analysis and more on deep knowledge of the situation studied. Thus the tools used for statistical and economic analysis are fairly simple, for example, descriptive statistics, regressions or correlations, and enterprise budget analysis.

Finally, the case studies presented here show that an entirely new set of analytical tools or methods are not needed to highlight the role that institutions play in determining production and market behavior. An institutional focus is largely about asking the right questions and seeking to uncover insights into the impacts that institutional apparatus has on such characteristics as productive efficiency, behavioral incentives, market power, and the distribution of profits among market players.

References

Dorward, A. R., J. Kydd, and C. Poulton. 2005a. Coordination risk and cost impacts on economic development in poor rural areas. Paper presented at the Agricultural Economics Society Conference, Nottingham, U.K., April.

———. 2005b. Beyond liberalisation: "Developmental coordination" policies for African smallholder agriculture. *IDS Bulletin* 36 (2): 80–85.

Dorward, A. R., J. G. Kydd, J. A. Morrison, and C. Poulton. 2005. Institutions, markets and economic coordination: Linking development policy to theory and praxis. *Development and Change* 36 (1): 1–25.

North, D. C. 1994. Economic performance through time. *American Economic Review* 84 (3): 359–368.

Chapter 4

Exchange, Contracts, and Property-Rights Enforcement

Eleni Gabre-Madhin

Even the simplest exchange is a species of contract; each of the parties is abandoning rights over the things that he sells, in order to acquire rights over the things he buys. Now it will happen, very early on, that the things to be exchanged are not physically present at the moment when the arrangement to exchange them is made. Thus the bargain has three constituents, which soon become distinguishable: the making of the agreement, the delivery one way, and the delivery the other. As soon as this distinction is made, the agreement itself becomes no more than a promise to deliver. Trading is trading in promises; but it is futile to exchange in promises unless there is some reasonable assurance that the promises will be kept.

(Hicks 1969, 34)

4.1 Introduction: Trading in Promises

Market exchange is fundamentally the voluntary exchange of private ownership rights over goods and services by individuals. Thus it is important to recognize all market transactions as a form of contract—be it for the transfer of goods, credit, or labor—with mutual obligations for both transacting parties. Contracts need not be formal or even explicit. However, because of the opportunistic nature of human beings, any form of contract is only as good as the belief that it can be enforced (Fafchamps 2004). This point is central to the analysis of market institutions and is at the heart of the notions put forward by North (1990) and Williamson (1985) regarding transaction costs and their role in shaping institutions. Hence this discussion starts with the premise that markets cannot exist without defined and protected property rights over goods and services. Even when property rights are defined and protected, there is room for cheating in the exchange process itself.

The work of Hayek (1945) suggests that economic actors never possess all the relevant information and hardly ever command complete knowledge of the available means to make rational economic decisions. As a result, economic systems are subject to information asymmetries, which generate problems of moral hazard and adverse selection. Information asymmetry further generates contract-enforcement problems, because compliance with contracts becomes hard to verify by external agents, such as the courts (Fafchamps 2004). Thus the presence of information asymmetry along with opportunistic behavior implies that institutions must and do emerge to enable contract enforcement in the market, without which market exchange cannot take place. These various institutions are the subject of this chapter.

If opportunities to exchange were limited to individuals directly bartering their own goods within their own community, where enforcement is more likely, the gains from exchange for economies would remain modest. North and Thomas (1973) conclude in their paper on the economic growth of nations that the transition from personalized to impersonal exchange is the key to the performance and growth of economies. Money and merchants emerge as intermediaries and facilitate the expansion of exchange beyond closed communities. However, to realize the gains from market exchange, the economic rules of the game that ensure the enforcement of private ownership rights must be specified. Critical questions are: How do trading individuals establish trust? Is a buyer's promise to pay at a future date reliable? Will a seller's promise to deliver certain goods at a certain date at a specified quantity and quality be kept? How can the buyer be sure that the goods are not "lemons" (Akerlof 1970)? (See Chapter 2 for a discussion on the market for lemons.)

In this chapter, these questions are addressed through the development of a thorough understanding of the various institutions that have emerged to enable contract enforcement and through an understanding of the conditions under which particular institutions emerge. The discussion is not limited to the study of formal contracts but considers all agreements that bind the transfer of goods and services, be they legally bound or informal, implicit or explicit. Nor is the concern solely with formal enforcement institutions, such as rules and laws, but broadly with all forms of enforcement means, such as trust, guilt, reputation, repeated interaction, and joint sanctioning in communities. Enforcement is therefore addressed using a multidisciplinary approach, drawing on law and economics, contract and contractual choice theory, theory of property rights, legal anthropology, social capital and trust theory, sociological approaches to community norms and generalized morality, and game theoretic approaches to incentive compatibility and self-enforcing strategies. This approach to understanding the market institutions for enforcement thus entails a broad view across a range of disciplines and concepts. Information asymmetry and opportunistic behavior lead to enforcement-related costs, which are minimized through a range of enforcement institutions that emerge out of the need by actors to lower the transaction costs related to the enforcement of agreements and contracts. This need can be met if such institutions are structured in an incentive-compatible manner, if actors exhibit dynamic strategic behavior, and if the past or history matters. This construct is then a simple one for framing the analysis of which, when, and how enforcement institutions emerge, the subject of the remainder of this chapter. At this stage, note that enforcement institutions can and do span the range of private actors, collective actors, and the state. Moreover, this process, which is inherently dynamic, matters enormously for development and growth. According to North (1990, 54): "The inability of societies to develop effective, low-cost enforcement of contracts is the most important source of both historical stagnation and contemporary underdevelopment in the third world."

Finally, it is important to recognize that, at the same time, information asymmetries and asset specificity can lead to other, nonenforcement-based transaction costs, such as those related to search and bargaining, that can give rise to coordination failure rather than contract failure.[1] However, often the same institutions can redress both contract and coordination failure.

4.2 The Problem of Contracting in African Agricultural Trade

In many developing economies in Sub-Saharan Africa and elsewhere, traders in liberalized agricultural markets, particularly for food grains, operate in a context in which prices are not publicly announced, goods are highly differentiated with no formal standardization and classification system, contracts are oral and nonstandardized, there is little inspection or certification, and there is virtually no recourse to legal means of contract enforcement (Fafchamps and Gabre-Madhin 2001; Gabre-Madhin 2001). Thus both producers and traders are highly vulnerable to being cheated with respect to market prices, qualities, and quantities of the delivered good, as well as other contractual terms (such as the timing of delivery and product spoilage or loss during transport).

Much like grain merchants in the mid- to late-nineteenth–century American Midwest, grain traders in Africa can, and do, often cheat their partners by delivering a lower quality of the product than promised at the time of sale (Box 4.1). Because there are no official inspections of grain, a trader who contacts a partner by telephone

Box 4.1 Contract failure in agricultural trade in Malawi and Benin

In an extensive survey of traders in Malawi and Benin, two countries with a contrasting history of private commercial exchange, agricultural commodity traders reported a high incidence of contractual nonperformance (up to 41 percent of traders in Malawi and up to 12 percent in Benin). In Benin, where trading networks are more extensive and traders have a longer tradition of commerce, traders only report a handful of cases of bad quality, disagreement over measures, or ex post price renegotiation with suppliers. In contrast, Malawian traders report close to 200 such occurrences per year—roughly 6 percent of purchases. For sales contracts, problems with the frequency of payment are much higher in Malawi than in Benin. Malawian traders are also more likely to mention efforts by clients to renegotiate prices ex post. One means of containing the failure of contracts is through reputation effects. The fear of losing one's reputation with others in the market appears to be a deterrent to nonpayment. Thus the majority of traders in both countries state that other suppliers would find out if a client fails to pay.

Contract enforcement and commercial disputes in Benin and Malawi

	Benin		Malawi	
	Number or percentage		Number or percentage	
Dispute	Mean	Standard deviation	Mean	Standard deviation
Supplier				
Bad quality	3%		41%	
Disagreement over measuring	7%		35%	
Renegotiate price	12%		25%	
Cases of bad quality per year	0.3	2.8	63.9	340.9
Cases of measuring dispute per year	2.3	12.4	99.5	410.9
Cases of price renegotiation per year	1.6	6.0	45.7	217.5
Place orders	6%		32%	
Proportion of purchases on order	1.2	6.4	6.3	12.7
Number suppliers from whom order	0.0	0.4	0.7	3.9
Late delivery	18%		41%	
Partial delivery	20%		31%	
No delivery	16%		27%	
Cases of late delivery per year	5.0	20.8	37.5	197.5
Cases of partial delivery per year	3.1	9.3	19.0	57.7
Cases of no delivery per year	0.3	0.8	31.3	148.0
Number of purchases per year[a]	10	14	3,345	12,315

| | Benin | | Malawi | |
| | Number or percentage | | Number or percentage | |
Dispute	Mean	Standard deviation	Mean	Standard deviation
Client				
Late payment	24%		42%	
Partial payment	21%		34%	
No payment	20%		25%	
Renegotiate price	5%		20%	
Cases of late payment per year	10.8	34.1	15.2	36.5
Cases of partial payment per year	9.8	62.2	14.9	71.8
Cases of no payment per year	0.9	3.4	7.1	62.4
Cases of price renegotiation per year	0.4	2.1	116.0	506.7
Number clients who order	0.1	0.6	0.5	1.6
Number of sales	3,102	4,433	7,898	9,140
Others know of nonpayment	53%		70%	
Number of people dealing with debt collection	1.1	1.0	0.7	0.6

Source: Fafchamps and Gabre-Madhin (2001).
[a]Number of purchases on order for Benin.

is forced to take the partner's word at face value. Furthermore, grain quality can deteriorate in the course of storage or transport to the buyer. Traders can deceive partners by misquoting or omitting information on any of the abovementioned parameters at the time of the oral agreement on grain price. Other opportunities for fraud are presented by the lack of standardized bags and the practice of cheating on the weights of traded goods. The commitment problem is also a function of the point at which ownership of grain is transferred between partners. When a seller retains ownership, and concomitant risk, for a shipment of grain until it reaches the final destination, the trader is highly vulnerable to reneging on the buyer's part. Similarly, if the buyer takes ownership of a load of grain at the seller's venue, the buyer is highly vulnerable to fraudulent representation of the grain or damage during transport.

4.3   Markets and Growth: A Series of Staged Stories

Economic history can be seen as a series of staged stories (North 1991). The earliest economies constitute local exchange in a village. Gradually trade expands beyond the village, beyond the region, and eventually expands to much of the world. Each stage involves increasing specialization and division of labor and more productive technology. When trade is local to the village, informal constraints govern exchange, and the costs of transacting are low. As trade expands across distance and time, transaction costs related to monitoring and enforcement increase sharply, and the dense social network of the village needs to be replaced by enforcement by the state. In societies in which the expansion of the market has brought about more specialized producers, economies of scale, and specialized merchants, North (1991) argues that impersonal contract enforcement is required, because personal ties and informal constraints are no longer effective. Thus market institutions aimed at contract enforcement evolve along the spectrum from highly personalized to highly impersonal exchange (Figure 4.1).

Communities and markets can be considered alternative modes of governing transactions (Greif 1999). A long tradition in economic development and economic history considers the former to be inferior, because it entails personalized exchange and limited division of labor. The transformation from community- to market-based governance requires a transition from contract enforcement based on repeated relations and personal ties in a community to formal, state-mandated legal contract enforcement. This view is largely based on the understanding of market expansion in premodern Europe. North (1991) invokes the Western experience in arguing that a legal system administered by the state is a necessary condition for an advanced division of labor and a market economy. Earlier, Weber (1927, 277) argued that for the European capitalistic form of industrial organization to emerge, it must be able to depend on "calculable adjudication and administration of the law."

In recent years, however, it has been recognized that even in modern, developed economies, contract enforcement based on personal and repeated relations, such as the Jewish diamond merchants in New York (Richman 2005), is important for effective enforcement and thereby reduces transaction costs and enhances economic efficiency. It is important, because even impartial legal enforcement entails transaction costs due to asymmetric information, incomplete contracts, and verification costs by the court. Within communities, informal enforcement mechanisms may economize on these costs. Greif (1999) argues that, rather than considering communities and markets as substitute forms of governance, they can be considered complementary. The emergence of markets can be facilitated by appropriate community structures rather than by impartial courts. He demonstrates in his analysis of market expansion in premodern Europe during the late medieval commercial revolution (between the eleventh and fourteenth centuries) that a particular system of intercommunity enforcement enabled impersonal exchange despite the absence of an impartial legal system. In the modern world, there are numerous examples of pervasive business networks that preclude the use of formal legal contracts. The guanxi in Taiwan, chaebol in Korea, and keiretsu in Japan are business networks rooted in a deep tradition of personalized relations and reciprocal commitments (Fukuyama 1995; Platteau 2000).

Figure 4.1   Spectrum of enforcement and market exchange

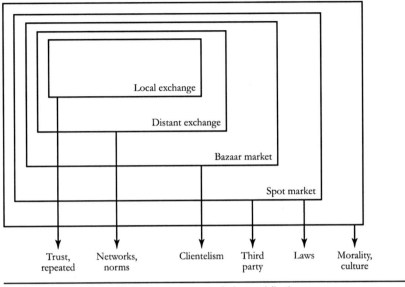

Enforcement costs, complexity, specialization

4.4   The Concept of Incentive-Compatibility for Self-Enforcement

An important concept developed in this chapter is that, with information asymmetries, contract enforcement through a formal legal system (the courts and police) is by definition imperfect and requires other supporting incentive-compatible self-enforcement institutions.[2] At the same time, the type of market system and the attributes of the traded goods and services matter. Thus, following North's economic history perspective, enforcement institutions evolve as trade expands and evolves, though not entirely to third-party rather than self-enforcement institutions. But third-party enforcement can involve private ordering as well as public institutions, or even hybrid private-public arrangements.

Consider self-enforcement or incentives for honest behavior. In game-theoretic terms, a commodity exchange opportunity involves a one-shot prisoner's dilemma:[3] two agents may each benefit from mutually honest trade (Table 4.1). However, if either agent unilaterally and solely cheats the other, there is even greater gain for that agent at the expense of the other. If both players are honest, the net gains from honest exchange (Γ) are divided equally. If both players cheat, both derive negative payoffs ($-\gamma$). If either party cheats unilaterally, the cheating player gets a higher advantage (α),

Table 4.1   Payoff consequences of trade game

Trader 2 \ Trader 1	Honest	Cheat
Honest	$\Gamma/2, \Gamma/2$	$-\beta, \alpha$
Cheat	$\alpha, -\beta$	$-\gamma, -\gamma$

Source: Aoki (2001).

while the cheated player suffers damage ($-\beta$). The unique Nash equilibrium when this game is played once in isolation is for both players to opt for no trade if they expect that the other player will cheat (Aoki 2001). The key question is then: What mechanisms constrain traders to choose honest exchange? Alternatively: Under what conditions would stable expectations be generated among traders to constrain their choice to honest trading? When trade expands beyond local, or personalized exchange, a third party may be necessary to govern exchange.

4.5   Private versus Public Ordering of Enforcement

With regard to third-party enforcement, a significant body of legal literature examines regulation by parties other than government (often referred to as private ordering): rules, norms, and institutions that are self-imposed by private parties to govern their behavior and transactions. Macaulay's (1963) seminal work in this field observed that few contractual disputes are litigated, and most are settled without resorting to government-enforced laws.

Much of the research following Macauley's observation on opting out of the governmental legal system examined bilateral, relationship-based transacting, in which reputational investments in the relationship serve as collateral against opportunism. This effort includes Geertz (1978) and Belshaw (1965), who noted that traders in traditional markets tend to personalize their exchange relations to mitigate contractual uncertainty (that is, opportunism). Posner (1980) pointed to a similar pattern of "barter friendships" in primitive societies, which oblige the parties to similar standards of loyalty as they owe their ethnic social group. Such a status and its attached obligations serve to mitigate opportunism despite the absence of public enforcement. Landa (1981) expanded Geertz's and Posner's observations by considering a wider, network relationship, which she identified as an ethnically homogenous middleman group. This group facilitates exchanges when government enforcement of law is deficient (and therefore the certainty of abiding to contracts is lacking) by taking advantage of the high barriers to entry into an ethnic social group (and therefore the need to stay on good terms with one's existing ethnic group).

Moving down the spectrum to more formal institutions, McMillan and Woodruff (2000) point to the role of private-ordering organizations in coordinating responses to opportunism, whereas Bernstein (1992) examines such mechanisms as arbitration and the maintenance of a common culture by which trade associations, diamond exchanges, and other trading networks enforce their private legal systems.

In the following sections, various contract-enforcement mechanisms and the conditions under which they become self-enforcing are considered. A distinction is made between private and public-order enforcement mechanisms, including third parties. Because private third parties are not neutral and exogenous, it becomes important to consider how the rules for the third party's actions are incentive-compatible to achieve a stable governance mechanism. However, there are important limitations of endogenous, self-enforcing mechanisms for achieving market order (Platteau 2000). Thus public-order third-party governance, such as the rule of law and the state, are also considered. Before doing so, however, it is first necessary to consider a typology of contract-enforcement institutions, particularly in the context of African agricultural trade.

4.6 A Typology of Contract-Enforcement Institutions in African Agriculture

In the African context, several key features of the marketing system are important for understanding the evolution of different enforcement institutions. First, agricultural producers are generally small and geographically dispersed. These conditions give rise to thin markets with dispersed buyers (traders), operating at low levels of working capital and buying in small lots (Morris and Newman 1989; Staatz, Dione, and Dembele 1989; Gabre-Madhin 2001). With generally small market transactions undertaken by small-scale trading firms, neither small firms nor small-scale farmers have assets that can be seized in the event of contract failure, rendering the threat of court action nonviable. As a result, firms in general opt for trading practices that have minimal potential for breach of contract. On the purchase side, most domestic agricultural markets are characterized by the marked absence of large processors and therefore have a much greater proportion of small buyers, made up of traders, retailers, and consumers themselves. So domestic food-grain markets can be characterized as markets with dispersed small producers, many small trading firms, and many buyers. The overwhelming prevalence and persistence of small firms in domestic markets is somewhat a puzzle, perhaps explained by diseconomies of scale in marketing (Fafchamps, Gabre-Madhin, and Minten 2005).

The picture changes somewhat in the case of agricultural exports, both traditional crops and nontraditional, high-value products. In the case of traditional crops, such as coffee, cotton, and tobacco, small-scale producers still persist, but the buyers are often a small number of large exporting firms, large agribusiness companies and/ or processors, or a government monopsony. Export certification and financing requirements often create a single channel at the border. In the case of nontraditional high-value exports, for which logistical and process requirements are considerably greater, small-scale producers and large exporters are much more tightly linked into contractual arrangements in supply chains. In each of these types of commodities, different enforcement mechanisms may emerge in response to the differences in the market arrangement.

Thus, because most market transactions are beyond the reach of the formal legal system, trading practices evolve to minimize the potential for contract failure, such as immediate cash sales rather than long-distance orders, supplier credit, and forward contracting (Fafchamps and Minten 2001; Gabre-Madhin and Negassa 2005).

There are also features of the agricultural product and production processes that matter. In the case of food grains, varieties produced are largely indigenous, implying a large number of local varieties and the absence of grades and standards. Moreover, agricultural commodities are largely unprocessed and come to market with highly uneven qualities. Not only are products not standardized, but it is also difficult to screen honest and dishonest market actors, because there are no viable systems for business registry or certification. In the case of both traditional and nontraditional exports, product standards are much more stringent and enforcement mechanisms are more developed. However, for all types of products and markets, these constraints lead to significant opportunities for cheating and contract failure. Without viable enforcement, the prospects for expanded market exchange remain dim, and markets remain in what Fafchamps and Minten (2001) consider a flea-market economy, that is, markets with no placement of orders across time or distance, no credit, no warranty, no check-based payments—essentially cash-and-carry markets with inspection, delivery, and cash payment on the spot.

A typology of contract enforcement that accounts for market and product attributes might look like the following. In the absence of costless legal enforcement, personal trust often prevails when screening costs are high and markets (such as those with large numbers of buyers and sellers) create significant opportunities for cheating. However, where does trust come from? Trust is based on successful repeated exchange, leading to what is considered relationship-based or relational contracting (Hayami and Kikuchi 1981). Thus trust-based exchange based on repeated interaction prevails when opportunities for collective action are weak. By definition, this type of enforcement limits the scope for market expansion, given that it is limited to individual repeated exchange among parties who know each other. This type of enforcement may dominate in markets in which product quality is unknown, with many dispersed buyers and sellers, such as the case of localized food-grain markets in many parts of Africa.

Fafchamps (2004) shows how *relational contracting* has become the primary contract-enforcement mechanism in African markets (Box 4.2). There is some evidence of information sharing to screen new clients, but little evidence of reputational penalties. Exchange is more difficult between strangers because of the lack of trust. As a result, many potential transactions cannot take place because agents are not connected. Therefore exchange only takes place among agents who have formal, long-lasting relationships (Fafchamps 2004). Thus markets with relational contracts are different from impersonal markets in which perfect contract enforcement exists.

But in markets where information about cheaters can be more easily transmitted and market actors are willing to collectively sanction or punish the cheater, then another mechanism prevails: the multilateral punishment strategy based on reputation (Greif 1993). Although this type of enforcement is limited because it is difficult for the group to know exactly what went on between two parties, network-based systems may dominate in markets for long-distance transfers of goods, either to export markets or across long distances within countries. In this case, tightly knit, ethnic-based export networks may emerge, as in the case of high-value agricultural exports from East Africa to European markets, much like the ethnic Chinese networks in East Asia.

A third alternative to trust- or reputation-based contract enforcement is third-party enforcement, which arises in the absence of repeated interactions or of dense social networks in which collective action is likely. The third-party institution requires that considerable information exist about market actors but does not require collective action among market actors. This third-party mechanism, such as a credit-reporting agency or trade association, can resemble the reputational mechanism in that information about individual cheating behavior is available, but it differs in that collective punishment is not required. This system prevails when information about past behavior can be recorded, usually in a centralized market, such as an export registration board or export auction.

Finally, when collective-action opportunities are high and information about actors' behavior is also available, contract enforcement can depend largely on a higher order set of norms and moral authority. This situation is also the arena in which laws and formal rules governing economic exchange are likely to be meaningful. This type of enforcement may prevail in formal commodity exchanges where many buyers and sellers collectively agree to abide by rules and laws established by the market and when information on behavior is readily available in a transparent way.

The typology developed is based on two key parameters: the availability and ease of obtaining information about market behavior and the extent to which market

Box 4.2 Middlemen of the middlemen: Grain traders and brokers in Ethiopia

In the absence of formal means to mitigate the risk of commitment failure, how do Ethiopian grain traders carry out long-distance transactions? Personalized exchange is one option, when they trade grain only with partners whom they know and trust, who may be associated to them by kinship, religion, or ethnicity. Alternatively, survey evidence reveals that traders use the services of brokers to conduct long-distance trade with anonymous partners.

With brokers acting on behalf of traders, the relationship is that of a principal and an agent. Like most such relationships, this one is characterized by information asymmetry, because traders have relatively less information on market prices and equally little information on the behavior of brokers. This asymmetry, exacerbated by the physical distance separating regional wholesalers and brokers, gives rise to moral hazard and opportunism by brokers. For the institution of brokerage to be sustained and be more efficient than the alternatives, norms must exist to provide incentives for brokers not to cheat their clients, the traders.

Characteristics of Trader-Broker Relations

Relations between traders and brokers appear to be based on repeated interaction and exclusive relations. Thus 87 percent of brokers' transactions are with long-term clients. On average, traders have worked with the same brokers for 6 years. Moreover, 59 percent of traders appear to work exclusively with a single broker. A particular feature of trader–broker relations is that not only do traders work exclusively with a broker, but also traders in a given location tend to work with the same broker. Thus brokers obtain 50 percent of their clients through traders' referrals and 43 percent from having other clients in the same region. It is generally uncommon for a broker to represent both a buyer and a seller in a given transaction, with only 7 percent of brokers' transactions falling into this category. Similarly, it is relatively rare for brokers to trade on their own account with their own clients. That is, if a partner is not found for a client, only 7 percent of brokers' transactions involve buying or selling grain directly to clients.

Norms Governing Relations

The sustainability of the brokerage institution over time depends on the extent to which brokers are prevented from abusing their clients' trust. Without institutional constraints limiting the possibility of opportunistic behavior by brokers, trader–broker relations would be characterized by a higher incidence of conflict and would not be self-enforcing. In the absence of any market regulation of their function and given the high costs of monitoring the activities of brokers, what norms prevail to limit cheating by brokers and to maintain long-term agency relations between brokers and traders?

Effective Reputation Mechanism

Agency relations are structured in a manner that provides a means for sanctioning brokers' actions. Thus although the practice of many traders in the same market working exclusively with the same broker appears to give brokers significant market power over individual traders in a market, this structure actually offers a safety net for these traders in that information provided by the broker flows freely among all traders in a given market. This flow enables a reputation system to work by the implicit threat that a broker who cheats one client will be considered as likely to compromise relations with all clients in that market and nearby markets in the region. Evidence suggests that traders actually do carry out sanctions and effectively boycott brokers.

The Absence of Market-Making

A second means of limiting opportunistic behavior by brokers lies in the incentive compatibility of brokers relative to their clients. A potential source of conflict in agency relations would exist if brokers, trading on their own account, bought and sold grain from their own clients. As noted earlier, it is not common practice for grain brokers to buy or sell clients' grain on their own account, at least overtly, in the interests of maintaining neutrality vis-à-vis their client traders. Brokers reiterated that trading on their own accounts was considered a serious breach of the implicit rules governing agency relations. Because information on purchase and sale orders is incomplete at any given time, traders cannot confirm a broker's information that a partner was unavailable. Brokers would only be willing to transact at a rate more favorable than the market, thus causing a strain in their relations with clients.

Flat Commission Rates

Ethiopian grain brokers are compensated for their services with a fixed commission that is a flat rate per quantity transacted, rather than a percentage of the final transaction price. This practice is common to all regions studied in

Ethiopia and is confirmed by 93 percent of brokers. The flat fee is fixed across brokers and time but varies with region. A flat brokerage fee is compatible with broker incentives for several reasons. First, brokers do not usually act as dual agents, and represent only one of the trading partners. Thus they receive a commission from only one party in the transaction. In a given transaction, the seller's agent and the buyer's agent each receive a commission from their clients. Second, the service for which brokers are compensated is not price search (given that there is a spot price that prevails in the market) but rather the search for buyers or sellers. For this reason, brokers maximize profit across a large volume of transactions in a short period of time, charging a small transaction fee. Third, a flat commission limits cheating by brokers. Because brokers themselves determine the market price in the price-discovery role described above, a percentage fee would bias the price-discovery process and provide brokers with incentives to fix prices to their advantage.

Source: Gabre-Madhin (2001).

actors are willing to engage in collective action. These dimensions determine the degree of private and public enforcement and also attempt to capture the specificities of the products and markets themselves (Figure 4.2).

4.6.1 Personal Trust

A well-known aspect of the prisoner's dilemma is the effect of reputation through repeated plays of the game. Over an infinite time horizon, the threat of terminating future trade in the event of unilateral cheating may mutually deter cheating (Sugden 1986). This type of personal or bilateral trust is distinct from the generalized trust mentioned above.[4] In a repeated game setting trust is reinforced by the threat of punishment if either party deviates from honest behavior.

Fundamentally, personal trust in the sense employed here implies that individuals continue to act in a self-interested way and that the consequences of repeated interaction deter dishonest behavior. The Folk theorem in game theory stipulates that for cooperation (or honest behavior) in the infinitely repeated game to be a Nash equilibrium in every subgame (known as a subgame perfect equilibrium), the same set of players must frequently play the same game over an infinite time horizon (Fudenberg and Maskin 1986). In addition, the punishment must be credible in the sense that each player would find it optimal to carry it out, players would need to be in continuous interaction, and they must be well informed about one another's actions and payoffs (Platteau 2000).

Figure 4.2   Typology of contract enforcement

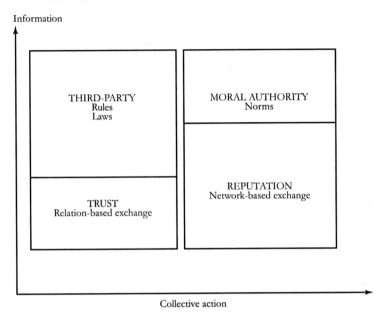

Examples of this type of enforcement mechanism are found in local market settings where repeated interaction is common. Empirical research in the context of agricultural markets in Madagascar by Fafchamps and Minten (1999) demonstrates that trading contracts are enforced mainly by the existence of trust-based relationships, in which trust is established primarily by repeated interaction. The incidence of theft and breach of contract is low, and recourse to the legal system is rare.

4.6.2   Traders' Community Norms

The bilateral reputation mechanism described above is limited in its enforcement potential, because retaliatory sanctioning only affects the mutual relationship of the two partners without affecting the relations of the cheater with other potential partners in the community. However, a multilateral reputation mechanism resolves this limitation (Platteau 2000). This mechanism requires that information about past dealings circulate effectively in a given social group or community. Thus, even if no two traders exchange together frequently, but if each trades frequently with other traders, then transferable reputations are an adequate bond for honest behavior if members of the community can be kept informed about one another's behavior (Milgrom, North, and Weingast 1990). In small communities characterized by dense networks, this informational condition is easily satisfied. In Hayami and Kawagoe's (1993, 167) analysis of rural markets in Indonesia, this is effectively the case:

> In the village community, everyone is watching everyone. Gossip about one's misconduct is circulated by word of mouth faster than any modern means of communication. In such an environment, a significant cost would be incurred to a person who would violate a contract with his fellow villager, not only would he lose benefits from the present contract but the resulting contract would deprive him of future opportunities to enter into other contracts with other villagers.

The specification of desirable behavior along with rules regarding sanctions in a community may be viewed as a social or a community norm (Kandori 1992). In small communities where members observe one another's behavior, the Folk theorem for personal enforcement can apply to community enforcement. The critical element is the transmission of information regarding past actions.

Richman (2005) provides a useful account of how small communities—in this case the network of diamond merchants in New York—go about enforcing contracts between different agents in the industry. He shows how long-term players and independent contractors are induced to cooperate and comply with contractual agreements through a combination of industry-based institutions (an industry arbitration system that publicizes information if promises are not kept), a family-based reputation mechanism (good behavior could mean inheriting the family business), and community-based enforcement institutions (the threat of being excluded from excludable community goods in the—in this case Jewish—community) allows the New York diamond industry to organize credible asynchronous exchange.

4.6.3 Clientelism

In a setting beyond small communities, with an expanded market in which traders are no longer bound in dense social networks that allow the free flow of information, anonymous exchange seems to prevail with an expanded and constantly changing scope of actors. Hence enforcement mechanisms based on personal trust and social norms are no longer viable. In the famous example of the bazaar economy in Morocco described by economic anthropologist Clifford Geertz (1979, 30), traders make use of clientelization, which he defines as "the tendency for repetitive purchasers of particular goods and services to establish continuing relationships with particular purveyors of them, rather than search widely through the market at each occasion of need. The apparent Brownian motion of randomly colliding bazaars conceals a resilient pattern of informal personal connections."

Thus, despite the many actors involved in the bazaar, trade in effect is not impersonal but is based on long-term relations and repeated interaction. However, in this case each trader has little access to information about the partner's past actions. As a result, more emphasis is placed on selecting the "regular" with whom one establishes a long-term relationship. Selection, or the signaling of future honest behavior, could be on the basis of appearance, habit, accent, mutual friends, or other signals (Aoki 2001).

In addition to the Moroccan bazaar economy, many examples of clientelization in developing and developed countries have been extensively studied, particularly by an earlier generation of economic anthropologists. These studies have covered relations between fishermen and dealers in the Maine lobster market (Acheson 1985); the *pratik* in Haiti (Mintz 1964); *onibara* relationships in Nigerian markets (Trager 1981); *suki* relations in the Philippines (Szanton 1972), and *cliente* relations between vegetable producers and middlemen in Guatemala (Swetnam 1978). Generally, these clientele-based relations have been characterized in this literature as a means of risk-sharing rather than contract enforcement. But if the concept of risk is clarified as the risk of contractual failure, which is generally true, then these practices constitute an effective enforcement mechanism.

Given the importance of ex ante selection of the regular partner, it is not clear from the anthropological literature what the basis of selection is. Platteau (2006) and Fafchamps (1992) suggest that ethnicity and kinship may play an important signaling role (Box 4.3).

Box 4.3 Enforcement of commercial contracts in Ghana: An example of clientelism at work

The enforcement of commercial contracts in Ghana is problematic for two reasons. First, there is no mechanism for sharing information about bad payers. As a result, each firm must screen every single firm and individual it wants to deal with. Second, many firms find it impossible to honor a contract because of shortages of critical inputs, difficulties in transport, and payment delays.

Fifty-eight Ghanaian firms were interviewed in 1993 by a team of Ghanaian and World Bank researchers. Firms were asked about nonpayment and late payment problems encountered with clients. More than half of the firms experienced nonpayment and nearly all had experienced late payment. Similarly, firms were asked about problems of late and nondelivery and deficient quality by suppliers. Although nearly half had experienced late delivery, far fewer had faced nondelivery. A high proportion experienced deficient quality of inputs delivered.

Incidence of contractual problems in Ghana

Problem	Number of observations	Number of individuals citing problems
Nonpayment by client	52	30
Late payment by client	50	41
Nondelivery by supplier	55	14
Late delivery by supplier	55	28
Deficient quality	54	31

Source: Fafchamps (1996).

Means of Avoiding Problems

Reputation per se plays a minor role in identifying reliable clients, because there is no mechanism to transfer information on past defaults. The use of legal recourse is rare: 13 percent of firms in the case of suppliers and 8 percent in the case of clients. One-fourth of the sample actively screens prospective clients by visiting their client's workplace and establishing a relationship with them. In the case of suppliers, two-fifths of the sample indicated that the best way to avoid problems is to trade repeatedly with the same supplier. Firms deal on average with only five suppliers, and have three regular suppliers who extend credit to them, with whom they have been working for an average of 8 years. Thus the use of regular suppliers is considered the dominant form of avoiding enforcement problems. Although this institutional response successfully enables firms to develop and gain trade credit, it leads to fragmentation of the market into networks, potentially limiting specialization and firm growth.

Source: Fafchamps (1996).

4.6.4   Cultural Beliefs and Self-Enforcing Employment Contracts

The case of expanded exchange across space, in which long-distance trade may imply that either buyer or seller or both cannot be physically present in the exchange market, should also be considered. In this case, the ability to transact long-distance depends on the presence of an agent. Further, it depends on the trustworthiness of the agent, who cannot be easily monitored by the trader. Historically, North (1991) suggests that this problem has been circumvented by the use of relatives to act as agents. But this analysis does not directly address the agency problem (see Chapter 2 for a definition).

Combining a game-theoretic approach to the historical analysis of the rise of long-distance trade in the Mediterranean basin in the medieval period, Greif (1994) compares the ways in which Maghribi traders in North Africa and Latin traders in Genoa dealt with this agency problem. The merchant's objective is to deter cheating, and his strategy is to start with a fixed wage in the first period and a decision to rehire or fire at the end of the game. This problem can be considered as a one-sided prisoner's dilemma (Aoki 2001). The payoff structure for the merchant–agent game is shown in Table 4.2.

The merchant must determine an efficiency wage ω that induces agents to be honest. In so doing, the merchant's employment strategy can take one of two polar cases: not employing an agent who has previously cheated another merchant, or employing any unemployed agent. Greif (1994) considers the former strategy to be the collectivist strategy and the latter to be the individualist strategy. Under the collectivist strategy, the efficiency wage that induces honesty is lower. He contrasts the Maghribi Jewish traders who had emigrated from Baghdad in the eleventh century as having had collectivist cultural beliefs, with the Genoese traders, who were highly individualistic and lacked the capacity for information sharing and collective punishment (Aoki 2001). In the face of expanding opportunities for economic exchange, the Genoese responded by extending their agent relations with non-Genoese, whereas the Maghribis expanded their activities only as far as other Maghribis became employable. Ultimately, these differences in cultural beliefs determined different paths of organizational development.

4.6.5 Private Third Parties
An alternative solution to the information problem that is posed when traders do not meet repeatedly and dense social networks are not present is that of a third party who monitors cheating and transmits information on past cheating behavior among traders. In this case, with the introduction of a third agent who serves as a repository of information over time, the prisoner's dilemma can be resolved in a market setting, even when pairs of traders only meet once (Aoki 2001).

Table 4.2 Payoff consequences of merchant–agent game

Agent	Merchant	
	Hire	Not hire
Honest	$\omega, \Gamma - \omega$	0, 0
Cheat	$\alpha, -\beta$	0, 0

Source: Aoki (2001).

The well-known historical example is the case of the law merchant in medieval Europe analyzed by Milgrom, North, and Weingast (1990). During the twelfth and thirteenth centuries, much trade between southern and northern Europe was conducted at Champagne fairs, in which merchants from all over Europe entered into contracts for long-distance shipments over time. Without the benefit of legal enforcement, merchants evolved their own commercial code, the *lex mercatoria* (law merchant), which governed commercial exchange and was administered by private judges drawn from commerce on a fee basis (Box 4.4). After any exchange, each trader could accuse the other of cheating and appeal to the law merchant, who adjudicated fairly and awarded damages. However, the payment of damages was voluntary, because the law merchant had no power to enforce payment. The law merchant kept a record of any unpaid payments. Finally, prior to finalizing a contract, any trader could query the law merchant for records of previous judgments about any other players (Aoki 2001).

Box 4.4 eBay.com

Modern corollaries to the law merchant can be found in cyberspace. Founded in 1995, eBay.com is the world's largest online auction website. The eBay community includes tens of millions of registered members around the world. The company's mission is to provide a global trading platform where anyone can trade anything. On any given day, there are more than 12 million items listed on eBay across 18,000 categories. In 2002, members transacted US$14.87 billion in annualized gross merchandise sales.

eBay.com maintains a record of trading experiences, positive and negative, of buyers regarding sales agents. These are available to anyone who trades on eBay.com. It also maintains and provides records of buyers' past assessments. Thus it is possible to obtain a considerable amount of information on the reliability of an otherwise completely anonymous trading partner. Most of the selling on eBay occurs in an auction or "buy it now" format. It all begins when the seller posts the item on eBay for a specified duration. Potential buyers search for items and place bids, which are recorded and available for anyone to see. The person who placed the highest bid or who chooses to "buy it now" wins the items, and the seller and buyer make private arrangements for payment and shipping. After the payment and delivery, both buyer and seller leave feedback on each other on eBay's Feedback Forum.

Anyone interested in knowing the seller or buyer's reputation can obtain the partner's trading history on eBay, from voluntary comments and feedback of previous partners. eBay has a feedback ratings star system, based on obtaining either negative or positive points for each comment received, which is used to standardize the feedback. Thus, next to an eBay member's user identification number, there is a feedback rating number. Because the feedback mechanism is critically important to the success of this auction, eBay has developed a set of rules regarding feedback, including the prohibition of "shill" feedback (that is, using other identification to artificially boost one's own feedback), extorting feedback, soliciting or trading feedback, and abuses of feedback. In addition, responses can be given to feedback, which are then also in the permanent record. Finally, users can choose to not make their feedback public. However, this is discouraged because, as the website states, "feedback is your valuable asset as a way to generate trust in you."

Secondly, eBay.com offers online dispute resolution called Square Trade. This is a free mediation service that records complaints from each side and mediates a solution. Although Square Trade has no means of guaranteeing compliance, the other party voluntarily responds in the majority of complaints to safeguard their reputation. In addition, a seller can obtain a Square Trade Seal to show buyers that they are committed to high selling standards and have their identity verified by a third party. To obtain a Seal, which is displayed along with their identification, sellers must agree to participate in Square Trade dispute resolution in the event of problems, have their identity verified, and commit to Square Trade's selling standards.

Sources: Aoki (2001); http://ebay.com/aboutebay.

4.6.6   Public Third Party: The Rule of Law

Eventually, the practice of the law merchant in premodern Europe gave way to formal legal codes administered by the state. Milgrom, North, and Weingast (1990) suggest that as the size of markets expanded, replacing individual payments to the law merchant with a tax system saved the cost of maintaining the law merchant. In addition, private third parties lack enforcement power. Although use of private third parties is voluntary, private agents cannot escape from the coverage of the national government without physical exit (Aoki 2001). At the same time, the role of the state in defining and enforcing property rights cannot be considered exogenous to the market system. This condition poses what Weingast (1995, 1) called the fundamental political dilemma of an economic system: "A government strong enough to protect property rights and enforce contracts is also strong enough to confiscate the wealth of its citizens. Thriving markets require not only the appropriate system of property rights and a law of contracts, but a secure political foundation that limits the ability of the state to confiscate wealth."

Further, in considering which law a given country should have, Schmid (1992) cautions against the idea that the rule of law can be externally driven. Thus countries in transition, which are modernizing their commercial codes, are patterning them on the laws of industrialized countries. But is all Western legal capital the same? In 1991, Czechoslovakia revised its prewar code by adding new material from German commercial law. Mali has the same modern commercial code that France does. But did France have this commercial code when it was in Mali's current stage of development?

4.6.7   Beyond Norms and Laws: Morality

Finally, something more than formal incentives or credible informal enforcement mechanisms are required to foster better relations within and among firms, collective action and cooperation, and economic transformation. The missing element is generalized trust (Gambetta 1988; Levi 1997; Ostrom 1998). First, the notion of self-enforcing equilibria has important limitations. In bilateral enforcement, the honest outcome of the tit-for-tat strategy of mutual retaliation is only one of several possible equilibria. Gambetta (1988) considers that a predisposition to trust is required to achieve the cooperative equilibrium in this game. As markets expand, giving rise to informational asymmetries, the need for formal third-party enforcement becomes apparent. But the rule of law also has its limits. For small transactions, legal costs are too high to justify recourse to legal procedures (Fafchamps 1996). Second, the existence of the law does not assure that rules will be followed. When fraud is widespread, an excessively authoritarian state may be called into being, creating high costs and a repressive climate. Recent empirical studies in the United States reveal that normative concerns are an important determinant of law-abiding behavior (Tyler 1990). Thus laws provide external validation of underlying social norms, and can only work as a supplement to, rather than a replacement of, informal enforcement of norms (Axelrod 1986).

Ultimately, beyond the different forms of bilateral and multilateral enforcement and even of the most efficient legal system, a social consensus must exist in society for impersonal exchange to expand and order to prevail. There must be consensus on what is fair behavior in economic exchange and on the structure of basic property rights (Platteau 1996). This social consensus is based on generalized moral norms. These norms are distinct from the endogenous trader community or network norms discussed earlier. Moral norms are cultural beliefs to which members of a society subscribe. How do these norms arise? How are they maintained? How do they change over time? How can they be manipulated? Research in cognitive science and experimental psychology suggests that answers to these questions depend on notions of reciprocity, identification, upbringing, and religion (Platteau 2000). The importance of generalized morality in fostering market order gives impetus to the idea that there is a greater role for public-order institutions than merely the provision of the rule of law.

4.7 Conclusions

In this chapter I developed a thorough basis for understanding the various institutions that have emerged to enable contract enforcement and the conditions under which particular institutions emerge. The chapter did not focus only on formal enforcement institutions, such as rules and laws, but also considered all forms of enforcement means, such as trust, guilt, reputation, repeated interaction, and joint sanctioning in communities.

Some of the key points of this chapter are:

1. Self-enforcement, collective, and third-party systems coexist and emerge for reasons related to specific markets and product attributes. Self-enforcement in trust-based systems is a less optimal market outcome and is a response to the absence of costless third-party enforcement. Information seems to be the key constraint to moving from trust-based to expanded markets with third-party enforcement. The policy implication is to design interventions that address the information constraint.

2. Policy can move in the direction of encouraging collective action. In the absence of other incentives, ethnicity is the basis for existing collective action. However, if other bases or incentives for collective action could be developed, such as membership in merit-based trade associations and firm-ratings systems, then collective action could enable higher order norms to govern the market. To this end policies to promote private third-party collective action would be desirable.

Notes

1. Coordination and "coordination failure" are examined in Chapter 5. "Coordination failure" refers to the fact that although coordination of the actions of economic actors could arise naturally, in many cases it does not happen. In the absence of institutions the only efficient institutional solution is for agents to coordinate their actions. If this does not happen, coordination failure occurs. One example of coordination failure is when firms fail to share information about bad payers, even though they would all collectively benefit from doing so. (See also Fafchamps 2004, 458, for his treatment of the concept and several other examples of coordination failure.)

2. Self-enforcement institutions are those that induce voluntary compliance because the expected gains from adherence to the agreement or contract exceed the current gain from violation of the agreement, thus providing incentives compatible with rational self-interest.

3. The prisoner's dilemma is a concept emerging from the game theory literature and refers to the classic decision problem for two players (agents) in a joint activity whose outcome has an impact on both. The prisoner's dilemma effectively illustrates the conflict between individual and group rationality. Agents or players are typically inclined to rational self-interest, but the outcome of the prisoner's dilemma illustrates that a group whose members pursue this behavior may all end up worse off than a group whose members act contrary to rational self-interest by putting the interest of the group first. In short, the prisoner's dilemma is a type of nonzero sum game in which each individual player is trying to maximize his or her own advantage without concern for the well-being of the other players.

4. Generalized (or moralistic) trust refers to an individual's trust in strangers, especially in people who are different from the individual. It is that in which moral norms of honest behavior, civic duty, and the like exist, regardless of repeated interaction but in the presence of some other enforcement mechanism.

Further Reading

Fafchamps, M 2004. *Market institutions in Sub-Saharan Africa: Theory and evidence.* Cambridge, Mass., U.S.A.: MIT Press. (Chapters 2 and 4–12 are especially recommended.)

References

Acheson, J. M. 1985. The social organization of the Maine lobster market. In *Markets and marketing,* ed. S. Plattner. Lanham, Md., U.S.A.: University Press of America.

Akerlof, G. 1970. The market for lemons: Quality uncertainty and the market mechanism. *Quarterly Journal of Economics* 83 (3): 488–500.

Aoki, M. 2001. *Toward a comparative institutional analysis.* Cambridge, Mass., U.S.A.: MIT Press.

Axelrod, R. M. 1986. An evolutionary approach to norms. *American Political Science Review* 80 (4): 1095–1111.

Belshaw, C. 1965. *Traditional exchange and the modern market.* Englewood Cliffs, N.J., U.S.A.: Prentice Hall.

Bernstein, L. 1992. Opting out of the legal system: Extralegal contractual relations in the diamond industry. *Journal of Legal Studies* 21: 1–12.

Fafchamps, M. 1992. Solidarity networks in preindustrial societies: Rational peasants with a moral economy. *Economic Development and Cultural Change* 41 (1): 147–174.

———. 1996. Market emergence, trust and reputation. Mimeo. Stanford, Calif., U.S.A.: Stanford University.

———. 2004. *Market institutions and Sub-Saharan Africa: Theory and evidence.* Cambridge, Mass., U.S.A.: MIT Press.

Fafchamps, M., and E. Gabre-Madhin. 2001. *Agricultural markets in Benin and Malawi: The operation and performance of traders.* World Bank Policy Research Working Paper 2734. Washington, D.C.: World Bank.

Fafchamps, M., and B. Minten. 1999. *Returns to social capital among traders.* Markets and Structural Studies Division Discussion Paper 23. Washington, D.C.: International Food Policy Research Institute.

———. 2001. Property rights in a flea market economy. *Economic Development and Cultural Change* 49 (2): 229–267.

Fafchamps, M., E. Gabre-Madhin, and B. Minten. 2005. Increasing returns and market efficiency in agricultural trade. *Journal of Development Economics* 78 (2): 406–442.

Fudenberg, D., and E. Maskin. 1986. The Folk Theorem for repeated games with discounting and incomplete information. *Econometrica* 54: 533–554.

Fukuyama, F. 1995. *Trust: The social virtues and the creation of prosperity.* New York: Free Press.

Gabre-Madhin, E. 2001. *Market institutions, transaction costs, and social capital in the Ethiopian grain market.* Research Report 124. Washington, D.C.: International Food Policy Research Institute.

Gabre-Madhin, E., and A. Negassa. 2005. Linking trading practices and arbitrage behaviour in the Ethiopian grain market. Mimeo. Washington, D.C.: International Food Policy Research Institute.

Gambetta, D. 1988. *Trust: Making and breaking cooperative relations.* New York: Basil Blackwell.

Geertz, C. 1978. The bazaar economy: Information and search in peasant marketing. *American Economic Review* 68 (2): 28–32.

———. 1979. The bazaar economy in Sefrou. In *Meaning and order in Moroccan society,* ed. C. Geertz, H. Geertz, and L. Rosen. New York: Cambridge University Press.

Greif, A. 1993. Contract enforceability and economic institutions in early trade: The Maghribi traders' coalition. *American Economic Review* 83 (3): 525–548.

———. 1994. Cultural beliefs and the organization of society: A historical and theoretical reflection on collectivist and individualistic societies. *Journal of Political Economy* 102 (5): 912–950.

———. 1999. On the study of organizations and evolving organizational forms through history: Reflection from the late medieval family firm. In *Firms, markets, and hierarchies,* ed. G. R. Carroll and D. J. Teece. New York: Oxford University Press.

Hayami, Y., and T. Kawagoe. 1993. *The agrarian origins of commerce and industry.* New York: St. Martin's Press.

Hayami, Y., and M. Kikuchi. 1981. *Asian village economy at the crossroads: An economic approach to institutional change.* Tokyo and Baltimore: University of Tokyo Press and Johns Hopkins University Press.

Hayek, F. 1945. The use of knowledge in society. *American Economic Review* 35 (4): 519–530.

Hicks, J. 1969. *A theory of economic history.* Oxford: Oxford University Press.

Kandori, M. 1992. Social norms and community enforcement. *Review of Economic Studies* 59: 63–80.

Landa, J. 1981. A theory of the ethnically homogeneous middleman group: An institutional alternative to contract law. *Journal of Legal Studies* 10: 349–362.

Levi, M. 1997. *Consent, dissent and patriotism.* New York: Cambridge University Press.

Macaulay, S. 1963. Non-contractual relations in business. *American Sociological Review* 28: 55–69.

McMillan, J., and C. Woodruff. 2000. Private order under dysfunctional public order. *Michigan Law Review* 98 (8): 2421–2458.

Milgrom, P., D. North, and B. Weingast. 1990. The role of institutions in the revival of trade: The law merchant, private judges, and the Champagne fairs. *Economics and Politics* 2 (1): 1–23.

Mintz, S. 1964. The employment of capital by market women in Haiti. In *Capital, savings and credit in peasant societies,* ed. R. Firth and B. S. Yamey. Chicago: Aldine.

Morris, M. L., and M. D. Newman. 1989. Official and parallel cereals markets in Senegal: Empirical evidence. *World Development* 17: 1408–1418.

North, D. C. 1990. *Institutions, institutional change and economic performance.* Cambridge: Cambridge University Press.

———. 1991. Institutions. *Journal of Economic Perspectives* 5 (1): 97–112.

North, D. C., and R. B. Thomas. 1973. *The rise of the Western world: A new economic history.* Cambridge: Cambridge University Press.

Ostrom, E. 1998. The institutional analysis and development approach. In *Designing institutions for environment and natural resource management,* ed. E. T. Loehman and D. M. Kilgour. Cheltenham, U.K.: Edward Elgar.

Platteau, J.-P. 1996. The evolutionary theory of land rights as applied to Sub-Saharan Africa: A critical assessment. *Development and Change* 27 (1): 29–86.

———. 2000. *Institutions, social norms, and economic development: Fundamentals of development economics.* Amsterdam: Harwood Academic.

———. 2006. Solidarity norms and institutions in village societies: Static and dynamic considerations. In *Handbook on gift-giving, reciprocity and altruism,* ed. S. Kolm and J. Mercier-Ythier. Amsterdam: North-Holland and Elsevier.

Posner, R. A. 1980. A theory of primitive society, with special reference to law. *Journal of Law and Economics* 23 (1): 1–53.

Richman, B. D. 2005. How community institutions create economic advantage: Jewish diamond merchants in New York. Duke Law Legal Studies Research Paper 65. http://www.law.duke.edu/fac/workingpapers.html. Accessed August 2005.

Schmid, A. A. 1992. Legal foundations of the market: Implications for the formerly socialist countries of Eastern Europe and Africa. *Journal of Economic Issues* 26 (3): 707–732.

Staatz, J. M., J. Dione, and N. N. Dembele. 1989. Cereals market liberalization in Mali. *World Development* 17 (5): 703–718.

Sugden, R. 1986. *The economics of rights, co-operation and welfare.* New York: Basil Blackwell.

Swetnam, J. 1978. Interaction between urban and rural residents in a Guatemalan marketplace. *Urban Anthropology* 7: 137–153.

Sykuta, M., and M. Cook. 2001. A New Institutional Economics approach to contracts and cooperatives. *American Journal of Agricultural Economics* 83 (5): 1271–1277.

Szanton, M. 1972. *Right to survive.* University Park, Penn., U.S.A.: Penn State University Press.

Trager, L. 1981. Customers and creditors: Variations in economic personalism in a Nigerian marketing system. *Ethnology* 20: 133–146.

Tyler, T. R. 1990. *Why people obey the law.* New Haven, Conn., U.S.A.: Yale University Press.

Weber, M. 1927. *General economic history,* trans. F. H. Knight. New York: Adelphi.

Weingast, B. 1995. The economic role of political institutions. *Journal of Law, Economics and Organization* 11 (1): 1–31.

Williamson, O. E. 1985. *The economic institutions of capitalism.* New York: Free Press.

Chapter 5

Coordination for Market Development

Colin Poulton and Michael C. Lyne

One major body of literature in the application of institutional economics to market development concerns economic coordination. This literature seeks to explain why market systems are structured as they are, thereby revealing fundamental challenges that have to be addressed if efficient markets (for goods and services) are to develop. On a practical level, interest in coordination has risen dramatically as supply chains have become increasingly globalized and have tried to respond to the greater demands placed on them by consumers and regulators. In the agro-food sector, the dramatic rise in the power of supermarkets in many countries (Reardon et al. 2003) is associated with moves away from product sourcing through traditional wholesale markets toward vertically coordinated chains. It is in this context that Jaffee (1995, 25) writes: "In commodity systems analysis, the central focus is on the problems and mechanisms for coordination."

The literature on economic coordination explores the potential for private-market actors to collectively contribute to market development, but it also examines the limitations of this potential, hence suggesting roles for the state that are taken up in Chapter 20. It explores the consequences of relaxing the following assumptions in the perfect-competition paradigm of neoclassical economics:

1. *Perfect information.* As in all economics of institutions, imperfect information makes economic actors vulnerable to opportunistic behavior by others. In this chapter, the implications for investment and the institutional arrangements devised

Eleni Gabre-Madhin made valuable contributions to this chapter. Parts of Section 5.3 draw heavily on Poulton, Dorward, and Kydd (2005).

to provide investment security under conditions of uncertainty are considered, as is the manner in which certain arrangements for economic coordination aid the process of contract enforcement (see also Chapter 4).

2. *Perfectly fungible capital.* In reality, capital is not costlessly transferable between uses. In this chapter, the consequences (under conditions of imperfect information) of the facts that assets are often lumpy, difficult to dispose of, or only realize their full value in the context of specific contracts is considered.

3. *Product homogeneity.* Few products are truly homogeneous, although some (including certain nonperishable agricultural commodities) more closely approximate to this ideal than others. Some of the consequences for agro-food sector organization are considered in this chapter.

4. *Private goods.* Most agricultural goods and services are indeed private goods. However, some support services required by agricultural producers (for example, technical and market knowledge) exhibit public good characteristics.

5. *A complete set of markets.* One manifestation of market failure is the near or complete absence of certain markets. Of most relevance to this chapter is the failure of the market for seasonal finance for agricultural producers. The ways that some actors overcome this problem and the challenge of providing the necessary seasonal financing are considered.

A useful starting point for studying economic coordination is to ask what coordination, if any, occurs in the perfect-competition paradigm of neoclassical economics. In this stylized world, characterized by spot-market transactions and unrestrained competition between atomistic agents, the "invisible hand of the market," operating through the price mechanism, coordinates demand and supply at each level of the supply chain. Markets clear, ensuring that what is demanded is what is supplied at the market-clearing price. However, there is no conscious coordinating activity on the part of any market actors. Rather, they make independent decisions, responding to price signals in pure competition with others.

The essence of the coordination discussed in this chapter is a move away from atomistic competition and spot-market transactions to a range of deliberately structured relationships among market actors that achieve one or more of the following:

- provide incentives for investment when assets are lumpy, difficult to dispose of, or specific to particular contracts (a concept that is explained in more detail below);

- equilibrate ("match") not just the quantity of goods or services that is supplied and demanded but also the quality and timing of supply of those goods or services; and

- assist in the enforcement of contracts (including those with third parties).

It can be argued that the perfect-competition paradigm assumes away these coordination challenges. However, North (1990) offers an alternative perspective: that actors in a stylized perfectly competitively market are able to focus solely on competing—and competing on price alone—because a perfect set of institutions underpins the market, handling all coordination challenges for them. Thus, to imagine an agricultural example, competition can focus on price alone because a set of perfectly functioning institutions determines—and ensures total compliance with—grades and standards for each commodity (hence creating product homogeneity in each product category). Indeed, commodity exchanges, such as SAFEX in South Africa (www.safex.co.za), KACE in Kenya (www.kacekenya.com) and the currently discontinued ZIMACE in Zimbabwe, seek not only to bring together buyers and sellers of particular agricultural commodities but also to ensure that common grades and standards are used in each transaction and transacting parties do not behave in an opportunistic manner. Thus trade on such exchanges can be conducted entirely on the basis of price.

Coordination is described by Poulton et al. (2004, 521) as the

> effort or measures designed to make players within a market system act in a common or complementary way or toward a common goal. This may also require effort or measures designed to prevent players from pursuing contrary paths or goals. Coordination may be undertaken by private agents acting collectively or may be orchestrated by state agents defining the boundaries within which private agents can act.

The SAFEX, KACE, and ZIMACE examples show that some coordination may be initiated, implemented, and even enforced entirely by private actors. However, public support for institutional development may also be required to lessen the coordination problems facing private actors, enabling them to concentrate their energies on market competition.

An additional variant on the concept of private coordination is that, rather than acting collectively, independent private agents may choose to merge ("integrate") their activities, handing all relevant decisionmaking to a single management team to reap the benefits that more effective coordination brings.

If an effective solution to coordination problems is not found, however, the market in question will likely fail to deliver particular goods or services (or deliver suboptimal quantities of these goods or services), because the incentives for the requisite investment in service delivery are not present.

In the sections that follow, various forms of coordination are examined, which are classified as

- vertical: coordination among actors at different points in a marketing chain;

- horizontal: coordination among actors (competitors) at a given stage of a marketing chain; or

- complementary: coordination among actors providing complementary services to producers at a given stage of a marketing chain.

These concepts are illustrated with reference to service provision for smallholder farmers in Africa, which also brings out:

- the importance of product and process attributes in structuring incentives for investment in service delivery;

- the public good attributes of certain services, most notably extension; and

- the significance of small transaction sizes (hence high per unit transaction costs) in discouraging market development.

In the context of service provision to smallholder farmers in Africa, there is also a clear theoretical role for collective action on the part of producers to

- reduce the transaction costs facing service providers and output buyers, a coordination role that can enhance market access and/or strengthen the competitive position of the producer group in the marketing chain;

- hold service providers (especially state service providers) to account for the types and quality of service that they deliver; and

- facilitate investment in lumpy and intangible assets that these farmers may require to access more reliable or profitable markets.

However, these requirements in turn raise the question of the internal organization and performance of farmer organizations, which is reviewed in the next section.

5.1   Vertical Coordination

In this section the discussion of transaction-cost economics (TCE) literature reviewed in Chapter 2 is expanded, focusing particularly on the work of Williamson and his analysis of the different forms of vertical coordination observed in market chains and how transaction costs determine the nature of these arrangements. Williamson set out to show that many contractual relationships between firms in a supply chain that were considered "nonstandard" by economists trained in the neoclassical tradition—and were thus criticized on the grounds of allocative efficiency— were in fact designed precisely to improve the efficiency of supply chains in delivering certain types of products. In doing so, he shed new light on key challenges to market development. After reviewing the work of Williamson, we consider applications of his theory to agricultural settings, along with criticisms leveled at the theory.

The foundation for analyzing market coordination and structure in terms of transaction costs is Coase's (1937) insight that, although reaching, modifying, and implementing agreements is essential to doing business and creating the conditions for investment, the costs of doing so also restrain the potential gains from trade. Thus in a world of transaction costs the relative merits of different organizational forms depend on a comparison of the costs of transacting.

As illustrated in Chapter 2, transaction costs—the costs of running the economic system—arise because individuals and firms are constrained by imperfect information and bounded rationality. Three types of transaction costs can thus be distinguished:

- Ex ante costs are those of searching for potential trading partners, then drafting and negotiating an agreement. These are mainly fixed costs (that is, they do not change with the volume of the goods being exchanged).

- Ex post costs are those of monitoring an agreement and negotiation when a circumstance arises that is not fully accounted for in the contract. Losses and the risk of losses resulting from a breach of contract are also ex post transaction costs. These, and some of the monitoring costs, increase with volumes traded, introducing a variable cost element to ex post transaction costs.

- "Bonding costs to securing commitment" (Williamson 1985, 22) do not fit neatly into the ex ante or ex post categorization. These costs are further discussed below.

5.1.1   Asset Specificity

TCE considers the most critical dimension of a transaction to be the degree of asset specificity involved. Asset specificity may take a number of forms, the two most important of which are physical and human specificity. Physical specificity occurs when, for example, a packinghouse invests in packaging equipment tailored to meet the specific requirements (such as pack size or labeling requirements) of a particular supermarket buyer. If the supermarket decides at a future date not to purchase from that packinghouse, then it may not be possible to use the same packaging equipment in supplying an alternative buyer.

Human specificity occurs when, to continue the previous example, supplying a specific supermarket chain may require that staff in the packinghouse are trained in specific procedures required by the supermarket to ensure the quality and safety of produce sold to that supermarket and/or to be able to trace produce back to its original source of supply. If the supermarket later decides not to purchase from that packinghouse, the training and experience in these procedures may not be transferable to another buyer.

Asset specificity can be conceptualized as having two dimensions:

- *Asset fixity* is a measure of the costs of exiting a particular investment (as noted in Chapter 2). Asset fixity can also be thought of in terms of the discount on the use value of the asset that would have to be accepted to dispose of it.

- *Transaction specificity* is the extent to which the use value of the asset is dependent on the continuation of a specific transaction or contract (such as the supermarket contract in the examples above).

In its strictest form, asset specificity requires that the asset have no alternative use outside of the contractual relationship to which it is specific and that there is no market for sale of the asset should the contractual relationship collapse. However, investment carries a specific risk element even if somewhat looser versions of these conditions hold:

- The asset produces goods for which the number of buyers is limited. Thus refusal by one buyer to buy the goods at a remunerative price forces the asset holder to engage in a costly search and/or negotiation process to start selling to an alternative buyer.

- Markets for sale of the asset exist, but limited numbers of buyers or high transportation costs to an alternative buyer mean that the asset owner would have to accept a discount in asset value if seeking to sell it.

Asset specificity can thus be thought of as a special case of a thin market; conditions prevailing in rural markets throughout much of Africa mean that a wide range

Figure 5.1   Conceptualizing asset specificity

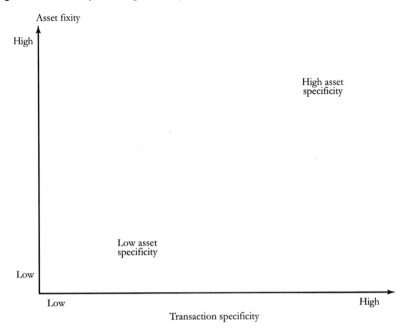

of assets exhibit a degree of specificity. Thus the nature of markets can confer specificity, whereas Williamson's (1985) original concept emphasized the attributes of the asset. Figure 5.1 illustrates the concept of greater or lesser asset specificity in terms of its two component parts. Market conditions are as important as the inherent properties of the asset in determining where a particular asset lies in this diagram.

5.1.2   What Determines Different Transaction Attributes?

Transaction-cost theory thus rests on the two key behavioral assumptions: (1) the bounded rationality and opportunism of humans and (2) asset specificity. It further assumes uncertainty and posits that the incidence of the three factors (bounded rationality, opportunism, and asset specificity) under conditions of uncertainty jointly determines the contracting process.

According to Williamson, the contracting process can take one of four forms (Table 5.1): planning, promise, competition, or governance. The objective of *planning* is to design mechanisms ex ante to cope with all potential opportunistic actions. (In the hypothetical situation of unbounded rationality, it is possible—and economical—to do this.) These mechanisms then kick in if a contractual partner attempts to act opportunistically, such that ex post transaction costs are minimized.[1] The essence of

Table 5.1   Attributes of the contracting process

Behavioral assumptions			
Bounded rationality	Opportunism	Asset specificity	Implied contracting process
0	+	+	Planning
+	0	+	Promise
+	+	0	Competition
+	+	+	Governance

Source: Williamson (1985).
Note: 0, attribute is absent; +, attribute is present.

promise is that contracts based on loyalty are sufficient in the absence of opportunism. This concept links to the discussion on relation-based contracting in Chapter 4: actors trade with few formal contractual safeguards with (a limited sphere of) partners whom they trust not to act opportunistically.

The key idea behind *competition* is that, when no specific assets are involved, actors can safely engage in competitive, spot-market transactions. If other actors in a particular market act opportunistically, the rest can simply shift their investment elsewhere, as assets are fully fungible and shifting investment is costless.

Governance here refers to the creation of a contractual and relational framework to manage trade and associated investment when all three factors (bounded rationality, opportunism, and asset specificity) are present. Planning is thus incomplete because of bounded rationality, promise breaks down because of opportunism, and conscious coordination between partners matters because of asset specificity. Although contracting partners may still depend on third-party (including court) arbitration or conflict resolution, the costs associated with such procedures force them to structure their own bilateral relationships in such a way that the incentives for opportunism are minimized (Williamson 1985).

5.1.3   Spot Markets, Bilateral Contracts, and Hierarchy

The probability of observing more-or-less vertically integrated forms of market organization depends on the underlying properties of contracts: higher asset specificity, greater uncertainty, more complexity, and greater frequency of transactions are associated with greater vertical coordination:

- Greater asset specificity increases the risk of entering into a given contract; hence the party investing in the specific assets is likely to seek reassurances in the terms of contractual relationships that other parties will continue to trade on terms that provide a fair return to the investment made.

- Greater uncertainty and/or complexity make it more likely that contracts will be incomplete, whereas higher frequency of transactions increases the costs associated with ex post negotiation when circumstances arise that are not fully accounted for in the contract. Thus parties are likely to seek to place their contracts in ongoing trading relationships that allow trust to be built and/or provide disincentives to short-term opportunistic behavior when unforeseen or otherwise difficult circumstances arise.

Williamson (1985, 1991) thus posits three main types of contracting relationship between actors at different points in a marketing chain: spot-market transactions, bilateral contracts, and vertical integration or hierarchy (Figure 5.2).

Spot markets.   Spot-market transactions are the normal form of transaction in basic neoclassical economics (although applications of neoclassical theory, of course, consider a range of alternative contractual forms, such as futures and options contracts). In spot-market transactions, two contracting parties, who may or may not have contracted with each other before, transact for a specific deal with no necessary expectation that they will transact again (that is, trade is impersonal). In addition, all dimensions of the transaction are completed simultaneously.

Figure 5.2   Vertical and horizontal coordination

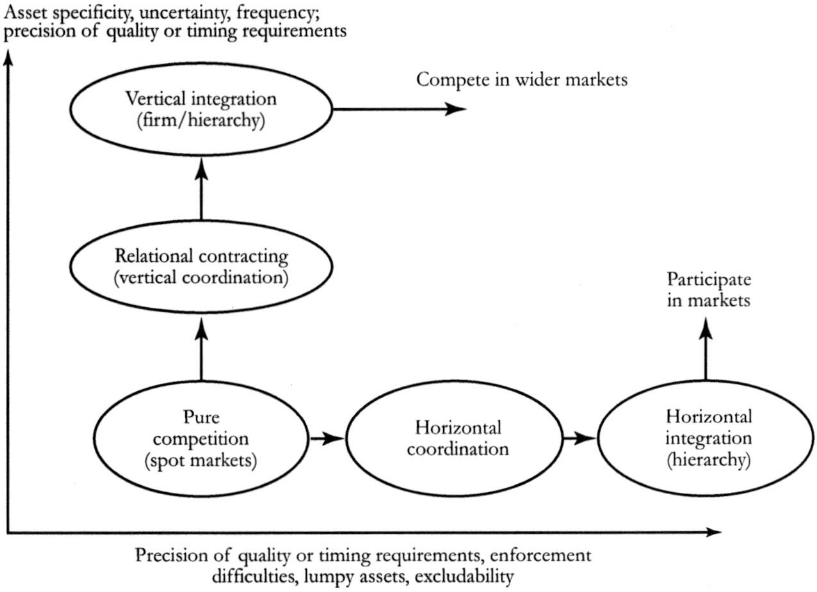

In such a situation, there is no conscious or deliberate coordination of economic activity by the contracting parties. However, as noted earlier, third-party institutions (such as commodity exchanges or auctions) may be created to facilitate spot-market transactions. A key insight of neoclassical economics is that, when the density of transactions is sufficient and information flows freely enough to all parties involved, spot markets generate clear price signals to equilibrate demand and supply of the commodities in question.

Even when all dimensions of the transaction are not completed simultaneously but trade is impersonal, price discovery can be efficient (commodity exchanges often also support futures and options contracts). However, in such cases there is also an additional enforcement challenge, as with credit contracts.

Williamson's (1985) central insight—why competition based on spot markets does not always prevail as the governing principle for exchange (see Table 5.1)—is that impersonal contracting in spot markets does not provide sufficient assurance for market actors to make asset specific investments. As the vector of asset specificity, uncertainty, and frequency increases (moving up the vertical axis in Figure 5.2), market actors thus move away from spot-market exchange to relational contracting (vertical coordination) and ultimately to vertical integration.

Vertical coordination (relational contracting). The key characteristic of relational contracting is that a pair of contracting parties enters into an agreement that stipulates the terms of their (often repeated) trading interaction. This agreement may be written or unwritten, but it is explicit. It sets out what is expected of each partner, the rewards for fulfilling these obligations (for example, continued opportunity to interact, perhaps on improved terms), penalties for failing to fulfil them, and the circumstances under which the agreement will continue (or cease to be) valid. Repeated interaction is one mechanism for ensuring contractual compliance, with the foreclosure of future opportunities for profitable transacting acting as a disincentive for contractual default. Thus an urban vegetable wholesaler may offer a rural producer group the promise of competitive prices and a guaranteed market in the face of severe price fluctuations for perishable produce in return for a promise of regular supply of that produce with reasonably reliable quality. A breach of this agreement, except under special circumstances, could result in the termination of the contract and loss of access to the guaranteed market or the assured supply of produce.

Williamson's (1985) additional insight is that relational contracting can provide the security necessary for one or both contractual parties to invest in specific assets. Thus, to take the earlier example of the packinghouse and the supermarket buyer, the packinghouse may only invest in tailored packaging equipment and staff training if it receives some form of assurance from the supermarket that the latter will buy from it on an ongoing basis at prices that will generate an acceptable return to its investment

(Boselie, Henson, and Weatherspoon 2003). Of course, the supermarket buyer may at some point wish to review its portfolio of supply sources and so will not commit to buying from the packinghouse (or even to paying a particular price) forever. However, some form of contractual continuity may be necessary to encourage suppliers to upgrade their facilities in response to evolving market conditions.

Relational contracting therefore seeks to ensure a mutually acceptable balance of costs and benefits between contracting parties. When the burden of investing in specific assets falls predominantly on party A, the onus is on party B to demonstrate their commitment to the contract to provide the necessary security for the investment in specific assets to take place. Depending on the size of the investment and the time taken to recoup it, party B may thus have to commit to buying from party A for a nonnegligible period and perhaps also to give some assurance on the prices that will be paid during this period. If the agreement is not legally binding or the costs of enforcing the agreement through the relevant legal channels are prohibitive, party B may have to undertake additional, costly measures (for example, building up a reputation for trustworthiness in contractual matters by eschewing opportunistic behavior over an extended period) to convince party A that the commitment to the contract is sincere. These are what Williamson (1985, 22) calls the "bonding costs to securing commitment."

Finally (following Williamson), the emphasis in this discussion on relational contracting has been on repeated trading interaction. However, similar principles can be applied to asynchronous transactions (that is, transactions, such as a credit contract, in which one party performs their obligations before the other), even when these turn out to be one-offs. Thus a lender looks for credible commitments from a new borrower (for example, in the form of collateral or the signature of a guarantor) that they will repay their loan before lending to them. Note that, although in one sense this is a straightforward case of contract enforcement, the credit contract can also be interpreted as the lender making an asset-specific investment in a deal with the borrower. In addition, a contract farming company usually has to provide some form of assurance that they will buy the output of contract farmers before the latter will invest their labor in the production process. This is because the products in question rarely have a reliable local market (snowpeas in rural Zimbabwe or Kenya, for example), in which case production involves a transaction-specific investment on the part of the farmer. The size of the transaction-specific investment is even greater if the crop is a perennial, so that the farmer has to commit scarce land and capital for several years before beginning to realize a return.

Firm/hierarchy (vertical integration). Although relational contracting may provide the necessary security for one or both contractual parties to invest in specific assets, there are also situations in which the size of asset-specific investment and/or level of uncertainty, complexity, or frequency of transactions are too great for a bilateral contract to deliver a sufficient degree of investment security. Under such circumstances, Williamson (1985) hypothesizes that relational contracting will give way to hierarchy, meaning that a contractual relationship between two independent parties will be replaced by the performance of the two activities by a single, vertically integrated firm.

In this case, a trade-off occurs. The management of the integrated firm now exercises full control over both activities. Therefore administrative control replaces the (incomplete) contract between the two independent parties as the means of ensuring that the returns to the asset-specific investment are not undercut by opportunistic behavior. However, the performance incentives facing employees in charge of these activities are likely to be weaker than they would be if the activities were carried out by two smaller firms in which managers also had a major ownership stake. (This logic obviously makes important assumptions about the ownership structures under both scenarios, an issue raised later in this chapter.) The dilution of incentives, according to Williamson (1985, 1991), is what discourages the creation of vertically integrated firms when there are few problems of asset specificity, uncertainty, and complexity, and/or low transaction frequency.

5.1.4   Other Reasons for Vertical Coordination

Although Williamson ascribes primacy to asset specificity as the driver of vertical coordination, there are other factors that also push actors in agro-food marketing systems in this direction. Perhaps the most important of these relate to product quality, that is, relaxing the assumption of homogeneous commodities in the perfect-competition paradigm of neoclassical economics. Two related, but distinct, aspects can be distinguished:

- Some agricultural products are highly perishable. Thus there is a need to coordinate the timing of supply with the pattern of demand, which may well require producers to stagger their planting of such products. Although market price signals may at times be sufficient to encourage producers to stagger plantings, specific investments may also be required if producers are to respond to demand for what might traditionally be considered out-of-season supplies. Examples of such investment include irrigation technology or knowledge of a new pest complex associated with a different time in the year. It may thus be that buyers cannot rely on spot markets to generate the timing of the supply flows that they desire, in which case they may seek to establish bilateral supply contracts with particular suppliers.

- Some buyers (for example, supermarkets) may also have particular quality requirements for food products that spot markets—given the inherent variability in agricultural products—cannot guarantee at all times. Increasingly, as food-safety legislation becomes more demanding,[2] supermarkets require not just reliably high-quality produce but also assurance from producers that the products are safe, along with the means of tracing produce to its original suppliers if any contamination occurs. Food safety (along with organic certification and environmental and animal welfare impacts of production) is a credence attribute—meaning one that cannot necessarily be verified by consumers even after consumption. Thus, given the prohibitively high costs of testing all products for all possible safety threats, assurance can only be provided through monitoring of the production process itself. Investment in such process monitoring can have high specific-asset dimensions. Moreover, the impersonal nature of spot markets militates against buyers knowing the production processes used by sellers. Although particular sellers in spot markets may decide to invest in reputation as suppliers of safe produce, spot markets alone cannot provide the assurances of food safety, environmental impact, and so on that such buyers as supermarkets are increasingly demanding.

5.1.5 Applications to Agriculture

Following a line of thinking similar to that of Williamson (1985, 1991), Binswanger and Rosenzweig (1986) considered how the technological attributes of crop production and processing influence the organization of production. Starting from the position that smallholder households generally enjoy advantages over large-scale agricultural enterprises in the supervision and motivation of unskilled labor (a critical input in most agricultural production in low-income economies), they argued that large-scale enterprises could nevertheless be active (and expected to dominate) in the production of

- crops involving important economies of scale in processing, combined with major coordination problems between harvesting and processing (for example, sugar cane); and

- perennial crops with high maintenance intensity (for example, rubber and tea, the latter combining perennialism with high perishability after harvest).

In the first case large companies become involved because it may prove prohibitively costly to organize numerous smallholder producers to stagger their production sufficiently to provide a year-round throughput of raw material to the processing operation. In the second, smallholders may not have the capital to invest in establishing plantations.

Binswanger and Rosenzweig (1986), however, accepted that other factors are also important in influencing actual sector structure. In particular, they noted the importance of land tenure and availability. Where large tracts of land are not available for estate production, owners of processing factories may seek to engage smallholder producers in contract-farming schemes, even when the nature of the production and processing steps otherwise favors large-scale production.

Work by Jaffee (1993) on Kenyan horticultural exports sought explicitly to test the predictions of Williamsonian theory in the context of agriculture. Jaffee scored a range of horticultural products on the basis of (1) asset specificity and economies of scale inherent in their postharvest handling and processing and (2) perishability, specificity of quality standards, and seasonal variability of product supply. (In conformity with Williams, Jaffee identifies these as indicators of uncertainty.)

Jaffee found that the combination of these attributes did have some predictive power in explaining the types of contractual arrangements observed in export supply chains for the different crops. In the case of processed products (with the highest asset specificity), a degree of vertical integration was often observed, with a typical arrangement being one whereby a European buyer had a stake in the Kenyan processing and exporting operations, which exported almost exclusively to the single buyer. Among fresh-produce exports, an important category was Asian vegetables. In this case less asset-specific investment was involved, but the highly perishable nature of the products meant that export trade often took place between one family member in Kenya and another in the United Kingdom or elsewhere. Trading within families meant that exporters were dealing with people whom they trusted—an important consideration, given that delays or obstructions in the trading process could lead to the produce being spoiled. In other words, the potential for opportunistic action was extremely high.

The relationships so far discussed were characteristic of large export operations, which sent consignments of produce year-round. Small-scale, occasional operators, by contrast, tended to work on a consignment (spot-market) basis, which highlights the importance of the frequency variable on the vertical axis of Figure 5.2.

However, Jaffee (1993) also found other factors to be important in determining the nature of contractual relationships within horticultural chains:

- patterns of land tenure;

- interventions by the government in land, input, and product markets; and

- resources of participating firms.

In the case of some horticultural crops, a wide range of forms of chain organization were observed, showing that the techno-economic attributes of the crops in question were at best one factor influencing institutional arrangements.

5.1.6 Critiques of TCE: The Issue of Power

One of the major critiques of TCE, as considered in Chapter 2, is that of naivety regarding the issue of power. As described earlier, TCE is built on the assumption that economic organization is driven by a desire to enhance efficiency. Thus an effort is made to minimize costs when aligning transactions that have different attributes with governance structures that have different costs and competencies. Indeed, one of the aims of Williamson's (1985, 1991) work was to defend "nonstandard" contractual forms against allegations (particularly from neoclassical economists suspicious of anything that could be a monopoly) that they were merely an abuse of market power. He did this by showing the transaction-cost economizing of non-standard contractual forms, such as various bilateral (relational) contracts. However, it is important to remember that his focus on industrial sectors in developed economies, characterized by high levels of competition in final markets, allowed him to downplay the power issue in his theoretical work. The horizontal arrow beside the term "vertical integration" in Figure 5.2 signifies that entire supply chains compete against one another. Hence, firms in these chains seek to develop contractual arrangements that enhance the competitive position of their particular chain through efficiency (transaction-cost) savings. In theory, when greater competitiveness brings benefits to a particular chain, these benefits can be shared equally among the members of the chain. In practice, it is unlikely that such sharing happens, but Williamson did not focus his attention on this issue.

In contrast, critics of the TCE approach studying marketing systems in developing countries have observed that contractual arrangements owe as much to unequal power relations as to transaction-cost minimization (Harriss 1993; Crow and Murshid 1994; Dolan and Humphrey 2000). Unlike the highly competitive final markets assumed by Williamson, the cases cited by the critics clearly feature both market power and vertical coordination through contracts. Thus Dolan and Humphrey (2000) argue that UK supermarkets and their agents offer few contractual guarantees to suppliers of fresh produce in developing countries but expect these suppliers to make significant investments in supply capacity, many of which are of a specific-asset nature. Both they and Crow and Murshid (1994), therefore, argue that contracts can be a way by which powerful actors in a marketing chain pass risk onto weaker actors who are, in fact, less well placed to bear it.

Undoubtedly power does affect the terms of contracts that are negotiated. The disputed issue is, therefore, whether it also affects their form. In other words, even in situations in which one party exercises power in key markets,[3] is the form of contractual relationship (for example, market, relational contract, hierarchy, or hybrid forms) still fundamentally affected by the nature of transaction costs, as posited by Williamson?

There does not seem to be a definitive answer, although it seems germane that it is the more powerful actors in a chain who are likely to exert more influence over both the form and the terms of contracts.[4] When parties to a contract have different preferences for contractual form, the preference of the more powerful party is likely to prevail. Form, therefore, is likely to be transaction-cost economizing first and foremost for them—and may not be for the other party. However, both parties have to believe that entering into the contract is in their interest (that is, it will generate a return greater than that which they would achieve if they did not enter the contract). Otherwise, no contract would take place.[5] Thus the choice of form should confer some benefits even on the weaker party. For instance, in his classic exposition of the institution of sharecropping, Stiglitz (1974) argued that this institution—long criticized for rewarding the tenant with only part of the marginal value product of his or her labor—actually struck a balance between the production incentives offered to the tenant and risk sharing between landlord and tenant in the case of bad years.

The implication of this discussion for researchers and policymakers is that they should look at both the form and the terms of contracts. As we argue in the next section, high levels of system performance generally require some balance to be struck between competition and coordination in a market system.

5.2   Horizontal Coordination

Despite advances in understanding vertical coordination, until recently institutional economics has shared with conventional industrial economics the view that horizontal relationships in supply chains essentially "relate to entry and competitive conditions prevailing at each industry stage" (Jaffee 1995, 24). In other words, actors at a given stage of a marketing chain are either competitors or they collude. This view is simplistic and needs to be modified. Specifically, the importance of horizontal coordination is highlighted and an understanding of horizontal coordination that is similar to the Williamsonian view of vertical coordination is suggested in this section.

5.2.1   Horizontal Coordination among Firms

Hall and Soskice (2001) have demonstrated the importance of horizontal coordination to the comparative advantage of a number of northern European economies (as well as Japan). They suggest that horizontal coordination—like vertical coordination—can assist in creating incentives for asset-specific investment. However, their argument might be recast more persuasively in terms of horizontal coordination assisting in contract enforcement and excluding free riders from the benefits of what might otherwise be common pool goods.[6] Thus one example concerns investment in employee training in German manufacturing (Hall and Soskice 2001). In certain high-tech manufacturing industries, employee training imparts a mixture of firm-specific skills and skills of sufficient relevance and value to other firms in the same industry that some successful trainees could obtain employment with competitors. Firms, however, only invest in training new workers if they have some confidence of keeping them once the training is completed. There is thus a horizontal coordination challenge in assuring a return on training investment, as competitor firms might be tempted to free ride on such investment by recruiting employees who have completed their training at other firms. To overcome this problem, strong employer and worker associations in Germany negotiate industrywide wage settlements for standard skill grades, such that the incentive for employees to switch firms is minimized (as they will receive essentially the same pay in any firm upon completion of their training). In other words, firms coordinate their activities in labor markets to protect the incentive to invest in human skills, even as they compete in output markets.

As explained by Poulton et al. (2004), the case of African cotton ginners providing preharvest loans to producers is directly analogous to the Hall and Soskice (2001) case. The provision of loans exposes ginners to free-riding actions by cotton-buying competitors. To tackle the side selling of cotton by producers, ginners are likely both to provide incentives directly to the producers (through the terms of the vertical relationship), so that they sell to the firm that provided them with preharvest services, and to seek ways of restraining the actions of competitors (horizontal coordination). Three examples from the cotton industry serve to illustrate how horizontal coordination may be pursued—sometimes successfully, sometimes not—to assist with contract enforcement.

In the years immediately after liberalization of the cotton sector in Ghana in 1985, all actors in the sector agreed to provide a common input package (tractor plowing, seed, fertilizer, pesticide spraying, and extension advice) to all producers. Until 1995 (by which time there were 12 companies in the sector) no explicit charge was made for this package, except for plowing costs. Instead, the per kilo price paid for seed cotton was adjusted downward to recoup the costs of inputs supplied, based on a notional average yield of 600 kg seed cotton per half-hectare unit. The main strength of this so-called free-input system was that, when combined with common pricing by all cotton companies for inputs and seed cotton, it removed almost all incentive for a producer to side sell. As a result, side selling was relatively rare. The two main disadvantages were that the more productive farmers subsidized the less productive ones and, more seriously, that common price setting reduced competition from price formation, so that the price of seed cotton fell steadily after liberalization in relation both to input costs and to competing crops, such as maize and groundnuts. In response, and on the basis of external advice, the sector moved during the mid-1990s to a more conventional system in which an explicit deduction was made for the inputs received by each producer. Although the intention was to raise effective prices for more productive producers, this change also removed the horizontal coordination that had been provided through the free-input system. As a result, side selling escalated dramatically in the second half of the decade, as producers now had a strong incentive to sell to a company other than the one that provided them with inputs (even though common pricing was retained). This experience led to pressure, by 2000, for a local monopoly system in which the state allocated concession zones to each company in which the latter would have the responsibility to invest in supporting smallholder cotton production but also the exclusive right to purchase the resulting output of seed cotton.

Meanwhile, in Zambia (from liberalization in 1995 to the present) and Zimbabwe (until 2001), two companies have dominated the cotton sector. In both countries the two companies have competed for the patronage of cotton producers, their international connections and ambitions driving them to offer reasonably attractive prices to farmers despite their duopoly positions in their respective national markets. At the same time as competing for the patronage of cotton producers—and offering incentives for the best farmers to stay with them from season to season—the two companies in each country have coordinated informally to ensure that seasonal credit can be recovered in the sector. In this case, coordination has amounted to a "gentleman's agreement" to respect each other's contracts with producers. Thus both countries boast successful credit schemes, with more than 70,000 producers obtaining credit in a given season in each country at their respective peaks. The major caveat to this story, however, is that the number of actors in the Zimbabwe sector increased dramatically after 2001. In the presence of new competitors, the sector's flagship credit scheme has had to be dramatically scaled back due to an explosion of side marketing. The previous informal coordination mechanisms have proven inadequate to the new sectoral composition, but it has so far proven impossible to gain agreement (particularly from the government) on the nature of a new, more formal regulatory system to enforce compliance by all actors in the sector to rules that ultimately should benefit all.

Finally, in the liberalized Tanzania cotton sector, with more than 30 ginners competing to buy seed cotton from farmers, it has proven impossible for individual firms to provide input credit to producers. As a result, an industrywide approach to the input-access problem has had to be adopted, with a leading role played by the state in the form of the Tanzania Cotton Board. Under the passbook system—a forced saving mechanism, rather than a credit system—when producers sell seed cotton, they receive stamps in their official passbooks recording how much they have sold. The buyer pays a levy to the sector-wide Cotton Development Fund per kilogram of seed cotton purchased (and the seed cotton price paid to producers is reduced accordingly). This money is then used to obtain chemicals that are distributed to producers (free of charge) at the start of the following season, with the quantity of chemicals received by each producer determined by the amount of seed cotton that they sold the previous season, as recorded in their passbooks.

These three cases thus contain examples both of horizontal coordination by private actors—the common adoption of the free-inputs system by all firms in Ghana prior to 1995 and the effective informal coordination between duopolists in Zambia and Zimbabwe (pre-2001)—and of intervention by the state when private firms failed to coordinate—Ghana post-2000 and Tanzania. In the former cases, the private actors continued to compete for farmers' patronage while coordinating on other matters. In the latter cases, in Ghana the effect of the state intervention was to reduce competition (in the interests of coordination), whereas in Tanzania it was to facilitate sectorwide coordination so that individual firms could concentrate on competing in output and export markets.

These cases thus suggest that, as problems of contract enforcement (with third parties) increase—in the cases considered, because of an increasing number of competing actors in the market—firms' first option is to strengthen contract enforcement through horizontal coordination. If this option proves inadequate, they may seek some form of intervention from the state to create the conditions conducive to investment. Thus in Ghana the major firms in the cotton sector successfully lobbied the regional government to introduce the system of local monopolies; in Zimbabwe the major firms in the cotton sector have been lobbying the government to introduce a new regulatory framework governing conduct in the sector, and in Tanzania leading ginners worked with the Cotton Board to devise an industrywide public response to the problem of input supply. We also note, however, that, as with private coordination, success is not guaranteed when firms seek intervention from the state. Although the introduction of the passbook system in Tanzania does seem to have been successful (albeit one with teething problems), the zoning allocations in Ghana were fiercely contested by some farmers and companies. As a result, cotton production fell dramatically and has yet to recover to its prezoning levels. Meanwhile, as of 2003, the Zimbabwe government and the major firms in the Zimbabwe cotton sector have not been able to agree on an appropriate new regulatory framework for the sector, despite private stakeholders drafting a bill for the state to consider.

Although these cases suggest a progression from market competition through horizontal coordination to state regulation as coordination challenges increase, other examples show that private hierarchy can be an alternative solution to coordination challenges. Thus when the three firms in the Tanzania tobacco sector found it impossible to recover input loans, despite the apparently low level of competition,[7] their solution was to create a common company to handle all dealings (input supply, output purchase, and credit recovery) with smallholder tobacco producers. The three processing companies are all shareholders in this combined venture and share the resulting tobacco leaf for processing on the basis of a mutually agreed formula.

Horizontal coordination can also be driven by the need to provide public (or club) goods in a sector, and the principles observed here are similar to those observed when the focus was on contract enforcement. Thus maintaining grading practices during the marketing of seed cotton (a critical issue if producers are to deliver high-quality seed cotton to ginners over time) has been a major challenge in all sectors so far discussed. In Zambia and (until 2001) Zimbabwe the two dominant companies in each country have again coordinated informally to ensure that comparable grading practices are maintained in the sector, so that producers do not run to the buyer who is willing to offer the highest grade for a given consignment of seed cotton. As a result, both sectors maintained (in the case of Zimbabwe prior to 2001) or established (in the case of Zambia) strong reputations for lint quality on the international market. Post-2001, however, in the presence of new competitors, Zimbabwe's grading system at primary marketing has collapsed. New entrants have offered to pay a standard price for seed cotton, irrespective of quality, in a bid to gain market share, and established companies have found that they must follow suit to defend their position. However, there is evidence that the quality of lint being produced as a result is declining, and the country's reputation for lint quality on the international market is expected to follow suit. (Zimbabwe was famed for the uniform quality of individual lint consignments, as a result of its rigorous grading practices.)

Similarly, in the liberalized cotton sector in Tanzania, it has so far proven impossible for individual firms to impose effective grading standards at primary marketing, as producers prefer to sell to buyers who impose less strict grading requirements.[8] Again, a solution is being considered that involves an active role for the Cotton Board: the establishment of local seed cotton auctions, at which all seed cotton produced in a given area must be sold. Under this system, sellers who attempt to adulterate seed-cotton consignments by adding water or sand risk exposure in front of the whole village, whereas quality-conscious buyers will be able to bid for high-quality consignments.

Another example of a public (or club) good that the industry needs to ensure its long-term competitiveness is an ongoing program of basic research, for example, the breeding of new, improved seed varieties. If the firms in a sector are to pay for this program, however, they need to reach agreement on such questions as: How will the appropriate contribution from each firm be decided? How will decisions about the use of these funds (for example, the priority areas to be researched) be taken? What will be the mechanism by which the firms can hold the researchers accountable for their use of funds? Will farmers also have a say in these matters? The firms, therefore, need to be able to coordinate on these matters of common interest while still competing in the day-to-day business of acquiring and ginning seed cotton. In a similar way, Harriss-White (1999) has observed that traders in Asian agricultural markets compete fiercely for business with producers, but, confronted by weak states that are reluctant to provide basic infrastructure for market operations (roads, physical market, and storage structures), have to come together to lobby for these matters of common interest.

In the introduction to this section, the argument was put forward that the traditional view of economists—that actors at a given stage of a marketing chain are either competitors or they collude—is simplistic and needs to be modified. However, this criticism does not mean that the danger of collusion should be ignored, especially when the number of firms in a sector is small. With horizontal relationships as with vertical ones, an awareness of transaction costs gives new insights into why relationships are structured as they are. However, transaction-cost minimization is not always the driving force behind economic organization. Relationships may also be structured to facilitate the exercise of power.

Horizontal coordination among (otherwise independent) firms may have positive outcomes in terms of service provision, if, for example, it enables contracts to be enforced, thereby providing incentives for investment. However, in the absence of effective state regulation, such coordination is most likely to be achieved when the number of firms concerned is small. Under such circumstances, there is clearly a danger that coordination among firms could result in collusion, keeping prices down to the detriment of farmers. Although the likelihood of this scenario will be influenced by a number of other factors (for example, the level of capacity utilization in the sector or the strength of demand from related firms down the supply chain), the few examples cited in this section show the potential for horizontal coordination also to be associated with depressed prices for producers. Poulton et al. (2004) therefore argue that the principal public policy objective with respect to major export cash-crop sectors should be to maintain a balance between competition and coordination in the sector. Depending on the circumstances in the sector (the number of actors being a key consideration), this balance may require interventions to facilitate coordination—as in Tanzanian cotton—or to encourage competition—as in Zambian cotton (Tschirley, Zulu, and Shaffer 2004).

Chapter 20 tackles the question of what the state might do to encourage market development. However, for now it is sufficient to note that state capacity may be considerably lower than state ambition. Considering that there is little expertise in the conduct of competition policy in most African governments, particularly not in relation to rural sectors, interventions to encourage competition may look quite different from a conventional competition policy in a developed economy. In the case of Zambian cotton, the state-funded Cotton Development Trust was given responsibility for administering a Cotton Outgrower Fund. This agency supplies funds to ginners for on-lending to producers, thereby assisting them to increase the number of producers that they are able to serve. The scheme has been administered in such a way as to disproportionately benefit smaller companies (even though, in absolute terms, the largest company in the sector has received the largest allocation), thereby promoting competition in what was otherwise close to being a duopolistic sector. At the same time, smaller companies receiving funds from the Cotton Outgrower Fund gain an incentive to compete responsibly (for example, not poaching seed cotton from outgrower producers served by other companies), as irresponsible behavior could lead to suspension of their access to funds.

5.2.2 Horizontal Coordination among Producers

So far the emphasis has been on horizontal coordination among companies. However, it is also an issue among producers, because the increasing specificity of buyers' quality and timing requirements—and the associated investment requirements (many of which are "lumpy")—can drive horizontal coordination and ultimately integration among small producers. Several results may follow. First, neighboring peri-urban smallholders supplying fresh produce to an urban wholesale market may decide to pool resources to hire a truck to take their produce to market. Second, if they want to negotiate a regular supply agreement with a particular wholesaler, they may instead have to commit to providing a certain minimum quantity of produce (of an acceptable quality) on a regular basis (once per week or perhaps month). This commitment may require some coordination of planting decisions. Third, if they wish to supply a more demanding buyer (say, an upmarket wholesaler) they may also have to exercise peer pressure in the group to ensure that more of their produce achieves higher quality. Fourth, to supply a supermarket chain (and especially to maintain a position as preferred suppliers in a fast-changing market), they may ultimately have to invest in common assets for sorting and handling produce, for cooling it during transport, and perhaps for assuring its quality through process monitoring. They may also have to appoint one of their members to manage their relationship with the supermarket chain. Such a person would inevitably end up telling members what they have to do to satisfy their client's quality and other requirements.

Finally, for many developing countries, such demands are driving smallholder producers—even those in well-organized groups—out of supermarket supply chains (Barham, Carter, and Sigelko 1995; Reardon et al. 2003; Raynolds 2004). Experience in industrialized economies suggests that survival may ultimately require individual members of farmer groups to cede their decisionmaking rights to delegated or hired managers, receiving instead shares in a more centralized enterprise and a production quota for sale through the new enterprise (which is also likely to specify the quality of produce to be supplied and the timing required). The vertical arrow above "horizontal integration" in Figure 5.2 signals that, although horizontal integration may reduce the number of actors in the immediate market (at first sight appearing to be anticompetitive), for small farmers it may actually be the only way that they can compete effectively in wider markets.

Traditionally, collective action[9] by producers has been seen primarily as a way of exercising countervailing market power against powerful agribusiness interests. Thus during the early 1900s, U.S. farmers, especially those producing perishable products, faced frequent hold-ups in negotiations with large processing companies. Under these circumstances, marketing cooperatives helped farmers to countervail opportunism and hold-up situations. However, the narrative above suggests that transaction-cost minimization may also be a motive for collective action by producers. For African smallholders, collective action on the part of producers can reduce transaction costs facing service providers and output buyers, as well as empower producers to hold service providers accountable for the types and quality of service that they deliver.

Whatever the objective of collective action, the internal organization of the farmer group or cooperative is an important determinant of its effectiveness. The collective action required to establish a viable organization—particularly one with control delegated to an accountable manager—is not costless, and farmer organizations have at best a mixed track record of performance. For example, cooperatives often require subsidies (especially cheap capital) to compete successfully with investor-owned firms (IOFs), such as private and public companies. The costs of collective action influence the likelihood of voluntary participation by farmers. This section focuses on relationships between the performance of farmer organizations and their organizational arrangements. Farmers could, for example, structure their marketing organization either as a private company (that is, an IOF) or as a cooperative. New Institutional Economics (NIE) helps explain why some types of business organization tend to be more successful than others.

In particular, NIE argues that, when (continued) effective participation in markets requires farmers to invest in lumpy assets to respond to the increasingly specific and demanding quality, timing, and process requirements of buyers, centralized management structures may outperform more traditional cooperative models.[10] These centralized management structures can be thought of as examples of horizontal integration, analogous to the Tanzanian tobacco case (among agribusinesses) mentioned earlier.

What then, are the institutional factors that contribute to differences in the performance of these organizations? It is widely accepted that the costs of collective action increase with the size of the group (Olson 1965). Consequently, user groups that succeed in making and enforcing rules that prevent unsustainable use of common pool resources tend to be relatively small, and those that succeed in making and enforcing more complex rules that encourage members to invest in shared improvements tend to be even smaller. Evidence presented by Olson (1965) suggests that significant investment is unlikely in user groups that have more than 6–10 members. However, if members of the group delegate control to a manager and define their property rights in terms of voting and benefit rights, a larger group may promote rather than constrain collective investment and generate the volume of output needed to enter markets without losing the advantages of decisive management.

Recent NIE literature analyzing the demise of conventional cooperatives and the sudden proliferation of "new generation" cooperatives in the United States explains the relative inefficiency of conventional cooperatives in terms of inadequate property rights (Cook and Iliopoulos 1999, 2000). The distinguishing features of property rights in conventional cooperatives can be summarized as follows:

- Returns to members are proportional to their patronage (for example, the amount of produce that they market through the cooperative) and not to their financial investment.

- Shares cannot be traded at their market value. They are repurchased at par value when a member exits the cooperative.

- Voting rights are egalitarian and not proportional to investment.

These property rights reflect the underlying Rochdale principle that cooperative enterprises should be controlled by their members and not by capital. This concept is quite distinct from an IOF, in which voting and benefit rights assigned to members (shareholders) are directly proportional to their individual investment and may be traded at their market value. Jensen and Meckling (1976), Porter and Scully (1987), Cook and Iliopoulos (1999, 2000), and Sykuta and Cook (2001) explain the consequences of inadequate property rights adopted by conventional cooperatives in terms of the following problems:

The *free-rider problem* discourages member investment because some of the gains from the cooperative accrue to individuals who did not fully invest in developing the gains. These free riders could be nonmembers who patronize an open cooperative, or new(er) members who acquire the same rights as initial investors without paying the appreciated (that is, market) price for their shares.

The *horizon problem* results from residual claims that do not extend as far as the economic life of the underlying asset. Under these conditions, cooperative members tend to underinvest in long-term and intangible assets (such as market research, product promotion, and brand loyalty) because they are prevented from realizing capital gains by retiring shares at their market value. New members therefore become free riders, as they benefit from past investments without paying fully for them in the form of higher share prices.

The *portfolio problem* results when cooperative members demand a premium on their investment, or underinvest relative to their IOF counterparts, because the cooperative's investment portfolio may not reflect the interests or risk attitudes of any given member. Members cannot trade shares at market prices and are therefore unable to diversify or concentrate their own asset portfolios to fully reflect personal risk preferences. This "forced-rider" problem is compounded by the cooperative principle of equal voting rights, because the portfolio preferred by those members who are willing to risk larger investments in the cooperative is likely to differ from that preferred by a risk-averse majority. In IOFs, voting rights are not egalitarian but are fair in the sense that shareholders receive proportionally more rights as their level of investment in the firm increases.

The *control problem* refers to the cost that members face in monitoring managers to ensure that they make prudent investment decisions and do not shirk or cheat. Although this principal-agent problem is not unique to cooperatives, it is less severe in IOFs, because

- larger investors are able to internalize the benefits of their policing effort (because dividends are proportional to investment),

- managerial performance is clearly signaled by the market or audited value of members' equity shares,

- members can sanction managers by disinvesting, and

- managers are often shareholders themselves and therefore have incentive-compliant employment contracts.

A study of Kenya's coffee cooperatives by Mude (2007) highlights a control problem compounded by flawed electoral procedures after 1998 and by political interference in the period prior to 1998.

Together, such problems have starved conventional cooperatives of equity capital, reducing their ability to finance the investments needed to maintain a competitive edge. Hendrikse and Veerman (2001) further contend that conventional cooperatives are at a disadvantage relative to IOFs when seeking capital from external sources to finance assets that have specific uses. Specific assets increase the financier's exposure to risk, and lenders find it difficult to predict and influence managerial decisions when numerous small investors hold a majority of votes. This *influence problem* tends to raise the cost of external equity and debt capital to finance assets that have specific uses. For this reason, a switch from cooperative to IOF status may be particularly beneficial when product markets become more differentiated (and hence assets become more specific).

In theory, a cooperative business structure that reduces the efficiency-robbing effects of inadequate property rights would require closed membership and equity contributions that are fully transferable, appreciable, and in direct proportion to an enforceable level of patronage (Cook and Iliopoulos 2000). To achieve these objectives without sacrificing the subsidies still enjoyed by agricultural cooperatives in the United States, new-generation cooperatives have substituted fully transferable and appreciable marketing (patronage) agreements for equity shares. In South Africa, where the deregulation of agriculture removed interest subsidies once enjoyed by agricultural cooperatives, the tendency has been for outright conversion from cooperative to company status (including the high-profile Cape Winegrowers Cooperative). Hendrikse and Veerman (2001) cite cases of leading marketing cooperatives in Ireland and the Netherlands changing their organizational arrangements to resemble that of IOFs by issuing some form of equity with proportional benefit and voting rights or by outright conversion to company status.

This NIE analysis offers exciting prospects for ways of influencing traditional user groups to encourage investment by members. Examples of equity-sharing joint ventures between communities and external investors have emerged in South Africa, especially in ecotourism enterprises, and are blurring the distinction between collective and private action. Renewed interest shown by African governments in conventional cooperatives seems to suggest an appreciation of the benefits of horizontal coordination but perhaps a poor understanding of adequate property rights and good corporate governance by officials when it comes to advising communities and supporting their efforts to organize.

Although the NIE arguments outlined in this section emphasize the importance of making voting and benefit rights tradable and proportional to individual investment, there are a host of other institutions that affect the relative performance of organizations. For example, rules governing electoral procedures and financial audits influence transparency and hence the accountability of managers, and incentive schemes influence the work effort of employees. Rules that provide for secret ballot and independent audit are often prescribed in national law (typically in legislation governing companies and cooperative societies). However, such rules are not always instituted, particularly when organizations are registered as trusts or informally constituted as farmer associations. In such cases, problems that discourage investment are likely to emerge if good institutional arrangements are not widely accepted by members and explicitly written into the organization's constitution. Of course, good institutional arrangements are not a sufficient condition for good performance. Box 5.1 draws attention to the need for training and mentoring.

Box 5.1 Equity-share schemes in South Africa

In South Africa, the recent advent of equity-share schemes in which previously disadvantaged employees acquire shares in the commercial farms on which they work is helping to redistribute wealth and income streams while empowering farmworkers and improving their productivity, retaining quality management, and preserving the creditworthiness of these farming enterprises. A cluster analysis of 35 measures of financial performance, worker empowerment, managerial quality, and organizational arrangements (Knight, Lyne, and Roth 2003) indicated that:

- A successful farmworker equity-share scheme should be operated as, or like, a company with voting and benefit rights proportional to the investment made by each member.

- Workers' interests in an equity-share scheme should not be diluted by a transfer of shares to nonworkers as a result of bequests or sales to outsiders. A unitized trust is sometimes created to warehouse and buy shares from workers who leave the scheme, disbursing the proceeds to the worker or, in the event of death, his or her estate. Only new and existing employees can acquire these shares.

- Although striving for the ideal of fully transferable shares, a temporary moratorium on the sale of shares—particularly by the previous owner—helps to preserve the creditworthiness of the enterprise by preventing sudden outflows of equity capital and managerial expertise. Most successful schemes also commit to a gradual, and therefore predictable, reduction in the proportion of equity held by the previous (white) owner.

- Workers should participate in the design of the equity-share scheme and its operating rules. Such participation is facilitated by training programs that transfer basic literacy, life, and technical skills to the workforce at large. Moreover, worker representatives should receive ongoing mentoring in financial, administrative, and managerial skills to help them participate meaningfully in policy decisions and perform their duties as office bearers.

- Farming requires decisive and accountable management. For directors and trustees, accountability is facilitated by transparency (for example, reporting externally audited financial statements) but is ultimately ensured by the mobility of capital and the electoral process.

- Successful equity-sharing schemes also tend to operate performance-based remuneration packages for managers and employees, observe a long-term business plan, entrench formal procedures to resolve disputes, and—without exception—have a history of good labor relations.

5.2.3 Summary of Horizontal Coordination

Both the organization of firms and producers may undergo a progression from pure market competition through horizontal coordination to horizontal integration with increasing buyer demand for produce quality or precision timing (often necessitating lumpy investments by suppliers) or increasing difficulties in contract enforcement (see Figure 5.2). Horizontal integration, however, can take two contrasting forms:

- It can replace the imperfectly coordinated actions of independent actors by a more centralized decisionmaking process in a single firm or enterprise. This approach is directly analogous to Williamson's (1985, 1991) hierarchy as the conclusion of vertical coordination in Figure 5.2.

- It can impose state or state-sanctioned regulation on the imperfectly coordinated actions of the same independent actors, so that they are forced to play by a common set of rules that is beneficial for the sector as a whole while remaining competitors in their core activities. Although apparently different from Williamson's private hierarchy, this approach still represents a move to a more centralized decisionmaking process. State hierarchy thus performs a similar function to private hierarchy.

It is also worth noting that a similar progression from market through collective action to private or state hierarchy can be traced in the literature on natural resource management (Chapter 14). In this case, the factors likely to drive actors to the right along the coordination continuum in Figure 5.2 include the extent of spatial externalities in the management of the resources, difficulties encountered in excluding free riders, and the intensity of public interest in the outcomes of the resource management (for example, because a protected or endangered species inhabits a particular area).

5.3 Complementary Coordination

Complementary coordination is critical for agricultural development in Sub-Saharan Africa but has thus far received insufficient attention. Complementary coordination fits neatly into Jaffee's (1995, 25) general definition of coordination as "a general problem of arranging interdependent activities which require linking the decisions and actions of different technical and ownership units when collective or overlapping tasks are performed."

In addition, the heart of the complementary coordination problem in agricultural development in Sub-Saharan Africa is one of investor "hold-up" in thin markets. There are thus similarities with Williamson's (1985, 1991) analysis of vertical coordination focusing on specific assets.

At a more general level, thinking on complementary coordination can be traced to Rosenstein-Rodan's (1943) arguments for a "big push" to catalyze early economic development. Rosenstein-Rodan argued for a strong role for state central planning in industrial development, so as to capture, through income growth in an essentially closed economy, the benefits of economies of scale in production of various industrial products. Although reaching very different policy conclusions, Hoff (2001, 39) reviews subsequent theoretical advances in institutional economics and recent, non-technological understandings of externalities[11] to argue that "coordination failures abound and are important. Neither the market alone nor government alone can solve them."

For Hoff, externalities (or spillovers) drive the need for coordination and explain why economic systems without appropriate coordination mechanisms get stuck in low-level equilibrium traps. So-called diffuse externalities—when large numbers of actors are affected (positively or negatively) by the actions of others—are the most challenging. When the number of actors affected by an externality is relatively small, the externality may be internalized by negotiation among the actors and/or by mergers among firms. This insight can also be applied to Williamson's (1985, 1991) explanation of vertical integration—two firms merge because the fortunes of each are critically dependent on the actions of the other. It is also consistent with the observation that duopolistic cotton sectors have often managed to solve their key coordination problems through informal agreement. In addition the insight explains why the three firms in the Tanzanian tobacco sector resolved their coordination problems through the formation of a unified service company handling interaction with smallholders, but the coordination problems in the Tanzanian cotton sector (with more than 30 ginners) have proven much more difficult to resolve.

In this chapter, the feature that distinguishes complementary from horizontal coordination is that it is coordination among providers of complementary services rather than among otherwise competitive providers of the same service(s). As the concept of complementary coordination is applied to the particular case of service delivery to smallholder agricultural producers in Sub-Saharan Africa, it will be clear that there is also a vertical dimension; namely, that the challenge is not only to coordinate the provision of preharvest services but also to ensure that this service provision is coordinated with access to remunerative output marketing opportunities. This particular expression of complementary coordination may thus be thought of as a hybrid between horizontal and vertical coordination. As shown in the next section, it is driven by factors similar to those for vertical coordination (for example, problems of asset specificity in the context of thin rural markets). In addition, complementary coordination problems may in some cases be resolved by private integration (whereby a single private firm provides all the services in question, capturing the positive externalities among them) or in other cases by state intervention. Thus the theoretical framework so far developed to explain horizontal and vertical coordination can readily be extended to cover complementary coordination.

To intensify agricultural production, smallholder households may require access to a range of support services, including improved seeds, inorganic fertilizers, credit, technical advice, market information, and output-market linkages. However, there is complementarity between support services in both their farm production and profitability impacts. Thus, producers' demand for one service depends on their expectation of reasonable (reliable and at acceptable cost) access to the supply of complementary services. Producers' demand for purchased inputs, for example, depends on their access to seasonal finance, and vice versa, and demand for these services also depends on expected access to output marketing services, demand for which in turn depends on prior input purchases. From the service providers' perspective, returns to their investments thus also depend on the availability of complementary services for producers.

Before the development of more intensive production systems in a given area, markets tend to be thin (characterized by low supply and demand). Hence there is limited investment in support services. In some parts of rural Africa key support services—especially seasonal finance, but also supply of improved seeds, fertilizers, and technical advice—are almost entirely absent. Thus pioneer investors face a dilemma: how will they obtain a return on their investment when complementary services are not available for their (potential) clients? Alternatively, how can the complementary investment decisions of multiple independent service providers (likely to include both private and public sector actors) be coordinated to increase the returns to all? As already mentioned, there is also a potential hold-up problem whereby, if one investor makes clear their desire to invest in a particular service, another can adopt a hard bargaining position before agreeing to put in a complementary investment.

Arguably, the reason that this problem of complementary coordination has failed to attract the attention that it deserves is that it disappears as market densities increase. Once there are several service providers of each type operating in a given area, new entrants can enter the market competitively without concern about complementary actions on the part of others. The challenge, therefore, is one of boosting agricultural production to a certain threshold level in a given area, so that spontaneous competitive investment in service provision will flourish.

The key question is how to overcome the challenge of complementary coordination to support service provision across different types of commodity chains in Africa. This problem serves to illustrate how the product and process attributes of particular commodity chains affect the incentives for investment and hence the institutional arrangements observed in different chains. The argument starts with an outline of the common problems to overcome if cost-effective commercial delivery of services to smallholder producers is to occur:

- *Public good* problems have been discussed briefly above. They arise when service providers are unable to capture the returns to investments in providing nonrival and nonexcludable services, for example, extension advice (Smith and Thomson 1991).

- *Strategic default* is the deliberate, opportunistic failure to complete a contract, for example, by failing to deliver produce or payment in a credit transaction (Poulton, Dorward, and Kydd 1998).

- *Commitment failure* is the corollary of the service complementarity just discussed but is less widely recognized. It is, however, a critical problem that arises from the complementarity among different support services. This feature can be seen at two levels: their farm production impacts and hence also the profitability to the service suppliers themselves. This mutual dependence poses a prisoners' dilemma for the development of new commodity chains that require investments in new sets of complementary services.

- *Specification opportunism* involves parties (having the possibility of) cheating through misinformation in a transaction. Small farmers are often perceived to be the victims of such opportunism, for example, the adulteration of inputs or fixing of scales or measures by traders. However, they can also engage in it, for example, by overstating quality of produce sold. The requirements of supermarket chains for assured safe food means that produce buyers in such chains must take great care to protect against such opportunism.

- *Small transactions* generally exacerbate the problems listed above, as transaction costs in addressing these problems tend to have high fixed costs per transaction or per transaction partner, so that small transactions incur high transaction costs per unit transacted.

These problems all directly reduce the incentives for commercial service delivery to small farmers and/or raise the costs of such service delivery. In addition, because of the interdependencies between services, dysfunctional service delivery or monopolistic pricing by one service supplier (again, in the context of thin markets) can indirectly reduce farmer demand for complementary services from other suppliers. Table 5.2 describes the ways in which different types of coordination may contribute to solving the problems of commercial service development and delivery discussed above. This table distinguishes between three basic types of coordination: vertical coordination along a supply chain, horizontal coordination among competitors performing the same function in a supply chain, and complementary coordination among providers of complementary services in a supply chain. We also identify focal coordination as a particular form of coordination that combines vertical and complementary coordination to facilitate a particular set of transactions supporting a critical link in a supply chain. Coordination mechanisms may be voluntary (soft) or enforced by some strong central coordinating body (hard). Hard coordination (local or extensive) may be initiated and enforced by the state, depending on its interests and capabilities. When this does not occur, establishment of coordinating mechanisms is voluntary, and there must be incentives for actors to invest in these mechanisms. These incentives, however, differ markedly across the three broad categories of commodity chains in Africa: traditional export cash crops, nontraditional exports, and food staples.

In the case of many traditional export cash crops, where buyers or processors need to invest in processing plant and/or downstream relationships, these investments may act both as a barrier to entry to small, undercapitalized traders[12] and, as fixed assets, provide buyers with an incentive to make further investments to increase reliable access to farm products so as to improve capacity utilization. Reliable access

Table 5.2   Coordination mechanisms for addressing service development and delivery problems

Problem	Coordination mechanism
Commitment failure	Complementary and focal arrangements
Monopolistic opportunism	Complementary and focal arrangements (must be strict enough to deal with incentives to renege on agreements)
Specification opportunism	Horizontal arrangements among farmers and among service providers for setting and enforcing standards; vertical, complementary, and focal arrangements to establish trust and compliance incentives (must be sufficiently strict and extensive to deal with incentives to shirk)
Strategic default	Horizontal arrangements (among farmers and/or among service providers) for penalizing defaulters; complementary and focal arrangements to establish trust, interlocking, and compliance incentives (must be sufficiently strict and extensive to deal with incentives to shirk)
Dysfunctional service delivery to farmers	Horizontal arrangements among farmers in bulking service demand; complementary coordination among service providers
Small-scale transactions	Horizontal arrangements among farmers (economies of scale); complementary coordination among service providers for economies of scope
Public goods	Horizontal arrangements among service providers to create club goods (concentrated market systems only); alternatively, complementary coordination among public providers of services with public good elements and private providers of other services
Limited farmer voice	Horizontal arrangements among farmers

Source: Poulton, Dorward, and Kydd (2005).

to farm products may be achieved by vertical integration (investing directly in commercial farm production), by establishing vertical coordination arrangements with large commercial farms, or by investing in service delivery to smallholder producers in exchange for rights to buy the resulting output. Commonly, processing firms provide a full package of preharvest services plus a guaranteed access to output market to smallholders with whom they work. As discussed in some detail earlier in this chapter, horizontal coordination is also needed among the companies concerned, so that they do not undermine one another's investments in service delivery through side buying. The incentives to work with small farmers thus tend to be strongest when output markets are more concentrated, because—in the absence of a strong state to facilitate coordination—horizontal coordination is easier the fewer the number of actors involved.

In the case of high-value, nontraditional products, investments to increase reliable access to farm products may be driven less by the need to achieve high utilization of expensive processing capacity and more by the need to assure consistent supply of high-quality produce as a prerequisite for participation in high-value marketing channels. However, the incentives for working with small farmers may be undermined when products have high credence attributes, as assuring these involves more-or-less fixed transaction costs per producer, posing major difficulties for intermediaries serving small farmers.

For staple food commodities (and some cash crop commodities with very low processing requirements) there tend to be large numbers of small buyers for whom limited capital is a major constraint to expansion, along with limited economies of scale and/or opportunities for value addition in processing. In such situations buyers face weak incentives to invest in service delivery to expand supply or to capture an increased market share of supply. Moreover, the multiple market channels for selling staples, plus the alternative of consuming them on farm, renders the provision of preharvest services on a credit basis unviable.

When the incentives do not exist for output buyers to also provide the full range of preharvest services, the challenge of complementary coordination for a number of (potential) independent service providers looms large. It is thus perhaps not surprising that all cases of successful Green Revolutions in smallholder agriculture in the twentieth century (mainly in Asia, but also several abortive revolutions in African maize) featured major state intervention. Dorward et al. (2004), in a review of policies in successful and partially successful areas of Green Revolution, found that the majority of smallholder agricultural transformations involved a staged process of state investment in institutional and economic development:

- Initial (stage 1) interventions involved basic investments to establish more favorable conditions for productive intensive cereal technologies: investments in physical infrastructure (roads and irrigation), in development of improved technologies, and (where necessary) in land-tenure systems providing smallholders with reasonably equitable and secure access to land. These investments improved access and potential productivity. Basically profitable new technologies would at this point be limited to a small number of relatively wealthy farmers with access to seasonal finance and markets.

- Stage 2 then involved state investment to "kick start" market and service development, enabling farmers to access seasonal finance and input and output markets at low cost and low risk. A common form of intervention was to subsidize the price of key inputs so as to increase market volumes, thereby attracting private service providers into the market.

When farmers became used to the new high-yielding cereal technologies and volumes of credit, and input demand and produce supply had built up, then thicker markets allowed per unit transaction costs to fall so that governments could then (in theory at least) withdraw from service coordination and let the market play an increasingly important role.

This model of state intervention was, however, very costly, and it failed if:

- Stage 1 physical investments did not establish the necessary conditions for intensive cereal-based transformations, such as some minimum level of access and productivity potential (caused, for example, by lack of irrigation, insufficiently high yielding technologies, or low population and road densities).

- Stage 2 institutional investments were ineffective in developing high volume and robust service demand and delivery (caused, for example, by poor political or technocratic management, corruption, or the failure to continue the system long enough for changes to become embedded).

In particular, failures of costly state intervention to stimulate agricultural transformation in much of Africa—and the need to reduce state intervention when it had been successful—contributed to donor pressures for market liberalization and structural adjustment policies. However, it has to be acknowledged that there are no clear-cut examples of smallholder agricultural transformation occurring after market liberalization. Thus market liberalization is a huge experiment. Can institutional arrangements be devised to support smallholder agricultural intensification in Africa in a liberalized market? There are divergent views on this question, which are elaborated in Chapter 20.

Decentralized planning may be one way of overcoming problems of complementary coordination, if multiple stakeholders are invited to make a genuine contribution to local development planning. Planning processes could thus create the deliberative forums in which different service providers develop a degree of mutual understanding and trust, so that they are willing to embark on complementary investments (Hall and Soskice 2001). The likelihood of this occurring would be heightened if local development plans also provided some direct incentives for investment of this nature. However, the reality of administrative decentralization, and with it decentralized planning, currently lags far behind the rhetoric, such that considerable progress will have to be made in most African countries before devolution has any notable impact on the complementary coordination problems afflicting service provision to smallholder producers.

Decentralized planning processes and more direct state intervention (as in many Asian economies in the second half of the twentieth century) are two alternative approaches to the problem of complementary service provision that can be thought of as the complementary equivalents of coordination and integration, respectively (see Figure 5.2).[13] Depending on the severity of the complementarity (externalities) problem, a facilitative role by the state in encouraging coordinated private activity may be sufficient. However, if the complementarity problem is too great, a directive role for the state may be required, with parallels to the centralized decisionmaking characteristic of vertical and horizontal integration.

5.4   An Integrated Framework for Thinking about Coordination

Figure 5.3 generalizes the insights from Figure 5.2 to encompass all three forms of coordination. The emphasis of the two axes is no longer on vertical and horizontal coordination but instead on the different forces that drive the need for coordination. As the vector of forces becomes stronger (moving away from the origin), first voluntary coordination responses are likely to be observed in response to the problems. However, there will also be cases for which voluntary responses are insufficient and coordination challenges can only be met by integrating previously discrete activities and/or organizations under a more centralized decisionmaking structure. When the number of actors that need to coordinate is few enough, private integration will sometimes occur. At other times, effective coordination will only be achieved through the intervention of an appropriate state agency.

Figure 5.3   Integrated conceptual framework

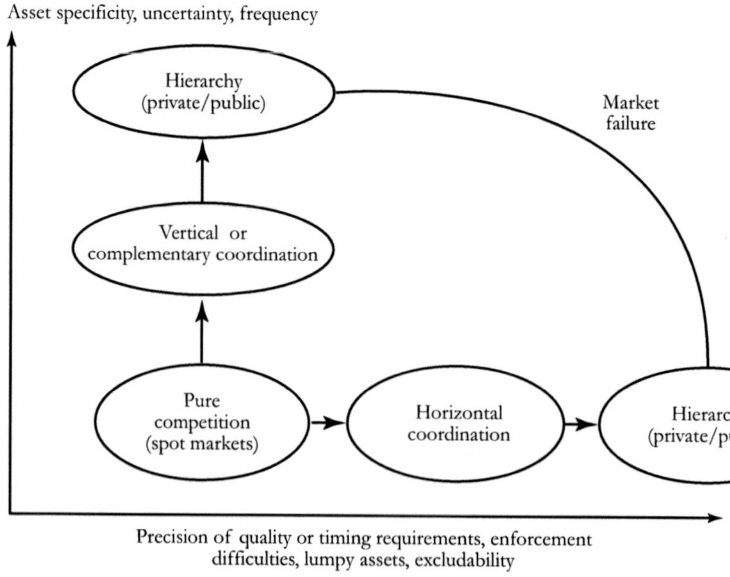

Asset specificity, uncertainty, frequency

Hierarchy (private/public)

Market failure

Vertical or complementary coordination

Pure competition (spot markets)

Horizontal coordination

Hierarchy (private/public)

Precision of quality or timing requirements, enforcement difficulties, lumpy assets, excludability

The new dimension introduced in Figure 5.3 is that, when neither of these responses occurs (perhaps because the state does not have the capacity to play the required coordination role), the outcome is market failure, and goods or services are not supplied to people who need or want them. Such failure is widely observed in the supply of critical services (for example, inputs and finance) to smallholder producers in Sub-Saharan Africa and constitutes an important part of the reason for the poor performance of the agricultural sector across the continent at present. In this chapter we suggest that this result is not the outcome of either market or state failure but of both. Smallholder producers in Africa are caught between the twin problems of poorly developed (and hence thin) markets on the one hand and ineffective states on the other.

Notes

1. This hypothetical case does illustrate some of the distinctions between the concepts of bounded rationality and imperfect information. However, following the logic of the rest of this book, we note that the scope for opportunism is minimized when information is perfect.

2. The increasing stringency of food-safety legislation is primarily a phenomenon of developed economies. However, as supermarket supply chains become first regionalized and then globalized, the same standards are rapidly being applied to producers in developing countries (Henson and Reardon 2005). This process is not advanced in Africa, but these trends will increasingly be seen there even during the lifetime of this textbook.

3. Another possibility is that the wealthier party also exercises some social control over the weaker party (Crow and Murshid 1994).

4. A literature known as global commodity chain analysis (Gereffi 1994; Gibbon 2001) defines a chain driver (the most powerful player in their chain) in large part according to ability to dictate the nature of other relationships in the chain and the terms on which other players in the chain do business.

5. The point beyond which a party will choose not to contract at all, rather than to accept the terms and conditions on offer, is known as the party's reservation position in a bargaining process. A party's reservation position is determined by its options for income or profit generation outside of the bargaining process in question.

6. In the Hall and Soskice (2001) example of employee training in the German manufacturing industry, similar issues would have arisen had all firms been required to pay a levy to fund an industry-wide training program. Had this alternative approach been taken, firms would be free to compete for the resulting trainees, but trainees would not gain the firm-specific element of training that they receive under the current arrangements. Arguably, this is why Hall and Soskice see this example as being about creating conditions for asset-specific investment rather than about contract enforcement or provision of public goods.

7. The difficulties of enforcing contracts in the tobacco sector may owe something to the heavy dependence on purchased inputs in this sector (even greater than in cotton).

8. Although in theory firms that maintain higher quality standards should be able to obtain higher prices for their cotton lint and hence pay higher seed cotton prices to producers who supply them with high-quality seed cotton, there are a number of reasons why this does not happen in prac-

tice. Firms wishing to maintain high quality standards thus struggle to pay more for seed cotton than do competitors who prioritize volume of seed cotton ginned over quality.

9. Modifying the definition of collective action provided by *A Dictionary of Sociology* (Marshall 1998), collective action is defined here as action taken by a group, involving some degree of collective decisionmaking, in pursuit of members' perceived shared interests. This contrasts with decision-making by a state regulator or by the management of a private firm, where responsibility for decision-making is delegated to the manager by the owners, who then have to hold the manager to account for his or her decisions.

10. The argument also holds when farmers want or need to invest in intangible assets (such as product branding) to defend or enhance the share of profits that they capture in rapidly changing market systems.

11. Such externalities can include information externalities, group-reputation effects, agglomeration effects, and knowledge spillovers.

12. This case holds only if players with processing capacity refuse to process on behalf of smaller traders without such capacity and/or if the state refuses to grant trading licences in particular sectors to traders who have not made specified investments in processing capacity.

13. Alternatively, Dorward and Kydd (2004) refer to them as soft and hard coordination, respectively.

Further Reading

Jaffee, S. 1995. Transaction costs, risk and the organization of private sector food commodity systems. In *Marketing Africa's high-value foods,* ed. S. Jaffee and J. Morton. Dubuque, Iowa, U.S.A.: Kendall Hunt.

Reardon, T., and C. P. Timmer. 2005. Transformation of markets for agricultural output in developing countries since 1950: How has thinking changed? In *Handbook of agricultural economics,* vol. 3: *Agricultural development: Farmers, farm production and farm markets,* ed. R. E. Evenson, P. Pingali, and T. P. Schultz. Amsterdam: Elsevier.

References

Barham, B., M. Carter, and W. Sigelko. 1995. Agro-export production and peasant land access: Examining the dynamic between adoption and accumulation. *Journal of Development Economics* 46: 85–107.

Binswanger, H., and M. Rosenzweig. 1986. Behavioural and material determinants of production relations in agriculture. *Journal of Development Studies* 22: 503–539.

Boselie, D., S. Henson, and D. Weatherspoon. 2003. Supermarket procurement practices in developing countries: Redefining the roles of the public and private sectors. *American Journal of Agricultural Economics* 85 (5): 1155–1161.

Coase, R. H. 1937. The nature of the firm. *Economica* 4 (16): 386–405.

Cook, M. L., and C. Iliopoulos. 1999. Beginning to inform the theory of the cooperative firm: Emergence of the new generation cooperative. *Finnish Journal of Business Economics* 4: 525–535.

———. 2000. Ill-defined property rights in collective action: The case of US agricultural cooperatives. In *Institutions, contracts, and organizations: Perspectives from the New Institutional Economics*, ed. C. Ménard. Cheltenham, U.K.: Edward Elgar.

Crow, B., and K. A. S. Murshid. 1994. Economic returns to social power: Merchants' finance and inter-linkage in the grain markets of Bangladesh. *World Development* 22: 1011–1030.

Dolan, C., and J. Humphrey. 2000. Governance and trade in fresh vegetables. The impact of UK supermarkets on the African horticulture industry. *Journal of Development Studies* 37 (2): 147–176.

Dorward, A. R., and J. Kydd. 2004. The Malawi 2002 food crisis: The rural development challenge. *Journal of Modern Africa Studies* 42 (3): 343–361.

Dorward, A. R., J. G. Kydd, J. A. Morrison, and I. Urey. 2004. A policy agenda for pro-poor agricultural growth. *World Development* 32 (1): 73–89.

Gereffi, G. 1994. The organization of buyer-driven global commodity chains: How U.S. retailers shape overseas production networks. In *Commodity chains and global capitalism*, ed. G. Gereffi and M. Korzeniewicz. Westport, Conn., U.S.A.: Greenwood Press.

Gibbon, P. 2001. Upgrading primary production: A global commodity chain approach. *World Development* 29: 345–363.

Hall, P. A., and D. Soskice, eds. 2001. *Varieties of capitalism: The institutional foundations of comparative advantage.* Oxford: Oxford University Press.

Harriss, B. 1993. *Markets, society and the state: Problems of marketing under conditions of smallholder agriculture in West Bengal.* Report to the United Nations University–World Institute for Development Economics Research. Development Policy and Practice Working Paper. London: Open University.

Harriss-White, B., ed. 1999. *Agricultural markets from theory to practice: Field experience in developing countries.* New York: St. Martin's Press.

Hendrikse, G., and C. Veerman. 2001. Marketing cooperatives and financial structure: A transaction cost economic analysis. *Agricultural Economics* 26: 205–216.

Henson, S., and T. Reardon. 2005. Private agri-food standards: Implications for food policy and the agri-food system. *Food Policy* 30 (3): 241–253.

Hoff, K. 2001. Beyond Rosenstein-Rodan: The modern theory of underdevelopment traps. In *Annual World Bank Economic Conference 2000*, ed. B. Pleskovic and N. Stern. Washington, D.C.: World Bank.

Jaffee, S. 1993. Contract farming in the shadow of competitive markets: The experience of Kenyan horticulture. In *Living under contract: Contract farming and agrarian transformation in Sub-*

Saharan Africa, ed. D. D. Little and M. J. Watts. Madison, Wis., U.S.A.: University of Wisconsin Press.

———. 1995. Transaction costs, risk and the organization of private sector food commodity systems. In *Marketing Africa's high value foods,* ed. S. Jaffee and J. Morton. Dubuque, Iowa, U.S.A.: Kendall Hunt.

Jensen, M., and W. Meckling. 1976. Theory of the firm: Managerial behaviour, agency costs, and ownership structure. *Journal of Financial Economics* 3: 305–360.

Knight, S. L., M. C. Lyne, and M. Roth. 2003. Best institutional arrangements for farm worker equity-share schemes in South Africa. *Agrekon* 42 (3): 228–251.

Marshall, G., ed. 1998. *A dictionary of sociology.* Oxford: Oxford University Press.

Mude, A.G. 2007. Institutional incompatibility and deregulation: Explaining the dismal performance of Kenya's coffee cooperatives. In *Decentralization and the social economics of development: Lessons from Kenya,* ed. C. B. Barret, A. G. Mude, and J. M. Omiti. Wallingford, U.K.: CAB International.

North, D. C. 1990. *Institutions, institutional change and economic performance.* Cambridge: Cambridge University Press.

Olson, M. 1965. *The logic of collective action: Public goods and the theory of groups.* Cambridge, Mass., U.S.A.: Harvard University Press.

Porter, P. K., and G. W. Scully. 1987. Economic efficiency in cooperatives. *Journal of Law and Economics* 30 (October): 489–512.

Poulton, C., A. R. Dorward, and J. Kydd. 1998. The revival of smallholder cash crops in Africa: Public and private roles in the provision of finance. *Journal of International Development* 10 (1): 85–103.

———. 2005. The future of small farms: New directions for services, institutions and intermediation. Paper presented at The Future of Small Farms Workshop, Imperial College, Wye, U.K., June.

Poulton, C., P. Gibbon, B. Hanyani-Mlambo, J. Kydd, M. Nylandset Larsen, W. Maro, A. Osario, D. Tschirley, and B. Zulu. 2004. Competition and coordination in liberalized African cotton market systems. *World Development* 32: 519–536.

Raynolds, L. 2004. The globalization of organic agro-food networks. *World Development* 32: 725–743.

Reardon, T., P. Timmer, C. Barrett, and J. Berdegue. 2003. The rise of supermarkets in Africa, Asia and Latin America. *American Journal of Agricultural Economics* 85 (5): 1140–1146.

Rosenstein-Rodan, P. 1943. Problems of industrialization of eastern and southeastern Europe. *Economic Journal* 53: 202–211.

Smith, L. D., and A. M. Thomson. 1991. *The role of public and private agents in the food and agricultural sectors of developing countries.* FAO Economic and Social Development Paper 105. Rome: Food and Agriculture Organization of the United Nations.

Stiglitz, J. E. 1974. Incentives and risk sharing in sharecropping. *Review of Economic Studies* 41 (2): 219–256.

Sykuta, M., and M. Cook. 2001. A new institutional economics approach to contracts and cooperatives. *American Journal of Agricultural Economics* 83 (5): 1273–1279.

Tschirley, D., B. Zulu, and J. Shaffer. 2004. *Cotton in Zambia: An assessment of its organization, performance, current policy initiatives, and challenges for the future.* Lusaka: Food Security Research Project.

Williamson, O. E. 1985. *The economic institutions of capitalism.* New York: Free Press.

———. 1991. Comparative economic organisation: The analysis of discrete structural alternatives. *Administrative Science Quarterly* 36: 269–296.

Chapter 6

The Role of Trust in Contract Enforcement: An Analysis of Smallholder Farmers and Sugar Millers in Swaziland

Micah B. Masuku

The purpose of this case study is to investigate the role of trust in a contractual relationship in agricultural commodity markets. This case study was conducted in the sugar supply chain in Swaziland and conceptualizes the supply chain as a series of connected activities concerned with planning, coordinating, and controlling the production of sugar, starting with the production of sugarcane by farmers, through its processing by millers, and finally its sale to consumers. Thus it can be broken into units, beginning with the cane growers who provide sugarcane to millers, who then process it into sugar and pass it on to the Swaziland Sugar Association (SSA), which then markets it on behalf of both farmers and millers.

Trust in this study was conceptualized as the farmers' or millers' confident belief in the other's honesty. Trust economizes on information search and transaction costs. It creates the conditions under which exchanges between technologically and legally separate entities can take the form of problem solving rather than bargaining. Therefore, trust is expected to improve the supply chain performance by improving information availability, reducing transaction costs, reducing opportunistic behavior, and diminishing the likelihood of free riding and other negative externalities. The main theme is that trust increases the propensity of people to cooperate and produce socially efficient outcomes and helps to avoid inefficient noncooperative traps.

6.1 Characteristics of Sugarcane Farming

Sugarcane farming has several characteristics that necessitate specific institutional arrangements, such as contracts to facilitate and coordinate exchange. First, it involves highly capitalized and highly specific investments, especially at the processing levels. Second, it takes about 12 months for the sugarcane crop to be ready for harvesting, and once it has been harvested it has to be processed within 24 hours to prevent loss in the sucrose yield of the cane. This timing requirement also has implications for the optimal distance between the mill and sugarcane fields. The distance between the farm and the mill not only affects the quality of the cane through the loss in sucrose but also has cost implications that could substantially reduce the net return to the farmer.

In addition, harvesting of sugarcane must be done according to a schedule that allows all growers the possibility of delivering a predetermined daily quantity during the crushing season. This daily quota is needed because the sucrose content of the crop is low at the beginning of the season and increases with time, but it decreases toward the end of the season because of increased rainfall. Thus delivery scheduling enables every farmer to go through all the stages of sucrose concentration in the crop without some farmers benefiting more than others. Given the high transaction costs in coordinating so many small growers, milling companies often resort to farming large estates to secure their own supply of cane at lower costs. The limited size of own estates plus the sociopolitical imperative to encourage development necessitates some procurement of cane from outgrowers, which brings about a set of different coordination and contractual challenges to the milling company. This case study highlights the impact of trust on these challenges and transaction costs, and thus on the performance of the supply chain.

6.2 Stakeholders and the Institutional Framework (Environment)

The main participants in the Swaziland sugar industry are the SSA, the millers, and the cane growers. The sugar industry is regulated by the SSA, as mandated by the Sugar Act of 1967 (Government of Swaziland 1967).[1] The SSA regulates the functions of the industry, the millers are responsible for producing sugar, and the cane growers for producing sugarcane and delivering it to the mills. Apart from producing sugar, the millers also own sugar estates from which they produce sugarcane (UNCTAD 2000).

Historically, most cane production and sugar processing in Swaziland has been vertically integrated in mill cum plantations, whereas outgrowers have never had a significant role in the industry. However, large private farmers and small cane growers have started to play an increasingly important role. Outgrower farmers absorb some production risks that would otherwise have been incurred by millers and, through their supply to the mill, they increase the mills' throughput. They now supply more than 36 percent of the national supply of sugarcane (UNCTAD 2000). The other 64 percent is produced by the milling companies' own estates.

The Sugar Act of 1967 specifies the structure of the Swaziland sugar industry and also provides the legal regulatory framework for the industry. The act specifies the composition of the SSA, which is made up of twelve members from the Swaziland Sugar Millers Association (SSMA) and twelve members from the Swaziland Cane Growers Association (SCGA). The two bodies are of equal status, and hence are both represented in the council of the Sugar Association, which administers the business and affairs of the association. The functions, powers, and duties of the SSA are set out in the Swaziland Sugar Industry Agreement (Government of Swaziland 1967).[2]

A quota or a license is required before a farmer can grow sugarcane. Each grower's delivery quota is set by the Swaziland Quota Board, which is a component of the SSA. The Quota Board consists of 10 members: three growers' representatives, three millers' representatives, three others nominated by the minister for Enterprise and Employment, and a chairperson nominated by the SSA. The quota in effect represents a contract between the grower and the miller. Growers are required to provide the full amount of their quota to the mill to which they are attached, and the mill in turn is required to accept all cane delivered to it up to each grower's quota. In essence the contract is limited to the amount of sucrose indicated in each farmer's quota. It is, however, silent about the price to be paid for the sucrose, as that is determined by the SSA. The contract is enforced through the rejection of cane or withdrawal of the quota for those who fail to meet the standards set out in the Sugar Agreement (Government of Swaziland 1967) as well as through price discrimination between quota cane and segregated cane. Quota cane refers to the amount specified in the quota, and segregated cane is any cane beyond that specified by the quota. The quota system is meant to ensure that the miller can handle the crop and that the grower has water rights and the right to use the land.

Each mill has a mill group committee, which consists of an equal number of representatives from the miller and growers attached to a particular mill. The mill appoints miller representatives, and the SCGA appoints the representatives for the cane growers. Although the mill group committee is accountable to the SSA, it is financed locally in a manner agreed upon by growers and mill representatives. One of the responsibilities of the mill group committee is to determine the quality standards of cane delivered to the mill to which growers are attached. If for any reason a grower delivers cane that does not meet these standards, the relevant mill group committee is entitled to reduce payment for cane produced by the defaulting grower(s) and to pay the amount deducted pro rata to the production of the remaining growers attached to the mill (Government of Swaziland 1967).

The mill group committee is also charged with making estimates of the quantity of cane that will be produced by each grower attached to the mill in its area. The grower has to supply his mill group committee with the accurate information it requires; otherwise, the mill group committee must make estimates. This information includes area of land available for cane production, estimated tonnage of cane, area of land under cultivation in the current year, and any area still to be planted (Government of Swaziland 1967; UNCTAD 2000).

In accordance with the Sugar Act (Government of Swaziland 1967), the SSA operates a pooled payment system in which the annual revenue earned from the sales of sugar is distributed to the millers and growers after deducting the industry obligation costs. This system of pooling revenues ensures that the payment per ton of sugar produced by millers is not affected by the timing of their sugar production. It also ensures that payment to the growers, per ton of sucrose delivered, is not affected by the timing of deliveries of cane over the season. Through the pooling system both millers and growers benefit from the best prices the industry receives from its preferential markets.

The SSA divides the total net payment to the mills according to quota sugar and segregated sugar. Quota sugar is that sugar produced during the year to the maximum aggregate of all quotas attached to the mill (the amount of brown and white sugar the mill should produce) plus any quota shortfall reallocated from another mill. The price that millers and growers receive for producing sugar and sugarcane, respectively, is determined by the SSA, which after identifying and projecting all revenue from the sale of sugar and sugar by-products (such as molasses) and deducting all industry obligations, passes the remainder to millers and growers. Millers and growers however, negotiate the ratio of the price split for sugarcane processing and production. The price split for the 2001/02 season was set at 67.5 percent to growers[3] and 32.5 percent to millers. Millers are paid on the basis of their sugar output, and payments are made a week after production. The millers, in turn, pay the cane growers based on the amount of sucrose extracted from their cane, and the growers are also paid a week after delivering their cane to the mill.

6.3   Context and Issues (Action Domain)

This case study focuses specifically on the interactions and contractual arrangements between the milling companies and the cane growers, that is, where a variety of institutional problems emerge that could influence the efficiency of the supply chain and thus the returns to growers and millers.

To coordinate the sugarcane supply across the industry, all cane growers, including the estates of the milling companies, are subject to delivery quotas. These are specified in terms of weight of sucrose in cane to be delivered to the mill. The aim of the quota is to ensure that (1) the national sugar production is restricted to the quantity that the market for sugar produced in Swaziland can accommodate at satisfactory prices, and (2) sufficient milling capacity is available to accommodate the deliveries.

Growers are required to provide the full amount of their quota to the mill to which they are attached in each season unless prevented by force majeure, such as fire, frost, floods, and strikes (Government of Swaziland 1967). The mill in turn is required to accept all cane delivered up to each grower's quota. Any cane above the grower's quota is paid a segregated price. In the event the grower ceases, for any reason, to deliver sugarcane to the mill, the Quota Board may cancel the quota and reallocate it to other growers who meet the requirements (Government of Swaziland 1967).

The delivery quota for each grower is set by the Quota Board. The Quota Board in a sense is not a third party, because it is composed of both millers and growers, who are the actors and stakeholders. As such the contract is an incomplete one that cannot be legally enforced, because there are no verifiable variables or quantified penalties. Thus using the definition provided by Milgrom and Roberts (1992, 330), the quota agreement/contract between the cane growers and the millers can be considered as a relational contract: "a contract that specifies only the general terms and objectives of a relationship and specifies mechanisms for decision making and dispute resolution." A relational contract must therefore be self-enforced, so that trust plays an important role to ensure that the arrangement works well for all parties. Formal, written, and complete contracts usually imply significant distrust between the contracting parties, whereas if one party trusts the other there is little need for contractually specifying actions. Thus trust reduces transaction costs by replacing contracts with handshakes, or in this case an agreement managed by the industry actors.

The contractual arrangement in the sugar industry signals a clear example of a hybrid governance structure (Williamson 1996), because the nature of the crop and its processing precludes the spot market from being a coordination mechanism, and vertical integration is only possible for the milling company's farming on its own estate. The arrangement with the outgrowers is thus a hybrid structure of the two extremes.

Despite the clear rules set out in the Sugar Act and the quota arrangements, perceptions of unfairness exist regarding this exchange relationship between cane growers and millers. Farmers argue that they are competing with millers, because millers not only process sugar but are also involved in cane production, which entrenches their power in the supply chain. This perception of unfair competition could be a result of misaligned goals of the actors in the chain, with actors trying to maximize their own goals. The millers' objectives involve profit maximization by maintaining their monopsonistic status. However, the cane growers want to increase their income through the sale of cane; maintain a food supply source; improve their standard of social services; ensure maximum use of their resources; and minimize exposure to risks, crop failure, and authority imposed by the processing firms.

Some farmers complain that at times millers deliberately record low levels of sucrose in their cane as a strategy to reduce the payment to producers. However, the sugar industry does allow farmers to verify the laboratory tests of their cane if they have any such suspicions. This suspicion by farmers implies that they have no confidence in the millers and therefore suspect opportunistic behavior by the millers. The perceived opportunistic behavior and associated power position of the millers is not conducive to strong cooperation between the actors in the chain. This perception often leads to acts of "counteropportunism" by growers. It is a clear indication of information asymmetry. Farmers in most cases are not well informed about the operations of the industry and the actual quality of the cane they deliver.

At every change of ownership along the value chain, competition occurs for returns between farmers and millers, thus resulting in negotiation of the "pricing of value added." This concept involves the negotiation of the farmer's cane input versus the miller's manufacturing input. Cane growers complain of an unfair distribution of the sugar industry's proceeds from sugar by-products. They argue that they are paid only on the basis of the cane they deliver, when in fact they are also entitled to the proceeds from by-products. Although the distribution of the industry's proceeds to farmers and millers is based on an agreed formula, the formula allows farmers to obtain proceeds only from the resulting sugar output stream. Outputs containing residual sugar after mill processing, such as molasses and bagasse (fibrous remainder of cane after processing), are treated as the property of the mill. Bagasse is regarded as an unpriced fuel source, and the mills use it for the generation of mill steam and electricity.

Economically, if millers were to operate the whole industry without outgrowers, there would be no debate about the sharing of the proceeds, and essentially each stage in the value chain would be treated as a cost center. Similarly, if the whole industry was in the hands of the farmers, value-adding stages up to the marketing of sugar would be treated as cost centers. Therefore, farmers would like to have their value-added share priced during the transfer of ownership of the cane, using a payment formula instead of a distribution of the surplus after the sale of the product. Farmers consider this distribution of proceeds as unfair and regard millers as being opportunistic. By-products, for instance, have some economic value but are used or sold by millers without paying anything to the cane growers.

The challenges in the sugar industry can thus be summarized as improving mutual understanding of each participant's goals and roles, avoiding the use of power to gain advantage, and ensuring smooth flows of cane and proceeds along the supply chain, as well as valuing the role of social capital in the exchange relationship.

The inherent conflicts in the sugar industry result from perceived opportunism and limited trust and cooperation between millers and cane growers, which in turn leads to poor performance by these farmers as a result of (1) perceived unfair pricing systems for sucrose, (2) perceived unfair value sharing of sugarcane by-products, (3) misunderstanding of rules and their enforcement in the industry, (4) lack of skills and information, and (5) conflicting objectives of cane growers and the millers.

6.4   Trust as a Self-Enforcement Mechanism in Contractual Arrangements

Agricultural contracts typically imply an agreement (written or oral, formal or informal) between a processing firm and an independent farmer to purchase the farmer's produce, and the terms of purchase are arranged in advance through the contract. These contracts can range from agreements that address nearly all contingencies (complete contracts) to simple, open-ended, informal agreements (incomplete or relational contracts). As argued above, the contracts (or rather the quota arrangements) in the sugar industry resemble a type of relational contract, because they are not verifiable by a third party and rely on the threat of termination to entice mutually satisfactory performance. For the exchange arrangement to work well for both actors, there is a need to rely on the good behavior of both and on social factors (such as trust) to enhance the success and sustainability of these types of contractual relationships.

Trust is considered to exist if one party believes that the other is honest or benevolent (Doney and Cannon 1997). Trust is the expectation that attenuates the suspicion that one party in the transaction will behave opportunistically (Gulati 1995). Thus if trust exists in a relational contract, the contracting parties will be convinced that they will not be victims of such behavior as adverse selection, moral hazard, hold-up, or any type of contractual hazard.

In Chapter 4 it was shown that the role of trust goes beyond just complementing incomplete contracts—it actually plays an effective role as an enforcement mechanism. It can be argued that the importance of law in contractual relations has been vastly overstated and that economic agents construct productive relationships mainly without reference to the legal system (Macneil 1985). Agents use a variety of purely private mechanisms, such as personal trust, calculative trust, reputation, and constructed mutual dependence. The main difference between relationship enforcement through legal institutions and through trust lies in the relative roles of trust and law in promoting cooperation (Deakin, Lane, and Wilkinson 1997).

Greif (1997) and Granovetter (1985) argue that relationships are embedded in a broader social structure. Therefore social or network relations affect the nature of interactions among traders and provide powerful enforcement mechanisms when a potential for dispute exists (Galanter 1974). Businesses rarely resort to legal remedies, and even when they do, they find that contract law is often not interpreted according to accepted social principles and mores.

Several empirical studies suggest that the main factors influencing efficiency in the supply chain include informal elements (such as trust or norms that support exchange relations), irrespective of contractual obligations and authority relations (Cullen and Hickman 2001). Authority relations are those exerted throughout the supply chain by individuals who have superior information or power in the market. Teegen and Doh (2002) concluded that trusting relationships are perceived to promote alliance performance and that the presence of authority relations has a negative effect on alliance performance, which is further worsened by the absence of trust.

Milford (2002), in a study of the value chain in the Australian sugar industry, found that millers perceive the level of trust between millers and growers to be better than that perceived by growers and harvesters. Milford attributed the perception of lack of trust by growers and harvesters to the poor performance of the industry in the past, individualism on growers' part, and perceived power and information imbalances. Similarly a study by Medina-Munoz and Medina-Munoz (2002) on the role of trust in the success of interorganizational relationships found that all types of trust used in the analysis were positively and significantly associated with the success of the relationship between tour operators and accommodation companies.

Scholars in chain relationships increasingly acknowledge the role of such interpersonal factors as trust on interfirm outcomes. Larson (1992), studying the governance of exchange relationships, found that personal relationships and reputations, coupled with knowledge of the firm's skills and capabilities, shape the context of new exchanges between firms by reducing uncertainties about the motives and intentions of the other firm. Several studies suggest that interpersonal trust operates in an independent yet complementary manner to many organizational variables (Anderson and Narus 1990). For example, it facilitates relational processes, such as collaboration and relational norms, but has limited impact on performance (Moorman, Zaltman, and Deshpande 1992). However, empirical results suggest that interpersonal trust is capable of safeguarding joint competitive advantages against varying levels of ex post opportunism. Thus the adverse effect of suspicions of opportunism may be limited to less tangible relational outcomes, such as expectations of continuity and evaluations of an exchange counterpart.

6.5 Methodology

Data collected in 2001 from a sample of 124 smallholder cane growers and representatives of farmers' associations who supply cane to the three sugar mills in Swaziland (Simunye, Ubombo, and Mhlume) were used in this study, following the theoretical framework outlined in Chapter 3. Data were collected by means of personal interviews. Trust was measured using proxy variables in a structured four-point Likert-type scale questionnaire, in which 1 was equal to strongly disagree and 4 equal to strongly agree (Table 6.1 shows the items used to measure trust).

Because the data selection criterion was to increase validity in addition to obtaining a representative sample (Carmines and Zeller 1988), purposive sampling was used, because it ensures that certain important segments of the target population are represented. The power of purposive sampling lies in selecting information-rich cases for study, that is, those cases that provide a great deal of insight into the issues of central importance to the research (Patton 1990). The sample incorporated 10 percent of the members from those farmer associations whose members mainly farm on individual plots of land and not on communal land. A farmer was only interviewed if he or she had sold sugarcane to the mill at least once.

Globalization, technological advancement, and increased instability and uncertainty of the competitive arena and the environment in which organizations operate has led to increased complexity of organizations (Kanter 1989). In response to these complexities, organizations have explored the use of social structures in which they operate by forging interorganizational relationships. In the past, few studies focused on the social context of organizations. Hence researchers paid little attention to the role of relationships among organizations and the effect that the social environment has on the outcomes of these relationships. This case study is concerned with the relationship of the smallholder cane growers and millers in the Swaziland sugar industry supply chain. It attempts to bring to light the role of relational factors, such as trust, in the performance of agricultural supply chains. The challenge is to find suitable proxies to measure the concept of trust.

Table 6.1   Survey items measuring trust

Response number	Response
1	The mill's decisions are meant to benefit both growers and the mill
2	The mill treats cane growers with care
3	There is a mutual understanding between the mill and the cane growers
4	The mill can be relied upon for its technical ability
5	The mill sometimes withholds some information that may be useful to cane growers (R)
6	The mill cheats on farmers (R)
7	One has to monitor and double-check whatever information the mill gives to growers (R)
8	One sometimes thinks of quitting sugarcane farming (R)
9	The way farmers are treated by the mill makes one think of changing to another mill (R)

Note: R indicates reversed coding. (The responses to these items were reversed before the analysis was conducted; for example, responses 1 and 4 were switched, and 2 and 3 were also switched.)

6.6   Farmers' Trust and Perceptions of Their Relationships with Millers

As argued above, trust is generally regarded as an important asset in an exchange relationship among actors in the supply chain. Its importance is rooted in the belief that trust leads to desirable attitudes of commitment, promotes cooperation, and reduces transaction costs associated with monitoring and providing safeguards in an exchange relationship. So what does the case study show about the levels of trust between millers and growers in the Swaziland sugar industry?

Every transaction involves some element of trust. The fact that transactors agree to exchange shows that there is some level of trust, however minimal. Trust in relationships is important, as it enhances cooperation among parties. The results in Table 6.2 show that less than half of the respondents (46.8 percent) trust the millers. Trust in an exchange relationship is important because it reduces opportunistic behavior and promotes cooperation and commitment in the relationship. The results indicate that farmers were nearly evenly divided on the issue of trust (46.8 percent trust versus 42.7 percent who do not).

It is also worth noting that trust can be built in three ways in an exchange relationship:

- Institutionally based trust is minimal trust based on formal controls, such as rules, procedures, and regulations in the industry. These controls specify the patterns of behavior and penalties or sanctions to be applied in cases of nonconformance by both growers and millers.

- Characteristic-based trust is based on the reputation of millers and farmers. Reputation results from the collection and distribution of aggregate feedback on past behaviors of millers and farmers. Because farmers believe that millers are cheating them, they do not believe millers have a good reputation.

- Process-based trust results from the intensity of interaction between millers and farmers. This interaction only occurs at the mill group committees and through representatives at the SSA.

The provision of an extension service by the government and the SSA contribute to the farmers' belief that millers are not making an effort to assist or interact with them. The risk involved in the interaction process becomes important in enabling trust. However, in the case of smallholder farmers and millers, there is no risk of either party defaulting on the contract, because it would be uneconomic for farmers to change mills or switch to other crops. The millers own estates from which they

Table 6.2 Sample cane growers' trust in millers

Trust level	Number of respondents	Percentage of respondents
No trust	53	42.7
Not sure	13	10.5
Trust	58	46.8
Total	124	100

supply their own cane to their mills. Hence they may not be affected by defection of some farmers. Therefore no risks are faced jointly by both parties, which hinders the development of trust. In addition, some farmers argue that millers refuse to employ farmers' representatives in laboratories, because they would ensure that farmers are not cheated during the testing of sucrose content. This argument clearly indicates limited trust by farmers in the millers.

Table 6.3 compares the perceptions of the cane growers who have some trust in the millers and those who do not trust the millers at all. The results indicate that almost all respondents are certain about their relationships with their millers. Nearly all respondents indicated that they are committed to their contractual relationships with their millers. The perception by farmers of lack of cooperation on the part of millers is evident in both types of farmers (84.9 and 62.0 percent, respectively, of those who do not and who do trust their millers). Both farmers who do not trust

Table 6.3 Cane growers' trust in millers and their perceptions of their relationship

Perception of relationship	Respondents without trust ($n = 53$)	Respondents with trust ($n = 71$)	Total respondents ($n = 124$)
Uncertain of relationship	1 (1.9)	1 (1.4)	2 (1.6)
Certain of relationship	52 (98.1)	70 (98.6)	122 (98.4)
No commitment	2 (3.8)	0 (0)	2 (1.6)
Commitment	51 (96.2)	71 (100)	122 (98.4)
No cooperation	45 (84.9)	44 (62.0)	89 (71.8)
Cooperation	8 (15.1)	27 (38.0)	35 (28.2)
No relative dependence	23 (43.4)	16 (22.5)	39 (31.5)
Relative dependence	30 (56.6)	55 (77.5)	85 (68.5)
No Influence by miller	6 (11.3)	16 (22.5)	22 (17.7)
Influence by miller	47 (88.7)	55 (77.5)	102 (82.3)
No opportunistic behavior	5 (9.4)	28 (39.4)	33 (26.6)
Opportunistic behavior	48 (90.6)	43 (60.6)	91 (73.4)
No satisfaction	19 (35.8)	6 (8.5)	25 (20.2)
Satisfaction	34 (64.2)	65 (91.5)	99 (79.8)

Note: Numbers in parentheses are percentages.

Table 6.4   Trust and profit making

Perception of relationship	Respondents without trust (*n* = 47)	Respondents with trust (*n* = 69)	Total respondents (*n* = 116)
Not making profit	13 (27.7)	4 (5.8)	17 (14.7)
Making profit	34 (72.3)	65 (94.2)	99 (85.3)

Note: Numbers in parentheses are percentages.

and those who do perceived their dependence on the millers (56.6 and 77.5 percent, respectively). The results also suggest that more than three-quarters of both types of farmers are influenced by millers. A majority of both types (90.6 percent of those who do not trust and 60.2 percent of those who do trust) perceives that millers exercise opportunistic behavior toward farmers. The majority of those who trust (91.5 percent) and those who do not trust millers (64.2 percent) are satisfied in their relationship with the millers. Satisfaction in this study was used as a proxy for performance.

These results show the importance of trust in complementing relational contracts. They reveal that farmers who trust their millers outperform those without trust. It is possible that those lacking trust develop an attitude toward millers and so cheat on their contract terms. For example, they may plant larger areas of land than specified in the contract, burn more cane than scheduled for delivery, and then report a runaway fire because they want to supply all their cane when the sucrose content is high.

It is a common phenomenon that the element of trust in relationships is linked to economic benefits. In most cases people who realize economic benefits in their relationships are likely to have developed trust in that relationship. Table 6.4 presents the perceptions of profit for the respondents who trust millers and those who do not. Nearly all farmers (94.2 percent) who trust the millers indicated that they make a profit from the sale of sugarcane. About three-quarters (72.3 percent) of those who do not trust the millers also indicated that they make a profit. Thus more of those who trust millers (compared to those who do not) perceive themselves to profit from sugarcane production, indicating the importance of trust in enhancing economic benefits.

6.7   Farmers' Trust and the Duration of Their Relationship with Millers

The relationship between exchange partners is expected to improve with time. Thus the level of trust in a relationship is expected to be increase as the duration of the relationship increases, which is largely a result of repetitive engagements. However, the

Table 6.5   Duration of relationship and farmers' trust in millers

Duration	Respondents without trust (n = 49)	Respondents with trust (n = 71)	Total respondents (n = 120)
Less than 10 years	19 (38.8)	41 (57.7)	60 (50.0)
More than 10 years	30 (61.2)	30 (42.3)	60 (50.0)

Note: Numbers in parentheses are percentages.

results in Table 6.5 show a negative relationship between the number of years in the exchange relationship and farmers' trust in their millers. More than half (57.7 percent) of the farmers who trust millers have farmed sugarcane for less than 10 years, whereas 61.2 percent of those who do not trust millers have more than 10 years in sugarcane farming. This result may reflect the poor relationships these farmers have experienced with the millers, which they regard as bad because they were not given all proceeds from the sugarcane, such as the value of the bagasse that is used as fuel by millers. The result suggests that trust changes over time, evolving through stages of development, build-up, and decline. Trust as an asset depreciates when one party senses opportunistic behavior on the part of the other party.

6.8   Conclusions and Implications

This study has shown that trust is important in enhancing the performance of members of a supply chain and hence that of the whole supply chain. Farmers who trusted their millers complied with the contract specifications because they do not anticipate cheating by the millers. This behavior may be associated with the good performance of these farmers. Farmers who do not trust their millers are outperformed by those who do.

Both smallholder cane growers and millers need to understand that trust cannot be created easily. It is not a simple factor that can be regarded as separate from other preconditions of an exchange. There is a need for (1) directness (honest and effective communication, and explanations and justifications for actions), (2) continuity (frequency of communication, taking time to explain, and investing time in the relationship), (3) multiplexity (mutual understanding of parties, roles, and responsibilities), (4) parity (fairness, impartiality, not acting opportunistically, integrity, good intentions, and honoring promises), and (5) common interests and diversity (shared values, purpose, and vision; setting expectations; successful handling of problems; and reconciliation). Overall, the smallholder cane growers and millers need to practice fairness, show integrity, ensure effective communication, and show commitment.

This study proposes that the development of relational contracts between supply chain participants embedded in a social system is an appropriate strategy for smallholder farmers. Relational contracts are more rewarding when undertaken in appropriate facilitating conditions. These conditions can be created by social control mechanisms, such as trust and cooperation. Such an environment would reduce the costs of transacting, because contracts characterized by trust and cooperation are self-enforcing. Hence there is no need for a third party, such as the courts.

Notes

1. The Sugar Act (Government of Swaziland 1967) consists of 16 paragraphs. Paragraph 3 defines the SSA and its functions:

> There is hereby established a body corporate, to be known as the Swaziland Sugar Association, which shall be capable of suing and being sued in its corporate name and of performing all such acts as prescribed from time to time in its constitution and as are necessary for, or incidental to, the carrying out of its functions under the Agreement and under this Act.

2. The Swaziland Sugar Industry Agreement is introduced in paragraph 6 of the Sugar Act of 1967 (Government of Swaziland 1967) and states that "The Agreement. . . . Shall be binding upon all millers, growers, miller-cum-planters, refiners, and any other persons engaged in any aspect of the sugar industry."

3. Growers in this case refers to cane-growing farmers and cum-mill planters.

References

Anderson, J. C., and J. A. Narus. 1990. A model of distributor firm and manufacturer firm working partnerships. *Journal of Marketing* 54 (1): 42–58.

Carmines, E. G., and R. A. Zeller. 1988. *Reliability and validity assessment.* Beverly Hills, Calif., U.S.A.: Sage.

Cullen, P. A., and R. Hickman. 2001. Contracting and economic alliances in the aerospace sector: Do formal contact arrangements support or impede efficient supply chain relationships? *Technovation* 21 (7): 525–533.

Deakin, S., C. Lane, and F. Wilkinson. 1997. Contract law, trust relations and incentives for cooperation: A comparative study. In *Contracts, co-operation and competition: Studies in economics, management and law,* ed. S. Deakin and J. Michie. Oxford: Oxford University Press.

Doney, P. M., and J. P. Cannon. 1997. An examination of the nature of trust in buyer-seller relationships. *Journal of Marketing* 61 (2): 35–51.

Galanter, M. 1974. Why the "haves" come out ahead: Speculations on the limits of legal change. *Law and Society Review* 9 (1): 95–160.

Government of Swaziland. 1967. Swaziland Sugar Industry Act. Mbabane, Swaziland.

Granovetter, M. 1985. Economic action and social structure: The problem of embeddedness. *American Journal of Sociology* 91 (3): 481–510.

Greif, A. 1997. Contracting, enforcement, and efficiency: Economics beyond the law. In *Annual World Bank Conference on Development Economics, 1996,* ed. M. Bruno and B. Pleskovic. Washington, D.C.: World Bank.

Gulati, R. 1995. Does familiarity breed trust? The implications of repeated ties for contractual choice alliances. *Academy of Management Journal* 38 (1): 85–112.

Kanter, R. 1989. *When giants learn how to dance.* New York: Simon and Schuster.

Larson, A. 1992. Network dyads in entrepreneurial setting: A study of the governance of exchange relationships. *Administrative Science Quarterly* 37: 76–104.

Macneil, I. R. 1985. Relational contract: What we do and what we do not know. *Wisconsin Law Review* 3: 483–525.

Medina-Munoz, R. D., and D. R. Medina-Munoz. 2002. The role of trust in inter-organizational relationships' control and success. Paper presented at the European Academy of Management Conference, Stockholm, May.

Milford, B. J. 2002. *The state of value chains in the Australian sugar industry.* CRC Sugar Occasional Publication. Townsville, Australia: Cooperative Research Centre for Sustainable Sugar Production.

Milgrom, P., and J. Roberts. 1992. *Economics, organisation and management.* London: Prentice-Hall.

Moorman, C., G. Zaltman, and R. Deshpande. 1992. Relationships between providers and users of market research: The dynamics of trust within and between organizations. *Journal of Marketing Research* 29 (3): 314–329.

Patton, M. Q. 1990. *Qualitative evaluation and research methods.* Beverly Hills, Calif., U.S.A.: Sage.

Teegen, H. J., and J. P. Doh. 2002. U.S./Mexican business alliance negotiations: Impact of culture on authority, trust and performance. Center for Latin American Issues working paper. Washington, D.C.: George Washington University. Available at http://www.gwu.edu/~clai/working_papers/Teegen_Hildy_04-02.pdf. Accessed April 2009.

UNCTAD (United Nations Conference on Trade and Development). 2000. *Policies for small-scale sugar cane growing in Swaziland.* Report for project SWA/99/A06. New York.

Williamson, O. E. 1996. *The mechanisms of governance.* New York: Oxford University Press.

Chapter 7

An Institutional Economic Appraisal of Worker Equity Schemes in Agriculture

A. S. Mohammad Karaan

T he importance of institutional innovation as a key determinant of economic growth has received much attention in the economic literature. Joseph Schumpeter in particular was concerned with this issue and the important role of the entrepreneur whose innovations advance growth (Demsetz 2000). Lewis (1955) later gave further attention to the institutional factors in society that determine economic performance, such as property rights, population, and capital. Hayami and Ruttan (1985) later introduced the concept of induced innovations: institutional changes tend to follow price signals. More recent work relates to the innovations occurring in firms and industries that enhance global competitiveness (Best 1990; Porter 1990).

Institutional innovation is discussed here in the context of the South African land reform program. In 1994 the newly elected democratic government of South Africa initiated a program of land reform, including redistribution of a portion of the country's commercial agricultural land, largely owned by white farmers. This program encompasses all agricultural land redistributed through the three pillars of the land reform program, namely, restitution for people and/or communities who were deprived of land rights under apartheid laws from 1913, a program of land redistribution to settle black people as commercial farmers, and a program to upgrade and protect the land rights of the most vulnerable people in South Africa's rural areas. Progress on the program has been slow, with less than 4 percent of land formerly owned by white commercial farmers transferred in its first decade, compared to a target of 30 percent before 2014.

Given that the majority of large commercial and white-owned farms targeted for land redistribution are too large for a single individual or small group of land-reform beneficiaries to purchase, innovative business models to facilitate greater participation have been developed. For agriculture, this implies among other things a focus on partnerships, contracts, joint ventures, and the like. Agricultural workers, considered to be one such disadvantaged group, are positioned as a target group for empowerment,[1] given their prevailing human (vocational) capital. Farmworker equity schemes (FES) similar to employee stock ownership plans (ESOPs) common in other industries, have thus emerged as one business model for such empowerment processes (see also Box 5.1). Whereas ESOPs appear to have labor productivity gains as their key objective, FES also have economic empowerment as an objective. In FES workers hold shares collectively, obtained mainly with state grants. Third-party investors are often involved, including others who qualify for state grants, such as black professionals and/or entrepreneurs, private investors, or equity warehousing financiers. Unfortunately, experience has shown thus far that these schemes have difficulty in overcoming the legacy of paternalistic labor relations that exists in commercial agriculture.

This case study is based on my participation in and observations and evaluations of about twelve FES over a period of 5 years. This effort involved several project visits, stakeholder interviews, reports to government departments (for example, Land Affairs, Water Affairs), and mentorship of selected schemes and key individuals. The research was prompted by continuous inquiries into the effectiveness and economic empowerment merits of FES. The reporting on FES is mixed and void of an appropriate framework for such appraisal. This chapter is an attempt to present such a framework using institutional economics to ensure that the evaluation is theoretically founded, sound, and objective. This framework is then applied in analysis to identify the aspects requiring further attention to improve the empowerment model. The development of the conceptual model is eclectic, drawing on theory from across economics and the social sciences. The analytical emphasis is on the extent to which the empirical observations conform to economic theory. Further empirical work could well draw on the conceptual framework developed in this chapter.

7.1   Theoretical Framework

The conceptual framework for appraising the institutional arrangements of these worker equity schemes is derived from Williamson's (1999) four-tier analysis of economic institutions presented in Chapter 2. The discussion in this section is organized in the following fashion. Social capital is first addressed, with emphasis on aspects of power and control. The focus then shifts to governance issues (basically levels two and three of Williamson's four tiers), including ownership and control, incomplete contracts, and empowerment. Finally, the more conventional neoclassical aspects are addressed by examining issues related to worker incentives and finance. This methodology is certainly not exhaustive, but the aspects addressed here were selected on the basis of their relevance to the equity schemes being appraised. This type of descriptive and deductive institutional economic analysis is uncommon in agricultural economics and agribusiness. The advances of new institutional economics (NIE) in agribusiness studies and the recent work of such prominent scholars as Alan Schmid (Robison, Schmid, and Barry 2002) and others clearly indicate the necessity of adding this type of analysis to the repertoire of methods and approaches.

7.2 Institutional Economic Appraisal

7.2.1 Embeddedness of Equity Schemes
Embeddedness is understood here as the extent to which an entity is subjected to its social environment. Assessing the social capital and embeddedness aspects of equity schemes requires, first, that the motives for the formation of this institution be examined, and second, that the nature of social capital and the social embeddedness of the institution be assessed. The alignment of motives to embeddedness and social capital will subsequently complete this (first-tier) appraisal. The purpose is to assess whether the motives for establishing worker equity schemes are adequately predicated on social capital and whether the social capital is likely to sustain the institution.

Motives.   The motives for embarking on an equity-sharing venture with workers must be assessed on the basis of a genuine innovation in the presence of transaction costs. The institution is primarily prompted by the sociopolitical imperatives for agrarian change toward greater equity in land ownership. The institution thus emerged from an attempt by the landowner to retain or secure his or her asset in the face of political uncertainty. Reciprocity is also alleged to be a motive, whereby landowners intend to compensate workers for loyalty and sustained contributions to the firm. The coincidence with political change, however, somewhat diminishes the institution's importance and lends greater weight to politics and the anticipated transaction costs. Attachment value to land (emotional goods) is not considered a strong motivator for equity schemes, because several schemes have focused on new land and new ventures (that is, a growth-oriented focus) with little emphasis placed on tenure security as a key motivator. Security of tenure is instead a consequence of the scheme. Another more meritorious motivation is access to alternative markets (for example, ethical trade). These markets compensate firms for applying ethical practices.

The nature of social capital and embeddedness.   Social capital can be assessed by examining (1) reciprocity and (2) networks of exchange and/or engagement. Schmid agrees, but also argues for social capital to be considered as sympathy or care

(Robison, Schmid, and Barry 2002; Schmid 2003). Reciprocity was treated above. The engagement between workers and employers is generally embedded in a history of slavery, racial policies, paternalism, land dispossession, colonialism, social inequality, social injustice, constrained unionization, and the like. This heritage in no way suggests that equity schemes are all equally disposed to these factors. On the contrary, the evidence suggests that equity schemes have a relatively better-than-average record in this context. The landowners are observably entrepreneurial and progressive individuals or firms with a propensity for innovation and pragmatism. Nonetheless, although there is evidence of positive and above-average engagement and care for labor, the entrepreneurial opportunism of the landowner is by far the key source of innovation and energy that brought about this institution.

Trust as an indicator of social capital is irrelevant here, because the relationship is de facto vertical, even though workers and employers are joint shareholders. Power and authority remain with the landowner, and if coupled with paternalism they become more entrenched. Workers are active in planning and decisionmaking processes in the initial stages of the venture, but their lack of human capital in this domain renders them increasingly marginalized over time. The initial collectivist orientation, mainly induced by a small government subsidy, begins to give way to authoritarian management. This finds form in the leadership among workers taking greater responsibility in decisions and interfacing with management. Information asymmetries grow, which leads to problems with collective action and in turn erodes the social capital among the group. Similarly, individuals in the group become less appreciative of delayed gratification associated with bulky investments, which further exacerbates the situation. The resulting intragroup and interpartner tensions have not induced any further innovations yet, which brings into question the merits of equity schemes as genuinely evolving institutions. However, this statement may be premature, given that little time has passed (by institutional standards) since their inception.

Aligning motives to social capital. Evidently some social capital is based on the relative traits of workers and landowners compared to the rest of the agricultural industry, despite the negative historical embeddedness. However, it is abundantly clear that the institutional innovation can mainly be attributed to the characteristics of the landowners and their subsequent motivations. The relative lack of human capital and collective-action problems experienced among the workers is further testimony to this observation. Hence, the motives do not appear to align with social capital. Progressive firms would, in other words, engage in ethical trade, and would favor more inclusive business models, based on a simple cost–benefit assessment. Hence, the institutional innovation of FES as a credible commitment remains in question. The arrangement could be interpreted as covert opportunism by landowners to secure their assets in the face of uncertainty or to enhance their returns in the marketplace. The opportunism is prompted by the initial trust of workers, who expose their equity (state grants) to such opportunism, given their lack of perceived alternatives.

7.2.2 Aspects of Governance

Appraising governance aspects or the institutional arrangements commences with examining the nature of the FES. This first involves an assessment of the extent to which the institutional arrangement resembles a separation of ownership and control. This trend is acknowledged in modern firms and can be anticipated even in agriculture, given the accelerated industrialization of the sector. Second, the agility of the arrangement is examined using incomplete contract theory, whereby the incompleteness of the contract is acknowledged. The purpose is to identify, by way of reality or conjecture, the incentives required to correct for incompleteness. Finally, the implications for empowerment are elicited.

The nature of the institutional arrangements in FES. The commercial agricultural sector of South Africa has faced economic pressures from domestic market deregulation and trade liberalization. Surviving firms are perpetually pressured to craft innovations that will enhance global competitiveness. Equity schemes coupled with ethical trade strategies are certainly a relevant innovation in this respect. Increased industrialization has gradually decimated the traditional family firm in favor of attracting nontraditional capital (Cook 1995). Equity schemes appear consistent with this trend of diversifying the shareholder composition to attract capital amid economic pressures.

Although ownership is diversified, control is increasingly in the hands of specialized managers who wield considerable power and influence and are often not from among the ranks of the workers. Although this arrangement appears best for the firm in terms of maximizing shareholder returns, it limits the economic development of workers to gains in labor efficiency. Furthermore, although gains in efficiency and productivity are initially evident, they are seldom sustained, due to delayed gratification problems. The latter have become a point of contention and frustration for workers, as their ability as principals (shareholders) to monitor the performance of agents (management) is limited because of the lack of human capital. This asymmetry makes worker shareholders vulnerable to opportunism and has fuelled distrust, especially given the history of racial prejudice.

In addition, the residual rights (for example, payment of dividends) and control of assets in modern firms should be seated with the shareholders. However, the evidence, especially from the few failed cases, indicates that such residual claims are not met, upon termination or at any other stage, partly because of missing markets for such equity. The equity is not easily transferable or tradable in the market, and when equity is reallocated it is mostly done for financial relief and risk management.

Nevertheless, the majority of cases have not shown capital appreciation, but the exceptions are notable.

Thus although the model appears to be consistent with the modern trend of separating ownership and control, the existing human capital and information asymmetries imply that workers are vulnerable to opportunism. Ex ante investment decisions of worker investors are subsequently subjected to opportunism in the ex post allocation of residual claims. As discussed earlier, trust is not sufficient to control this problem, especially in an environment that is historically embedded in the exploitation of low-skilled labor. The innovation thus seems better suited to less asymmetric situations.

Several observations can be made regarding equity schemes as a means of worker empowerment:

1. It can be seen as a means of constructive engagement with much latitude for opportunism, given human and information asymmetries.

2. In the absence of effective ex post monitoring systems, opportunism will inevitably manifest because of the relative lack of social capital.

3. The model is vulnerable to collective-action problems mentioned by Olson (1972, 1982).

4. There seems little incentive to alter the model (Bardhan 2000), so that Schumpeterian entrepreneurial internal dynamism (creative destruction) drives economic performance (Best 1990; Dietrich 1994).

5. Government agencies responsible for supporting the model employ individuals with little incentive to ensure that the model works once supported.

As a result, the model suffers from poor financial performance, worker frustrations, and increased dissatisfaction (Fast 2000; Tregurtha and Karaan 2001; Karaan 2002). The problems experienced can be summarized as a combination of a lack of internal dynamism, covert opportunism, collective-action problems, and generally incomplete design. The latter specifically refers to the inclusion of high-powered incentives that encourage entrepreneurship and the problem of missing markets. The most important missing market is that for empowerment equity, which, once created in the firm, can hardly be traded in the open (or concessionary) market.

Hart and Moore (1988) propose a timeline for analyzing incomplete contracts and governance structures. This model is adapted to equity schemes in Table 7.1.

Table 7.1   Phases of contractual evolution

Pre-investment period		Investment period	Post-investment period		
Phase 1 (initial contract)	Phase 2 (investment)	Phase 3 (initial state)	Phase 4 (renegotiation)	Phase 5 (delivery)	Phase 6 (payment)
Landowner offers shares to workers Coerced worker collectivization Facilitation services Obtain state grants Equity sharing arrangement Limited worker entrepreneurship		Human capital by exposure Collective-action problems Eroding of trust and social capital Institutional rigidity Gratification problems Mixed financial results Suspicions of oppor- tunism Lack of verifiability Asymmetric power No countervailing power Unproven residual claims	Dispersion of expectations Labor mobility Third-party monitoring and/or enforcement Develop countervailing power Adapt grant mechanism Entrench residual claims Dynamic institutional evolution Include incentives for efficacy		

Source: Adapted from Brousseau and Fares (2000).

The table depicts six stages of contractual evolution that can also be aggregated into pre-investment, investment, and post-investment periods. The pre-investment period continues up to the point of investment. The investment period elicits the key factors that show contractual incompleteness of the present situation. This enables the key challenges to be identified in the post-investment period in an attempt to guide the requisite renegotiation that will deliver more appropriate institutions.

Empowerment implications.   The empowerment objectives of FES have not yet been reached despite the initial intentions. The value of the acquired asset (shares) has not been sufficiently realized and the shares have no trade value outside the firm. Real ownership as a means of power over residual claims and control has hence not materialized. This failure may also stem from the absence of markets for such equity, which is unconventional and not generally associated with promising financial returns. Empowerment must, however, be built on adequate human capital, which remains insufficient, despite some improvement due to the experience gained by workers in the venture. In addition, the heterogeneity of the group is not sufficiently acknowledged, as human capital and entrepreneurial talents can vary considerably. Workers at the lower levels are frustrated and confused about the benefits of equity sharing, whereas those in or aspiring to management and entrepreneurship feel professionally trapped. This dispersion effect indicates the need for institutional adaptation.

7.2.3 Marginal Conditions

In this chapter marginal conditions relate mainly to those that affect the microperformance of the firm. In equity schemes these center on worker incentives and finance. Equity is expected to be a key incentive to encourage trust, productivity, loyalty, commitment, and the benefits of worker gratification. However, the absence of worker's perceived power over residual claims, coupled with the short horizon of workers for gratification, has dampened these incentives. Although worker participation in operational, tactical, and strategic decisionmaking occurs, it is reactive and is limited by their ability to participate effectively at high levels in the company. As a result, the process (participation) has been compromised in favor of the product (management targets). Leading workers often clamor for greater management responsibility, which indicates a need for greater vertical mobility of professional labor and talented workers. Human resource development plans require more attention.

Finance is a key determinant for the establishment of equity schemes, either as state grants or concessionary loans. Hence it is important to determine whether schemes are established merely to access these funds. The evidence proves that ventures in which the landowner invests first and the rest remains bankable perform better than ventures requiring concessionary funding. Opportunism is also limited in this way. Similarly, equity portfolios including multiple (private) investors with differing gratification horizons also perform better, given the respective pressures that investors are able to exert. State intervention by way of grants and concessions should thus be complementary to private investment, as opposed to being the trigger for empowerment investments.

7.3 Conclusions

The institutional economic appraisal conducted in this case study confirms that equity schemes are subject to institutional incompleteness, as proposed in incomplete contract theory. The incompleteness stems from the lack of verifiability related to social capital, embeddedness, governance, and microperformance. In addition, they lack the requisite pre-investment incentives to enable post-investment adaptation, countervailance over opportunism, and distribution of residual claims and control. The first reason for incompleteness emanates from the motivations of the initiators, which is opportunism by landowners to secure their assets in the face of uncertainty and/or to enhance their returns in the marketplace. The lack of worker effort and options in the early stages of implementation raises credible commitment questions. Examining the governance aspects of equity schemes reveals that they are consistent with modern trends to separate ownership and control. However, a key concern is the asymmetry in human capital and subsequently in power, residual control, gratification, and ultimately economic empowerment. The analysis is aimed at identifying the incentives and innovations required to make equity schemes, as a type of shareholder contract, more complete and credible in an empowerment context.

7.4 Recommendations

The conclusions from the institutional appraisal of farmworker equity schemes suggest a set of recommendations that should be taken into account for the successful implementation of such schemes in the future:

1. *Project selection.* Selection should favor the following economic criteria to ensure long-term institutional sustainability:

   - proven human and social capital;

   - bankable, irrespective of subsidies;

   - progressive and entrepreneurial initiators;

   - accommodating growth and equity approaches; and

   - dynamic worker participation from the start.

2. *Power.* The venture should ensure that workers have real residual control and rights that can be exercised. It is just as important to encourage mechanisms by which workers can develop and exercise countervailing power to offset asymmetries in the allocation of power. In the context of information asymmetries, real or effective power should lie with those who possess more information. Operational information advantages often reside with workers, which encourages them to shirk and exert control over operational productivity. The extent of shirking or productivity gains is a function of social capital, including such aspects as trust and the consequent devotion to the ideals of the firm. Because power in the firm is relative, empowerment is more effective when the emphasis is on ensuring a credible process rather than having a premature focus on product or outcome.

3. *Incentives.* Introduce pre-investment incentives to enable appropriate post-investment adaptation and control over residual rights. Incentives and penalties are

critical to encouraging entrepreneurial behavior. Entrepreneurship is the essential force required to sustain economic institutions. These incentives include

- providing short-term gratification or returns,

- ensuring upward labor mobility,

- investing in human capital,

- assisting talented workers to take advantage of supplementary auxiliary entrepreneurial opportunities, and

- encouraging dispersion in heterogeneous groups.

4. *Finance.* Only those projects with committed private investment that will remain sustainable with private funds should be launched. Multiple investors constituting a varied investment portfolio should be preferred, which can at most be supplemented by government-assisted program or institutions. Aggressive financial leverage is initially attractive when empowerment results must be achieved hastily. This tactic is, however, too risky in the long term because of the volatile nature of agricultural investments. Concessionary equity investments that are backed by credible asset and/or fund management are a key requirement for financial success of empowerment ventures.

5. *Monitoring.* Third-party monitoring is required to curtail opportunism and provide mentoring.

6. *Government support.* Support should be varied and flexible to adapt to circumstances initially and over time as the project evolves. Government should complement the private sector instead of leading the way. It should incentivize private action and provide safeguards against market failure and opportunism associated with private action.

7. *Models.* Equity ventures are but one model; and several other models should be sought and allowed to emerge from these schemes. Hence the further evolution of equity schemes should also be encouraged, firmly keeping in mind the real purpose of worker equity schemes.

Note

1. Black economic empowerment is an integral part of South Africa's transformation process, encouraging the redistribution of wealth and opportunities to previously disadvantaged communities and individuals, including blacks, women, and people with disabilities. In the agricultural context this goal implies, among other things, increasing the number of black people who manage, own, and control enterprises and productive assets in the sector.

References

Bardhan, P. K. 2000. The nature of institutional impediments to economic development. In *A not so dismal science: A broader view of economies and societies*, ed. M. Olson and S. Kähkönen. New York: Oxford University Press.

Best, M. H. 1990. *The new competition: Institutions of industrial restructuring.* Oxford: Polity Press.

Brousseau, E., and M. Fares. 2000. Incomplete contracts and governance structures: Are incomplete contract theory and New Institutional Economics substitutes or complements? In *Institutions, contracts, and organizations: Perspectives from the New Institutional Economics,* ed. C. Ménard. Cheltenham, U.K.: Edward Elgar.

Cook, M. L. 1995. The future of US agricultural cooperatives: A neo-institutional approach. *American Journal of Agricultural Economics* 77 (5): 1153–1159.

Demsetz, H. 2000. Dogs and tails in the economic development story. In *Institutions, contracts, and organizations: Perspectives from the New Institutional Economics,* ed. C. Ménard. Cheltenham, U.K.: Edward Elgar.

Dietrich, M. 1994. *Transaction cost economics and beyond.* London: Routledge.

Fast, H. 2000. Farmworker equity schemes. Mimeo. Capetown: Surplus Peoples Project.

Hart, O., and J. Moore. 1988. Incomplete contracts and renegotiation. *Econometrica* 56: 755–786.

Hayami, Y., and V. Ruttan. 1985. *Agricultural development: An international perspective.* Baltimore: Johns Hopkins University Press.

Karaan, A. S. M. 2002. Evaluation of Goedemoed and Lutouw Equity Schemes. Cape Town: Department of Water Affairs and Forestry.

Lewis, A. 1955. *The theory of economic growth.* Homewood, Ill., U.S.A.: Richard D. Irwin.

Olson, M. 1972. *The logic of collective action.* Cambridge, Mass., U.S.A.: Harvard University Press.

———. 1982. *The rise and decline of nations: Economic growth, stagflation and social rigidities.* New Haven, Conn., U.S.A.: Yale University Press.

Porter, M. 1990. *The competitive advantage of nations.* New York: Free Press.

Robison, L. J., A. A. Schmid, and P. J. Barry. 2002. The role of social capital in the industrialization of the food system. *Agricultural and Resource Economics Review* 31: 15–24.

Schmid, A. A. 2003. Discussion: Social capital as an important lever in economic development policy and private strategy. *American Journal of Agricultural Economics* 85 (3): 716–719.

Williamson, O. E. 1999. The New Institutional Economics: Taking stock and looking ahead. Address to the International Society for New Institutional Economics. *ISNIE Newsletter* 2 (2): 9–20.

Chapter 8

From Statutory to Private Contracts: Emerging Institutional Arrangements in the Smallholder Tea Sector in Malawi

Ephraim W. Chirwa and Jonathan G. Kydd

This case study addresses the issues of institutional change and the need for collective action in a commodity, tea, which requires high fixed investment in processing facilities. In the wake of political and economic changes, the case study illustrates how asset specificity and commodity characteristics facilitate vertical integration as discussed in Chapter 5 and how exogenous changes have influenced institutional arrangements and contract enforcement in the Malawian tea industry. The case study raises such issues in contract farming as enforcement of contracts and compatible incentives when the state is a major player, and it shows the consequences of state failure, an issue that is discussed further in Chapter 20.

Tea was Malawi's main export crop in the 1960s and 1970s but has recently fallen to the third most important export-earning commodity. Prior to the country's independence in 1964, tea was grown only on estates owned by expatriate-owned and multinational corporations. The estates are vertically integrated, owning both tea plantations and processing facilities. After independence, the state intervened to open up the industry to smallholder farming through outgrower schemes, managed and coordinated by a purpose-built state enterprise. The state enterprise was essential in facilitating the vertical integration of the smallholder sector in the supply chain, by coordinating smallholder output from production to marketing. However, because of problems created by the inefficiencies inherent to state enterprises, the state-coordinated system collapsed, and the state could not honor its obligations to smallholder farmers. As a result of problems of contract enforcement, smallholder farmers are now seeking new ways of directly engaging with commercial estates in the marketing of green leaf and of gaining access to an array of agricultural services. It appears that there is incentive compatibility between the estates and smallholder farmers in the short- to medium-term, which enhances enforceability of contracts, as discussed in Chapter 4. On the one hand, estates demand smallholder clonal tea (which is of better variety) to improve the tea quality and capacity use of their factories, as they are replanting their seedling tea with clonal tea. On the other hand, because of the technological and commodity characteristics of tea, smallholder farmers require a reliable market for the perishable green leaf.

Tea farming has special characteristics that necessitate state intervention and institutional arrangements. Tea farming requires high fixed investment for production and processing, and it also requires large economies of scale in factory operations. Tea bushes have a 5-year period to full maturity for farmers to start plucking at economic levels and a short time span between harvesting and processing. At the farm level, cultivation requires continued financing to pay for inputs and labor. At the processing level, a steady flow of green leaf is required to support expensive specific investments in processing plants. Thus the tea industry makes major financial demands at the establishment stage that cannot be met by capital-constrained smallholder farmers. In such cases, the market may limit the participation of smallholder farmers in a high-value export crop.

Such market failures have often been addressed through state intervention. In agriculture, outgrower schemes and contract farming have been justified as institutions that address market failure in similar cash crops (Key and Runsten 1999; Kirsten and Sartorius 2002). Governments have created outgrower schemes with special institutions to link the smallholder growers with private multinational companies. Private firms that opt not to vertically integrate use contract farming to obtain raw materials for processing or marketing to reduce transaction costs and minimize supply uncertainties. Kirsten and Sartorius (2002) argue that contract farming can become an important institution for empowering poor smallholder farmers in developing countries and can improve their access to technology and high-value markets. Singh (2002) also notes that contract farming leads to increases in incomes in agriculturally backward regions.

8.1   Methods and Data

The structure of the smallholder tea sector is a good example of market coordination through vertical integration that is conditioned by asset specificity and commodity characteristics, such as perishability of green tea leaves. Smallholder tea farmers enter into a relational contract with either a state enterprise or private commercial farmers; such contracts can be formal, statutory, or informal. These relational contracts have evolved over time. In this case study we sought to understand the institutional changes that have taken place in the smallholder tea sector in Malawi and the socio-political factors that have led to such changes. To study institutional arrangements that involve processes (formal and informal rules of the game, some of which cannot be adequately covered using methodologies in economic studies), we used a combination of quantitative and qualitative research methods.

For the quantitative research, data were collected through questionnaire interviews with 190 smallholder tea outgrowers. The quantitative approach is more useful for understanding the existing economic conditions and management of smallholder tea farms but is inadequate for understanding the institutional changes. In contrast, the qualitative approach is more suitable for studying the nature of institutions and the drivers of institutional change over time. For the qualitative research, several tools were used, including focus group interviews with smallholder farmer groups, life histories of those farmers who have witnessed events over time, and interviews with managers of tea factories and commercial estates in two tea growing districts in southern Malawi. The face-to-face interviews and discussions with various stakeholders, in a historical perspective, helped us to understand the evolution of the smallholder tea sector, the institutional arrangements at different stages of smallholder tea development, the economic and political factors that led to changes in the institutional arrangements, and the relative performance of the sector under different institutional arrangements.

8.2   Political Economy of Smallholder Tea Farming in Malawi

8.2.1   Origin of Smallholder Tea and Institutional Arrangements

Smallholder tea farming in Malawi started through state intervention in 1967. According to TAML (1974) the response from Malawians to participate in tea farming was rather disappointing, such that by 1966 only 30.8 ha of land, mainly in Mulanje, were under smallholder tea cultivation. The government of Malawi purchased land for the introduction of tea to smallholder farmers, but in 1966 there was high demand from farmers to cultivate tea on customary land. This increase in demand led to the establishment of the Smallholder Tea Authority (STA) in 1967, as a quasi-commercial statutory corporation, to oversee the development of the smallholder tea subsector. STA was established by the Special Crops Act of Parliament to foster and promote the growing and marketing of tea by smallholder indigenous Malawians (STA 1998). STA was initially funded by the government of Malawi, which provided extension services and field staff on secondment, and the Commonwealth Development Corporation financed the planting of 760 ha of smallholder tea between 1967 and 1971 in Phase I, and a further 1,660 ha in Phase II through a loan agreement (TAML 1974).

The big expansion phase of the smallholder tea sector occurred between 1970 and 1979, during which about 130 ha were planted per year and the total area under smallholder tea cultivation expanded from 287 ha in 1970 to 1,995 ha in 1980 (and subsequently to 2,902 ha in 2002; Chirwa and Kydd 2005). The average holding size was 0.5 ha, and the number of smallholder tea farmers rose to 4,904 in 1990 (TAML 1991).

Originally, smallholder green leaves were sold to tea estates that had factories, but farmers were paid by STA. However, with the expansion in the smallholder tea sector, it became apparent that the capacity of processing factories was not adequate to handle the volume of tea (TAML 1991). In 1975 the government established the Malawi Tea Factory Company, Limited (MATECO), as a joint venture of STA and the Agricultural Marketing and Development Corporation (ADMARC), in which ADMARC owned 40 percent of the share capital. MATECO was conceived as a commercially viable enterprise responsible for purchasing green leaf from smallholder farmers and marketing of processed smallholder tea. The high quality of smallholder tea and modern technology enabled MATECO to achieve prices well above the average prices for the industry (TAML 1991).

The transaction costs of dealing with small farmers were minimized by the organization of smallholder farmers into tiered groups (the organization of farmers into different groups varied from clubs to blocks to district committees). The smallholder tea growers were organized into area (blocks) and district committees consisting of five members in each committee elected by growers. The committees were responsible for selecting potential growers, informing smallholder farmers of policy decisions of STA, and advising and assisting STA in management through their representation on the STA Board (TAML 1974). The smallholder tea growers were under "statutory" contract to STA, such that all smallholder tea farmers were required to register with STA, and, by association, all smallholder tea farmers belonged to STA. There was no formal contract between STA and smallholder growers—the contractual arrangements were embedded in the statutes that established STA, in which smallholder farmers were voiceless on the terms of the contract and only trusted that the state would always work in their best interests. STA was accountable to the government of Malawi as one of the statutory corporations, and smallholder growers did not have any voice in policies affecting smallholder farmers.

The statutory contract obliged STA to provide services and benefits to smallholder farmers, including

- free tea seedlings financed by the government-sponsored development program under the auspices of the EU Export Earnings Stabilisation Scheme facility;

- input credit (fertilizers and chemicals) and expansion loans;

- market access to estate factories and a state-owned factory (STA purchased green leaf from smallholder farmers at predetermined prices, with the first payment usually made within 10 days from month end and the potential for a second payment, depending on the final market outcome);

- collection and weighing of the green leaf from smallholder blocks and transportation of the green leaf to the factories;

- extension services guiding smallholder farmers on tea farm management; and

- provision of maize on credit to smallholder tea farmers as an incentive to substitute tea for maize farming.

Smallholder farmers in return sold their tea to MATECO and estates through STA. The statutory contract was essentially a marketing contract in which smallholder farmers sold green leaf to STA at specified prices, with the farmer retaining full autonomy on production decisions, although the buyer provided inputs on credit and other incentive services.

8.2.2   State Failure and the Smallholder Sector Crisis

The performance of STA was initially satisfactory, especially in delivering services, between 1967 and 1985. This period coincided with the highest expansion phase in the smallholder tea sector. Nonetheless, STA never showed convincing evidence that it was financially sustainable. Financial performance was erratic, and it incurred losses, especially in the 1980s, with some intermittent recovery in the early 1990s. The financial position worsened in the late 1990s with a loss of US$0.53 million. The deteriorating financial position led to massive debt accumulation by STA. By 2002 STA owed the government of Malawi US$16 million and US$14.7 million on loan interest payments and principal, respectively.

Several factors contributed to the poor performance of STA, including conflicting objectives that resulted in operational inefficiency (Kaluwa 1989; Lawson and Kaluwa 1996); overstaffing and mismanagement; growing political intervention in operational issues with the appointment of politicians on the boards of STA and MATECO; the labor crisis and disputes in 1992 that led to the introduction of a multiparty political system, with the result that smallholder farmers demanded higher prices for tea; and increasing costs of fuel, leading to high transport costs of collecting green leaf (some smallholder farms were located more than 70 km away from the factory). The political pressure was more damaging in the less repressive multiparty political culture of the late 1990s. For instance, the vehicles of STA and MATECO were increasingly being used without compensation for political activities while smallholders' plucked green leaf was left wilting at the collection points. Most smallholder farmers believed that STA and MATECO had neglected their cause since the introduction of multiparty government in 1994, and therefore they did not trust that the organization was operating in smallholders' interest. STA and MATECO became more corrupt and were overstaffed with ghost workers and high levels of political interference. There was also neglect of equipment at the factory, and MATECO and smallholder farmers had no legal mandate to influence the management of STA (Chirwa and Kydd 2005).

These factors led to a crisis in the organization of smallholder farmers. STA failed to honor its statutory obligation of paying smallholder farmers in time for their green leaf, but farmers were powerless to enforce the statutory contract. Some farmers experienced delays of up to 6 months in receiving payments, although the factories had paid STA in time. These delays impacted negatively on the livelihoods of smallholder farmers—for most farmers, tea farming was their main source of livelihood. The input credit program that operated in the 1980s and 1990s collapsed because of the financial problems that led to the failure of STA to pay its debts. According to STA (1997), although loans were recovered from growers, the loan was not repaid to the financing company because funds were diverted to bonus payments in spite of the losses MATECO made in the 1995/96 financial year. In 1998, the financing company only financed 350.5 tons of fertilizers out of the required 616 tons.

The financial problems in STA also led to the erosion of the services that the organization was providing, such as input and maize credits and extension services. According to STA (1997), frontline extension workers were removed in the 1993/94 season, and the extension service was virtually nonexistent in the 1996/97 season. The quality of transport facilities eroded, and smallholder-plucked green leaf wilted because of delays in transport. The erosion of extension services and lack of inputs in turn led to a decline in the quality of tea leaves and low productivity in the smallholder tea sector. With deteriorating access to inputs and extension services, smallholder productivity slumped to 810 kg/ha in 2002 compared to 2,129 kg/ha on the estates (GoM 2004).

Most growers lost faith in STA and MATECO and started demanding changes in the statutory contract with the state-owned enterprises. Most growers sought alternative marketing relationships with other factories, especially with commercial estates.

The estates, though willing, would only deal with smallholders with the authorization of STA. Initially, estates were allowed to purchase green leaf from smallholder farmers around their estates, but the proceeds were paid to STA. Although commercial estates were paying STA regularly, smallholder farmers continued to experience delays in receiving payments from green leaf sales. This situation further strengthened the resolve of smallholder farmers to completely detach from their statutory contract with STA and MATECO.

MATECO lost most of the smallholder farmers to commercial estates, so that by 2002, of about 8,000 smallholder growers, only 800 were still selling green leaf to MATECO. With a reduction in the supply of green leaf, MATECO was only using 30 percent of its installed capacity. Its financial performance deteriorated further, and it had accumulated a debt of US$0.6 million, the factory equipment was rarely maintained, and vehicles and tractors that were donated by the EU had worn out and were poorly maintained. STA and MATECO had a combined operating loss of US$1.3 million in the 2002 financial year after farmers were paid their arrears.

8.2.3 Reforms in the Smallholder Tea Sector

The management crisis and the operational inefficiency of STA and MATECO triggered a reform process by the government through the Privatisation Commission, in preparation for the eventual privatization of STA and MATECO (Privatisation Commission 2002, 2003). STA was merged with MATECO. A trust, the Smallholder Tea Growers Trust (STGT), was registered in April 2002 as a holding company of MATECO. The Trust has seven trustees, three of whom are growers, two traditional chiefs, two from professional bodies (the Society of Certified Accountants of Malawi and the Law Society of Malawi). Under the restructuring, all smallholder tea growers were designated as members of STGT, reinstating the statutory contract.

In June 2002 MATECO completed a rationalization program in which excess employees were laid off. MATECO became known as the Smallholder Tea Company (STECO) as a government enterprise in a transitional arrangement and was entrusted to STGT. The creation of STGT and its mandate to manage STECO was a 3-year transitional arrangement that culminated in STECO's privatization in 2007/08. Smallholder farmers now have an ownership stake in the factory. According to the Privatisation Commission (2003), the shares of STECO are held by the trust for ultimate disposal to growers, management, and staff. STGT is responsible for managing STECO through the appointment of the board, and effectively STECO became a quasi-farmer-operated processing factory. The board of STECO has nine members with four growers (two of whom are STGT trustees) and five individuals appointed for their competence. An important point to note is that

STGT is dominated by farmers, whereas the board of STECO is dominated by individuals appointed for their professional competence. However, the disproportionate representation of smallholder growers on STGT and the board of STECO has been a source of discontent about the proposed privatization or rationalization of STA and MATECO among some powerful growers, who felt left out in the management of the smallholder tea sector.

The restructuring of STA and MATECO led to recruitment of new management for STECO. These reforms have brought substantial improvements in performance in an environment without access to finance from the banking system. The number of farmers selling green leaf to STECO increased from 800 growers in 2002 to 2,500 by 2004, mainly because of improvements in payments to farmers and the timely provision of inputs. As a result of improvements in service delivery, factory capacity increased from 30 percent in 2002 to 62 percent in 2004. STECO has also managed to secure forward contracts with buyers in Malawi, providing the necessary working capital. STECO has managed to pay part of the debt inherited from MATECO, to the tune of US$0.16 million, from tea proceeds, and it has invested in upgrading factory equipment and has paid growers' bonus payments (Chirwa and Kydd 2005).

8.3   Emerging Institutional Arrangements

8.3.1   Reorganization of the Smallholder Tea Sector

The strategy of the Privatisation Commission and the government of Malawi was to unify all smallholder tea growers under one association—STGT—as was the case under the defunct STA. The smallholder growers were organized into clubs as the smallest unit. The clubs form the business centers (formerly blocks) and the business centers form zones. Three zones constitute STGT. Under the restructuring, smallholder tea growers that had abandoned STA and MATECO were expected to resume selling green leaf to STECO. STECO in turn was expected to purchase tea from them and honor its obligations to pay the farmers in time and to provide inputs on credit. However, the issue of providing extension services did not form part of the postrestructuring statutory contract.

Nonetheless, some of the smallholder farmers, especially those who were larger scale, better educated, and more powerful, were unhappy about the restructuring and the privatization process, believing that the process was irrational. For some smallholder farmers, the creation of STGT was seen as the maintenance of the status quo in which smallholder farmers were forced into an association not of their own making. Exacerbated by the inefficiency of STA and MATECO and the political dispensation, and encouraged by the fact that they were doing well in their engagement with commercial farmers, the elite farmers started influencing other farmers to form their own associations.

8.3.2   Formation of New Smallholder Tea Associations

Smallholder farmers started forming their own association while maintaining the club and business-center structures of STGT. Three other associations have emerged as breakaways from STGT. Some of the smallholder farmers have maintained their loyalty to STECO despite the difficulties the company has experienced. Others that used to sell to estates have resumed selling the green leaf to STECO. Although STGT has retained 2,500 growers, one of the new associations has 4,807 growers and is leasing a small tea factory (with a processing capacity of 40 tons/day of green leaf) from the Tea Research Foundation, assuming responsibility for provision of input credit and other services.

It is apparent that there have been dramatic changes in the organization of smallholder tea growers since 2002. The financial and management crises both at STA and MATECO, freedom of association, and a democratic political dispensation have contributed to the changing structure of smallholder organizations in the tea sector. The top-down approach of creating farmer organizations has not been sustainable, and smallholder farmers are seeking alternative ways of organizing themselves into smaller associations. However, the elite smallholder farmers have been instrumental in the formation of these new associations. The opening up of the marketing of smallholder green leaf has widened the choice of market channels for smallholder farmers. Farmers are able to switch between different marketplaces based on the quality of services offered by factories.

8.3.3   Smallholder Associations and Tea Factory Relations

The high investment needs of tea production meant that those farmers who had abandoned the statutory contract had to seek alternative private contracts with tea processors. The new associations started negotiating contractual relationships directly with commercial estates that own processing factories. The commercial estates are willing partners partly because of their interest in seeing the smallholder sector grow in Malawi and the desire to improve their factory capacity use. Furthermore, smallholder tea is perceived to be of a higher quality, being mainly from clonal varieties, which in turn has improved the quality of processed seedling tea produced by the estates.

The tea factories have signed private contracts with smallholder associations whose nature is similar to the statutory contract with STA or STGT. The factories provide input credit (for fertilizers, including such high-yielding fertilizers as NPK, and for seedlings for infilling), market access through direct contracts with respective smallholder associations, leaf collection and transport facilities, and extension services with commercial estates employing dedicated officers to guide smallholder farmers in farm management. In contrast, smallholder farmers that have maintained the statutory contract with STECO do not have access to extension services. Under the private contract, the smallholder associations commit business centers (farmer groups) to sell their green leaf to the respective estates as a way of facilitating credit repayments, and estates guarantee to purchase smallholder green leaf and to pay farmers in good time. The estates pay smallholder farmers directly without going through the association or other intermediary.

The commercial estates are also providing an array of services to the surrounding communities, including social development work, such as providing access to health care, education, and other social services. Most of the estates are active in construction and rehabilitation of education facilities, provision of clean water, and provision of health services. One commercial estate has an HIV clinic for the community while another has extended its water supply to the communities and also provides transport facilities to the hospital.

8.3.4　Response of the Commercial Tea Industry

The tea industry has responded positively to the changes that have taken place in the smallholder sector. The formation of smaller associations also means that smallholder farmers have become more fragmented and are not speaking with one voice. Consequently it is difficult to channel external support to smallholder farmers as they used to receive from STA. The associations are new and will take some time to demonstrate good governance and accountability to potential donors and local farmers. The estates saw the fragmentation of smallholder groups as a disadvantage to the development of the smallholder sector, potentially leading to increases in transaction costs, and therefore they want the sector to be better organized. The Tea Association of Malawi (TAML), the umbrella association for commercial tea growers, is increasingly involved in smallholder growers' issues.

The active engagement of estates in smallholder tea issues has brought benefits that would not have existed when farmers were bound by the statutory contract. First, TAML initiated involvement of smallholder farmers in the setting of prices for green leaf and agreed to make second payments based on the marketing outcome of processed tea. Larger estates pay relatively more than the smaller estates or farmer-operated factories (such as STECO) that are leased by a smallholder association. The consultative pricing has resulted in reversing the downward trend in real farmgate prices for green leaf (Chirwa and Kydd 2005). Second, TAML has facilitated the formation of the National Steering Committee of Smallholder Tea Growers as an umbrella organization. TAML sponsored meetings with smallholder associations, including STGT, at which a 10-member committee was elected, and TAML insisted on the involvement of women in the committee. Women form a significant proportion of smallholder farmers (35 percent of the sample farmers in the study), and their involvement in the growers' committee is vital for the development of the tea sector. This pressure from estates has resulted in the inclusion of 2 women farmers in the 10-person steering committee. Third, TAML has created a smallholder desk at TAML head offices with a smallholder manager responsible for the affairs of smallholder tea growers. The smallholder desk was created to promote the organization of smallholder farmers and as a vehicle of channeling donor assistance to smallholder farmers through a more transparent and accountable body.

Are these new institutional arrangements beneficial to smallholder farmers? Most smallholder growers rely on tea farming as their primary source of income and livelihood, and tea farming provides some income security throughout the year (although because of rain-fed agriculture the peak period is the rainy season). Chirwa and Kydd (2005), in their analysis of the relative profitability of different contractual arrangements, find that growers that sell to estates earn twice as much profit as those selling to STECO, which still operates on the basis of a statutory contract with growers. Only 27 percent of growers selling to STECO, compared to 44 percent of growers selling to estates, thought that tea had become more profitable than in the pre-reform period.

Most farmers attributed such changes to better tea prices and lower costs of inputs obtained from the estates. The factory leased by a smallholder association pays higher prices to its growers than do the estates and STECO. However, there are also differences in terms of the levels of second payments, with large estates paying relatively higher second payments than do STECO and the factory leased by the smallholder association. The quality of services also varies: growers selling to the smallholder-leased factory experienced transport problems and delays in payments, whereas those selling to estates are receiving better services.

8.4 Conclusions

This case study has demonstrated the important role of institutions in the tea industry in Malawi and has also highlighted how changes in the policy and governance environment influenced the nature of the institutions that facilitate the coordination of exchange. Tea farming is a high-investment activity that requires vertical integration between farming and processing. Commercial estates, mainly foreign and multinational companies, are vertically integrated, but smallholder farmers with an average land holding of 0.5 ha of tea cannot afford processing facilities. In addition, green tea leaves require immediate processing soon after harvest. These features necessitate proper coordination for the exchange of tea and other services between smallholder farmers and estates. Estates benefit from lower transaction costs through outgrower contracts—statutory or private—by engaging with smallholder associations. The case study has also demonstrated the vulnerability of the smallholder farmers to a statutory contract in which they have very little enforcement powers. State-sanctioned institutions may not serve the best interests of smallholder farmers. Contractual issues with smallholder farmers are not well defined, and typically smallholder farmers do not have any effective voice in such contracts.

State failure in smallholder tea has led to some changes in contractual arrangements in the Malawian tea industry. STA became too inefficient, and its financial performance deteriorated significantly, such that it could not even provide efficient transport services and failed to pay farmers in time for their green leaf. Although there have been attempts to reorganize the smallholder tea sector, many smallholder farmers have broken away from the statutory smallholder growers association and are forming their own associations. The statutory association is selling its green tea to STA, reformed as a government trust, whereas the new associations have sought alternative markets by direct contracts with estates.

Smallholder farmers who have moved from the statutory contract to direct private contracts with estates and the smallholder-leased factory are performing much better than those who have maintained the statutory contract. Smallholder farmers who are dealing with estates are receiving better services, and their tea farming has become more profitable. The compatibility of incentives as a mechanism of enforcing the contract between estates and smallholder farmers is strong in the short to medium term, driven by the desire for estates to improve factory capacity as they embark on a replanting program and the desire to improve the quality of processed tea. For the smallholder farmers, the technological characteristics of tea and regular working capital needs require a more reliable and guaranteed market for green leaf. However, as the new and replanted tea plantations of the estates mature and the productivity of smallholder farmers improves (because of improved services), the existing capacity of factories, if not expanded, has the potential to weaken incentives for contract enforcement in the long run. These issues have started emerging in a factory that is leased by a group of smallholder farmers, where farmers are experiencing delays in payments and the factory has been battling to cope with the supply of green leaf.

References

Chirwa, E. W., and J. G. Kydd. 2005. *Study on farmer organisations in smallholder tea in Malawi. Report of the Farmer Organisations and Market Access Study.* London: Imperial College.

GoM (Government of Malawi). 2004. *Malawi economic growth strategy.* Lilongwe, Malawi: Ministry of Economic Planning and Development.

Kaluwa, B. 1989. An interim report on aspects of the objectives, management and performance of the Smallholder Tea Authority. Department of Economics Working Paper 9. University of Bath/University of Malawi Joint Project on Parastatals. Zomba: University of Malawi.

Key, N., and D. Runsten. 1999. Contract farming, smallholders, and rural development in Latin America: The Organization of Agroprocessing Firms and scale of outgrowers production. *World Development* 27: 381–401.

Kirsten, J. F., and K. Sartorius. 2002. Linking agribusiness and small-scale farmers in developing countries: Is there a new role for contract farming? *Development Southern Africa* 19 (4): 503–529.

Lawson, C., and B. Kaluwa. 1996. The efficiency and effectiveness of Malawian parastatals. *Journal of International Development* 8 (6): 747–765.

Privatisation Commission. 2002. *Annual report.* Blantyre, Malawi.

———. 2003. *Quarterly newsletter* 7 (3). Blantyre, Malawi.

Singh, S. 2002. Contracting out solutions: Political economy of contract farming in the Indian Punjab. *World Development* 30: 1621–1638.

STA (Smallholder Tea Authority). 1997. *Annual report 1997.* Thyolo, Malawi.

———. 1998. *Annual report 1998.* Thyolo, Malawi.

TAML (Tea Association of Malawi, Limited). 1974. *Malawi tea.* Blantyre, Malawi.

———. 1991. *Tea: A handbook to Malawi's tea industry.* Blantyre, Malawi.

Chapter 9

Institutional Changes and Transaction Costs: Exchange Arrangements in Tanzania's Coffee Market

Anna A. Temu

This case study presents an assessment of institutional and organizational changes in Tanzania's coffee market following market liberalization. It provides an understanding of how institutions can influence transaction costs in the exchange of agricultural commodities. The discussion is based on the literature on industrial organization, institutional economics, and transaction-costs theory discussed in previous chapters. Market liberalization policies have been implemented in several countries in Africa since the mid-1980s. In this study the structure of the coffee market before and after liberalization is examined and market conduct, institutions, and organizational linkages that influence market performance are identified. The aim is to assess the performance of the market after liberalization, identify sources of transaction costs, and identify constraints on market performance.

Liberalization of an industry may change the sources of transaction costs in the market. Prior to market liberalization, extensive government intervention characterized Tanzania's coffee industry through state-controlled marketing cooperatives and marketing boards. The government set prices and provided guidelines on exchange arrangements. Farmers and cooperatives had no alternative marketing channels or arrangements for exchange. These market conditions have changed since liberalization. In the free market, farmers and traders now have to consider the costs of exchange under alternative market arrangements, and they cannot precisely predict the actions of other farmers or traders. And in the emerging marketing system after liberalization of the coffee market, cooperatives continued to enjoy a positive image, whereas private traders were perceived negatively by the growers, creating an uneven playing field for these new traders. This perception was largely due to the political and ideological history of Tanzania, where private traders were considered to be exploiters.

Transaction costs may arise from poor market coordination or lack of necessary institutional support for least-cost information sharing, monitoring, and negotiation. In addition, market arrangements may increase risks for all market participants or shift risks to participants who are less able to manage them. Since liberalization, marketing costs in Tanzania's coffee industry decreased because of competition among market intermediaries, resulting in more effective use of labor and other inputs. However, transaction costs may have increased because of (1) reduced flow of information on coffee quality and prices, (2) increased uncertainty stemming from regulations governing exchange, (3) missing markets that are important to the coffee industry, and (4) poor services from other sectors of the economy.

This case study chapter is structured as follows. Section 9.1 discusses the methods used, and Section 9.2 presents an overview of the exchange arrangements before and after liberalization. Section 9.3 discusses the performance of coffee markets in the postliberalization period, and Section 9.4 discusses institutional arrangements, highlighting the change and sources of transaction costs following liberalization.

9.1 Research Methodology

In terms of the analytical framework described in Chapter 3, this study identifies and describes the characteristics of the major actors (individual producers, traders, and their organizations; the state; and various exchange nodes) in the coffee-marketing chain and then describes at length the various exchange arrangements as well as the rules, regulations, and entities governing exchange. The hypothesis to be tested here is that institutional changes after liberalization would lead to different arrays of transaction costs to the participants in the market. Marketing costs after liberalization may decrease because of increased competition, but transaction costs may also increase stemming from the breakdown of institutions that guided exchange.

The research methodology includes surveys of 160 farmers and 18 traders (exporters, processors, and parchment coffee buyers); observations of auction proceedings; discussions with cooperative officials, village leaders, and Ministry of Agriculture officials; visiting coffee outlets and curing factories; and discussions with private traders' associations. Secondary information was obtained from various documents (research reports, reports from organizations, and records from various nodes in the marketing chain). Checklist questions and a structured questionnaire were used to collect information. Back-to-back discussions with participants in the market ensure further understanding of the institutional issues and their relation to transactions costs.

Transaction costs considered in the analysis are monitoring, negotiation, and search and information costs, which are defined as follows in the context of the Tanzanian coffee market:

- *monitoring costs:* the costs of ensuring product quality handling, quality and grade uncertainty, and observation of the grading process;

- *negotiation costs:* the costs in the negotiation process stemming from the presentation of product for inspection, viewing, and quality assessment; the frequency of auctions, and the order in which lots are sold; the bargaining disadvantage of the growers relative to that of the trader; and payment arrangements; and

- *search and information costs:* the costs associated with price discovery and information and price uncertainty (for example, auction prices depend on the number of bidders and on product-information costs, among other things).

In this case study the institutional changes that were brought about by the change in market environments are also described. These institutional changes provided a series of different exchange arrangements that affected the nature and extent of transaction costs.

9.2 Liberalization in the Tanzanian Coffee Industry

This case study focuses on the exchange arrangements in Tanzanian coffee markets. To understand the nature of these arrangements and the sources of transaction costs related to exchange, this section provides an overview of the economic changes in the Tanzanian coffee industry that shaped the domain in which the actors in the coffee industry engage.

9.2.1 Markets before Liberalization

Prior to liberalization, two- and three-tier systems existed for export-crop marketing in Tanzania.[1] In both systems, private traders were not allowed to perform domestic marketing functions. For major export crops (coffee, cotton, sisal, tea, and tobacco), farmers' participation in the market was coordinated by primary cooperative societies, regional cooperative unions, crop authorities, and marketing boards. To strengthen the government role in agricultural marketing, farmer-based cooperatives were dissolved in 1976, but re-established in 1982 as government-led cooperatives.

Between 1976 and 1982, the Coffee Authority of Tanzania held the mandate to market all coffee produced by farmers throughout the country. It used village government to coordinate coffee buying activities at the farm gate.

The reorganization of the market in the 1970s resulted in a marketing system with different organizations, but its institutional characteristics were largely unchanged. The government set producer prices, established marketing firms, and ensured that transactions between producers and marketing firms were completed. Public marketing firms performed all domestic marketing functions between the farm gate and the export market on behalf of farmers. The intermediary collected parchment from farm-assembly points, processed, and sold the coffee to exporters at auction. Farmers were paid based on extractable coffee quality and realized auction or world-market prices, minus the agents' marketing costs. In theory, all marketing risks were borne by farmers, but in practice government subsidies were used to guarantee price floors.

The state-controlled marketing channel accommodated the interlocking exchange between farm input credit and the output market. These institutions were important to farmers, creditors, and cooperatives. In addition, the function of the government as a guarantor was important. Moreover, loyalty to the government and government support, trust, and reputation played a significant role in sustaining coffee farming. These institutions facilitated exchanges in the coffee industry in the 1970s and 1980s. The interlocking exchanges and three-part payment institutions were important to coffee farmers because of the failure of financial markets in rural Tanzania. These institutions are discussed in more detail below.

9.2.2 Markets in the Postliberalization Period

Liberalization of the coffee industry was undertaken parallel with reforms in all other sectors of the Tanzanian economy. At a macrolevel, the Structural Adjustment Programs emphasized tighter budgetary control, devaluation of the currency, the establishment of a flexible exchange-rate regime, and reforms in the financial sector. Reforms in the financial sector constrained the cooperative system. The cooperative unions had accumulated large amounts of debt that rendered them ineligible for credit at the new commercial banks. Because cooperatives failed to access credit for purchasing coffee from farmers, coffee exporters were presented with a business opportunity to buy coffee directly.

The new marketing policy and the newly structured Tanzania Coffee Board (TCB) facilitated the involvement of private traders in parchment buying by introducing regulations and guidelines for a private trader's operations. Table 9.1 shows that within 6 years of liberalization, five large private companies and a few small private coffee buyers (PCBs) had successfully entered the market, gaining considerable market share in parchment buying. The shares of quasi-government firms in parchment buying dropped from 21 percent in 1994/95 to 1 percent in 1997/98 as the new private traders gained more market share. The five largest private companies accounted for 59 percent of auction deliveries in 1996/97 and 45 percent in 1997/98. Market shares for primary societies and the unions declined from 58 percent in 1994/95 to an average of 25 percent in the 1996/97 and 1997/98 seasons. TCB established the Tanzania Coffee Establishment (TCE) to buy coffee from remote areas of the country. TCE was intended to address concerns that it might not be commercially feasible for private traders, especially in their early establishment phase, to enter into the market in remote areas and thus the government should take on the responsibility for these areas. Table 9.1 treats TCE and TCB as quasi-government firms.

9.3 Performance of the Coffee Market in the Postliberalization Period

At the beginning of the liberalization process, the primary societies and the cooperative unions were facing liquidity problems, but they had well-established networks with farmers, good market infrastructure, and well-developed institutional arrangements for effective buying and processing of coffee. Interviews with new entrants into the market revealed that the cost of entry for private traders was high because of the capital required to pay for licenses, taxes, levies, and establishing contacts with farm-

Table 9.1   Share of coffee deliveries to the auction by agents, northern Tanzania, 1994/95–1997/98 (percent)

Company[a]	1994/95	1995/96	1996/97	1997/98
1	6	12	22	16
2	6	7	11	8
3	0	9	10	8
4	0	5	13	9
5	0	0	1	4
Primary cooperative societies and unions	58	44	22	27
Estates	8	4	6	7
Quasi-government	21	11	2	1
Other private coffee buyers	1	8	12	22
Total deliveries (kg)	10,901,298	18,777,394	14,368,514	7,108,984

Source: Constructed from Tanzania Coffee Board, Coffee Management Unit (1994–1998).
[a]The analysis treats companies with the same board of directors (sister companies) as one entity. Companies numbered 1–5 are the five largest companies based on deliveries. All five companies listed had invested in milling factories within 4 years of liberalization.

ers. In addition, there was a lack of supporting services, especially credit services, and it was more costly for private traders to operate if they continued to depend on the cooperative curing facilities. Primary societies and the unions were given preferential access to the curing factory. As a result, private traders complained that their coffee was unfairly delayed and that they were charged higher curing fees than the primary societies and the unions. In reality the high fees were partly due to the inefficiencies in running the curing factory and technical problems with the old technology.

Several initiatives were taken by PCBs to enable them to enter the market successfully. These included opening buying points at the village level, establishing private curing factories, developing relationships with farmer groups and primary societies, securing foreign financing and offshore services, and initiating coordination among traders and dialogue between market participants and the government. Along with these initiatives, new exchange arrangements and coordination mechanisms developed. Among these were marketing agreements between farmers and private traders, networking between coffee traders, the Tanzania Coffee Association, the Annual Coffee Industry Conference, the National Input Voucher Scheme, and bilateral relationships between input suppliers and coffee buyers.

9.3.1   Performance of Parchment Buying and Processing

Although the primary cooperative societies have the advantages of reputation, trained manpower, and established buying posts, private buyers usually have better access to credit through international sources and have achieved lower processing costs by investing in new curing factories. By 1996/97, traders owning curing factories accounted for more than 50 percent of the market. The new factories are technically and economically more efficient than the existing cooperative factory. According to private traders, curing costs decreased by an average of TSh 14/kg. After liberalization, coffee is now moving faster from the farm gate to the export market (Figure 9.1).

In interpreting Figure 9.1, note that the coffee-marketing season begins in September and ends in August. For example, in 1996/97 more than 80 percent of the coffee produced in northern Tanzania was auctioned in the first 6 months of the marketing season, September to March. Before liberalization, only about 50 percent of the coffee crop was marketed in the first 6 months. Accelerated processing means that capital is tied up for a shorter period than before and that Tanzanian fresh coffee gets to the international market early, enabling exporters to receive price premiums for freshness. Traders are also now much more timely in fulfilling their contractual obligations abroad.

In the 1996/97 and 1997/98 seasons, the private curing factories processed 43 and 51 percent, respectively, of the coffee produced in the northern zone. The new

Figure 9.1   Auction deliveries by marketing month

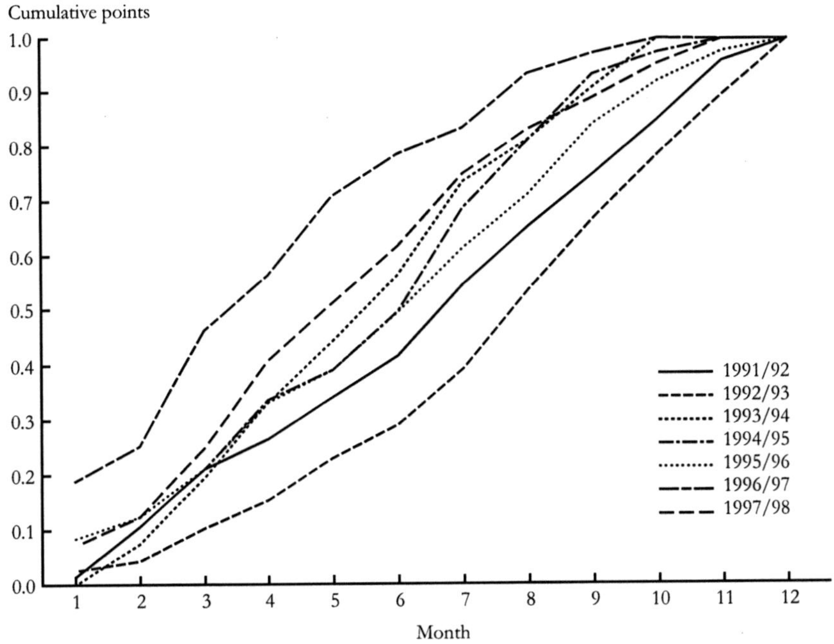

Cumulative points

Month

Note: The numbers on the horizontal axis denote the months of the coffee marketing year, where 1 = September and 12 = August.

factories that operated for the entire seasons of 1996/97 had capacity use of between 23 and 32 percent, which is rather low, but the decrease in the marketing costs justified the investment. The new factories have the latest technology and perform better than the Tanzania Cooperative Coffee Curing Company (TCCCCO). Before the new private curing factories were established, TCCCCO operated at about 70 percent capacity. This number dropped to below 30 percent by 1997/98 following the introduction of the new five factories. In addition, the new curing technology and new management have led to better grading, lower curing losses, and more economical use of the by-products. According to the interview with one curing factory operator, the old TCCCCO grading process penalized grades A and AA (coffee bean grade is determined by the size of the coffee bean; AA is the largest, followed by A and B, which are successively smaller). The differences in grading are reflected in the percentage of grades realized by the new factories compared to TCCCCO (Table 9.2). The new technology coupled with better management has also resulted in lower processing costs. The advantages of the new curing factories over the TCCCCO services are presented in Table 9.2.

Table 9.2   Comparison of new and TCCCCO curing factories, northern Tanzania

New factories	TCCCCO factories
Higher extraction rates (80–81 percent)	Lower extraction rates (78 percent)
Lower curing cost (average, TSh 35/kg)[a]	Higher curing costs for private coffee buyers (TSh 56/kg)[b]
Grading system gives higher percentage to grades AA (27 percent) and A (28 percent)	Grading system penalizes grades AA (26 percent) and A (23 percent)

Note: TCCCCO, Tanzania Cooperative Coffee Curing Company.

[a]The cost reduction is mainly due to better factory management.

[b]High cost is attributed to poor management that led to overemployment, poor scheduling of shifts, and delays in processing, which led to high inventory costs.

The monetary evaluation of the advantages of the new factories for 1996/97 is shown in Table 9.3. The monetary benefit from a 2 percent increase in extraction rate is based on the three new curing factories that process about 7,800 tons of coffee, and the price of parchment of TSh 1,200/kg. The benefit due to lower curing costs is based on the difference in curing cost of TSh 21/kg and the same amount of coffee processed by the three companies. The benefit from grading is calculated based on 3,117,572 kg—the amount processed by two factories that have different grading technology from that of TCCCCO. Machinery costs of the medium-sized factory were about US$300,000. Other costs are building and consultation fees. According to traders, the investment in new factories can be recovered in two seasons because of cost efficiency and better grading.

The additional value stemming from advanced technology is US$0.209/kg, equivalent to TSh 115/kg of parchment bought by the three companies (Table 9.3). Cost savings may trickle down to producers, but the degree to which this happens

Table 9.3   Advantages of new technology over TCCCCO technology, 1996/97

Advantage	Quantity (kg)	Value (U.S. dollars)[a]	Value (U.S. dollar/kg)
Lower curing loss[b]	7,832,053	1,004,791	0.128
Lower curing cost[b]	7,832,053	299,052	0.038
Grading[c]	3,848,854	166,271	0.043
Total (U.S. dollars)		1,470,114	0.209

Source: Author's analysis using Tanzania Coffee Board, Coffee Management Unit (1996/97) and information from private traders.

Note: TCCCCO, Tanzania Cooperative Coffee Curing Company.

[a]Exchange rate US$1 = TSh 550.

[b]Applies to three new factories.

[c]The three new factories considered in this evaluation indicated that the new technology has a different grading process that leads to larger percentages in the higher grades.

depends on the competitiveness of the market at the farm gate. Market intermediaries are able to pay higher producer prices because they have lower marketing costs resulting from efficient processing, better timing of the export market, better coordination of domestic and export trading, and better evaluation of product quality. Higher prices offered by private traders are partly due to these cost savings.

9.3.2 Coordination Mechanisms and Performance

Liberalization offered coffee-exporting companies opportunities for better control and new risk-management avenues. The cooperative system failed to meet exporters' needs for timely supply of coffee to satisfy their contracts on the international market. Vertical coordination by exporters allowed them better control of the supply of coffee. Initially, this integration took the form of ownership of parchment-buying businesses and processing factories. Further developments were taking place in which exporters were initiating marketing contracts with farmers through farmer groups. These agreements simply specify price and delivery conditions. Consequently, the amount of coffee that was procured, processed, and exported by vertically coordinated traders increased. In 1996/97 and 1997/98 the top seven vertically coordinated companies bought more than 50 percent of the parchment produced in the northern zone of Tanzania. The companies perform all domestic marketing functions (that is, parchment assembling, transporting, warehousing, and processing), purchase clean coffee from the auction, and export it. In addition, two or more of these companies receive finance and managerial services from the same multinational coffee company, indicating that the vertical integration goes beyond Tanzania's borders.

9.4 Institutional Changes in the Tanzanian Coffee Market after Liberalization

Policymakers foresaw that the exchange arrangements used in the state-controlled channel would not be able to facilitate exchange between private traders and farmers in the immediate postliberalization period because of potential failure in enforcing exchange. This potential for failure was partly because of the parallel existence of two exchange arrangements, namely, the three-part payment and interlocking exchanges. The latter was based on trust, reputation, loyalty, and government guarantees. These exchange arrangements reduced the cost of lack of information about quality, poor risk management, lack of banking institutions, and cost of enforcing credit repayments.

The presence of multiple output traders undermined the enforcement mechanisms in the interlocking contracts, as producers sold their crops to traders with whom they did not have any interlocking contract. TCB regulations that include licensing, at-delivery payment, and rules guiding payment of local levies and taxes were instituted to accommodate the change in market structure and the institutional vacuum. Policymakers and cooperative unions did not anticipate that postliberalization regulations, which defined exchange arrangements between private traders and farmers, would influence a change in the exchange arrangements of cooperatives. They did not anticipate that these changes would lead to malfunctioning of the auction as a price-setting institutional mechanism. In addition, they expected that three-part payment arrangements as an instrument of quality-based price determination and interlocked exchange as a credit-delivery institution could be maintained. But increased transaction costs confounded these expectations. The following sections describe the changes along the coffee chain from the farm gate to the exchange at the auction floor, with an emphasis on the changes in transaction costs resulting from the change in exchange arrangements.

9.4.1 Producer Price Discovery

Both the auction and the payment arrangement were price-discovery instruments that worked fairly well before liberalization. At that time the government set producer prices. Auction prices were used as base prices, because coffee was competitively exchanged and prices were discovered based on buyers' competitive bids. The bids were based on full information about the quality of coffee on sale. Producer prices were determined as a residual after deducting the estimated costs of marketing agents, and transactions with producers were completed after the coffee was auctioned. After liberalization the regulations required traders to complete transactions at delivery (that is, pay farmers for their parchment coffee at delivery) and allowed exporters to have multiple licenses along the marketing chain.

The payment-at-delivery arrangement now led to prices being determined at parchment exchange (the farm gate) on the basis of presumed quality, instead of at auction exchange on the basis of realized quality. This shift implies that in the absence of well-established grades and standards at farm gate, producer prices were determined without enough information about the product quality. In addition, allowing multiple licenses to exporters and increased competitive pressures in the market and on the auction floor led many exporters to move away from spot-market exchange toward vertical coordination arrangements to ensure greater control over price and quality. These vertical coordination arrangements typically involved exporters purchasing coffee directly from the farmers, giving the former a claim of ownership on the coffee before it was auctioned. Because of the decreased levels of competition and crop share at the auction, it was no longer the appropriate institution for price discovery in the coffee chain. Lack of competition at the auction added problems to quality-based payment, because price formation at the auction might not reflect quality differences.

9.4.2 Payment at Delivery versus Three-Part Payment

Before liberalization farmers were paid in three parts: the first payment at parchment exchange, and additional payments, commonly referred to as second and third payments. The second payment was a premium for quality, and the third payment was arrears, which followed from a higher realized price at the auction than that predicted. Quality and auction price information was transmitted through the cooperative system. The three-part payment arrangement had two main potential advantages. First, the price of the product was determined after knowing its attributes. Second, the system could be used to provide farmers with interseasonal earnings, eliminating the need for farmers to sell in installments to solve liquidity problems within a season. However, despite the price floors set by the government, this payment system transferred the entire market and price risk back to the farmers. The risks were due to changes in prices, costs of marketing, and poor product handling that could result in low quality. The fact that the three-part payment system transferred all marketing risks to farmers suggests that the transaction costs could be relatively high, because risks are shifted to market participants who are relatively poor at managing them.

After liberalization limited dissemination of quality and price information created a situation in which traders had more information about the quality of the coffee they purchased than did the farmers. Thus at-delivery payment arrangements increased negotiation costs because of the rather obvious increase in information asymmetry; while traders could use the information they had about the quality of previously bought parchment coffee (which is determined after curing and cup tasting) to more precisely predict the quality of the parchment coffee they were buying, farmers did not have similar information to use as a basis for negotiations. Farmers failed to trust traders on the at-delivery prices they offered for parchment coffee because of a lack of access to information on auction prices and the actual quality of their coffee after curing and cup tasting, thus creating considerable suspicion about the price the traders were offering.

However, the at-delivery payment affected how risk was shared between farmers and traders. With this type of arrangement, marketing risks were shifted from the farmers to the traders. On the one hand, private traders paid farmers based on traders' prediction of coffee quality, and thus they absorbed the market risk due to changes in both price and variation between the actual and predicted quality of coffee. On the other hand, it was noted that after repeated exchanges traders could be charging farmers a risk premium based on knowledge of possible quality variations. It is logical to assume that traders can manage market risks more effectively than small-scale farmers. If this is true, then the at-delivery payment arrangement could be better than the three-part payment in terms of risk management, and thus it may offer improved efficiency.

In addition to transaction costs originating from the payment arrangements in the postliberalization period, competition at the farmgate level was not based only on price but also included various nonprice benefits, such as the provision of (1) transport services for farm and nonfarm supplies, (2) farm input distribution services, and (3) financial services. These services are provided selectively based on the quantity and quality of the coffee a farmer can supply to the trader. These strategies made farmers select buyers based on factors other than price alone and so increased farmers' search costs for finding the best buyer in terms of value-added services. Although prices are widely known from the traders' price postings, information on provision of these services is not openly known.

9.4.3 The Auction

Before liberalization, TCB ran an open auction floor where coffee exporters bought coffee for the international market. Exporters bid competitively for coffee lots placed for auctioning. Figure 9.2 illustrates the bidding at the auction. None of the exporters were involved in other stages in the chain. The procedures of the coffee auction stayed the same following the reforms and largely involve the following steps. Before the auction commences, TCB distributes auction catalogs to all participants (licensed parchment buyers and exporters). The catalog specifies each lot, indicating the supplier, grade, class, warehouse, and lot size. International standards for grades and classes are followed. TCB sets the ceiling price for each grade, but this information is not revealed to buyers. TCB ceiling prices are based on prices for 3-month New York (for Arabica coffee) and London (for Robusta coffee) futures contracts.

Auction participants assemble in one room, taking their assigned seats. Bids for each lot are presented orally until the highest bidder is found. Participants directly observe all bids and the number of contestants for each lot, as exporters bid against one another until the bidding stops. The auctioneer declares a lot sold to the highest bidder only if the bid exceeds the reserve price by at least US$0.10.[2] If the highest bid is below the reserve price, the auctioneer records the bid as a noted price, which is used by TCB to administer a selling price.

After liberalization, exporters became increasingly vertically coordinated from exporting, back to processing, and then back to parchment buying, as explained earlier. As the market share of vertically coordinated coffee increases, the auction has lost its institutional ability to set coffee prices, because exporters were simply at the auction to repossess the coffee that they already have a contract to supply to an international importer. The frequency with which price is determined by bidding is lower for exporter-owned coffee lots. From 1994/95 to 1997/98 the share of exporter-owned coffee lots that were freely bid ranged from 6 to 19 percent, whereas share of other coffee lots that was freely bid ranged from 15 to 44 percent (Table 9.4).

Figure 9.2   Tanzania coffee auction: Price-discovery paths

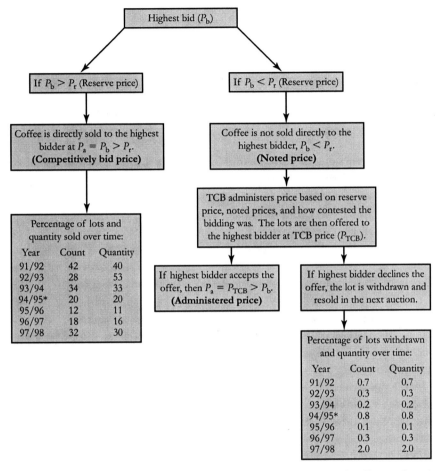

Notes: P_a = auction price (selling price); P_b = highest bid price; P_r = reserve price; P_{TCB} = price set by TCB; P_w = world market price. TCB, Tanzania Coffee Board; *, season in which the liberalization policy was adopted.

On average only 19 percent of coffee lots were priced through competitive bidding in the period after liberalization. This is 23 percentage points below the average for the 3 years before liberalization. The share of coffee whose price was determined by competitive bidding drops by 15 percentage points when exporter-owned coffee is excluded. Overall the trend shows that prices of coffee lots were more and more frequently administered by TCB; exporter-owned lots became less and less frequently priced through competitive bidding. Descriptive statistics that compare

Table 9.4   Share of coffee sold through competitive bidding, northern Tanzania, 1994/95–1997/98 (percent)

Year	Free coffee	Private coffee	Average
1994/95	20	19	20
1995/96	15	6	11
1996/97	27	5	16
1997/98	44	16	30
Average	27	12	19

Source: Author's analysis using Tanzania Coffee Board, Coffee Management Unit (1994–1998).

noted and administered prices show that competitively bid and administered prices were statistically different at a 95 percent level of significance. These results suggest that administered and freely bid prices carry different information (Temu, Winter, and Garcia 2001). Thus information-access costs increased as it became difficult to understand how prices were derived.

However, vertical coordination has several advantages in terms of reducing marketing costs. The major cost savings are due to the reduced time between farm gate and auction, and improved timeliness in delivering to the world market.

9.4.4   Interlocking Exchanges between Output and Input Markets

Like small-scale farmers, primary cooperative societies are often excluded from commercial credit facilities because either their financial requirements do not warrant the transaction costs or they have no assets to use as guarantees.[3] Interlocking exchange between product and input markets is a key exchange arrangement that guarantees credit repayment and provides an important alternative avenue for accessing the credit market. Before liberalization, interlocking exchange was possible due to the monopsonistic power of the lender in coffee buying. The interlocking exchange minimized enforcement costs, and it was scale neutral, because all coffee farmers— rich or poor, small or large scale—had equal access to the required inputs.

Although interlocking exchange was an efficient way of providing input credit to farmers, fundamental problems persisted in the procedures used to distribute input credit in the coffee sector. First, farmer repayment was based on coffee delivered and not on the cost of inputs purchased. This policy encouraged free riding, as all farmers were required to pay for inputs regardless of the amount they collected. Some farmers paid even when they did not receive inputs. Second, because of input distribution procedures, farmers believed that inputs were free of charge. This problem led to resource allocation inefficiencies: farmers never felt the need to use them effectively. Third, the unions deducted total expenses for inputs distributed to the primary cooperative society and not the actual amount collected by farmers. Thus, farmers paid for uncollected inputs still in cooperative stores, even for inputs that were not made available on time or not of the right kind. Very few well-informed farmers understood the arrangements sufficiently to take full advantage of the services. It has been claimed that some farm inputs, which were fully paid by farmers in Tanzania, were resold across the borders at relatively low prices (Coffee Authority of Tanzania 1985). Other problems in input distribution included timeliness and the appropriateness of inputs, which also led to inefficiencies in input use.

After liberalization, primary cooperative societies started keeping records of input credit obtained by individual farmers to deduct input costs based on inputs collected by each farmer. Farmers responded by reducing the amount of inputs collected from the cooperative society. Thus farmers previously had been misallocating resources, because when farmers were given a chance to decide how much input to purchase, the demand for input decreased. In addition, credit repayment for those who received the inputs was relatively low, as farmers strategically defaulted by not selling through the cooperative channel. Unions faced high enforcement costs when they attempted to enforce repayment because of the presence of alternative buyers in the market.

The breakdown of the interlocking exchange institution led to difficulties in obtaining input credit but made marketing participants address the problems of inefficient resource use that resulted from input distribution and procedures for credit allocation and recovery. The National Input Voucher Scheme (NIVS),[4] which requires farmers to prepay for the inputs, addresses some of these problems but leaves other distribution problems to be solved by the forces of market supply and demand. However, farmers have to appreciate the economic benefits of using inputs before they can effectively demand input services. NIVS was partly designed to force farmers to save for input purchases; thus it does not allow farmers to make independent decisions on how to allocate their coffee income. In some cases the vouchers were insufficient for farmers to purchase the recommended amounts of inputs because of the small scale of their operations, thus leading to misallocation of resources.

9.5   Conclusions

This case study illustrates how information, negotiation, and monitoring costs may change with changes in market organizations and institutions. Because of economic reforms and market liberalization in Tanzania, the information demands of producers and market participants differed considerably from those required in the state-controlled market. The three-part payment arrangement in the state-controlled channel had lower negotiation and information costs, as interim payment was based on quality and primary cooperative societies received reports on grade realization and auction prices for the season. In addition, the monitoring costs were relatively lower than those incurred after liberalization, because the farmers' coffee was processed in the cooperative curing factory. This difference in costs suggests that if information on quality-based prices and quality attributes of coffee from specific locations is disseminated, it will reduce noncompetitive behavior resulting from information asymmetries. However, practical problems exist, especially for small-scale farmers who market individually. Traders pool coffee from different sources, which makes it costly to target quality incentives. Farmers' groups may pool volumes to make it less costly for traders to preserve the identity of the supplier from assembly to auction. Unless the volume of coffee pooled economically justifies separate processing and grading, the free-rider problems could be more severe after reforms, fundamentally because private traders buy parchment from several regions, whereas cooperative unions are bound to their regions.

The methodologies applied in this study show complementarities between the methodologies of neoclassical economics and those of new institutional economics (NIE). Neoclassical methodologies were used to analyze market performance as measured using price relationships among markets that are integrated and arbitraging. The methodology views firms as in the category of a market, contrary to standard microeconomic theory, in which firms are actors very much like consumers and whose individual behaviors are emphasized. The method extends beyond the individual actor, traditionally either a consumer or a firm maximizing utility or profit, respectively. It describes the institutional framework, which examines what options individual actors have and what outcomes they receive as a function of the actions of others. Greater emphasis is given to the institutions that establish "price." In traditional models of microeconomics, prices in an impersonal marketplace constitute the institutional framework; the NIE analysis in this study defines prices as outcome of more complex institutional set-ups.

The institutional concepts and aspects that are used in this study include organization arrangements, transaction costs, missing markets, social norms, enforcement mechanisms, human assets, social capital, contractual safeguards, asset specificity, monitoring costs, incentive to collude, opportunism, and bargaining strength. All these are aspects in the NIE analyses.

Analyzing price behavior in markets without considering the institutional framework may lead to misinterpretation of the results. Without institutional analyses, the behavior of Tanzanian auction market prices could have been interpreted as the collusion of self-interested individual firms as they contest for coffee. However, this research found that auction prices are determined by the organizational arrangement of the market and the auction itself. Furthermore, the uncertainties in the at-delivery and three-part payment system and interlocking exchanges are mainly due to high enforcement costs and missing financial markets, respectively.

Notes

1. The three-tier system comprised primary cooperative societies, cooperative unions, and the marketing board as intermediaries between farmers and the export market. This system operated from 1962 to 1976 and from 1984 to 1991. The two-tier system was made up of village and crop marketing boards as intermediaries between farmers and exporters. This system operated from 1976 to 1983, when cooperatives were dissolved.

2. Prices are quoted in U.S. dollars per 50-kg bag of clean coffee.

3. Historically, commercial banks have failed to lend small-scale farmers because of the high risk of default and high negotiation and monitoring costs, largely attributed to the small sizes of the farms, lack of security, and low level of farmers' business education. The problems of formal credit systems and the importance of informal lending in Tanzania have been topical issues since late 1980s (Von Pischke, Adam, and Donald 1983; Temu and Hill 1994).

4. To solve the problem of liquidity and unavailability of credit for purchasing input, TCB initiated NIVS, in which traders would pay farmers partly in cash and partly in input vouchers that should be used to purchase inputs from registered farm input retailers.

References

Coffee Authority of Tanzania. 1985. *Tanzania coffee marketing study.* Project 5100.031.50.010. Moshi, Tanzania.

Tanzania Coffee Board, Coffee Management Unit. Various years. Auction catalogs. Moshi, Tanzania.

Temu A. A., A. Winter-Nelson, and P. Garcia. 2001. Market liberalization, vertical integration and price behaviour in Tanzania's coffee auction. *Development Policy Review* 19 (2): 205–222.

Temu, A. E., and G. P. Hill. 1994. Some lessons from informal finance practices in rural Tanzania. Special issue: African review of money, finance and banking. *Savings and Development* 1–2 (supplement): 141–166.

Von Pischke, J. D., D. W. Adam, and G. Donald. 1983. *Rural finance markets in developing countries, their use and abuse.* Economic Development Institute Series in Economic Development. Baltimore: Johns Hopkins University Press.

Chapter 10

A Transaction-Cost Approach to Enterprise Modeling and Coordination between Small Growers and a Large Firm: The Case of Mussel Mariculture in South Africa

A. S. Mohammad Karaan

The challenge of growing the agricultural sector in South Africa entails, among other things, the creation of livelihoods for previously disadvantaged farmers by facilitating their integration into established farming. It is argued that small start-up firms face considerable transaction costs in commencing business and establishing business relations with dominating large firms, even though small-scale farming brings significant efficiency gains (principally by the use of family labor), which suggests that small firms should dominate this industry.

However, such factors as risk, asset specificity, information asymmetry, and opportunism tend to favor large firms, which contend with these aspects through hierarchy. This explains the existence of large firms. Nevertheless, sociopolitical imperatives to promote growth and economic empowerment through active advancement of the emerging sector prompted the participants in the mussel industry to reconsider the efficiency and political gains associated with promoting small growers.

This case study addresses both these challenges to start-ups by first motivating the idea of small-scale mussel farming as an innovative farming venture with significant small-scale efficiency merits. Second, appropriate farming models that facilitate the big–small business interfaces in mussel mariculture are analyzed based on transaction-cost theory. Four relevant farming models are considered: (1) small independent operators, (2) contract farming, (3) franchises, and (4) large vertically integrated firms. Transaction costs are then identified and discussed for each model: in preproduction, in production, in marketing and processing, as well as in the political and economic environment. In this way a suitable model for mussel farming is identified. It is postulated that the appropriate model is one that is subjected to lower transactions and risks and has the ability to advance through perpetual adaptation.

10.1   Background and Characteristics of the Mussel Mariculture Industry

South Africa has a coastline stretching for mote than 3,000 km, which is highly exposed, although a few protected bays offer excellent opportunities for mariculture.[1] Saldanha Bay on the west coast is the largest sheltered bay and the most suitable for shellfish farming. The bay is fed by the nutrient-rich Benguella stream, and is largely free of marine infestations, such as red tide. Mussel farming here commands a global comparative advantage in terms of excellent mussel growth rates. Mussels grow to marketable size in 6–8 months, compared to 12–18 months in New Zealand, 24 months in Spain, and 30 months in The Netherlands.

The world consumption of mussels is increasing amid an increased demand for seafood. Quality mussels remain globally in short supply of about 30 percent of demand, and South Africa remains a net importer of mussels. Local production has a competitive edge on cheaper imported mussels (for example, China and New Zealand), as the fresh mussels command a premium in local markets.

Some fishing companies have been farming mussels successfully in Saldanha Bay since the early 1990s, and despite early difficulties and the exit of some firms, the industry shows potential for growth. Mussel farming involves growing mussels clustered on ropes, which are suspended from floating wooden rafts. Rafts are stocked at about one per hectare. The local Port Authority administering the bay has allocated a specific area for mussel mariculture by small growers. In the late 1990s, a fishing company, which also farms mussels in the bay, implemented a pilot project involving three workers. The company provided the assets on a cost-recovery basis to the growers, as well as extension services, guaranteed markets, inputs on credit, and other logistical assistance. The success of the pilot project encouraged an extended program in which new growers are included each year.

The nature of the relationship between the growers and the large company was of concern because of the following factors:

1. lack of trust stemming from an absence of prior transactions and business history;

2. information asymmetries between new growers and an established firm;

3. expected dependency between parties, given the risks and transaction costs;

4. a history of problematic race relations;

5. ex-workers weaned from the authority of their previous employer;

6. concerns about a prisoner's dilemma by the large company; and

7. mutual suspicions over opportunism.

10.2 Transaction-Cost Analysis

10.2.1 Theoretical Premise

Transaction-costs economics forms the theoretical base of this study. It is accepted that high transaction costs essentially constrain the participation of small farmers in the open market economy (Binswanger and Rosenzweig 1986; Hoff, Braverman, and Stiglitz 1993). Hence it is posited that transaction costs associated with mussel farming account for the prevailing preference for larger firms or vertical and horizontal coordination among firms. It follows on Williamson's (1985) tradition of identifying transactions costs with a view of attending to pretransaction incentives and related posttransaction governance adaptations to facilitate and safeguard transactions and interfirm relations.

The case study also follows the arguments and methodology of Delgado (1999), who advocates for market reforms aimed at eradicating barriers to smallholder participation in the market economy. He acknowledges that such measures have often failed to confront the hidden reasons for lack of market participation, such as information asymmetry, unenforceable contracts, lack of skills, and ability to engage effectively. The methodology employed is derived from Alston and Gillespie (1988), who developed a framework to model the effects of transaction costs on the relationships between firms (Table 10.1). Transaction costs are classified by crossing three factors of production with the three stages in the production process. The factors appearing under the "preproduction" and "postproduction" categories are factors that encourage production within firms. The factors appearing under the "production" category are costs of using the firm.

10.2.2 Transaction-Costs Framework

This framework is used to construct Table 10.2, which categorizes and analyzes transaction costs associated with the mussel industry. Table 10.2 depicts the transaction

Table 10.1 Structure of transaction costs

Factor of production	Production process		
	Preproduction	Production	Postproduction
Physical and financial capital	Asset specificity	Abuse and agency costs	n.a.
Human capital	Information constraints and asset specificity	Coordination costs	Measurement of output and contract enforcement
Work intensity	n.a.	Shirking and contract enforcement	n.a.

Source: Alston and Gillespie (1988).
Note: n.a., not applicable.

costs as well as some factors that induce transaction costs in mussel mariculture and in inter- and intra-firm relations. Four models are compared, based on the respective effects of these factors, to obtain the most suitable model that is least encumbered by transaction costs. The various farming models are (1) independent small growers, (2) contract farming between small operators and processors/marketers, (3) agricultural franchises, and (4) vertically integrated and specialized large firms.

The concept of agricultural franchising is less well known in agriculture compared to the other models. *Business-format franchising*, as opposed to product or brand franchising, is defined as a contractual relationship between two or more businesses when the following conditions hold (Rudolph 1999):

1. A franchisor provides inputs and/or services to franchisees.

2. In return, franchisees pay the franchisor an initial sum as well as royalties that are tied to sales or profits.

3. For at least one of the services provided by the franchisor, which covers an essential administrative or managerial function, the following set of conditions must hold simultaneously: (a) the service is subject to economies of size; (b) although there need not be rivalry in consuming the service, other firms in the industry who have not bought the franchise can be excluded from consuming it; (c) the provision of this service gives the franchisees a competitive advantage; and (d) the productivity of this service for the franchisee requires a long-term contractual relationship.

4. Although the franchisee is not employed by the franchisor and has some discretion in decisionmaking, the franchisor has the right to monitor those actions of the franchisee that might cause negative external effects for other franchisees with respect to the conditions listed above.

Table 10.2   Transaction costs in mussel farming and effects on relevant farming models

Transaction cost and possible cause	Independent small growers	Contract farming	Agricultural franchises	Vertically integrated, specialized large firms
Preproduction				
Asset specificity of rafts and equipment	–	+	++	++
Interfirm information asymmetry	–	–	+	+
Bureaucracy to obtain water tenure	–	–	+	+
High investment requirements	–	–	+	+
Adverse selection of growers	–	–	++	+
Production				
Diseconomies of scale	+	+	+	–
Returns to research and development	–	+	++	++
Entrepreneurial and managerial capacity	–	+	++	+
Moral hazard	–	–	+	++
Shirking	–	+	+	–
Hold-up from underperformance	–	–	+	++
High value-to-weight commodity	–	+	+	++
Product losses from lack of coordination with processor	–	+	+	+
Ability to enforce contracts	–	–	+	++
Processing and marketing				
Economies of scale in marketing	–	+	++	++
Marketing opportunism (prisoner's dilemma)	–	+	+	+
Export market penetration	–	–	+	+
High investment cost or risk	–	–	–	+
Information asymmetry	–	+	++	++
Quality specificity (form utility)	–	+	+	–
Economic and political environment				
Land access costs	+	+	+	–
Poorly integrated output markets	–	+	+	++
Stringent financial markets	–	–	–	+
Deficient input or factor markets	–	+	++	++
Economic empowerment imperatives	+	+	+	–

Notes: —, unfavorable; +, favorable; ++, highly favorable.

5. The franchisees do not share in the ownership of the franchisor firm.

6. There is limited growth potential for individual franchisees.

7. A high degree of asset specificity of the production technology exists.

8. A more or less vertically integrated structure must be less efficient.

The franchisor could be an existing large corporate entity with which the existing farmers have contracts or a joint venture between relevant organizations. Prospective franchisees could be expected to pay a joining fee, which entitles them to the range of requisite services. Some flexibility and creativity is required, given that emerging growers have limited resources. Royalties may also be recovered from sales on a feasible basis. Growers would enter into this arrangement because it brings economies of scale in marketing, processing, research and development, and input procurement, and it improves their competitiveness by providing access to expertise and/or extension services, greater price certainty, synchronized harvesting, and certainty on factor markets. The conditions on asset specificity and limited growth potential are also satisfied, because only conventional mussel rafts are used, which have hardly any alternate uses.

In Table 10.2, transaction costs and factors are identified in production, processing and marketing, and the economic and political environment. The intention was not to identify the absolute values but rather to compare their relative values, as advised by Williamson (1985). Business decisions are often made based on relative rather than absolute positions and values. The depicted transactions costs were identified through observation, studies, and discussions with industry stakeholders over an extended period of about 3 years and continued involvement with this venture since 1996.

Preproduction transaction costs.   The floating rafts on which the mussels are produced do not have any alternate use and, once constructed, cannot easily be changed. Thus they have a high degree of asset specificity.[2] Informational constraints (asymmetry) are also considered to add preproduction transaction costs because they influence the way in which transactions are forged for the purposes of production. In this case, transaction costs arise because of the cost of information transmission from the corporate entity, which is more knowledgeable about the technology and production techniques, to the novice growers. In addition it also involves maladaptation costs, given that novice growers lack the requisite experience and are thus more prone to error. The bureaucratic costs are rather high for individual farmers who wish to acquire a lease over an area of water from the local and port authorities, as well as all the other requisite elements of project support (for example, extension services, inputs, markets, technology, and equipment). Investment costs are particularly high for individual operators because of the cost of screening, bargaining, and monitoring as well as the adverse selection problems that usually accompany credit provision.

The selection of beneficiaries (novice growers) has been a tedious process over 3 years. The first grower who commenced the pilot phase exhibited a high level of technical competence and subsequent efficiency, surpassing industry average yields per rope by a significant margin. Unfortunately there was failure in managerial ability and responsible behavior (moral hazard), causing hold-up problems. The cumbersome public participation and awareness endeavors aimed at eliciting interest and identifying prospective growers, few of whom had any entrepreneurial experience, increased the risk of adverse selection of beneficiaries. The original purpose of attracting entrepreneurs to engage in mussel farming did not yield sufficient interest or ended in opportunistic behavior and debilitating problems with cooperation.

In conclusion, the transaction costs identified under the preproduction category tend to favor a higher degree of vertical integration or coordination as opposed to small independent growers or contract farming. Franchises, as the more sophisticated form of contracting, appear to have somewhat equal merit to specialized vertical integrated firms. Franchises were selected (before the project commenced) as a form of idealized design in which all risks are usually catered for in a contract.

Production-based transaction costs. At the inception of the project, it was expected that small growers would have production efficiency advantages compared to larger enterprises. Experience to date has confirmed this expectation, as the first grower was able to achieve an average rope yield of 64 kg per rope, which is significantly higher (42 percent) than the 45 kg per rope achieved on rafts managed by the large corporation. The absolute yields could fluctuate with the nutritional status of the water resource, but the yield efficiency margin between big and small could be retained. This difference is mainly due to the ability of small growers to more effectively monitor and manage the growth of the mussels on-raft. Besides the incentives to monitor, thereby attaining better quality product and prices, small growers are also able to exert more individual and family effort at lower cost compared to larger firms. Transaction costs (among other things) therefore increase with a higher degree of vertical integration, thus favoring smaller enterprises. Larger firms are, however, better at investing in and internalizing the costs of research and development, placing them at an advantage over smaller firms. New entrants lack managerial and entrepreneurial ability, which under most circumstances encourages vertical integration. The political challenges of economic empowerment, livelihood creation, and the like do not favor large and vertically integrated firms. In addition, moral hazard and subsequent hold-up problems have occurred with contract farming to date. These problems mainly stem from the lack of enforceability of contracts among large companies, growers, and other service providers. Large companies bear the risks of shirking[3] by employees, which partly explains the efficiency of smaller enterprises. Shirking is an intrafirm principal-agent problem that can be solved through smallholder contract farming and franchises.

The marketable yield per rope is about 20 percent of total production, indicating low value to weight in primary production. Once sold to the processor, the situation changes to high value to weight, which favors vertical linkages and coordination between growers and processors. The same holds for the high perishability of the product. The lack of contract enforcement again favors vertical integration. This lack of enforcement stems, first, from the sociopolitical environment in which white-dominated firms are prompted to contribute to the economic development of previously disenfranchised people and which requires gestures of goodwill on their part. Second, when contract growers default, both formal (legal) and informal (peer penalties) mechanisms are ineffective in the short run because of a general lack of business history and precedent. Franchises have the advantage of enabling individual growers (franchisees) with less enforcement risks than the contract growers but require higher levels of technical competence.

In conclusion, the transaction-cost factors considered under the production category mostly favor vertical integration, with the important exception of diseconomies of size, which favor small-scale farming. Hence franchising seems to be the favored model for production.

Processing- and marketing-based transaction costs.   In this section the transaction costs in the processing and marketing stage of the supply chain are highlighted. Economies of scale in marketing emanate from the importance of grading and quality assurance. Individual growers attain yields that are too varied with regard to size and quality to be able to individually penetrate more lucrative local, export, and other niche markets. Processing equipment (excluding grading) is also subject to scale efficiencies and is best employed in large and better-endowed enterprises. Some postharvest activities, such as cleaning, declumping, and grading, can be done on raft by the grower and improve price margins for growers. There is also informational asymmetry on processing techniques, marketing channels, contacts, and processing-related services. The asymmetry originates from the fact that the experience of growers is in production rather than further up the chain, where the large firms dominate. Marketing of mussels presents a real case of a prisoner's dilemma, in which individual growers are often tempted to sell directly at higher premiums to retailers, restaurants, and other buyers. Direct selling occurs at the expense of an interlinked contract and marketing arrangement with a large processor, whose interest is best served by procuring the best sizes and quality of mussels from growers. In return the processors also provide other support services (for example, extension services, raft construction, seed, some equipment, and goodwill based on ad hoc assistance). For this category, franchises and vertically integrated firms are generally preferred, whereas contract growers and franchises are better at maintaining quality.

Political and economic transaction costs. The high cost of agricultural land acquisition in South Africa necessitates that innovative and alternative livelihood opportunities in agriculture be sought. Small-scale mariculture, requiring little land, is certainly such an opportunity, because the cost of access to a water lease is negligible compared to the cost of land. The reality that small-scale farming is largely under-developed in South Africa means that input and output markets are consequently underdeveloped for this sector. However, these markets do exist for large-scale com-mercial agriculture and mariculture. The challenge is to identify and if necessary appropriate these markets for small growers. This strategy has not been problematic in mussel farming. Without such integration, access to input and output markets would result in high transaction costs for small growers. The prevailing politico-economic dispensation in South Africa favors the creation and support of small and medium-sized enterprises, which are supported by large corporate entities, as opposed to vertical integration by the corporations. In this context franchises, contract farm-ing, and independent small growers are more acceptable than vertical integration.

It generally appears that increased levels of vertical integration produce better economic results, but contract farming and especially franchises have compelling merits as well. Three factors militate against specialized, vertically integrated firms in favor of franchises and contract farming: diseconomies of size, shirking, and qual-ity specificity. From a transaction-cost point of view, franchises appear to be more advantageous than contract farming. This conclusion is evident in practice—contract farming failed to adequately address all the transaction costs, manifested in the lim-ited replicability of the existing contract-farming model, although other factors (such as the inaccessibility of the allocated site) also contributed. However, it is considered easier to incorporate measures into the design of the franchise to cater for transac-tion costs than is the case for contract farming. Franchisees are more reactive to risk and are better at dealing with contract enforcement, export market penetration, high investment costs, informational asymmetry, and deficient input factors. Franchises are also less prone to hold-up problems, moral hazard, adverse selection, and bureaucracy.

10.3 Conclusions

This case study considers the action domain (see Figure 3.2) of mariculture and reflects on the most appropriate institutional arrangements for coordination between new entrants and existing corporate enterprises. The case is an illustration of transaction-costs analysis that emphasizes the identification of transaction costs and comparison of their manifestations across four institutional arrangements (business models) for ensuring effective participation of small farmers in agribusiness. It was found that the efficiency advantages of small-scale farming are outweighed by the transactions costs that such farming has to contend with. This result partly explains the dominance of large, vertically integrated firms. However, political imperatives and competitive pressures to capture the benefits of small intensive farming worked in favor of a reconsideration of small-scale farming. The success of the pilot project added to the merits of the case. The franchising model was found to be the most efficient model, as it combines a large degree of vertical coordination coupled with the merits of small-scale farming. It is also better at dealing with contract enforcement, export market penetration, high investment costs, informational asymmetry, and deficient input factors. In addition, it is less prone to hold-up problems, moral hazard, adverse selection, and bureaucracy. This model is considered rather sophisticated, given the considerable informational asymmetries that persist between emerging small and experienced large operators. The contract-farming model is therefore considered to be the most suitable alternative, as it is more conducive to incremental adaptation (the remediableness criterion) through learning and the subsequent reduction in transaction costs and information incompleteness.

Notes

1. *Mariculture* refers to the cultivation of marine species.

2. Asset specificity is relevant when one party in a transaction makes an investment that cannot be fully recovered if the transaction is terminated (Williamson 1981).

3. *Shirking* is defined as a deviation from expected behavior by employees (Alston and Gillespie 1988) that reduces the productivity of the firm (Yarbrough and Yarbrough 1988).

References

Alston, L. J., and W. Gillespie. 1989. Resource coordination and transaction costs: A framework for analyzing the firm/market boundary. *Journal of Economic Behavior and Organization* 11 (2): 191–212.

Binswanger, H., and M. Rosenzweig. 1986. Behavioural and material determinants of production relations in agriculture. *Journal of Development Studies* 22: 503–539.

Delgado, C. 1999. Sources of growth in smallholder agriculture in Sub-Saharan agriculture: The role of vertical integration of smallholders with processors and marketers of high value–added items. *Agrekon* 38 (May, special issue): 165–189.

Hoff, K., A. Braverman, and J. E. Stiglitz. 1993. *The economics of rural organization: Theory, practice and policy*. New York: Oxford University Press.

Rudolph, D. W. 1999. Vertical organization of agribusinesses in transition economies: Hungarian production systems or agricultural franchising? *Agribusiness* 15 (1): 25–40.

Williamson, O. E. 1981. The economics of organization: The transaction cost approach. *American Journal of Sociology* 87: 549–577.

———. 1985. *The economic institutions of capitalism*. New York: Free Press.

Yarbrough, B. V., and R. M. Yarbrough. 1988. The transactional cost structure of the firm. A comparative survey. *Journal of Economic Behavior and Organization* 10 (1): 1–28.

Chapter 11

An Analysis of Animal Healthcare Service Delivery in Kenya

Leonard Oruko and Leah Ndung'u

One important objective of agricultural polices and interventions in developing countries is to commercialize and intensify agricultural production. As argued in Chapter 5, to intensify their agricultural production, smallholder households may require access to a range of support services, including improved seeds, inorganic fertilizers, credit, technical advice, market information, and linkages to output markets. In this case study one of the critical inputs for animal production—animal healthcare services—is analyzed. The control of animal diseases and the promotion and protection of animal health through efficient and reliable animal healthcare services are essential components of any effective animal breeding and production program and constitute an essential prerequisite to livestock development. Despite remarkable technical advances in the diagnosis, prevention, and control of animal diseases, the condition of animal health throughout the developing world remains generally poor, causing substantial economic losses and hindering any improvement in livestock productivity.

In many developing countries, animal healthcare services were established with the main objective of controlling major contagious and infectious diseases, such as foot-and-mouth disease, rinderpest, and contagious bovine and caprine pleuro-pneumonia, as well as parasitic diseases (such as trypanosomiasis and tick-borne diseases). This goal was obviously the first priority, because the control of these diseases is a prerequisite for any successful livestock development program. The successful control of disease depends initially on its timely and accurate recognition and on the presence of sound diagnostic capabilities based on effective working links between laboratories and field services. Emergencies created by outbreaks of major infectious diseases demonstrate the need for establishing and improving such diagnostic services. Particular attention should also be given to the development of an efficient animal disease information system.

In the immediate postcolonial period of the 1960s, the public-sector veterinary services of most developing countries were engaged in delivery of the full range of veterinary activities and services, with little or no participation by the private sector. By the mid-1980s, many of these countries were experiencing serious economic difficulties and were left with little choice but to accept structural adjustment policies (SAPs), linked to International Monetary Fund and World Bank loans. These SAPs sought to increase the role of the private sector in providing commercially based services that had previously been provided by the public sector. The rationale behind this policy was that market-oriented economies and any form of private enterprise would be likely to outperform the public sector. In the agricultural and especially the livestock sectors, SAPs have resulted in reduced investment in capital and recurrent expenditures. This outcome in turn led to a drive for the privatization of veterinary services, with the aim of diminishing the role of the state in these activities. Animal health was seen as a private good, and veterinary services were seen essentially as providing an animal healthcare delivery system. The sale of veterinary medicines and vaccines and the provision of clinical services or vaccinations were thus at the forefront of privatization programs. Surveillance, early warning, laboratory diagnostic services, planning, regulation, management of disease-control programs, and assurance of the quality and safety of animal products became secondary considerations (FAO 2002).

Thus an institutional vacuum developed in the supply of animal healthcare services and veterinary inputs in the rural and more remote areas of most developing countries, where the majority of livestock is to be found. The casual stance adopted by many governments, allowing the privatization process to evolve passively, has resulted in this vacuum being filled by informal delivery systems (or by donors and nongovernmental organizations). These informal systems give livestock keepers ready access to prescription-only medicines, often of questionable quality, which they administer to their animals themselves with insufficient regard for informed diagnosis or correct treatment regimens.

It is against this general background that this case study presents an analysis of the emerging pattern of animal healthcare services delivery after liberalization in Kenya. Largely following from the neoliberal market thinking of the 1980s, service delivery through the private sector was considered more or less a panacea for redressing government failure in delivering animal healthcare services. The case study illustrates how the process of reform in this crucial input market was informed by a good understanding of the economic characteristics of animal healthcare services.

The reforms focused on defining clear roles for both the public and private sectors in the delivery of these services: the public sector would be responsible for provision of services with public goods characteristics, leaving those with private goods characteristics to the private sector. This case study illustrates how the framework for the analysis of institutions developed in Chapter 3 can also be used in analyzing the market for inputs and service delivery to farmers.

11.1   Characteristics and Attributes of Animal Health Services

It is useful to discuss the economic characteristics and attributes of animal healthcare services to help define the distribution of responsibilities between the public and private sectors, because these services can be delivered both by government veterinary staff (completely or partly free of charge) or by private veterinarians (usually at cost). Broadly speaking, the spectrum of animal healthcare services includes preventive and control and/or inspection programs and the treatment of sick animals. The most important tier of the animal healthcare service structure is the field animal healthcare service, which is in direct contact with producers, animals, and their products. The work done at the village, farm, herd or flock, and individual animal levels is decisive for any animal healthcare program.

Animal healthcare services can typically be classified as private or public goods, depending on who receives the benefits (Leonard 1993). At one extreme are purely private goods, which (1) only benefit the animal owner receiving the service; (2) can be enjoyed exclusively by that owner (the exclusion principle); and (3) when provided, exclude somebody else from that service at that particular time (the rival principle). For example, clinical treatment for a wound or worms would qualify as a pure private good, because the treatment benefits only the owner of that animal, and it excludes other farmers from the services of the veterinarian at that time. In contrast, such services as quarantine and meat inspection are pure public goods, as they do not directly benefit the owner of the animal and do not exclude other producers from that service.

As a rule, the higher the private benefit, the more justified it is to have the beneficiary pay for the service directly and to transfer the service to the private sector. Public-sector management of private-good services is justified if economies of scale are an important consideration or if sophisticated expertise or equipment is needed. In such cases, the services should be financed through direct payment from the beneficiaries and not from general revenue.

Pure public good services typically involve market failures, externalities, or moral hazards and should be managed by the public sector (although subcontracting to private operators is always possible) and financed by the general public revenue. Such activities as meat inspection approximate a purely public service and should therefore be financed and managed by public resources. Other examples of pure public goods include veterinary public health care and prevention, control, or eradication of major epidemic livestock diseases that have the potential to affect the national economy through high production losses, losses in export trade, or food insecurity at a national level. Individual farmers (particularly poor and marginalized farmers) and private providers of animal health care are relatively powerless to protect themselves from these diseases, which require a national or even international approach for their control. This approach should also include the prevention and control of zoonotic diseases and other food-safety issues that could cause substantial public health concerns in communities. The control of the tsetse fly, which transmits cattle trypanosomiasis, is one important example.

Between these extremes, there is a continuum of diseases and animal health concerns with varying public and private attributes. Brucellosis, for example, is a classic zoonotic disease with high infection rates in rural populations. It frequently affects whole families in a short time, causing severe disability and family crisis, because most of the wage earners will be sick simultaneously. If medical treatment is not sought or available, the disease results in significant economic loss to individuals and countries. There is a clearly recognized public good in controlling this disease in livestock, the only source of infection for humans. Brucellosis species cause abortion and decreased lactation in female cattle or small ruminants, so prevention is clearly a private good for livestock owners. Both individual owners and the public sector could have obligations to pay the costs of controlling this disease.

One important aspect of animal healthcare service delivery that complicates the decision on who should provide or pay for the service relates to the externalities produced by these services. Externalities are spillover effects from production or consumption of a given service. Markets may be ill equipped to allocate resources optimally when externalities exist. Typically, therefore, either too little (in the case of a positive externality) or too much (in the case of a negative one) is produced or consumed in the absence of a price mechanism to determine the value of these externalities. A vaccination for control of epidemics is an example of a service with a positive externality. Controlling the spread of foot-and-mouth disease or rinderpest in a given region checks the spread to other regions. As another example, cattle dips designed for the treatment of ticks and tick-borne diseases (especially East Coast fever in East Africa) produce predominantly private benefits. However, if participation is low, the population of ticks resistant to the acaricide may increase and pose a threat to all farmers, including those participating in the program. Because of these externalities, there is a public element in a dipping program, suggesting the need for some state involvement.

An additional attribute of animal healthcare services is the existence of economies of scale, which relate to the research and production of vaccines, veterinary drugs, and supplies and to individual veterinary practices. All entail significant indivisible fixed costs that are diminished with increasing scale of operation and sales. The cost of input delivery is at times increased substantially as a result of widely dispersed farmers. Under such circumstances, natural monopolies enjoying economies of scale deliver the inputs at a comparatively lower cost. However, net welfare losses arise from monopolistic market structures, leading to a suboptimal allocation of resources.

Furthermore, the limited skills and knowledge of farmers about animal diseases and their diagnoses confirm a typical situation of information asymmetry, in which one party is better informed about the details of a given transaction than the other, providing scope for opportunistic behavior. An animal healthcare service provider is capable of administering expired vaccines or drugs to an animal without detection, because the farmer is not able to evaluate the quality of the drugs. Likewise, a service provider can recommend a more costly course of therapy to reap higher returns from a transaction.

Thus the roles of the private and public sectors in the delivery of animal healthcare services are not so clear-cut. Although recognizing the broad spectrum of animal healthcare services and the varied economic characteristics of different animal healthcare services, Gros (1994) points to the possible complementarities of the public and private sectors in the provision of animal healthcare services. In addition, Gros (1994) observes that although most services can be classified as private goods, public goods, or services that confer externalities, the original design of the animal healthcare services delivery system and the nature of most animal diseases in Africa mar this distinction. Most contagious diseases in Africa, such as foot-and-mouth disease or rinderpest, cannot be cured. However, vaccinations exist, and in some countries it is mandatory that the animal health authorities and farmers are alerted in the case of an outbreak. Whereas the diagnosis of such a disease by an animal healthcare specialist exhibits the rivalry principle, the control measures instituted, including vaccinations, confer positive externalities on neighboring farmers. According to Gros (1994), therefore, some curative services in Africa assume the character of a public good rather than a pure private one. Nevertheless, some curatives (such as treating a case of trypanosomiasis or a surgical intervention for delivering a calf by caesarean section) exhibit pure private good characteristics, because only the herd owner benefits and there are no externalities. Thus there is a need to take the characteristics of the disease, the intervention technology needed for prevention and cure, and the economic benefits flowing from the delivery of the service (all collectively referred to as the techno-economic characteristics of the activity or good) into account to determine the optimal delivery mode of animal healthcare services.

11.2   Case Study Method

Using the framework presented in Chapter 3, this case study examines the effects of changes in the policy and economic environment (the environment) on the delivery of animal healthcare services to two smallholder dairy production regions in Kenya, namely, Kilifi in the coastal lowland zone and Meru in the upper midland zone (the action domain). Data were obtained through a survey of 320 farm households selected through a random sampling technique. In addition, information was obtained from the population of animal healthcare service providers in the survey area and a review of secondary data.

Ndung'u (2002) followed a similar approach in analyzing the structure of the animal healthcare delivery market in the Kiambu, Nakuru, and Nyandarua districts of Kenya, and the results are also reported here. Both studies recognize the imperfect market structure as a key characteristic of the animal healthcare delivery market.

11.3   Structure of the Market for Animal Healthcare Services in Kenya

Although both the public and private sectors are involved in the delivery of animal healthcare and artificial insemination services in Kenya, there has been an increase in the number of private-sector players, especially in the importation and distribution of pharmaceutical products, in the postliberalization period (Ndung'u 2002). Most of these pharmaceutical companies import semifinished products for reconstitution or finished products for repackaging. In addition, most have specialized in the distribution of human medicine as a product line, although some also have distributed agrochemicals used in crop protection. Save for semen for artificial insemination services, where the government-owned Central Artificial Insemination Services remains a key player, most of the pharmaceutical and veterinary vector-control products are imported or manufactured and distributed by private companies. Likewise, at the lower channel levels, upcountry distributors and private retailers are the main source of these products (Figure 11.1).

The state regulatory authorities (the Pharmacy and Poisons Board or the Pest Control Products Board) should register all pharmaceutical products. At this level of the delivery chain, the role of the state is largely regulatory. The pharmaceutical companies use a network of distributors and retailers for their line products. More often than not, a single upcountry-based distributor serves several pharmaceutical companies, implying some degree of coordination. Likewise, a single retailer serves as a retail outlet for a variety of products from different pharmaceutical companies. The distributors and retailers are the main source of veterinary inputs to service providers and farmers.

Figure 11.1   Market intermediaries and delivery channels for veterinary products

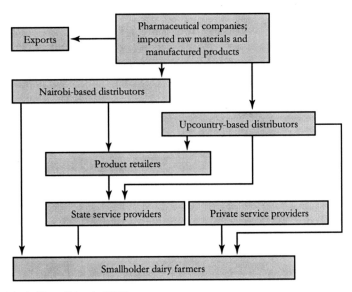

Source: Adapted from Ndung'u (2002).

At the point of delivery, both the private and public sectors are involved in the delivery of a variety of animal healthcare services. Although both sectors provide clinical services, advice on vector control is mainly provided by the government. The level of formal training of service providers varies from professional veterinarians to animal healthcare technicians. Animal healthcare specialists in the public sector are posted according to geographical region, following a clear hierarchical structure based on level of professional qualification. Professional veterinarians supervise a number of paraprofessionals or veterinary technicians, thereby complementing one another in delivering services to livestock producers. Although some services remain the responsibility of professional veterinarians—including complicated clinical diagnosis, cases requiring major surgery, and prescription of veterinary drugs (classified as "ethicals")—minor clinical cases, collection of samples, and routine herd health management are handled by paraprofessionals. Government records indicate that the ratio of professionals to paraprofessionals is 1:10 in Meru and 1:7 in Kilifi. Likewise Ndung'u (2002) indicates a ratio of veterinarians to paraveterinarians of 1:4, 1:2, and 2:3 for Nyandarua, Nakuru, and Kiambu, respectively. Undeniably, therefore, the paraprofessionals are the predominant service provider at the farm level.

Figure 11.2 indicates the main sources of animal healthcare services by service provider type and level of formal qualifications in Meru and Kilifi. These include professional veterinarians, who are trained to degree level; paraveterinarians, who usually hold a certificate of training ranging from a few months to 2 years from animal healthcare training institutes and may be animal healthcare assistants (AHA) or junior animal healthcare assistants (JAHA); and village animal health scouts with no formal training, but who have acquired their skills through years of experience, otherwise known as *wasaidizi* (Kiswahili for "helper"). Other sources of animal healthcare services include fellow farmers and relatives.

The two studies reveal that there are very few private veterinary practices operating in the smallholder dairy production systems of Kenya. However, some paraprofessionals are increasingly setting up unlicensed practices with the minimum equipment required for the delivery of clinical services. Veterinary professionals in the public sector have traditionally engaged in private clinical work since the pre-independence period. Even with the advent of subsidized government clinical services, budgetary constraints limited the capacity of the government clinics. Therefore, most of the public-sector service providers have gradually expanded routine moonlighting[1] into fully-fledged private activities. Consequently, routine government work turned into private activity during office hours. The survey work in Kilifi and Meru revealed that animal healthcare practitioners in the government service spend a significant proportion of their time on private clinical practice using government facilities.

Figure 11.2   Sources of animal healthcare services

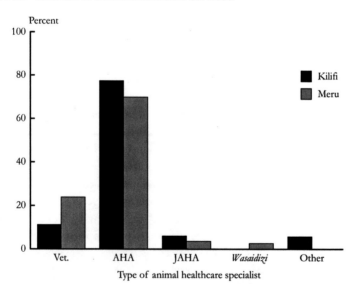

Notes: AHA, animal healthcare assistant; JAHA, junior animal healthcare assistant; *wasaidizi*, helper; vet., veterinarian.

Access to government-owned equipment and facilities by public-sector service providers operating in their private capacity causes a distortion in the animal health-care delivery market. Table 11.1 indicates that even in those cases when service providers in the public sector own some equipment, their levels of investment are far lower than that of their counterparts in private practice. Arguably, the public sector may be obliged to provide a form of production subsidy to animal healthcare service providers, especially where markets are too thin to support fully fledged private practices. In the present case, however, this policy is not that of the government, because private veterinary practices are not subsidized. Instead, the practice is a typical agency problem, in which service providers engage in hidden action, because the government does not condone their extraction of economic rent from their privileged positions. Besides their salaries and allowances, the public-sector service providers have access to government facilities and equipment that could create barriers to entry for private practitioners (Table 11.2).

Table 11.1 Average levels of investment by professional veterinarians (U.S. dollars)

Asset	Private sector		Public sector	
	Meru	Kilifi	Meru	Kilifi
Motor vehicle	3,000	2,667	0	0
Surgical kit	500	750	83	50
Refrigerator	1,167	250	0	0
Furniture	833	333	0	0
Other items	333	333	100	0
Total	5,833	4,333	183	50

Source: Oruko (1999).

Table 11.2 Items provided by the public sector

Item	Nature of unintended subsidy
Office rent and furniture	Public-sector practitioners operate from a government office
Telephone	Clients mostly call; specialists just receive
License fees	Public-sector practitioners do not need a license
Vehicle purchase and maintenance	Where available, the government meets the cost of purchase and maintenance
Fuel	Farmers often meet the fuel cost when specialists attend a case
Laboratory and refrigeration facilities	Practitioners based at Veterinary Investigation Laboratories or at the district headquarters with a functional laboratory
Surgical equipment	Usually provided by the government
Client base	Public-sector practitioners are posted in a geographical area with a ready client base (no monetary value attached)

11.4   Market Imperfections and Asymmetric Information in the Animal Healthcare Market

The effects of asymmetric information on prices has been extensively analyzed in the human healthcare economics literature. A large number of studies in the United States have documented wide dispersions in physicians' fees in seemingly competitive markets (Feldstain 1970; McCarthy 1985; Rizzo and Zeckhauser 1992). These large dispersions have been interpreted as indicative of incomplete market information. Chawla (2002) indicates that for a variety of reasons, including information asymmetries and the urgent nature of consumption, patients in the market for human healthcare services face high search costs and therefore balance the prospect of finding a physician willing to accept lower fees against the cost of gathering the information and searching for the physician. The physician may also balance between charging a lower fee against losing the patient. In such a market, stable market equilibria may exist, with different physicians charging different prices for the same product (Chawla 2002). In New Institutional Economics (NIE) terms, both patients and doctors face transaction costs. The magnitude of costs may, however, not be sufficiently high to result in market failure in the developed world.

The framework of incomplete market information can be applied to the animal healthcare sector to analyze the service-seeking behavior of livestock farmers. In a full-information market, dairy farmers seeking healthcare services of a given quality should obtain them at the lowest cost possible. Likewise, income-maximizing animal healthcare service providers should be able to assess the farmers' willingness to pay and charge the maximum fees possible. However, in a market with information imperfections, dairy farmers may have a general knowledge of the price spread but not of the actual fees charged by each service provider. Consequently, they choose an optimal amount of search, balancing the cost of search with the amount of savings from finding a lower price. This strategy is especially common when there is a wide spectrum of service providers to choose from.

The animal healthcare service providers interviewed indicated that the cost of clinical and prophylactic services depended on a number of factors, including the nature of the disease, qualification of the healthcare practitioner, means of transportation, and perceived wealth of the client. A client's ability to pay—assessed by such criteria as type of housing, breed of animals, and farm layout—influences the fees for clinical services. Accordingly, the fees charged for a given service vary a great deal both within and across different service providers. This observation appears to be consistent with the behavior of physicians reported in Chwala (2000).

Most livestock farmers are either unable (or do not bother) to assess the professional qualification of animal healthcare service providers. The title "doctor," meant for a qualified professional veterinarian, is therefore used for all service providers, irrespective of their qualifications. The paraprofessionals working with the professionals often observe the rates charged by their supervisors for given cases and subsequently use these as guidelines for their own fee structures. Given the farmers' inability to differentiate between a professional veterinarian and a paraprofessional, uniform charges are often levied to specific clients. By the same token, most animal healthcare practitioners do not clearly itemize their charges into transportation costs, professional fees, and margins on drugs. In fact, few professional veterinarians and paraprofessionals fix their professional fees for cases, even though guidelines are provided by the Kenya Veterinary Association (KVA). The general trend is to consolidate the charges into a single fixed fee, and farmers are often made to believe they are paying for the drugs rather than for a professional service.

As a result, dairy farmers face ex ante search and information costs in the animal healthcare delivery market. It is hypothesised that transaction cost is one of the key factors influencing the choice of animal healthcare service provider. Several studies have analyzed the effect of transaction costs on market participation and choice of market outlet in the product markets (Goetz 1995; Hobbs 1997). Most of these studies employ binary choice econometric models using indicator variables to capture the elements of transaction cost. Oruko (2001) employed a probit model to examine the probability that a farmer will consult a veterinarian. Distance to the nearest alternative clinic run by a paraprofessional and frequency of use of animal healthcare services positively influenced the probability of consulting a veterinarian (Table 11.3). Similar results were obtained with paraveterinarian specified as the dependent variable. These results suggest that professional qualification is not critical in the choice of service provider.

Likewise, Ndung'u (2002) employed a probit model, specifying both the frequency of previous contact and ethnicity—key information-indicator variables—as explanatory variables to predict a farmer's probability of using a veterinarian. Density of veterinarians in a particular zone, ethnicity of a service provider, and frequency of previous contact all positively influenced the probability of consulting a professional veterinarian. By the same token, ethnicity and density positively influenced the probability of farmers consulting paraveterinarians (Table 11.4). Irrespective of the level of professional qualification, service providers of similar ethnic background to their clients commanded a higher degree of trust from the farmers. The above results appear to be consistent with the findings by Ahuja et al. (2000), who examined the quality of veterinary services from three categories of service providers in three provinces of India using two indicators: degree of accuracy in diagnosis and prescription, and the success rate of the services (measured by the proportion of total service provider visits that result in the animal's recovery). Results showed no significant differences among government, private, and cooperative services, and the study concluded

Table 11.3   Significant variables influencing the probability of using a veterinarian

Significant variable	Coefficient (β)	Standard error	z-Score
Region (Kilifi)	−0.261***	0.008	−2.541
Distance to alternative source of animal healthcare services	0.051**	0.030	4.215
Frequency of use of animal healthcare services in the past 12 months	0.122**	0.201	2.838
Household head educated to tertiary level	−0.318*	0.524	3.568

Least likelihood = −237.711
Pseudo R^2 = .1220
Model c^2 = 26.28

Notes: * indicates significance at the 10 percent level, ** at the 5 percent level, and *** at the 1 percent level.

that characteristics of the service provider do not explain variations in the quality of services.

As indicated earlier, the scope for opportunistic behavior does exist in the presence of information asymmetries. The Oruko (2001) and Ndung'u (2002) studies reveal that frequency of transactions and ethnicity are key factors determining the choice of service provider. Following repeated transactions, farmers are better able to assess the quality of services provided by a given provider. Trust based on reputation is thus built among the transacting parties. Likewise, members of a similar ethnic group belong to the same social networks. Accordingly, trust is viewed as a source of social capital. According to Dyer (1997), noncontractual trust, such as goodwill, eliminates the need for formal contracts, which are costly to write, monitor, and enforce. When trust exists, transacting parties spend less time and resources on ex ante contracting and monitoring to see whether the other party is shirking, because they trust that pay-off will be divided fairly.

Table 11.4   Transaction-cost variables and use of a vet (Kiambu, Nyandarua, Nakuru)

Significant variable	Coefficient (β)	Standard error	z-Score
Farmer perception of service quality	0.207*	0.108	1.907
Density of veterinarians in the area	0.117**	0.030	3.950
Travel time to the nearest veterinarian	−0.004**	0.001	−3.330
Veterinarian belongs to the same ethnic group as client	0.604**	0.218	2.766

Least likelihood = −199.288
Pseudo R^2 =.1124
Model c^2 = 50.49

Source: Ndung'u (2002).

Notes: * indicates significance at the 10 percent level and ** at the 5 percent level.

11.5   Challenges of Regulation

The responsibility for regulation and quality control is vested in the public sector and the Kenya Veterinary Board. Only qualified veterinary surgeons with a degree in veterinary medicine are allowed to practice by law. Private veterinary practices are registered only after meeting the recommended standards in terms of equipment and location of clinic. Based on these recommendations, KVA provides investment guidelines for start-up clinics. In addition, KVA provides periodic fee guidelines for private practitioners. Table 11.5 shows the recommended minimum level of investment by KVA. The majority of the start-up clinics operated by professional veterinarians barely meet the minimum registration requirements. Even the highly capitalized clinics (Table 11.1) do not meet the recommended levels of investment. Clearly there is a need to review these requirements, because some of the equipment, especially diagnostic facilities, could be provided by government laboratories at a fee.

The greater regulatory challenge is posed by the paraprofessionals in private practice. Traditionally, paraprofessionals provided services under the supervision of a professional veterinarian and, as indicated earlier, they are limited to handling less complicated cases. However, the case study reveals that, except for cases requiring surgical procedure, the paraprofessionals do indeed attend to more complex cases, and farmers are largely satisfied with their performance. This development has caused concern at the policy level and among professionals. Given their level of training, paraprofessionals might not appreciate the possible impact of externalities generated by their activities, especially those associated with drug resistance. And in a bid to undercut the professional veterinarians, the paraprofessionals could adopt a price-competition strategy that is harmful to the industry. Evidence from the present

Table 11.5   Estimates by the Kenya Veterinary Association of the minimum recommended costs for establishing a clinic (U.S. dollars)

Item	Estimated cost
Motorcycle	4,167
Laboratory equipment	1,667
Drugs and vaccines	10,000
Salaries	3,000
Clinic rent	600
Telephone, electricity, and water	600
Fuel and repairs	1,000
Stationery	1,000
Sundries	1,000
Total	23,034

study indicates that these fears are largely unfounded. The paraprofessionals provide a much-needed service to smallholder farmers. Furthermore, there is more complementarity than competition between private- and public-sector paraprofessionals. However, the existing harmony tends to be based on goodwill rather than a clear institutional framework and could provide scope for opportunistic behavior.

Undeniably, the distribution of paraprofessionals exceeds that of professional veterinarians among smallholder farmers. However, although paraprofessionals live closer to farming communities and are therefore more accessible to farmers than professional veterinarians, they are only allowed to deliver a limited range of services, and legislation presently creates entry barriers to their participation in private practice. One way to use their service potential more effectively is to better develop their interface with veterinarians as a way of increasing penetration into rural communities and improving service quality. Veterinarians would have their clinics in their preferred locations and would support paraprofessionals in the more rural areas that the former would visit routinely to supply with drugs and attend to any cases that require their expertise. This coordination would also minimize transaction costs associated with service quality through the supervisory role of professionals. In addition, there is need for the formation of a regulatory professional body that includes the paraprofessionals in the animal healthcare market to address the potential of exploitation of paraprofessionals by professional veterinarians.

11.6 Methodological Note

This case study employed the NIE framework to analyze markets for animal healthcare services in Kenya. The study hypothesizes the existence of thin markets, widely distributed cattle keepers each with a small number of animals, poor infrastructure, and information asymmetry in the market. Accordingly, market reforms in the animal healthcare sector that presume the existence of competitive market structure are unlikely to generate the desired outcomes—effective and efficient mechanisms for coordinated exchange. Standard neoclassical economic analysis of input markets is therefore not suitable for this case study.

The case study uses cross-sectional data from a survey of farm households and animal healthcare service providers to analyze the market structure and delineate the significant transaction-cost elements in the exchange process. A binary choice model is estimated with proxies for transaction costs. Undeniably, the probit model is not robust enough to delineate the transaction costs faced by dairy farmers in Kenya. In addition, the proxy variables for transaction costs could be improved, given the current status of knowledge.

We therefore recommend that future empirical research in this area should employ more recent models, such as the linear selectivity model, to capture the sequential nature of farmer decisionmaking in the choice of animal healthcare service provider. We also recognize the limitations of cross-sectional data from a relatively small sample of households and market intermediaries. We recommend a study design that uses panel data from repeated transactions that distinguish transaction costs from variables for general marketing costs. Despite these areas for improvement, the case study provides an informative analysis based on the NIE principles of the animal healthcare market in Kenya.

Note

1. *Moonlighting* refers to working outside office hours for additional income.

References

Ahuja, V., P. S. George, S. Ray, K. E. McConnell, M. P. Kurup, V. Gandhi, D. L. Umali-Deininger, and C. de Haan. 2000. Agricultural services and the poor: Case of livestock health and breeding services in India. Ahmedabad, India; Washington, D.C.; Berne, Switzerland: Indian Institute of Management; World Bank; Swiss Agency for Development and Cooperation.

Chawla, M. 2002. Estimating the extent of patient ignorance of health care markets. *World Bank Economists Forum* 2: 3–24.

Dyer, J. H. 1997. Effective interfirm collaboration: How firms minimize transaction costs and maximize transaction value. *Strategic Management Journal* 18: 535–556.

FAO (Food and Agriculture Organization of the United Nations). 2002. *Improved animal health for poverty reduction and sustainable livelihoods.* FAO Animal Production and Health Paper 153. Rome.

Feldstain, M. 1970. The rising price of a physician's service. *Review of Economics and Statistics* 52 (5): 121–133.

Goetz, J. S. 1995. Markets, transaction costs and selectivity models in economic development. In *Prices, products and people: Analyzing agricultural markets in developing countries,* ed. J. Scott. Boulder, Colo., U.S.A.: Lynne Rienner.

Gros, J. G. 1994. Of cattle, farmers, veterinarians and the World Bank: The political economy of veterinary services privatization in Cameroon. *Public Administration and Development* 14: 37–51.

Hobbs, J. E. 1997. Measuring transaction costs in cattle marketing. *American Journal of Agricultural Economics* 79 (4): 1083–1095.

Leonard, D. K. 1993. Structural reform of the veterinary profession in Africa and the New Institutional Economics. *Development and Change* 24: 227–267.

McCarthy, T. R. 1985. The competitive nature of primary care physician's market. *Journal of Health Economics* 4 (2): 93–117.

Ndung'u, L. W. 2002. Assessing animal health delivery for tick and tick-borne diseases in Kenya: An application of the New Institutional Economics. Ph.D. thesis, University of Pretoria, South Africa.

Oruko, L. O. 1999. Delivery of animal health services in Kenya. Ph.D. thesis, University of Reading, U.K.

————. 2001. *Animal health services–seeking behaviour: The case of smallholder dairy producers.* Research report. Nairobi: Kenya Agricultural Research Institute.

Rizzo, J. A., and R. K. Zeckhauser. 1992. Advertising and the price, quantity and quality of primary care physician service. *Journal of Human Resources* 27 (3): 381–421.

Chapter 12

Networks and Informal Mutual Support in 15 Ethiopian Villages

John Hoddinott, Stefan Dercon, and Pramila Krishnan

Many factors inhibit the development of the agricultural sector in much of Sub-Saharan Africa: poor infrastructure, limited dissemination of new technologies, inappropriate government policy, and so on. One factor that is again receiving attention is that of uninsured risk. It is well understood that smallholders in Africa are exposed to a wide range of risks, including those deriving from climatic events, economic shocks (such as sudden drops in output prices or increases in input prices), illness and death, and social and political conflicts.[1] Not only is the threat of such adverse events pervasive, but also formal credit and insurance mechanisms in much of the subcontinent are badly underdeveloped.

Why should uninsured risk matter? A small but growing body of evidence points to the role that risk and shocks play in perpetuating poverty. Specifically, uninsured shocks—adverse events that are costly to individuals and households in terms of lost income, reduced consumption, or the sale or destruction of assets—are a cause of poverty. For example, even if shocks do not reduce asset holding, the threat of shocks discourages innovation and risk taking. It is true that many households

We thank the Food-For-Peace Office of the United States Agency for International Development and the World Food Programme for generously funding the survey work, and the Department for International Development (DfID) and Systemwide Program on Collective Action and Property Rights (CAPRi) for funding the analysis that underlies this chapter; in particular, we thank P. E. Balakrishnan, Robin Jackson, Ruth Meinzen-Dick, Malcolm Ridout, and Will Whelan for their support. We have benefited from superb research assistance from Yisehac Yohannes. The data used in this paper were collected in collaboration with the Economics Department, Addis Ababa University. It is a pleasure to acknowledge our primary collaborator, Tassew Woldehanna. Errors are ours.

have developed ways of insuring themselves against risk. But these methods come with high opportunity costs. Using household-level data from India, Bliss and Stern (1982) showed that a 2-week delay in planting following the onset of seasonal rains is associated with a 20 percent reduction in rice yields. Walker and Ryan (1990) find that in semi-arid areas of India, households may sacrifice up to 25 percent of their average incomes to reduce exposures to shocks. The liquidity of these assets may also affect entry into activities. For example, Dercon (1996) and Dercon and Krishnan (1996) find that in Ethiopia and Tanzania, the possession of more liquid assets, such as livestock, is a precondition for entry into higher return—but higher risk—activities. Further, the threat of shocks can make households reluctant to access credit markets, because they fear the consequences of an inability to repay. In one survey of the Amhara region of Ethiopia, 44 percent of households indicated that they did not borrow money, because they were concerned that they could not repay these loans (Gilligan, Hoddinott, and Taffesse 2007). Others are simply unable to obtain credit because they are perceived to be at risk of default.

Given the absence of formal mechanisms for dealing with shocks, is there a role for informal institutions? The large body of literature on collective action in developing countries (as discussed in Chapter 5) has run in parallel to a different literature that focuses on another means by which households cope with shocks—the use of networks and other forms of collective action. Although much of this literature initially focused on villages in their entirety as the means by which the adverse impacts of shocks were smoothed out (see Townsend 1995), such approaches were clearly a simplification. There is now considerable interest in the role that subvillage local networks play in protecting members from fluctuations in their incomes.

Why might such networks matter? And why are they of interest in a volume such as this? All societies rely on a mix of informal network-based institutions and more formal market-based exchanges. Sociologists and anthropologists have extensively documented the role of informal networks in Africa, but there is little understanding of the interlinkages among them and more formal government and market activities. Informal networks are, for example, where much of rural insurance and credit activity takes place. As Chapter 1 explains, they lie at one end of a continuum of institutional arrangements. They are, however, by their nature personalized and exclusive. Why and under what circumstances some people might be excluded from social networks is not known; when exclusionary, networks might not be benign.

Furthermore, as Dasgupta (2003) points out, transactions in informal networks have effects that spill over to other areas of economic activity. Some spillovers reflect synergies between the operations of networks and markets, for instance; but when markets and networks are substitutes, they will be antagonistic. When markets or other formal interventions displace networks, there might be people who suffer, but equally, this observation has a converse. Some kinds of networks might prevent markets from functioning well or even from coming into existence. These issues therefore call for careful design of economic interventions.

In short, if one accepts that addressing risk is an important component of any strategy designed to strengthen African agriculture, then understanding informal institutions—such as informal networks—is important, particularly for the development of effective antipoverty, agricultural, and rural development policies. A misunderstanding of the roles of these networks can lead to policy changes that have unintended consequences on the functioning of these networks, with potentially damaging effects on the capacity of the poor to mitigate, and cope with, the effects of shocks. At the same time, a better understanding of such networks can lead to the identification of policies that complement existing networks that already serve the poor well and to policies that can substitute for networks that simply are not reaching the poor.

This chapter provides a descriptive assessment of the role played by collective action through informal social networks that helps rural Ethiopians manage their exposure to risks and cope with shocks to their livelihoods. It describes the extent and correlates of these networks and the role played by credit in redressing the pernicious effects of shocks. Following the work by Dercon et al. (2004), it also describes the extent of *iddirs,* insurance institutions indigenous to Ethiopia that are used to cope with the high cost of funerals.

12.1 Data

Ethiopia is divided into 11 regions, each subdivided into zones. The zones are partitioned into *woredas* that are roughly equivalent to a county in the United States or the United Kingdom. *Woredas,* in turn, are divided into Peasant Associations (PAs) or *kebeles,* an administrative unit consisting of a number of villages. Our data are taken from the Ethiopia Rural Household Survey (ERHS), a unique longitudinal household dataset. Data collection started in 1989, when a survey team visited 6 PAs in central and southern Ethiopia. The survey was expanded in 1994 to encompass 15 PAs across four regions, yielding a sample of 1,477 households. An additional round was conducted in late 1994, with further rounds in 1995, 1997, 1999, and 2004.

As part of the survey redesign and extension that took place in 1994, the sample was rerandomized by including the same percentage of newly formed or arrived households in the sample as in the previous survey, as well as by replacing households lost to follow-up by those that were considered by village elders and officials as broadly similar in terms of demography and wealth. The nine additional PAs were selected to better account for the diversity in the farming systems found in Ethiopia. The sampling in the PAs newly included in 1994 was based on a list of all households, constructed with the help of the local PA officials. The sample was stratified within each village to ensure that a representative number of landless households was included. Similarly, the same percentage of female-headed households as in the previous survey was included by stratification.

Table 12.1 gives the details of the sampling frame and the actual proportions in the total sample. It shows that the population distributions in the sample are broadly consistent with the those in the three main sedentary farming systems—the plough-based cereals farming systems of the northern and central highlands, mixed plough/hoe cereals farming systems, and farming systems based on *enset* (a root crop) that is grown in southern parts of the country. In this way, the sampling frame was stratified by the main agro-ecological zones with one to three villages selected per strata. Furthermore, sample sizes in each village were chosen to approximate a self-weighting sample in terms of farming system: each person (approximately) represents the same number of persons found in the main farming systems as of 1994. However, results should not be taken as being nationally representative. The sample does not include pastoral households or urban areas. In addition, the practical aspects associated with running a longitudinal household survey when the sampled localities are as much as 1,000 km apart constrained sampling to only 15 communities in a country of thousands of villages. Therefore, although these data can be considered broadly representative of households in nonpastoralist farming systems as of 1994, extrapolation from these results should be done with care.

12.2 Networks: Basic Descriptive Statistics

In the 2004 survey round, households were asked to provide information on the five most important people, whether within or outside the village, on whom each household would rely for support. In addition, they were asked whether there were other

Table 12.1   Distribution of households in the Ethiopian Rural Household Survey, by agro-ecological zone

Zone	Population share in 1994 (percent)	Sample share in 1994 (percent)	Number of villages
Cereal plough complex: northern highlands	21.2	20.2	3
Cereal plough complex: central highlands	27.7	29.0	4
Cereal plough: Arsi/Bale region	9.3	14.3	2
Sorghum plough/hoe: Hararghe region	9.9	6.6	1
Enset (with or without coffee or cereals)	31.9	29.9	5
Total	100	100	15

Source: Dercon and Hoddinott (2004).

Note: There are 1,368 households in the sample. Percentages of population share relate to the rural sedentary population; they exclude pastoralists, who account for about 10 percent of total rural population.

people, beyond these five, who could be relied on for help in time of need. The links among each household and its friends describe a network, in which each person is a node, and the positions they occupy with respect to one another define the shape of the network.[2] Here descriptive statistics are provided on three dimensions of these networks: correlations between network size and observable household characteristics, characteristics of individuals in a household's network, and the extent to which networks consist of like or dissimilar households.

Virtually all households—91 percent—report that there is at least one person they can rely on for assistance. The median number of people in a households' network is 5, with about a quarter of households reporting that they have 2 or fewer people in their network and a smaller percentage (16 percent) reporting 10 or more people in their network. There is some evidence that households do indeed call on these networks. Respondents indicate that they received help from 86 percent of the individuals they list as part of their network. Furthermore, there is some evidence of reciprocity in these relationships: in 75 percent of the individuals listed as being in a household's network, households had both received and provided assistance in the past. Fewer than 10 percent of individuals listed as part of a network neither rendered nor received assistance.

Does access to networks vary by observable household characteristics? Although it is possible to construct descriptive tables, their interpretation is difficult. For example, female-headed households have smaller networks—a mean size of 5.8 compared to a mean size of 7.3 for male-headed households. However, larger households tend to have larger networks, and female-headed households have, on average, fewer members than male-headed ones, so that it is unclear whether the smaller network size of the former is due to their being female-headed or being smaller. For this reason, regression analysis was used to assess the associations between household characteristics and the likelihood that a household has a network as well as the size of that network.

Results are presented in Table 12.2. The first column reports the results of estimating a probit in which the dependent variable equals 1 if the household has at least one person in its network and is 0 otherwise. To make the coefficients readily interpretable, the marginal effects of the regressors are reported in column (1). In columns (2) and (3), the determinants of the size of the household's network are reported. Because the estimates must account for the censoring at 0 of the dependent variable, a tobit estimator is used, which is reported in column (2). However, estimates derived from a tobit are suspect if the underlying disturbance terms are non-normally distributed, so the results of estimating Powell's (1984) censored least absolute deviations model are also reported.

The first result that can be deduced from Table 12.2 is that few household characteristics are associated with an increased or decreased likelihood that a household

Table 12.2   Correlates of the presence of networks and their sizes

Variable	(1) Probit[a]	(2) Tobit[b]	(3) Censored least absolute deviations[c]
Household is in second landholding quintile[d]	0.037	0.039	0.607
	(1.11)	(0.04)	(1.21)
Household is in third landholding quintile[d]	0.038	0.527	0.685
	(1.40)	(0.60)	(1.32)
Household is in fourth landholding quintile[d]	0.052	1.904	1.856
	(1.97)**	(2.18)**	(3.97)**
Household is in highest landholding quintile[d]	0.028	3.037	1.726
	(1.18)	(3.07)**	(2.52)**
Log of age of household head	−0.039	0.357	−0.114
	(1.34)	(0.34)	(0.17)
Female-headed household[d]	−0.004	−0.938	−0.212
	(0.31)	(1.29)	(0.51)
Household head has schooling[d]	0.022	2.081	0.951
	(1.16)	(2.57)**	(1.78)*
Log of household size	−0.009	1.302	0.443
	(0.70)	(2.15)**	(1.27)
Household head born in this village[d]	0.0002	−1.164	−0.682
	(0.02)	(1.59)	(1.57)
Mother or father was important person in social life of village[d]	−0.008	0.814	0.977
	(0.53)	(1.24)	(2.52)**
Relative holds official position	0.021	1.378	1.111
	(1.42)	(2.22)**	(2.72)**
Father belonged to an *iddir*[d]	0.047	2.395	0.878
	(2.12)**	(3.38)**	(2.13)**
Household belongs to an ethnic minority in Peasant Association[d]	−0.012	−0.582	0.309
	(0.51)	(0.60)	(0.52)
Household belongs to a religious minority in Peasant Association[d]	−0.004	0.988	0.100
	(0.30)	(1.22)	(0.20)

Notes: * indicates significance at the 10 percent level and ** significance at the 5 percent level. Peasant Association dummies are included but not reported. Sample size is 1,227.

[a]Dependent variable is: household has at least one person in network. Results of probit are presented in terms of marginal effects of regressors; dummy variables measure marginal impact of switching from 0 to 1. Absolute values of z-statistics are in parentheses. Standard errors are robust to locality cluster effects.

[b]Dependent variable is: number of people in household's network. Absolute values of t-statistics are in parentheses.

[c]Dependent variable is: number of people in household's network. Absolute values of t-statistics are in parentheses. Standard errors use a bootstrap with 1,000 replications.

[d]Covariate is a dummy variable.

has at least one person in its network. The only statistically significant characteristics are whether the household's landholdings lie in the fourth (second highest) quintile in the village and whether the father of the household head belonged to an *iddir*. These characteristics marginally increase (by 4.7 percent) the likelihood that the household has at least one person in its network. Second, being wealthier, defined in terms of landholdings, is associated with bigger networks. Using the parameter estimates reported in column (3), households in the fourth and top landholding quintiles have one or two more people in their networks compared to households in the bottom quintile of landholdings. Third, larger households have larger networks. Fourth, family background plays some role in influencing network size. Having a parent who was an important person in the social life of the village, a relative who holds an official position in the village, and having a father who belonged to an *iddir* all increase the mean number of persons in a household's network. Households belonging to ethnic or religious minorities do not appear to have smaller networks.

Table 12.3 provides descriptive statistics on some of the characteristics of individuals found in these networks. Most individuals in these networks are neighbors (60 percent) or, if not neighbors, live in the same village (27 percent). Just over a quarter have at least one plot of land adjacent to a plot held by the household. Only 13 percent of individuals in a household's network reside outside the village. The most common relationship is that of being a relative or being a member of the same *iddir;* indeed, only 12 percent of network members are neither relatives nor members of the same *iddir*. Network members are often (49 percent) individuals whom previously the household had borrowed from or lent to. They are unlikely to be individuals with whom the household sharecrops, hires in or hires out labor, or buys or sells crops.

Table 12.4 provides additional descriptive statistics. Here the focus is on the extent to which other network members are similar or dissimilar to the respondents, where comparative measures of wealth and age are considered. Slightly more than 40 percent of other network members have more land than the respondent household,

Table 12.3 Characteristics of individuals in a household's network (percent)

Characteristic of other individuals in network	Proportion of members with characteristic
Neighbors	60
Not neighbors, but in same village	27
Not neighbors, live outside village	13
Have plot(s) of land next to plots belonging to this household	28
Members of the same social group	21
Relative	66
Belong to same *iddir*	57
Neither relative nor member of same *iddir*	12
Members of same labor-sharing group	43
Partners in sharecropping or land-renting arrangement	6
Partners in oxen-sharing arrangement	23
Members of same *iqqub*	7
Borrow or lend money	49
Do wage work	7
Buy or sell crops	4

Note: A total of 1,368 households reported information on 4,951 individuals who form part of their networks.

about a quarter have the same amount, and a third have less. The top panel in Table 12.4 cross-tabulates land ownership (by quintile) against the amount of land held by the household in the network. Poorer households tend to have relatively better-off households in their networks, and richer households tend to have relatively poorer households in theirs. The bottom panel compares household ownership of oxen to that of individuals in the household's network. Unlike land, there appears to be some sorting by asset ownership: households with no oxen or only one animal tend to have as network partners similar households. Households with two or more oxen typically have as network partners other households with two or more oxen.

The analysis on the distribution of the differences in age between the household head and other individuals in the network who are either relatives or members of the same *iddir* shows that the modal age differences for both are close to 0. However, although the distribution for age differences among *iddir* members is more peaked than for relatives, both are characterized by a considerable spread around this mode.

To summarize, nearly all households in the ERHS report that they have a network of individuals whom they can call on for help. These networks consist largely of other households in the same village, which suggests that the scope for addressing covariate risks is likely to be limited. Individuals in these networks appear to engage in reciprocal assistance. Furthermore, they typically have other ties; in particular, they are relatives, members of the same *iddir*, or members of the same labor-sharing group.[3] Better-off households tend to have larger networks, as do households whose relations (parents or other relatives) had either status or connections in the village. Network heterogeneity is mixed: network members tend to be varied when measured by age or land ownership but not by ownership of oxen.[4]

Table 12.4   Wealth characteristics of other individuals in networks: land and oxen (percent)

	Other household in network has		
Quintile of landownership of respondent household	More land	About the same	Less land
Poorest quintile	53	21	26
Second quintile	43	22	35
Third quintile	40	24	36
Fourth quintile	36	25	39
Richest quintile	31	25	44

	Other household in network owns		
Respondent household owns	No oxen	One ox	Two or more oxen
No oxen	49	21	30
One ox	26	34	40
Two or more oxen	18	17	65

Note: Household landownership quintiles are listed in ascending order of wealth.

12.3   Informal Credit

Credit as insurance can be a means by which households can use networks to smooth out the adverse effects of shocks that might otherwise lead to reductions in consumption, asset depletion, or both.[5] More than half the households in the ERHS report borrowing at least 20 birr (equivalent to payment for 2–3 days of unskilled agricultural labor) in the previous 12 months from either formal or informal sources. Among households that borrowed, about three-quarters obtained one loan, another 19 percent borrowed twice, and the remaining 7 percent had three or more loans.

The most common reason for borrowing money was to purchase inputs, such as seeds, fertilizers, and pesticides. Here we focus on loans that were largely used for consumption: to buy food or other goods for the household or to pay for travel, health, education, or wedding or funeral expenses. Descriptive data are provided in Table 12.5. The dominant use of these consumption loans is to either buy food or other goods or to pay for health-related expenses. Median loan size is 100 birr for the former and 80 birr for the latter, although a small number of loans are taken out for larger amounts. Loan sizes are given in fixed amounts, as seen in the peaks in the distribution of loan sizes around 100, 200, 300 birr, and so on. Virtually all these loans were from informal sources. Just over a third (37 percent) came from relatives, 28 percent came from friends or relatives, 15 percent from an *iddir*, 11 percent from moneylenders, and 9 percent from other sources.

Among the 46 percent of households who did not borrow, half stated that they did not need to borrow, 32 percent did not borrow because they were concerned that they could not pay back a loan or feared losing their collateral, 9 percent indicated that there was no one from whom they could borrow, 2 percent either expected to be rejected so that they did not try to borrow or believed they had no collateral necessary for a loan, and the remaining 8 percent gave a variety of other reasons. A

Table 12.5   Characteristics of consumption loans

Loan purpose	Mean loan size (birr)	Median loan size (birr)	Share of consumption loans used for this purpose (percent)	Share of all loans used for this purpose (percent)
Buy food or goods for household	172	100	48	18
Pay travel expenses	146	100	3	1
Pay health expenses	117	80	27	10
Pay education expenses	335	120	7	3
For wedding	393	230	6	2
For funeral	139	80	9	4

Notes: There were 375 loans taken out for consumption purposes by the 1,368 households in the sample. Loan size calculations exclude the 5 percent of loans taken out in-kind.

question that arises is whether households who wished to borrow, but did not, also experienced shocks that caused them to lose income, reduce consumption, or sell assets. Table 12.6 provides some details.

Table 12.6 indicates that between 16 and 20 percent of households reported being adversely affected by insufficient rainfall, pests that attacked crops or livestock, death, or illness. Between 50 and 60 percent of households who were affected by these shocks borrowed money. However, a significant percentage of households—40 to 63 percent, depending on the shock—who did not borrow indicated that they wished to borrow funds but either did not (largely out of fear that they could not repay the loans) or could not. These credit constraints were most severe among poorer households. Forty-one percent of households with no oxen who were affected by one of these shocks and who did not borrow indicated that they wished to do so but did not or could not, compared to 15 percent of households with two or more oxen.

12.4 Membership in *Iddirs*

A widespread institution in Ethiopia is the *iddir,* a funeral association that pays out to the family of the deceased, in cash or in kind, when a member or a relative of a member dies. These payouts are funded by contributions made to the *iddir* by its members. A striking feature of these organizations is their degree of formality; often there are written rules and records of contributions and payouts (Dercon et al. 2004; see also Dejene 1993; Pankhurst 2003).

Outside of Tigray (a region in northern Ethiopia), *iddir* membership is widespread, with nearly 90 percent of households reporting that they belong to at least one *iddir.* Among households who report belonging to an *iddir* (and again excluding Tigray, where *iddirs* do not exist), just fewer than 60 percent report belonging to one *iddir,* 21 percent belong to two, and another 20 percent belong to three or more. Of the 132 households (11 percent of the sample) indicating that they did not belong to an *iddir,* 49 (37 percent) stated that they had no need for *iddir* membership, and 51

Table 12.6 Shocks and credit constraints (percent)

Shock	Share of households reporting this shock in last 12 months	Share of households reporting shock who borrowed for any purpose	Share of nonborrowing households reporting shock who would have liked to borrow but did not
Insufficient rain	20	60	63
Crop or livestock pests	17	58	47
Death	16	55	40
Illness	19	54	49

Note: There are 1,368 households in the sample.

(39 percent) claimed that they could not afford to join. Virtually all *iddirs* (93 percent) are situated in PAs. Two-thirds of *iddirs* appear to have no restrictions on membership beyond paying the necessary dues and fees, 14 percent were restricted to members of the same church or mosque, 6 percent were restricted to women, and 14 percent had some other restriction. All villages had at least one *iddir* that was open to anyone.

Table 12.7 uses probits and ordered probits to examine the correlates of membership in *iddirs*. Wealthier households are more likely to join an *iddir* and to join

Table 12.7   Correlates of membership in *iddirs*

Variable	(1) Probit[a]	(2) Ordered probit[b]
Household is in second landholding quintile[c]	0.014	0.248
	(0.23)	(2.02)**
Household is in third landholding quintile[c]	0.028	0.269
	(1.93)*	(2.22)**
Household is in fourth landholding quintile[c]	0.030	0.348
	(3.58)**	(2.53)**
Household is in wealthiest landholding quintile[c]	0.018	0.190
	(1.66)*	(1.47)
Log of age of household head	0.011	0.105
	(0.55)	(0.53)
Female-headed household[c]	−0.008	−0.018
	(0.61)	(0.15)
Household head has schooling[c]	0.030	0.213
	(1.77)*	(2.23)**
Log of household size	0.069	0.576
	(5.31)**	(6.12)**
Household head born in this village[c]	−0.007	−0.166
	(0.57)	(1.69)*
Mother or father was important person in social life of village[c]	−0.0005	0.036
	(0.04)	(0.42)
Relative holds official position	0.015	0.177
	(1.35)	(2.39)**
Father belonged to an *iddir*[c]	0.055	0.210
	(2.91)**	(2.24)**
Household belongs to an ethnic minority in Peasant Association[c]	−0.017	0.102
	(1.35)	(0.53)
Household belongs to a religious minority in Peasant Association[c]	0.014	0.141
	(0.66)	(0.70)

Notes: * indicates significance at the 10 percent level and ** significance at the 5 percent level. Absolute values of *z*-statistics are in parentheses. Standard errors are robust to locality cluster effects. Peasant Association dummies are included but not reported. Sample size is 1,132.

[a]Dependent variable is: household has at least one person in an *iddir*. Results are presented in terms of the marginal effects of the regressors. Dummy variables measure marginal impact of switching from 0 to 1.

[b]Dependent variable is: number of *iddirs* household belongs to. If the number of *iddirs* is more than three, then the variable is set to 3.

[c]Covariate is a dummy variable.

Table 12.8   Events for which *iddirs* make payouts or offer loans (percent)

Event	Share of *iddirs* that give a cash transfer	Share of *iddirs* that offer a loan
Funeral	100	9
Fire	20	9
Loss of oxen or other livestock	7	3
Destruction of house	6	4
Wedding	5	5
Illness	10	15
Harvest loss	3	2
Other event	6	1
Any event	34	25

Notes: There are 1,368 households in the sample. Households report membership in 1,967 *iddirs*.

more of them. However, the magnitude of these effects is not large; a household in the fourth land-owning quintile in a village is only 3 percent more likely to belong to an *iddir* than a household in the omitted category (households in the poorest land-owning quintile). Larger households and households in which the father of the head had been an *iddir* member are more likely to join *iddirs*. Being a female-headed household or belonging to either an ethnic or religious minority appears to have no statistically significant impact on the likelihood or extent of *iddir* membership.

Iddirs provide cash in the event of a funeral. The median amount that is paid out by the *iddirs* that our households belong to is 100 birr. However, a third of the *iddirs* these households belong to also provide cash payouts to their members when they have experienced other types of adverse shocks, and a quarter offer loans. As Table 12.8 shows, the most common form of assistance, apart from funerals, is cash payouts in cases of fire. Ten percent of *iddirs* provide cash in case of illness, and 15 percent provide loans. A smaller percentage of *iddirs* provide cash transfers or loans if the member has lost oxen or other livestock, lost their house, or are paying for a wedding or some other event.

12.5   Summary

Addressing risk is an important component of any strategy designed to strengthen African agriculture. Given the failures in markets for credit and insurance, understanding how informal institutions—such as informal networks—help small farmers cope with risks and shocks is of value. As explained in the introduction, a misunderstanding of the roles of these networks can lead to policy changes that have unintended consequences. Conversely, a better understanding of such networks helps identify policies that complement existing pro-poor networks or substitute for nonexistent ones.

This chapter discusses a case study of networks in rural Ethiopia—institutions that, as described in Chapter 1, lie at one end of a continuum of institutional arrangements. It shows that many Ethiopian households belong to some type of network that provides assistance in times of need. These networks are composed primarily of other individuals who live in the same geographical location. Often, members of these networks share characteristics, such as kinship, or membership in other organizations, such as *iddirs* or labor-sharing groups. These networks are well suited for providing mutual insurance against idiosyncratic shocks. For example, *iddirs* are a form of life insurance—paying out money to the family of the deceased, in cash or in kind, when a member or relation of a member dies. Some *iddirs* provide assistance in the event of other shocks, such as fire and illness. The overlap of network membership with other interactions provides opportunities to monitor behavior and thus address concerns over moral hazard (an exception being shocks affecting crops, because relatively few network members share adjoining fields, and so monitoring of crops and harvests is less easy) but not against covariate shocks, given that few network members reside outside the village. Some households do use these networks as a means of obtaining credit for food or health expenses. However, a number of households, especially poorer ones, do not borrow even when they experience a shock, out of fear that they cannot repay the loan.

Notes

1. Dercon, Hoddinott, and Woldehanna (2005) describe the incidence of shocks and their consequences in rural Ethiopia.

2. Krishnan and Sciubba (2004, 2005) examine the role of both connections and structure of networks on outcomes, arguing that the number of connections alone cannot capture the impact of networks. Krishnan and Sciubba (2005) explore the formation of informal insurance networks, arguing that the architecture and size of such networks is driven by both the level and distribution of individual endowments.

3. Krishnan and Sciubba (2004) examine the formation of labor-sharing networks and find that heterogeneity in endowments is associated with asymmetric network architecture (as predicted), whereas homogeneity is associated with symmetric structures in which network partners have similar numbers of links. Furthermore, they find that the impact of wealth on connections varies by network architecture and that correcting for endogeneity raises the impact of network membership on outcomes. In contrast to the current literature, we emphasize the critical role of both number of links and architecture in determining the impact of social networks on outcomes.

4. De Weerdt (2005) obtained similar results in Tanzania.

5. Another form of mutual insurance, informal transfers and gifts, appears to be relatively unimportant in this sample.

References

Bliss, C., and N. Stern. 1982. *Palanpur.* Oxford: Clarendon Press.

Dasgupta, P. 2003. Social capital and economic performance: Analytics. In *Foundations of social capital,* ed. E. Ostrom and T. K. Ahn. Cheltenham, U.K.: Edward Elgar.

Dejene, A. 1993. *The informal and semiformal financial sectors in Ethiopia: A study of the iqqub, iddir and savings and credit cooperatives.* AERC Research Paper 21. Nairobi: African Economics Research Consortium.

Dercon, S. 1996. Risk, crop choice, and savings: Evidence from Tanzania. *Economic Development and Cultural Change* 44: 485–513.

Dercon, S., and J. Hoddinott. 2004. The Ethiopian rural household surveys: Introduction. Mimeo. Washington, D.C.: International Food Policy Research Institute.

Dercon, S., and P. Krishnan. 1996. Income portfolios in rural Ethiopia and Tanzania: Choices and constraints. *Journal of Development Studies* 32: 850–875.

Dercon, S., J. Hoddinott, and T. Woldehanna. 2005. Consumption and shocks in 15 Ethiopian Villages, 1999–2004. *Journal of African Economies* 14: 559–585.

Dercon, S., J. De Weerdt, T. Bold, and A. Pankhurst. 2004. *Group-based funeral insurance in Ethiopia and Tanzania.* Working Paper 227. Oxford: Centre for the Study of African Economies, University of Oxford.

De Weerdt, J. 2005. Risk sharing and endogenous network formation. In *Insurance against poverty,* ed. S. Dercon. Oxford: Oxford University Press.

Gilligan, D., J. Hoddinott, and A. S. Taffesse. 2007. The impact of Ethiopia's Food Security Program on household food security and wellbeing: An interim assessment. Mimeo. Washington, D.C.: International Food Policy Research Institute.

Krishnan, P., and E. Sciubba. 2004. Endogenous network formation and informal institutions in village economies. Cambridge Working Papers in Economics 0462. Cambridge: Faculty of Economics, University of Cambridge.

———. 2005. The structure of social networks and informal insurance: Evidence from Ethiopia. Mimeo. Cambridge: Cambridge University.

Pankhurst, A. 2003. The role and space for *iddirs* to participate in the development of Ethiopia. In *Iddirs: Participation and development,* ed. A. Pankhurst. Addis Ababa: Agency for Cooperation and Development.

Powell, J. 1984. Least absolute deviations estimation for the censored regression model. *Journal of Econometrics* 25 (5): 303–325.

Townsend, R. 1995. Consumption insurance: An evaluation of risk-bearing systems in low-income countries. *Journal of Economic Perspectives* 9 (3): 83–102.

Walker, T., and J. Ryan. 1990. *Village and household economies in India's semi-arid tropics.* Baltimore: Johns Hopkins University Press.

Part 3

Natural Resource Management

Institutions for Natural Resource Management

In this part of the book the focus is on the institutions relevant to natural resource management (NRM), and the action domain (in the parlance of Chapter 3) now becomes the natural resources or natural capital that are so important to developing countries. Whereas Part 2 focused on the exchange of goods and services, this part is concerned with how people, communities, and societies engage with their natural resource bases. The natural resource base is critical in developing countries, because farmers, fishermen, and cattle herders all earn their livings from the use of such renewable natural resources as land, water, air, forest, grazing areas, irrigation water, plants, and animals.

Concerns about the degradation of these resources have stimulated scholars to find the reasons for degradation. The destruction of natural capital has vast implications for livelihoods, poverty alleviation, and food security. It also has great implications for sustainable development and the commercial use of these resources. Without sustainable development, the efforts highlighted in Part 2 to improve the exchange of the goods produced using these resources will be futile.

The two theoretical chapters in this section (Chapters 13 and 14) provide an in-depth overview of the literature on the institutional issues in NRM. Issues related to property rights and how they influence the management of natural resources are addressed in Chapter 13; Chapter 14 reviews the various institutional mechanisms (arrangements) relevant to coordination in NRM.

There has been a great deal written about the "constraints to adoption" of improved production technologies and NRM practices in developing-country agriculture. Much of the literature on this subject has focused on the lack of infrastructure, information, labor, wealth, and access to credit of smallholder farmers across the continent. Other factors that have received attention are agro-ecological conditions and price policies that create environmental and economic risks or low profitability of agriculture. However, these technical and economic factors tell only part of the story; equally important is the institutional environment under which farmers, fishers, herders, and other rural producers operate (Otsuka and Place 2001; Barrett, Place, and Aboud 2002; Meinzen-Dick et al. 2002).

In particular, the institutions governing property rights play a key role in shaping rural producers' choices of production practices and outputs, and hence affect food security and poverty reduction. Their effects are seen both directly (on adoption) and indirectly on a range of other conditions, including many of the other factors that have been identified as constraints to adoption. This part of the volume provides background on these institutions, particularly as they apply to NRM in Africa.[1]

Identifying the Role of Property Rights and Coordination

Although property rights and coordination are vital, they are not always the highest priority factors to consider in NRM. Other institutions or technical factors may be more important. For agriculture and NRM, the Systemwide Program on Collective Action and Property Rights (CAPRi) framework[2] provides a means of identifying the conditions under which these two key institutions are likely to play major roles in the adoption of technologies or practices.

As illustrated in Figure P3.1, agricultural technologies or NRM practices can be plotted according to their temporal and spatial scales. The horizontal axis moves from practices with short-term to those with long-term payoff periods. Those that yield returns in a single season would therefore be on the left, and those long-term investments, with payoff periods that may extend over generations, would be on the right. On the vertical axis, plot-level technologies or practices are at the bottom, and technologies that need to be practiced at a regional scale for them to be effective appear at the top.

Accordingly, new varieties of maize or an annual crop would plot in the lower-left corner. They provide the returns in a single season, so even a farmer with insecure tenure can adopt the technology without coordinating with anyone else. In this case, neither property rights nor coordination are likely to be a constraint to adoption. This argument is borne out empirically: Holden and Yohannes (2001) found that tenure insecurity in Ethiopia (derived from fear of land redistribution) did not have a significant effect on the use of purchased inputs, such as seeds and chemical fertilizers. However, as the time between adoption and returns lengthens, property rights become more critical. Hence people with insecure tenure have less incentive to invest in long-term soil fertility.

Figure P3.1   Role of collective action and property rights in natural resource management

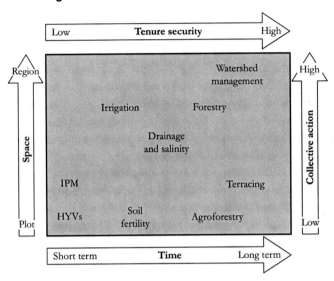

Source: Knox McCulloch, Meinzen-Dick, and Hazell (1998).

Moving up the vertical scale, integrated pest management (IPM) yields returns in a season, but it is usually not effective if a farmer adopts such practices as reduced spraying and release of beneficial insects alone, while neighbors continue to spray with pesticides. The harmful insects (which do not respect property boundaries) will be drawn to the unsprayed field, and the beneficial insects may be killed by the adjacent spraying. Some form of cooperation is required for effective adoption of IPM practices. Swallow et al. (2002) studied the role of coordination in adoption of pour-on treatments that would control tsetse fly and other insects in Ethiopia. The treatments would be most effective if all cattle were treated, but there was a potential free-rider problem: If all surrounding cattle were treated, then insect problems would be reduced for untreated cattle as well. Analysis of cooperation patterns identified that crossing land of a different ethnic group to reach a treatment center was a local cultural problem, which the program solved by opening treatment centers in areas of each ethnic group (Swallow et al. 2002). Thus economies of scale associated with positive or negative spatial externalities call for wider nonmarket coordination mechanisms.

Most NRM practices have elements that are long-term and operate above the farm level. Hence, both property rights and coordination become important.

Watershed management programs call for investments in re-vegetation (either by planting trees or grasses, or reducing the use of the land to allow natural regrowth), structures to reduce lateral flows of water and soil, or both. Moreover, because they operate at the landscape level, there is a need to coordinate the practices of those who use the land for farming, grazing, collecting wood, and the like (Swallow, Johnson, and Meinzen-Dick 2001). Rangelands and forests are also used by many people, and investments in improving the state of these resources do not yield returns in the short term. Hence people who do not have confidence that they will receive the benefits are unlikely to want to invest in those improvements. Even if there are short-term returns, but individuals are not sure they will receive what they consider their fair shares in those returns, they will not have the incentive to invest. This lack of incentives has been a problem in many forestry management programs in which communities are expected to care for the forest resources without being given clear rights over the improved forests. Insecure property rights shorten people's time horizons and thereby discourage the adoption of improved NRM practices.

Similarly, most surface irrigation systems in developing countries serve many farmers, and the payoff period is over several years or even decades. Farmer-managed irrigation systems are therefore generally found where there is both relatively secure tenure and good cooperation among farmers. Even if the state undertakes to build the infrastructure, farmers still need to make an investment in their own plots to make effective use of the irrigation, and experience has shown that few governments can afford to provide irrigation services to smallholders down to the farmgate level without some form of collective action among farmers to at least share the water, and often, to undertake some maintenance activities. Thus irrigation projects that resettle people from many different backgrounds, without social bonds between them, are likely to face greater management challenges than systems that serve pre-existing communities.

Note that a particular technology may not always appear at the same place in Figure P3.1 for several reasons. First, the spatial scale is relative to farm size. Hence, a technology or practice covering 100 ha could serve hundreds of farms in an area of very small farm size or serve less than one farm where holdings are very large. Second, any particular technology can vary with scale. Irrigation may be a large canal system serving thousands of hectares or may be a small treadle pump providing enough water for only one small plot. Agroforestry can include a community nursery (short-term, but collective), as well as planting fruit or timber trees on an individual plot (long-term, but individual; Place, Otsuka, and Scherr 2004). Finally, even technologies that can be adopted on an individual farm may require coordination for crop improvement, dissemination, or marketing, as discussed in Part 2 of this volume.

Despite these complications, this framework provides a useful way of identifying whether property rights and/or coordination problems are likely to be a constraint to the adoption of new agricultural or NRM practices. Most programs that seek to disseminate new crop varieties or inputs that give a short-term return would not need to look at the extent of tenure insecurity and could be adopted regardless of whether neighbors get along well with one another. However, such programs as watershed management would do well to examine the incentive structure and cost patterns that result from existing property rights and coordination institutions. Just as crop varieties need to be adapted to the biophysical environment in which they are applied, so also NRM practices need to be adapted to their institutional environment. Thus, if an area has high tenure insecurity, it would be well to look for component practices that give returns in the short term, such as leguminous vegetative barriers, instead of planting trees or building stone terraces that yield returns only in the long term.[3] If an area has many different ethnic groups with a poor history of getting along with one another, then trying to coordinate activities at the landscape level would be more likely to fail than approaches that can be divided into practices on individual farms. The chapters of this section provide greater detail on ways of analyzing property rights and coordination.

Case Study Chapters

Some of the first applications of the New Institutional Economics (NIE) framework were related to the management of common property resources and public goods—the standard market failures. Whereas the case studies in Part 2 highlighted the application of NIE to the nontraditional terrain of exchange in goods and services, the four case studies prepared for this part (Chapters 15–18) return to more familiar terrain. They nevertheless provide innovative applications to different issues related to natural resources, that is, property rights to land and management of water resources.

Chapter 15 discusses the internal processes and decisions that characterized the transition from collectively held group ranches to individualized property systems among the Maasai pastoralists in Kenya. The case study focuses especially on explaining how property rights change. Significant attention is given to the politics and power relations in the assignment of the new property rights. In addition, aspects related to path dependence, timing, the role of actors, history, and the role of the state in the process of changing a property-rights regime is carefully described.

The case study examines who the main actors were during subdivision of the group ranches, their interactions, and the outcomes of these interactions. Unsurprisingly, the narrative shows how the process of land allocation was captured by the elite. Regardless of the reasons motivating individuals to seek a reassignment of rights, the process of reassignment itself is characterizd by conflict over the eventual distribution of rights, because the losers contested the outcome. Similarly, those with power and influence employed their resources to ensure their preferred outcome. In the end, it is the wealthy group that wins, and resources that had been collective become concentrated in the hands of a subset of the original claimants. Such an outcome is particularly likely when the state abandons its enforcement role and transfers decisionmaking powers to self-interested management committees. Chapter 15 thus effectively illustrates how the activities (or in this case the lack thereof) of state actors may impede the attainment of equitable outcomes, regardless of whether ensuing property arrangements are efficient.

Chapter 16 also considers institutional change with respect to land rights and shows how such change can be initiated to bring about increased allocative efficiency. The case study on changing property rights in South Africa uses participatory research techniques to develop a rental market for cropland in an area characterized by customary land rights. The researchers used an adaptive strategy, facilitating gradual adjustments to existing institutions to strengthen tenure security and reduce transaction costs that constrained rental transactions. Results observed over a period of 10 years indicate that minor interventions can increase the supply of appropriate institutional change when well managed and based on good information. In this example, rental market activity increased dramatically with significant gains in both efficiency and equity.

Chapter 16 thus leads to a better understanding of why endogenous institutional change is unpredictable and presents alternative approaches to exogenous institutional change. In addition it also provides an appreciation of why policy may be better informed by second-best efficiency solutions.

Chapter 17 considers the role of collective action in ensuring coordination in the operation and maintenance of irrigation schemes in Uganda. The case study is set against the background of a general belief that the devolution of NRM from governments to user groups is a good practice on the premise that local users have comparative advantage and self-interest over government agents in managing and monitoring such resources. The success of the devolution policy in improving NRM is, however, highly dependent on the ability and willingness of the farmers to organize into successful farmers' associations—which cannot be assumed, especially if devolution calls for considerably more time and cash contributions from the farmers. The need to examine farmers' willingness to participate in collective action after the withdrawal of government support motivated this case study, because their cooperation is critical for effective implementation of the devolution policy and the development of strategies for sustainable collective action.

The authors of Chapter 17 examined the incentives (benefits and penalties) for participation in collective action and found major failures in the enforcement of rules and delivery of benefits that will likely diminish the effectiveness of the devolution policy, which was intended to improve the management of the irrigation scheme. To stimulate greater participation in collective action, stronger and more effectively enforced bylaws governing user-fee payments, collection procedures, and efficient use of resources must be undertaken along with evidence of improved delivery of services and benefits.

Once again this case study illustrates the multilevel focus of the NIE approach to specific problems. Collective action was considered, but then issues related to enforcement were seen to play an important role. In analyzing the situation, the characteristics of the actors were clearly understood, which assisted in designing appropriate coordination mechanisms for the improved delivery of irrigation water that can ultimately ensure sustainable use of a scarce resource.

Implicit to the NIE philosophy is an understanding of structural issues and power and social relations. Thus gender considerations are fundamental to the NIE paradigm and form part of the effort to understand reality. Chapter 18 illustrates why it is so important to pay attention to gendered production relations in farming and stresses the necessity of mainstreaming gender in agricultural policy. Understanding the attributes of actors, their relationships, and their relative power positions helps in understanding and predicting economic and social outcomes.

The effective use of the NIE perspectives should by definition always include a gender focus. This statement is confirmed by Chapter 18, which highlights the dilemma of intervening agencies (and especially their expatriate experts and donors) when they not only fail to recognize the productivity of customary gendered small-holder agriculture but also destroy what exists, at the expense of all parties involved.

This case study underlines what is basically common sense: women farmers, like their male counterparts, are more highly motivated to increase their productivity when they control the output of their efforts. Long-term use rights to the land cultivated, as offered in customary land tenure (and to some extent to women), are an important condition for such control. These basics have been widely recognized in the case of male tenants and land-poor men, especially in Asia. This recognition has also been translated into policies and programs for land reform and tenure security that "vests land in the tiller." Productivity considerations were as important as equity considerations in this case study. The same needs to be applied to gender relations in agriculture in general.

Notes

1. This introductory part draws on Meinzen-Dick et al. (2002), particularly the conceptual framework in Chapter 2 of that volume, and Meinzen-Dick and Di Gregorio (2004).

2. The CAPRi framework was developed by the Systemwide Program on Collective Action and Property Rights—see Knox McCulloch, Meinzen-Dick, and Hazell (1998); Meinzen-Dick and Di Gregorio (2004), and www.capri.cgiar.org.

3. Note, however, that making investments in the land, including tree planting, can provide a mechanism to strengthen property rights, as discussed in Chapter 13.

References

Barrett, C. B., F. Place, and A. A. Aboud, eds. 2002. *Natural resources management in African agriculture: Understanding and improving current practices.* Wallingford, U.K.: CAB International.

Holden, S. T., and H. Yohannes. 2001. Land redistribution, tenure insecurity, and intensity of production: A study of farm households in southern Ethiopia. CAPRi Working Paper 21. Washington, D.C.: International Food Policy Research Institute.

Knox McCulloch, A., R. S. Meinzen-Dick, and P. Hazell. 1998. Property rights, collective action, and technologies for natural resource management: A conceptual framework. CAPRi Working Paper 1. Washington, D.C.: International Food Policy Research Institute.

Meinzen-Dick, R. S., and M. Di Gregorio, eds. 2004. *Collective action and property rights for sustainable development. 2020 Focus 11.* Washington, D.C.: International Food Policy Research Institute. Available at http://www.ifpri.org/2020/focus/focus11.htm.

Meinzen-Dick, R. S., A. Knox, F. Place, and B. Swallow, eds. 2002. *Innovation in natural resource management: The role of property rights and collective action in developing countries.* Baltimore: Johns Hopkins University Press.

Otsuka, K., and F. Place, eds. 2001. *Land tenure and natural resource management: A comparative study of agrarian communities in Asia and Africa.* Baltimore: Johns Hopkins University Press.

Place, F., K. Otsuka, and S. Scherr. 2004. Property rights, collective action and agroforestry. In *Collective action and property rights for sustainable development,* ed. R. S. Meinzen-Dick and M. Di Gregorio. 2020 Focus 11. Washington, D.C.: International Food Policy Research Institute. Available at http://www.ifpri.org/2020/focus/focus11.htm.

Swallow, B. M., N. L. Johnson, and R. S. Meinzen-Dick. 2001. Working with people for watershed management. *Water Policy* 3 (6): 449–456.

Swallow, B. M., J. Wangila, W. Mulatu, O. Okello, and N. McCarthy. 2002. Collective action in space: Assessing how collective action varies across an African landscape. In *Innovation in natural resource management: The role of property rights and collective action in developing countries,* ed. R. S. Meinzen-Dick, A. Knox, F. Place, and B. Swallow. Baltimore: Johns Hopkins University Press.

Chapter 13

Understanding Property Rights in Land and Natural Resource Management

Esther Mwangi and Ruth S. Meinzen-Dick

A better understanding of the role of property rights in land and natural resource management requires attention to several basic questions: What are property rights? Where do they come from? What are they good for? Why and how do they change, with what outcomes? This chapter is an attempt to answer these questions.

13.1 What Are Property Rights?

In Chapter 2, property rights were defined as those actions that individuals can take in relation to others regarding some thing. If one individual has a right, someone else has a commensurate duty to observe that right. Although many individuals influenced by Western concepts think of property rights in the narrow sense of ownership—the right to exclusively control and alienate a resource—property rights are better understood as overlapping bundles of rights. Indeed, because of the complex interrelations among these individual rights and rights-holders, they could even be considered as a web of interests (Arnold 2002; Hodgson 2004). There are many combinations of such rights, but they can often be grouped as (Schlager and Ostrom 1992)

- *use rights,* such as the right to access the resource (for example, to walk across a field), withdraw from or consume a resource (pick some wild plants), or exploit a resource for economic benefit (graze cattle on common pastures); and

- *control* or *decisionmaking rights,* such as the rights to management (plant a crop), exclusion (prevent others from accessing the field), and alienation (rent out, sell, bequeath, or give away the rights).

For example, a farmer may have the right to plant a crop on a piece of land, but anyone can cross that land to get water, pastoralists may have the right to graze their herds on that land in the fallow season, family elders may have the right to allocate or reallocate that land, and the state may claim ultimate ownership of the resource. Such multiple, overlapping rights and claims to the same resource are characteristic of African tenure systems (Okoth-Ogendo 1976, 1991; Bruce and Migot-Adholla 1994).

To these use rights may be added the *rights to earn income* from a resource, which Roman legal traditions have referred to as usufruct rights (see also Alchian and Demsetz 1972; Eggertson 1990). Rights to earn income from a resource (even without using it directly) can be separate from use and management of the resource, as when government departments collect revenue from water users or when communities in parts of East and Southern Africa collect a charge from tour operators in their common lands.

Although most discussions of property rights focus on rights over land, the rights over other natural resources must also be examined. Land and water are inextricably linked, but in many cases water and land rights do not coincide, which can complicate such efforts as watershed management programs (Hodgson 2004; Swallow, Onyango, and Meinzen-Dick 2005). Fortmann and Bruce (1988) have even established that tree tenure may be separate from the underlying land itself. Even rights to specific plants or genetic resources, such as medicinal plants, may be distinct. Thus it is important to look at the rights over each resource.

Property-rights regimes are often classified as public (rights held by the state), private (rights held by individuals or legal individuals, such as corporations), or common property (rights held by a defined group).[1] However, because different stakeholders can have different rights over the same resource, these three types of property rights are often not so neat in practice. Individuals and communities frequently have rights of access, use, and sometimes even decisionmaking on land that is officially government (public) land. Individuals similarly have use rights on common property, whereas the state may have some regulatory or decisionmaking rights over it. Even on private property, others may have certain use rights, and the state may claim the right to regulate the resource. The important issue is not to classify resources into one or another rigid category but to be aware of the different types of rights holders (individuals, groups, and the state). Moreover, public, private, and common property stand in contrast with open access—the condition under which no one has clearly defined rights over the resource, and hence everyone can use it as they like (see Chapter 14 for a fuller analysis of the implications of open access).

Each property-rights structure has a corresponding set of costs and benefits, which are linked to the nature of the resource under investigation or of the technology that determines the use of the resource (Dahlman 1980; Bromley 1991; Kirk 1999; Ostrom 2001). Three types of costs have been identified for common property (Dahlman 1980; Eggertson 1990, 1996; Ostrom 1990): costs of establishment and protection, internal governance costs, and the costs of excluding nonmembers. Governance costs include those of decisionmaking with respect to resource use, of establishing organizations to facilitate production and exchange, and of monitoring use. Governance costs are likely to vary with group size and heterogeneity. They increase when rights holders violate or circumvent collective decisions on resource use (Baland and Platteau 1996; Platteau 2000; Ostrom 2001). Governance costs also increase with population increase. By increasing the number of users, population pressure raises both the likelihood of externalities and their magnitudes (Platteau 1996). In addition, because population pressure enhances the scarcity value of resources, it also induces a corresponding increase in the aggregate losses from collective exploitation (Platteau 2000). Under these circumstances, private, individual property appears to be beneficial, as it internalizes these externalities without involving any governance costs.

However, private, individual property is also not without cost. These include the costs of boundary demarcation, recording and transferring titles, and fencing or excluding others (Bromley 1989). When there are economies of scale that can be realized by maintaining collective ownership but that ownership is instead individualized (as in the Maasai example in Chapter 15), several costs emerge. In the case of hunting or grazing, for instance, owners need to reach a joint decision on keeping the range open and accessible (Dahlman 1980; Platteau 2000). This decision increases transactions costs in two ways. First, it requires considerable interaction among individuals, to either negotiate compensation for mutual use of grazing or for the damage to one another's property. Second, because each individual owns a geographically defined piece of soil, some may acquire a strong bargaining position and threaten withdrawal. Under conditions of economies of scale, collective rights in grazing save on transactions costs.

This review of the benefit–cost structure of different property arrangements demands a more careful reflection on the relationship between biophysical aspects of resources and the property regime. These are issues that have been only incompletely addressed in the property-rights debate (Dahlman 1980; Ostrom 1990, 2001, 2005b; Nugent and Sanchez 1991, 1995, 1998; Bromley 1992). The existence of a wide diversity of property-rights arrangements across space and through time—sometimes in the same cultural and socioeconomic community—begs questions that are not necessarily answered by a strict consideration of economic calculations alone.

According to Dasgupta (2005, 1612), "privatisation is an alternative system of property rights to communal ownership in those cases where the resource is divisible without productivity loss." However, in addition to potential returns to scale, it is often the case that such resources as water, rangelands, or forests are highly variable over time and space. It is therefore often better for a user to have a share of a larger area that may include land that provides good pasture in the dry and wet seasons, water points, and mineral licks rather than to have an exclusive right to a smaller portion of the resource, which might not have all requisite features.

Studies of property rights under a range of conditions, such as the high mountainous regions of the world, may help illustrate the complexity of factors influencing the choice of property regimes. In Torbel in the Swiss Alps, for example, where population, technology, and political factors remained relatively stable for close to five centuries, the patchiness of high alpine pastures and the labor economies of collective herding necessitated a communal structure to access and management (Netting 1976). In contrast, lower altitude pastures, grain fields, and vineyards (that is, resources of dependable productivity that can be improved in different ways and may be exploited by individual or family labor) were held under individual tenure. A similar situation—in which both communal and private property rights coexist and are practiced by the same people—occurs in the central Andean Alps (Guillet 1981). Joint control, which is strongly correlated with pasture, is found at higher altitudes. Private, individual control is found in lower altitudes, where continuous irrigated agriculture and specialized horticulture take place. The vertical gradient imposes constraints to land intensification, such as the introduction of irrigation and ox-drawn ploughs. Stevenson (1984) cited in Picht (1987), working in the Bernese Alps, similarly finds that areas with better soil, fewer swampy spots, better grass quality, and higher exposure to the sun are more likely to be individual property. But areas with poor precipitation conditions, strong prevailing winds, and poor exposure to the sun discourage individual property. These results are reiterated by Mendes (1988) for the Moroccan Atlas Mountains. This relationship between environmental conditions and institutional choice follows a similar pattern in the arid and semi-arid regions of the tropics, which although culturally distinct, share commonalities in supporting pastoral modes of land use and in which property regimes, at least for land, are more often than not collective in nature (Sandford 1983; Khazanov 1984; Galaty and Johnson 1990).

The examples outlined above seem to indicate that common property might have certain distinct advantages over private, individual property in certain biophysical situations. These advantages are related to minimizing risk in highly variable environments, promoting equitability of variable resources, and minimizing production and transactions costs (Dahlman 1980; Sandford 1983; Galaty and Johnson 1990; Niamir-Fuller 1995, 1998, 1999; Scoones 1995). In the African rangelands, where rainfall is low and variable and productivity marginal, the costs of privatization may far exceed the benefits (Ostrom 1990; Bromley 1989, 1991; Behnke, Scoones, and Kerven 1993). Collective rights to land and land resources are a more equitable way of distributing variable resources and minimizing risk. In these regions common property arrangements spread these risks and serve as an insurance against individuals incurring frequent financial expenses to mitigate the consequences of environmental variability. In addition, not only does common property allow a more equitable distribution of a variable, though critical, resource for herders, it is also associated with considerable savings on transactions and production costs. Economies of scale in herding and infrastructure are also important. In addition, where a well-defined community of users exists, they will be able to exclude outsiders, and the costs of establishing and protecting their collective rights are much lower than those of establishing rights for a large number of individually owned parcels. In the latter situation, each individual would have to find and transact with every other individual owner for every issue that arises. Furthermore, compensation may need to be considered when resources and facilities are unevenly distributed. In addition, even when individual owners may cooperate, there remains the possibility that some individuals may follow a hold-out strategy and try to appropriate gains by withdrawing from joint obligations.

It is worth pointing out that private joint ventures, in which group members surrender resource control to an expert manager but retain benefit and voting rights, may have similar advantages to common property arrangements. In this case risk minimization and scale advantages are achieved through an organizational structure that is horizontally integrated (for an example, see Box 14.1 in Chapter 14).

13.2 Where Do Property Rights Come From?

There are multiple sources of property rights, including

- international treaties and law;

- state (or statutory) law;

- religious law and accepted religious practices;

- customary law, which may be formalized (written) custom or living interpretations of custom;

- project (or donor) law, including project or program regulations;

- organizational law, such as rules made by user or nonuser groups; and

- the marketplace.

In Africa for example, state and customary institutions have been principal mechanisms for the creation and allocation of rights in society. In promoting their policy objectives in agriculture, political stabilization, political control, resource management, and land redistribution, the African states in Ethiopia, Burkina Faso, Mali, Nigeria, Senegal, Tanzania, and even South Africa have at various points in their histories attempted to extinguish or suppress private property to pave the way for collectivization or national ownership. Similarly, to encourage agricultural production, colonial Kenya privatized parts of the settler-occupied highlands that were under indigenous tenure systems. The end of the colonial era saw the same state encouraging land privatization in the African Reserves to defuse escalating political tensions stemming from landlessness. Thus, apart from supplying enforcement, registration, survey, and titles in a market-based framework where individuals can buy, sell, or contract for rights, the state actively influences property assignment.

The market and the state are just part of a diverse complex of systems for the creation of rights and access to land. In many parts of Africa indigenous forms of rights to land still persist. Land under customary tenure currently comprises about 60 percent of Africa's land (Bruce 1989, 1998). Having evolved in particular environments among specific ethnic or linguistic groups, such systems accordingly exhibit great diversity. Nonetheless, certain commonalities exist. Such attributes as ethnic identity and kinship, in concert with status, gender, seniority, and residence, feature prominently in the determination of access and use rights (Berry 1989, 1993, 2002; Bruce and Migot-Adholla 1994). Group control over land is fairly common. The group may be an extended family, lineage, clan, village, or tribe; it can be defined by common descent, common residence, or both. Membership in the group often determines the nature and strength of the rights. Rights over land are allocated for the relatively exclusive use of individuals or families in the group; such rights are not dissimilar to private ownership. The rights are allocated and administered by a local, indigenous authority, such as lineage elders, tribal chiefs, or land priests. Rights are held in trust for future generations by the local authorities, and the only rights possible are use rights; land transfers are rarely allowed. Rights may be allocated to nonmembers if they are affiliated to the group through residence or marriage and are granted temporary use rights subject to relatively strict controls. Thus the rights of use, transfer, allocation, control, and administration lie in different hands (Downs and Reyna 1989). More importantly, Berry (1993) documents how the negotiability of social identities introduces fluidity in the nature of indigenous land-rights systems that may at times result in insecure rights.

The influence of religion on defining property rights is seen particularly in the designation of sacred groves, such as the Malshegu sacred groves in Ghana. Traditional forms of tenure in Islamic countries represent another variation in this range (Payne 2001). For example, *Waqf* land is land "held for God," whereas state-controlled land carries *tassruf* or usufruct rights to resources. *Musha* are communal lands, where resources are jointly shared and managed.

The coexistence and interaction of multiple types of law is referred to as legal pluralism. Claims to property rights are only as strong as the institution that stands behind them. Thus the different types of law may be regarded as overlapping "force fields," as illustrated in Figure 13.1: each type of law exerts a different level of influence, which can vary over space and time (Meinzen-Dick and Pradhan 2002). For example, in a diverse migrant community near the capital city or in areas of high-value agriculture, statutory law may be strong and customary law weak, but in remote areas customary law might be much stronger than state law. Not only the rules but also their enforcement mechanisms need to be considered when examining property rights. That property rights must be enforced to be meaningful is illustrated by forest management and sustainability in the Mpigi District of southwestern Uganda (Banana and Gombya-Ssembajjwe 2000). An investigation into the relationship between forest disturbance and property regime (state, individual, and common property) across a sample of 16 forests found that some forests in all three property regimes are overused whereas others are sustainably managed. The distinguishing feature between overharvested and sustainably managed forests is not the property regime but rather the ability to monitor the forest and sanction rule breakers (that is, enforcement). A broader, global study across almost 200 forests reiterates this finding—that regular monitoring and sanctioning results in better forest conditions (Gibson, Williams, and Ostrom 2005).

Security of tenure[2] is generally associated with several components, including excludability (the ability to exclude those without rights), duration (temporal extent of one's rights), assurance (an institutional framework capable of enforcing an individual's rights), and robustness (the number and strength of the bundle of rights an individual possesses; Roth, Wiebe, and Lawry 1993). Although extensive academic and policy work has been done to create titles and registries, particularly in Africa, customary law regarding property rights can provide just as much tenure security for agriculture (Place and Hazell 1993; Bruce and Migot-Adholla 1994). In some cases, titling and formalization of tenure can strengthen property rights, particularly against outside threats, but in many cases the experience has been that registration

Figure 13.1   Coexisting multiple legal orders (legal pluralism)

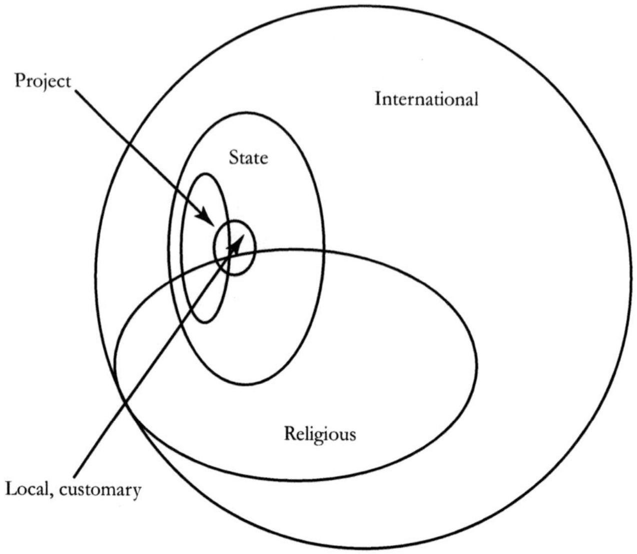

Source: Meinzen-Dick and Pradhan (2002).

and titling processes have created opportunities for elite capture and a loss of customary use rights by marginalized groups, particularly women (Lastarria-Cornhiel 1997; Toulmin and Quan 2000). In addition, formalization may lead to conflicting claims, particularly where customary rights are strong, creating uncertainty and reducing tenure security. Nevertheless, title is meaningless without the full backing of the state, implying that the state stands ready to protect assets defined by that title. Thus it is important to look beyond simplistic notions of property rights to understand rights as they exist in practice.

13.3   What Are Property Rights Good For?

The rationale for attention to property rights can be summarized in terms of the "four Es": efficiency, environment, equity, and empowerment. In terms of efficiency, arguments are often made that secure property rights are needed to provide incentives to invest in a resource. In the case of agricultural land in particular, scholars have elaborated demand-side (incentives to farmers) and supply-side (incentives to lenders) aspects of tenure security (Place, Roth, and Hazell 1994). Because tenure security increases the likelihood that a farmer will capture her investment returns and reduce the incidence of disputes, an enhancement of tenure security is expected to raise the demand for investments in land improvements over the longer term and ultimately increase yields. On the supply side, increased tenure security is expected to enhance the land's collateral value. Moreover, both rental and sales markets are facilitated by tenure security, as potential buyers are assured that the seller is indeed the holder of the rights.

Environmental arguments are closely related: property rights provide incentives to protect the resource, and without property rights that are enforced, resources often become degraded. Equity relates to the distribution of the resource and can be defined in terms of equality of access, particularly for meeting basic needs, of distribution of rights in proportion to investment that people make, or some combination thereof. The way in which rights are defined determines whether people are included or excluded in the control of a vital resource for their lives. Holding property rights is thus empowering to individuals or groups, particularly control rights that recognize authority over the management of the resource.

But how do these theoretical justifications for property rights hold up empirically? Do property rights, and in particular private, individual property, increase efficiency, sustainability, equity, or empowerment? Empirical outcomes are mixed. Migot-Adholla et al. (1991) and Bruce and Migot-Adholla (1994) demonstrate that the presence of titles does not automatically result in increased land productivity in cultivated regions of Ghana, Kenya, Rwanda, and Uganda. However, in Ghana, Goldstein and Udry (2005) found that those with higher status and better political connections have greater tenure security compared to those of lower status (including women). The greater security allows those men to leave more land fallow, and reap higher productivity when they do farm, but at the expense of denying land to others. In Uganda, Deininger and All (2007) found that overlapping land rights between land owners and tenants was a significant source of insecurity and limited tenants' investments in the land. In Ethiopia, Deininger et al. (2007) found that a cost-effective land certification program had preliminary positive effects, although the overall evidence of links between land tenure and investments in natural resource management is mixed (see Pender, Place, and Ehui 2006). In Thailand, a comparison of the performance of squatters on state land (who lack titles to their farms) with that of titled farmers demonstrated that the latter had greater investment, higher likelihood of land improvements, more intensive use of variable inputs, and higher output per unit of land (Feder and Feeny 1991). As Roth et al. (1989) note, in this case, title was a proxy for tenure security (which is not always the case), and much of the impact of title ownership stemmed from the fact that titles increased farmers' access to formal credit. Private-property systems in land are most likely to make a difference in productivity gains when there is a somewhat dense population, so that competition for use is present, as well as improvements in infrastructure, marketing, credit institutions, input supply, and extension services (Migot-Adholla et al. 1991).

In pastoral areas, where systematic studies are few, privatization programs have neither resulted in substantial increases in pastoral (livestock) productivity nor in decreased land degradation in different parts of East, Southern, and West Africa (de Carvalho 1974; Njoka 1979; Evangelou 1984; Rutten 1992). In fact, privatization programs have resulted in considerable inequity, as women and youths are excluded in emerging land titles, whereas individuals and groups with better connections to politicians, land administration, and court systems often end up acquiring larger parcels of land at the expense of those with fewer connections. The case study in Chapter 15 demonstrates the equity implications of privatization processes.

13.4 Complexity and Dynamics of Property Rights

Although the security of property rights has been identified as a key constraint to the adoption of long-term investments in agriculture and natural resource management, the relationship is not always unidirectional, because of the complex and dynamic nature of property-rights institutions. Agroforestry provides a clear illustration of some of these complexities.

Planting trees on a plot is a long-term investment; hence those with insecure tenure would be less likely to plant trees, either because they do not have the incentive or they are not authorized to do so. Indeed, the right to manage a resource—to change it in some way, including by planting a tree—is an important component in the bundle of property rights. Studies in Cameroon, Kenya, Mali, Uganda, and Zambia have found that tenants without long-term land rights are restricted in their rights to plant or harvest from trees because of insecurity of tenure (Place 1994).

Differences in tenure security can even be significant within the household. In communal areas of Zimbabwe, Fortmann, Antinori, and Nabane (1997) found that the potential for loss of land and trees following widowhood or divorce was a significant source of insecurity for women that limited tree planting on household land: women and men were equally likely to plant trees on community woodlots, because rights over those trees derived from community membership and investment, not marital status, and hence there were fewer gender differences in tenure security. However, differences in the socioeconomic status of households were a bigger factor than gender differences alone in explaining tree-planting behavior overall: the poorest households had least ability to plant and tended to focus on trees for subsistence needs rather than for commercialization—a useful reminder that institutions are not always the biggest constraint on improving agriculture.

But a closer examination of the links between tree planting and tenure security illustrates some of the complexities involved in examining such institutions as property rights: they are dynamic, so that relationships are not always one-way. For example, Otsuka and Place (2001) found that in many places the planting of trees strengthens individual land rights.[3] Indeed, it is to prevent such enhanced claims on the land that tenants and women are often prohibited from planting trees. Thus not only do property rights affect adoption, but adoption of tree planting can also affect one's property rights. These same processes are seen at larger scales: many devolution programs grant communities stronger rights over forest resources when they have planted trees or made other improvements to the resource base.

On an even broader scale, adoption of new farming practices can change property-rights regimes. For example, Quisumbing and Otsuka (2001) describe how customary systems of acquiring land in western Ghana by clearing forests came under pressure from the increasing population. As a result, agroforestry—particularly cocoa production—became more profitable than shifting cultivation, which created local pressure to individualize land tenure. Though individualization of tenure frequently led to women losing their customary access to land (Lastarria-Cornhiel 1997), in this case the introduction of cocoa increased the demand for women's labor. Men needed to provide incentives for their wives to work in the cocoa fields. Although land was customarily held only by men, women acquired use rights through their relationships with men, and traditional "gifting" ceremonies, witnessed by the community, were adapted so that husbands could transfer individual land rights to their wives in exchange for labor on the cocoa fields. Thus, with the introduction of cocoa, customary practices were used to adapt the land tenure and give women relatively secure rights to land and trees.[4]

Property rights affect access to credit when banks or other lenders require land as collateral for loans. This link is often cited as a major reason for land titling programs (for example, De Soto 2000). However, having land as collateral does not guarantee that credit will be available, unless there are banks accessible to rural areas and willing to lend to farmers (Toulmin and Quan 2000). Other mechanisms are available for securing credit, including using the crop itself as collateral or using social capital through microfinance groups. Hence, transferable land titles are not always a necessary or sufficient condition for access to credit.

13.5 Why and How Do Property Rights Change?

The development of exclusive property rights over land and related natural resources is an increasingly common trajectory in the development of agricultural systems in

Africa. The shift toward more exclusive property rights is triggered by changes in the economy, such as technological innovation, changes in relative factor scarcities, and the creation of new markets (Demsetz 1967; North and Thomas 1973). These changes in the external economy cause the benefits of claiming rights in the new and privatized situation to exceed the costs of negotiating and enforcing those rights (Demsetz 1967). Individuals thus seek to adjust property rights to capture these new opportunities.

In a study of the introduction of private ownership of beavers among Indian hunters in Eastern Canada, Demsetz (1967) demonstrates that, because of the development of the commercial fur trade, the hunting of beavers increased. Consequently, to foster sustainable use and an increase in community wealth, individual hunters introduced exclusive rights. North and Thomas (1973) and North (1981) provide a historical account of changing property rights in the Middle Ages. They show that plentiful land and scarce labor during the ninth century led to the feudal manorial system, which institutionalized property rights over labor services. By the twelfth century, a growing population led to a change in the relative factor scarcities, resulting in a shift of property rights toward land instead of labor. The result was the beginning of the enclosure movement. Similar tendencies toward sharper articulation of individual interests with technological change have been documented for Africa. The introduction of tree crops, enclosures, and innovations involving large capital investments (such as grade cattle in the 1950s) resulted in a strengthening of individual rights among agricultural communities in parts of East, Southern, and West Africa (Uchendu 1970).

Demsetz and colleagues have also defined the incentive structures that emerge with privatization (Alchian and Demsetz 1972). The ability to exclude others encourages individuals to invest in the quality of the resource, because the person who bears the costs also reaps the rewards. In addition, the transferability of rights under private-property arrangements creates an opportunity cost that drives resources to the most effective users. Privatization is thus expected to increase land or agricultural productivity and the wise use and conservation of resources.

These arguments crystallize around the notion of efficiency. Private, individual property rights to land are considered to be efficient, and rights are assumed to evolve toward greater efficiency. Property regimes other than private property for land are considered by many economists to be inefficient and prone to overuse. The model of property change outlined here also ignores the collective-action problem. It assumes that simply because economic conditions for change are present and new arrangements are demanded, individuals will automatically organize to effect change and that the change required will be executed. In reality, for change to occur, the interests of individuals must be aggregated in some way and there must be a capability and willingness of the political order to provide new arrangements—the supply side of institutions. In Thailand, for example, when government officials anticipated benefits from public investments, they met the demands for exclusive rights, yet declined to do so when institutional interventions would have been harmful to the interests of influential officials. Such rulers as the paramount chief of Akyem Abuakwa of Ghana have also manipulated political institutions to meet their own objectives (Firmin-Sellers 1995, 1996). The case study in Chapter 16 indicates that not until tribal chiefs in South Africa credibly committed to uphold written lease agreements did rental markets for land begin to function. But economic gains on their own are not necessary or sufficient to induce the implementation of alternative property-rights arrangements. Instead, distributional conflicts and, as discussed earlier in this chapter, political intervention are crucial determinants of how property rights change (Libecap 1989, 2003; Eggertson 1990; North 1990; Platteau 1998, 2000; Greif 2006). Property rights may sometimes be created to serve specialized interests, particularly those who have the power to devise new rules (North 1990). Distribution refers to how wealth and political power are assigned among individuals in society because of a change in property rights (Libecap 1989, 2003). How property rights change depends on the nature of conflicts over distribution, who the winners and losers are, and how conflicts between the winners and losers are resolved (Libecap 1989, 2003; Knight 1992; Firmin-Sellers 1996). Conflict over distribution is shaped by the formula used to allocate assets during privatization (Libecap 1989, 2003), which often depends on social norms of equity and fairness that prevail in a community (Ensminger 1996).

Because different allocation mechanisms distribute assets in different ways, actors attempt to influence the process of property-rights change in ways that accord them maximum advantages. Those likely to be disadvantaged organize to oppose change. Those likely to benefit under the new arrangement support it. Actors engage those institutions, both formal-legal and customary, that they perceive will be responsive to and best articulate their claims. Conflict is reduced and change more likely when the anticipated aggregate benefits are large, interests are more homogenous, and the distribution of wealth under the proposed change is equalized (Libecap 1989, 2003). Change may be slowed and even blocked when the distribution of benefits is concentrated.

To end distributional conflict and realize new property arrangements, some actors may call on the authority of the state (Firmin-Sellers 1996). Alternatively, powerful actors with a relative bargaining advantage may constrain others to comply with new institutional rules (Knight 1992). Because of their resources, powerful actors can make credible commitments during bargaining and may even threaten retaliation. Weaker parties may thus be pressured to accept a less preferred property-rights alternative.

The addition of distributional issues greatly enriches the analysis of property-rights change. By acknowledging and extending the notion of individual benefit–cost calculus, distributional arguments capture the heterogeneity of societal actors, their differential endowments, their competition for scarce resources, and the processes through which they resolve conflict.

Many analysts of property rights focus on the importance of scarcity of the resource as a driving force toward clearer definition and enforcement of property rights, particularly private property (Demsetz 1967). Scarcity arises from a conjunction of physical conditions (limitations of the resource itself) and its demand, which in turn depends on population growth rates and the livelihood strategies of the users, market integration, prices, and the like. Although there is certainly evidence of growing privatization of property rights under customary systems as well as state titling systems (Otsuka and Place 2001), the establishment and enforcement of property rights—whether public, private, or common—entails substantial transaction costs that depend, in turn, on the nature of the resource and the technology used. Moreover, institutional history and cultural norms play a major role in shaping both the nature and distribution of property rights. The concept of path dependence (see Chapter 2) is particularly relevant: property-rights systems brought in from one context will not operate in the same way in another context, as seen, for example, in Kenya's experience with privatization and land-titling programs in the colonial and postcolonial eras.

Much has been debated about the notion of replacement as opposed to adaptation with regard to African land tenure systems (Bruce and Migot-Adholla 1994). Replacement arguments were based on now-discredited assumptions that African indigenous or customary tenures did not provide sufficient security to enable individual investment, but customary inheritance practices also resulted in fragmentation of land holdings. Replacement of these tenure systems with individualization, titling, and registration programs would provide the tenure security necessary for investment in agriculture. Following this argument, state-led privatization schemes were implemented in different parts of Africa, often with the support of donors. However, the dismal performance of titling schemes has been reviewed by various scholars (Okoth-Ogendo 1976, 1991; Coldham 1978; Haugerud 1983; Barrows and Roth 1990; Platteau 1992, 1996; Shipton and Goheen 1992; Ensminger 1997). In contrast, adaptation arguments draw from a wide range of studies in Africa (Migot-Adholla et al. 1991; Place and Hazell 1993; Platteau 2000) and suggest that under conditions of high population pressure, customary tenures spontaneously evolve toward exclusive, Western-style property rights characterized by ownership. State-led programs to induce privatization are thus not necessary; the state should instead focus on providing support services, such as administration and registration, where such processes are under way or when demanded by individuals and/or groups.

Both the replacement and adaptation arguments favor Western-style private, individual property rights, yet studies from both sides indicate that titling programs cannot be unambiguously associated with tenure security in Africa. The implications of privatization in the context of multiple, sequential rights over resources have been outlined in earlier sections of this chapter. It is more useful to focus on how farmers and administrators have modified various titling programs to satisfy their needs for tenure security, and what their actions mean for customary tenure and for policy more generally (Firmin-Sellers and Sellers 1999). Following the imposition of the 1974 Lands Ordinance in Cameroon, for example, farmers used the ordinance to receive concrete boundary markers, rather than formal title. Although the boundary markers grant no legal right or protection and do not give access to credit, community members recognized the markers as symbols of effective land occupation. At the same time, administrators modified the ordinance to protect customary tenure by selectively registering underdeveloped and undeveloped lands, because custom obligates family heads to preserve land for family members' future use (Firmin-Sellers and Sellers 1999). Thus state law cannot eliminate or replace customary law, because community norms remain important, even after custom begins to evolve. Nowhere is this more evident than in Kenya, where customary law is applied under the Land Disputes Tribunal Act of 1991 even for the lands where rights have been adjudicated and are now governed by the Registered Land Act of 1962 (McAuslan 1998). Thus the adaptation–replacement debate should be reframed to consider whether titles meet the needs of a wide range of resource users (including farming and nonfarming communities), why or why not, how, and with what consequences.

13.6 Conclusions

Property rights exist as multiple bundles of rights that are claimed by individuals, extended families, villages, and the state, not as some neat variable for "ownership" of resources. Instead of rights that derive from state law only, many different types of law and rule systems provide the basis for property-rights claims. Instead of clearly defined rights, there are usually ambiguity and negotiation over rights. And instead of rights that are defined once and for all, property rights are dynamic, changing over time.

How can such complexity be addressed? Rather than avoiding analysis of these institutions, or simplifying them to some "ideal" (often Western) system of property rights, there is a need to come to grips with complexity. To go beyond the limitations of many conventional treatments of property rights, it is useful to turn the analysis upside down. Instead of beginning with statutory law and regarding all behavior as either following or deviating from those regulations, it is more useful to start from the perspective of people's experience with access and control, in which individuals draw on a range of strategies for claiming and obtaining resources (Von Benda-Beckmann, Von Benda-Beckmann, and Spiertz 1997). From this vantage point the interplay of legal frameworks becomes visible, as does the manner in which the institutions themselves—the shared understandings among people—evolve. When a new state law is passed, it is interpreted at the local level, and it is ultimately this (varying) local interpretation that goes into practice. At the same time, when local people discuss new state laws or appeal to them, local custom is also likely to change. Finally, no one property regime is suitable in all situations. The costs and benefits of establishing, adapting, and enforcing a property arrangement vary both with the physical nature of a resource and the characteristics of communities appropriating the resource.

Notes

1. Some authors add communal property as a fourth category of tenure regime, which may be defined as "primary forests and uncultivated woodlands are owned communally and controlled by an authority such as a village chief, whereas exclusive use rights of cultivated land are assigned to individual households of the community, and its ownership rights are held traditionally by the extended family" (Otsuka and Place 2001, 12) However, this system can also be analyzed as different parties (individuals and families) holding different bundles of rights—that is, individual use and some decisionmaking rights—while the group or extended family holds the alienation rights.

2. Security of tenure refers to the ability of an individual to appropriate resources on a continuous basis, free from imposition, dispute, or approbation from outside sources, as well as the ability to claim returns from investment in the resource (Migot-Adholla et al. 1991).

3. Conversely, in heavily forested areas, clearing of trees to make agricultural fields gives one a claim over the land. In either case, it is the investment in "improving" the land that strengthens property rights.

4. Although this trend represents a significant advance in women's rights to land, it does not represent full equality. Women had to plant 40–50 percent of the land to cocoa before receiving rights to it, whereas men had to plant only 20–25 percent of the land before receiving their rights.

Further Reading

Bruce, J. W., and S. E. Migot-Adholla, eds. 1994. *Searching for land tenure security in Africa.* Dubuque, Iowa, U.S.A.: Kendall Hunt.

Ensminger, J. 1996. *Making a market: The institutional transformation of an African society.* Cambridge: Cambridge University Press.

Firmin-Sellers, K. 1996. *The transformation of property rights in the Gold Coast: An empirical analysis applying rational choice theory.* Cambridge: Cambridge University Press.

Greif, A. 2006. *Institutions and the path to the modern economy: Lessons from medieval trade.* Cambridge: Cambridge University Press.

Juul, K., and C. Lund, eds. 2002. *Negotiating property in Africa.* Portsmouth, N.H., U.S.A.: Heinemann.

Otsuka, K., and F. Place, eds. 2001. *Land tenure and natural resource management: A comparative study of agrarian communities in Asia and Africa.* Baltimore: Johns Hopkins University Press.

References

Alchian, A. A., and H. Demsetz. 1972. Production information costs and economic organization. *American Economic Review* 62 (9): 777–795.

Arnold, C. A. 2002. The reconstitution of property: Property as a web of interests. *Harvard Environmental Law Review* 26 (2): 281–364.

Baland, J.-M., and J.-P. Platteau. 1996. *Halting degradation of natural resources: Is there a role for rural communities?* New York and Oxford: Food and Agricultural Organization of the United Nations and Clarendon Press.

Banana, A. Y., and W. Gombya-Ssembajjwe. 2000. Successful forest management: The importance of security of tenure and rule enforcement in Ugandan forests. In *People and forests: Communities, institutions, and governance,* ed. C. C. Gibson, M. A. McKean, and E. Ostrom. Cambridge, Mass., U.S.A.: MIT Press.

Barrett, C. B., F. Place, and A. A. Aboud, eds. 2002. *Natural resources management in African agriculture: Understanding and improving current practices.* Wallingford, U.K.: CAB International.

Barrows, R. L., and M. Roth. 1990. Land tenure and investment in African agriculture: Theory and evidence. *Journal of Modern African Studies* 28: 265–297.

Behnke, R. H., I. Scoones, and C. Kerven, eds. 1993. *Range ecology at disequilibrium: New models of natural variability and pastoral adaptation in African savannahs.* London: Overseas Development Institute.

Berry, S. 1989. Social institutions and access to resources. *Africa* 59 (1): 41–55.

———. 1993. *No condition is permanent: The social dynamics of agrarian change in Sub-Saharan Africa.* Madison, Wis., U.S.A.: University of Wisconsin Press.

———. 2002. The everyday politics of rent-seeking: Land allocation on the outskirts of Kumase, Ghana. In *Negotiating property in Africa,* ed. K. Juul and C. Lund. Portsmouth, N.H., U.S.A.: Heineman.

Bromley, D. W. 1989. Property relations and economic development: The other land reform. *World Development* 17: 867–877.

———. 1991. *Environment and economy: Property rights and public policy.* Cambridge, Mass., U.S.A.: Blackwell.

———, ed. 1992. *Making the commons work: Theory, practice and policy.* San Francisco: ICS Press.

Bruce, J. B. 1989. A perspective on indigenous land tenure systems and land concentration. In *Land and society in contemporary Africa,* ed. R. E. Downs and S. P. Reyna. Hanover, N.H., U.S.A.: University of New Hampshire Press.

———. 1998. *Country profiles of land tenure: Africa, 1996.* Research Paper 130. Madison, Wis., U.S.A.: Land Tenure Center, University of Wisconsin.

Bruce, J. W., and S. E. Migot-Adholla, eds. 1994. *Searching for land tenure security in Africa.* Dubuque, Iowa, U.S.A.: Kendall Hunt.

Coldham, S. 1978. The effect of registration of title upon customary land rights in Kenya. *Journal of African Law* 22 (2): 91–111.

Dahlman, C. J. 1980. *The open field system and beyond: A property rights analysis of an economic institution.* Cambridge: Cambridge University Press.

Dasgupta, P. 2005. Common property resources: Economic analytics. *Economic and Political Weekly* 40 (16): 1610–1622.

De Carvalho, E. C. 1974. "Traditional" and "modern" patterns of cattle raising in southwestern Angola: A critical evaluation of change from pastoralism to ranching. *Journal of Developing Areas* 8 (January): 199–226.

Deininger, K., and D. A. All. 2007. Do overlapping property rights reduce agricultural investment? Evidence from Uganda. Policy Research Working Paper WPS4310. Washington, D.C.: World Bank.

Deininger, K., D. A. All, S. Holden, and J. Zeverbergen. 2007. Rural land certification in Ethiopia: Process, initial impact, and implications for other African countries. Policy Research Working Paper WPS4218. Washington, D.C.: World Bank.

Demsetz, H. 1967. Toward a theory of property rights. *American Economic Review* 57 (2): 347–359.

De Soto, H. 2000. *The mystery of capital: Why capitalism triumphs in the West and fails everywhere else.* New York: Basic Books.

Downs, R. E., and S. P. Reyna. 1989. Introduction. In *Land and society in contemporary Africa,* eds. R. E. Downs and S. P. Reyna. Hanover, N.H., U.S.A.: University of New Hampshire Press.

Eggertson, T. 1990. *Economic behaviour and institutions.* Cambridge: Cambridge University Press.

———. 1996. The economics of control and the cost of property rights. In *Rights to nature: Ecologic, economic, cultural and political principles of institutions for the environment,* ed. S. S. Hanna, C. Folke, and K. Maler. Washington, D.C.: Island Press.

Ensminger, J. 1996. *Making a market: The institutional transformation of an African society.* Cambridge: Oxford University Press.

———. 1997. Changing property rights: Reconciling formal and informal rights to land in Africa. In *The frontiers of the New Institutional Economics,* ed. J. N. Drobak and J. V. C. Nye. San Diego: Academic Press.

Evangelou, P. 1984. *Livestock development in Kenya's Maasailand: Pastoralists' transition to a market economy*. Boulder, Colo., U.S.A.: Westview Press.

Feder, G., and D. Feeny. 1991. Land tenure and property rights: Theory and implications for development theory. *World Bank Economic Review* 5 (1): 135–153.

Firmin-Sellers, K. 1995. The politics of property rights. *American Political Science Review* 89 (4): 867–881.

————. 1996. *The transformation of property rights in the Gold Coast: An empirical analysis applying rational choice theory*. New York: Cambridge University Press.

Firmin-Sellers, K., and P. Sellers. 1999. Expected failures and unexpected successes of land titling in Africa. *World Development* 27: 1115–1128.

Fortmann, L., and J. W. Bruce, eds. 1988. *Whose trees? Proprietary dimensions of forestry*. Boulder, Colo., U.S.A.: Westview Press.

Fortmann, L., C. Antinori, and N. Nabane. 1997. Fruits of their labors: Gender, property rights, and tree planting in two Zimbabwe villages. *Rural Sociology* 62 (3): 295–314.

Galaty, J. G., and D. L. Johnson, eds. 1990. *The world of pastoralism: Herding systems in comparative perspective*. New York: Guilford Press.

Gibson, C. C., J. T. Williams, and E. Ostrom. 2005. Local enforcement and better forests. *World Development* 33: 273–284.

Goldstein, M., and C. Udry. 2005. The profits of power: Land rights and agricultural investment in Ghana. Working Paper 929. New Haven, Conn., U.S.A.: Economic Growth Center, Yale University.

Greif, A. 2006. *Institutions and the path to the modern economy: Lessons from medieval trade*. Cambridge: Cambridge University Press.

Guillet, D. 1981. Land tenure, ecological zone, and agricultural regime. *American Ethnologist* 8 (1): 139–157.

Haugerud, A. 1983. The consequences of land tenure reform among smallholders in the Kenya Highlands. *Rural Africana* 15–16: 65–89.

Hodgson, S. 2004. Land and water—The rights interface. FAO Legal Papers Online 36. Rome: Food and Agriculture Organization. http://www.fao.org/legal/prs-ol/lpo36.pdf. Accessed January 3, 2004.

Holden, S. T., and H. Yohannes. 2001. Land redistribution, tenure insecurity, and intensity of production: A study of farm households in southern Ethiopia. CAPRi Working Paper 21. Washington, D.C.: International Food Policy Research Institute.

Khazanov, A. 1984. *Nomads and the outside world*. New York: Cambridge University Press.

Kirk, M. 1999. The context for livestock and crop-livestock development in Africa: The evolving role of the state in influencing property rights over grazing resources in Sub-Saharan Africa. In

Property rights, risk, and livestock development in Africa, ed. N. McCarthy, B. Swallow, M. Kirk, and P. Hazell. Washington, D.C.: International Food Policy Research Institute.

Knight, J. 1992. *Institutions and social conflict.* New York: Cambridge University Press.

Knox McCulloch, A., R. S. Meinzen-Dick, and P. Hazell. 1998. Property rights, collective action, and technologies for natural resource management: A conceptual framework. CAPRi Working Paper 1. Washington, D.C.: International Food Policy Research Institute.

Lastarria-Cornhiel, S. 1997. Impact of privatization on gender and property rights in Africa. *World Development* 25: 1317–1333.

Libecap, G. D. 1989. *Contracting for property rights.* New York: Cambridge University Press.

———. 2003. Contracting for property rights. In *Property rights: Cooperation, conflict, and law,* ed. T. L. Anderson and F. S. McChesney. Princeton, N.J., U.S.A.: Princeton University Press.

McAuslan, P. 1998. Making law work: Restructuring land relations in Africa. *Development and Change* 29: 525–552.

Meinzen-Dick, R. S., and M. Di Gregorio, eds. 2004. *Collective action and property rights for sustainable development. 2020 Focus 11.* Washington, D.C.: International Food Policy Research Institute. Available at http://www.ifpri.org/2020/focus/focus11.htm.

Meinzen-Dick, R. S., and R. Pradhan. 2002. Legal pluralism and dynamic property rights. CAPRi Working Paper 22. Washington, D.C.: International Food Policy Research Institute.

Meinzen-Dick, R. S., A. Knox, F. Place, and B. Swallow, eds. 2002. *Innovation in natural resource management: The role of property rights and collective action in developing countries.* Baltimore: Johns Hopkins University Press.

Mendes, L. 1988. Private and communal land tenure in Morocco's western high Atlas Mountains: Complements, not ideological opposites. Paper 26a. London: Overseas Development Institute, Agricultural Administrative Unit, Pastoral Development Network. Available at http://www .odi.org.uk/networks/pdn/papers/26a.pdf. Accessed August 2005.

Migot-Adholla, S. E., P. Hazell, B. Blarel, and F. Place. 1991. Indigenous land rights systems in Sub-Saharan Africa: A constraint on productivity? *World Bank Economic Review* 5 (1): 155–175.

Netting, M. C. 1976. What alpine peasants have in common: Observations on communal tenure in a Swiss village. *Human Ecology* 4: 135–146.

Niamir-Fuller, M. 1995. A new paradigm in African range management policy and practice. Invited presentation at the fifth International Rangeland Congress, Salt Lake City, Utah, U.S.A., July 1995.

———. 1998. The resilience of pastoral herding in Sahelian Africa. In *Linking social and ecological systems: Management practices and social mechanisms for building resilience,* ed. F. Berkes and C. Folke. Cambridge: Cambridge University Press.

———. 1999. A review of recent literature on pastoralism and transhumance in Africa. In *Managing mobility in African rangelands: The legitimization of transhumance,* ed. M. Niamir-Fuller.

Report for the Food and Agriculture Organization of the United Nations and Beijer Institute of Ecological Economics. London: Intermediate Technology Publishers.

Njoka, T. J. 1979. Ecological and socio-cultural trends of Kaputiei group ranches in Kenya. Ph.D. dissertation, University of California, Berkeley.

North, D. C. 1981. *Structure and change in economic history.* New York: W. W. Norton.

———. 1990. *Institutions, institutional change and economic performance.* Cambridge: Cambridge University Press.

North, D. C., and R. B. Thomas. 1973. *The rise of the Western world: A new economic history.* Cambridge: Cambridge University Press.

Nugent, J. B., and N. Sanchez. 1991. Tribes, chiefs and transhumance: A comparative institutional analysis. Paper presented at the Annual Meeting of the Middle Eastern Economic Association, Washington, D.C., December 1990.

———. 1995. The local variability of rainfall and tribal institutions: The case of Sudan. *Journal of Economic Behavior and Organization* 39 (3): 263–291.

———. 1998. Common property rights as an endogenous response to risk. *American Journal of Agricultural Economics* 80 (3): 651–657.

Okoth-Ogendo, H. 1976. African land tenure reform. In *Agricultural development in Kenya,* ed. J. Heyer. Nairobi: Oxford University Press.

———. 1991. *Tenants of the crown.* Nairobi: African Center for Technology Studies Press.

Ostrom, E. 1990. *Governing the commons: The evolution of institutions for collective action.* Cambridge: Cambridge University Press.

———. 2001. The puzzle of counterproductive property rights reforms: A conceptual analysis. In *Access to land, rural poverty, and public action,* ed. A. de Janvry, G. Gordillo, J.-P. Platteau, and E. Sadoulet. New York: Oxford University Press, for the World Institute for Development Economics Research of the United Nations University.

Otsuka, K., and F. Place, eds. 2001. *Land tenure and natural resource management: A comparative study of agrarian communities in Asia and Africa.* Baltimore: Johns Hopkins University Press.

Payne, G. 2001. Urban land tenure policy options: Titles or rights? *Habitat International* 25: 415–429.

Pender, J., F. Place, and S. Ehui, eds. 2006. *Strategies for sustainable land management in the East African highlands.* Washington, D.C.: International Food Policy Research Institute.

Picht, C. 1987. Common property regimes in Swiss alpine meadows. Initial draft. Paper prepared for the Conference on Advances in Comparative Institutional Analysis, Inter-University Center of Post-graduate Studies, Dubrovnik, Yugoslavia, October.

Place, F. 1994. The role of land and tree tenure on the adoption of agroforestry technologies: A summary and synthesis. Madison, Wis., U.S.A.: Land Tenure Center, University of Wisconsin–Madison.

Place, F., and P. Hazell 1993. Productivity effects of indigenous land tenure systems in Sub-Saharan Africa. *American Journal of Agricultural Economics* 75 (1): 10–19.

Place, F., K. Otsuka, and S. Scherr. 2004. Property rights, collective action and agroforestry. In *Collective action and property rights for sustainable development,* ed. R. S. Meinzen-Dick and M. Di Gregorio. 2020 Focus 11. Washington, D.C.: International Food Policy Research Institute. Available at http://www.ifpri.org/2020/focus/focus11.htm.

Place, F., M. Roth, and P. Hazell. 1994. Land tenure security and agricultural performances in Africa: Overview of research methodology. In *Searching for land tenure security in Africa,* ed. J. W. Bruce and S. E. Migot-Adholla. Dubuque, Iowa, U.S.A.: Kendall Hunt.

Platteau, J.-P. 1992. *Land reform and structural adjustment in Sub-Saharan Africa: Controversies and guidelines.* Report prepared for the Policy Analysis Division of the Economic and Social Policy Division. Rome: Food and Agriculture Organization of the United Nations.

———. 1996. The evolutionary theory of land rights as applied to Sub-Saharan Africa: A critical assessment. *Development and Change* 27 (1): 29–86.

———. 2000. *Institutions, social norms, and economic development: Fundamentals of development economics.* Amsterdam: Harwood Academic.

Quisumbing, A. R., and K. Otsuka. 2001. *Land, trees, and women: Evolution of land tenure institutions in western Ghana and Sumatra.* Research Report 121. Washington, D.C.: International Food Policy Research Institute and Tokyo Metropolitan University.

Roth, M., K. D. Wiebe, and S. W. Lawry. 1993. Land tenure and agrarian structure: Implications for technology adoption. In *Proceedings of the Workshop on Social Science Research and the CRSPS,* ed. USAID. Washington, D.C.: United States Agency for International Development.

Roth, M., R. Barrows, M. Carter, and D. Kanel. 1989. Land ownership security and farm investment: Comment. *American Journal of Agricultural Economics* 71 (1): 211–214.

Rutten, M. M. E. M. 1992. *Selling wealth to buy poverty: The process of the individualization of land-ownership among the Maasai pastoralists of Kajiado District, Kenya, 1890–1900.* Nijmegen Studies in Development and Cultural Change 10. Saarbrücken, Germany: Verlag Breitenbach.

Sandford, S. 1983. *Management of pastoral development in the Third World.* Chichester, U.K., and London: John Wiley and Sons, and Overseas Development Institute.

Schlager, E., and E. Ostrom. 1992. Property-rights regimes and natural resources: A conceptual analysis. *Land Economics* 68 (3): 249–262.

Scoones, I. 1995. Integrating social sciences into rangeland management: Chairperson's summary and comments. Invited presentation at the Fifth International Rangeland Congress, Salt Lake City, Utah, U.S.A., July 1995.

Shipton, P., and M. Goheen. 1992. Introduction: Understanding African land-holding: Power, wealth and meaning. *Africa: Journal of the International African Institute* 62 (3): 307–325.

Swallow, B. M., N. L. Johnson, and R. S. Meinzen-Dick. 2001. Working with people for watershed management. *Water Policy* 3 (6): 449–456.

Swallow, B. M., L. Onyango, and R. S. Meinzen-Dick. 2006. Catchment property rights and the case of Kenya's Nyando Basin. In *Preparing for the next generation of watershed management programmes and projects: Africa,* ed. B. Swallow, N. Okono, M. Achouri, and L. Tennyson. Proceedings of the African Regional Workshop, Nairobi, Kenya, October 8–10, 2003. Rome: Food and Agriculture Organization of the United Nations. Available at http://www.fao.org/docrep/009/a0380e/a0380e00.htm. Accessed April 2009.

Swallow, B. M., J. Wangila, W. Mulatu, O. Okello, and N. McCarthy. 2002. Collective action in space: Assessing how collective action varies across an African landscape. In *Innovation in natural resource management: The role of property rights and collective action in developing countries,* ed. R. S. Meinzen-Dick, A. Knox, F. Place, and B. Swallow. Baltimore: Johns Hopkins University Press.

Toulmin, C., and J. Quan, eds. 2000. *Evolving land rights, policy and tenure in Africa.* London: International Institute for Environment and Development Drylands, DFID.

Uchendu, V. C. 1970. The impact of changing agricultural technology on African land tenure. *Journal of Developing Areas* 4: 477–486.

Von Benda-Beckmann, F., K. Von Benda-Beckmann, and H. L. J. Spiertz. 1997. Local law and customary practices in the study of water rights. In *Water rights, conflict and policy,* ed. R. Pradhan, F. Von Benda-Beckmann, K. Von Benda-Beckmann, H. L. J. Spiertz, S. S. Kadka, and K. A. Haq. Proceedings of a workshop, Kathmandu, Nepal, January 22–24, 1996. Colombo, Sri Lanka: International Irrigation Management Institute.

Chapter 14

Coordination in Natural Resource Management

Ruth S. Meinzen-Dick

Because of their spatial scale, most irrigation systems, forests, rangelands, and fisheries cannot be managed at the individual or household level (Knox McCulloch, Meinzen-Dick, and Hazell 1998). They require some form of coordinated regulation to limit overuse and ensure that there is sufficient investment to sustain the resource base. Even the adoption of "lumpy" technologies (such as equipment) that are not cost effective for a single farm requires some form of coordination.

Carving up resources into holdings that are individually managed without coordination is often not appropriate for natural resources, such as water systems, rangelands, or forests, in which each unit of the resource has a great deal of internal variation (Thompson and Wilson 1994) and is interdependent with other units, making it difficult to provide all claimants and users with a viable piece of the resource. This difficulty poses serious problems for individualization policies, as demonstrated by externally induced programs to divide and privatize rangelands in Kenya and Botswana (Lane and Moorehead 1994; Peters 1994; Kirk 1999; Niamir-Fuller 2000), as discussed in Mwangi's case study in Chapter 15.

A further reason that coordination is needed is that there are generally multiple uses, as well as multiple users, of these natural resources. Irrigation systems are used not only for field irrigation but also for domestic purposes, fishing, livestock, and home gardens (Bakker et al. 1999); forests are used for kindling, fodder, resins, and other minor forest products as well as timber (Dewees and Scherr 1996); the same land may be employed for crops, a few trees, and grazing by different groups or in different seasons (Swallow et al. 1997). Many of these "secondary" uses have high economic value or are essential to the livelihood strategies of various types of households. Outside approaches that focus on resource management to maximize a single use are not likely to be as appropriate in these situations as rules that are locally developed through negotiation among different users (Steins and Edwards 1999). Local collective action can be instrumental in finding rules and allocations of the resource among different users in a way that is seen as equitable by the users themselves. Thus there are equity as well as productivity arguments for coordination in natural resource management (NRM).

Critical coordination tasks in NRM include developing rules for resource use; monitoring compliance with the rules and sanctioning violators; and mobilizing the necessary cash, labor, or material resources to invest in maintenance and improvements in the resource base. The need for coordination is particularly marked for common pool resources that are shared by many users. Hardin's (1968) article on "The Tragedy of the Commons" was influential in highlighting how unregulated access to resources could lead to degradation of the resource base, because each individual user would have an incentive to be a free rider, taking advantage of others.[1] Being a free rider can take two forms: (1) to overuse the resource because the individual receives the full gains from use of the resource but only shares the cost of its degradation; or (2) to underinvest because the individual bears the full costs of the investment but only receives a share of the benefits. The "tragedy of the commons" is unfortunately a misnomer, which has led to numerous calls for either privatization or nationalization of many shared natural resources, so that either the market or state would provide coordination. However, what Hardin refers to is more accurately called the "tragedy of open access," because the situation he describes is the lack of effective regulation. An examination of the empirical experience can provide thousands of examples of successful common property resource management around the world, in which collective action provides effective coordination among users and even investment in improving the resource. There are also thousands of examples in which the state or individuals have not been effective in regulating the use of resources held as public or private property. What is critical is the degree of coordination among users and enforcement of property rights.

As in the case of exchange of goods and services, this coordination may take place through the state, market, or collective action. However, the exchange of goods and services often deals with items that are characterized by high excludability and high subtractability. They therefore can be treated as private goods, and the market is a suitable coordination institution for managing the exchange of private goods and services. But many natural resources are characterized by the high costs of excluding others. Hence, they fit more as public goods, when there is low subtractability, or common pool resources, when there is high subtractability. Thus coordination for such resources is more commonly achieved through the state or collective-action institutions than through the market. State coordination is exemplified in government-managed forests and irrigation systems. Collective action is seen in many types of user groups. Market coordination for technologies or NRM practices above the level of the farm is relatively less common, but groundwater markets in which well owners sell their surplus water (above what their farm needs) to neighboring farms provide one example (Shah 1993; Meinzen-Dick 1996).[2] The following sections of this chapter focus on the factors that are likely to facilitate or constrain the functioning of state and collective action institutions for coordination of NRM.

Much of the coordination that takes place is embedded in broader social institutions. Coordination may not even be intentional but may come about through people adhering to social rules and norms or through using their social networks. Totems, taboos, proverbs, religious teaching, and myths about water or tree spirits all influence how people relate to their natural environment. In many cases, even an instrumental view of land, water, and trees as economic resources is not consonant with local world views, and applying a narrow economic analysis of maximizing profits from the resources will not lead to an accurate understanding of local practices. Thus there is a need to go deeper: in terms of Williamson's (1999) levels, certainly to the levels of governance and institutional analysis, but perhaps even to the level of embeddedness.

14.1 State Coordination

Land, water, forests, and other natural resources generate not only vital livelihood benefit streams for the farmers and other families who use them directly but also critical environmental services, such as biodiversity, regulation of soil and water flows (watershed functions), and carbon sequestration, that affect others who may not even live in the community where the resources are located. Indeed, many environmental services are of global importance. The critical nature of the resources and the high degree of externalities generated by their use have provided a rationale for a strong role for the state in coordination as a matter of public trust. In many cases, this role has extended to the state claiming public ownership of the resource, entrusting its management to a government agency and even excluding citizens from entering or using the resource.

Such "fines and fences" approaches to state protection of natural resources has come under criticism on two grounds. First, it has often denied customary property rights of resource-dependent communities, threatening both their culture and livelihoods. Second, the state is often not effective in its coordination role, particularly at the local level. Irrigation agencies, for example, frequently lack the personnel and financial resources needed to operate and maintain the extensive canal networks, and the forestry department may not be able to patrol and monitor forest use. Involving local resource users can lead to more effective coordination, because they have a stronger interest in managing the resource and more detailed local knowledge of both the resource and of local users.

In response to growing recognition of the limitations of the state in coordination of natural resources and the fiscal crisis of the state in many countries, there has been a major policy trend toward devolving control over natural resources from government agencies to user groups.[3] This type of devolution has not only cut across countries from Asia, Africa, and the Americas, but also across natural resource sectors, encompassing water (especially irrigation), forests, rangelands, fisheries, and wildlife. The process of devolution of resource management involves programs that shift responsibility and authority from the state to nongovernmental bodies—a "rolling back [of] the boundaries of the state" (Vedeld 1996, 137).

Devolution programs go by a range of names. When control over resources is transferred more or less completely to local user groups, it is often referred to as community-based resource management (CBRM). In these cases, the government generally withdraws from a role and either cuts or redeploys agency staff. When the state retains a large role in resource management, in conjunction with an expanded role for users, it may be referred to as joint management or co-management. However, these cases are often not clear-cut, with most involving some form of interaction between the state and user groups. Specific terms vary by sector and country. For example, in irrigation, irrigation management transfer generally refers to programs that go farther in divesting state agencies of their role, whereas participatory irrigation management programs seek to increase user involvement, usually as a supplement to the state's role. Joint forest management and fisheries co-management are other examples of programs that transfer responsibility for some management tasks to user groups, in conjunction with state agencies.[4]

Devolution is often part of a number of related policy reforms in which central government agencies transfer rights and responsibilities to more localized institutions,[5] as illustrated in Figure 14.1:

- *Deconcentration* transfers decisionmaking authority to lower level units of a bureaucracy or government line agency. It represents the least fundamental change, because authority remains with the same type of institution, and accountability is ultimately still upward to the central government, which is sometimes taken to represent society at large (Agrawal and Ribot 1999).

Figure 14.1 Devolution in the context of decentralization and other institutional reforms

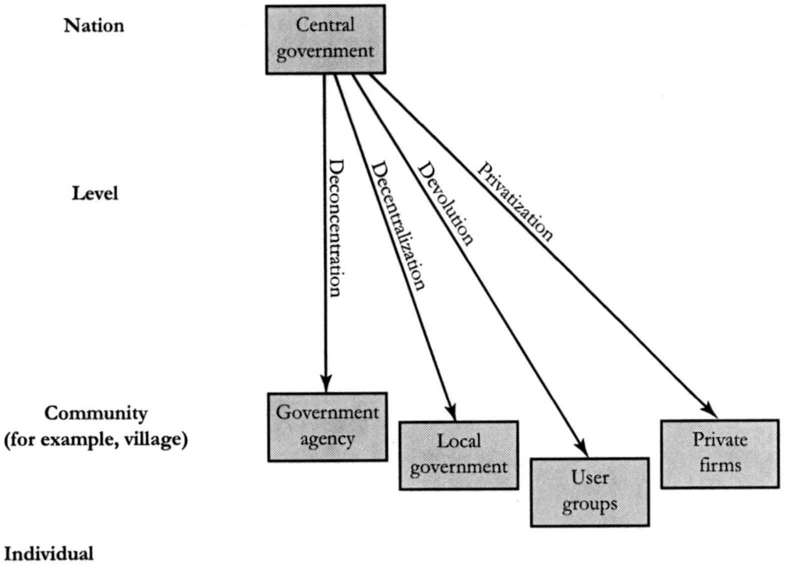

Accountability	Central government	Local populace	Resource and service users	Shareholders
Sector	Government		Collective	Private

Source: Meinzen-Dick and Knox (2001).

- *Decentralization* transfers both decisionmaking authority and payment responsibility to lower levels of government. Although authority still resides in the government, decentralization provides a stronger role for local bodies, which are presumed to have greater accountability to the local populace, including both users of the resource and others who live in the area.

- *Devolution* involves the transfer of rights and responsibilities to user groups at the local level. These organizations are accountable to their membership (usually those who depend on the resource) but do not represent others in the local community or society at large (Ribot 1999).

- *Privatization* broadly refers to transfer from the public sector to private groups or individuals. This transfer can include firms that are responsible to their shareholders as well as nonprofit service organizations (grassroots or external nongovernmental organizations) that are accountable to their donors (Uphoff 1998).

Behind these trends is the broad principle of *subsidiarity*, which requires that the distribution of power and responsibility should be in favor of lower level governmental institutions and smaller jurisdictions, and that political authority should always be allocated at the lowest possible institutional level, that is, close to the citizens, who are the ultimate sovereigns (Ngaido and Kirk 2001). Accordingly, the central state should not withdraw decisionmaking power and authority from the private sector and civil society organizations or local government. When lower level capacity is weak, the state should provide temporary help and transfer more complete rights when local capacities are developed. Thus devolution does not mean a total withdrawal of state involvement, but it often implies the need for the state to engage with other institutions in different ways.

A key to effective decentralization is increased broad-based participation in local public decisionmaking. For decentralization to effectively improve the welfare of local communities as well as the environment, it should be "downwardly accountable" to the community (Agrawal and Ribot 1999, 474). The different accountability mechanisms present in various types of devolution and decentralization do not always include all stakeholders affected by the management of the targeted resource. The greater the degree of divergence, the greater is the need for a countervailing regulation mechanism. For example, if responsibility for water management is transferred to an irrigators' association, other water users in the local community will be affected but may not be included in the decisionmaking. When examined in detail, community-based forms of local NRM often lack representation and downward accountability, and hence they are susceptible to elite capture (wherein the benefits go primarily to the elites). In his research Ribot (1999) showed that decentralizations in the Sahel, for example, are transferring decisionmaking powers to various unaccountable local bodies, threatening local equity and the environment. Decentralization to local government bodies may include more of the local stakeholders but not those living downstream, who are affected by the management of the resource. A local government agency is accountable to the central government, which may be accountable to the entire citizenry, but in fact sectoral divisions (and principal-agent problems; see Chapter 2) often limit their accountability to all stakeholders. For example, an irrigation agency may not be as concerned with biodiversity or the impact of water management on fisheries. Privatization is likely to have the greatest divergence between stakeholders and the accountable body. To take an extreme example, there is very little overlap between shareholders in a multinational corporation that takes on management of municipal water supply and the people who are affected by how that water supply is managed. In this case, a strong regulatory body is required to ensure that the needs of those who are directly and indirectly affected are taken into account in the system management (for a review of experiences in developing countries, see Parker and Kirkpatrick 2005). In most cases regulation is vested with the state as the representative of the citizenry, but it maintains separate regulatory boards with representatives of key stakeholder groups (for example, farmers, fishers, and environmental agencies or groups).

A second key to successful devolution is that the local organizations being vested with greater responsibility should have sufficient incentive and capacity to manage the resource. Incentives include both rewards and deterrents that would motivate actors to manage the resource in a sustainable and equitable manner. Capacity refers to the potential or actual ability to manage the resource, which may include knowledge about the resource (from formal training or local knowledge), and the requisite labor, finances, tools, and other requirements. Ribot (1999, 2003) highlights the importance of local bodies having sufficient discretionary powers, but in a review of decentralization in Africa, he found that the governments in Burkina Faso, the Gambia, Mali, and Senegal were devolving insufficient powers and benefits to carry out decentralization or to motivate local actors to take on new environmental management responsibilities. Appropriate accountability structures may help to create incentives for lower level government agencies, local governments, and private-sector contractors, but it is essential to check that their capacities are appropriately matched with their new roles. In the case of user groups, the incentive and capacity to manage the resource are often assumed, based on their dependence on the resource and past experience with it. However, if the groups are not given sufficient rights, or if using the resource is not profitable (because of poor terms of trade for agriculture, forestry, or fishing), then the users will not have the incentive. In addition, the capacity of user groups should also be examined, because conditions are likely to have changed compared with traditional management conditions.

Most empirical cases involve some combination of public, private, and collective-action arrangements. These are often referred to as co-management. For example, a large-scale irrigation system could have government agency staff operating the reservoir and main canal system, water users' associations (user groups) operating the lower level distribution canals, and a private company providing management services. There could be central government agencies, local governments, user groups, and private contractors all involved in joint forest management (Box 14.1).

Although the theoretical advantages of user management have been convincing and the impetus for devolution policies strong, the actual outcomes of devolution programs in various sectors and countries have been mixed. The stated objectives of such programs in terms of positive impact on resource productivity, equity among stakeholders, poverty alleviation, and organizational and environmental

Box 14.1 State, private, or collective action?

The flowchart below generalizes the organizational structure of joint ventures among previously disadvantaged communities, private investors, and the state that are emerging in South Africa. The previously disadvantaged community is often the sole or majority shareholder in a trust or communal property association that owns fixed improvements (or land and fixed improvements) and is a minority shareholder in the operating entity. Private investors usually buy a majority interest in the operating company that rents assets from the community at a pre-agreed rate. The state provides grants to finance the community's equity and concessions to the operating company if the latter owns the land. The private investor also contributes expertise and a credit history that, together with the community's equity, leverages additional capital from commercial banks. Such hybrids contain elements of state, private, and collective action, and of both horizontal integration and vertical coordination. They are becoming attractive options for white-owned firms in South Africa, partly because the government provides grants for black economic empowerment (BEE) in the agricultural and tourism sectors, and partly because these firms are expected to comply with sector-wide BEE charters.

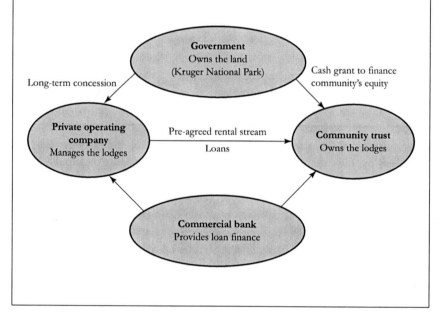

sustainability are often not met. When user groups are created, they sometimes set up a second set of informal institutions that work in parallel to the officially responsible bodies (especially if the user groups do not have a clear legal status and external money is involved). Decentralization schemes can create several layers of institutions that compete with rather then complement one another. Resources have not always been used more efficiently than under state management, nor have the benefits been distributed equitably. In some cases the resource base has been depleted. Experience has shown that the outcomes of devolution programs depend on the strength of collective-action institutions as well as on effective coordination with other institutions.

14.2 Coordination through Collective Action

The term "collective action" often conjures up images of formal organizations, but much collective action takes place through less formal arrangements, and the mere presence of an organization does not automatically imply that there will be collective action—many formal organizations are ineffective or even moribund. The presence of an organization with regard to collective action is analogous to having an electricity connection to a house: it does not guarantee that there will be electricity (collective action). However, there can be electricity in a house through batteries or even lightening bolts, even without an electric connection, just as there can be collective action without an organization, through social networks or some form of spontaneous action.

The concept of collective action is related to the term "social capital," which has received much attention in the development literature over the past decade, but the two are not identical. As defined by Putnam (1995, 67), social capital is "features of social organisation such as networks, norms and social trust that facilitate cooperation and coordination for mutual benefit."[6] Accordingly, social capital can provide the basis for collective action, but something must be done to mobilize this capital to achieve collective action.

Collective action is important in many aspects of life, but it has gained particular prominence in development discourse in recent years as a supplement to—or even substitute for—weak states and missing markets. Groups or communities come together to provide infrastructure and services, ranging from water supplies and roads to schools, health care, and even policing, when their government does not provide these services adequately. Through a range of institutional arrangements, including formal cooperatives, self-help groups, and social networks, people come together to help overcome the missing markets by providing forms of credit, insurance, marketing assistance, and labor, as well as to provide the basis for greater bargaining power in transactions. Collective action also plays a critical role in many cases of NRM (as discussed below).

Examples of successful collective action in various areas (especially irrigation, forestry, rangeland management, and fisheries) have contributed to policies to devolve NRM to a range of local organizations (Meinzen-Dick, Knox, and DiGregorio 2001). Collective provision of other services, including water supply and sanitation, health care, and education, has also provided the basis for a variety of community-driven development projects (Mansuri and Rao 2004).

But collective action is not found everywhere and is not available for every type of public good. And even where collective action is found, it is not always inclusive, particularly of the poor. Programs that rely heavily on collective action as a solution to market or state failure may be setting up for failure if they do not take into account the extent of such action or the potential for local provision of services. Thus a clear understanding of the capacity for collective action under different conditions is needed as well as a clear recognition of its limitations.

The comparative advantage for coordination in NRM between state and collective-action institutions likely depends on the level of aggregation, with collective action at the level of the village community or subgroup and the state having an advantage at higher levels, such as the management of river basins. The costs of state involvement at lower levels are very high, particularly when government employees are required to do all resource monitoring. Local users may have an advantage over government agents through their detailed knowledge of the resource—especially important when the resource is highly variable over space and time. By living and working in the area, users may also have a comparative advantage over government agents in monitoring resource use and rule compliance. Furthermore, because their livelihoods depend on the resource, local users are often assumed to have the greatest incentives to maintain the resource base over time. Although it is possible for collective-action institutions to operate at higher levels (for example, through federated structures, even to the level of a national forest user group), the transaction costs of collective action increase with broadening scope. At these levels, scientific knowledge and information (for example, remote sensing and computer-assisted models) often play an important role, giving government agencies a comparative advantage.

14.3 Complexity and Dynamics in Coordination Institutions

Just as property rights can change with the introduction of new technologies, so technical or socioeconomic change can influence coordination institutions, especially in agriculture. The process of jointly developing an irrigation system can, for example, forge linkages among farmers (Coward 1986). There are also many examples of the erosion of collective-action institutions by technologies that allow individual farmers to become more independent. Such a breakdown is particularly common if the wealthier farmers are able to opt out of dependence on the shared resource. The introduction of mechanized pumps that provide alternatives to shared sources of surface water can, for example, erode cooperation on irrigation.

Property rights and collective action can even have an effect on each other. As noted above, property rights require some type of enforcement mechanism, which is often a form of collective action. Common property regimes particularly require collective action, or they deteriorate into open access. Similarly, holding property rights in common can provide the impetus and incentive for collective action.

The coordination institutions not only have a direct influence on technology adoption, but they also have strong interactions with other critical factors in agriculture, particularly credit, markets, and information (for example, agricultural extension).[7] The rise of microfinance programs illustrates how collective action can be used to access credit: group members stake their reputations and social relations with others as the guarantee or collateral. Similarly, through agricultural cooperatives, smallholder farmers can use collective action to improve their access to markets. Extension programs are also linked to property rights, because they often give more attention to landowners than to other farmers. However, the use of farmer groups for technology dissemination, and even for demanding technologies, indicates the potential for collective action to improve access to information (Place et al. 2002).

The interactions among property rights, collective action, and credit, marketing, and information are some of the complex linkages that influence both the institutions themselves and the outcomes in terms of equity, efficiency, or environmental sustainability.

14.4   Factors Affecting Coordination Institutions

Although the capacity to work together plays a crucial role in the outcomes of NRM, these conditions are not found in every situation. There is a large body of literature on the factors hypothesized to affect collective action institutions, particularly as exemplified in common property regimes (for example, Olson 1971; Ostrom 1990; Rasmussen and Meinzen-Dick 1995; Baland and Platteau 1996; Agrawal 2001). Consistent with the conceptual framework in this book, these factors, which are derived from examination of case studies and game theory, can be broadly grouped in terms of (1) physical and technical characteristics of the resource, (2) social and economic characteristics of the resource users, and (3) policy and governance factors. The specific factors cited by several key authors are summarized in Table 14.1.

Table 14.1 Factors affecting local organizations for natural resource management

	Reference				
Factor	Ostrom (1990, 1992)	Wade (1988)	Bardhan (1993)	Nugent (1993)	Oakerson (1992)
Physical and technical characteristics of the resource	Size Clarity of boundaries Flow patterns (predictability of quantity over time and space) Condition Technologies for extraction and for exclusion	Boundedness Size Cost of exclusion Technology	Boundedness	Nature of resource Excludability	Capacity Excludability Subtractability/jointness Divisibility Physical boundaries
Social and economic characteristics of the users	Number of members Time horizon Proximity to resource and distance between users Extent and nature of interaction (individualized or collective action) Skills and assets of leaders Homogeneity versus heterogeneity of interests Norms of behavior and culture	Size of user group Boundaries of group Location of resource and residence of users Users' knowledge Users' demands Power structure Mutual obligations	Size of user group Shared norms Group identification Egalitarian structures/homogeneity Openness Stability (migration and mobility possibilities)	Competition among alternative organizations Tradition and norms	n.a.
Policy and governance arrangements	Design principles Member and access rules Resource boundary rules Appropriation (withdrawing) and provision rules Collective-choice arrangements Monitoring and sanctioning rules	Existing arrangements for discussion of resource problems Punishment rules Relationships between users and state (external rules and intervention)	Structures of punishment and sanctions Monitoring mechanisms External authorities' recognition of local norms	Rules for monitoring and sanctioning Ability to change rules Governance structure (internal and external)	Decisionmaking arrangements Operational rules Collective-choice rules External arrangements
Relationships	n.a.	Noticeability (ease of detection of free riders)	Ecological stress	n.a.	n.a.

Source: Rasmussen and Meinzen-Dick (1995).
Note: n.a., not addressed.

14.4.1   Physical and Technical Factors

Among physical and technical factors, many authors stress the importance of the degree of excludability and subtractability (or rivalry) of the resource, as described in Chapter 3. Excludability and subtractability, which are critical factors in defining whether goods are best treated as public, private, common pool, or toll goods, are influenced by the size of the resource system and the natural boundedness of the resource—the degree to which it is easy to designate boundaries (Uphoff 1986; Ostrom 1992; Oakerson 1993). For example, it is easier to place a boundary around a crop field than around a rangeland, and water or fisheries are still more difficult to designate within boundaries.

The technology used for the extraction of resources and for enclosing will, according to Wade (1988) and Ostrom (1990), affect the possibility of interaction between the individuals as well. Animal traction, tractors, or chainsaws enable each person to exploit more crop or forest land, increasing the pressure on the resource and the need for coordination. The type of irrigation canals affects the way water is shared among farmers and determines the plausibility of cutting off water to those who do not contribute, as described in the case study in Chapter 17. In Nepal, Lam (1996) found that farmer-managed irrigation systems with temporary diversion structures that needed to be replaced each year meant that even farmers at the head of the canal needed the labor of other farmers to repair the headworks each year and hence had an incentive to provide equitable water sharing with the tail enders. But when the headworks were replaced with concrete, head enders did not need the tail-enders' labor as much and so did not share the water as much. Fencing provides another classic example: without fences, livestock need to be herded, resulting in more human interaction, but with the introduction of fencing, there is less interaction (positive or negative) between the livestock keepers and farmers. However, it is not only technology for production that matters. Transportation and communication technologies have not received as much attention in NRM, but they play a vital role in reducing the costs of covering a large area, for example, when patrolling the forest against encroachers.

The underlying agro-ecological conditions and the technologies used are essential to the flow or supply of the resource, which can be described by the extent of predictability in quantity over time and space (Ostrom 1990). High variability and unpredictability of the resource increase the need for coordination among users, but these conditions may also increase the difficulty in reaching agreement over rules and their application. For example, transhumant pastoralists may move their animals over extensive areas to take advantage of seasonal differences in the availability of fodder and water. This effort requires coordination among the herders to decide who will move to which areas, as well as coordination with farmers in those areas.

Moreover, the risk of drought prompts many pastoralists to develop access options, whereby herders from one tribe can go to another tribe's territory during drought or other crises, with reciprocal expectations. These access options require considerable negotiation among groups, but they provide an important source of security.

14.4.2 Socioeconomic Factors

Among the socioeconomic characteristics of the resource users, analysts have focused on the user demand for, dependence on, and knowledge of the resource as important in increasing incentives for organization for NRM (Wade 1988; Stern et al. 2002). Local coordination efforts are more likely to take place for resources that are important to the livelihoods of a substantial number of people in an area. Here history also matters: effective irrigation associations are more likely to be found in areas where farmers have been irrigating for a long time than in a new scheme where they are less familiar with the requirements of irrigation (and thus have less knowledge of the resource).

The number of users in the resource system also influences the possibility of voluntary organization. The general hypothesis claims that with an increasing number of participants, the possibility of voluntary organization decreases (Olson 1971; Ostrom 1990; Bromley 1992; Bardhan 1993; Nugent 1993). One of the arguments used to support this hypothesis is that the smaller the group, the easier it is to monitor one another's behavior, but larger groups have higher communication and bargaining costs. As groups increase in size, formalization of rules for contributions or extraction and for monitoring and sanctioning are often needed to assure members that others are contributing their fair share, but at some level, collective action is no longer sufficient, because too many people are involved over too large an area. Thus collective action is more likely to occur for spring protection or local watershed management, but management of full river basins requires some state involvement (and, in many of the transboundary river basins, such as those found throughout Africa, even international coordination). The transaction costs of developing common rules for management also increase with the number of people participating, which may lead to more delegated decisionmaking, such as when a group hires managers who are responsible for monitoring and enforcement (and sometimes even development) of the rules that the group adopts.

In the context of NRM, similarity in resource access and perceptions of the risk of long-term resource exploitation enhance the possibility of cooperation (Ostrom 1992). Consistency in norms in general has also been identified as a crucial factor affecting the degree of organization (Ostrom 1990; Bardhan 1993; Nugent 1993; White and Runge 1995). Common norms of sharing, social solidarity, or the value of the natural resource provide a motivation to contribute and something to which members can appeal. Hence a study of the ideology related to social relations and to natural resources (for example, determining whether they are viewed as a gift from God or a purely instrumental resource) can help in understanding the potential for local coordination efforts.

Though several authors identify homogeneity as an important factor facilitating organization, Olson (1971) and Baland and Platteau (1994, 273–284) question the validity of this idea. Ostrom (1992) makes the same point, claiming that heterogeneity in asset structure can actually favor the possibility of organization, particularly when there is a need for leadership and entrepreneurship. The presence of some wealthier members who have a strong interest in the collective good and of some members with strong connections to outsiders can be useful for stimulating and supporting collective action. For example, in western Kenya farmers with more land may be persuaded to set aside part of that land for spring protection that benefits others living nearby (as well as their own households). A sense of noblesse oblige or social prestige may help motivate the wealthier members to take on such leadership roles. Indeed, for some "privileged goods" the benefits to the wealthier members may be sufficient that they will provide them, even without the contributions of other members—a condition that Olson (1971, 169) referred to as "exploitation of the great by the small."

It is easier to invoke collective action to manage resources when people live near one another, and when they live close to the resource, because such proximities increase the regular interaction of people with one another and with the resource (Wade 1988; Ostrom 1990). The social capital literature also suggests that the extent of interaction and organizational experiences or organizational density in other types of activity than NRM would increase the likelihood of collective action for NRM. However, this is not necessarily the case. Disputes from other aspects of social life can spill over into NRM, and people may not want to sanction a relative or neighbor for taking too much water if it will cause ill-will over other matters.

The expectations about the time horizon of the activity are hypothesized to be positively related to the possibility of organization for NRM (Ostrom 1990). If people do not expect to benefit, they are less likely to contribute. This factor is related to the openness and stability of the community in general as a crucial determinant of cooperating. Migration, occupational mobility, and market development provide alternatives for some people to opt out of dependence on the natural resources and on others in the community, and hence reduce their incentives to cooperate in managing the resource. This possibility is particularly problematic when it is the richer members who have access to better exit options compared to those of the poor, because then the rich may not abide by the rules, even if they would gain the most in absolute terms from cooperation (Bardhan 2004). Thus the higher the rate of migration, mobility, and market integration, the lower is the possibility of voluntary cooperation or organization (Ostrom 1990; Bardhan 1993; Baland and Platteau 1994).

14.4.3 Policy and Governance Factors

Policy and governance factors refer to the rules applied in a local group as well as to external forces, particularly state influences. Among internal arrangements, it is especially important to consider the extent of formal and informal rules regarding boundary and access, which define the resource system in terms of area and members; allocation, inputs, and contributions; monitoring and sanctioning; and mechanisms for conflict resolution. If the rules can be described by a high degree of simplicity, flexibility, and fairness, it seems to enhance the possibility of local organization for NRM (Baland and Platteau 1994, 265–267).

The external arrangements include any public regulation of relevance, such as property rights, delegation of decisionmaking to the local level, rights of reorganization, and environmental and natural resource regulation. As noted above, stronger rights for local groups enhance both their incentives and authority for managing the resource. The form of the relationship between external arrangements and the degree of organization depends on the specific content of the former. Generally, recognition by the external authorities of local practices and norms are emphasized as facilitating effective local NRM (Wade 1988; Bromley and Cernea 1989; Ostrom 1990; Bardhan 1993; Stern et al. 2002). Local organization becomes easier when the arrangements in the external environment support the process, because it can reduce the transaction costs of organizing, as well as strengthen local authority over group members and outsiders who might try to break the rules and overexploit the resource.

Finally, it has been argued that organizational activity is positively affected by links to other organizations. Both horizontal and vertical linkages play a vital role; existing organizations seem to be better off when they are a part of a larger organizational system than when they are isolated (Uphoff, Ramanurthy, and Steiner 1991; Uphoff 2000). Similarly, Ostrom (1990) finds the use of "nested enterprises" consisting of a number of organizations on different levels to be a design principle for stable NRM in more complex systems. This structure is exemplified by the Kenya Dairy Goat Association (Box 14.2).

Although the literatures on case studies and game theory have been instrumental in identifying the factors that affect coordination institutions for NRM, in practice these factors cannot be taken as independent variables because of the high degree of interaction among them. More recent work has attempted to link these factors causally, particularly by looking at which resource conditions contribute to adherence to shared norms, monitoring, and enforcement (Agrawal 2002; Stern et al. 2002). Other researchers are testing the effect of these factors empirically, using data

Box 14.2 Kenya Dairy Goat Association

The introduction of improved dairy goat stock in Kenya has been facilitated by the formation of associations of local farmers who learn about dairy goat production and share in the ownership of a breeding buck used to cross breed with their local goats. However, after approximately 2 years, the buck would be mating with its own offspring, and hence should no longer be used by that group of farmers. To overcome this problem, local groups have formed a federation that keeps records on improved goats and rotates bucks among the various local groups.

from a sufficiently large sample of sites to be able to make quantitative tests of these hypothesized variables. Nkonya et al. (2005) examined the determinants of whether a community had passed and followed certain types of NRM rules, and the awareness and compliance with those rules for a sample of 271 communities in Uganda. They found that access to all-weather roads, credit, education, and higher agricultural potential contributed to awareness and compliance with NRM rules, whereas poverty reduced compliance. In a study of NRM in an agropastoral area of Burkina Faso, McCarthy, Dutilly-Diane, and Drabo (2004) examined the role of such variables as rainfall, group size, heterogeneity, education, migration, and distance from the capital on two different types of capacity to cooperate (network capacity and implementation capacity). These investigators found that the two types of capacity had different determinants and outcomes. As evidence from such comparative studies accumulates, the picture that emerges is one of complexity rather than simple prescriptions about these key institutions.

Moreover, rather than viewing state *or* collective action *or* markets as the appropriate institutions for coordinating NRM, a range of hybrid co-management arrangements are likely to be appropriate. Under co-management, the state can provide coordination at supracommunity levels and can support the authority of local organizations that have a large role in managing the resources on a daily basis. Such arrangements allow each type of institution to support the others, rather than expecting any one to stand on its own—rather like a tripod or three-legged stool in contrast to a single pillar. The advantage of a tripod is that no leg needs to be perfectly straight or strong, as it will be supported by the others, and it can be stable on a more variable terrain than can a solid pillar. However, such an institutional arrangement does entail considerable transaction costs and negotiation between state and local organizations—for coordination among coordinating institutions.

14.5 Conclusions

Institutions certainly play an important role in shaping how people interact with one another and with their natural environment. However, neither the institutions nor their influences are simple, and no prescriptions can be written for setting up the "right" institutions. There has been too much zigzagging of policy emphasis, from heavy reliance on the state, to user groups, and even to markets. A major cause of this vacillation is the tendency for analysts to compare the actual performance of one type of institutions (for example, the state) with the ideal performance of another type (for example, user groups). In fact, none of the institutions is likely to meet all expectations, and even if specific institutions show very high performance, they cannot be replicated in every village and for every resource. Rather than expecting perfection from any single type of institution, it is essential to look realistically at the performance of each and consider how they can be combined so that they complement one another. Because of the dynamic nature of resource management and changes in the external environment, adaptive co-management, rather than blueprint approaches, is needed.

Coordination is multifaceted, depending on a range of conditioning factors and social relations; it is not a simple cost–benefit analysis of the returns to cooperation. To understand coordination, it is necessary to look beyond formal organizations, particularly those set up by the government, and to recognize the range of ways in which people work together. Social networks may be more important than membership in designated groups. As with property rights, it is not only rules that matter but also their legitimacy and enforcement. Although we can identify factors that are likely to facilitate or constrain cooperation for NRM, there is no single policy lever that will turn on effective coordination. However, a more accurate understanding of these institutions as dynamic entities is more likely to lead to appropriate strategies than merely applying rigid formulations of institutional engineering—particularly those that import and impose foreign institutions. The state, collective action, or markets acting alone are not "the" solution—instead, a combination of institutional types and hybrid forms of coordination are likely to be needed for effective NRM.

Notes

1. Gordon (1954) showed that even with open access, resource degradation is not inevitable if the costs of exploiting the resource are greater than its average product.

2. Interestingly, such market coordination often seems to be applied when mechanical equipment is involved in extracting or managing the resource. It may be that the level of technical sophistication of machinery is such that it is preferable to have one person responsible for the management.

3. This discussion of devolution draws heavily on Meinzen-Dick and Knox (2001).

4. For reviews of experience with CBRM, see Murombedzi (1998) and Uphoff (1998); for irrigation management transfer, see Subramanian, Jagannathan, and Meinzen-Dick (1997); for fisher-

ies co-management, see Jentoft and McCay (1995), Hanna (1998), and Pomeroy, Katon, and Harkes (1999); and for joint forest management and similar approaches, see Ostrom (1999).

5. These different types of reforms are often referred to under the broad heading of decentralization or devolution. For discussions of such reforms, see Rondinelli, McCulloch, and Johnson (1989); Ostrom, Schroeder, and Wynne (1993); Van Zyl, Kirsten, and Binswanger (1996); Vedeld (1996); Carney and Farrington, (1998); and Agrawal (1999). For an analysis of the types of institution involved, see Uphoff (1998) and Ribot (1999). Although the same broad reforms are described in many sources, the terminology used is not always consistent. For a review of decentralization and land tenure, see Meinzen-Dick, Di Gregorio, and Dohrn (2008).

6. This collective definition of social capital as belonging to a society or group is consistent with that used by UNDP (1997) and the World Bank (http://www1.worldbank.org/prem/poverty/scapital/index.htm), but differs from the more individualistic definition of social capital as social connections that individuals cultivate in pursuit of their own particular objectives, such as that used by Coleman (1988) or Carney (1998).

7. For a more complete discussion of these and other interactions, see Knox McCulloch, Meinzen-Dick, and Hazell (1998).

Further Reading

Agrawal, A. 2001. Common property institutions and sustainable governance of resources. *World Development* 29: 1649–1672.

Baland, J.-M., and J.-P. Platteau. 1996. *Halting degradation of natural resources: Is there a role for rural communities?* New York: Food and Agriculture Organization of the United Nations and Clarendon Press.

Dietz, T., E. Ostrom, and P. C. Stern. 2003. The struggle to govern the commons. *Science* 302: 1907–1912.

Meinzen-Dick, R. S., A. Knox, F. Place, and B. M. Swallow. 2002. *Innovation in natural resource management: The role of property rights and collective action in developing countries.* Washington, D.C., and Baltimore: International Food Policy Research Institute and Johns Hopkins University Press.

Meinzen-Dick, R. S., A. Knox, and M. Di Gregorio, eds. 2001. *Collective action, property rights, and devolution of natural resource management: Exchange of knowledge and implications for policy.* Feldafing, Germany: Zentralstelle für Ernährung und Landwirtschaft.

Ostrom, E., R. Gardner, and J. M. Walker. 1994. *Rules, games and common-pool resources.* Ann Arbor, Mich., U.S.A.: University of Michigan Press.

Ostrom, E., T. Dietz, N. Dolsak, P. C. Stern, S. Stonich, and E. U. Weber, eds. 2002. *The drama of the commons.* Washington, D.C.: National Academy of Sciences Press.

References

Agrawal, A. 1999. *Greener pastures: Politics, markets, and community among a migrant pastoral people.* Durham, N.C., U.S.A.: Duke University Press.

————. 2001. Common property institutions and sustainable governance of resources. *World Development* 29: 1649–1672.

————. 2002. Common resources and institutional sustainability. In *The drama of the commons*, ed. E. Ostrom, T. Dietz, N. Dolsak, P. C. Stern, S. Stonich, and E. U. Weber. Washington, D.C.: National Academies Press.

Agrawal, A., and J. C. Ribot. 1999. Accountability in decentralization: A framework with South Asian and West African cases. *Journal of Developing Areas* 33: 473–502.

Bakker, M., R. Barker, R. S. Meinzen-Dick, and F. Konradsen, eds. 1999. Multiple uses of water in irrigated areas: A case study from Sri Lanka. System-Wide Initiative on Water Management Paper 8. Colombo, Sri Lanka: International Water Management Institute and International Food Policy Research Institute.

Baland, J.-M., and J.-P. Platteau. 1994. Coordination problems in resource conservation programs. Cahiers de la Faculté des Sciences Économiques et Sociales 142. Namur, Belgium: Facultés Universitaires Notre-Dame de la Paix, Centre de Recherche en Économie du Développement.

————. 1996. *Halting degradation of natural resources: Is there a role for rural communities?* New York and Oxford: Food and Agricultural Organization of the United Nations and Clarendon Press.

Bardhan, P. K. 1993. Analytics of the institutions of informal cooperation in rural development. *World Development* 21: 633–639.

————. 2004. *Scarcity, conflicts and cooperation: Essays in political and institutional economics of development*. Cambridge, Mass., U.S.A.: MIT Press.

Bromley, D. W., ed. 1992. *Making the commons work. Theory, practice and policy*. San Francisco: ICS Press.

Bromley, D. W., and M. Cernea. 1989. The management of common property natural resources. Some conceptual and operational fallacies. Discussion Paper 57. Washington, D.C.: World Bank.

Carney, D., ed. 1998. *Sustainable rural livelihoods: What contribution can we make?* London: Department for International Development.

Carney, D., and J. Farrington. 1998. *Natural resource management and institutional change*. New York: Routledge.

Coleman, J. S. 1988. Social capital in the creation of human capital. *American Journal of Sociology* 94 (supplement): 95–120.

Coward, W. E. 1986. Direct and indirect alternatives for irrigation investment and the creation of property. In *Irrigation investment, technology, and management strategies for development*, ed. W. K. Easter. Boulder, Colo., U.S.A.: Westview Press.

Dewees, P. A., and S. J. Scherr. 1996. *Policies and markets for non-timber tree products*. Environment and Production Technology Division Discussion Paper 16. Washington, D.C.: International Food Policy Research Institute.

Gordon, H. S. 1954. The economic theory of a common-property resource: The fishery. *Journal of Political Economy* 62: 124–142.

Hanna, S. 1998. Co-management in small-scale fisheries: Creating effective links among stakeholders. Paper presented at the International Workshop on Community-Based Natural Resource Management, Washington, D.C., May.

Hardin, G. 1968. The tragedy of the commons. *Science* 162: 1243–1248.

Jentoft, S., and B. McCay. 1995. User participation in fisheries management: Lessons drawn from international experiences. *Marine Policy* 19 (3): 227–246.

Kirk, M. 1999. The context for livestock and crop-livestock development in Africa: The evolving role of the state in influencing property rights over grazing resources in Sub-Saharan Africa. In *Property rights, risk, and livestock development in Africa,* ed. N. McCarthy, B. Swallow, M. Kirk, and P. Hazell. Washington, D.C.: International Food Policy Research Institute.

Knox McCulloch, A., R. S. Meinzen-Dick, and P. Hazell. 1998. Property rights, collective action, and technologies for natural resource management: A conceptual framework. CAPRi Working Paper 1. Washington, D.C.: International Food Policy Research Institute.

Lam, W. F. 1996. Improving the performance of small-scale irrigation systems: The effects of technological investments and governance structure on irrigation performance in Nepal. *World Development* 24: 1301–1315.

Lane, C. R., and R. Moorehead. 1994. Who should own the range? New thinking on pastoral resource tenure in drylands Africa. Pastoral Land Tenure Series Paper 3. London: International Institute for Environment and Development, Drylands Programme.

Mansuri, G., and V. Rao. 2004. Community-based (and driven) development: A critical review. Policy Research Working Paper 3209. Washington, D.C.: World Bank.

McCarthy, N., C. Dutilly-Diane, and B. Drabo. 2004. Cooperation, collective action and natural resources management in Burkina Faso. *Agricultural Systems* 82: 233–255.

Meinzen-Dick, R. S. 1996. *Groundwater markets in Pakistan: Participation and productivity.* Research Report 105. Washington, D.C.: International Food Policy Research Institute.

Meinzen-Dick, R. S., and A. Knox. 2001. Collective action, property rights, and devolution of natural resource management: A conceptual framework. In *Collective action, property rights, and devolution of natural resource management: Exchange of knowledge and implications for policy,* ed. R. S. Meinzen-Dick, A. Knox, and M. Di Gregorio. Feldafing, Germany: Zentralstelle für Ernährung und Landwirtschaft.

Meinzen-Dick, R. S., M. Di Gregorio, and S. Dohrn. 2008. Decentralization, pro-poor land policies and democratic governance. CAPRi Working Paper 80. Washington, D.C.: International Food Policy Research Institute.

Meinzen-Dick, R. S., A. Knox, and M. Di Gregorio, eds. 2001. Collective action, property rights, and devolution of natural resource management: Exchange of knowledge and implications for policy.

Feldafing, Germany: Zentralstelle für Ernährung und Landwirtschaft. Available at http://www
.capri.cgiar.org/workshop_devolution.asp.

Murombedzi, J. C. 1998. The evolving context of community-based natural resources management in
Sub-Saharan Africa in historical perspective. Paper presented at the International Workshop on
Community-Based Natural Resource Management, Washington, D.C., May.

Ngaido, T., and M. Kirk. 2001. Collective action, property rights and devolution of rangeland man-
agement. In *Collective action, property rights, and devolution of natural resource management:
Exchange of knowledge and implications for policy,* ed. R. S. Meinzen-Dick, A. Knox, and M. Di
Gregorio. Feldafing, Germany: Zentralstelle für Ernährung und Landwirtschaft.

Niamir-Fuller, M., ed. 2000. *Managing mobility in African rangelands: The legitimization of transhumance.* London: Intermediate Technology Publishers.

Nkonya, E., J. Pender, E. Kato, S. Mugarura, and J. Muwonge. 2005. Who knows, who cares?
Determinants of enactment, awareness and compliance with community natural resource man-
agement bylaws in Uganda. CAPRi Working Paper 41. Washington, D.C.: International Food
Policy Research Institute.

Nugent, J. B. 1993. Between state, markets and households: A neo-institutional analysis of local organizations and institutions. *World Development* 21: 623–632.

Oakerson, R. J. 1993. Reciprocity: A bottom-up view of political development. In *Rethinking institutional analysis and development: Issues, alternatives, and choices,* ed. E. Ostrom, D. Feeny, and
H. Picht. San Francisco: ICS Press.

Olson, M. 1971. *The logic of collective action: Public goods and the theory of groups.* New York: Shocken
Books.

Ostrom, E. 1990. *Governing the commons: The evolution of institutions for collective action.* Cambridge:
Cambridge University Press.

———. 1992. *Crafting institutions for self-governing irrigation systems.* San Francisco: ICS Press.

———. 1999. Institutional rational choice: An assessment of the institutional analysis and development framework. In *Theories of the policy process,* ed. P. A. Sabatier. Boulder, Colo., U.S.A.:
Westview Press.

Ostrom, E., L. Schoeder, and S. G. Wynne. 1993. *Institutional incentives and sustainable development:
Infrastructure policies in perspective.* Boulder, Colo., U.S.A.: Westview Press.

Parker, D., and C. Kirkpatrick. 2005. Privatisation in developing countries: A review of the evidence
and the policy lessons. *Journal of Development Studies* 41 (4): 513–541.

Peters, P. 1994. *Dividing the commons: Politics, policy, and culture in Botswana.* Charlottesville, Va.,
U.S.A.: University Press of Virginia.

Place, F., G. Kariuki, J. Wangila, P. Kristjanson, A. Makauki, and W. Neale. 2002. Assessing the factors
underlying differences in group performance: Methodological issues and empirical findings from

the highlands of central Kenya. CAPRi Working Paper 25. Washington, D.C.: International Food Policy Research Institute.

Pomeroy, R. S., E. Katon, and I. Harkes. 1999. Fisheries co-management in Asia: Lessons from experience. Manila: International Center for Living Aquatic Resources Management.

Putnam, R. 1995. Bowling alone: America's declining social capital. *Journal of Democracy* 6 (1): 65–78.

Rasmussen, L. N., and R. S. Meinzen-Dick. 1995. *Local organizations for natural resource management: Lessons from the theoretical and empirical literature.* Environment and Production Technology Division Discussion Paper 11. Washington, D.C.: International Food Policy Research Institute.

Ribot, J. C. 1999. Decentralization, participation and accountability in Sahelian forestry: Legal instruments of political-administrative control. *Africa* 69 (1): 23–65.

———. 2003. Democratic decentralization of natural resources: Institutional choice and discretionary power transfers in Sub-Saharan Africa. *Public Administration and Development* 23 (1): 53–65.

Rondinelli, D., J. S. McCulloch, and R.W. Johnson. 1989. Analyzing decentralization policies in developing countries: The case for cautious optimism. *Development Policy Review* 4 (1): 3–23.

Shah, T. 1993. *Groundwater markets and irrigation development: Political economy and practical policy.* Mumbai: Oxford University Press.

Steins, N. A., and V. M. Edwards. 1999. Platforms in collective action in multiple-use CPRs. *Agriculture and Human Values* 16 (3): 241–262.

Stern, P. C., T. Dietz, N. Dolsak, E. Ostrom, and S. Stonich. 2002. Knowledge and questions after 15 years of research. In *The drama of the commons,* ed. E. Ostrom, T. Dietz, N. Dolsak, P. C. Stern, S. Stonich, and E. U. Weber. Washington, D.C.: National Academy Press.

Subramanian, A., N. V. Jagannathan, and R. S. Meinzen-Dick. 1997. User organizations for sustainable water services. Technical Paper 354. Washington, D.C.: World Bank.

Swallow, B. M., R. S. Meinzen-Dick, L. A. Jackson, T. O. Williams, and T. A. White. 1997. *Multiple functions of common property regimes.* IFPRI Environment and Production Technology Workshop Summary Paper 5. Washington, D.C.: International Food Policy Research Institute.

Thompson, G. D., and P. N. Wilson. 1994. Common property as an institutional response to environmental variability. *Contemporary Economic Policy* 12 (3): 10–21.

UNDP (United Nations Development Programme). 1997. *Governance for sustainable human development: A UNDP policy document.* New York. Available at http://magnet.undp.org/policy/glossary.htm.

Uphoff, N. T. 1986. *Local institutional development: An analytical sourcebook with cases.* West Hartford, Conn., U.S.A.: Kumarian Press.

———. 1998. Community-based natural resource management: Connecting micro and macro processes, and people with their environments. Plenary presentation, International Community-

Based Natural Resource Management Workshop, Washington, D.C., May. Available at http://www.cbnrm.net/pdf/uphoff_001.pdf.

———. 2000. Understanding social capital: Learning from the analysis and experience of participation. In *Social capital: A multifaceted perspective*, ed. P. Dasgupta and I. Serageldin. Washington, D.C.: World Bank.

Uphoff, N. T., P. Ramanurthy, and R. Steiner. 1991. *Managing irrigation: Analyzing and improving the performance of bureaucracies*. New Delhi: Sage.

Van Zyl, J., J. F. Kirsten, and H. P. Binswanger, eds. 1996. *Agricultural land reform in South Africa: Policies, markets and mechanisms*. Cape Town: Oxford University Press.

Vedeld, T. 1996. Enabling local institution building: Reinventing or enclosing the commons of the Sahel. In *Improved natural resource management: The role of formal organizations and informal networks and institutions*, ed. H. S. Marcussen. Occasional Paper 17. Roskilde, Denmark: International Development Studies, Roskilde University.

Wade, R. 1988. *Village republics: Economic conditions for collective action in south India*. New York: Cambridge University Press.

White, T. A., and C. F. Runge. 1995. The emergence and evolution of collective action: Lessons from watershed management in Haiti. *World Development* 23: 1683–1698.

Williamson, O. E. 1999. The New Institutional Economics: Taking stock and looking ahead. Address to the International Society for New Institutional Economics. *ISNIE Newsletter* 2 (2): 9–20.

Chapter 15

What Happens during the Creation of Private Property? Subdividing Group Ranches in Kenya's Maasailand

Esther Mwangi

This case study discusses the internal processes and decisions that characterized the transition from collectively held group ranches to individualized property systems among the Maasai pastoralists of the Kajiado district in Kenya. It examines who the main actors were during subdivision, their interactions (including their degree of latitude in crafting and changing rules), as well as the outcomes of these interactions.

Although scholars have focused quite extensively on the motivations and outcomes of such change, much less has been done to explain and illustrate *how* property rights change (see Chapter 13 for some preliminary explanations). More particularly, the significance of politics and power relations in the assignment of property rights is increasingly acknowledged (Libecap 1989, 1998, 2003; Eggertson 1990; North 1990; Knight 1992; Firmin-Sellers 1995, 1996). In this regard the role of state enforcement (often assumed) and other interactions in the political arena are also analyzed in processes of transformation, over and above the initial economic motivations for institutional change. Understanding the process of change is important, because the process may itself influence outcomes. Protracted conflict over distribution may, for instance, undermine the efficiency gains that are often anticipated in property-rights transformations (Banner 2002). Tracking processes of change also provides insights into the design of future reforms.

15.1 Context

The Maasai are located in Kajiado and Narok Districts of southwestern Kenya. They have for a long time practiced transhumant pastoralism: livestock forms the basis of their economic livelihoods. It is the focus of their social relations and a critical element of their ethnic self-definition. Prior to major transformational changes, the Maasai sociopolitical structure comprised an age-set system, and decisionmaking authority was vested in the council of elders. Economically, the Maasai livestock enterprise was defined by collective use and ownership of pasture and water, with individual ownership of livestock.

15.1.1 Maasai Group Ranches

A group ranch is land that has been demarcated and legally allocated to a group, such as a tribe, clan, section, family, or other group of persons (Republic of Kenya 1968). It is composed of a body of members to whom legal title has been jointly awarded and a management committee that is elected by the members. Group ranches were introduced in 1968 by the government of Kenya. By shifting land tenure from traditional common ownership to smaller portions owned by groups under a common title, group ranches were anticipated to provide tenure security, create incentives for the Maasai to invest in range improvement, and ultimately reduce the tendency to overaccumulate livestock (Republic of Kenya 1974). These objectives were to be achieved by implementing the following:

- registration of permanent members in each ranch, who were to be excluded from other ranches;

- allocation of grazing quotas to ranch members;

- development of shared ranch infrastructure (such as water points, dips, stock-handling facilities, and fire breaks) using loans;

- management of their own livestock by members, who have access to loans for purchasing breeding stock; and

- election of a group-ranch committee to manage all affairs of the group ranch, including infrastructure development, loan repayments, enforcement of grazing quotas, grazing management, and exclusion of nonmembers.

A separate law, the Land (Group Representatives) Act of 1968 (Republic of Kenya 1968), was passed to provide a legal framework for ranch operation. Under this law the entire group holds the title to the ranch, which cannot be sold by any of its members. Each individual has residency rights, but the group as a corporate body, through an elected group-ranch committee, controls resource use (that is, grazing, water, and tillage) and may establish mechanisms for resource allocation. The Department of Land Adjudication and the Registrar of Group Representatives (subsequently referred to as the registrar of group ranches), both in the Ministry of Lands and Settlement, were extensively involved in the initial establishment of group ranches. The Range Management division of the Ministry of Agriculture played a key role in drawing up group-ranch development plans. The Ministry of Water Development coordinated water development. The Agricultural Finance Corporation administered the loans provided by donors.

The group-ranch concept is now close to its fourth decade, yet there is consensus among scholars and planners that it has been a dismal failure (Munei 1987; Rutten 1992; Galaty and Ole Munei 1999). Not only has it failed to meet its stated objectives, but it has also jeopardized the socioeconomic welfare of the Maasai (Kipuri 1989; Kituyi 1990; Fratkin 1994). There is a growing trend toward subdivision of group ranches into individual plots and frequent sale of portions of individual holdings to prevent foreclosure on development loans (Kimani and Pickard 1998).

15.1.2 Recent Studies

Recent research on different group ranches in Kajiado District point to a diverse set of pressures that motivated Maasai to support the subdivision of their group ranches. These motivations are generally consistent with the efficiency and distributional explanations highlighted in Chapter 13. In the better watered areas of the district (more than 800 mm annual rainfall), for instance, individuals were eager to acquire individual land titles to access capital markets (Grandin 1986; Rutten 1992; Kimani and Pickard 1998; Galaty 1999a). Internal population increase in the face of a fixed land resource was also a motivator for subdivision (Galaty 1992, 1994, 1999b; Kimani and Pickard 1998). In other cases the allocation of group land to unauthorized individuals by the management committee prompted calls for subdivision (Galaty 1992; Rutten 1992; Simel 1999). Other factors motivating the transition included difficulties in enforcing the collective interest in resource allocation and a need for protecting individuals' land claims against threats of appropriation by both internal and external actors (Mwangi 2007). Although these studies provide useful insights into what may have motivated subdivision of the group ranches, the process of subdivision, the method of land allocation and distribution, the identity of the decisionmakers, and the outcomes need to be studied in more detail. This case study illustrates processes and interactions during subdivision of the group ranches.

15.2   Research Sites and Methods

Four group ranches were selected to represent variations in size, location (in terms of proximity to the main livestock marketing center of Bissel), and progression in the subdivision process (Table 15.1). Fieldwork was conducted from January 2001 to January 2002 and from June to August of 2002. Structured interviews were conducted with elders of different categories, youths, widows, and married women to find out whether they participated in the decision to subdivide, how parcel sizes and locations were determined and distributed, whether dissatisfied individuals contested committee allocations, how they organized such contestation, and with what success. Table 15.2 illustrates the individuals and categories interviewed. Those formally registered group-ranch members who were interviewed included retired elders (that is, those belonging to the Ilterito and Ilnyankusi age sets), senior elders (those belonging to the Iseuri and Ilkiseiya age sets), younger elders (of the Irang Irang and Ilkingonde age sets), and widows. Group-ranch nonmembers—those not registered as formal members (for example, married women and some youth in the Ilmajeshi and Ilkilaku age sets)—were also interviewed; however, this case study does not report on their findings.

Interviews were supplemented with archival material, such as records of group-ranch meetings and disputes files, which contained information on membership,

Table 15.1   Basic information on Enkaroni, Meto, Nentanai, and Torosei group ranches

Group ranch	Date group ranch was incorporated	Size (ha)	Number of members	Date of agreement to subdivide	Number of titles issued by October 2002	Distance from Bissel (km)
Enkaroni	April 1975	11,378	356	May 1988	310	8
Meto	December 1977	28,928	645	September 1989	400	65
Nentanai	December 1977	3,696	57	March 1987	42	18
Torosei	June 1977	45,445	300	September 1989	0	56

Table 15.2   Number of interviews by age set and gender

Group ranch	Ilterito	Ilnyankusi	Iseuri	Ilkiseiya	Irang Irang	Ilkingonde	Ilmajeshi	Ilkilaku	Widows	Married women
Enkaroni	0	4	11	20	8	12	2	1	3	17
Meto	1	6	17	22	13	22	0	1	15	12
Nentanai	0	5	10	6	4	1	0	0	6	6
Torosei	0	1	16	13	12	33	11	1	4	15
Total (331)	1	16	54	61	37	68	13	3	28	50
Percentage of total	0.30	4.83	16.31	18.43	11.18	20.54	3.93	0.91	8.46	15.11

Note: Age sets are defined in the text.

minutes of annual general meetings, minutes of committee meetings, communications with the bureaucracy, boundary disputes, and complaints about the conduct of the subdivision.

15.3 Subdividing the Group Ranch: Decisions and Procedures

The four group ranches adopted similar decision rules and procedures for subdivision. One set of procedures originated from the registrar of group ranches, a government official in the Ministry of Lands and Settlement, whereas the other was crafted and authorized by group-ranch members when they resolved to subdivide at separate annual general meetings.

15.3.1 Formal Procedures

The following points describe the formal procedures prescribed by the government for a subdivision application:

1. Formal application is made for group-ranch dissolution to the registrar of group ranches, which includes a KSh 100 (about US$1.20) processing fee and the Minutes of the Annual General Meeting at which members voted to dissolve their group ranch.

2. The registrar verifies that the group ranch has no outstanding loans. If it does not, the registrar authorizes the subdivision and subsequent survey and demarcation of group ranch.

3. The group ranch then applies to the district's Land Control Board[1] for further consent to subdivide. The Land Control Board verifies that the title deed to the group ranch is not encumbered by loans, confirms the size of land to be subdivided and reasons for its proposed subdivision, establishes the number of parcels that will result from subdivision, and confirms which public utilities will be set aside from the land. If satisfied, the board gives its consent for the group ranch to undertake subdivision.

4. After the group ranch has completed demarcation, surveying, and mapping, the Land Control Board provides its consent for the collective title to the group ranch to be discontinued and converted into a series of individual titles by the District Land Registrar. However, before doing so the board must once again verify that all registered group members have been allocated parcels and that they

are relatively equal; it must determine that there are no disputes over the subdivision; and it must verify on the surveyor's site map that public utility areas, such as schools, trading centers, water points, health centers, and access roads, have been set aside. If satisfied, the board consents to the transfer of title from the collective to the individuals and the District Land Registrar is allowed to process the individual land titles.

5. Group-ranch representatives (that is, the committee chair, vice-chair, and secretary) sign the title transfers to individual members once each member has paid the necessary processing fees. The District Land Registrar bears witness to this transfer process.

6. Once all individuals' titles have been transferred to each member, the registrar of group ranches officially dissolves the incorporated group and its representatives. To date, however, this final step has not happened for any group ranch.

15.3.2   Procedures Internal to the Group Ranch

The procedures internal to the group ranch involve the following steps:

1. Members resolve that subdivision be conducted to ensure that all parcels are approximately equal in size, except where land is distinctly marginal, such as on hills or near stream beds, or for exceptionally large families, in which case larger parcels are to be issued. This allocation formula draws from the Group (Land Representatives) Act, which specifies that group-ranch land is the property of the registered collectivity, held by each member in equal, undivided shares. It also draws from shared customary understandings, which consider land an indivisible territory to which all recognized users have equal access.

2. Members select an additional group of up to 10 individuals to assist the official management committee in the physical task of demarcating the group ranch. This demarcation committee lasts only for as long as it takes to physically mark parcel boundaries.

3. Members indicate to the official committee their preferred parcel locations.

4. Members resolve to remain at their current locations until completion of subdivision to safeguard against opportunistic relocation to choice areas prior to subdivision.

5. After receiving consent to subdivide from the registrar, the group ranch engages a certified surveyor to conduct on-ground demarcation. Prior to formal survey, however, the official committee and the temporary demarcation committee mark out individual parcel boundaries using natural features, such as trees, rivers, rocks, and hills, as markers. Surveyors formalize these boundaries,[2] after which the management committee shows members the locations of their parcels. Individuals then obtain their titles, at a fee, from the District Land Registry.

15.4   The Subdivided Group Ranch

Table 15.3 below provides a synopsis of the parcel sizes and their distribution among members following subdivision. The results indicate that, contrary to members' expectations, the subdivision did not result in equal or nearly equal parcels.[3] In the three group ranches where subdivision was completed (that is, in Enkaroni, Meto, and Nentanai) two-thirds or more of the registered members have parcel sizes that fall below the average parcel size in each group ranch. More than 25 percent of former group-ranch land is owned by 9 percent of its registered members. Moreover, committee members who spearheaded the subdivision exercise ended up with between 25 and 35 percent of the land that they were entrusted to subdivide. The average sizes of committee members' parcels following subdivision were 100 ha for

Table 15.3   Distribution of parcel sizes in Enkaroni, Meto, and Nentanai group ranches

Characteristic	Enkaroni[a]	Meto[b]	Nentanai[c]
Total area (ha)	11,802.5	27,358.02	4,038.48
Number of members	332	548	56
Average parcel size after subdivision	35.56	49.92	72.12
Largest parcel (ha)	200.5	152.79	214
Smallest parcel (ha)	3.6	4.27	14.21
Standard deviation	27.23	21.87	51.06

[a]A total of 64 percent of members have less-than-average parcel sizes; 25 percent of former group-ranch land is now owned by 9 percent of the former members. Thirteen individuals have parcels less than 10 ha in size. Committee members (10 individuals) own 9 percent of former group-ranch land (average size of committee-member parcels: 100 ha).

[b]A total of 60 percent of members have less-than-average parcel sizes; 35 percent of former group-ranch land is now owned by 9 percent of the former members. One individual has a parcel less than 10 ha in size. Committee members (10 individuals) own 4 percent of former group-ranch land (average size of committee-member parcels: 113 ha).

[c]A total of 63 percent of members have less-than-average parcel sizes; 26 percent of the former group-ranch land is now owned by 9 percent of the former members. Committee members (10 individuals) own 30 percent of former group-ranch land (average size of committee-member parcels: 133 ha).

Enkaroni (compared to an Enkaroni average of 36 ha), 113 ha for Meto (compared to a Meto average of 50 ha), and 133 ha for Nentanai (compared to a Nentanai average of 72 ha). Committee parcels were more than twice the average size of ordinary members' parcels.

Committee members allocated larger parcels to themselves, to individuals with close ties to them, and to individuals rich in livestock. The latter were alleged to have given committee members gifts of livestock.[4] Livestock-poor herders ended up with considerably smaller parcels. Widows also received small parcels, as they were unable to defend their claims.[5] Those individuals that had prior disagreements with the committee had no space to negotiate—they were punished with smaller parcels. The outcome of the subdivision process clearly favored wealthy cattle owners and the committee members.

15.5   Contesting the Outcome

In Enkaroni, those dissatisfied with the outcome organized to challenge the committee's allocations. They included widows, men with small parcels, and others who had altogether missed being allocated parcels. This group of about 50 was referred to as the *kikundi cha malalamiko ya beacon* (or beacon complainants' group). They approached the committee to renegotiate parcel size but were told that "the fingers on one hand are not equal," so how then did they expect everyone to get equal-sized parcels? The committee was unwilling to discuss the complaints about unequal-sized parcels.

The complainants' group then approached the elders and asked them to appeal to the committee about the unequal allocations. The elders' *barazas* (public meetings) were unfruitful. The elders had insufficient powers to override committee decisions; in any case they had a vested interest in the outcome.

The complainants then appealed to officials in the Department of Lands Adjudication and Settlement. But the department adopted an attitude of noninterference in matters of group-ranch subdivision. On two prior occasions the district land adjudication officer had stated that the determination of parcel sizes depended entirely on the group ranch and that complaints be directed to the committee and not to his office because "all facts related to cases are present in Enkaroni."[6] The district officer of Kajiado Central Division reiterated this position.

Many individuals believed that their appeals to government officials went unheeded because of a lack of accountability. One letter of 19 February 1990 from a widow to the district commissioner is instructive. Not only does she complain of an exceedingly small parcel size (her 15 ha compared to committee members' average of 300 ha), but she also states that "government officers are corrupt and take bribes."[7]

She also accused the committee of corruption and abuse of powers. General evidence of members' dissatisfaction comes from a letter dated 9 February 1990, written jointly by an unidentified number of members, which was addressed to a broad range of government officials, including the district range officer, the district commissioner, district officer of central division, member of parliament of Kajiado central, the location councillor, district land adjudication officer, and the chief of Enkaroni. In this letter the members alleged that:[8]

- People in leadership (that is, committee members and chiefs) allocated themselves huge chunks of land.

- Committee failed to subdivide the ranch in an equitable manner.

- Close friends, relatives, and in-laws of the committee were given bigger portions of land.

- Committee members are never ready to listen to members' complaints (heavy-handedness).

- Chiefs are blocking people from seeking redress at alternative forums.

- The chairman is demanding that those with personal differences with him must kneel down and beg for mercy.

- There is bribery.

- Some members are allowed to participate in committees' private meetings; others are not.

- Some unregistered people have been given ranches by the committee without members' knowledge.

This letter went unheeded, and the complainants appealed to the High Court as a final recourse. Six members out of the initial group of 50 eventually took their case against the group-ranch committee (the legal representatives of Enkaroni group ranch) to the High Court.[9] They demanded the following:

- Land be allocated equally among all its members.

- The land subdivision that had been carried out on the group ranch be declared null and void.

- Subdivision should be halted until suit is heard.

A ruling by the High Court dismissed, with cost, the plaintiffs' application for an injunction.[10] The justice ruled that:

1. The plaintiffs should show, prima facie, why it was wrong that they had been allocated smaller land parcels than other members. The burden was on the plaintiffs to show that the discriminatory subdivision was for some cogent reason, for instance, wrong, unlawful, or contrary to the objections of the defendant. This had not been shown.

2. The annexure to the affidavit of the plaintiff seemed to show that it was rather the district land adjudication and survey officer, the surveyor, and the local chief who might be accused of unfair distribution of land.

3. The plaintiff must show beyond mere allegation that they had been given smaller portions of land than those given to others. No evidence on the actual sizes of the portions of land involved had been provided.

4. The plaintiffs had not made a prima facie case with a probability of success. They had shown no reason to support their allegation of discriminatory subdivision and why they should not have been allocated what they were given.

As a result, the plaintiffs' application for injunction was dismissed with cost. Following this defeat, the complainants did not reorganize to appeal the High Court's ruling. In fact, their advocate advised them to give up the case because "everybody was against them, including the Registrar of the High Court, who is a member of Enkaroni and whose *shamba* is among the big ones."[11]

During this contestation, the committee threatened to withdraw land that had already been allocated to the complainants and their supporters, or to reduce further the size of parcels allocated to them. The committee also allegedly secretly increased the parcel sizes of some selected individuals within the group of complainants. These selective allocations eroded group cohesion and resulted in a systematic decline of the complainants' group size from about 50 individuals to about 6, who eventually launched the appeal to the courts.

In Meto, individuals dissatisfied with their parcel sizes complained individually. Those who confronted the committee were threatened with reduction or total loss of their parcels. Some individuals chose not to confront the committee, because they knew of other members with even smaller parcels and felt they were better off not complaining. The Meto group-ranch committee also reminded members that by raising objections, subdivision might be suspended as in several neighboring group ranches. Organizing to contest committee decisions was a big challenge in Meto, not only because of committee intimidation but also because it is a large group ranch over which people are thinly scattered.

In Nentanai individuals did not contest unequal allocation. The Nentanai group ranch borders on the Ilpartimaru group ranch, where the process of subdivision had been delayed for close to a decade owing to distributional conflict. Indeed, Nentanai has provided refuge to residents fleeing escalating conflict in Ilpartimaru. Even if discontented individuals wanted to organize, it would have been difficult. Many of those allocated small parcels were the poorest and had migrated to urban areas, where they were pursuing alternative livelihoods.

15.6 Discussion

Subdividing a total of about 90,000 ha of variously endowed group-ranch land among 1,400 registered members by about 40–80 committee members of the respective group ranches of Enkaroni, Meto, Nentanai, and Torosei, is a difficult task. However, when the exercise was completed, parcels were found to be unequal, with more than 60 percent of registered members having holdings substantially smaller than the average. Land was concentrated in the hands of committee members, their friends, relatives, and wealthy herders. Group members dissatisfied with this outcome contested the decision by local means of arbitration, such as through the council of elders or government administration, as well as in the courts. They did not win. Others, fearing retribution by a vengeful committee or lacking resources, did not organize to contest the outcome.

The process of group-ranch subdivision had components that were internal to the group ranch in which rules, procedures, and decisions were crafted by group members and/or their representatives. It also had an external component designed and controlled by state representatives and/or individuals selected by them. The external component included dispute resolution or arbitration by government officials, including the High Court.

The internal processes were set in motion by a members' majority vote to subdivide. There was a shared understanding of the principles of subdivision that would lead to a desired outcome (an equal or nearly equal allocation of parcels), an endorsement of their management committee to oversee the process of subdivision, and the election of a temporary demarcation committee to assist it. Customary norms of trust, reputation, and a good track record led members to believe that their expectations would be fulfilled.

The subdivision component external to the group ranch involved acquiring consent from relevant actors (primarily government officials) to enable the formal survey and the registration and titling of individual parcels, to ensure that all registered members received parcels, and to provide arbitration in the event of disputes. The group-ranch committee mediated between the internal and external components. It is important to note that following the decision by group-ranch members to subdivide the ranch, most other critical decisions were made outside of the group ranch by government officials (verification of land sizes and elements of dispute resolution) and/or internally by the committee (parcel sizes and locations). The points of intersection between internal and external decisions were few, and in any case involved member representation by means of the group-ranch committee. The committee had legal recognition through the Group Ranch Act and state sponsorship. It also derived influence and authority from traditional institutions. In addition, it had privileged knowledge and understanding of the process—a process that is unprecedented in Maasai history.

The government left extensive discretion to the committee, which unilaterally determined the size and location of each individual's parcel after subdivision, and most importantly, ensured the new owners' role as signatories to the emerging land titles. The Land Control Board in particular failed to discharge its obligation of ensuring an equitable allocation of resources. In addition, government administrators referred disputes and complaints back to the group-ranch committee, whose members were direct beneficiaries of the subdivision process. Moreover, the High Court placed the burden of proof on the complainants. Quite clearly, the state abrogated its enforcement role, recklessly vesting power in a self-interested management committee.

15.7   Conclusions

As suggested by property-rights theorists (Knight 1992), conflict is resolved by credible threats from powerful community actors directed against weaker individuals. The committee was able to threaten those complaining about the distribution with confiscation of their assets. But in some instances the committee was unable to sufficiently intimidate individuals, and some parties organized to contest the inequitable distribution through the judiciary. In this case the court ruled against the plaintiffs, and the power of the state was used to coerce the acquiescence of those opposed and to insist on the implementation of the new property structure. This behavior conforms to the arguments of Firmin-Sellers (1995, 1996) that state coercion is crucial in terminating conflict.

What insights might this case offer for the conduct and/or reform of agricultural policy in Africa? That the process of land allocation would be captured by the elite in society is not new. Regardless of the reasons motivating individuals to seek a reassignment of rights, the process of reassignment itself is characterized by conflict over the eventual distribution of rights, because the losers will contest the outcome. Similarly, those with power and influence will employ these resources to ensure their preferred outcome. In the end, the powerful group wins, and prior collective resources become concentrated in the hands of a subset of the original claimants. Such an outcome is particularly likely when the state abandons its enforcement responsibilities and transfers decisionmaking powers to self-interested management committees. In sum, contrary to the vague, often unstated assumption in property-rights theory, state enforcement cannot be taken for granted. The activities (or lack thereof) of state actors may actively impede the attainment of equitable outcomes, regardless of whether ensuing property arrangements are efficient or not. Indeed, a strong case can be made for the involvement of multiple actors (such as the community, state, and development partners) in the design and implementation of land reforms, each of whom may serve as a check against arbitrary decisionmaking and opportunism. Finally, a lottery system for parcel allocation would have worked to maintain disinterest among the committee.

Notes

1. The Land Control Board, consisting of 8–12 individuals, is chaired by the district commissioner, who is also the head of government administration in the district. Other technical officials on the Land Control Board include the district land adjudication officer, the District Land Registrar, and a representative from the local Kajiado County Council. Landowners in the district must comprise three-quarters of the board, to include both men and women from the Maasai community.

2. Individuals are expected to pay surveyor fees as a precondition to being shown their parcels. The fees varied from 1,500 KSh (about US$19), in Enkaroni (which was surveyed by a government surveyor) to 4,500 Ksh in Meto and 5,000 KSh in Nentanai (both of which were surveyed by private surveyors). The committee and the surveyor negotiated survey fees.

3. Torosei is not included in these results, because they have not formally subdivided; thus parcel sizes are not confirmed.

4. Interviews, Enkaroni, July and August 2001.

5. Of the 17 widows that were allocated land in Enkaroni, 12 have land sizes below the group-ranch average. The committee members were hesitant to issue any land to widows because of the fear that if the widow were to remarry, their land would be lost to the deceased's family. This fear was more acute in the event that the widow remarried an outsider.

6. Minutes, Enkaroni Annual General Meeting, 10 July 1991. Meetings File, Enkaroni Group Ranch. Department of Land Adjudication, Kajiado District.

7. Letter written by Nenkitai ene Lolkinyei, 19 February 1990. Disputes File, Enkaroni Group Ranch. Department of Land Adjudication, Kajiado District.

8. Unnamed author, 9 February 1990. Disputes File, Enkaroni Group Ranch. Department of Land Adjudication, Kajiado District.

9. Plaint, Civil Suit 3956 of 1992, 22 July 1992. High Court of Kenya.

10. Ruling, Civil Case 3956 of 1992. 31 July 1992. High Court of Kenya.

11. Interview, Enkaroni, October 2002.

References

Banner, S. 2002. Transitions between property regimes. *Journal of Legal Studies* 31: S359–S371.

Eggertson, T. 1990. *Economic behaviour and institutions.* Cambridge: Cambridge University Press.

Firmin-Sellers, K. 1995. The politics of property rights. *American Political Science Review* 89 (4): 867–881.

———. 1996. *The transformation of property rights in the Gold Coast: An empirical analysis applying rational choice theory.* New York: Cambridge University Press.

Fratkin, E. 1994. Problems of pastoral land tenure in Kenya: Demographic, economic and political process among the Maasai, Samburu, Boran and Rendille, 1950–1990. Working Paper 177. Boston: African Studies Center, Boston University.

Galaty, J. G. 1992. The land is yours: Social and economic factors in the privatization, subdivision and sale of Maasai ranches. *Nomadic Peoples* 30: 26–40.

———. 1994. Ha(l)ving land in common: The subdivision of Maasai group ranches in Kenya. *Nomadic Peoples* 34/35: 109–121.

———. 1999a. Property in the strict sense of the term: The theory and rhetoric of land tenure in East Africa. Arid Lands and Resource Management Alarm Network in Eastern Africa Working Paper 4. August. Kampala, Uganda: Center for Basic Research.

———. 1999b. Grounding pastoralists: Law, politics and dispossession in East Africa. *Nomadic Peoples* 3 (2; special issue): 56–73.

Galaty, J. G., and K. Ole Munei. 1999. Maasai, land, law and dispossession. *Cultural Survival Quarterly* 22 (4): 68–71.

Grandin, B. E. 1986. Land tenure, subdivision and residential change on a Maasai group ranch. *Bulletin of the Institute for Development Anthropology* 4 (2): 9–13.

Kimani, K., and J. Pickard. 1998. Recent trends and implications of group ranch subdivision and fragmentation in Kajiado District, Kenya. *Geographic Journal* 164 (2): 202–213.

Kipuri, N. 1989. Maasai women in transition: Class and gender in the transformation of a pastoral society. Ph.D. dissertation, Temple University, Philadelphia.

Kituyi, M. 1990. *Becoming Kenyans: Socio-economictransformation of the pastoral Maasai.* Nairobi: African Center for Technology Studies Press.

Knight, J. 1992. *Institutions and social conflict.* New York: Cambridge University Press.

Libecap, G. D. 1989. *Contracting for property rights.* New York: Cambridge University Press.

———. 1998. Distributional and political issues modifying traditional common-property institutions. In *Law and the governance of renewable resources: Studies from Northern Europe and Africa,* ed. E. Berge and C. Stenseth. Oakland, Calif., U.S.A.: ICS Press.

———. 2003. Contracting for property rights. In *Property rights: Cooperation, conflict, and law,* ed. T. L. Anderson and F. S. McChesney. Princeton, N.J., U.S.A.: Princeton University Press.

Munei, K. 1987. Grazing schemes and group ranches as models for developing pastoral lands in Kenya. In *Property, poverty and people: Changing rights in property and problems of pastoral development,* ed. P. T. W. Baxter and R. Hogg. Manchester, U.K.: Department of Social Anthropology and International Development, University of Manchester.

Mwangi, E. 2007. The puzzle of "perverse" property rights: Explaining property rights transitions in Kenya's Maasailand. *Development and Change* 38 (5): 889–910.

North, D. C. 1990. *Institutions, institutional change and economic performance.* Cambridge: Cambridge University Press.

Republic of Kenya. 1968. Land (Group Representatives) Act. Chapter 287 of the Laws of Kenya. Nairobi: Government Printer.

———. 1974. *Development Plan 1974–1978.* Ministry of Finance and Planning. Nairobi: Government Printer.

Rutten, M. M. E. M. 1992. *Selling wealth to buy poverty: The process of the individualization of landownership among the Maasai pastoralists of Kajiado District, Kenya, 1890–1900.* Nijmegen Studies in Development and Cultural Change 10. Saarbrücken, Germany: Verlag für Entwicklungspolitik.

Simel, O. J. 1999. Premature land subdivision, encroachment of rights and manipulation in Maasailand—The Keekonyokie Clan Section. Arid Lands and Resource Management Alarm Network in Eastern Africa Working Paper 8. Kampala, Uganda: Center for Basic Research.

Institutional Change to Promote a Rental Market for Cropland in the Communal Areas of KwaZulu-Natal, South Africa

Michael C. Lyne

This case study identifies institutional problems that constrain efficient use of cropland in the communal areas of KwaZulu-Natal, describes interventions to address some of these problems, and demonstrates the outcomes of appropriate institutional change in the areas studied. It deals with aspects of institutional change introduced in Chapter 2 and highlights relationships between property rights to land and land use discussed in Chapter 13. Participatory research techniques were used to adapt existing institutions in the study areas. Cross-sectional survey data gathered from households in follow-up surveys were then analyzed using linear discriminant and regression techniques to identify efficiency and equity outcomes of the institutional changes. The surveys delivered useful information about the impacts of institutional change, and the participatory elements of the case study exposed critical problems and provided valuable insights into policy interventions to improve customary institutions. The findings also have implications for the Consultative Group on International Agricultural Research Systemwide Program on Collective Action and Property Rights (CAPRi) framework described in the introduction to Part 3.

16.1 Context

The province of KwaZulu-Natal stretches along the eastern seaboard of South Africa and covers an area of 9.2 million ha. Historically, the province was split into two regions: Natal and the self-governing homeland of KwaZulu. Merging these regions under a single provincial administration after the country's first democratic election in 1994 did not alter fundamental differences in their institutional environments. Natal is characterized by large privately owned commercial farms and KwaZulu[1] by smallholdings and customary land rights administered by Traditional Authorities (that is, district chiefs and their counselors). Rural households in KwaZulu hold overlapping rights to land. Primary rights permit a household to exclude other households from land that it cultivates during the summer growing season, and secondary-use rights allow neighboring households to graze cattle on land that is not cultivated. Thus land planted to seasonal crops in summer becomes communal grazing in winter. Land rights are enforced by tribal courts and tribal police, but the level of enforcement differs among Traditional Authorities.

16.1.1 The Problem

Land use in KwaZulu is paradoxical. Although the region is characterized by very small farms and a high rate of unemployment, arable land is farmed extensively, and large tracts are left fallow. Lyne and Nieuwoudt (1991) attribute this anomaly to the absence of a rental market for cropland. They argue that both allocative efficiency and equity would improve if land could be rented. Allocative efficiency is expected to improve because the market imposes an opportunity cost on underused and idle farmland. Households would rather lease their land out than forego rental income. Equity improves because voluntary rental transactions benefit both lessor and lessee. Land is transferred to those households short of land for subsistence or commercial farming purposes, while rental income accrues to those households who cannot, or prefer not to, farm. Furthermore, renting does not create a landless class, nor does it oblige lessors to relocate their homes (Lyne and Thomson 1998).

Considering their potential advantages, it is curious that rental markets for cropland are so imperfect or are missing altogether in the communal regions of South Africa (Lyne, Roth, and Troutt 1997). An efficient land rental market requires security of tenure and low transaction costs (Nieuwoudt 1990). It is often claimed that customary tenure is secure, but it is only in the sense that individuals who comply with customary rules will not easily be dispossessed of their land. However, the situation is entirely different when tenure security is measured by economic yardsticks, such as the ability to internalize the benefits of an investment.

As explained in Chapter 13, property rights are insecure when the breadth of rights is inadequate. In KwaZulu, customary law prohibits the sale of land, and individuals seldom enjoy fully exclusive rights to farmland. In most cases the individual's right to exclude others is a primary right that can be exercised only on land that is cultivated during the summer growing season. Other individuals can exercise secondary-use rights on this land once the crop is harvested. Thomson (1996, 90) reports a case in KwaZulu in which the Traditional Authority fined a progressive farmer who attempted to remove stover from his land to feed his own livestock during winter. In the economic sense, property rights to cropland are insecure, because they lack both breadth and duration.

When assurance is lacking, property rights and their duration are rendered uncertain, even if they are well defined in national or customary law. According to customary law in KwaZulu, the Traditional Authority announces a date after which farmers are allowed to start plowing and planting operations. Stockowners are then supposed to remove their cattle from the cropland. However, this law is not well enforced. Almost half the households surveyed by Thomson (1996, 92–94) in rural KwaZulu reported crop losses caused by livestock straying into in their fields after planting. Crop farmers were reluctant to seek compensation in the tribal court because (1) court fees, penalties, and compensation are unpredictable; (2) it is difficult to establish who owns the livestock; and (3) stockowners are a relatively wealthy and politically influential group.

Viewed from another perspective, this legal uncertainty raises the risk premium built into transaction costs. Transaction costs that are high relative to the value of the transaction could shift the potential buyer's offer to a point where it no longer exceeds the reservation price of the seller. It is useful to distinguish between ex ante and ex post transaction costs (Williamson 1985, 20). Ex ante transaction costs are mainly fixed costs associated with the search for trading partners and with negotiating and drafting agreements. These costs increase when physical infrastructure (especially roads and telecommunications) is poor, and they affect the decision to participate in the market. Ex post transaction costs are mainly variable costs associated with moral hazard, that is, the risk of a breach of contract. These costs vary directly with the quantity transacted (the more land transacted, the more each party stands to lose if the contract is breached) and, together with fixed transaction costs, affect volumes traded and the type of contracts drawn up.

In summary, transaction costs are likely to increase when physical infrastructure is inadequate and when contractual parties face severe moral hazard—for instance, when transactions take time to complete and the legal infrastructure is weak. It follows that tenure security and transaction costs are inversely related: assurance strengthens tenure security and reduces ex post transaction costs. Household surveys conducted in Lesotho (Lawry 1993) and KwaZulu (Thomson and Lyne 1991) revealed a general perception that tenants might claim land rented from lessors, or that lessors might claim crops produced by tenants. This lack of assurance helps to explain why so few rental transactions were observed in these surveys and why these transactions tend to be highly personalized agreements between family relatives and close friends.

16.1.2 Institutional Change

Chapter 13 and the case study in Chapter 15 illustrate the argument that farmers will assert increasingly exclusive rights to land as population pressure grows and farming prospects improve (Uchendu 1970; Ault and Rutman 1979; Hecht 1985). This Evolutionary Theory of Land Rights is consistent with the Coasian transaction-cost model of endogenous institutional change (Bardhan 1989b), which postulates that tenure becomes more secure when land becomes scarce, because farmers have an incentive to invest but are unable to internalize the benefits of rising product prices or new technology unless they can exclude free riders.

However, the transaction-cost model of institutional change presumes that farmers are able to organize an effective lobby for more exclusive land rights and that their demands are accepted by government authorities. Curiously, the transaction-cost approach ignores problems of collective action, such as high transaction costs in large groups (Olson 1971, 34) and vested interest groups opposed to changes in the distribution of income caused by a restructuring of existing property rights (Hayami and Ruttan 1985, 95). These problems influence the supply of institutional change.

A shift toward more exclusive land rights is bound to attract resistance in communal areas where stockowners rely heavily on secondary-use rights to graze cattle on land that is not cultivated by its primary holder. For example, the Traditional Authority may sympathize with (poor) households who depend on secondary-use rights to subsist, or they may identify with (wealthy) stockowners who graze cattle freely on land that is not theirs to cultivate.

Platteau (1995, 6) argues that tensions generated by demands for more exclusive land rights result in efficiency losses and social unrest that, in turn, encourage national governments to carry out administrative reforms, including the formal registration of private property rights. In theory, land titling is expected to increase tenure security, stimulate investment, and allow the emergence of a land market (Barrows and Roth 1990). In practice, attempts to replace customary tenure with title deeds have seldom delivered these outcomes in rural areas owing to the reality of imperfect information.

Thomson (1996, 47–49) reviewed a number of rural titling programs in African countries and concluded that they had aggravated tenure insecurity by creating conflicting claims to land. Customary law continued to operate de facto, because Traditional Authorities were generally regarded as the only credible source of information about property rights, and customary institutions were more familiar and cheaper for people to use. To avoid the pitfalls of replacement strategies like titling, Bruce and Freudenberger (1992) recommend the use of adaptive strategies to bring about gradual but predictable changes in local customs, laws, and regulatory institutions that define the tenure system.

Establishing precedents that reinforce tenure security is an important element of the adaptive approach. Identifying potential losers and finding ways of compensating them is also important, because institutional change is likely to be resisted by those who benefit from the existing structure of property rights. If tenure is secured at the expense of households who rely on secondary-use rights, acceptable compensation may involve alternative forms of social security, such as adequate pension and unemployment benefits or options to exchange use rights for serviced residential sites (Lyne, Thomson, and Ortmann 1996). Adaptive strategies would have to be accepted and endorsed by traditional leaders, and the principle of compensation may have to extend to these leaders when institutional changes recommended by an external agent impose economic or political costs on them.

16.2 Research Design

This case study set out to test three basic propositions; first, that rental transactions in cropland were constrained primarily by a perception that land rented out could be lost permanently owing to the customary "use it or lose it" rule; second, that customary institutions could be modified in a predictable way by engaging with traditional leaders and communities; and third, that the processes used to adapt local institutions could be replicated in other parts of KwaZulu. To test these propositions, the research design used a sequence of participatory and survey research strategies spread over a sufficiently long period to modify local institutions, observe outcomes, and replicate the changes in a different area. In total, the case study spanned a period of 10 years.

The first phase (Phase 1) ran from 1993 to 1996 and started with consultations to identify a supportive Traditional Authority and a manageable research site in Okhahlamba District, an area used for both livestock and crop production. Two sub-wards in the Amangwane Tribal Ward were selected, one as an experimental site (Moyeni) and the other as a control (Dukuza) where institutional changes would not be initiated. Unfortunately, successful institutional change is not easily confined to an experimental area once the benefits become apparent to people in neighboring areas. In this study, the institutional changes initiated in Moyeni spilled over to Dukuza, and their impacts could be assessed only by monitoring market activity and outcomes over time.

A baseline survey of 80 households, representing approximately 7 percent of the population of households in the study area, was conducted during the 1993/94 summer growing season. A structured questionnaire was applied to de facto household heads to elicit information on household and farm characteristics, participation in land rental transactions, contract types, disputes, and indicators of transaction costs.

Questions relating to perceived and actual land rights were also included. Sixty-four of the original 80 respondents were successfully located and paneled in a follow-up survey conducted in 1995/96 after 2 years of participatory research with communities, leaders, and government agencies to promote rental transactions through institutional change. The participatory elements of Phase 1 are described in Section 16.3. Changes in the level of market activity were quantified by comparing sample statistics, such as the proportion of households participating in rental transactions. In contrast, market outcomes were inferred by comparing the characteristics of all known lessors and lessees. This comparison included all market participants identified in the surveys and any other lessors and lessees that the researchers encountered in the study area.

Phase 2 of the case study involved a second follow-up survey of 80 households in 2000 to establish whether the institutional changes introduced in Phase 1 had sustained a rental market in cropland, and—if so—whether the outcomes for market participants had changed with the passage of time. A panel survey of the original respondents would have been ideal, but this was not possible, as the Phase 1 respondents were guaranteed anonymity, and no record was kept of their names. The approach used was to identify and panel as many of the original respondents as possible and then to make up the balance of the sample by random selection from the remaining households. Almost one-quarter of the original respondents were located and included in the sample. As in Phase 1, this representative sample was used to quantify changes in the level of market activity, and a census survey of all known market participants was used to draw inferences about market outcomes. Key findings are presented in Section 16.4.

Phase 3 ran from 2000 to 2003 and set out to test whether the strategies developed in Phase 1 (to modify customary institutions) could be replicated on a larger scale. Lima, a local nongovernmental organization (NGO) specializing in rural development, was awarded a United States Agency for International Development (USAID) contract to extend the pilot rental market in 1999. By 2002 Lima had replicated the institutional changes in six communal areas in the Bergville and Estcourt Districts of KwaZulu-Natal and—in 2003—commissioned the author to assess its progress. Surveys were conducted at two sites, one in each district, and included both Lima clients and nonclients. Lima clients had all participated in at least one land rental transaction facilitated by the NGO during 2000–03. Random samples were drawn from lists of households at each site. For clients, the lists were extracted directly from records maintained by Lima. Nonclients were listed by matching each client with a nonclient neighbor identified by Lima staff. A total of 149 de facto household heads, evenly distributed across the two districts and across Lima clients and nonclients, were interviewed. Clearly, these survey data provide no information about changes in market activity over time. Nevertheless, by sampling both clients and nonclients, it was possible to determine whether Lima's efforts to replicate institutional change had succeeded in converting nonparticipants into market participants and to quantify the impact that rental transactions had on investment in crop production. The findings are summarized in Section 16.5.

16.3 Phase 1 of the Case Study

Initially it was assumed that the risk of losing land was the most important factor constraining rental transactions. The following strategies were employed to reduce transaction costs, including risk (Lyne and Thomson 1998):

1. Permission to promote a rental market for arable land was granted by the Traditional Authority. The chief and his counselors agreed (on public radio broadcast) to uphold written lease agreements in tribal courts, and they established clear procedures to settle disputes.

2. The tribal secretary endorsed written lease agreements.

3. Willing lessees and lessors were identified, and their names were publicized to reduce private search costs.

4. An extension officer organized voluntary meetings attended by small groups of potential lessors and lessees to discuss the rights and obligations of contractual parties, and to clarify procedures used to establish contracts and settle disputes.

5. Willing lessors and lessees were encouraged to negotiate their own contractual terms but were assisted in preparing written lease agreements.

Many households were willing to lease land out after this first round of institutional changes. However, the changes did little to encourage potential lessees. Few farmers were prepared to hire additional land, because they perceived land tenure to be insecure for the following reasons (Lyne and Thomson 1998):

1. Households do not have exclusive rights to cropland for the whole year. In winter all land becomes communal, and stockowners are entitled to graze their livestock on crop residues. This practice prevented farmers from internalizing the full benefits of their investment in crop production.

2. The limited duration of exclusive rights to arable land also constrained managerial decisions relating to land use. According to customary law, farmers cannot plow before a planting date specified by the chief.

3. Although stockowners are supposed to remove their cattle from arable land after the prescribed planting date, most farmers suffered crop damages caused by stray livestock. In short, customary rights of exclusion were not assured.

Following in-depth discussions with the Traditional Authority, the chief and his counselors agreed to enforce new grazing rules, provided that the community made the rules. A series of community workshops was convened to discuss existing problems and possible solutions, and a committee was elected to propose new rules and penalties. Members represented the two main interest groups—crop farmers and stockowners. This Rules Committee hosted a series of public meetings to test proposals, and the Traditional Authority accepted the following recommendations (Lyne and Thomson 1998):

1. Plowing may commence on 1 October every year. After this date all livestock must be removed from arable allotments.

2. Households may claim compensation for crops damaged by stray livestock after 1 October. Rates of compensation and legal fees imposed by the tribal court were also set.

3. These rules were advertised on radio, poster displays, and pamphlets distributed through local schools.

The incidence of crop damage caused by stray cattle fell from 50 to 25 percent during the following season, and the proportion of households engaged in rental transactions increased from 4 percent in 1993 to 25 percent in 1996. Most of the growth in rental market activity occurred after 1994 when the new rules reinforcing exclusive rights to arable land were introduced and advertised (Lyne and Thomson 1998).

Table 16.1 presents indicators of efficiency and equity changes observed across all contractual parties identified in the study area. The data show that lessees farmed their land more intensively than did lessors. Lessees applied variable inputs at more than five times the rate that lessors did, and grossed much higher crop incomes per hectare. The incidence of investments in farm implements, tractors, and fencing was also substantially higher among lessees.

Table 16.1   Efficiency and equity advantages of land rental, 1993–96

	Lessees ($n = 36$)	Lessors ($n = 24$)	t-Value
Farm size (ha)	0.85	2.11	3.73***
Area operated (ha)	2.02	1.21	1.99**
Input expenditure (R/ha)	606	113	3.93***
Crop income (R/ha)	494	105	2.02**
Rental income (R/ha)	—	80	—
Own tractors (percent)	50	0	4.92***
Number of implements	1.22	0.17	5.05***
Invest in fencing (percent)	61	25	2.95***
Number of livestock	5.33	2.42	2.72***
Off-farm income (R/month)	861	764	0.28
Pensioned widows (percent)	0	17	2.14**
Age of household head (years)	47	56	2.70***

Source: Lyne and Thomson (1998).
Notes: ** indicates significance at the 5 percent level and *** at the 1 percent level; — indicates not applicable.

From an equity perspective, households that negotiated cash lease agreements earned a mean annual rental of R 80/ha from land that previously lay idle. Rental transactions tended to equalize farm sizes—land was transferred from land-rich to land-poor households. However, income transferred from households wealthy in cash and nonland assets (especially livestock) to households strapped for liquidity. Although lessors and lessees appear to have similar off-farm incomes, the sample estimate for lessees (R 861) is biased downward. Sixty percent of the lessees were self-employed and did not declare their incomes. Overall, the results confirm Bell's (1990) view that renting gives people who have land but little else (for example, widows) an opportunity to generate income.

16.4   Phase 2 of the Case Study

Because institutional change is a long-term process, more time and data were needed to establish the outcome of Phase 1. This prompted a second follow-up survey in 2000 to establish whether the earlier efforts to reduce transaction costs and improve tenure security had sustained a rental market in cropland. Crookes and Lyne (2003) found that both the number of market participants and the area of cropland rented were substantially higher in 2000 than in 1993, before the adaptive strategies were initiated. However, the number of market participants had fallen after reaching a peak in 1995, the year in which the participatory aspects of Phase 1 were completed.

Viewed from the perspective of transaction costs, the data highlight an apparent anomaly. On the one hand, the number of market participants had declined after

1995, suggesting an increase in transaction costs. On the other hand, the quantity of land traded had continued to increase, suggesting a decline in transaction costs. Areas hired by lessees grew from 0.71 ha in the 1995/96 season to 2.01 ha in the 1999/2000 season.

One explanation for this apparent anomaly lies in the distinction between fixed and variable transaction costs. Evidence presented by Crookes and Lyne (2001) indicates that variable ex post transaction costs associated with uncertain contract enforcement had declined for those successful participants who remained in the market. As a result, the total area transacted increased, even though the number of participants did not. That the number of participants did not increase suggests that prospective lessees and lessors were prevented from entering the rental market by high fixed ex ante transaction costs. These costs had been subsidized by the research project during Phase 1, as the researchers identified prospective lessors and lessees and brought them together. This service was discontinued after 1995, shifting search and transport costs to new participants.

In essence, this follow-up study found that the adaptive strategies implemented in Phase 1 had sustained rental transactions in cropland, and that the market—although imperfect—was still producing gains in both allocative efficiency and equity. Crookes and Lyne (2003) estimated a linear discriminant model to examine the rental market's allocative efficiency and equity outcomes. The model hypothesized that lessees would have more family farm labor available, larger investments in agricultural implements and fixed improvements (fencing), higher agricultural education, and more liquidity than did lessors. Lessors, in contrast, would have a higher incidence of widowed household heads (typically poorer in labor and liquid assets), and their arable lands would be larger and of better quality than those owned by lessees.

Results of the discriminant analysis are presented in Table 16.2. The estimated model classified approximately 91 percent of lessors and 82 percent of lessees correctly. Four of the coefficients estimated for the predictor variables were statistically significant at the 1 or 5 percent level of probability, and two at the 15 percent level. The signs of these coefficients supported expectations. Allocative efficiency improved in 2000, because the rental market transferred cropland to households better equipped with the complementary resources (agricultural education, implements, and fencing) needed to farm it. From an equity perspective, land transferred to households with relatively small areas of low-quality cropland, and rentals earned by those unable or unwilling to farm their land increased (from R 103/ha in 1996 to R 147/ha in 2000 when expressed in constant 2000 prices) as variable transaction costs declined. The rental market was establishing a core of emerging farmers with allocative efficiency and equity gains still evident 4 years after the minor interventions introduced in Phase 1.

Table 16.2   Discriminant function distinguishing between lessors and lessees, 2000

Discriminating variable	Standardized coefficient	Group means	
		Lessors	Lessees
Attended agricultural training course	0.55***	0.17	0.71
Household head is a widow	0.54**	0.39	0.00
Natural logarithm of farm size measured in hectares	0.53***	0.83	0.08
Quality index for own land[a]	0.48*	6.63	5.42
Number of farm implements owned	0.45**	0.39	1.94
Household has fenced its cropland	0.29*	0.39	0.65
Number of on-farm adult-equivalents	NS	2.67	2.71
Liquidity proxied by number of income earners	NS	2.00	1.82
Number of cases		23	17
Correct classification (percent)		91	82
Overall correct classification (percent)		88	
Wilk's l		0.42**	
Canonical correlation		0.76	

Source: Crookes and Lyne (2003).

Notes: * indicates significance at the 15 percent level, ** at the 5 percent level, and *** at the 1 percent level; NS, not significant.

[a]The land quality index was calculated by summing objective measures of land slope and aspect. The resulting index scores ranged from –4.81 to 12. For example, a gentle northeast-facing slope scored 7.5, whereas a steep southwest-facing slope scored –3.81.

16.5   Phase 3 of the Case Study

Between 2000 and 2003 the adaptive strategies developed in Phase 1 were replicated in two other districts by Lima, the local NGO contracted by USAID to check their effects on participation in the rental market and to assess market outcomes, including the market's impact on investment in agriculture.

Descriptive statistics (Lyne 2004) indicated that the recipe of institutional changes developed in Phase 1 and implemented by Lima had indeed drawn prospective participants into a broader market. Growing confidence in the integrity of land rental contracts was also indicated by findings that more than 25 percent of Lima's clients had negotiated their latest (2003/04) contracts privately, and that contractual terms had matured from cash rentals with payments made in advance to transactions involving credit and risk sharing. The land rental market had become a partial substitute for imperfect credit and insurance markets.

Again, the data indicated efficiency and equity gains in rental transactions, and regression analysis of investments made by farmers in operating inputs provided useful information about the market's contribution to the productive use of cropland. Investment in crop production is expected to increase in the presence of an active rental market. An obvious reason is that the market attaches an opportunity cost to underused land, which tends to improve allocative efficiency by transferring land to farmers who are willing and able to use it. Another reason is that the market allows farmers to increase the scale of their operations, which—in the presence of size economies created by fixed transaction, information, and management costs— strengthens incentives to invest. The following regression model was estimated using ordinary least squares to identify important determinants of investment in operating inputs (Lyne 2004):

$$\text{INVESTMENT} = f(\text{LAND, DISTRICT, LESSEE, LIQUIDITY,}$$
$$\text{EDUCATION, AGE OF HEAD, HOUSEHOLD SIZE}),$$

where INVESTMENT is the total expenditure on fertilizer, chemicals, seed, and hired labor; LAND is the area operated measured in hectares; DISTRICT is a dummy variable scoring 1 for Bergville and 0 for Estcourt; LESSEE is a dummy variable scoring 1 for lessees and 0 otherwise; LIQUIDITY is the natural logarithm of monthly off-farm wage income measured in Rands; EDUCATION is a dummy variable scoring 1 if the household head has higher than primary schooling and 0 otherwise; and AGE OF HEAD and HOUSEHOLD SIZE are measured appropriately.

The results of the regression analysis are presented in Table 16.3. The estimated model is statistically significant and has an adjusted R^2 of 77 percent. There was no evidence of multicollinearity, the largest variance inflation factor being 1.47. As would be expected, area operated (LAND) is the most important determinant of total investment. LAND has by far the largest standardized regression coefficient (b = 0.738). Of course, some of the investment attributed to LAND should be attributed to the presence of a rental market, as most of the land cultivated by lessees had previously been idle. After farm size, the land rental market (represented by the variable LESSEE, with b = 0.254) makes the next most important and positive contribution to investment in operating inputs. According to its unstandardized regression coefficient (B), a lessee spends R 2,160 more on operating inputs each year than do other respondents, other things being equal. This amounts to an additional investment of R 470/ha, as lessees operated a mean area of 4.6 ha (of which 4.0 ha were rented). DISTRICT ranks third, ahead of smaller contributions made by EDUCATION and LIQUIDITY. Investment gains associated with an active rental market are therefore made up of at least two parts: the first can be attributed to an increase in the area of land cultivated (R 432/ha), and the second to the more intensive use of land farmed by lessees (R 470/ha). This finding suggests that the CAPRi framework is somewhat naive, as it shows that even short-term investments in seasonal inputs made by individuals at the plot level increase with improved tenure security if tenure is not secure enough to sustain an efficient land rental market.

Table 16.3   Regression analysis of investment in farm operating inputs

Explanatory variable	Unstandardized coefficients		Standardized coefficients	
	β	Standard error	β	t-Statistic
(Constant)	−4955.554	2095.559		−2.365**
LAND	432.357	32.098	.738	13.470***
DISTRICT	1167.229	351.347	.175	3.322***
LESSEE	2159.641	472.507	.254	4.571***
LIQUIDITY	580.536	355.766	.099	1.632*
EDUCATION OF HEAD	820.111	415.698	.110	1.973**
AGE OF HEAD	4.239	16.787	.016	0.253
FAMILY SIZE	−44.782	57.404	−.042	−0.780

Source: Lyne (2004).

Notes: * indicates significance at the 10 percent level, ** at the 5 percent level, and *** at the 1 percent level; NS, not significant. The sample number is $n = 145$.

16.6   Conclusions

This case study shows that adaptive strategies that are well researched and judiciously implemented in a participatory manner by an external agent can improve tenure security, reduce transaction costs, and promote a more efficient rental market for cropland in areas characterized by customary forms of land tenure. The findings also show that rental markets tend to produce both efficiency and equity gains, and they bring into question the CAPRi framework, which ignores relationships among tenure security, the rental market, and investment in agricultural inputs.

Quick and visible responses to the minor interventions described in this chapter suggest that emerging farmers had not been able by themselves to address problems (of collective action and political influence) obstructing an endogenous shift to more secure land rights. This difficulty suggests an important role for government. In addition, the study highlights roles that government and extension staff could play in reducing transaction costs confronting prospective lessees and lessors. Rental market participation is expected to be highly sensitive to fixed transaction costs when areas transacted are severely constrained by small farm sizes. Public investment in physical infrastructure would help to reduce fixed transaction costs. Extension staff could help to reduce fixed and variable transaction costs by maintaining lists of willing lessors and lessees, supplying copies of pro forma lease agreements, witnessing rental contracts, and disseminating information about procedures for contracting and settling disputes as part of their regular duties. Of course, government must provide a dependable judicial system to uphold rental contracts and to enforce penalties and compensation for crop damage caused by stray livestock. Although such interventions are meaningful in KwaZulu, they should not be regarded as a blueprint for all communal areas; rental markets for cropland may be inhibited by other institutional problems as well as noninstitutional constraints.

The broader African experience suggests that adaptive strategies are likely to outperform replacement strategies (such as titling programs) as ways of changing customary institutions in rural areas where there is a demand for change. However, they must be well informed and well managed, and may not be any cheaper to implement than replacement strategies. This case study hints at a substantial commitment from government to conduct research, train and mobilize extension staff, support negotiations with local authorities and communities, document transactions and disputes, publicize procedures and precedents, and provide quality physical and legal infrastructure. Losers may also have to be identified and compensated; for example, when farmers require fully exclusive land rights to better internalize the benefits of long-term investments in fixed improvements.

Note

1. In this case study, the term "KwaZulu" refers to the communal areas of KwaZulu-Natal.

References

Ault, D. E., and G. L. Rutman. 1979. The development of individual rights to property in tribal Africa. *Journal of Law and Economics* 22 (1): 163–182.

Bardhan, P. K. 1989a. The New Institutional Economics and development theory: A brief critical assessment. *World Development* 17: 1389–1395.

———. 1989b. Alternative approaches to the theory of institutions in economic development. In *The economic theory of agrarian institutions,* ed. P. Bardhan. Oxford: Clarendon Press.

Barrows, R. L., and M. Roth. 1990. Land tenure and investment in African agriculture: Theory and evidence. *Journal of Modern African Studies* 28: 265–297.

Bell, C. 1990. Reforming property rights in land and tenancy. *World Bank Research Observer* 5: 143–166.

Bruce, J. W., and M. S. Freudenberger. 1992. Institutional opportunities and constraints in African land tenure: Shifting from a "replacement" to an "adaptation" strategy paradigm. Draft paper. Madison, Wis., U.S.A.: Land Tenure Center, University of Wisconsin.

Crookes, T. J., and M. C. Lyne. 2001. Improvements in the rental market for cropland in a communal region of KwaZulu-Natal. *Agrekon* 40: 669–677.

———. 2003. Efficiency and equity gains in the rental market for arable land: Observations from a communal area of KwaZulu-Natal, South Africa. *Development Southern Africa* 20 (5): 579–593.

Hayami, Y., and V. Ruttan. 1985. *Agricultural development. An international perspective.* Baltimore: Johns Hopkins University Press.

Hecht, R. M. 1985. Immigration, land transfer and tenure changes in Divo, Ivory Coast, 1940–1980. *Africa: Journal of the International African Institute* 55 (3): 319–336.

Lawry, S. W. 1993. Transactions in cropland held under customary tenure in Lesotho. In *Land in African agrarian systems,* ed. T. J. Basset and D. E. Crummey. Madison, Wis., U.S.A.: University of Wisconsin Press.

Lyne, M. C. 2004. *Findings of a survey to assess a programme implemented by Lima Rural Development Foundation to promote a rental market for arable land in two communal areas of KwaZulu-Natal.* Pietermaritzburg, South Africa: Lima Rural Development Foundation.

Lyne, M. C., and W. L. Nieuwoudt. 1991. Inefficient land use in KwaZulu: Causes and remedies. *Development Southern Africa* 8: 193–201.

Lyne, M. C., and D. N. Thomson. 1998. Creating opportunities for farmers in communal areas: Adapting institutions to promote an efficient rental market in arable land. In *The agricultural democratisation of South Africa,* ed. J. Kirsten, J. van Zyl, and N. Vink. Cape Town: Francolin Publishers.

Lyne, M. C., M. Roth, and B. Troutt. 1997. Land rental markets in Sub-Saharan Africa: Institutional change in customary tenure. In *Issues in agricultural competitiveness: Markets and policies,* ed. R. Rose, C. Tanner, and M. Bellamy. Aldershot, U.K.: Dartmouth Publishing.

Lyne, M. C., D. N. Thomson, and G. F. Ortmann. 1996. Advantages of a rental market for land in developing regions of Southern Africa and institutions necessary for its operation. *Agrekon* 35 (1): 12–19.

Nieuwoudt, W. L. 1990. Efficiency of land use. *Agrekon* 29: 210–215.

Olson, M. 1971. *The logic of collective action: Public goods and the theory of groups.* New York: Shocken Books.

Platteau, J.-P. 1995. *Reforming land rights in Sub-Saharan Africa: Issues of efficiency and equity.* Discussion Paper 60. Geneva: United Nations Research Institute for Social Development.

Thomson, D. N. 1996. A study of land rental markets and institutions in communal areas of rural KwaZulu-Natal. Ph.D. dissertation, University of Natal, Pietermaritzburg, South Africa.

Thomson, D. N., and M. C. Lyne. 1991. A land rental market in KwaZulu: Implications for farming efficiency. *Agrekon* 30: 287–290.

Uchendu, V. C. 1970. The impact of changing agricultural technology on African land tenure. *Journal of Developing Areas* 4: 477–486.

Williamson, O. E. 1985. *The economic institutions of capitalism.* New York: Free Press.

Chapter 17

Collective Action in the Management of Canal Irrigation Systems: The Doho Rice Scheme in Uganda

Dick Sserunkuuma, Nicholas Ochom, and John H. Ainembabazi

evolution of natural resource management (NRM) from governments to user groups has often been justified on the premise that local users have comparative advantage and self-interest over government agents in managing and monitoring such resources. Examples of successful collective action in various areas have also fuelled the drive to devolve NRM to local users (Meinzen-Dick, Raju, and Gulati 2000). It is on this basis that the government of Uganda decided to devolve management of the irrigation system at the Doho Rice Scheme (DRS) to the DRS Farmers' Association. The operation and maintenance of such irrigation schemes requires a high degree of coordination, yet with devolution, the state withdraws from this role. Therefore, the success of the devolution policy in improving NRM is highly dependent on the ability and willingness of the farmers to organize successful collective action, but this outcome cannot be assumed—the more so when devolution calls for more time and cash contributions from the farmers. The need to examine farmers' willingness to participate in collective action after the withdrawal of government support motivated this case study, because it is critical for effective implementation of the devolution policy and the development of strategies for sustainable collective action at DRS.

17.1 The Problem

DRS was constructed by the Uganda government between 1976 and 1989 to promote rice production in the area through the provision of irrigation water, improved rice seeds, farm tools, and marketing and milling services. DRS is divided into six blocks, with a total area of 1,012 ha. Following its completion, the government partitioned each block into smaller plots (0.10–0.40 ha) and allocated them to individual farmers on a first come, first served basis, but it kept the role of maintaining the irrigation structures, farm tools, and milling plant. The irrigation water used at DRS comes from the Manafwa River, which originates from Mt. Elgon. Its main stream is 70 km long and covers a catchment area of 570 km², an agriculturally rich region. Some of these agricultural activities are carried out on land with steep slopes, which causes erosion and deposits of silt into the river and the main irrigation canal supplying DRS. The silt in turn reduces the amount of water reaching the rice fields and negatively affects rice yields. In the past the canals were regularly de-silted by the government, but starting in the early 1990s, the government withdrew its support, except for payment of salaries of a skeleton staff composed of irrigation engineers and agricultural extension agents. As a result, the silting of irrigation canals worsened.

To address the siltation problem, a meeting was held in January 1994 among farmers, the DRS management, and local and district authorities, and a decision was made to require farmers to pay an irrigation user fee of USh 12,350/ha per season. A committee was set up to collect the funds and de-silt the canals. A bylaw was enacted stating that those who did not comply with the user-fee payment in any cropping season would have their plots of land withdrawn from them the following season and rented out to willing farmers, and the money realized would go toward the cost of de-silting. The de-silting started in May 1994 using hired excavators but was halted in November 1994 because of a shortage of funds caused by alleged misappropriation and noncompliance of some farmers with the user-fee payment bylaw. As a way of increasing their involvement in management affairs of the irrigation scheme, the DRS farmers formed the Doho Rice Scheme Farmers' Association in December 1994, to which the government is transferring responsibility of managing the scheme.

17.2   Research Questions and Methods

17.2.1   Research Questions
The questions addressed by this study draw from the literature on the factors hypothesized to influence collective action in NRM. These include (1) physical and technical characteristics of the resource (degree of excludability and subtractability; see Chapter 3); (2) social and economic characteristics of the resource users that affect their demand for and dependence on the resource, and enable or prevent

them from privately benefiting from it; and (3) policy and governance factors (rules or bylaws and their enforcement). This study addresses three main questions. First, what are the existing benefits (incentives) for participation in collective action or payment of irrigation user fees at DRS and what is their potential for motivating collective action? Second, how effective is enforcement of the existing bylaw on user-fee payment and to what extent does it foster collective action? Third, assuming sufficient incentives and effective bylaw enforcement, why do some farmers comply with the bylaw and others do not?

17.2.2 Research Methods

Data sources.   The data were obtained from a survey of 411 households selected using a stratified random sampling technique from among DRS rice producers in 2001. Participation in collective action is measured by degree of compliance with the bylaw requiring all DRS farmers to pay the irrigation user fee. Household and plot-level data were gathered on several variables relating to the physical and technical environment and socioeconomic characteristics of the users, including money paid as irrigation fees; plot distance from the irrigation canals; household endowments of physical assets (farm size, number of plots, livestock, and the like), human capital (education, agricultural training and extension education, farming experience, labor, and the like), social capital (membership in organizations, family and ethnic relations, and so on), and financial capital (savings, credit, and so on); and other household characteristics.[1]

Analysis.   In this study, participation in collective action was measured by the degree of compliance with the user-fee bylaw. The surveyed households were grouped into three categories based on level of compliance (no, partial, and full compliance). The noncompliance category (I) consisted of households (3 percent) that did not comply at all in the first or second cropping season of 2001. The partial-compliance category (II) consisted of households (31 percent) that paid irrigation fees in only one of the two cropping seasons of 2001. Also included in this category were households that did not comply at all for some plots but partially or fully complied on others. The full-compliance category (III) consisted of households (66 percent) that paid irrigation fees for all plots operated at DRS in both the first and second cropping seasons of 2001. Descriptive statistics were used to address the first two study questions, and an ordered logit model (OLM) was estimated to address the third study question. In the OLM, an ordinal measure of compliance constructed from three levels of compliance (1 2 3) was regressed against household and plot-level variables hypothesized to affect compliance, including incentives and governance issues that are partly addressed using descriptive statistics.

17.3   Results and Discussion

17.3.1   Descriptive Statistics

Table 17.1 shows that nearly all (99 percent) of the surveyed DRS farmers reported irrigation water as their greatest benefit from DRS, followed by extension and technical advice (50 percent). Because they have access to irrigation water, DRS farmers have two crop seasons of rice a year compared to one crop season for those outside DRS, whose production is entirely dependent on rain. Rice milling and marketing were also mentioned as benefits by 41 and 21 percent of the respondents, respectively, though these are services not offered directly by DRS but by private enterprises operating at DRS. There was no significant difference in the proportions of farmers mentioning all types of benefits across the three categories of compliance. Most DRS farmers (68 percent in the first season and 60 percent in the second season) perceived

Table 17.1   Benefits received by farmers in the Doho Rice Scheme and their perceptions of the benefits relative to costs

Benefit or service	All households (n = 411)	Noncompliance category (n = 14)	Partial-compliance category (n = 128)	Full-compliance category (n = 269)
	Percentage of households reporting			
Irrigation water	98.5	100.0	99.2	98.14
Rice milling	40.87	21.43	41.41	41.64
Extension and technical advice	50.36	50.0	54.69	48.33
Marketing/collection center	22.38	14.29	21.88	23.05
Perception of benefits in relation to costs				
First season				
Benefits are less than costs	20.4	28.57	17.97	21.19
Benefits equal costs	11.9	7.14	14.84	10.78
Benefits exceed costs	67.6	64.29	67.19	68.03
Average yield (kg/ha)	1,474.6	1,394.3[ab]	1,387.9[a]	1,516.2[b]
	(31.25)	(148.9)	(62.4)	(36.5)
Number of plots used in analysis	614	15	185	414
Second season				
Benefits are less than costs	26.7	42.86	30.47	24.16
Benefits equal costs	13.3	7.14	18.75	11.15
Benefits exceed costs	59.9	50.0	50.78	64.68
Average yield (kg/ha)	1,570.8	1,562.7[ab]	1,445.9[a]	1,634.9[b]
	(32.78)	(86.1)	(57.3)	(42.6)
Number of plots used in analysis	589	34	187	368

Notes: n, number of households reporting. Superscripts a and b indicate that the difference between numbers marked with differing superscripts is statistically significant. A number marked with both a and b is not significantly different from the numbers marked with only a or b. Numbers in parentheses are standard errors.

the benefits from DRS to outweigh the costs they incur, which include payment of user fees and additional labor supplied to de-silt the irrigation canals when funds are insufficient. The proportion of those perceiving the benefits to be lower than the costs was 20 percent in the first season and 27 percent in the second season; and those perceiving the benefits to be equal to the cost constituted 12 and 13 percent in the first and second seasons, respectively. That one-fifth to one-quarter of farmers perceived the benefits derived from DRS not to be worth the cost incurred is suggestive of insufficient incentives for payment of user fees and could partly explain why one-third of the farmers did not comply fully with the bylaw.

Most farmers felt that benefits from DRS, except for marketing,[2] had deteriorated in the past 10 years, with supply of irrigation water and provision of extension and/or technical advice being most affected (Table 17.2). They blamed the former on frequent breakdown of the DRS excavator and the resultant siltation of the canals and reduction of the amount of water supplied. Inadequate water supply is associated with reduced rice yields (Table 17.3), which reduces compliance with the user-fee bylaw (see Table 17.1).[3] Other reasons that farmers cited for nonpayment include inadequate income and poor or nonexistent rice harvests.

Table 17.2   Farmers' perceptions of the change in benefits and services, user-fee collection procedure, and performance of the current DRS administration (percentage of households)

Characteristic	Response	
Perceived change in benefits and services in the past 10 years	Improvement	Deterioration
Irrigation water ($n = 375$)	1.9	98.1
Rice milling ($n = 122$)	41.8	58.2
Extension and technical advice ($n = 156$)	17.3	82.7
Marketing and collection center ($n = 37$)	56.7	43.2
Perception of user-fee collection procedure	First season	Second season
	($n = 373$)	($n = 289$)
Very good	1.6	1.0
Good	53.9	50.9
Fair	27.6	31.1
Poor	15.3	14.9
Very poor	1.6	2.1
Perception of performance of current DRS administration ($n = 411$)		
Very good		0.5
Good		25.5
Fair		17.3
Poor		48.2
Very poor		8.5

Notes: DRS, Doho Rice Scheme; *n*, number of households reporting.

Table 17.3   Adequacy of irrigation water received by household and its correlation with rice yield in the first and second seasons, 2001

	Percentage of households reporting		Correlation with rice yield	
			First season	Second season
Adequacy of irrigation water received	First season	Second season	(N^p = 614)	(N^p = 589)
Adequate water throughout season	85.4	48.2	0.098**	0.091**
Adequate water part of season and inadequate water the other part	12.9	24.1	−0.036	0.005
Inadequate water throughout season	7.5	31.4	−0.046	−0.039
Inadequate water part of season and no water for the other part	1.9	8.3	n.a.	−0.022
No water throughout season	1.2	5.6	n.a.	n.a.

Notes: The figures add up to more than 100 percent because some respondents had more than one plot of land. The number of households reporting is 411. N^p, total number of plots used in the analysis; n.a., not applicable; ** indicates significance at the 5 percent level.

As mentioned earlier, there is a bylaw requiring all farmers to pay user fees, and the penalty for nonpayment is denial of rights to use or to own land the following season. But as indicated in Table 17.2, more than 44 percent of the farmers ranked the irrigation-fee collection procedure as unsatisfactory (fair to very poor), which could be why some farmers failed to pay their fees. In addition, only one-quarter of the farmers (25 percent) understood the correct interpretation and penalty of the bylaw. Nkonya, Babigumira, and Walusimbi (2001) observed that it is difficult to effectively enforce bylaws and restrictions that are not clear to farmers. Also observed was poor and selective enforcement of the bylaw, being soft on enforcers themselves and their relatives or friends. These circumstances perpetuate non-compliance. Some 20 percent of the surveyed farmers said that since the establishment of this bylaw in 1994, they knew of five defaulters (on average) who were not punished for nonpayment. Three-quarters of the farmers rated the current DRS administration as poor to fair, mainly because of poor maintenance of irrigation facilities and corruption. These administrative weaknesses result in inadequate fee collection, irrigation canals not being effectively de-silted, reduced water supply, poor rice harvests, and a vicious cycle of reduced irrigation water delivery and nonpayment of fees. Thus weaknesses in enforcement of the rules weakens farmers' confidence in the institution, and breaking this vicious cycle requires guaranteeing the delivery of irrigation water first, without which it may be difficult to enforce the payment of user fees.

However, the administration at DRS attributes the abovementioned administrative weaknesses to the physical characteristics of the irrigation system. First, there is no means of blocking water supply to individual defaulters, making it hard to enforce the fee-payment bylaw. Elsewhere, successful collective action has been achieved by effective enforcement that enabled administrators to cut off water supply to defaulters. For instance, Meinzen-Dick, Raju, and Gulati (2000) found that farmers in India abstaining from communal activities had to pay a penalty of 30–60 rupees/day per person. If a farmer refused to pay, the users' group stopped water supply to their plots and doubled the penalty, thus increasing compliance. There are no such mechanisms at DRS. Second, most DRS farmers own their land in perpetuity, such that threatening repeated defaulters with permanent confiscation of land is not possible, except to those who rent or borrow land (Table 17.4). The worst that could happen to them is to be denied access for a season, but even this penalty is poorly enforced. Tenure security may thus be a disincentive to compliance with the bylaw, implying a need for alternative compliance-enhancing mechanisms. In other schemes where farmers do not own the land but land is allocated for use at the beginning of each season, the user-fee bylaw has been effectively enforced by not allowing farmers to plough the plots allocated to them before paying irrigation fees for that season (Fred Malinga, personal communication, February 2002).

Table 17.4 Land ownership and methods of land acquisition by DRS farmers

Characteristic	Entire sample ($n = 411$)	Noncompliance category ($n = 14$)	Partial-compliance category ($n = 128$)	Full-compliance category ($n = 269$)
Land ownership				
Average number of plots owned	1.6 (0.042)	1.93 (0.322)	1.60 (0.076)	1.58 (0.05)
Average total area of land owned	1.27	1.74[a]	1.28[ab]	1.25[b]
at DRS (ha)	(0.054)	(0.433)	(0.096)	(0.065)
Methods of land acquisition				
Purchase	34.1	35.71	32.81	34.57
Gift or inheritance	40.4	28.57	43.75	39.41
Government or DRS administration	38.4	50.0	35.16	39.41
Rented	7.1	0.0	6.25	7.81
Borrowed	0.7	—	—	—
Share-cropped	0.2	—	—	—

Notes: Superscripts a and b indicate that the difference between numbers marked with differing superscripts is statistically significant. A number marked with both a and b is not significantly different from the numbers marked with only a or b. Numbers in parentheses are standard errors. DRS, Doho Rice Scheme; n, number of households reporting; —, insufficient data to conduct difference of proportion tests.

17.3.2 Regression Results

Table 17.5 presents the results of regression analysis on the determinants of participation in collective action, measured by level of bylaw compliance. The income share of rice was perceived to be potentially endogenous, thus its inclusion in the model explaining participation in collective action would likely produce biased estimates, because of its high correlation with the error term. To solve this problem, a two-step approach was used: (1) estimating an ordinary least squares regression model on determinants of the share of household income from rice;[4] and (2) regressing the level of compliance against predicted values of rice income share from step 1 and other exogenous variables (Table 17.5) in the OLM.

The descriptive results show that irrigation water is the primary benefit that farmers derive from DRS, as it enables them to produce rice for two seasons in a year compared to one season for rice growers outside DRS. Thus perceived direct economic benefits from de-silting in the form of increased irrigation water supply likely motivates user-fee payment as a collective action. However, the amount of irrigation water receivable is directly proportional to the distance of one's rice plot from irrigation canals, such that an inverted U-shaped relationship (measured by distance and the square of distance) is expected between this distance and participation in collective action (Bardhan 1993). That is, farmers receiving plenty of water because of their proximity to irrigation canals are expected to be less compliant, which is also true for those expecting too little water because of excessive distance from irrigation canals. The regression results show that distance and the square of distance from the main irrigation canal to the rice plot had insignificant relationships with payment of user fees; but having a rice plot on blocks 1, 2, 3, and 5 positively affects payment of user fees. This result suggests that other block-level (locational) differences in the scheme (possibly differences in administration and effort directed to user-fee collection) and not just distance of blocks or plots from the canals are important in influencing compliance.

Theory predicts that users' demand for and dependence on a resource influences their participation in the collective management of that resource. The regression results show that households that depend on rice for a large part of their cash income are more likely to pay the user fee to reduce the risk of irrigation water scarcity and its negative impact on rice harvests and income. In addition, the sale of other crop produce (besides rice) as the primary income source increases compliance, probably because the income from these alternative sources increases the ability to pay the user fee. However, rice being a major subsistence food crop does not seem to affect compliance, suggesting that producing rice primarily for subsistence needs of the household does not provide the cash for payment of the user fee.

Agricultural training in soil and water conservation and access to formal credit sources increase compliance. These correlations are likely because training in soil and

Table 17.5   Determinants of participation in collective action

Explanatory variable	Coefficient	Robust standard error
Physical characteristics of irrigation scheme		
Average distance from subirrigation canal to rice plot(s) (km)	0.218	1.058
Square of the average distance from subirrigation canal to rice plot(s) (km^2)	−0.282	0.546
Household operated a rice plot on block 1 in 2001 = 1; 0 otherwise	0.873*	0.467
Household operated a rice plot on block 2 in 2001 = 1; 0 otherwise	1.046**	0.457
Household operated a rice plot on block 3 in 2001 = 1; 0 otherwise	1.058**	0.474
Household operated a rice plot on block 4 in 2001 = 1; 0 otherwise	0.700	0.435
Household operated a rice plot on block 5 in 2001 = 1; 0 otherwise	0.654**	0.325
Household operated a rice plot on block 6 in 2001 = 1; 0 otherwise	0.462	0.391
Socioeconomic characteristics of the resource users (farmers)		
Predicted proportion of household income contributed by rice in 2001	8.712***	1.611
Sale of crops other than rice as primary income source = 1; 0 otherwise	4.693***	1.067
Importance of rice as a subsistence crop = 1 if rice constitutes at least 50 percent of household food consumption; 0 otherwise	0.111	0.372
Training in soil and water conservation = 1 if household received training; 0 otherwise	1.153*	0.651
Access to formal credit = 1 if household applied for credit from at least one formal source; 0 otherwise	0.964***	0.371
Total number of extension visits received by the household in 2001 on the subject of irrigation water management	0.182	0.195
Agricultural training organization = 1 if household had membership in agricultural training program or organization; 0 otherwise	0.869	0.681
Education of household head (years of schooling)	−0.078	0.137
Perception of costs exceeding benefits of participation in collective action = 1; 0 otherwise	−0.556**	0.242
Gender of the household head = 1 if male; 0 otherwise	0.968*	0.545
Dependency ratio (number of children and adult dependents divided by number of working adults in household)	0.200**	0.099
Number of separate rice plots owned by the household at DRS	−0.484***	0.164
Tenure security = 1 if household owned at least one of the rice plots it operated at DRS in 2001; 0 otherwise.	−1.000**	0.513
Experience in rice growing at DRS (years)	−0.336***	0.123
Governance (enforcement) issues		
Number of unpunished defaulters known by the household since 1994	−0.012	0.240
Number of observations	398	
Log likelihood χ^2 value	76.940***	
Log likelihood	−259.987	
Pseudo R^2	0.1289	
Value of cut1	0.911	1.513
Value of cut2	4.005	1.517

Notes: Dependent variable is the level of compliance with the user-fee bylaw. * indicates significance at the 10 percent level, ** at the 5 percent level, and *** at the 1 percent level; DRS, Doho Rice Scheme. Cut1 and cut2 stand for intercepts (constants) for "partial-compliance" and "full-compliance" categories, respectively. These cut results are produced by STATA automatically for categories considered in the model.

water conservation increases farmers' awareness of siltation problems and appreciation of the need to pay the user fees to overcome the problems, and credit increases
their ability and desire to pay to reduce water scarcity and increase rice yield—and
thus their ability to pay back the credit. However, number of agricultural extension
visits did not have a significant effect, nor did membership in an agricultural training organization or general formal education. The perception that the costs of participation exceed the benefits is negatively related to compliance, as expected. This
perception may be due to the deterioration in the level and quality of benefits derived
from DRS, which negatively affects rice yields and willingness to pay irrigation fees.
Male-headed households are more compliant, and a higher household dependency
ratio (defined as the ratio of children or adult dependents to productive household
members) increases compliance, yet one would expect households with a high dependency ratio to be overburdened with the subsistence needs of their members and thus
less likely to pay user fees.

Influence or external recognition is a leadership attribute considered to be
essential for organization of successful collective action (Meinzen-Dick, Raju, and
Gulati 2000). However, in the case of DRS, several factors that one would expect to
epitomize influence and recognition—such as security of land tenure (owning land
versus renting), number of separate rice plots owned (measure of wealth and influence), and experience in rice growing at DRS—have significant negative effects on
compliance. In other words, more influential households are less likely to comply,
which corroborates the descriptive statistics presented earlier, with 7 percent of the
respondents saying that the most notorious defaulters who go unpunished are rich
and influential individuals. Farmers with a longer experience of rice growing at DRS
are less compliant, probably because they have learned that the marginal benefit of
their contribution is low when others do not contribute or that the money is often
not put to proper use. However, one could also argue that more experienced farmers
started growing rice at DRS when the government met the maintenance costs and,
therefore, changes that required them to pay for maintenance might be perceived as
unfair, whereas newcomers, always faced with the charge, may have different perceptions of fairness over who is responsible for maintenance. This argument illustrates
path-dependence issues discussed in the theory chapters in Part 1.

The number of rice plots owned negatively affects compliance, which could be
a result of the wealth effect: for wealthy farmers, the relative importance of potential
benefits from compliance is lower than for poor farmers with limited alternatives
sources of food and income. It is also possible that those owning many plots of land
tend to rent out some of them, which makes the owners unavailable or unwilling to
comply. The negative relationship between owning the rice plot operated (versus
renting) and compliance is probably because those who own land know that the

worst that could happen to them is to lose access for one season, but the likelihood of loss is very low because of poor enforcement of the bylaws. In contrast, those who rent land have a higher incentive to pay for two possible reasons. First, they want to reduce the risk of water scarcity for the season when they are renting the land to ensure a sufficiently high harvest to at least recover the rental cost of land. Second, they view prompt payment of all fees (rental and irrigation) as one way of appeasing their landlords to enhance their prospects for renting the land in subsequent seasons. Thus prompt payment may be one way of acquiring some level of security over the land, suggesting feedback between compliance and tenure security. Finally, the impact of bylaw enforcement (governance) on compliance—as measured by the number of defaulters identified by the household who were not punished for noncompliance since the establishment of the bylaw in 1994—is negative, as expected, but statistically insignificant.

17.4 Conclusions

This study examined the incentives (benefits and penalties) for participation in collective action at DRS and found major problems in enforcement and delivery of benefits that will likely diminish the effectiveness of the devolution policy, which was intended to improve the management of the irrigation scheme. To stimulate greater participation in collective action, stronger and more effectively enforced bylaws governing user-fee payment, collection procedures, and efficient use of resources must be coupled with evidence of improved delivery of services and benefits.

Currently there is limited awareness and poor enforcement of the user-fee bylaw. Only 25 percent of the surveyed farmers understand the bylaw as it is written, and nearly 20 percent said that since the establishment of this bylaw in 1994, they knew of five defaulters (on average) who were not punished for nonpayment. Furthermore, the benefits of irrigation water and extension received by farmers from DRS, which could serve as an incentive for compliance, have deteriorated over the years to the extent that one-quarter of DRS farmers perceived the benefits of compliance to be lower than the costs. This perception, coupled with limited awareness and poor enforcement of the bylaw, partially explains why some farmers do not pay the user fee even when it is meant for their own benefit. Indeed, the regression results show a significant negative relationship between compliance and the perception that benefits are lower than the costs, suggesting a need to improve water supply to change this perception.

The challenge remains that, without enough farmers paying the fees, the irrigation system cannot be adequately de-silted, which in turn lowers the amount of irrigation water supplied to the rice plots, hampering rice yields and farmers' ability to pay the user fees in the following season. Therefore, failure to adequately de-silt the canals sets up a cycle of failure. Breaking this cycle requires rehabilitation of the entire irrigation system to increase water supply to farmers, who will then have an incentive to improve agricultural productivity as well as their willingness and ability to pay the user fee. The study results show significant differences in compliance across the six blocks that make up DRS, which suggests block-level differences in enforcement and incentives for compliance. Further research on the nature and extent of these block-level differences and how they influence compliance is needed to provide information on how to increase compliance on blocks where it is currently low.

The regression results show that households that depend on rice for a large part of their cash income are more likely to comply, supporting the theory that users' dependence on a resource increases the incentives for organization for collective management of that resource. Agricultural training in soil and water conservation and access to credit increase compliance, which underscores the importance of providing support services (extension and credit) to increase farmers' awareness of the need—and enhance their ability—to contribute to the cost of supplying water.

Influence and recognition are leadership attributes that can facilitate organization for successful collective action. However, at DRS, such attributes are negatively associated with compliance. In other words, more influential people are less likely to comply, which is a further manifestation of the failure to enforce the bylaw, which in turn results in failure to collect sufficient funds to de-silt the canals. This observation suggests that after rehabilitating DRS to increase water supply as suggested above, stronger bylaws must be enacted and awareness and enforcement of these laws improved. Alternative ways of enforcing payment, such as use of private collection agencies, may also be useful.

Renting the rice plot versus owning it increases compliance, likely because those who rent land pay promptly as a means of increasing water supply and rice harvests to enable them to recover the rental cost of land. Other studies in Uganda have found higher intensity of labor use on rented than on purchased plots of land (Nkonya et al. 2004) and higher use of improved seed and fertilizer on maize plots acquired through renting than on purchased plots (Sserunkuuma 2003). These findings also suggest that intensification is more likely to occur on rented plots than on owner-operated plots. Thus development of a land rental market could improve efficiency by permitting access to land for those who have none but are likely to use it more efficiently and profitably.

Notes

1. Although policy factors are also important and are included in the scheme-level (qualitative) analysis, they do not vary among households and are therefore not included in the quantitative analysis.

2. The reason farmers perceive marketing services to have improved could be attributed to the government policy of market liberalization.

3. Rice yield in the full-compliance category is higher than in the partial-compliance and non-compliance categories.

4. Results of the income-share model show that payment of irrigation fees (compliance) and number of rice plots owned at DRS significantly increases the percentage of household income generated by rice. Education of the household head, having a male household head, number of livestock (cattle and oxen) owned, savings in the form of cash or noncash precautionary savings (such as storable agricultural produce), access to formal credit, and having a salary or wage employment or sale of crops other than rice as primary income source have significant negative relationships with income share of rice. The adjusted R^2 for the rice income-share model was 0.25.

References

Bardhan, P. K. 1993. Analytics of the institutions of informal cooperation in rural development. *World Development* 21: 633–639.

Meinzen-Dick, R. S., K. V. Raju, and A. Gulati. 2000. *What affects organization and collective action for managing resources? Evidence from canal irrigation systems in India.* Environment and Production Technology Division Discussion Paper 61. Washington, D.C.: International Food Policy Research Institute.

Nkonya, E., R. Babigumira, and R. Walusimbi. 2001. Soil conservation by-laws: Perceptions and enforcement among communities in Uganda. Mimeo. Washington, D.C.: Environment and Production Technology Division, International Food Policy Research Institute.

Nkonya, P., J. Pender, P. Jagger, D. Sserunkuuma, C. K. Kaizzi, and H. Ssali. 2004. *Strategies for sustainable land management and poverty reduction in Uganda.* Research Report 133. Washington, D.C.: International Food Policy Research Institute.

Sserunkuuma, D. 2003. The adoption and impact of improved maize and land management technologies in Uganda. Paper presented at the Workshop on Green Revolution in Asia and Its Transferability to Africa, Durban, South Africa, August.

Chapter 18

Gender, Resource Rights, and Wetland Rice Productivity in Burkina Faso

Barbara van Koppen

W omen are acknowledged to be responsible for 70–80 percent of food production in Sub-Saharan Africa. They operate within the institutional arrangements of the farm household, the single most important institution for agricultural production. This chapter illustrates why and how the ways in which production and related resources rights are organized along gender lines are critical to smallholder agricultural growth in the continent. It also illustrates how policies and intervention programs based on an inadequate understanding of gender relations are bound to fail.

Such failure was the experience of the wetland rice improvement project in Comoé Province in southwestern Burkina Faso, presented here. The project Développement de la Riziculture dans la Province de la Comoé, or in short Opération Riz (OR), was a conventional formal infrastructure development project, attached to the Ministry of Agriculture and Livestock of Comoé Province and financed by the government of Burkina Faso and the EU. France and the Netherlands provided technical assistance during the period studied. The project aims were to improve swamp rice cultivation in the small valleys in this area that were already used for rice cultivation by constructing infrastructure for better water control and introducing high-yielding varieties, fertilizer, and pest management. The technical construction of the central drains and contour bunds was accompanied by the expropriation of land and reallocation of the improved land.

In the first project phase of OR from 1979 to 1986, which is the period studied, seven schemes totaling 860 ha were constructed. Technically, the intervention was largely the same for all schemes. Socially, however, the land-expropriation and reallocation processes, which implicitly also determined membership of water users associations and targeting of other project benefits, differed. In the first two schemes (A and B),[1] improved land was reallocated to male household heads, based on the notion of the unitary farm household—which also shows that farm-household concepts and analysis are not just academic exercises but touch deep-rooted beliefs that profoundly shape concrete action on the ground. Those schemes collapsed.

However, in schemes C and D and in all later schemes this reallocation policy changed, and expropriated land was reallocated to existing plot holders, mainly women. These schemes were productive, illustrating that interventions based on an adequate gender analysis of household and community production relations and resource rights are win-win for all involved. Such gender-sensitive intervention provides incentives to the producers and considerably reduces transaction costs for the agency. In spite of two decades of further gender analysis and mainstreaming since this project in the 1980s, the concrete operationalization of gender analysis into intervention and the empirical evidence of positive impacts on productivity are still scarce—and hence, still worth emphasizing.

18.1 Concepts

As mentioned, the concept of the farm household is central in this case study—and in much of the literature on gender and agriculture (Safiliou 1988; Haddad and Hoddinott 1995; Quisumbing 1996; Haddad, Hoddinott, and Alderman 1997; Quisumbing and Mallucio 2000). In particular, the incentives that appear to be key to higher productivity are control over labor and over the fruits of one's labor and secure resource rights. These requirements may seem evident—and are widely acknowledged to be so for men. Women producers appear no different. Hence, intrahousehold bargaining over labor and its fruits and over resource rights are at the heart of institutional economics that seeks to understand agricultural production. These bargaining processes are much more adequately described by the new model of household relations (accounting for bargaining by the different members) than by the model of the "unitary household" (in which intrahousehold dynamics are supposed to be insignificant).

The intrahousehold aspects of family labor—the most critical production factor in Africa's smallholder agriculture—determine whether production relations are antidevelopment by fostering rent seeking, in this case by (elder) males from women's labor, or prodevelopment by optimizing incentives for all household members, including the youth, to enhance labor productivity. Indeed, many studies (Jones

1986; Carney 1988; Quisumbing 1996) corroborated how African women's incentives to enhance productivity are strongly related to their control over the output. This case study confirms that relationship.

This study also corroborates how land tenure affects the outcome of the bargaining processes over labor and outputs. Thus it underpins the growing recognition of the need for enhanced land-tenure security for women in land reform in Sub-Saharan Africa, which seeks to redress gender-inequitable customary arrangements through support by formal institutions. However, this case study shows that even the opposite of the desired result can occur: the formal institutions, the project itself, completely eroded the customary land rights that women had, at least in the first two schemes. In later schemes, the women (but also the men and community leaders) themselves reinstated and then formalized women's customary resource rights. Avoiding weakening of women's customary land rights is in itself a major contribution that formal organizations can make to women's land security.

Gendered production relations at the household level, including labor obligations and norms about the control over produce, are entirely embedded in wider customary resource rights and other arrangements, as elaborated in Section 18.3. Therefore, formal institutions' blindness to gender issues goes hand in hand with the project's general lack of appreciation of customary production relations and resource rights. The case study illustrates the risk that African governments, intervening agencies, and especially their foreign experts and donors, not only fail to recognize the productivity of customary gendered smallholder agriculture but also destroy what exists at the expense of every party involved (Sections 18.4.1 and 18.4.2). Section 18.4.3 presents the resilience of customary arrangements, leading to project redesign, to the benefit of all.

18.2 Methodology

The case study is based on interviews with female and male rice producers; male and female local authorities and administrative authorities; project field officers; sociological, agronomic, and technical project staff; and project direction and expatriate assistants for all schemes. Project archives at the project's office in Banfora, Burkina Faso, and the head office of the Delegation of the Commission of the EU in Ouagadougou, Burkina Faso, were also studied. The fieldwork was carried out between 1991 and 1994. This field study was part of the Research Program Aménagement et Gestion de l'Espace Sylvo-Pastoral au Sahel of Wageningen Agricultural University, Wageningen, the Netherlands. In this chapter, quotations from project documents in French are translated by the author.

18.3   Context: Local Farming and Land and Water Tenure in Comoé Province

18.3.1   The Gendered Farming System

Agriculture is the main source of income in Comoé Province; off-farm employment, especially for young men, is limited to the province capital and Côte d'Ivoire. In the uplands, rain-fed maize, millet, sorghum, sesame, groundnuts, and the cash crop cotton are grown. In the low-lying wetlands swamp rice is cultivated using flooding from runoff and rising shallow or deep subsoil water sources.

The organization of agriculture is gendered. Men are the farm decisionmakers in upland cropping, where they also hold the customary primary land titles. They mobilize the labor of their women and children according to culturally defined norms. Men are obliged to give part of the food harvests to their wives. Men sell food and cash crops partly for family needs and partly to spend as they like. Most men in Comoé who need rice for their own needs (for ceremonies, visitors, or during the Islamic fast) buy or exchange it on the market or with their wives. Few land chiefs hold their own rice plots, which are cultivated by their wives. With the exception of one valley, very few men have their own rice plots, which is never their primary activity. As one respondent commented, "if one sees a man going down into the valley, one knows he has finished upland cropping."

Women up to their mid-40s both cultivate their rice plots and work on their husbands' upland fields. Especially among two ethnic groups, the Turka and Gouin, labor obligations on men's fields are intensive and compete with women's own rice cultivation. In the customary "week" (of five days) of these ethnic groups, there is one "day of the woman," which women can devote to their own activities, and one day for the local market. During the other three days men can command their wives' labor. Senoufo and most Dioula women, in contrast, have fewer obligations and are free to start rice cultivation even when the plowing and sowing of rain-fed upland crops have not yet finished. Younger wives use their rice to feed themselves, their children, and their husbands, as well as to sell. It is also used for gifts, especially to their maternal kin, and for ceremonies.

Elder women are "liberated" when sons or nephews become adults and take over women's labor obligations on their husbands' fields. From then on, these women can dedicate themselves full-time to their own rice cultivation, and, incidentally, to upland cropping. However, as women stop providing labor on their husbands' fields, the latter are no longer obliged to share their food with them. Rice cultivation then becomes women's main source of food and income.

Both younger and older women mobilize labor for their plots in multiple forms of mutual help among daughters, mothers, and maternal aunts, as well as of unpaid and paid working groups or laborers. The time that men, especially sons, assist (mainly during harvesting and threshing) is less than 3 percent of total time input required for rice cultivation (Van Koppen et al. 1987).

Women's general predominance in swamp rice cultivation in Comoé Province and elsewhere in Africa is probably related to the fact that swamp rice is labor intensive compared to dryland crops. As men control cropping and land tenure in uplands, women as a gender chose the second-best option of valley cultivation.

18.3.2 Female and Male Land and Water Chiefs

Typically for Sub-Saharan African land tenure, uplands and wetlands in Comoé Province belong to what could be called a large family, with many members who have died, some who are alive, and innumerable members still to be born (Bachelet 1982; Ouedraogo 1986). The clans that came first assumed the authority of land chief. In these matrilineal clans, the function of land and water authority in rice valleys is often carried out by women, such as the married sisters or daughters, mothers, or sisters' daughters of the male land chiefs. Land inheritance is also matrilineal. Sons inherit uplands from the brothers of their mothers, and daughters inherit their mothers' plots in the valleys. Nowadays matrilineal inheritance is gradually changing to patrilineal inheritance, especially in the uplands and among the Senoufo.

Women and men land chiefs protect collective interests. Their first function is in land coordination and allocation. Chiefs are the living memory and administrators of land titles (Le Roy 1982, 55). Fallow upland or valley land can be cleared by anyone, including newcomers, but the norm is that the land chief concerned has to be informed and must give formal permission for new land use. Such permission is always given, because as many respondents said, "one cannot deny people to feed themselves and their children." Actual land use strengthens the users' claims on the land over years and generations. Land chiefs cannot take land back, because by so doing one is seen to go against the will of his father (Ouedraogo 1978). Yet proprietors are not allowed to transfer or sell land to persons outside the group.

A second function is dispute resolution, often over inheritance. In valleys, land chiefs also intervene in water disputes between neighbors. Water management conflicts arise, for example, when neighbors continue enlarging their own fields from both sides at the expense of the small earthen bunds or ditches that separate their fields to the point of collapsing. Also, neighbors may suffer from overdrainage and the sand and weeds coming from an upstream user. Conflict resolution at the lowest level possible is fostered by the rule that both parties have to pay if the case has to be taken for conflict resolution, even the party who is judged to be right. A rule with a similar effect is that the land will be taken away from both if they fail to find a solution.

A third function of land chiefs, particularly in rice valleys, is to give the sign to start rice cultivation as soon as hydrological conditions seem fit. This authorization contributes to a more-or-less simultaneous cropping calendar, which is important to harmonize crop water requirements, to avoid the concentration of attacks of birds on isolated early maturing crops, and to allow for early entrance of animals into the valleys after the growing season. Land chiefs also indicate when fishing from ponds, a male activity, can start. Water from ponds or shallow wells in the valleys is used for drinking and domestic purposes during the whole year.

Finally, land chiefs play a central role in several socio-religious customs, such as fixing totem days on which no hoe may touch the soil and making sacrifices. Special sacred bushes or woodlots in the valleys and uplands are reserved to this end. Meant as a recognition of the authority and functions of the land chief, the land users in his or her area give some 10 percent of the harvest and provide labor on the chief's rice plots during one or two days per year.

In the valleys, women land chiefs perform most functions, although women who want to request a rice plot may have to address themselves first to the male land chief, who then delegates the actual work to his female relatives. His agreement may also be required in dispute settlement. He can have a say over the crop shares offered and over the harvest of the rice field to be cultivated by the users on the land under his command. In other cases women are the decisionmakers. In some villages, there is even a taboo on male chiefs going down into the valleys during the cropping season. "This would cause inundations and make cultivation impossible; a sacrifice would be needed to put things right," reported a female chief. However, the slaughtering of animals is strictly forbidden to women chiefs "because women give life," as several respondents asserted. If there are public meetings, women may take their sons, with the justification that "he has to slaughter the animal." Neither are women allowed to participate in the village council of elders (Ouedraogo 1990), so when land issues are discussed there, they depend on mediation by their male relatives. Moreover, male land chiefs often keep representing the clan to outsiders—including those implementing projects.

18.3.3 Women's Land Rights
There are three ways in which a woman obtains rice plots: through maternal relatives, her husband's family, and the land chief. As one rice cultivator expressed it, "women have two to four plots: one from the mother, one from the maternal aunt, one from the husband, and one the woman herself asked from the land chief." This flexibility allows women to adapt the total size of land to their labor availability during their life cycle. In all of these cases women control the output of their lands. This benefit is accompanied by specific obligations to partially or fully feed her children,

herself, and sometimes her husband. Often husbands are not even aware of where the plot is located.

Mother's lineage: women's independent rights. In this case the rice plot passes from mother to daughter without interference of male kin or land chiefs. Rice plots are a treasure that women pass on to their daughters. Women keep these plots in case of divorce, during illnesses when the plot can lie fallow for several years, or after neglect of obligations to work on the land chief's field (Somé 1991).

Husband's lineage: women's exclusive use rights. If there are no plots in the matriclan to inherit or if a woman marries far away in these virilocal (living with husband's family) societies, she receives a rice plot from her husband's family, especially when she grows older. Her husband—but even more so her husband's mother, sisters, and aunts—are obliged to find this plot for her. Generally husbands prefer their own wives to grow rice rather than their sisters, who are going to feed another family. However, husbands can refuse their younger wives' land requests, if that would jeopardize their wives' labor obligations on the men's upland fields.

Request to the land chief: establishing new rights. The growing population pressure in Comoé Province increasingly leads to clearing unused land. In that case women ask the land chiefs for permission to occupy such land. Women themselves (or their mothers on behalf of their daughters) negotiate with a land chief (Van Etten 1992). In several villages and ethnic groups, husbands accompany their wives in their formal requests, or brothers accompany their sisters. However, one male land chief commented, "nowadays women should not bother their husbands any more and should address themselves directly to the land chief."

In some areas where the demand for land is high, land chiefs increasingly prevent people from establishing longer term use rights by allocating land for 1–4 years only. In one such case, all 20 women interviewed, including the wife of the land chief, criticized him for keeping a reply to a request for a plot too long in suspense, imposing the choice of the site, and demanding crop shares that were too high. Therefore, two of the women interviewed preferred the state to come and manage the valley (Somé 1991).

18.4 Project Intervention

18.4.1 Project Design Phase

As in many infrastructure projects in the 1980s, the initial planning by OR took place with hardly any knowledge of the abovementioned farming system and arrangements for land and water tenure. The limited information available was not used in the design. Thus the project imposed concepts and practices that were completely alien to the rice-growing communities in Comoé Province.

In 1978 the project started with a hydro-technical study by a French engineering bureau, which was largely incorporated into the project document. The engineer visited 11 valleys over 10 days (OR 1980a) and selected eight sites totaling 1,000 ha (Faye 1978). Without further explanation, he proposed a plot size of 0.25 ha, assuming that each cultivator would get one plot and that the total number of beneficiaries would be 4,000. When phase II of OR was formulated in the mid-1980s, similar hasty technical appraisals were carried out, either in the field (OR 1985) or, later, on the basis of satellite photography (CEDRAT 1989). On the basis of these technical criteria, sites were selected where the project was to first construct central drains for quick evacuation of floods, with storage and irrigation facilities for dryer periods, and then build bunds according to the contour lines for improved dispersal of peak floods and water retention in dryer periods. The project paid all construction costs, including paid wage labor for men. As in most construction projects, funds were allocated on the basis of a rapid technical preliminary design and an estimate of the construction costs. Construction constituted 72 percent of the budget.

After the site selection and construction plans had been decided upon, sociologists were appointed to solicit people's buy-in and to assist in the required procedure for land expropriation and reallocation (Ouedraogo 1978; SAED 1978). These researchers communicated mainly with male village chiefs, male land chiefs, and other men but with only a few women rice cultivators. The report of the first sociological study failed to mention matrilineal inheritance and ignored the role of female land chiefs. Instead, husbands were categorically ascribed a decisive role in both the distribution of land to women and in management of rice plots. Women were seen as cultivators only. Male land chiefs were recognized to be critical for regulating the upcoming intervillage problems regarding changing the land tenure in the valleys (Ouedraogo 1978).

Without explaining where the idea originated, the sociologists in this first study somehow thought "that perhaps the selection criteria will not leave any chance to have a plot allocated to women." They sought reactions to such reallocations of land from women to male household heads or to young unmarried men—and raised men's expectations and women's fears accordingly. For example, one man reacted positively: "We, the men, do not cultivate rice and are obliged to buy rice from our women. If the scheme comes we will take plots and devote some of our time to the rice in order to have rice for marriages and funerals." But the report also mentioned that "more than half of the men interviewed agree that their wives will have plots for themselves." Young men were "very interested to get a plot. They find that after the improvement, women should rejoin their husbands in the collective plots enabling them to benefit from plot allocation. Then they [the men] would not have to go and suffer in Côte d'Ivoire." In contrast, all women interviewed disagreed. "During one interview the men and women almost started fighting because one man (the village chief) wished that the women would rejoin their husbands on one single plot. Some women got really worried when I raised the problem of common plots or individual plots. One woman said to me: "If my husband obliges me to cultivate rice with him that will not work out. I will never agree because he himself was born finding that women cultivate rice'" (Ouedraogo 1978).

The notion of collective plots in which women join their husbands, reflecting the unitary household model, re-emerged in the second sociological study, which further refined allocation criteria (SAED 1978). Unlike the first study, this report clearly stated that new rice plots would be allocated to the former rights holders and cultivators—thus predominantly to women. This decision was justified on the basis of women's existing role in rice cultivation and the willingness that women had expressed to adopt new practices. The authors also seriously doubted whether male family heads would be willing to spend their efforts in labor-intensive rice cropping, because they already cultivated food crops and groundnuts as a profitable cash crop (SAED 1978, 41). In addition, allocation to women was expected to be the outcome if the mode of allocation was left to the villagers (SAED 1978). This opinion was the conclusion of their discussions in almost all valleys.

The authors of this second report had problems in reconciling the numbers of new plots that the engineers had decided on, of existing rice cultivators, and of potential holders of new plots. This third category was assumed to be all women between 20 and 60 years old, so on the basis of the limited demographic data available, it was calculated that there were 6,748 rice cultivators. But this estimate outnumbered the planned 4,000 plots. As the authors realized that the population would react badly if only some of the actual rice cultivators could benefit from a plot, they proposed two solutions (SAED 1978). One was simply to reduce the plot size from 0.25 to 0.15 ha, which would easily fit the entire target group. The other solution was to re-engineer social farm units to fit the 4,000 plots (SAED 1978). Taking the available demographic data on extended families and reviving the notion of the family plot, they imagined the allocation of so-called family farms (*exploitations familiales*). But the calculated 2,167 family farms were far below the planned number of 4,000 plots. Taking demographic data on nuclear households (*ménages*) to be 6,301, the required number of "nuclear household plots" was again too high. The report (SAED 1978) stopped at this point and failed to propose a procedure for the reallocation of the improved plots. The later project document, however, promised without any ambiguity that the women, who already cultivated rice in the valleys to be improved, would be the primary beneficiaries (DCCE 1978).

18.4.2   Project Implementation in Schemes A and B

In 1979 OR simultaneously started implementation of schemes A and B. The major job to be done under great time pressure to achieve the ambitious construction goals was to refine the technical design, expropriate land, and undertake construction. With the support of male village chiefs, land chiefs, and the administrative leaders, women's rice lands were readily put at the disposal of OR. Many male wage workers earned good wages. For the unpaid construction of field bunds, the project engineers also asked men to assist and supervised them (SNV 1984).

At the moment of expropriation for construction, the women had been led to believe that they would receive individual plots on the day of land distribution. The project never discussed the reallocation procedure in these women's groups. This oversight is even more remarkable, because by 1981 the project had organized women into 58 extension groups, out of which 57 groups were exclusively female. The groups focused on labor and agronomic skills, completely parallel to decision-making about resource rights (OR 1980d, 1981b, 1984).

Only in 1980 did the project's expatriate management, an engineer and an agronomist, start any procedure for the reallocation of land. They initiated formal demographic surveys with the aim of evaluating the total population concerned, to get an idea of the number of men and women cultivators in the valleys in order to proceed to what the authors saw as a more rational redistribution of plots after the construction (OR 1980b). The questionnaires were addressed to the male household heads and comprised questions on the number and ages of all family members, the number of adult men and women, and sons and daughters, active on the family field and on individual fields, including rice plots. It was also asked whether the family had a rice plot in the valley to be improved or wanted to have one. Some field officers complemented this information with the tax lists of the tax offices, which included liberated women who had to pay tax individually.

In scheme A, the survey found that in 191 families there were 243 older women, 498 younger women, and 50 men cultivating rice, giving a total of 791 (OR 1980c). Although the survey data did not reveal that there were family rice plots, the project management made a new distinction in its interpretation of the survey results. It referred to 191 families who were cultivating a rice plot in the valley and 791 persons who also cultivated an individual plot. On this basis the project management reasoned that one could reasonably allocate 0.25 hectare to each family and 0.125 hectare to those who cultivated an individual plot (OR 1980b). Without empirical grounding, the family rice plot was invented.

In 1981, just before construction was finished and schemes A and B were to be handed off to the farmers, the project management's "family plot" came up again, but now, critically, as the only criterion used to allocate the improved plots. In scheme

A it was reported that information and sensitization meetings on the land distribution and cultivation requirements had been held in scheme A in the presence of the village chiefs, land chiefs, and authorities. Those meetings led to the decision, which the authors claim to be unanimous, that one or more plots would be allocated to the family heads according to the number of active members (OR 1981a,c). Not surprisingly, the small group of land chiefs and men present agreed to any form of distribution. Thus the project managers proposed, if not imposed, to vest local chiefs and men with power and control over land they had never had before.

In scheme B land was also reallocated as family plots to men, ironically, in the name of equity and fairness. Before the project there were 484 rice cultivators, almost exclusively women. Their number was greater than the number of plots designed by the engineer, which was 360 (OR 1980d). However, male heads of households were fewer in number. So to distribute a scarce resource among a large number of eligible claimants, the rights of these eligible claimants were nullified and vested in a smaller category of people with hardly any existing rights. Again, this blatant gender discrimination was underpinned by the concept of the household as a unit, in which the male head can dispose of all "family resources" according to his discretion and cultural norms.

The land distribution itself in both schemes A and B did not use any demographic list. The project's field officers, the village chiefs, administrative authorities, and male candidates passed through the valley. Plots were allocated on the spot to any man who presented himself. This process was closely witnessed by the land chief of that portion of the valley. Rumors abounded that people sent others in their name, that the same person presented himself twice, and that the most powerful land chiefs put their own families on their portions and even allocated plots to babies.

Women had not been informed of how and when the actual land distribution would take place. When women saw the group of men passing through the valley, a number of them came themselves to negotiate for land. In scheme A, a few widows were able to obtain plots, and they immediately paid their contributions to the maintenance fund to confirm their claims. All women felt that the men had betrayed them. In scheme B the two sisters of the most powerful land chief commented:

> Our brother, and the village chief, and the people from the project told us that there would be a list of the women wanting a plot. We thought that each woman would select her own plot. The day of the distribution we came too late, because we were not informed. Part of the plots had already been distributed. Then they told us that the plots would not have been enough for all women, because many women would have wanted them, including those who had no plot before. Therefore, they had decided to allocate to the chiefs of the extended households. Our brother had already

selected our plots. But he does not know the good sites, and he selected a bad site. We are women. We could not do anything. Then the chiefs of the families divided the plots they had received. First they took a part for themselves, and the rest they divided into small parts for the older women in their family. We have never seen a list.

The project reports either did not mention the actual process of distribution or stated that the plots had been distributed in alphabetical order (SNV 1984, 19).

As predicted by the sociologists, the newly imposed gendered organization of rice cultivation was totally counterproductive. Neither in scheme A (Ouedraogo 1990) nor scheme B did men abandon their upland food and cash crops to cultivate rice. On virtually all plots, rice cultivation remained exclusively women's work. In scheme A, most often, women were obliged to cultivate their husbands' plots. Yet, on their husbands' plots, women could not dispose of the harvest as they could before the project was implemented (Ouedraogo 1990). In scheme B, it was equally observed that, after plot allocation to family heads, the latter divided those among their women after taking a portion for themselves. Thus the women cultivated half or two-thirds of the plot for the men, and they themselves had only a small portion. This gave women very little, in comparison with the labor burdens they were bearing. The project realized that it needed to revise their status, as the women wanted to be owners of the plots they cultivated. This would motivate them more strongly (OR 1987).

As formal plot holders, men were also responsible for infrastructure maintenance, but most of them refused to do it. Moreover, the male village elite in schemes A, B, and C used the project's maintenance fund to repair a school (schemes A and C), a road, and a prefect's office (scheme B). Other funds completely disappeared (scheme B), or were said to be used by the land chief for his pilgrimage to Mecca (scheme C).

Frustrations rose further when the technical "improvements" turned out to be no improvements at all in parts of scheme A and in the whole of scheme B. Oversizing of the central drain, inadequate leveling, and earthen constructions that could not resist the force of floods had spoiled the valley to the point that all cultivators interviewed wished the project "to fill up this bad hole and leave." In 1988 parts of scheme A were rehabilitated. Scheme B is now called the lost scheme. One wonders whether women rice producers would have accepted the technical design had they been involved in construction work (Dey 1980).

18.4.3 Gender-Sensitive Land Allocation in Later Schemes

After 3 years of project implementation, the project management still had no idea how to prevent women's frustration in the subsequent two schemes (C and D). In

1983, the director of the regional department of the Ministry of Agriculture and
Livestock of Comoé Province, who was also formally in charge of the OR, made the
most accurate in-depth study on women in rice production and clearly highlighted
the role of women land chiefs and the widespread matrilineal heritage in rice cultivation. However, he thought that formal state administrative law was more important
than productivity and well-being (Sérémé 1983, 7):

> Before land improvement, rice cultivation was almost the exclusive domain
> of women, who are both actors and beneficiaries as a result of the original
> land allocation. After public intervention, the administrative allocation
> ignores women whose juridical existence is only through the family head.
> This new distribution of rice land induces a new nature of land operation in
> which the woman is still the principal actor but no longer the exclusive ben-
> eficiary. The improvement worsens the situation of women, and, as a conse-
> quence, the situation of children whose care is fully delegated to women.

It is significant indeed that the win-win solution for all parties involved in the
next two schemes, C and D, emerged from the communities themselves: women,
their husbands, and land chiefs alike, in consultation with receptive local project
staff. They developed land expropriation and reallocation procedures according to
the productivity and equity considerations embedded in customary arrangements.
Local project staff did so in spite of their management's instructions. The crucial
enabling factor was simply time: 2 years elapsed between the first contacts with
the projects, in which the more equitable allocation to both men and women was
announced, and the actual start of construction.

Moreover, in Scheme C the Senoufo women rice cultivators had been warned by
the events in both scheme B (at some 8 km distance) and one of the earlier irrigation
schemes (more than 30 km away) that women had been pushed out (Ouedraogo
1978). As Senoufos "they are not ashamed to express themselves in front of men,
unlike the Gouins." Senoufo women also have fewer labor obligations on men's
fields and devote themselves fully to their rice plots. Furthermore, the women were
already organized in a women's group by the regional department of the Ministry of
Agriculture and Livestock. And last but not least, the women had time to negotiate.

In an interview, the woman leader of scheme C narrated the course of events
after OR established its first contacts:

> The field officer registered all women per quarter. Some men asked for
> plots, because the field officer said that if it succeeds everybody will have
> rice. But men do not like the work of rice. Some abandoned them and left

them to their women. If you do not work you cannot take the benefits. During the land distribution women negotiated their own plots while men observed, because the women cultivate. For the collective maintenance work, men help. Everybody eats the rice.

Thus in scheme C every woman with former land rights received a plot; many daughters got individual plots as well. Although the project had given ample opportunity to men to apply for land, only 4 percent of the new title holders were male (OR 1986).

In scheme D, the project's field officer took the initiative to visit the land chief immediately upon his arrival in 1980. He asked the chief about the actual plot users. Registering the inventory of existing rights holders took only a couple of hours. Although the roundabout demographic surveys were still compiled, they were never used during the actual plot distribution in 1984.

This bottom-up approach for identifying existing plot holders and reallocating first to them before assigning plots to others (both men and women) further crystallized in the three schemes constructed from 1984 to 1986. From 1987 on the project gradually committed these tested, consistent, equitable, and transparent procedures for land expropriation and reallocation to paper (*cahier des charges*). In the next three schemes, constructed under phase II of OR, this process was further refined and documented. It effectively guided the interactions between the project and villagers and between project and prefects and other administrative authorities.

The procedures stipulate that, first, open meetings are to be organized, to which the current farm decisionmakers and anyone else interested are invited. The participants at the meetings are then informed about the project—the technical aspects, the land redistribution, and proposed organizational design. Before any construction is started, field officers make an inventory of current plot holders in the field. They register name, sex, age, quarter or village, ethnic group, whether a woman is liberated or nonliberated, number of plots cultivated, and number of plots held in neighboring schemes that have already been improved. The names are checked with the male or female land chiefs.

The project retains the authority to determine the plot size, and thus how many landless individuals can also benefit from the intervention. Interested new candidates register with the field officer. In practice, women appear to remain the majority of new applicants. In some cases male land chiefs submitted requests. Only in a few regions where fertile uplands have become scarce are men increasingly reported to register and start cultivating rice (OR 1997). These men have to negotiate their wives' labor and also to pay women wage laborers. Their upland crops remain their priority.

Rice cultivators from the same quarter or village are placed in the same portion of the improved scheme for reasons of social cohesion. Further plot selection is at random. On the days of distribution, plots are distributed according to lists of rights holders and topographical maps. A committee of project staff and male village and administrative authorities—but still not the female land chiefs or other women users —supervises the process (OR 1991).

After construction and land reallocation, plot holders become members of the new water users associations, fulfill their maintenance obligations, and elect their leaders. Men remain overrepresented in the committees. The increasing role of the state has led to a decrease in the crop shares that cultivators give to the land chiefs. Land chiefs regret this erosion of their traditional power (SAED 1988; Ouedraogo 1990).

Overall, the procedure, which begins at the start of intervention, is considerably shorter, has considerably lower transaction costs, and is seen as legitimate. Local knowledge, like the knowledge of the land chiefs, is used.

18.4.4 Again: The Family Farm

In 1988 phase I of the OR was evaluated to formulate recommendations for the next phase (SAED 1988). This report adequately described the prevailing production relations, in which both older and younger women cultivate rice and older women have no labor constraints. Male land chiefs were reported to insist on the continuing inclusion of older women, as they depend on rice for their survival. Local men do not disagree with plot allocation directly to their wives. The report explicitly acknowledged that the concept of the family farm is problematic in the local farming system. It was found to be difficult to distinguish between family fields and individual fields of men, because both types of field are cultivated by the same family members (SAED 1988).

However, contrary to all evidence cited, the imaginary family rice plot, managed by the male head of household, suddenly emerged again in the concluding recommendations (SAED 1988, 35–36, author's translation from French):

> The field studies show that traditional rice cultivation is a quasi-exclusive women's affair, especially of older women. Should such a situation be continued by allocating land exclusively to women? This raises the following questions:
>
> • The problem of infrastructure maintenance. Could one count on their contributions to ensure maintenance of the infrastructure?
>
> • What attitude would men have if they saw economic power concentrated in women's hands?
>
> • What future would the project have if it is only carried out by older women? Would the objective of production increase be achieved? Could the cooperative spirit be initiated?

- Would the objective of self-management be possible?

In fact, the basis should be laid now for a progressive elimination of presently predominant production forms (exclusively female) in favor of familial and collective forms. Those forms would allow growth in production by installing a credit system. Therefore, we suggest that in plot allocation one allocates both individual plots and family plots. Individual plots of 0.25 ha will be allocated to the women already present in the valleys that will be improved. Family plots will cover 0.50 ha. With the expected profits, the production conditions [*cahier de charges*] that will be imposed on men to work on the plot will bring rice cultivation to a higher level than that of secondary crop, as it is at present.

This recommendation was never implemented, but illustrates the persistent prejudice that agricultural productivity can only *really* be enhanced through a mode of production that subjugates women's labor to men and erodes women's resource rights.

18.5   Conclusions

How representative is the case of OR? How important are the findings of intra-household and intracommunity institutional arrangements in Burkina Faso for the design of agricultural policy in Sub-Saharan Africa as a whole? Is the mode of agricultural growth in this area, which profoundly differs from northern agricultural patterns characterized by the male-dominated family farm, more generally applicable to the continent as a whole? Has past inertia in operationalizing policy intentions and gender analysis in implementation programs contributed to the well-documented stagnation of smallholder agriculture in Sub-Saharan Africa? Will stagnation persist if the gender relations are persistently ignored?

If one accepts that 70–80 percent of agricultural production is the responsibility of women and that labor is the key production factor, the answer is clearly: yes. Existing and especially potential land-tenure arrangements, as currently promoted in land-reform measures, vary, but they are in many cases (certainly in matrilineal societies) not so different from the rice valleys in Burkina Faso as they seem at first glance. The related key questions are: Do African women farmers produce in their own right, or as unpaid family laborers without incentive to increase their productivity? What does this mean for their productivity?

The answer to the last question from past literature and this case study boils down to the common-sense observation that women are human beings, too, and that farmers who control the output of their efforts are more motivated to increase their productivity than those who do not. Long-term use rights to the land cultivated are important but are not the only condition for such control. In Asia, these basics of institutional economics have not only been widely recognized for male tenants and land-poor men, but have also been operationalized in policies and programs for land reform and tenure security that "vests land in the tiller." In Sub-Saharan Africa, a similar approach to gender relations in the farm household and in other informal and formal institutions would contribute considerably to agricultural growth and gender equity.

Note

1. Scheme A is the scheme of Koutoura, scheme B is the scheme of Dakoro, scheme C is that of Moadougou, and scheme D that of Niofila.

References

Bachelet, M. 1982. Titulaires de droits fonciers coutumiers. In *Encyclopédie juridique de l'Afrique,* vol. 5: *Droit des biens,* ed. A. Bourgi. Abidjan, Ivory Coast: Les Nouvelles Editions Africaines.

Carney, J. 1988. Struggles over land and crops in an irrigated rice scheme: The Gambia. In *Agriculture, women and land. The African experience,* ed. J. Davison. Boulder, Colo., U.S.A.: Westview Press.

CEDRAT and Ministère de l'Agriculture et d'Elevage. 1989. Direction des etudes et de la planification. Projet Opération Riz-Comoé (2ième phase). L'aménagement de 550 ha de plaines alluviales dans la Province de la Comoé. Projet d'Exécution. Mémoire Agro-socio-économique. Mimeo. Project archives, Ministère de l'Agriculture et d'Elevage, Banfora, Burkina Faso.

DCCE (Délégation de la Commission des Communautés Européennes en République de Haute Volta). 1978. *Proposition de financement développement de la riziculture dans l'Organisme Régional de Développement (ORD) de la Comoé.* 4ème Fonds Européen de Développement. Brussels.

Dey, J. 1980. Women and rice in the Gambia: The impact of irrigated rice development projects on the farming system. Ph.D. thesis, University of Reading, Reading, U.K.

Faye, B. 1978. Expertise sur les aménagements rizicoles de l'Organisme Régional de Développement de la Comoé. In *Etudes socio-économiques des plaines rizicoles dans l'Organisme Régional de Développement de la Comoé.* Société Africaine d'Etudes de Développement, République de la Haute Volta, et Fonds Européen de Développement. Paris: Bureau pour le Développement de la Production Agricole.

Haddad, L., and J. Hoddinott. 1995. Women's income and boy-girl nutrition outcomes in the Côte d'Ivoire. *World Development* 22: 543–553.

Haddad, L., J. Hoddinott, and H. Alderman. 1997. *Intrahousehold resource allocation in developing countries: Models, methods and policy.* Baltimore: Johns Hopkins University Press.

Jones, C. W. 1986. Intra-household bargaining in response to the introduction of new crops: A case study from North Cameroon. In *Understanding Africa's rural households and farming systems,* ed. J. L. Moock. Boulder, Colo., U.S.A.: Westview Press.

Le Roy, E. 1982. Caractères des droits fonciers coutumiers. In *Encyclopédie juridique de l'Afrique,* vol. 5: *Droit des biens,* ed. A. Bourgi. Abidjan, Ivory Coast: Les Nouvelles Editions Africaines.

OR [Opération Riz, Organisme Régional de Développement de la Comoé, Ministère du Développement Rural, République de Haute Volta]. 1980a. *Rapport annuel d'activités du 1er Avril 1979 au 31 Mars 1980.* Banfora, Burkina Faso.

————. 1980b. *Rapport d'activités du 1er Janvier 1980 au 31 Mars 1980.* Banfora, Burkina Faso.

————. 1980c. *Rapport d'activités du 1er Juillet 1980 au 30 Septembre 1980.* Banfora, Burkina Faso.

————. 1980d. *Rapport d'activités du 1er Octobre 1980 au 31 Décembre 1980.* Banfora, Burkina Faso.

————. 1981a. *Rapport trimestriel du 1er Janvier au 31 Mars 1981.* Banfora, Burkina Faso.

————. 1981b. *Rapport trimestriel du 1er Avril au 30 Juin 1981.* Banfora, Burkina Faso.

————. 1981c. *Rapport semestriel nr. 4. Avril 1981.* Banfora, Burkina Faso.

————. 1984. *Rapport d'activités de la section Animation Féminine 1979–1984.* Banfora, Burkina Faso.

OR [Opération Riz, Organisme Régional de Développement de la Comoé, Ministère du Développement Rural, Burkina Faso]. 1985. *Données sur la mise en culture. Mars 1985.* Banfora, Burkina Faso.

OR [Opération Riz, Organisme Régional de Développement de la Comoé, Ministère de l'Agriculture et d'Elevage, Burkina Faso]. 1986. *Rapport de la première phase du projet Opération Riz.* Banfora, Burkina Faso.

————. 1987. *Rapport des rencontres avec les structures organisationnelles sur l'évaluation de leur participation à l'exécution du Projet. Mars 1987.* Banfora, Burkina Faso.

OR [Opération Riz, Centre Régional de Production Agro-Pastorale de la Comoé, Ministère de l'Agriculture et d'Elevage]. 1991. *Recensement sur la situation foncière avant aménagement Lomangara, Badini Aval I et Badini Aval II.* Banfora, Burkina Faso.

OR [Opération Riz, Centre Régional de Production Agro-pastorale de la Comoé, Ministère de l'Agriculture et des Ressources Animales]. 1997. *Rapport annuel Janvier–Décembre 1996.* Banfora, Burkina Faso.

Ouedraogo, C. 1978. *Etude sur les plaines aménagables de Banfora. Mars–Avril et Avril–May 1978.* Ouagadougou, Burkina Faso: Délégation de la Commission de Communautés Européennes en République de Haute-Volta.

Ouedraogo, E. 1990. *Etude socio-économique concernant les exploitants(es) touché(es) par le projet "Opération Riz Comoé."* Ouagadougou, Burkina Faso: Projet Opération Riz Comoé, Ministère de l'Agriculture et de l'Elevage et Association Néerlandaise d'Assistance au Développement.

Ouedraogo, H. 1986. Le droit de la terre et les enjeux du développement. Approche comparative des transformations foncières au Burkina (ex-Haute Volta). Ph.D. thesis, Université de Paris, Pantheon-Sorbonne, Paris.

Quisumbing, A. R. 1996. Male-female differences in agricultural productivity: Methodological issues and empirical evidence. *World Development* 24: 1579–1595.

Quisumbing, A. R., and J. Maluccio 2000. *Intrahousehold allocation and gender relations: New empirical evidence from four developing countries.* Food Consumption and Nutrition Division Discussion Paper 84. Washington, D.C.: International Food Policy Research Institute.

SAED (Société Africaine d'Etudes de Développement, République de la Haute Volta, and Fonds Européens de Développement). 1978. *Etudes socio-économiques des plaines rizicoles dans l'Organisme Régional de Développement de la Comoé. Juin 1978.* Ouagadougou, Burkina Faso.

SAED (Société Africaine d'Etudes de Développement, Ministère de l'Agriculture et de l'Elevage, Projet Opération Riz). 1988. *Etude socio-économique pour l'exécution de la phase II du projet "Opération Riz Comoé."* Ouagadougou, Burkina Faso.

Safiliou, C. 1988. Farming systems and gender issues: Implications for agricultural training and projects. Wageningen: Ministry of Agriculture and Fisheries of the Netherlands and the International Agricultural Centre.

Sérémé, M. 1983. *Rôle des femmes dans la production vivrière à la Province de la Comoé.* Banfora, Burkina Faso: Organisme Régional de Développement.

SNV (Netherlands Development Association) Burkina Faso. 1984. *SNV-project verslag over de inzetten bij het project Opération Riz 1979–1984.* Ouagadougou, Burkina Faso.

Somé, J. 1991. Survey: Women and land tenure in Guéra, Comoé. Mimeo. Opération Riz, Banfora, Burkina Faso.

Van Etten, J. 1992. Le changement du régime foncier par l'influence d'un aménagement dans la plaine de Kawara, Burkina Faso. M.S. thesis, Wageningen Agricultural University, Wageningen, The Netherlands.

Van Koppen, B., J. Somé, A. Gnanou, K. Hié, F. Koné, D. Sauratié, M. Somda, M. Tiéba, P. Traore, and D. Zamba. 1987. *Champs personnels des femmes dans la Province de la Comoé: Etude socio-économique.* Banfora, Burkina Faso: Bureau Economie Familiale Rurale de l'ex-Organisme Régional de Développement de la Comoé.

Part 4

An Institutional Perspective on the State: Its Role and Challenges

Chapter 19

Agricultural Research

Colin Poulton

lthough the majority of the material, including the case studies, in this volume focuses on institutional arrangements for either market development or natural resource management, the provision of relevant public goods (transport and communications infrastructure, irrigation investment, and agricultural research and investment) is also a key challenge for agricultural development policy in Africa. In this chapter I consider the challenge of improving the performance of agricultural research systems in Africa from an institutional perspective as an important example of the types of issues that arise in public good investments.

Chapter 1 noted the need for both institutional and technical changes if agricultural development is to proceed. In this chapter I explore the institutional reasons that technology generation and adoption does not happen more frequently than it does. Following the analytical framework developed earlier in the book, this chapter illustrates how the nature of agricultural research influences the way that research is commonly organized. However, prefiguring arguments developed more fully in the next chapter, it also illustrates the importance of the wider institutional environment as a determinant both of appropriate institutional arrangements for and the performance of agricultural research.

19.1 Investment in Agricultural Research in Africa: A Puzzle?

Much of the literature on agricultural research in Africa highlights a puzzle. There is a large literature on returns to public investment in agricultural research (and extension) in Africa and elsewhere. These studies produce highly variable estimates of returns that center around a very high mean. Thus Alston et al. (2000) reviewed 292 studies published since 1953—reporting a total of 1,886 estimates of rates of return—and found mean (median) rates of return on investment of 100 percent (48 percent) for agricultural research, 85 percent (63 percent) for extension, and 48 percent (37 percent) for analyses of combined investments in both research and extension. For the 188 estimates reported for Africa, the mean and median rates of return were 50 and 43 percent, respectively.

There are, of course, methodological challenges in arriving at such estimates. Alston and Pardey (2001) consider two attribution problems: how one should assess the contribution to observed research outcomes from spillovers of research efforts elsewhere, and how one should assess the contribution to current research outcomes of (distant) past research investments. On this second point, Alston and Pardey (2001, 149) affirm other findings that "long lags—at least 30 years—may be necessary to capture all of the impact of research on agricultural output." Specifying shorter lags in econometric studies will tend to overestimate returns to recent research investment through omitted-variable bias. Nevertheless, even taking these qualifications into account, the general picture that emerges from the literature on returns to public investment in agricultural research is that these returns are high.

The puzzle then is that investment in agricultural research in Sub-Saharan Africa was static or declining during the 1990s. Beintema and Stads (2004) report that most African nations, assisted by donors, expanded their agricultural research capacity in the decades after independence. However, the rate of growth in both number of researchers employed and expenditure on research declined over time, such that growth in aggregate expenditure was just 0.8 percent per year during 1991–2000 and only –0.3 percent per year if Nigeria and South Africa (the two biggest research systems in Sub-Saharan Africa) are excluded. This stagnation in research investment occurred at a time when Asian countries, most notably China and India, plus Brazil, were investing heavily in research. Thus Evenson and Gollin (2007) report that between 1985 and 1995 (the latest period for which they had data), investment in agricultural research increased by 48 percent in China, 88 percent in the rest of Asia, but only 8 percent in Sub-Saharan Africa.

When considered as a share of the value of agricultural gross domestic product (GDP), investment in agricultural research in Sub-Saharan Africa does not look too bad. According to Evenson and Gollin (2007), so-called agricultural research intensity in Sub-Saharan Africa was 0.85 percent of agricultural GDP in 1995,[1] compared with just 0.43 percent for China and 0.62 percent for developing countries as a whole. However, research programs in many African countries are very small—Beintema and Stads (2004) report than more than half of Sub-Saharan African countries have fewer than 100 full-time equivalent staff employed in agricultural research,[2] and there are significant economies of scale in such research. Moreover, the heterogeneity of agro-ecological conditions in Sub-Saharan Africa argues for a higher-than-average research intensity. Expert recommendations for optimal research intensity in Sub-Saharan Africa are generally in the range of 1–2 percent (Beintema and Stads 2004).

An immediate reason for the stagnation in research investment in Sub-Saharan Africa has been the stagnation or fall in research investment by major donors, such as the World Bank and the United States Agency for International Development (Evenson and Gollin 2007, 2426). However, a deeper cause is the weakness of domestic political support for agricultural research.[3] The main reason that Evenson and Gollin (2007) advance for this lack of support is the long-term nature of agricultural research. Thus when finances are tight, governments protect expenditures on items that are considered more pressing. A fuller explanation for this phenomenon is perhaps found in the nature of many African states (the subject of the next chapter). So-called developmental states—a term used to describe many Asian states—have a strong political commitment to economic growth and recognize the importance of investments in science and technology, including in agriculture, to achieve this goal. In contrast, many African states are characterized as "neopatrimonial" (van de Walle 2001). A major reason for acquiring power is to obtain control over state resources, and the distribution of patronage is important for remaining in power once it has been acquired. The long-term and highly technical nature of agricultural research makes it difficult for individual politicians to claim credit for research outputs, and it is difficult to use research spending for patronage purposes—unlike, say, the distribution of subsidized fertilizer or food aid.

A second reason for low investment is linked to the first. The high rate-of-return estimates on selected success stories notwithstanding, there is a widespread perception that agricultural research in Africa has often failed. Thus Evenson and Gollin (2007: 2458) conclude that:

> The agricultural research system—IARCs [international agricultural research centers] and NARS [national agricultural research systems] alike—has . . . failed Sub-Saharan Africa. Farmers in Sub-Saharan Africa have paid a high price for these failures. Farmers in the rest of the world have received significant cost reductions over the past 50 years. . . . But farmers in many Sub-Saharan African countries have received little in the way of cost reductions. They have been delivered price reductions without cost reductions.

Lack of investment is one important reason for this perceived failure, but the perception of failure also contributes to the lack of investment. In the remainder of this chapter I use an institutional perspective to look at why agricultural research in Africa is perceived to perform poorly and what can be done about it.

19.2   Private Agricultural Research

At the start of the chapter I described agricultural research as a public good. Once generated, it is difficult to exclude people from new knowledge on agronomic practices or ways to control pests and diseases (although poor communications systems mean that millions may never hear about these improvements). And the fact that one person acquires such knowledge does not prevent others from acquiring it, too.

In some cases (for example, seeds, crop-protection chemicals, veterinary drugs, or vaccines), research output is embodied in a product. Hence private companies can capture returns to research efforts through the sale of the product. In some cases, competitors may be prevented from incorporating the same scientific advance in their products by patents, although the tradition in seed varietal research (at least, prior to the rise of the large biotechnology multinationals) was for a much more open property rights regime that recognized continued evolution in crop varieties. Meanwhile, in the case of seed, farmer retention and reuse of seed is rendered less attractive by hybrid technology (for which traits are gradually lost and performance declines with replanting). However, from an organizational perspective, the high fixed costs, long lags, and inherent uncertainty associated with agricultural research result in high risks. Thus only large companies are likely to conduct their own basic research, although smaller ones may undertake some adaptive research on technologies sourced from others. In turn, big investments will only be made where markets are large and secure, which means that little private research is undertaken on many of the crops and problems most important to poor people or on open-pollinated seed varieties, which farmers can freely reuse and distribute once they have acquired them (Pray and Ramaswami 1991; Pingali and Traxler 2002). Consequently, in the 2000 survey of 27 Sub-Saharan African countries reported by Beintema and Stads (2004), the private sector accounted for only 2 percent of total investment in agricultural research.

A number of innovative institutional arrangements can be considered to encourage greater private investment in agricultural research in Africa. These include:

- Provision of a guaranteed market for a particular technology of importance to African smallholders. This idea has its roots in health policy, where governments or donors might plausibly commit to buy a given quantity of a new vaccine every year for a specified time period—sufficient to make it worthwhile for a private company to undertake the necessary research and development. However, in the agriculture sector, it is much less clear who might provide such a guarantee, for what type of product, and why. Governments sometimes distribute subsidized fertilizer or improved seed, but rarely on the scale or for the duration necessary to make dedicated research on a new product or variety worthwhile.

- Prizes paid ex post to research "innovators" (organizations or individuals) according to the social benefits derived from adoption of their innovations (Masters 2005, 60–62; see also http://www.agecon.purdue.edu/prizes). These need not be confined to private companies but could also provide esteem incentives for top scientists (in either private or public sectors) who want to do more than simply work for money. Note, however, that rewarding innovators according to the social benefits derived from adoption of their innovations requires clear rules and high technical capacity for the management of the prize funds. Masters (2005) envisages prizes as being a mechanism primarily for donors to provide additional incentives to agricultural research effort in Africa.

- Forms of public–private partnership, whereby public (probably donors or private foundations) actors partner with private research to share the risks and costs at key stages in the new product development chain. In the health field, such approaches have had a dramatic impact on the amount of research undertaken into drug development for so-called neglected diseases in the past 10 years (Moran et al. 2005). However, in addition to the availability of funding from private foundations (now also available for African agriculture), a factor that has contributed to private-sector participation has been the growing pressure from the global civil society on leading health multinationals to make affordable drugs available to citizens of poor countries, including those in Sub-Saharan Africa. At present there is much less pressure for agricultural multinationals to supply low-cost agricultural technologies to poor farmers in Africa.

Although the situation could change rapidly in the coming years, these ideas are at present largely still at the proposal stage. For the rest of this chapter, therefore, I concentrate on public-sector agricultural research in Africa, as up to now state organizations have dominated agricultural research in the continent.

19.3 Public-Sector Agricultural Research

As noted above, public sector agricultural research encompasses both national agricultural research systems (NARS) and international agricultural research centers (IARCs). The main IARCs are the member centers of the global Consultative Group

on International Agricultural Research (CGIAR) research network (http://www
.cgiar.org). Fifteen main centers make up this network. Four of these have their head-
quarters in Sub-Saharan Africa, and others also have regional offices there. According
to Evenson and Gollin (2007), in 1995 the total expenditure of the CGIAR system
worldwide was about US$400 million (in 2001 dollars). This amount compares with
US$1,270 million aggregate expenditure by NARS in Sub-Saharan Africa. Because
of the changing priorities of donors who fund the CGIAR system, the share of total
CGIAR expenditure incurred in Africa has risen from about one-third in 1995 to
45 percent in 2003. Thus the CGIAR system accounts for a significant minority
share of total expenditure on agricultural research in Africa. In terms of impact,
its contribution is arguably greater,[4] although such commentators as Evenson and
Gollin (2007) clearly believe that CGIAR could do more. Scientists in CGIAR
centers are paid internationally competitive salaries and, periodic uncertainties over
budgets notwithstanding, have good facilities and vehicles to assist them in their
work. Moreover, the organizational culture generates expectations of performance,
and international networking and engagement with the wider research community
generate incentives for good performance through peer recognition. Major research
breakthroughs, such as higher yielding, mealybug-resistant cassava varieties and New
Rice for Africa (NERICA) rice varieties, have come from individual CGIAR centers
(Dalton and Guei 2003; Nweke 2004).

In contrast, in most NARS the inherent challenges of agricultural research are
combined with generic problems of public-sector management and funding (a highly
undesirable aspect of the institutional environment) to seriously depress performance incentives. Consider the following:

- Staff members in most NARS are paid according to nationally determined pay
  scales for public-sector workers. The real value of these salaries has eroded over
  time, as staffing levels in African civil services have increased more rapidly than
  budgets (van de Walle 2001)—a trend also seen in agricultural research systems
  (Beintema and Stads 2004). Many scientists, therefore, seek to leave NARS and
  find jobs either in IARCs or in other, nonresearch occupations.

- As with other civil service positions, decisions on hiring, relocation, and firing
  are often taken centrally, with little input from the manager who best knows the
  performance of the staff member concerned. Administrative and other considerations may dominate questions of individual merit in determining who fills
  which post. Thus effort and achievement may go unrewarded, and shirking or
  even absenteeism may not be disciplined, reducing the incentives to work hard.
  Following a study of 29 public-sector organizations[5] in six developing countries

(including the Central African Republic, Ghana, and Tanzania in Sub-Saharan Africa), Grindle (1997, 491) concluded that "autonomy in personnel matters" was "consistently associated with good performance."[6] At a more senior level in African bureaucracies (such as the directorships of NARS or the ministers to whom they are accountable), van de Walle (2001) argues that the politicization of appointments in the decades after independence was the main factor undermining the capacity of the African state:

- Not only are salary scales low, but also the operational funds that NARS researchers have to work with have been progressively squeezed, as salaries have occupied an increasing share of available funding. Beintema and Stads (2004) estimate that funding per research scientist in African NARS fell by half in real terms over the period 1971–2000. Furthermore, this funding can be highly erratic, depending on the state of the wider national and agricultural sector budgets, making it difficult to mount a sustained research effort.

- The long-term nature of much agricultural research, inherent uncertainty in any research process, plus the erratic funding make it more difficult even for diligent managers to monitor individual performance and attribute outcomes to effort.

As with efforts to encourage greater private investment in agricultural research, institutional arrangements can be sought that enhance performance incentives for public-sector agricultural researchers. These may be thought of as institutional innovations that (partially) compensate for weaknesses in the wider institutional environment, in particular, the negative influence of public-sector management and funding. I discuss three arrangements here, two of which have wider benefits in enhancing the effectiveness of agricultural research beyond simply strengthening performance incentives for individual researchers.

One currently popular mechanism is the establishment of competitive research funds at the organizational, national, or regional level. These can be funded by donors or out of the budget of the organization or ministry concerned. At the organizational or ministry level, these funds can provide managers with valuable information on the activities and productivity of individual staff. When donor funding is involved, successful bids can augment the funds available to particular researchers, teams, or institutes. The discipline of deliverables and deadlines can provide a more effective incentive to productivity than prevailing public-sector management and supervisory processes. On the downside, the transaction costs of preparing applications (for researchers) and assessing them, entering into contracts, and then monitoring subsequent performance (for research fund managers) can be large: 25 percent of the value of funds disbursed would not be uncommon as management overhead. These are funds that could otherwise have been used for research activities directly, so the additional performance engendered by competitive funding has to be significant to justify the costs entailed. As with all attempts to introduce a market where none has existed before, there is also the question of how effective the competition is. If a fund is not accessible to a sufficiently large pool of researchers, competition will be limited, as will be the enhancement of performance engendered by competitive funding. However, increasing the coverage of a fund raises the costs of searching for and validating information (about the capabilities of applicants and the activities of those who eventually receive funding). There may, therefore, be an optimal scale to get the best balance between competition and information.

A second mechanism, also currently popular (although not new) is the establishment of research networks, typically at the regional level. These networks contribute to information exchange among researchers working on similar problems, compensating in part for the small size of individual research establishments. A proactive network management can also introduce new concepts and best practice to all members of the network, for example, in establishing linkages with other stakeholders or monitoring and evaluating the impact of research work. Returning to the theme of researcher motivation, however, participation in a wider network can increase the esteem in which a researcher is held beyond her/his immediate institution, and opportunities to travel to network gatherings can provide a nonsalary incentive to supplement the meager remuneration available through civil service salaries.

Third, increasing client involvement in research activities can benefit research effectiveness in a number of ways. Engagement with clients, be they farmers or agribusiness enterprises, assists priority setting. However, it can also contribute to performance incentives for researchers if forums are created at which researchers have to present their results to clients and/or account for lack of success. I return to this issue below.

19.4   Agricultural Innovation Systems

So far I have focused on performance incentives in public-sector agricultural research as a key cause of poor overall performance of research. However, in recent years there has also been increasing attention paid to systemwide issues. Traditionally, research proceeded along a more-or-less supply-driven, linear route, with research outputs being passed onto extension agents for dissemination to farmers. The importance of two-way communication along this chain was then recognized: researchers could learn from farmers not just in terms of specific feedbacks on disseminated research (to make it suitable for their farming systems), but also as innovators in their own right, who experiment with their own responses to the challenges that they face. More recently, thinking on agricultural research has recognized the importance of engaging with other actors, including nongovernmental organizations (NGOs) involved in agricultural development and—perhaps most importantly—the private sector.

There are at least three ways in which the private sector and linkages to agricultural markets are critical for the uptake and impact of agricultural research:

1. Farmers adopt new technologies only if it is profitable to do so, and market demand for new products or for expanded production of existing products is a major determinant of profitability. Private buyers and processors may be able to explain and predict market demand for a particular product more accurately than can farmers who have only limited experience in selling that product. They may also be able to inform researchers of particular product attributes that the market values, which will enhance competitiveness of producers able to supply them.

2. As explained in Chapter 5, farmers require a number of complementary services if they are to intensify production and/or to invest in new crops. Many are unlikely to adopt a more expensive, improved seed variety if they cannot obtain complementary inputs (for example, fertilizer), which may in turn require access to credit (Feder, Just, and Zilberman 1985). Hence researchers need to communicate with the private sector and possibly with NGO suppliers of these complementary services to ensure that they are available to support the uptake of new research outputs.

3. As a specific case of the second method, public-sector researchers must coordinate with both public- and private-sector seed suppliers to ensure that promising new seed technologies are commercialized and marketed to farmers. At the least, seed suppliers need to be aware of farmer response to research trials as one early indicator of future market demand for new varieties.

Box 19.1 illustrates some of these points.

Academic thinking about agricultural research increasingly emphasizes the existence of national innovation systems, rather than simply agricultural research organizations and their linkages to extension agencies and farmers (Hall et al. 2004; Spielman 2005). According to Spielman (2005, 12–15):

- "An innovation system is defined as a set of interrelated agents, their interactions and the institutions that condition their behaviour with respect to the common objective of generating, diffusing and utilizing knowledge and/or technology."

Box 19.1 Poor uptake of past agricultural research

The traditional linear process by which the products of research are passed on to extension services for dissemination to farmers has produced many important advances, such as the control of cassava mealy bug and of rinderpest. Much more common, however, are technologies that do not leave the research station shelves. Scientists have attributed this problem to the failure of the extension services, but such (real or perceived) shortcomings have not prevented farmers from adopting viable technologies such as hybrid maize, livestock vaccination, and smallholder dairying.

Now there is increasing recognition that some "solutions" remain on the shelves because, although they show technical potential, they are poorly adapted to the complex situations within which they are intended to be adopted. Farming systems research, which emphasizes on-farm experimentation, has had considerable success locally. With farmers involved in testing, many innovations have been shown to work on participating farms. But these innovations have typically failed to spread even to neighbouring localities—as exemplified by the case of the ox-drawn broadbed maker in Ethiopia, which was designed to make raised seedbeds with intervening furrows that drain the land to permit early planting. With the right seed varieties and fertilizer, this method raises crop yields significantly. The implement was developed over many years of on-farm testing, but after initial promise it failed to be adopted as widely as had been anticipated.

One plausible explanation for the poor uptake of research products is the existence of critical gaps in the knowledge of research teams. If farming communities had been more involved in designing and validating the research on the broadbed makers (in addition to providing fields and labour), local farmers may well have predicted the poor uptake of this technology. They would have known about the unreliability of essential inputs such as fertilizer and the effects of market failures on the price of grain in case of local production increases.

Source: Jones (2004, 2–3).

- Agents include "individuals and firms as well as public institutions and non-state actors." They are viewed "not as rational maximizers responding to price signals, but as strategists, responding to other agents' behaviours and their institutional context."

- Knowledge is understood broadly to include scientific/technical and organizational/managerial knowledge, knowledge that is embodied in a good or service as well as knowledge that is not, knowledge that is codified or explicit, and knowledge that is tacit or implicit.

- Knowledge may be generated by "the conventional providers of advanced research: public research organizations, private laboratories and universities," but "may also emerge from the practices and behaviours of individuals, households and civil society organizations."

- Understanding the interactions among actors is emphasized. These may include "spot market exchanges of goods and services that embody new knowledge or technology; costless exchanges of non-rival, non-excludable knowledge made available in the public domain; long-term durable exchanges that incorporate complex commitment mechanisms and related transaction costs; collusive arrangements among oligopolistic firms, and hierarchical/command structures that govern the exchange process." In these interactions, modes of cooperation are of particular interest (especially "relationships that blur the traditional roles of distinct actors—for example, partnerships between public and private research entities"), as are the institutions that promote or impede cooperation.

- The "institutions that affect the process by which innovations are developed and delivered" are integral to the innovation system. As might be expected from discussions in the earlier chapters of this volume, these institutions include "the laws, regulations, conventions, traditions, routines and norms of society that determine how different agents interact with and learn from each other, and how they produce, disseminate and utilize knowledge."

More practically, new methodologies for best practice in agricultural research are being developed that recognize the importance of establishing linkages among researchers, farmer clients, and relevant private-sector organizations. One of these—the Integrated Agricultural Research for Development (IAR4D) concept that is being promoted by the CGIAR system—is described in Box 19.2.

Box 19.2 An integrated approach to agricultural research

The CGIAR Challenge Program concept is a response to the need for innovative, high impact research involving a wider array of partners and attracting new funding sources. The Integrated Agricultural Research for Development (IAR4D) concept, adopted by the proposed Sub-Saharan Africa Challenge Program led and coordinated by FARA [Forum for Agricultural Research in Africa], provides an example of how such an approach can work. IAR4D carries out research in a demand-driven mode, with impact measured in terms of meeting that demand, rather than in the supply-driven mode that has characterized much agricultural research in the past. IAR4D asks fundamental questions about the type of research needed and the social organization and attitudes and behaviours of the participants.

Past research has frequently failed to accommodate the complexity of the situations in which products must be adopted. IAR4D attempts to overcome this failure by addressing the following key elements:

- integrating levels of analysis

- merging disciplinary perspectives

- guiding research on component technologies while making use of a wide range of technological options

- generating policy, technological, and institutional options

- improving the adaptive capacity of stakeholders to manage the resilience of the agro-ecosystem

- moving from training to social learning

- advancing knowledge management

- increasing awareness of the environmental costs of poor natural resource management.

IAR4D projects are to include specific measures to ensure that the research benefits will scale out and up. Projects will involve community members beyond those on the farms or premises where the research is conducted, in order to get their intellectual input and to ensure that they are aware of and take ownership of the emerging research products. Special attention will be paid to overcoming gender bias and finding ways to institutionalize modes of scaling out and up that target female as well as male farmers. Policymakers at national and regional levels will also be involved and kept informed of the outcomes of IAR4D projects. This wide scope aims to help spread research benefits to neighbouring communities, and to internalize such benefits in institutions at local, national, and regional levels. These objectives influence the biophysical, socioeconomic, and institutional aspects of IAR4D at all levels. . . .

IAR4D also requires teams of scientists from many disciplines to work together as learning organizations with farmers and the full range of other stakeholders in highly adaptive ways. The formation of such teams demands institutional flexibility and willingness to change. It also implies a substantial need for capacity building, with funding for team building as a primary element of proposal development and project implementation. It will also require professional facilitation to enable partners from different cultures, dissimilar educational backgrounds, and unequal endowments to collaborate effectively.

Source: Jones (2004, 3–4).

19.5   Institutionalizing Stakeholder Involvement

New methodologies for agricultural research, such as IAR4D, are being introduced to African NARS by CGIAR centers with which they collaborate and by other donor initiatives. However, it remains an open question whether the impetus generated by such initiatives can be sustained, given the weak incentives for individual research performance discussed previously. Fundamentally, IAR4D still relies on researchers reaching out to other stakeholders and inviting them to contribute to the research and adoption process. Researchers at CGIAR centers have the necessary internal incentives to do so. However, will NARS researchers have sufficient incentives once CGIAR collaboration or donor funding—and the additional external accountability that such funding implies—has ended?

Earlier I noted that increasing client involvement in research activities can both assist the setting of research priorities and contribute to performance incentives for researchers, in the latter case by creating new accountability mechanisms. Institutionalizing such client involvement is required if these performance benefits are to be sustained. In their review of African agricultural research, Beintema and Stads (2004) note the modest growth of what they call nonprofit research, particularly in southern Africa. In this category, clients (farmer organizations and/or agribusiness) have been given a role in the management of a research organization, often in some form of public–private partnership. All cited examples are found in traditional cash crop sectors: tea in Kenya, Malawi, and Tanzania; coffee in Kenya, Tanzania, and Uganda; cotton in Zambia; and sugar in Mauritius and South Africa. In exchange for their enhanced influence over research management, the stakeholders in the sector are often expected to pay for part or all of the research effort, commonly through a levy on crop marketing, processing, or export.

The organizations concerned (for example, the tea and coffee research institutes in Tanzania) are often among the best performing in their respective countries. In addition to improving priority setting and accountability, a condition commonly imposed by private stakeholders when entering into the new management partnerships is that the new management gains the ability to hire and fire staff and to pay them at rates more typical of commercial salaries. Beintema and Stads (2004, 242) comment that "generally agricultural scientists employed by the non-profit organizations had almost double the financial resources to hand compared with their colleagues working at government or higher education agencies. This is reflected in the relatively higher salary packages offered by the non-profit organizations."

Why are such cases found only in traditional cash crop sectors? Following the logic of Chapter 5, I suggest that a critical factor is the relatively concentrated output markets found in many of these sectors. Where a few medium-sized to large firms dominate processing and/or export in a sector, such firms may have the necessary incentives to invest time in improving the quality of research activity. As the major buyers, they will be major beneficiaries of improved quantities or quality of raw material supplied by producers (see also Box 19.3). In contrast, in the case of many food crops, there are numerous small primary buyers and even processors and wholesalers. Individual agents, therefore, lack the incentives to engage in research management, as most of the benefits of improved performance would be captured by others. There may be only a few importers, but they do not have an interest in increasing the productivity of local producers. And farmer organizations that could credibly represent food-crop producers rarely exist. In other words, effective demand for enhanced research performance is lacking.

It therefore appears that institutional arrangements can be devised for traditional cash crop sectors to overcome some of the weaknesses observed in conventional pub-

Box 19.3 An example of private agricultural research: Quton Seed Company in Zimbabwe

Zimbabwe has a strong tradition of public sector cotton research, dating back to an era when the Commercial Farmers' Union advocated strongly for public investment to support the interests and competitiveness of the country's white commercial farmers. After Independence close links were maintained between the parastatal Cotton Marketing Board (CMB) and the Cotton Research Institute (CRI). Following liberalization, Quton Seed Company, a wholly owned subsidiary of CMB's privatized successor Cottco, was granted monopoly rights to multiply and sell to the whole sector seed varieties produced by CRI, in exchange for which Quton makes royalty payments to CRI. As state funding for CRI collapsed post-2001, these royalty payments became increasingly important, albeit inadequate to sustain a dynamic program. Quton, therefore, began to invest in its own research capability, which is now reckoned to surpass that of CRI. As of early 2007 Quton was preparing to release the first products of its in-house research activity and there was also talk of Quton taking over the assets of CRI. Quton's investment first in CRI and later also in its own research capacity reflects the strong recognition within the Zimbabwe sector of the importance of productivity-enhancing research. However, it is no coincidence that it has occurred in a concentrated sector where Cottco, as the largest firm, is also the biggest beneficiary of national research outputs.

Source: Tschirley et al. (2008, 84).

lic research organizations (weaknesses that can be attributed to deficiencies in the prevailing institutional environment). However, although institutional arrangements are being devised for food crop systems research, it is questionable whether enhanced performance will be sustained once CGIAR collaboration or donor funding is ended, because the underlying difficulties in the prevailing institutional environment will once again assert themselves. Reform of the institutional environment—a topic addressed in more detail in Chapter 20—may be required before performance of agricultural research for food crops in Africa can improve considerably. In the meantime, the challenge of crafting institutional arrangements to raise performance within the constraints of the prevailing institutional environment remains.

Notes

1. Beintema and Stads (2004) report a figure of 0.7 percent for 2000.

2. Similarly, Evenson and Gollin (2007, 2425) observe that some national agricultural research systems in Sub-Saharan Africa have only "notional" budgets (less than US$20 million per year) and many employ fewer than 50 research scientists. They comment that "these programs are unlikely to be able to conduct original research—particularly if the research effort is spread (as is typical) across a range of crops and animal species."

3. Beintema and Stads (2004) report that it is common for donors to provide one-third to half of the budget for national agricultural research systems in Africa, although the share is lower in some cases.

4. Comparisons between IARCs and NARS are not meant to convey the impression that the two are totally separate. Indeed, CGIAR centers see one of their aims as being to complement, collaborate with, and supply resources to NARS in their countries of operation.

5. These organizations were engaged in macroeconomic management, delivery of agricultural extension services, or delivery of maternal and child healthcare services.

6. "This autonomy meant that organizations could identify positions, advertise for candidates, establish routines for hiring people to fill positions, promote people on the basis of organizationally defined standards and priorities, and punish those who did not meet those standards" (Grindle 1997, 491).

References

Alston, J., and P. Pardey. 2001. Attribution and other problems in assessing the returns to agricultural R&D. *Agricultural Economics* 25 (2–3): 141–152.

Alston, J., C. Chan-Kang, M. Marra, P. Pardey, and T. Wyatt. 2000. *A meta-analysis of rates of return to agricultural R&D: Ex pede Herculem?* Research Report 113. Washington, D.C.: International Food Policy Research Institute.

Beintema, N., and G. Stads. 2004. Sub-Saharan African agricultural research: Recent investment trends. *Outlook on Agriculture* 33 (4): 239–246.

Dalton, T., and R. Guei. 2003. Productivity gains from rice genetic enhancements in West Africa: Countries and ecologies. *World Development* 31: 359–374.

Evenson, R., and D. Gollin. 2007. Contributions of national agricultural research systems to crop productivity. In *Handbook of agricultural economics*, vol. 3: *Agricultural development: Farmers, farm production and farm markets*, ed. R. Evenson and P. Pingali. Amsterdam: Elsevier.

Feder, G., R. Just, and D. Zilberman. 1985. Adoption of agricultural innovations in developing countries: A survey. *Economic Development and Cultural Change* 33: 255–298.

Grindle, M. 1997. Divergent cultures? When public organizations perform well in developing countries. *World Development* 25: 481–495.

Hall, A., B. Yoganand, R. Sulaiman, R. Raina, G. Prasad, G. Naik, and N. Clark, eds. 2004. *Innovations in innovation: Reflections on partnership, institutions and learning*. Patancheru, India: International Crops Research Institute for the Semi-Arid Tropics.

Jones, M. 2004. Strengthening agricultural research in Africa. 2020 Africa Conference Brief 9. Washington, D.C.: International Food Policy Research Institute. http://www.ifpri.org/pubs/ib/ib25.pdf. Accessed April 2008.

Masters, W. 2005. Paying for prosperity: Investing in international agricultural R&D. *Journal of International Affairs* 58 (2): 35–64.

Moran, M., A. Ropars, J. Guzman, J. Diaz, and C. Garrison. 2005. *The new landscape of neglected disease drug development. Pharmaceutical R&D Policy Project.* London: George Institute for International Health, London School of Economics, and Wellcome Trust.

Nweke, F. 2004. *New challenges in the cassava transformation in Nigeria and Ghana.* Environment and Production Technology Division Discussion Paper 118. Washington, D.C.: International Food Policy Research Institute.

Pingali, P., and G. Traxler. 2002. Changing locus of agricultural research: Will the poor benefit from biotechnology and privatization trends? *Food Policy* 27 (3): 223–238.

Pray, C., and B. Ramaswami. 1991. *A framework for seed policy analysis in developing countries.* Washington, D.C.: International Food Policy Research Institute.

Spielman, D. 2005. *Innovations systems perspectives on developing country agriculture: A critical review.* International Service for National Agricultural Research Discussion Paper 2. Washington, D.C.: International Food Policy Research Institute.

Tschirley, D., C. Poulton, P. Labaste, J. Baffes, J. Dana, G. Estur, and N. Gergely. 2008. *Comparative analysis of organization and performance of African cotton sectors: Learning from reform experience.* Washington, D.C.: World Bank.

Van de Walle, N. 2001. *African economies and the politics of permanent crisis.* Cambridge: Cambridge University Press.

Chapter 20

A New Institutional Economic Analysis of the State and Agriculture in Sub-Saharan Africa

Jonathan G. Kydd

The state, an all-encompassing term taking in all layers of government from the local to supranational level,[1] is an important actor in most spheres of economic life and is dominant in some. It is a key source of law and has a legal monopoly over the harsher mechanisms of enforcement, such as arrest, prosecution, fining, and loss of liberty. The rules made and upheld by the state are core features of the institutional environment. But the state is also seen as an indispensable provider of certain services, including law and order, physical infrastructure, education and heath, and regulation of the economy, for which it has to raise taxes. There is constant debate about which services the state should provide and the manner of their provision. Economists (both orthodox and those who pursue New Institutional Economics [NIE]) find that the concepts of public goods, market failure, merit goods, and redistribution (Box 20.1) provide useful guidance in this debate, as they focus attention on needs that would not be met adequately, if at all, were provision left solely to the market.

These concepts, although very useful, are far from sufficient. In some of the literature on development policy, they can become part of an unrealistic technocratic discourse that assumes the existence of a rational, development-oriented state, backed by political leaders with similar motivation, and with adequate capacity. Certainly it is helpful to identify and rank the importance of public goods, market failures, and merit goods and to debate the possibilities for asset and income redistribution. But if this effort is done without considering key issues in the wider context, the result will

Box 20.1 Public goods, market failure, merit goods, and redistribution

Public goods are those that are supplied by the market or are supplied in insufficient quantity. A pure public good has two key properties: (1) it does not cost anything for an additional individual to enjoy its benefits (nonsubtractability) and (2) it is impossible, or at least difficult, to exclude individuals from enjoyment of its benefits (nonexcludability).

Welfare economics has a fundamental theorem: resource allocations with the property that no one can be made better off without someone else being made worse off are Pareto efficient (or optimal). There are factors that may cause markets to be Pareto inefficient, and these provide rationales for government activity:

1. *competition* in the market, or at least the realistic threat of potential competition;

2. *public goods;*

3. *externalities* (the actions of one individual or firm imposes an uncompensated cost or benefit on other individuals or firms);

4. *incomplete markets* (private markets fail to provide a good, even though the costs of provision are less than what individuals would be willing to pay; incomplete markets are said to be common in insurance and finance);

5. *information failures* (the market may not supply business and consumers with sufficient information); and

6. *high unemployment* of people and also of machinery.

Category 6, which might be called systemic market failure, has been the basis of much controversy in macroeconomics and development economics.

Arguments for merit goods are based on the proposition that there are cases when governments should intervene to provide the good, because individuals do not know what is in their own best interests. Thus perhaps consumers are not well informed, or suffer from "bounded rationality" or, even if well informed, still make bad decisions. Government provision of universal and compulsory primary education is often cited as a merit good. The argument is that if primary school attendance were optional, pupils (and their parents) may decide not to go to school, even though this is against their longer run interests.

The argument is that Pareto efficiency (optimality) is silent about the distribution of incomes, even though the working of markets, interacting with government, may lead to a distribution of incomes that is ethically unacceptable, particularly if a significant proportion of members of the society have incomes below poverty levels. In these circumstances governments should tax wealthier groups and spend the funds on (1) pro-poor public and merit goods, (2) subsidies to the economic activities of the poor (for example, credit subsidies), and (3) direct income transfers to the poor.

be unbalanced assessments underpinning what could prove to be dysfunctional policy advice. So it is critical to examine sections of the state (that is, state organizations) in their broader social, political, economic, and cultural settings. This examination includes determining whose interests state organizations serve, for example, those of politicians, different grades and professions of state employees, interest groups in society at large, and foreign aid donors. Related matters are the internal cultures of state organizations: how are staff members motivated and their actions regulated, and what are their accepted norms of behavior? The financial resources available to state organizations and the mechanisms of accountability are also very important.

Many writers see successful development in poorer countries as stemming from the presence of a "developmental state," in other words, a system of politics and governance able to define and enforce rules that reassure investors while also encouraging efficient resource allocation, investing in infrastructure and human capital, and overcoming market failures. With Sub-Saharan Africa in mind, most of the authors in this book see a critical role for the state in kick-starting development, to overcome low-level equilibrium traps (LLETs). LLETs may exist in subsectors that could be made much more productive by increased investment and/or more efficient use of capital stock, but there are impediments that cannot be overcome solely by the market and/or by existing collective-action organizations. As the phrase "kick-starting" suggests, the challenge of overcoming LLETs points to the need for what may be called the stage of development-defined public goods. This stage consists of pro-poor interventions to promote development through markets and/or collective action that will cease to be required, at least in their initial forms, after successful escape from the trap. The case studies in this book describe various attempts to provide public interventions to support agriculture, with varying degrees of success.

There are institutional perspectives to all of these topics, which have been discussed in earlier chapters. The rules of the state are central features of the institutional environment and come out of a complex interplay of history (path dependency), culture (or habits of mind), and influences of powerful elements in society (generally, but not exclusively, the richer segments). The rules of the state can be considered as layered from the higher levels (which structure the ways in which politics affects government and property rights are recognized and enforced) to lower levels (which define the rules detailing entitlements to rights and to state services). However, the rules of the state are only one component of the institutional environment. As Chapter 13 has explored, we live in a world of legal pluralism, with multiple sources of rules.

In discussing the state and the challenges facing Sub-Saharan African agriculture, there are acute difficulties in defining the boundaries of embeddedness (between exogeneity and endogeneity). This is because there is a broad consensus across the political spectrum that most Sub-Saharan African countries lack "developmental states," even though there is heated controversy among different political positions as to what a developmental state might look like. The growing literature on this topic is fascinating and compelling reading (for a review, see Lockwood 2005, Chapters 5–10). However, for NIE to make a distinct contribution, this literature has to be treated as largely exogenous, providing the context of NIE analysis of the state and agriculture, not the content. The content is about the insights that NIE can provide into reforms that can be made in the setting of what are at best weakly developmental—and often antidevelopmental—states. Put another way, there is a need to be aware of the political-economy literature on the state and to take it fully into account in thinking through the exogenous (embedded) setting for applying NIE analysis to the roles and performance of state organizations. But the NIE analysis is a distinct and useful additional contribution to the larger picture.

NIE analysis of the roles and performance of the state and possible improvements in Sub-Saharan African agriculture is a difficult topic:

1. Although for a given country there may be wide agreement that much of the state is anti- (or at best weakly) developmental, there is likely to be considerable disagreement on the details of how and why.

2. As noted earlier in this chapter, much of the existing technocratic discourse (about public goods and the like) has been naive about politics, governance, and organizational cultures. This oversight does not invalidate the concepts employed (for example, public goods and market failure), but it does require that such ideas as public goods and market failure be iterated with analysis of state motivation and capacity.

Nevertheless, NIE can be applied to these difficult questions with some confidence. As the earlier chapters in the volume have shown, NIE has insights to offer into contracts, the nature of market failures in early-stage agriculture, incentives, and forms of economic and social coordination (for example, hierarchy; market, hybrid, and private firms versus cooperatives and mutual organizations).

20.1 Developmental and Antidevelopmental States: An Outline

As noted above, analysts from across the political spectrum tend to agree that most Sub-Saharan African countries lack a developmental state, even thought there is much disagreement on what a developmental state might look like.[2] Nevertheless, there is a consensus that in general the situation has become worse in the past quarter-century, despite large investments in capacity building (Lockwood 2005, 84). Van de Walle (2001, 133) uses the concepts of neopatrimonialism and clientelism to argue that this erosion in the developmental impact of the state "is a direct consequence of the formal and informal practices of governments for which a developmental state apparatus is not a priority" (Box 20.2). This conclusion highlights politics, but before turning to this topic, it is useful to consider briefly the possible characteristics of a developmental state in Sub-Saharan Africa.

Analysts have tended to tackle this question by interrogating the history of different categories of developed countries to gain insights that may be relevant to Sub-Saharan Africa. The most obvious distinction seems to be between the successful East Asian pattern of development (for example, Japan, Taiwan, and Korea, presently being followed rapidly by the giant of mainland China) and the North American–European pattern. The East Asian pattern came later, being a prominent feature of the second half of the twentieth century, and it included as a central stage rapid expansion of export-oriented manufacturing, which required much coordinated investment and a willingness to learn international best-practices and then improve on these.

Lockwood (2005, 35) summarizes priorities and activities of a stylized "capitalist development state" model of East Asia:

- Economic development rather than welfare is the top state priority. Thus investment (private and public, efficiently allocated) and the resulting productivity and international competitiveness are emphasized.

- The state is committed to private property and the market, but it guides the market with instruments formulated by an elite economic bureaucracy.

Box 20.2 The politics of neopatrimonialism and clientelism

According to van de Walle (2001), the essence of neopatrimonialism can be captured in the following four characteristics.

1. *Clientelism:* a position of power is valued primarily for the resources procured for the office holder's own family and kin. Although clientelism is a system of redistribution of the benefits of office to a wider group, the benefits are not widespread. Van de Walle (2001, 119) quotes Gavin Williams and others: "What is striking about many African countries is how little trickles down to the worse off through the patronage network and how much sticks to a few hands at the top." The core argument here is that there is little accountability in this system: clients have weak influence over their patrons, who are often "big men" to whom they must be grateful for a junior job or small contract.

   Van de Walle's argument that in weak Sub-Saharan African states clients have little influence over patrons sits uneasily with Khan's (2005) insight that the problem is rather that patrons have insufficient control over clients (who use benefits gained on consumption rather than on investment that promotes development). It may be that the paradox can be resolved by assuming that these observers are referring to different levels of governance. Both agree that at a high level the central state is too weak to adequately control rent seeking by "big men" and to enforce economic development performance in return for rents. Furthermore, both views fit with the proposition that in the lower levels of clientalist systems subordinates obtain small benefits and have very little influence over their benefactors. Thus in neopatrimonial and clientalist systems the "big men" experience weak pressure for accountability, either from below or above.

2. *Control over state resources:* such control is the primary purpose of politicians (as opposed, for example, to what van de Walle (2001, 120) calls a "development project," which could be the objective of elements of the bureaucracy and/or aid agencies). Thus corruption, sanctioned at the highest level, becomes a systemic feature, substantially lowering government revenues, and there is little impetus from the political sphere to supply public and merit goods.

3. *Centralization of power around the president and in the capital city:* large shares of the government budget are controlled by the president, with little transparency and/or oversight by senior bureaucrats. Outlays to local government are very small. Cabinet ministers have little autonomy and are frequently shuffled between portfolios.

4. *Hybrid regimes:* informal institutions of personal rule and plunder coexist uneasily with a modern bureaucracy and its distinct logic. There is constant tension between the patrimonial shadow state and the rational-legal elements in the bureaucracy. In some countries the latter elements may be no more than small pockets, whereas in others the power and scope of the rational-legal bureaucracy is considerable.

It is possible to draw excessively pessimistic conclusions from discussions of neopatrimonialism. For van de Walle (2001, 128), intellectual debates within Africa about public policy "are meaningful, and cannot be reduced to rent seeking motivations. . . . No state in Africa can claim to have entirely avoided neopatrimonial tendencies at its apex. The two tendencies [neopatrimonial and rational-legal] coexist, overlap, and struggle for the control of the state in most countries."

- The state consults and coordinates with the private sector through numerous institutions, and this is an essential part of the policymaking process.

- "State bureaucrats rule while politicians reign." Thus politicians allow substantial space for senior bureaucrats or technocrats to operate in the interests of national economic development. In return, bureaucrats must be responsive to the interest groups on whom the stability of the system rests. As has been shown by the work of Mushtaq Khan, discussed below, there is considerable corruption but, in the context of a strong state and elite commitment to national economic development, it does not act as a barrier to economic development.

- There is heavy and consistent investment in education, and the state devotes considerable attention to ensuring the acquisition of literacy, numeracy, and other key work skills.

Of course, an (ideal) effective African developmental state would look somewhat different and presumably would meld the best from African and foreign traditions.

Many Western (that is, North American and European) advisers to Africa would contest items in the list above. Orthodox economists would be worried about the proposition that an elite bureaucracy should guide the market's and the state's roles in coordination, which might be interpreted as anticompetitive behavior inhibiting market entry. However, as earlier chapters have shown, many NIE-influenced economists would advocate a substantial role for the state in coordination in contemporary Sub-Saharan Africa, providing that it can be done with acceptable competence. The emphasis on economic development and the downplaying of immediate poverty reduction could well attract disapproval from most Western aid agencies and development nongovernmental organizations (NGOs). The lack of emphasis on democracy, accountability, and transparency and the implicit tolerance of some corruption would also meet with disapproval.

Wade (1990), in contrasting North America–Europe with East Asia, identifies two key dimensions of difference: (1) the authoritarian state versus the democratic state and (2) corporatism versus pluralism. The East Asian experience has been authoritarian and corporatist whereas the North American–European experience has been democratic and pluralist (in its later years at least). Lockwood (2005) makes explicit a third dimension, which is the quality of leadership—that is, do the leading politician(s) and bureaucrats have a commitment to a viable development project? (To put it another way: what factors motivate and regulate the political leaders and bureaucrats? This important topic is examined further in Section 20.3). In "strong but corrupt states" there is what Khan has called the patrimonial settlement, under which

> Bureaucrats and politicians in a politically dominant state dispense rights and resources (licences, government contracts, subsidised credit, etc) and get a share of the benefits as bribes, or additional political support, but they can still enforce performance from the client company, and they are not dependent on that client. This form of corruption may add some cost to the taxpayer or the company, but it does not disrupt the process of investment and accumulation. (Lockwood 2005, 88, summarizing Mushtaq Khan)

In contrast, in Sub-Saharan Africa the state is weaker and has more need for the political support of clients. The center (usually the president) is in a more precarious position than in the authoritarian corporatist East Asian state and needs to buy off individuals representing various factional, regional, and ethnic constituencies. Thus the state tends to multiply the rights and resources available. The expansion of ministries and cabinet posts is symptomatic of this as each represents an opportunity for rent seeking. In summary, two critical contrasts between the East Asian authoritarian corporatist state and most contemporary Sub-Saharan African states are that: (1) the

African states are generally much weaker and (2) the results of corruption are different, in that the authoritarian state is strongly oriented to ensure that most resources get invested in the national project. In Sub-Saharan Africa, rulers are less interested in channeling resources into the necessary investment and economic coordination for national development. Even if they wished to do so, they would have less power to enforce their will. Instead, as van de Walle (2001; see Box 20.2) shows, resources are siphoned off from the state by what is usually a small group of individuals and is spent largely on consumption. So, although many Sub-Saharan African states exhibit authoritarian and corporatist tendencies, they are less able to produce the necessary investment in health and education, to intervene intelligently to deal with market failures, and to spur private investment in productive capacity.

Of course there is considerable variation in the quality of the state in Africa. Two writers have used striking images that were not developed for specific application to Sub-Saharan Africa but which can nevertheless be applied:

- Mancur Olson (2000) identified an early positive step in development as being the point at which "mobile bandits" become stationary. Once stationary, the bandits become interested in developing the territory they control. Particularly if they feel that their control is relatively secure, they have incentives to invest in infrastructure and other public goods.

- Wade's (1990) distinction between the "vampire state" and the "ruminant state." The vampire extracts blood and debilitates, whereas the ruminant grazes the resource base, and its processes of digestion and excretion provide nourishing fertilizer.

Clearly the African developmental state will emerge at the stationary/ruminant end of the spectrum, although in contemporary Sub-Saharan Africa there are unfortunately large areas where the state has collapsed and to which images of banditry and physical conflict for spoils are apposite. Allen (1995) makes the point that among the relatively stable states a key factor is whether ruling regimes have been able to centralize power to form what he calls centralized bureaucratic states, which he believes have prospects of evolving into effective developmental states.[3]

Two further issues for the Sub-Saharan African developmental state require mention. First is the major role of aid agencies in funding government expenditure, in some cases to the extent of being the main underpinning of the financial viability of the state apparatus. Second is democracy and multiparty politics, which is connected to the first, because in recent years aid has been used as a lever to press for the introduction of more democratic forms of politics.

Aid has enabled a more rapid expansion of the "service state" than would otherwise have been possible, for example, expanding numbers of teachers, health workers, agricultural researchers, and extension staff. This aid is often delivered through time-limited projects under which donors fund salaries for an initial period, with responsibility for payroll eventually being transferred to central and local governments. Although aid has facilitated expansion of the public sector, it has had distinctly less influence on public-sector management, including conditions of employment and the ratio of salary to nonsalary costs. The result has been a relatively large but seriously under-resourced state service system. The counterfactual of a smaller but better paid and incentivized public sector has considerable attractions (see Section 20.7). Further problems include the phenomenon of aid donors competing with one another for projects and staff, sidelining government officials, and sometimes failing to agree with the government and among themselves on a coordinated approach. Then, in the era of structural adjustment, which began in the early 1980s, donors pushed an agenda of liberalization, privatization, and public expenditure restraint, even though a few years earlier they had financed the creation or expansion of the very organizations that were now seen as problematic. In summary, Sub-Saharan African politicians and bureaucrats have experienced a disjointed and uncoordinated set of external funders, with a propensity for indulging fashions and rapid policy reversal. These episodes of pumping up the state apparatus and then criticizing and abandoning much of it (notably the services systems, which had been put in place to support small farmers) have acted against the emergence of a developmental state, undermining the confidence and commitment of civil servants.

A further feature of high levels of aid dependency is that government funds have often been easier to obtain from aid agencies than from domestic taxation. Moore (1992), among others, has pointed out that taxation may create a principal-agent relationship between the taxpayer and the state (as spender of their taxes) and that the development of such relationships of accountability may be powerfully developmental. The concern is that the emergence of the taxpayer–government principal-agent relationship is inhibited (see Sections 20.4 and 20.7 for more on principal-agent theory).

Aid agencies have taken account of such criticisms and have sought to improve the way they do business. Presently there is an emphasis on direct budgetary support in cases where governments are considered to be sufficiently effective, that is, sending a large consolidated check to the national treasury. There are intermediate arrangements for states that are not yet considered to be sufficiently effective but are showing signs of evolving in a positive direction. This practice avoids micro-intervention and lets governments manage while also reducing the likelihood of donors sending mixed messages at sector level. Unlike earlier aid models, this one may prove more conducive to the emergence of a Sub-Saharan African developmental state. Much will depend on the criteria selected to determine eligibility for and volumes of aid. If these are mainly process criteria (for example, Is the country democratic? Is the budget transparent? and Are robust mechanisms of accountability in place?), then effectiveness will depend on the selected criteria being good proxies for the types of performance to be expected from an evolving developmental state.

The earlier discussion of East Asian versus Western models suggests that there is a real possibility that external funders may mis-specify some of the key tendencies that need to be encouraged in a developmental state. Possibly this trap could be avoided by an approach that focuses purely on outcomes. In current debates measured progress in poverty reduction over a given period of time is the favored candidate. Again there may be a danger of mis-specification of the key ingredients of success, as short-term progress in poverty reduction might most effectively be achieved by spending a high proportion of aid on direct welfare, at the expense of investment in infrastructure, the supply of public goods, and the creation of capacity for intelligent economic coordination. Perhaps an aid agency dominated by the East Asian tradition would focus more on the quantity and quality of education, investment, and growth, assuming that successful expansion of these will, after some time, bring poverty reduction.

Lockwood (2005, 114–119) summarizes expert opinion on the extension of multiparty politics in Sub-Saharan Africa. There is a general welcome for an evolution that provides some protection against oppression and, in the longer run, ought to foster more accountable government. But this approval is tempered by knowledge that governments have been able to manipulate the electoral process, in the worst cases by fixing votes.

A key question is whether in the short term democracy can erode clientelism, or alternatively, even reinforce it and further weaken the state. The dilemma is that the literature reviewed above suggests that in the Sub-Saharan African state, weakness inhibits the emergence of a developmental state. Various commentators are concerned that intensified electoral competition may weaken the power of the center to resist rent seeking, and that government will be composed of a merry-go-round of personalities forming opportunistic alliances, purely for personal gain rather than to meet the needs of economic interest groups. The experiences of Zambia and Malawi since the end of the one-party state provide evidence of this idea: several parties are significant in their respective parliaments, and the result has been unstable coalitions. However there are other states, such as Tanzania, where the advent of multiparty democracy has enhanced freedom of expression and political action but has not seriously challenged the dominant position of the ruling party. Yet it is in Tanzania, where political competition has been restrained, that some observers detect early signs of the emergence of a developmental state. However, Lockwood (2005, 108) is far from complacent about the evolution of the Tanzanian state, noting that its experience poses a key dilemma because

> its state had a degree of central autonomy, and it currently has a leadership interested in economic growth. *It may even develop sufficient bargaining power with donors to experiment with interventionist policies.* However, there are signs that the power of the centre may not hold, and that Tanzania's stability (which underlies its economic performance) may be in jeopardy from political liberalisation and decentralisation [emphasis added].

Booth et al. (2005) tackle this dilemma by arguing that democracy will have prodevelopmental effects when civil society is strong, this being the result of people having strong "horizontal" affinities based on economic interest groups (farmers' organizations, business associations, trades unions, and the like). These organizations may cut across patron–client relations and lead to an interest group–based politics whereby politicians come under pressure to provide collective resources (including public goods) rather than individual payoffs. Booth et al. suggest that Ghana may be in the process of developing accountable interest-group politics. For example, the state may be responsive to the needs of some small farmers because of the strength of cocoa farmers' organizations.

20.2 Incentives, Economic and Social Coordination, and the State

Earlier discussion touched on the question of what motivates the actions of the state. It was noted that Weber (1946) coined the term "rational bureaucracy" to describe norms in the state that stress the broader public interest rather than the narrow interests of its employees. Much technocratic discussion of policy assumes, at least implicitly, that policymakers and their staffs are primarily motivated by the broader public interest. However, subsequent discussion of the failure of a developmental state to emerge in most Sub-Saharan African countries is based on radically different assumptions about motivations, that is, that actors in the state are largely concerned with personal and narrow sectional advantage, are ineffectively regulated, and do not find themselves in a normative framework that stresses the public good. In reality, both of these approaches are ideal types: the purely unselfish politician or bureaucrat is rare indeed, anywhere in the world. Even in the weaker Sub-Saharan African states it is possible to encounter politicians and civil servants who are primarily driven by a concern for the public good, and pockets of rational bureaucracy can be located in generally dysfunctional states.

The essential practical issue for the design of state interventions (for example, to regulate markets, protect natural resources, and overcome market failures) is to understand the balance of motivations in any particular situation. Moore (1992; Table 20.1) provides a useful framework for thinking about this balance. The Weberian model of public administration is based on hierarchical organization, motivated by duty and regulated authority, and closely supervised. Almost all bureaucracies are organized in a way that pays at least lip service to these elements. Moore (1992, 67) comments that Weber was keenly aware of the limits and dysfunctions of bureaucracy but tended to stress its advantages over preceding forms of state organization.

The third column in Table 20.1 might be described as the "public organization as disguised self-interest" approach, sometimes known as new public management. Tullock (1965, 26) is an extreme exponent of this view, arguing that bureaucracies "give special emphasis to the behaviour of an intelligent, ambitious and somewhat unscrupulous man in an organisational hierarchy." The steps in his argument are: (1) the main goal of bureaucrats is career progression; (2) bureaucracies provide wide scope for the concealment and manipulation of information; (3) those promoted most rapidly are the most effective in manipulating information; and (4) bureaucracies are ineffective, because the top ranks are filled with people whose key attributes are skills in the manipulation of information and untrustworthiness.

This extreme view fails to explain why policymakers could not devise methods of obtaining better information about bureaucratic performance. Other criticisms of bureaucracy stress an innate conservatism (or risk aversion) and lack of openness to new ideas, technologies, and working practices. Furthermore, even very accountable bureaucracies may be less concerned about minimizing costs and operating flexibly

Table 20.1 Models of economic and social coordination

Mechanism at the societal level	Model		
	Hierarchical control	Dispersed competition	Solidarity
Principle motivating microlevel interactions	Duty	Self-interest	Affectivity
Principle regulating microlevel interactions	Authority	Contract	Mutuality
Associated institution	Organization	Market (or democratic election)	Community
Associated mechanism for staff control in the institution	Feedback control (under close supervision)	Material incentive control (payment by results)	Preprogrammed control (socialization)
Associated mechanism for state to shape society	Authority	Market	Persuasion
Major exponents	Weber	Tullock, neoliberals	Wade
Program for public bureaucracy	Traditional bureaucracy	New public management	Organization as community

Source: Adapted from Moore (1992).

compared to profit-motivated firms. In summary, for a mixture of reasons, some valid and some probably overstated, distrust of bureaucracy is a background theme in current public administration. The general policy response to distrust of bureaucracy is to try to move from hierarchical to market and quasi-market relations in the delivery of public services. The NIE framework for analyzing the relative benefits of hierarchical, market, and hybrid forms of economic organization has a powerful contribution to make here. Many states are presently reforming by creating internal markets for services (including agriculture and rural services), whereby private firms, civil society organizations, and even parts of the civil service may compete for contracts to provide specified services. This experimentation with the boundaries between the public and private spheres has some similarities to Williamson's analysis of the fluid boundaries between markets and firms (or hierarchies) discussed in Chapter 2.

Finally, Table 20.1 shows a third mindset about public administration: solidarity or "organization as community." Here the ideal is neither bureaucratic command–obedience relationships nor the contractor–client relationship of the new public management approach. The bureaucratic approach of close supervision is thought to be expensive and likely to create workplace relationships that are not motivating. If staff members have a strong commitment to the goals of the organization through relationships of mutuality, then they will be creative, flexible, and open to technical innovation. Moore (1992) points out that much research on this approach has been undertaken in high-tech companies with well-educated and well-paid employees. In some ways the organization-as-community model is an evolution of bureaucracy but is based on the idea that employees can be trusted to show considerable self-discipline and to proactively share rather than hide information. Because of its cultural specificity, there must be doubts as to whether this model can be the starting point for evolution of Sub-Saharan African developmental states. However, NGOs are an increasingly important supplier of public services in Sub-Saharan Africa—sometimes as subcontractors to the state and sometimes independently of the state—and the ethos of most Sub-Saharan African NGOs and their Northern partners tends to be that of organization as community. An interesting question here is whether the internal cultures of these NGOs, which are influenced by those of their Northern partners, are trailblazing toward models for the development state. Or are they too insulated from the realities of the wider society? Section 20.7 provides some concepts for thinking about this matter.

20.3   State (Government) Failure: Arguments from Economics

It is useful at this point to review concepts from economics, including NIE, related to the above discussion. There are important issues in institutional arrangement concerning how the state configures itself to provide services. In the language of principal-agent theory (see Chapter 2), the broad objective is to design and implement institutional arrangements that, to the extent feasible, cause state agents (public servants) to deliver what their principals (for example, citizens or ministers) want. The challenge is that state agents have their own objectives. Sometimes they have a stronger commitment to the public interest than their political masters and possibly a different understanding of what is in the public interest. But state agents can be selfish, exhibiting such behavior as demanding bribes, shirking duties, and colluding with rent seeking by firms (Box 20.3). At this level, the challenges of state performance have many similarities with those analyzed for the private and collective spheres earlier in this book, and solutions in the search for better governance may often be found along broadly the same lines.

Box 20.3 Rent seeking

The term "rent seeking" does not have a precise meaning, as it is sometimes difficult to distinguish from profit-seeking behavior based on parties obtaining value by engaging in mutually beneficial transactions. The essence of rent seeking is the manipulation of the institutional environment in ways that cause the benefits to be mainly or exclusively one-sided. Thus a firm that lobbies for policies or regulations that favor it at the expense of consumers and/or taxpayers could be said to be rent seeking. If the firm is successful in its lobbying, then politicians and government officials could be said to be rent supplying. However, if the government officials initiate proposals to favor a particular firm, hoping for personal gain, then they are engaging in corruption. In contrast, rent seeking can be based on entirely legal activity, although sometimes it is not.

When government regulates a sector, or delegates this task to specialist agencies, the key challenges are that firms in the sector (1) often have better knowledge about relevant markets and technologies and (2) will (legitimately) lobby for a better deal from the regulator. An industry-captured regulator is one who has been unduly influenced by lobbying and therefore has conceded an excessively generous settlement to rent seekers.

When governments are excessively open to rent seeking, there can be large costs in terms of foregone investment and efficiency improvements. This is because firms may judge that they can get a better return on their resources by devoting them to lobbying and/or bribery rather than to outlays in new machinery and improved organization.

Many writers have made the point that market failures and arguments for the provision of public and merit goods and some asset and income redistribution do not justify government intervention. The benefits that may result from government action have to be weighed against the costs. The costs can be considerable, due in part to systemic failures of government to achieve objectives. The reasons for government failure are various. First, there are effects on incentives: the resulting unsought reactions of private agents to the levying of taxes. These effects include (1) discouraging activity and investment in heavily taxed sectors; (2) driving activity into the informal economy, where the requirements for invisibility may clash with the need for investment; and (3) creating opportunities for corruption between taxpayers and collectors.[4]

Second, insufficient information may be made available. The consequences of interventions are difficult to foresee, even when a major effort is put into prior analysis of the effects of policy, which is often not the case. To take some examples from African agriculture, what may be the effects of

1. a new government commitment, made before planting, to purchase postharvest all quantities of the staple grain crop offered for sale to a government agency at a specified price?

2. a government decision to write off all loans owned by small farmers to the state agricultural bank?

3. the introduction (and withdrawal several years later) of a program of free distribution of packs of seed and fertilizer to all smallholder farmers?

4. the removal of quotas and other quantitative restrictions on food imports and their replacement with a low external tariff?

Clearly these changes are hard to predict, and even the best teams of analysts can get it wrong. Some economists draw from this experience the conclusion that it might have been better if government had not intervened in the first place.

Third, there is limited control over bureaucracy. This failing is a manifestation of the principal-agent problem discussed above. Parliamentarians and government ministers set the broad objectives of policy but are often unclear and/or divided in their goals. Furthermore, they have to delegate the drafting of the detailed legislation to government agencies, raising the question touched on above about the internal culture and motives of the bureaucracy.

Finally, van de Walle (2001, 127) warns against an excessively politically naive technocratic analysis, mocking the public-policy community for playing down the patrimonial and clientalist dimensions of Sub-Saharan African regimes, by treating these traits as

> little more than an odd atavism, which a couple of additional "capacity building" projects promoting greater administrative hygiene will soon entirely do away with. It refuses to accept the idea that clientelism in these states is more than incidental. For example, a striking reality is that most anti-corruption strategies being devised in the policy community simply assume that there is a rational-legal logic at the apex of these states that will be available to carry out the strategy; in fact, all too often, leaders at the apex of the state choose to undermine these strategies, which threaten practices which they find useful and profitable.

20.4   The Impact of Adjustment and Liberalization on the Developmental State

Fukuyama (2004a) develops arguments about different aspects of "stateness," and from them creates a penetrating critique of structural adjustment and liberalization policies that developing countries, including those of Africa, have implemented since the mid-1980s. These policies were strongly advocated by the International Monetary Fund and the World Bank based on an analysis that the state was overextended and ineffective, and that the budgetary resources were not available to sustain state operations at the scale to which they had developed. Furthermore, relatively high levels of public expenditure were, through a variety of mechanisms, crowding out private-sector activity and investment.

Figure 20.1 shows state strength (for example, the ability to protect property rights) versus the scope of state functions (illustrated by how much the state is disposed to engage in the intermediate and activist functions listed in the lower part of Table 20.2). To summarize, most countries fall within one of the four quadrants shown in Figure 20.1:

1. quadrant I—strong state and limited scope (neoclassical ideal—for example, the United States);

2. quadrant II—strong state with extensive scope (good examples are France and Japan; bad examples from the past are the countries in the Soviet Union);

3. quadrant III—weak state, limited scope (for example, present-day Sierra Leone, which has recently been subject to serious internal conflict); and

Figure 20.1   Stateness and efficiency

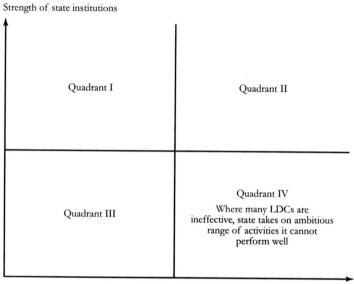

Strength of state institutions

Quadrant I

Quadrant II

Quadrant III

Quadrant IV
Where many LDCs are
ineffective, state takes on ambitious
range of activities it cannot
perform well

Scope of state functions

Source: Adapted from Fukuyama (2004a).

Table 20.2   Functions and scope of the state

Scope of functions	Function	
	Addressing market failure	Improving equity
Minimal	Providing pure public goods	Protecting the poor
	Providing for defense	Instituting antipoverty programs
	Securing property rights	Providing disaster relief
	Providing law and order	
	Providing public health services	
Intermediate	Addressing externalities	Providing social insurance
	Providing education	Providing redistributive pensions
	Protecting the environment	Providing family allowances
	Regulating monopolies	Providing unemployment insurance
	Regulating utilities	
	Enforcing antitrust laws	
	Overcoming imperfect information	
	Regulating insurance	
	Regulation the financial sector	
	Providing consumer protection	
Activist	Coordinating private activities	Instituting redistribution programs
	Fostering markets	Instituting asset redistribution programs
	Supporting cluster initiatives	

Source: Adapted from World Development Report (World Bank 1997).

4. quadrant IV—weak state, extensive scope (for example, many developing countries that have taken on an ambitious range of activities that are not performed well).

The core of Fukuyama's argument is that in reforming the state, the optimal path of structural adjustment might have been to decrease state scope while extending strength. However, in practice both have fallen, often with very damaging results. "The problem for many countries was that in the process of reducing state scope they either decreased state strength or generated demands for new types of state capabilities which were either weak or non-existent" (Fukuyama 2004a, 9).

Referring to the concept of neopatrimonialism, Fukuyama cites van de Walle (2001), finding that in cutting back state expenditure in the 1990s, African governments did not seriously try to protect core social expenditures. Indeed, the opposite tended to occur, with governments more interested in maintaining "sovereignty expenditures," often focused on the office of the head of state.

In summary, many African states took path II in Figure 20.2, as state capacity as well as state scope declined. For van de Walle, a major element in this deterioration was intensified competition between the two key sectors of politics and the state: the

Figure 20.2 Possible reform paths under structural adjustment

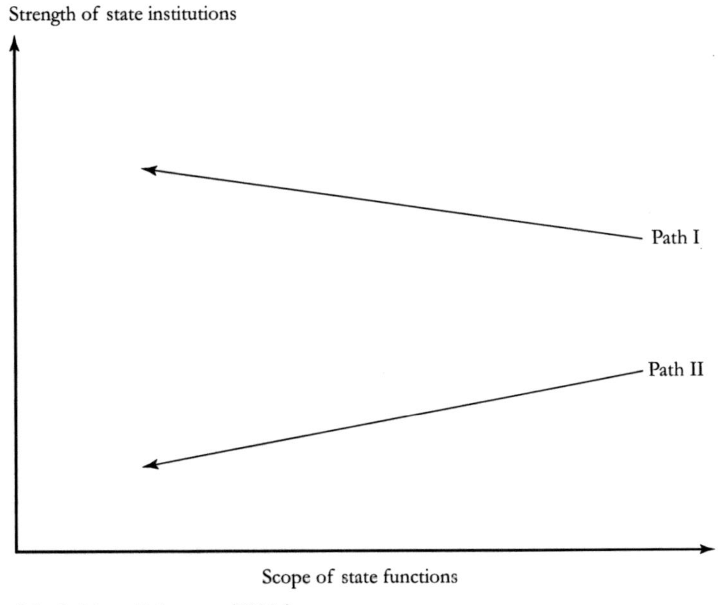

Source: Adapted from Fukuyama (2004a).

Weberian rational bureaucracy versus the neopatrimonial network. In this competition the modern state has lost out disastrously, with big reductions in expenditures on basic infrastructure, primary education, agriculture, and so on. Meanwhile, in the 1990s, sovereignty expenditures actually increased (for example, military, diplomatic services, and jobs connected to the office of the president).

Fukuyama (2004a, 11) argues that none of the donors wanted this outcome "yet none were able to structure their conditionality in a way to prevent it from happening because of their inability to control local political outcomes." According to Fukuyama, in retrospect many in the Washington Consensus say they understood the importance of institutions, the rule of law, and proper sequencing of reforms. Nevertheless "Y-axis questions of state capacity and state building were largely absent from early structural adjustment discussions" and "there were very few warnings issued from Washington-based policy makers about the dangers of liberalisation in the absence of proper institutions. Indeed, the general inclination among policymakers at the time was that any degree of liberalisation was likely to be better than no liberalisation at all" (Fukuyama 2004b, 27)

According to Fukuyama, the general philosophy of the Washington Consensus began to shift in the face of unsatisfactory privatizations:

- The Asian financial crises of 1997–98 as well as the problems of the post-communist countries prompted a rethinking: it was clear that a little liberalization could be more dangerous than no liberalization.

- Privatization in Russia required capacity and political will to deal with information asymmetries, and it is the job of governments to correct them. Essentially, assets and ownership rights have to be identified, valued, and transparently transferred, and the rights of new minority shareholders have to be protected to prevent asset stripping and tunneling.

Evidence summarized in Lockwood (2005) suggests that privatization in Sub-Saharan Africa during the 1990s often suffered from the some of the same problems, thus Fukuyama's (2004b, 28) comment about the nub of the problem—"while privatisation involves a reduction of state functions, it requires functioning markets and a high degree of state capacity to implement"—would appear to apply to some extent to Africa. The absence of these conditions in Russia's privatization resulted in the theft of state resources by the oligarchs.

To conclude this section, the key point is the importance of state strength and state capacity, even if the long-run objective is a state that is democratic, pluralist, and strongly based on the market. However, in the early stages of emergence of a developmental state, it is likely that the strength and capacity of the state will stem from an effective bureaucracy operating in a constructive relationship with a political system that has some authoritarian-corporatist characteristics. If this conclusion is correct, then it is somewhat at odds with much Western advice to Africa, which is currently based on democratic pluralism coexisting with a minimalist role for the state and with highly motivated "organizations as communities" contracting with the state for the delivery of public services.

20.5 The Agricultural Development Paradox

Chapters 1–3 in this book have explained the pressing nature of market failures in agriculture and rural development. Table 20.2 shows a summary of the functions of the state in developing countries, set out in the 1997 *World Development Report* (World Bank 1997). The table suggests that consideration should be given to governments undertaking some of the activities shown, which can perhaps be justified with reference to the arguments for state intervention explored earlier in this chapter. It shows a spectrum ranging from minimal through intermediate to activist functions. The implication is that minimal functions represent tasks that the state must try to undertake, even when resources are limited and political processes unhelpful. Indeed, it can be argued that when the dominant political processes in the country are very antidevelopmental, then those who wish to build up the state's capacity for service provision must concentrate strongly on the minimal functions. This is not just because these functions are the most important, but also because extending the state into intermediate or even activist functions creates further opportunities for predatory behavior by the political elite. Furthermore, predatory behavior may be encouraged by the likelihood that principal-agent problems will be more severe with the more activist functions. For example, it is probably easier to determine whether state agents (police and courts) are effectively protecting property rights than whether a state agency is effectively fostering markets. The issue of capacity—meaning the technical capability of government staff—is also relevant here, but is perhaps often overemphasized, for reasons summarized by van de Walle's (2001, 127) scornful reference to "a couple of extra capacity-building projects."

With respect to the agricultural and rural sector in Africa, a major question that arises is whether the general priorities in Table 20.2 are appropriate to this sector. The theory and case studies presented earlier in this book raise a major issue, namely that "coordinating private activity" and "fostering markets" is a critical early activity in smallholder development, as was the case for the South Asian Green Revolutions (Dorward et al. 2004).

Birner and Resnick (2005a) have summarized the reasons that early government activism is necessary for agricultural development. The argument stems from the specific material conditions of agricultural production, which include:

1. The level of effort required by many activities, which, combined with spatial dispersion across fields, poses acute principal-agent problems. Workers need to be motivated and trusted, as their labor is hard to monitor in detail. These considerations are thought to favor family- or household-based farming, causing the optimal organization to be based on small units.

2. Economies of agglomeration will be less accessible, because of the dispersed pattern of family and household farms. So there will inevitably be relatively high costs in delivering services and inputs and marketing output.

3. Dependence on biological processes and weather conditions make harvests unpredictable, especially when there is little control over water.

4. Covariance of risk across the territory of countries and regions poses problems of generalized shortages (with high prices and possibly threats to food security) or gluts (with very low prices and hence low farm incomes and possible inability to repay debts).

5. Idiosyncratic knowledge (that is, knowledge specific to a locality, often down to the characteristics of a particular parcel of land) creates knowledge asymmetries.

A further set of arguments relevant to the role of the state in agriculture is provided by Hall and Soskice's (2001) investigation into varieties of capitalism in advanced economies. They argue that the advanced economies can be differentiated into those with liberal market economies (LMEs) and those with coordinated market economies (CMEs). Empirical evidence shows that all the advanced English-speaking economies are LMEs, whereas the rest are CMEs. The essence of Hall and Soskice's conclusion is that LMEs have an institutionally based advantage in economic sectors characterized by discontinuous (disruptive) technical change. However, CMEs have an institutionally based advantage in sectors characterized by continuous or incremental technical advance.

The basis of Hall and Soskice's (2001) argument is that the challenge of asset-specific investment (discussed in Chapter 5) requires a number of parties to coordinate to gain assurance that specialized and (in some cases) long-term investments will be worthwhile. The parties include workers who have to invest in their own human capital, businesses that have to invest in plant and machinery, and governments that have to invest in infrastructure, research, and training capacity. To gain assurance that these investments will be worthwhile, the economy must develop a culture of *nonmarket coordination*. There are two key aspects to nonmarket coordination:

1. Deliberative forums are required for intrasector discussion and the development of understanding and confidence. In examining differences among LMEs, Hall and Soskice (2001) note variations in the roles of government and conclude that these arrangements tend to work best when government is a co-equal rather than a dominant partner. In particular, if governments are heavy handed (for example, changing policy precipitously without due discussion and prior consensus building), private-sector investment might be discouraged.

2. Some limitations must be placed on intrasectoral competition, in the long-run interests of the sector as a whole. However, certain key activities with longer-term payoffs may be allowed to access capital on preferential terms through interlinked capital markets (firms and banks tend to own equity shares in each other).

CMEs tend to try to protect workers and firms from disruptive change, for example with employment protection and restrictions on takeovers and market entry. Thus they may be well adapted for industries characterized by incremental technical change that remain at the forefront of technology. But CMEs are unattractive for industries characterized by risky, discontinuous, or disruptive technologies. In LMEs the costs of taking such bets, and then failing, or partly failing, are less.

Agriculture is a sector characterized by continuous technical change. With the possible exceptions of the ongoing supermarket revolution and the introduction of genetic modification (GM) technologies, compared to other sectors it is not generally subject to discontinuous technological change. Therefore the CME institutional set may provide the basis for competitive advantage in agriculture. Thus the emphasis should be on nonmarket coordination; deliberative forums; and a state that is activist, intelligent, and not dominant. Of course, trying to meet these requirements is hugely ambitious, and they are very much at odds with the current motivation and capacity of politics and state services in much of Africa.

Figures 20.3 and 20.4 show an example, based on transactions-cost analysis, of a transition in the role of the state in agriculture based on a CME orientation. Initially, in the early stages of development, state provision is superior to provision by the private sector, supervised by farmers' organizations. In these early stages (Phase 1 in Figure 20.3) the set-up and maintenance costs of systems based on private farms collaborating through farmers' organizations are higher than those of state provision, so the implication is that the state must intervene. In the next stage (Phase 2 in Figure 20.3) the capacity of state organizations increases, with lower cost and more extensive provision of services. Finally, the volume of service activity increases to the point that private markets and farmers' organizations can take over. Thus Birner and Resnick (2005a, 302) are critical of views that early-stage agricultural development is

Figure 20.3 Processes and conditions for agricultural transformation

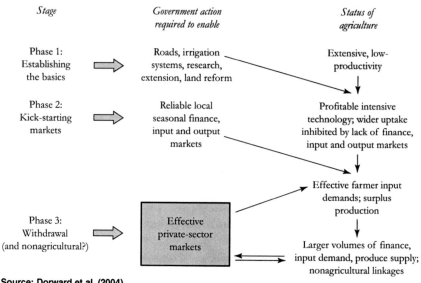

Source: Dorward et al. (2004).

Figure 20.4 Analyzing the role of the public, the private, and the third sectors (in extension)

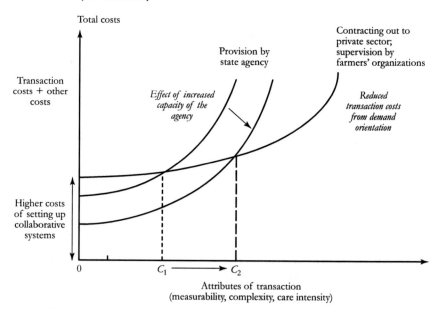

Source: Birner and Resnick (2005b).

Note: The lower axis indicates the efficient boundaries of the state.

not a core function of the state and can be left to the private sector. Quoting Robert Paarlberg, they note that if M. S. Swaminathan were to propose "the policy package that made the Green Revolution in India possible to the World Bank today, it would never [be] accepted due [to] its public sector focus."

In conclusion, there is an agricultural development paradox: the need for pro-poor state services is high when state failure is profound.

However, presently a pressing need exists for research on public-sector management for agriculture, because effective public administration is essential for pro-poor agricultural development. For Birner and Resnick (2005a), a consequence of general failure by development specialists to understand the core early-stage role of the state in agricultural development is that public-sector management specialists do not give adequate attention to agriculture, while agricultural sector specialists do not pay sufficient attention to public-sector management reform.

20.6 NIE Applied to the Reform of Agricultural Services

This section addresses the gap in communication between specialists in agricultural development and public-sector management reform, adding NIE into the picture. The general arguments explored in this chapter can be integrated with reference to interventions in agriculture. A useful starting point is Klitgaard's (1997) application of NIE to the challenge of public-sector reform, with Sub-Saharan Africa particularly in mind. Klitgaard argues that the central challenge is to find ways of improving performance incentives. He is careful to stress that the NIE issues that he selects (information and incentives) provide just one of a range of insights, and other matters, such as the norms and behavior of bureaucracy and the nature of the political system, are also important. Klitgaard (1997, 495) comments on a review by Ostrom and colleagues of rural credit and extension programs:

> in each case, if one asks whether government officials have the incentives to carry forth the programmes as designed (and whether information is available to which incentives can be tied) the answer is usually no. And in some cases when incentive reforms have been tried, such as in some public enterprise reforms, a careful reading shows that the incentives were not credible to employees and were small in any case—no surprise then, that they failed.

According to Milgrom (1988, 58–59), the key principle of efficient organizational design is "to do what the system of prices and property rights does in neoclassical economics: to channel the self-interested behaviour of individuals away from purely redistributive activities into well coordinated socially productive ones."

Table 20.3 has a column summarizing prevalent approaches to improving performance incentives in the civil service. Klitgaard (1997) states that these approaches

Table 20.3   Two approaches to incentives in the reform of public-service delivery

	Prevalent approach	Proposed approach
Objectives	Across-the-board pay increases; horizontal equity across jobs	Selective pay increases that eventually spread; incentives linked to performance targets
Means	Small cuts in personnel based on long-term studies; learning by planning; supply-side strategies	Experiments in which civil servants and clients help define measures of success; user charges; learning by doing; deep cuts in personnel; demand-side strategies
Constraints	Budgetary austerity; donor pressure to reduce wage bill	n.a.
Facilitating conditions	Studies; technical assistance; political will to reduce the size of the public-service sector	Institutional adjustment, including better information, more client feedback, and more competition

Source: Adapted from Klitgaard (1997, 497).
Note: n.a., not applicable.

generally fail, being too gradual while not providing sufficiently high incentives to retain well-motivated and highly skilled personnel. Its most critical failing, however, is that it is inflexible and fails to link pay to performance. In contrast, his two ideas for change are (1) experimentation with performance-based incentives and (2) system-wide investment in better information about outcomes. He suggests that financial constraints to civil service reform could be overcome by starting with revenue-raising and cost-saving experiments that could pay for themselves. Aid could also be used to fund reform experiments.

Turning to the challenges of designing experiments in improving incentives, the right-hand column of Table 20.4 summarizes the difficulties, which are often considerable. Applying principal-agent theory, the essence of the problem is that once performance pay is introduced, agents (employees/public servants) and principals (employers/managers) can take steps that undermine incentives and information:

- Agents may shift their efforts from important but hard-to-measure activities to those that are easily measured, and they may hide or distort information or influence evaluators. The use of relative rankings can undermine teamwork or even cause agents to sabotage the efforts of others.

- Principals may try "ratchet effects," constantly moving the goalposts and thereby leaving agents worse off than before. Intermediate layers in the hierarchy may collude with, or extract rents from, subordinate levels, thereby distorting information.

However, the prospects for improving incentives are not universally unpromising. The center column in Table 20.4 sets out conditions under which principal-

Table 20.4   Conditions favorable and unfavorable to incentives based on performance

Dimension	Favorable to incentives based on performance	Unfavorable to incentives based on performance
Marginal social benefits of more effort by agent	Additional efforts by public servants lead to big gains in effectiveness	Because of other constraints, additional efforts by public servants yield no gains in effectiveness
Agent's risk aversion	Agents are risk neutral, perhaps because plentiful opportunities exist and they are already well paid	Agents are risk averse, perhaps because they are poor
Ease of measurement of agent's effort	Effort and results are easy to measure	Effort and results are hard to measure
Responsiveness of agent's effort to incentives	Effort is very responsive to incentives (agents have high discretion)	Effort is not responsive to incentives (fixed-pace activity)

Source: Adapted from Klitgaard (1997, 498).

agent problems are less severe. In essence, the prospects for reform depend on (1) the nature of the task (in particular, whether it is possible to set targets that are good proxies for the service delivery desired) and (2) the general political and economic background (for example, average income levels, the nature of the state, and the size of and relative pay in the civil service).

Klitgaard (1997) recommends beginning with reforming areas of the state that have good prospects for a favorable outcome (center column in Table 20.4). Activities here might include (1) strengthening links between employees' efforts and government agencies' value added (by, for example, better task definition and team-based analyses of performance) and (2) improving performance measures though client surveys and benchmarking.

This book gives examples of agricultural and rural intervention by the state that include (1) providing credit, inputs, and output marketing services (on the argument of overcoming market failure); (2) agricultural extension services; (3) support for the establishment of cooperatives; (4) natural resource management; (5) nonmarket coordination with the participation of the state to raise long-term incentives for investors (along lines suggested by the work of Hall and Soskice 2001); and (6) regulation of the agricultural sector.

Some of these activities are amenable to the introduction of payment based on performance, particularly marketing services, where volume and quality targets can be set and monitored. The issue here is perhaps whether there is sufficient political determination to set and enforce targets. If these services were to be privatized, then it is likely that tougher targets and their monitoring would be introduced. The dilemma is that the private organization might not deal appropriately with market failures, so the challenge to those who are skeptical of privatization is to bring better performance management into the public sector.

Other state agricultural activities are less susceptible to efficient performance monitoring. A good example is agricultural extension, whose aim is to help poor farmers: it is very hard to collect information about the clients and their interactions with extension to determine whether that service is as effective as possible. Regulatory and nonmarket coordination require highly skilled individuals with incorruptible values based on public interest. Such coordination is perhaps best done by the higher levels of a classic Weberian bureaucracy, although these roles can be transferred to regulatory agencies with contracts that insulate them from lobbying.

20.7 Summary and Conclusions

This chapter started by reviewing how economists (both orthodox and NIE) analyze which services the state should provide. Concepts including market failure, public goods, merit goods, and redistribution are useful but tell only part of the story, because they do not analyze the motivations and capabilities of the state. If the state serves less the public interest and more the narrow sectional interests of individual politicians, businesses, or state employees, then the interventions may be, at best, ineffective and, at worst, damaging. Furthermore, interventions can fail even when the state has convincing public-interest motivations, because of the absence of such factors as adequate information, appropriate management methods, and technologies. In other words, when considering arguments for state intervention, the possibilities of a cure that is worse than the disease—that is, state failure—have to be kept firmly in mind.

Much of the analysis in this book has pointed to the need for varied state interventions in the early stages of agricultural development, including the creation of infrastructure; the arrangement of services for credit, inputs, and outputs to overcome market failure; research and extension; and intelligent coordination. A state that is able to supply these with tolerable efficiency would be a developmental state, with appropriate conditions for the early stages of agricultural development. The questions then are how developmental states might emerge in Sub-Saharan Africa and what form they might take. It was argued that although the central questions here are not those of NIE, nevertheless NIE has a role in these debates for the following reasons:

1. By specifying what a state needs to do to foster agricultural development, NIE can contribute usefully to determining the criteria for a developmental state.

2. If insights from NIE are to be used in the design of public-service delivery, then some notions about what kinds of developmental state may be expected to emerge are required, to fit the design of policies and organizations to the likely motivations and capabilities of the state.

Thus this chapter examines evidence from two distinctly different models of the developmental state. First, there is a Western model based on democratic pluralism and a reliance on markets. Second, there is the East Asian model, which is authoritarian and corporatist but committed to safeguarding private property and to reliance on markets. The East Asian model is more interventionist and depends on a strong bureaucracy committed to national economic development. The bureaucracy works in a policy space provided by a political framework that can be corrupt but, because of the strength of the state and the depth of its commitment to economic development, does not allow personal and narrow sectional interests to gain rents to an extent that seriously undermines economic development.

Drawing implications from this discussion for Sub-Saharan Africa, some authors have shown that patrimonial and clientalist politics lead to a weak state and forms of corruption through which resources are siphoned off into consumption by a small political and business elite. Foreign aid plays an ambiguous role here: increasingly, aid flows are dependent on compliance with principles of "good government" and the reform and reduction in scope of the state. Yet at the same time aid supports governments and may weaken the emergence of accountable (that is, principal-agent) relations, such as those between taxpayers and government. If this view, of which van de Walle is an exponent, is valid, then it follows that most Sub-Saharan African states affected by this form of politics will be, at best, only partly developmental. Except when large, long-term foreign aid commitments are available, Sub-Saharan African states will make only weak investments in education and infrastructure, mainly acting as a channel for aid, and will probably not be up to the job of supporting agriculture with specialist infrastructure and services to overcome market failures. When interventions are attempted, the possibilities for state failure are considerable. This scenario is the essence of the agricultural development paradox, which is that the need for pro-poor state services is highest when state failure is most profound.

Can multiparty democracy—through the space it provides for open debate, the formation of civil society organizations (for example, independent farmers' organizations), and the ability of electorates to dismiss corrupt and/or ineffective government —encourage the rapid emergence of a developmental state? Expert opinion is somewhat skeptical, because of a concern that multiparty politics will further weaken the state. What is required is a state that has sufficient strength to overcome personal and sectional rent seeking and yet uses its strength to follow a national development project with consistent institutions and policies designed to encourage investment.

These conclusions again raise the question of the motivation of the state and possible reasons for state failure. This is first discussed in terms of the models of economic and social coordination, and then the relevant economics arguments are brought together. Following Moore (1992), three broad categories can be distinguished: traditional bureaucracy (based on hierarchy), new public management (based on dispersed competition), and organization as community (based on solidarity). There is general agreement on the desirability of a bureaucracy motivated by the public interest, but disagreement as to whether this goal is realistic. In contrast to the Weberian view of the ideal bureaucrat being motivated by duty, a currently influential critique stresses the self-interest of public-sector staff members and their ability to evade accountability through hiding information about performance. The policy implication is that to obtain better quality and value in the supply of public goods, the state should contract out delivery, paying by results. However, public-interest values are an essential requirement for those in the state responsible for letting and supervising contracts, and information problems remain. The core questions are motivation and information; the relative merits of each approach are likely to change with the evolution of management methods and technologies.

The organization-as-community model is in some ways an evolution of bureaucratic values with an emphasis on staff identification with organizational goals, which, in the public sector, should be public goals. The model is found in parts of public, private, and voluntary sectors of developed countries, but there must be doubt as to whether its values of trust, self-discipline, and the sharing of information can be rapidly transferred to the public sector of most Sub-Saharan African countries. Possibly this model is a highly culture-specific one that in Sub-Saharan Africa is mainly adopted by NGOs.

In the past two decades most Sub-Saharan African states have been forced by a mixture of economic weakness and changes in the strategic thinking of aid agencies to engage in processes of liberalization, privatization, and the pruning and reform of the state (including experiments in contracting out service provision). Too often the result has been further erosion of the strength of the state coupled with an increasingly ambitious—and untenable—increase in state scope.

This chapter argues that smallholder development needs some services that are in the "activist category" of state scope, including coordinating private activity and fostering markets. Two lines of argument are also advanced to explain the importance of government intervention at the early stages of agricultural development: kick-starting agricultural development and overcoming market failures.

Obviously, if this picture of states weakening in scope, strength, and commitment to public services is correct, then the outlook for governments providing the kinds of support that agriculture needs is bleak. Policy proposals must be designed to fit the real circumstances in Sub-Saharan Africa. The final section of the chapter gives examples of how NIE concepts may be used to design better incentives for the public sector in situations in which government has been performing badly. To end on an optimistic note, it is argued that application of NIE thinking (mainly about information and the principal-agent relationship) can help improve the performance of some state agencies, even against an unpromising general background.

Notes

1. Max Weber (1946) defined the state as "a human community that (successfully) claims the monopoly of the legitimate force within a given territory." Thus for Weber the essence of "stateness" is ability to enforce. The term "the state" is a useful abstraction for certain kinds of general discussion, but for practical policy analysis it is necessary to focus on particular components of government. Furthermore, the boundaries of the state are fuzzy. For example, is a government-owned firm providing services in a market in which it competes with the private sector part of the state? Another example is provided by supranational organizations (such as COMESA [Common Market for Eastern and Southern Africa]), in which governments have pooled sovereignty in certain areas (such as the collection of border taxes).

2. South Africa, with its distinctly different history, level of development, and economic structure, is normally excluded from the generalizations about Sub-Saharan Africa discussed in this section of the chapter.

3. Examples of relatively successful centralized bureaucratic states include Kenya under Jomo Kenyatta, Tanzania under Julius Nyerere, Malawi under Hastings Banda, and Ivory Coast under Félix Houphuoët-Boigny. However, it may be argued that at present one, or at most two, of these four examples have had sustained success—Tanzania being the least controversial example.

4. For example, in Uganda, decentralization has necessitated an increased revenue effort by local government, often contracted out to private agents. But a high proportion of the tax collected is extracted by tax collectors and the politicians and officials who have contracted them. A disappointingly small proportion of funds is used to finance public services (Bahiigwa et al. 2003).

Further Reading

Fukuyama, F. 2004. *State building: Governance and world order in the twenty-first century*. London: Profile Books.

Lockwood, M. 2005. *The state they're in: An agenda for international action on poverty in Africa*. Bourton-on-Dunsmore, U.K.: ITDG.

van de Walle, N. 2001. *African economies and the politics of permanent crisis*. Cambridge: Cambridge University Press.

References

Allen, C. 1995. Understanding African politics. *Review of African Political Economy* 65: 301–320.

Bahiigwa, G., F. Ellis, O. H. Fjeldstad, and V. Iversen. 2003. *Rural taxation in Uganda: Implications for growth, income distribution, local government revenue and poverty reduction*. EPRC Research Series 35. Kampala, Uganda, and Norwich, U.K.: Economic Policy Research Centre and Overseas Development Group, University of East Anglia.

Birner, R., and D. Resnick. 2005a. Policy and politics for smallholder agriculture. Paper presented at a workshop on the future of small farms, Imperial College at Wye, June 26–29, Wye, U.K. Available at http://www.ifpri.org/events/seminars/2005/smallfarms/sfproc.asp. Accessed May 2009.

———. 2005b. Policy and politics for smallholder agriculture. PowerPoint presentation at a workshop on the future of small farms, Imperial College at Wye, June 26–29, Wye, U.K. Slide 13.

Booth, D., R. Crook, E.Gyimah-Boadi, T. Killick, and R. Luckham, with N. Boateng. 2005. What are the drivers of change in Ghana? CDD/ODI Policy Brief 1. London: Centre for Democratic Transition/Overseas Development Institute.

Dorward, A. R., J. G. Kydd, J. A. Morrison, and I. Urey. 2004. A policy agenda for pro-poor agricultural growth. *World Development* 32: 73–89.

Fukuyama, F. 2004a. *State building: Governance and world order in the twenty-first century.* London: Profile Books.

———. 2004b. The imperative of state-building. *Journal of Democracy* 15 (2): 17–31.

Hall, P. A., and D. Soskice, eds. 2001. *Varieties of capitalism: The institutional foundations of comparative advantage.* Oxford: Oxford University Press.

Khan, M. H. 2005. Social transformation and the state. Lecture given at SOAS Research Seminar Series on State and Development, London, spring. Available at http://mercury.soas.ac.uk/users/mk17/Docs/Social%20transformation%20and%20the%20state.pdf. Accessed April 2009.

Klitgaard, B. 1997. Cleaning up and invigorating the civil service. *Public Administration and Development* 17: 487–509.

Lockwood, N. 2005. *The state they're in: An agenda for international action on poverty in Africa.* Bourton-on-Dunsmore, U.K.: ITDG.

Milgrom, P. 1988. Employment contracts, influence activities and efficient organization design. *Journal of Political Economy* 96 (1): 42–60.

Moore, M. 1992. Competition and pluralism in public bureaucracies. *IDS Bulletin* 23 (4): 65–76.

Olson, M. 2000. *Power and prosperity: Outgrowing communist and capitalist dictatorships.* Oxford: Oxford University Press.

Tullock, G. 1965. *The politics of bureaucracy.* Washington, D.C.: Public Affairs Press.

Van de Walle, N. 2001. *African economies and the politics of permanent crisis.* Cambridge: Cambridge University Press.

Wade, R. 1990. *Governing the market: Economic theory and the role of government in East Asian industrialization.* Princeton, N.J., U.S.A.: Princeton University Press.

Weber, M. 1946. *From Max Weber: Essays in sociology.* New York: Oxford University Press.

World Bank. 1997. *World development report 1997: The state in a changing world.* Oxford: Oxford University Press.

Contributors

John H. Ainembabazi Ph.D. student in Development Economics at the Norwegian University of Life Sciences, Aas; formerly master's student in the Department of Agricultural Economics and Agribusiness, Makerere University, Kampala, Uganda

Ephraim W. Chirwa Professor in the Department of Economics, Chancellor College, University of Malawi, Zomba, Malawi

Stefan Dercon Professor of Development Economics, Queen Elizabeth House, Oxford University

Andrew R. Dorward Professor of Development Economics, Centre for Development, Environment and Policy, School of Oriental and African Studies, University of London

Eleni Gabre-Madhin CEO, Ethiopian Commodity Exchange, Addis Ababa, Ethiopia; formerly leader, Ethiopia Country Strategy Support Program, International Food Policy Research Institute, Addis Ababa, Ethiopia

John Hoddinott Senior research fellow, Food Consumption and Nutrition Division, International Food Policy Research Institute, Washington, D.C.

A. S. Mohammad Karaan Dean, Faculty of AgriSciences, University of Stellenbosch, Stellenbosch, South Africa

Johann F. Kirsten Professor and chair, Department of Agricultural Economics, Extension and Rural Development, University of Pretoria, Pretoria, South Africa

Pramila Krishnan University lecturer and fellow, Jesus College, Department of Economics, University of Cambridge

Jonathan G. Kydd Dean, University of London External System, formerly professor of Agricultural Development Economics and director, Wye External Programme, Imperial College at Wye, Wye, U.K.

Michael C. Lyne Associate professor, International Rural Development, Farm Management and Agribusiness Agriculture and Life Sciences Division, Lincoln University, New Zealand, and honorary professor, Agricultural Economics, School of Agricultural Sciences and Agribusiness, University of KwaZulu-Natal, Pietermaritzburg, South Africa

Micah B. Masuku Head, Department of Agricultural Economics and Management, University of Swaziland, Swaziland

Ruth S. Meinzen-Dick Senior research fellow, International Food Policy Research Institute, and coordinator, Consultative Group on International Agricultural Research Systemwide Program on Collective Action and Property Rights, Washington, D.C.

Esther Mwangi Postdoctoral fellow, Sustainability Science Program, Center for International Development, Kennedy School of Government, Harvard University, Cambridge, Mass., U.S.A.

Leah Ndung'u Research management officer, International Livestock Research Institute, Nairobi, Kenya

Nicholas Ochom Researcher, Department of Agricultural Economics and Agribusiness, Faculty of Agriculture, Makerere University, Kampala, Uganda

S. Were Omamo President, New Growth International, Nairobi, Kenya, and Palo Alto, Calif., U.S.A., and visiting scholar, Center for African Studies, Stanford University, Stanford, Calif., U.S.A.

Leonard Oruko Senior technical officer, Monitoring and Evaluation, Association for Strengthening Agricultural Research in Eastern and Central Africa Secretariat, Entebbe, Uganda

Colin Poulton Research fellow, Centre for Development, Environment and Policy, School of Oriental and African Studies, University of London

Dick Sserunkuuma Lecturer, Department of Agricultural Economics and Agribusiness, Faculty of Agriculture, Makerere University, Kampala, Uganda

Anna A. Temu Senior lecturer, Department of Agricultural Economics and Agribusiness, Sokoine University of Agriculture, Morogoro, Tanzania

Barbara van Koppen Principal researcher, rural sociologist and poverty and gender specialist, Southern Africa Regional Office, International Water Management Institute, Pretoria, South Africa

Nick Vink Professor and chair, Department of Agricultural Economics, University of Stellenbosch, Stellenbosch, South Africa

Index

3236983

Made in the USA